24th Conference on Computational Linguistics and Speech Processing

(ROCLING 2012)

Chung-Li, Taiwan
21-22 September 2012

Editors:

Richard Tzong-Han Tsai
Liang-Chih Yu
Chia-Ping Chen
Cheng-Zen Yang
Shu-Kai Hsieh
Min-Yuh Day

ISBN: 978-1-62748-392-6

Printed from e-media with permission by:

Curran Associates, Inc.
57 Morehouse Lane
Red Hook, NY 12571

Some format issues inherent in the e-media version may also appear in this print version.

Printed by Curran Associates, Inc. (2013)

For permission requests, please contact the Association for Computational Linguistics at the address below.

Association for Computational Linguistics
209 N. Eighth Street
Stroudsburg, Pennsylvania 18360

Phone: 1-570-476-8006
Fax: 1-570-476-0860

acl@aclweb.org

Additional copies of this publication are available from:

Curran Associates, Inc.
57 Morehouse Lane
Red Hook, NY 12571 USA
Phone: 845-758-0400
Fax: 845-758-2634
Email: curran@proceedings.com
Web: www.proceedings.com

Preface

Welcome to the 24th Conference on Computational Linguistics and Speech Processing at Yuan Ze University. Sponsored by the Association for Computational Linguistics and Chinese Language Processing (ACLCLP), ROCLING is the oldest and most comprehensive conference to focus on computational linguistics and speech processing. This year we received 45 valid submissions, each of which was reviewed by at least two experts on the basis of originality, significance, technical soundness, and relevance to the conference. In total, 15 papers were accepted for oral presentation and 19 for poster presentation. These papers cover a broad range on topics in natural language processing and speech technology and maintain the consistent quality of papers presented at ROCLING. The publications of these papers represent the joint effort of many researchers, and we are grateful to the efforts of the review committee for their work.

We are honored to have two distinguished invited speakers: Dr. Kenneth Church (President of ACL), speaking on "Towards Google-like Search on Spoken Documents with Zero Resources", and Dr. Li Deng (Principal Researcher, Microsoft Research), speaking on "Deep Learning and A New Wave of Innovations in Speech Technology". In addition, Prof. Jhing-Fa Wang will be organizing a panel discussion on "Research & Application of Speech & Language Technology for Orange Computing".

We would also like to thank our sponsors, including the Ministry of Education, the National Science Council, the Academia Sinica (Institute of Information Science), Chunghwa Telecom Laboratories, the Institute for Information Industry, the Industrial Technology Research Institute (Information and Communications Research Laboratories), Cyberon Corporation, and Behavior Design Corporation.

Finally, we appreciate your active participation and support to ensure a smooth and successful conference.

Richard Tzong-Han Tsai
Liang-Chih Yu
ROCLING 2012 Conference Chairs

Chia-Ping Chen
Cheng-Zen Yang
Shu-Kai Hsieh
ROCLING 2012 Program Chairs
September 2012

ROCLING XXIV (2012)
Organization

Conference Chairs

- Richard Tzong-Han Tsai, Yuan Ze University
- Liang-Chih Yu, Yuan Ze University

Advisory Committee

- Jason S. Chang, National Tsing Hua University
- Hsin-Hsi Chen, National Taiwan University
- Keh-Jiann Chen, Academia Sinica
- Sin-Horng Chen, National Chiao Tung University
- Wen-Lian Hsu, Academia Sinica
- Chu-Ren Huang, Hong Kong Polytechnic University
- Chin-Hui Lee, Georgia Institute of Technology
- Lin-Shan Lee, National Taiwan University
- Hai-zhou Li, Institute for Infocomm Research
- Chin-Yew Lin, Microsoft Research Asia
- Helen Meng, Chinese University of Hong Kong
- Jian Su, Institute for Infocomm Research
- Keh-Yih Su, Behavior Design Corporation
- Hsiao-Chuan Wang, National Tsing Hua University
- Jhing-Fa Wang, National Chen Kung University
- Chung-Hsien Wu, National Chen Kung University

Steering Committee

- Chia-Hui Chang, National Central University
- Jing-Shin Chang, National Chi Nan University
- Berlin Chen, National Taiwan Normal University
- Kuang-Hua Chen, National Taiwan University
- Jen-Tzung Chien, National Cheng Kung University
- Hung-Yan Gu, National Taiwan University of Science and Technology
- Zhao-Ming Gao, National Taiwan University
- Chih-Chung Kuo, Industrial Technology Research Institute
- Jeih-Weih Hung, National Chi Nan University
- Jyh-Shing Jang, National Tsing Hua University

- Yuan-Fu Liao, National Taipei University of Technology
- Chao-Lin Liu, National Chengchi University
- Jyi-Shane Liu, National Chengchi University
- Wen-Hsiang Lu, National Cheng Kung University
- Feng Zhu Luo, Yuan Ze University
- Chin-Chin Tseng, National Taiwan Normal University
- Yuen-Hsien Tseng, National Taiwan Normal University
- Hsin-Min Wang, Academia Sinica
- Hsu Wang, Yuan Ze University
- Ming-Shing Yu, National Chung Hsing University

Program Chairs

- Chia-Ping Chen, National Sun Yat-Sen University
- Cheng-Zen Yang, Yuan Ze University
- Shu-Kai Hsieh, National Taiwan University

Organization Chairs

- Wei-Tyng Hong, Yuan Ze University
- Jen-Wei Huang, National Cheng-Kung University
- Chin-Sheng Yang, Yuan Ze University
- Chien Chin Chen, National Taiwan University

Publication Chair

- Min-Yuh Day, Tamkang University

Publicity Chairs

- Shih-Hung Wu, Chaoyang University of Technology
- Lun-Wei Ku, Academia Sinica

Program Committee

- Guo-Wei Bian, Huafan University
- Ru-Yng Chang, National Cheng Kung University
- Tao-Hsing Chang, National Kaohsiung University of Applied Sciences
- Yu-Yun Chang, National Taiwan University
- Yi-Hsiang Chao, Chien Hsin University of Science and Technology
- Li-Mei Chen, National Cheng Kung University
- Pu-Jen Cheng, National Taiwan University

- Tai-Shih Chi, National Chiao Tung University
- Chaochang Chiu, Yuan Ze University
- Chih-Yi Chiu, National ChiaYi University
- Donghui Feng, Google Inc.
- Shu-Ping Gong, National ChiaYi University
- June-Jei Kuo, National Chung Hsing University
- Yi-Chun Kuo, National ChiaYi University
- Wen-Hsing Lai, National Kaohsiung First University of Science and Technology
- Bor-Shen Lin, National Taiwan University of Science and Technology
- Chuan-Jie Lin, National Taiwan Ocean University
- Shou-De Lin, National Taiwan University
- Shu-Yen Lin, National Taiwan Normal University
- Chao-Hong Liu, National Cheng Kung University
- Cheng-Jye Luh, Yuan Ze University
- Wei-Yun Ma, Columbia University
- Philips Kokoh Prasetyo, Singapore Management University
- Ming-Feng Tsai, National Chengchi University
- Wei-Ho Tsai, National Taipei University of Technology
- Gin-Der Wu, National Chi Nan University
- Jiun-Shiung Wu, National Chung Cheng University
- Jui-Feng Yeh, National ChiaYi University

Sponsored by:

Association for Computational Linguistics and Chinese Language Processing
Yuan Ze University

Co- Sponsored by:

Ministry of Education
National Science Council
Institute of Information Science, Academia Sinica
Chunghwa Telecom Laboratories
Institute for Information Industry
Industrial Technology Research Institute
Cyberon Corporation
Behavior Design Corporation

ROCLING XXIV (2012)

Program Overview

September 21, 2012 (Friday) 9:00 ~ 20:00		
09:00-09:50	Registration	
09:50:10:00	Opening Ceremony	Prof. Jin-Fu Chang Chair: Prof. Richard Tzong-Han Tsai Prof. Liang-Chih Yu
10:00-11:00	Invited Talk: How Many Multiword Expressions do People Know?	Speaker: Dr. Kenneth Church, President of ACL Chair: Dr. Wen-Lian Hsu
11:00-11:30	Coffee Break	
11:30-12:30	Oral Session 1: Speech Processing I	Chair: Dr. Yu Tsao
12:30-13:15	Lunch	
13:15-14:00	ACLCLP meeting for future directions	
14:00-15:20	Oral Session 2: Sentiment Analysis and Semantics	Chair: Dr. Lun-Wei Ku
15:20-15:50	Coffee Break / IJCLCLP editors meeting	
16:00-17:00	Panel Discussion: Research & Application of Speech & Language Technology for Orange Computing	Panelists: Prof. Chung-Hsien Wu Dr. Chih-Chung Kuo Dr. Bo-Wei Chen Chair: Prof. Jhing-Fa Wang
17:00~18:00	YZU — Banquet place (Hotel Kuva Chateau)	
18:00-20:00	Banquet	

September 22, 2012 (Saturday) 9:30 ~ 16:20		
9:30-10:30	Invited Talk: Deep Learning and A New Wave of Innovations in Speech Technology	Speaker: Dr. Li Deng, Microsoft Research Chair: Prof. Chung-Hsien Wu
10:30-11:00	Coffee Break	
11:00-12:00	Oral Session 3: Speech Processing II	Chair: Prof. Yuan-Fu Liao
12:00-13:00	Lunch	
13:00-14:00	Poster Session	
14:00-15:00	Oral Session 4: NLP Applications	Chair: Prof. Chao-Lin Liu
15:00-15:20	Coffee Break	
15:20-16:00	Oral Session 5: Machine Translation and Information Retrieval	Chair: Prof. Shou-De Lin
16:00-16:20	Closing Ceremony and Best Paper Award	

Proceedings of the Twenty-Fourth Conference on Computational Linguistics and Speech Processing ROCLING XXIV (2012)

TABLE OF CONTENTS

Preface iii

Organization iv

Program Overview vii

Invited Speech I: How Many Multiword Expressions do People Know? xi
Kenneth Church

Invited Speech II: Deep Learning and A New Wave of Innovations in Speech Technology xii
Li Deng

Oral Session 1: Speech Processing I

Improved Histogram Equalization Methods for Robust Speech Recognition 1
Hsin-Ju Hsieh, Jeih-Weih Hung and Berlin Chen

A Voice Conversion Method Mapping Segmented Frames with Linear Multivariate Regression 3
Hung-Yan Gu, Jia-Wei Chang and Zan-Wei Wang

Acoustic Variability in the Speech of Children with Cerebral Palsy 15
Li-Mei Chen, Han-Chih Ni, Tzu-Wen Kuo and Kuei-Ling Hsu

Oral Session 2: Sentiment Analysis and Semantics

Domain Dependent Word Polarity Analysis for Sentiment Classification 30
Ho-Cheng Yu, Ting-Hao Huang and Hsin-Hsi Chen

Attachment of English Prepositional Phrases and Suggestions of English Prepositions 32
Chia-Chi Tsai and Chao-Lin Liu

Associating Collocations with WordNet Senses Using Hybrid Models 47
Yi-Chun Chen, Tzu-Xi Yen and Jason S. Chang

Measuring Individual Differences in Word Recognition: The Role of Individual Lexical Behaviors 61
Hsin-Ni Lin, Shu-Kai Hsieh and Shiao-Hui Chan

Oral Session 3: Speech Processing II

Recurrent Neural Network-based Language Modeling with Extra Information Cues for Speech Recognition 75
Bang-Xuan Huang, Hank Hao, Menphis Chen and Berlin Chen

A Prediction Module for Taiwanese Tone Sandhi Based on the Decision Tree Algorithm 92
Neng-Huang Pan, Ming-Shing Yu and Pei-Chun Tsai

Development of a Taiwanese Speech and Text Corpus 102
Tzu-Yu Liao, Ren-Yuan Lyu, Ming-Tat Ko, Yuang-Chin Chiang and Jyh-Shing Jang

Oral Session 4: NLP Applications

The Design of Chinese Character Learning System Based on Phonetic Components 112
Chia-Hui Chang and Wen-Pen Wu

Automatic Correction for Graphemic Chinese Misspelled Words 125
Tao-Hsing Chang, Shou-Yen Su and Hsueh-Chih Chen

Exploiting Machine Learning Models for Chinese Legal Documents Labeling, Case Classification, and Sentencing Prediction 140
Wan-Chen Lin, Tsung-Ting Kuo, Tung-Jia Chang, Chueh-An Yen, Chao-Ju Chen and Shou-de Lin

Oral Session 5: Machine Translation and Information Retrieval

Detecting and Correcting Syntactic Errors in Machine Translation Using Feature-Based Lexicalized Tree Adjoining Grammars 142
Wei-Yun Ma and Kathleen Mckeown

An Improvement in Cross-Language Document Retrieval Based on Statistical Models 144
Longyue Wang, Derek F. Wong and Lidia S. Chao

Poster Session:

English-to-Traditional Chinese Cross-lingual Link Discovery in Articles with Wikipedia Corpus 156
Liang-Pu Chen, Yu-Lun Shih, Chien-Ting Chen, Tsun Ku, Wen-Tai Hsieh, Hung-Sheng Chiu and Ren-Dar Yang

Skip N-gram Modeling for Near-Synonym Choice 163
Shih-Ting Chen, Wei-Cheng He, Philips Kokoh Prasetyo and Liang-Chih Yu

Metaphor and Metonymy in Apple Daily's Headlines 176
Chih-Lin Chuang

Phonetics of Speech Acts: A Pilot Study 185
Chih-Lin Chuang

Convolutive Blind Source Separation Based on Sparse Component Analysis 192
Hsiang-Lung Chuang, Yu-Shiun Shie, Chang-Hong Lin and Jia-Ching Wang

Disambiguating Main POS tags for Turkish 202
Razieh Ehsani, Muzaffer Ege Alper, Gulsen Eryigit and Esref Adali

Automatic Time Alignment for a Taiwanese Read Speech Corpus and its Application to Constructing Audiobooks with Text-Speech Synchronization ..214
Wei-jay Huang, Jhih-rou Lin, Ren-yuan Lyu, Yuang-chin Chiang, Jyh-Shing Roger Jang and Ming-Tat Ko

Study on Keyword Spotting using Prosodic Attribute Detection for Conversational Speech 231
Yu-Jui Huang, Yin-Wei Chung and Jui-Feng Yeh

Translating Collocation using Monolingual and Parallel Corpus 246
Ming-Zhuan Jiang, Tzu-Xi Yen, Chung-Chi Huang, Mei-Hua Chen and Jason S. Chang

A Possibilistic Approach for Automatic Word Sense Disambiguation 261
Oussama Ben Khiroun, Bilel Elayeb, Ibrahim Bounhas, Fabrice Evrard and Narjès Bellamine Ben Saoud

Applying Association Rules in Solving the Polysemy Problem in a Chinese to Taiwanese TTS System 276
Yih-Jeng Lin, Ming-Shing Yu and Wei-Lun Li

Context-Aware In-Page Search 292
Yu-Hao Lin, Yu-Lan Liu, Tzu-Xi Yen and Jason S. Chang

Implementation of Malayalam Morphological Analyzer Based on Hybrid Approach 307
Vinod P M, Jayan V and Bhadran V K

A Light Weight Stemmer in Kokborok 318
Braja Gopal Patra, Khumbar Debbarma, Swapan Debbarma, Dipankar Das, Amitava Das and Sivaji Bandyopadhyay

Implementation and Comparison of Keyword Spotting for Taiwanese 326
Chung-Che Wang, Che-Hsuan Chou, Liang-Yu Chen, Yu-Jhe Li, Jyh-Shing Jang, Hsun-Cheng Hu, Shih-Peng Lin and You-Lian Huang

Applications of Parallel Corpora for Chinese Segmentation 341
Jui-Ping Wang and Chao-Lin Liu

Concatenation-based Method for the Synthesis of Engine Noise with Continuously Varying Speed 356
Ming-Kuan Wu and Chia-Ping Chen

Collaborative Annotation and Visualization of Functional and Discourse Structures 366
Hengbin Yan and Jonathan Webster

Improving Chinese Textural Entailment by Monolingual Machine Translation Technology 375
Shan-Shun Yang, Shih-Hung Wu, Liang-Pu Chen, Wen-Tai Hsieh and Seng-Cho T. Chou

Invited Speaker: Kenneth Church

How Many Multiword Expressions do People Know?

Abstract

What is a multiword expression (MWE) and how many are there? What is a MWE? What is many? Mark Liberman gave a great invited talk at ACL-89 titled "How many words do pe ople know?" where he spent the entire hour que stioning the question. Many of these same questions apply to multiword expressions. What is a word? What is many? What is a person? What does it mean to know? Rather than answer these questions, this paper will use these questions as Liberman did, as an excuse for surveying how such issues are addressed in a variety of fields: computer science, web search, linguistics, lexicography, educational testing, psychology, statistics, etc.

Biography

Kenneth Church was a researcher at Microsoft Research in Redmond, before moving to Hopkins, and before that he was the head of a data mining department in AT&T Labs-Research (formally AT&T Bell Labs). Prof. Kenneth Church received BS, Masters and PhD from MIT in computer science in 1978, 1980 and 1983, respectively. He enjoys working with very large corpora such as the Associated Press newswire (1 million words per week) and larger datasets such as telephone call detail (1-10 billion records per month). He has worked on many topics in computational linguistics including: web search, language modeling, text analysis, spelling correction, word-sense disambiguation, terminology, translation, lexicography, compression, speech (recognition and synthesis), OCR, as well as applications that go well beyond computational linguistics such as revenue assurance and virtual integration (using screen scraping and web crawling to integrate systems that traditionally don't talk together as well as they could such as billing and customer care).

Invited Speaker: Li Deng

Deep Learning and A New Wave of Innovations in Speech Technology

Abstract

Semantic information embedded in the speech signal manifests itself in a dynamic process rooted in the deep linguistic hierarchy as an intrinsic part of the human cognitive system. Modeling both the dynamic process and the deep structure for advancing speech technology has been an active pursuit for over more than 20 years, but it is not until recently that noticeable breakthrough has been achieved by the new methodology commonly referred to as "deep learning". Deep Belief Net (DBN) and the related deep neural nets are recently being used to replace the Gaussian Mixture Model component in the HMM-based speech recognition, and has produced dramatic error rate reduction in both phone recognition and large vocabulary speech recognition while keeping the HMM component intact. On the other hand, the (constrained) Dynamic Bayesian Net has been developed for many years to improve the dynamic models of speech while overcoming the IID assumption as a key weakness of the HMM, with a set of techniques and representations commonly known as hidden dynamic/trajectory models or articulatory-like models. A history of these two largely separate lines of research will be critically reviewed and analyzed in the context of modeling the deep and dynamic linguistic hierarchy for advancing speech recognition technology. Future directions will be discussed for the exciting area of deep and dynamic learning research that holds promise to build a foundation for the next-generation speech technology with human-like cognitive ability.

Biography

Li Deng received the Ph.D. from Univ. Wisconsin-Madison. He was an Assistant (1989-1992), Associate (1992-1996), and Full Professor (1996-1999) at the University of Waterloo, Ontario, Canada. He then joined Microsoft Research, Redmond, where he is currently a Principal Researcher and where he received Microsoft Research Technology Transfer, Goldstar, and Achievement Awards. Prior to MSR, he also worked or taught at Massachusetts Institute of Technology, ATR Interpreting Telecom. Research Lab. (Kyoto, Japan), and HKUST. He has published over 300 refereed papers in leading journals/conferences and 3 books covering broad areas of human language technology, machine learning, and audio, speech, and signal processing. He is a Fellow of the Acoustical Society of America, a Fellow of the IEEE, and a Fellow of the International Speech Communication Association. He is an inventor or co-inventor of over 50 granted patents. He served on the Board of Governors of the IEEE Signal Processing Society (2008-2010). More recently, he served as Editor-in-Chief for IEEE Signal Processing Magazine (2009-2011), for which he received the 2011 IEEE SPS Meritorious Service Award. He currently serves as Editor-in-Chief for IEEE Transactions on Audio, Speech and Language Processing.

改良式統計圖等化法於強健性語音辨識之研究

Improved Histogram Equalization Methods for Robust Speech Recognition

謝欣汝 Hsin-Ju Hsieh[1,2], 洪志偉 Jeih-weih Hung[2], 陳柏琳 Berlin Chen[1]
[1] 國立臺灣師範大學資訊工程學系
[2] 國立暨南國際大學電機工程學系
hsinju@ntnu.edu.tw, berlin@ntnu.edu.tw, jwhung@ncnu.edu.tw

摘要

統計圖等化法(Histogram Equalization, HEQ)[1]是一種概念簡單且有效的語音特徵處理技術，近年來被廣泛地研究與應用於強健性語音辨識的領域。在本論文中，我們延續統計圖等化法的研究，提出一系列使用語音特徵的空間－時間之文脈統計資訊(Spatial-Temporal Contextual Statistics)的語音特徵強健方法，這些方法主要的架構是利用一個簡易的差分(Differencing)和平均(Averaging)的處理方式，對語音之倒頻譜特徵的空間域與時間域加以分割，以擷取出語音特徵在空間域與時間域上不同頻率成分之統計資訊後，將其分別作統計正規化處理並結合，來達到降低雜訊對語音特徵所造成的影響。其所用的差分和平均的公式如下所示:

$$x_{s-diff}(d,t)=\begin{cases}\dfrac{x(d,t)-x(d-1,t)}{2}, & 2\le d\le D\\ x(d,t), \quad d=1 & \end{cases}$$

$$x_{s-avg}(d,t)=\begin{cases}\dfrac{x(d,t)+x(d-1,t)}{2}, & 2\le d\le D\\ 0, \quad d=1 & \end{cases}$$

其中 $x_{s-diff}(d,t)$ 與 $x_{s-avg}(d,t)$ 分別表示從原始語音特徵之空間域上所擷取出的高頻和低頻的統計資訊。同樣地，將此處理方式作用於同一維度之任意兩個相鄰的音框，亦可得到原始語音特徵在時間域上之高頻 $x_{t-diff}(d,t)$ 和低頻 $x_{t-avg}(d,t)$ 的文脈統計資訊。此外，本論文另外提出一個變型的方法，將空間域和時間域上所求得的高頻特徵 $x_{diff}(d,t)$ 及低頻特徵 $x_{avg}(d,t)$ 以線性加權的方式結合，來觀察辨識率是否有進一步提升的空間。

有別於傳統運用於語音特徵時間序列上之各別維度獨立正規化(Dimension-Wise)的方法例如:倒頻譜平均值消去法(Cepstral Mean Subtraction, CMS)[2]、倒頻譜平均值與變異數正規化法(Cepstral Mean and Variance Normalization, CMVN)[3]等，本論文所提出的一系列新方法能進一步地正規化不同空間與時間之間的特徵分布資訊，能更有效的降低不同聲學環境所產生的偏差並且嘗試消除傳統之統計圖等化法無法補償的問題，亦即隨機性雜訊對語音所產生的影響。值得注意的是，對於語音特徵之時間域或空間域上的正規化處理方式，過去已有學者提出概念類似的語音特徵之單一域的正規化處理技術[4-5]，而本論文所提出之結合式統計圖等化法使用語音特徵的空間－時間之文脈統計資訊的技術，於目前為止則是相對較少被研究與探討的議題。

本論文的辨識實驗是作用於國際通用的語音語料庫 Aurora-2[6]上，我們驗證了所提出之新方法能夠大幅提升各種雜訊環境下之語音辨識的精確度。其辨識效能都明顯高於許多傳統作用於語音特徵之時間序列上的正規化處理技術與只單獨正規化語音特徵之時間域或空間域的結果。此外以線性加權空間域與時間域上所求得的高頻特徵 $x_{diff}(d,t)$ 及低頻特徵 $x_{avg}(d,t)$ 的組合方式，使得辨識率從原始未加權的 83.33%進步至 85.05%，其絕對錯誤降低率為 1.72%。最終進一步地結合進階式前端標準(Advanced Front-End Standard, AFE)[7]強健性語音特徵，足足能使辨識率從原始的 87.17%提升至 88.22%，相對錯誤降低率約有 8%，足見這些新方法能有效提升語音特徵的強健性。

關鍵詞：自動語音辨識，雜訊強健性，統計圖等化法，特徵文脈的統計

Keywords: automatic speech recognition, noise robustness, histogram equalization, feature contextual statistics.

致謝：本論文之研究承蒙教育部－國立台灣師範大學邁向頂尖大學計畫（101J1A0900 和 101J1A0901）與行政院國家科學委員會研究計畫(NSC 101-2221-E-003 -024 -MY3 和 NSC 99 -2221-E-003 -017 -MY3)之經費支持，謹此致謝。

參考文獻

[1] Angel de la Torre, Antonio M. Peinado, Jose C. Segura, Jose L. Perez-Cordoba, Ma Carmen Benitez and Antonio J. Rubio, “Histogram equalization of speech representation for robust speech recognition”, IEEE Transactions on Speech and Audio Processing, Vol. 13, No. 3, pp. 355-366, 2005.

[2] S. Furui, “Cepstral analysis technique for automatic speaker verification”, IEEE Transactions on Acoustics, Speech and Signal Processing, Vol. 29, No. 2, pp. 254-272, 1981.

[3] O. Viikki and K. Laurila, “Cepstral domain segmental feature vector normalization for noise robust speech recognition”, Speech Communication, Vol. 25, No. 1-3, pp. 133-147, 1998.

[4] J. W. Hung and H. T. Fan, “Subband feature statistics normalization techniques based on a discrete wavelet transform for robust speech recognition”, Signal Processing Letters, IEEE, Vol. 16, No. 9, 2009.

[5] V. Joshi, R. Bilgi, S. Umesh, L. Garcia and C. Benitez, “Sub-band level histogram equalization for robust speech recognition”, 12th Annual Conference of the International Speech Communication Association (Interspeech), 2011.

[6] H-G. Hirsch and D. Pearce, “The Aurora experimental framework for the performance evaluation of speech recognition systems under noisy conditions”, Automatic Speech Recognition: Challenges for the Next Millennium, pp. 181-188, 2000.

[7] D. Macho, L. Mauuary, B. Noé, Y. M. Cheng, D. Ealey, D. Jouvet, H. Kelleher, D. Pearce and F. Saadoun, “Evaluation of a noise-robust DSR front-end on Aurora databases”, 3th Annual Conference of the International Speech Communication Association (Interspeech), 2002.

以線性多變量迴歸來對映分段後音框之語音轉換方法
A Voice Conversion Method Mapping Segmented Frames with Linear Multivariate Regression

古鴻炎 Hung-Yan Gu　　張家維 Jia-Wei Chang　　王讚緯 Zan-Wei Wang

國立臺灣科技大學 資訊工程系
Department of Computer Science and Information Engineering
National Taiwan University of Science and Technology
e-mail: {guhy, m9815064, m10015078}@mail.ntust.edu.tw

摘要

基於 GMM 對映之語音轉換方法常遇到的一個問題是，轉換出的頻譜包絡會發生過於平滑(over smoothing)的現象，因此本論文嘗試以線性多變量迴歸(linear multivariate regression, LMR)來建構另一種頻譜對映的方法，希望能夠改進頻譜過平滑的問題。首先，我們推導了 LMR 對映矩陣的解析求解公式，然後我們錄製平行語料，採用離散倒頻譜係數作為頻譜特徵，分割語音信號成聲、韻母之音段，再使用 LMR 對映方法來建造出一個語音轉換系統。應用此系統，我們就可進行內部、外部之平均轉換誤差的量測，並且和傳統 GMM 對映法所量測出的誤差距離作比較，量測的結果顯示，本論文研究的 LMR_F 對映法，不論是在內部或外部之測試情況，都可以獲得比傳統 GMM 對映法較小的平均轉換誤差。此外，我們也進行了主觀的語音品質聽測之實驗，聽測實驗的結果顯示，我們研究的 LMR_F 對映法，其轉換出的語音品值，能夠比傳統 GMM 對映法的稍好一些。

關鍵詞：語音轉換，線性多變量迴歸，高斯混合模型，離散倒頻譜係數

一、緒論

語音轉換(voice conversion)研究的目標是，要把一個來源語者(source speaker)的語音轉換成另一個目標語者(target speaker)的語音。這種語音轉換的處理，可應用於銜接語音合成處理，以獲得多樣性的合成語音音色，此外亦可應用於作戲劇配音的處理，以讓一個配音員可以為多個角色配音。過去在語音轉換領域，先前研究者提出的轉換方法包括了: 頻譜特徵之向量量化(VQ)對映(mapping)[1]，共振峰(formant)頻率對映[2, 3]，基於高斯混合模型(Gaussian mixture model, GMM)之對映[4, 5]，基於類神經網路(artificial neural network, ANN)之對映[6]，基於隱藏式馬可夫模型(hidden Markov model, HMM)之對映[7, 8]等。

最近幾年有不少研究者採取基於 GMM 對映之方向來作語音轉換，並且嘗試去解決

原始 GMM 對映方式[4]所碰到的問題，例如轉換出的頻譜包絡(spectral envelope)會出現過於平滑(over smoothing)的現象，一個例子如圖一所示，虛線曲線代表目標語者一個音框的頻譜包絡，實線曲線則代表由來源語者音框轉換出的頻譜包絡，明顯可看出虛線曲線的 F2、F4、F6 等共振峰(formant)的頻寬變寬了很多，也就是山鋒至山谷的深度減少了，這種過於平滑的頻譜包絡，將使得據以合成出的語音信號，發生語音品質衰退的情況，也就是語音聽起來，會讓人覺得悶悶的、不夠清晰。

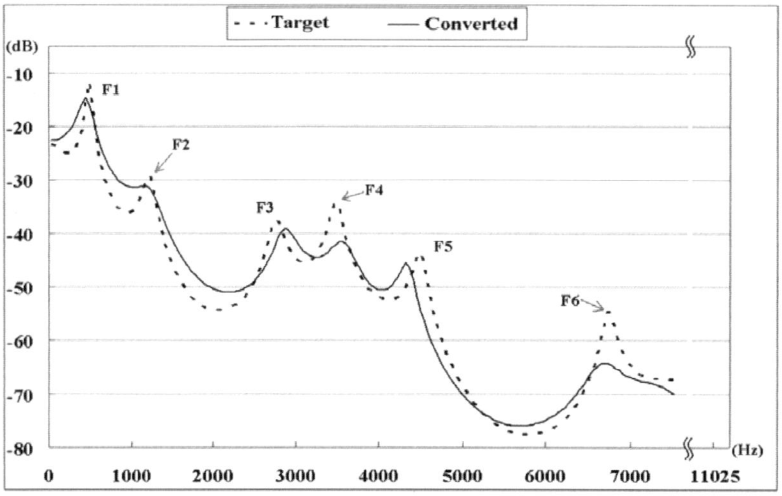

圖一、過於平滑之轉換出的頻譜包絡

為了避免發生頻譜過於平滑的情況，而造成音質的衰退，在此論文裡我們遂決定採取以最小均方(least mean square, LMS)誤差為準則，去研究線性多變量迴歸(linear multivariate regression, LMR)方式的頻譜對映方法，希望用以提升轉換出語音的音質。線性多變量迴歸對映(簡稱為 LMR 對映)的觀念是，在訓練階段使用平行語料，以訓練出一個 $d \times d$ 的線性對映矩陣 M， d 表示一個音框頻譜特徵係數的維度，然後在轉換階段，就可將來源語者第 k 個音框的頻譜特徵向量 S_k (維度為 $d \times 1$)，作 LMR 對映而得到轉換出的頻譜特徵向量 V_k，即令 $V_k = M \cdot S_k$。雖然 Valbret 等人已於 1992 年提出使用 LMR 對映來作頻譜轉換的想法[9]，但是他們對於前述矩陣 M 的數值的求解，只提出了一個逼近的作法，因此在本論文裡，我們遂去研究、推導矩陣 M 的解析(analytic)求解公式，詳細情形在第二節裡說明。

另外，我們由前人的研究得知[5, 10]，所採取的頻譜對映機制，如果不先依據語音內容(如音素或音節)來建立分段式(segmental)的對映模型，則容易發生一對多(one to many)對映的問題[10]，而造成某些相鄰的音框之間，相鄰音框所轉換出的頻譜卻出現劇烈的頻譜形狀差異(即頻譜不連續)，以致於怪音(artifact sound)被合成出來。為了減少發生怪音的機會，因此我們決定以聲、韻母為單位，對訓練用的語音作音段切割，並且各音段(segment)裡的語音音框就交由所屬之聲、韻母去收集，然後使用各個聲、韻母所收集到的音框，去分別訓練出專屬的 LMR 對映矩陣。至於在轉換階段，一個輸入的語音音框如何知道它是屬於那一個聲、韻母的？這樣的問題是一種語音辨識的問題，不過它不需要像語音辨識那樣嚴厲地被對待，因為選取到錯誤但近似的聲、韻母是可以容忍的。過去，我們研究分段式 GMM 對映之語音轉換方法[5]，曾提出一種自動挑選音段 GMM 的演算法，該演算法也可以搬過來使用。

關於頻譜係數的選擇，我們仍然採取先前研究過的離散倒頻譜係數(discrete

cepstrum coefficients, DCC)[11, 12]，階數設為 40 階，即一個音框要計算出 $c_0, c_1, c_2, \ldots, c_{40}$ 等 41 個係數，但是只拿 $c_1, c_2, \ldots, c_{40}$ 去作頻譜轉換的處理，所以維度 d 的值是 40。當轉換出各個音框的 DCC 係數之後，我們就可依據各音框的 DCC 係數去計算出頻譜包絡[11, 12]，然後再依據頻譜包絡、轉換出的基頻值，去設定該音框的諧波加雜音模型(harmonic plus noise model, HNM)之諧波參數和雜音參數[12, 13]，之後就可拿這些參數去合成出語音信號 [12, 13]。

二、LMR 對映矩陣

在訓練階段，把平行訓練語料各音框算出 DCC 係數之後，再經由動態時間校正(DTW)，就可得知一個來源語者音框(來源音框)所對應的目標語者音框(目標音框)。在此令某一個聲、韻母類別所收集到的 N 個來源音框是: $S_1, S_2, \cdots, S_N$，而其對應的 N 個目標音框是: $T_1, T_2, \cdots, T_N$，也就是 d×1 大小之 DCC 向量 T_k 經由 DTW 被匹配到 DCC 向量 S_k。為了方便推導，我們在此令矩陣 $S = [S_1, S_2, \cdots, S_N]$，而矩陣 $T = [T_1, T_2, \cdots, T_N]$，很明顯地矩陣 S 和 T 的大小都是 $d \times N$。理想上，我們希望找出一個大小為 $d \times d$ 的 LMR 對映矩陣 M，來讓如下的關係式獲得成立，

$$M \bullet S = T \quad . \tag{1}$$

實際上，由於 N 的值通常都比 d 大很多，所以不會存在理想的 M 矩陣，也就是會出現對映的誤差，在此令 E 表示大小為 $d \times N$ 之誤差矩陣，其定義是

$$E = M \bullet S - T . \tag{2}$$

若要找出最佳的對映矩陣 M，就相當於要把矩陣 E 的所有元素的絕對值都加以最小化。由於矩陣 E 有 $d \times N$ 個元素，而矩陣 M 只有 $d \times d$ 個元素，所以我們採取 LMS 準則，先去計算誤差平方和矩陣 $\boldsymbol{\mathcal{E}}$ ，其定義是:

$$\boldsymbol{\mathcal{E}} = E \cdot E^{\mathrm{t}} = (M \cdot S - T)(M \cdot S - T)^{\mathrm{t}}, \quad \text{t: transpose.} \tag{3}$$

然後拿 $\boldsymbol{\mathcal{E}}$ 的跡數(trace)，即 $\mathrm{tr}(\boldsymbol{\mathcal{E}}) = \boldsymbol{\mathcal{E}}_{1,1} + \boldsymbol{\mathcal{E}}_{2,2} + \ldots + \boldsymbol{\mathcal{E}}_{d,d}$ ，去對 M 作偏微分，並且令偏微分的結果為 0 矩陣 [11, 12]，公式如下，

$$\frac{\partial\left(\mathrm{tr}(\boldsymbol{\mathcal{E}})\right)}{\partial M} = 2(M \cdot S - T) \cdot S^{\mathrm{t}} = 0 \quad , \tag{4}$$

上式中矩陣形式之 $\partial\left(\mathrm{tr}(\boldsymbol{\mathcal{E}})\right) / \partial M$ 其實是表示 $\partial\left(\mathrm{tr}(\boldsymbol{\mathcal{E}})\right) / \partial M_{i,j}$ ，j=1, 2, …, d，i=1, 2, …, d，也就是分別拿 M 矩陣第 i 列第 j 行的元素 $M_{i,j}$ 去對 $\mathrm{tr}(\boldsymbol{\mathcal{E}})$ 作偏微分。公式(4)經過移項整理後，就可解出 M 的數值，公式如下，

$$M \cdot S \cdot S^{\mathrm{t}} = T \cdot S^{\mathrm{t}} , \tag{5}$$

$$M = T \cdot S^{\mathrm{t}} \cdot (S \cdot S^{\mathrm{t}})^{-1} \quad . \tag{6}$$

現在，我們已可使用公式(6)來找出 LMS 準則下局部最佳的 M 矩陣，說它僅是局部最佳，其原因可以圖二(a)所示的單變量線性迴歸的例子來說明，也就是如公式(1)的 M

矩陣的定義，相當於是在單變量線性迴歸情況下，限定迴歸之直線必須通過原點，因此迴歸所導入的誤差，會比圖二(b)情況或圖二(c)情況的都大。若要作改善，第一種作法是，設法把圖二(a)的情況轉變成圖二(b)的情況，如此公式(6)則仍然可繼續使用，作轉變的實際方法是，先計算出來源音框 $S_1, S_2, \cdots, S_N$ 的平均向量 S^m，再以 $S_k - S^m$ 取代原先的 S_k，同樣地對於目標音框 $T_1, T_2, \cdots, T_N$，也要去計算平均向量 T^m，然後作類似的取代。採用此種作法時，平均向量 S^m 與 T^m 必須儲存下來，如此在轉換階段才可拿出來使用。

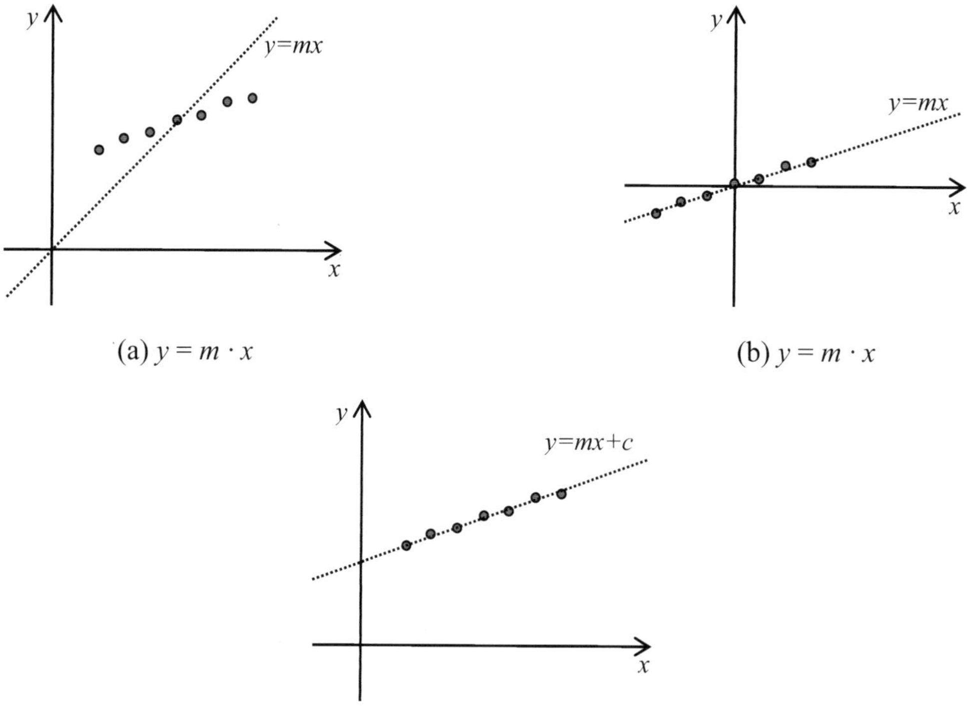

(a) $y = m \cdot x$　　(b) $y = m \cdot x$

(c) $y = m \cdot x + c$

圖二、單變量線性迴歸例子

在本論文裡，我們不希望另外作儲存平均向量的動作，因此研究了把圖二(a)情況轉變成圖二(c)情況的作法，也就是要導入常數項。我們想到的一個作法是，先依照下列公式把原先公式(1)裡的矩陣 M、S、T 的定義作擴充，

$$\tilde{M} = \begin{bmatrix} & & M_{1,d+1} \\ & M & M_{2,d+1} \\ & & \vdots \\ & & M_{d,d+1} \\ 0, 0, \ldots, 0, & & 1 \end{bmatrix}, \qquad \tilde{S} = \begin{bmatrix} S_1 & S_2 & \ldots & S_N \\ 1, & 1, & \ldots & 1 \end{bmatrix}, \quad \tilde{T} = \begin{bmatrix} T_1 & T_2 & \ldots & T_N \\ 1, & 1, & \ldots & 1 \end{bmatrix}, \tag{7}$$

第一步把 M 矩陣擴充成大小為$(d+1)\times(d+1)$之 $\tilde{M}$ 矩陣，亦即在原先的 M 矩陣裡加入第$(d+1)$列和第$(d+1)$行，而新增的元素如公式(7)所示；然後在 S 矩陣內加入第$(d+1)$列，並且把該列的元素值全設為常數 1，因此擴充後的 $\tilde{S}$ 矩陣大小為$(d+1)\times N$；接著以類似的擴充方式也把 T 矩陣擴充成 $\tilde{T}$ 矩陣。之後，就可以把擴充後的 $\tilde{M}$、$\tilde{S}$、$\tilde{T}$ 矩陣代入公

式(6)，去求取 $\tilde{M}$ 矩陣的數值。如此，當應用求得的 $\tilde{M}$ 矩陣於公式(1)時，就可以讓線性迴歸所導入的誤差減小。

三、系統製作 -- 訓練階段

我們製作的語音轉換系統，在訓練階段主要的處理步驟如圖三所示。首先我們邀請了二位男性和二位女性錄音者，其中二位男性，在此以 M_1 和 M_2 作代號，而另二位女性，則以 F_1 和 F_2 作代號。我們請四位錄音者分別到隔音錄音室去錄製 375 句(共 2,926 個音節)之國語平行語料，取樣率設成 22,050Hz。在本論文裡，我們實驗了四種語者配對方式，分別是(a)M_1 至 M_2、(b)M_1 至 F_1、(c)F_1 至 M_1、(d)F_1 至 F_2，這四種配對方式裡，前者就當來源語者，而後者則當目標語者。

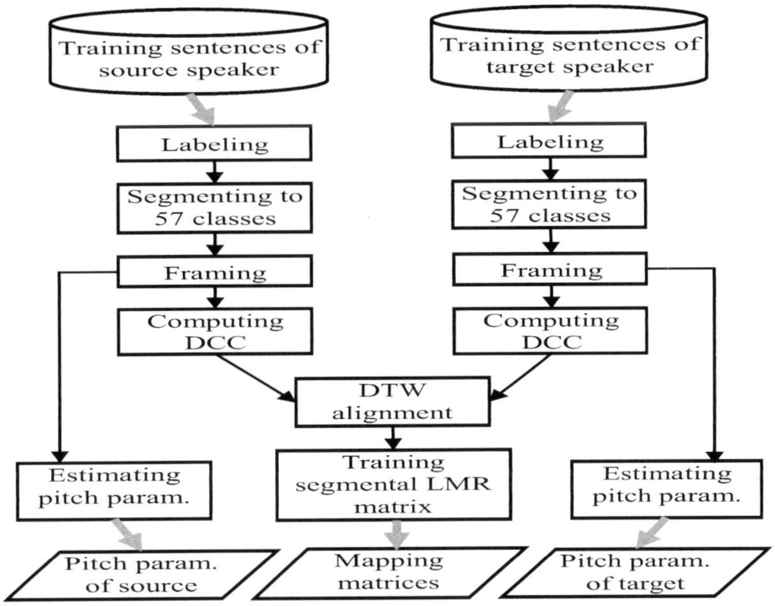

圖三、訓練階段之主要處理步驟

3.1 標音與切割音段

對於各個語者所錄的訓練語句(即前 350 句之平行語句)，我們先操作 HTK (HMM tool kit) 軟體，經由強制對齊(forced alignment)來作自動標音，把一個語句的各個聲母、韻母的邊界標示出來。由於自動標記的聲、韻母邊界有許多是錯誤的，因此我們再操作 WaveSurfer 軟體，以人工檢查自動標記的邊界是否有錯，有錯則加以更正。

接著，依據各個聲、韻母的拼音符號標記和邊界位置，就可作音段切割和分類的動作。對於各個訓練語句，依據其所屬的標記檔案，一一讀出各個音段(即聲、韻母)的資訊，就可依拼音符號將該音段作分類，我們一共分成 57 類(21 類聲母和 36 類韻母)，分類後再將該音段所在的語句編號、時間邊界資料寫出至分類記錄檔案。

3.2 DCC 係數計算

在本論文裡，我們採用離散倒頻譜之頻譜包絡估計方法[11, 12]，並且以 DCC 係數作為頻譜參數。對於一個語音音框，我們使用先前發展的 DCC 估計程式[12]來計算出 41 維的 DCC 係數。在此一個音框的長度設為 512 個樣本點(23.2ms)，而音框位移則設為 128 個樣本點(5.8ms)。

3.3 DTW 匹配和 LMR 矩陣計算

由於平行語料已經過音段切割和分類，所以在此就逐一對各個聲、韻母類別所收集的平行發音音段作 DTW 匹配，再依匹配出的音框對應序列去計算各類別的 LMR 對映矩陣。由於來源語者和目標語者的發音速度會有差異，因此對於兩人發音同一個句子所取出的平行音段(如/a/)，必需先作 DTW 匹配，以便為來源語者音段所切出的各個音框 S_k，去目標語者之平行音段內找出正確的音框來對應。如此，經由平行音段之間作 DTW 匹配，就可建立兩語者的平行音段內的音框對應關係(S_k, $T_{w(k)}$)，k=1, 2, ⋯, K_n，K_n 表示第 n 個平行音段之來源語者發音的音框數量。接著，把各個平行音段的音框對應關係作串接，就可求得一個聲、韻母類別的一序列的來源音框和目標音框的對應組合。

關於 LMR 矩陣的求取，在此也是逐一對各個聲、韻母類別去計算，先把各類別求得的一序列的來源音框和目標音框的對應組合，拿去建造如公式(1)裡的 S 和 T 矩陣，然後代入公式(6)以計算出基本型 LMR 對映所需的 M 矩陣。此外，我們也依據公式(7)，把矩陣 S 和 T 擴充成 $\tilde{S}$ 和 $\tilde{T}$，再代入公式(6)，以算出完整型 LMR 對映所需的 $\tilde{M}$ 矩陣。

3.4 音高參數

我們先計算零交越率(ZCR)，以把 ZCR 很高的無聲(unvoiced)音框偵測出來；再使用一種基於自相關函數及 AMDF (absolute magnitude difference function)的基週偵測方法[14]，來偵測剩餘音框的音高頻率。之後，把一個語者發音中有聲(voiced)音框偵測出的音高頻率值收集起來，據以算出該語者音高的平均值及標準差，而平均值及標準差就是本論文所使用的音高參數。

四、系統製作 -- 轉換階段

我們製作的語音轉換系統，在轉換階段的主要處理流程如圖四所示。當一句測試語句輸入後，它首先會被切割成一序列的音框，至於音框長度和位移則和 2.2 節裡使用的一樣，分別是 512 點和 128 點。然後，在圖四的左邊流程，系統會去偵測各音框的音高頻率，如果一個音框被偵測為無聲時，圖四中的三個灰色方塊就被直接跳過，也就是不作音高頻率的調整，且 DCC 頻譜參數也不會被轉換。相對地如果一個音框被偵測為有聲時，系統就會使用如下的音高調整公式，

$$q_t = \mu^{(y)} + \frac{\sigma^{(y)}}{\sigma^{(x)}}(p_t - \mu^{(x)}) \tag{8}$$

來調整音高頻率，其中 p_t 表示偵測出的音高頻率值，$\mu^{(x)}$和 $\sigma^{(x)}$分別表示來源語者音高頻率的平均值和標準查，而 $\mu^{(y)}$和 $\sigma^{(y)}$則是目標語者的。

4.1 聲、韻母音段辨識

當進行實驗以比較不同型式的 LMR 對映矩陣時，重點是放在 LMR 矩陣本身，所以我

們跳過此步驟(聲韻母音段辨識)的處理，而直接依據各語句所屬的標記檔案，來讀出各音段的拼音標記和時間邊界資料。

如果要處理一個線上即時輸入的語句，那麼”聲韻母音段辨識”步驟就必須實際地執行，關於這個步驟的製作，目前我們是透過呼叫 HTK 所提供的辨識命令來達成。不過，在能夠呼叫 HTK 的辨識命令之前，要先操作 HTK 的 HMM 訓練命令，以便拿 350 句來源語者的訓練語句去訓練出各個聲、韻母的 HMM 模型。

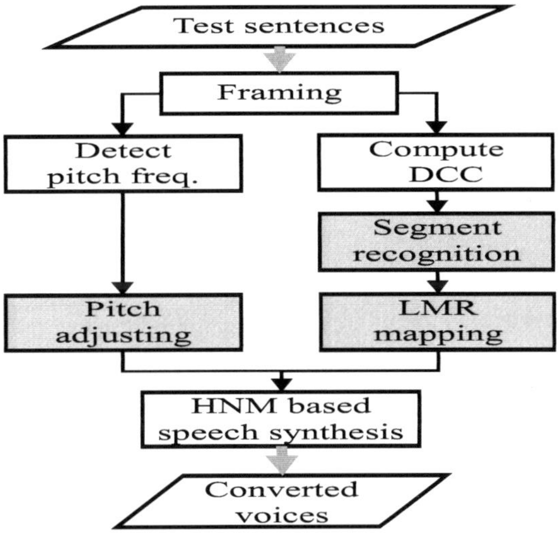

圖四、轉換階段之主要處理步驟

4.2 基於 HNM 之語音信號合成

在諧波加雜音模型(HNM)中，一個有聲音框的頻譜被分割成低頻的諧波部分和高頻的雜音部分，而分割這兩部分的邊界頻率稱為最大有聲頻率(maximum voiced frequency，MVF)[13]。為了簡化語音信號合成處理的程序，在此我們把各個有聲音框的 MVF 值都直接設為 6,000Hz。

使用 HNM 來對轉換出的頻譜包絡作語音信號合成，觀念上是分別去合成出諧波部分的信號，及合成出雜音部分的信號，然後把兩部分的信號加總，即是所合成的語音信號。由於我們在先前發表的論文裡[5, 12]都已說明 HNM 語音信號合成方法的細節，所以在本論文裡就不再重複敘述。

五、測試實驗

在第二節中我們說明了兩種 LMR 對映的作法，第一種作法是，採取如公式(1)定義的 M 矩陣來作為對映的矩陣，這種作法稱為基本型 LMR 對映，在此以 **LMR_B** 表示；至於第二種作法是，採取如公式(7)定義的 $\tilde{M}$ 矩陣來作為對映的矩陣，這種作法稱為完整型 LMR 對映，在此以 **LMR_F** 表示。

此外，我們也研究了一種把向量量化和 LMR 對映作結合的作法，稱為 **LMR_FC**，該作法的細節是，訓練階段時，在圖三中的”DTW alignment”和”Train LMR matrix”兩方塊之間，增加一個”VQ clustering”方塊，先對一個聲韻母類別所收集到的 DCC 接合向量(joint vector, 維度 80)作 K-means 分群的處理，以分成 L 群的 DCC 接合向量，並且記錄 L 群向量的中心向量，之後對各群的 DCC 向量分別去訓練出一個對應的 LMR 對映矩陣 $\tilde{M}$ ，在此我們只將群數 L 設為 4，因為設太多群時，有一些聲韻母會發生音框數過少的情況。

接著在轉換階段時，圖四中的”LMR mapping”方塊之前就必須增加一個”Select mapping matrix”方塊，以從 L 個對映矩陣中挑選出一個，我們採取的挑選方法是，將輸入音框的 DCC 向量(維度 40)和訓練階段記錄下來的 L 個中心向量的前 40 維，逐一量測幾何距離，然後把距離最小的那個中心向量所對應的對映矩陣，選取出來再用以作 LMR 對映。

5.1 誤差距離量測

由於 375 句平行語句中，只有前 350 句拿去訓練 LMR 對映矩陣，因此對於轉換出的 DCC 向量和目標 DCC 向量之間的誤差距離，我們分成內部測試(使用前 350 句)和外部測試(使用後 25 句、共 209 個音節)兩種情況分別去量測。設 $R = R_1, R_2, \cdots, R_N$ 為一序列被轉換出的 DCC 向量，而 $T = T_1, T_2, \cdots, T_N$ 為 R 所對應的目標 DCC 向量序列，在此我們以如下公式,

$$D_{avg} = \frac{1}{N} \sum_{1 \le k \le N} dist(R_k, T_k)\,, \tag{9}$$

去量測轉換誤差之平均距離，公式(9)中 $dist(\,)$表示幾何距離之量測函數。

對於前述三種對映方法，我們分別在內部測試與外部測試兩種情況下，去量測四組語者配對各自的平均轉換誤差距離，然後再取四組語者配對之平均轉換誤差的平均值，結果得到如表一所列的數值。從表一前二欄的數值可知，完整型的 LMR 對映方法(LMR_F)比起基本型的對映方法(LMR_B)，不論在內部測試或外部測試皆可讓轉換誤差減小(分別是 1.6%和 1.7%)，這樣的改進和我們預期的一致；不過，比較表一後二欄的數值，我們發現內部測試和外部測試出現不一致的情況，結合 VQ 和 LMR 對映的方法(LMR_FC)，在內部測試時獲得了非常顯著的改進，平均轉換誤差由 0.4956 降低至 0.4672，即改進 5.7%，然而在外部測試時，平均轉換誤差卻由 0.5382 變大成 0.5493，即變差了 2.1%。另一個觀點是，我們覺得 LMR_FC 法之內部測試的平均誤差值 0.4672 有一個含意，它表示將來我們有機會把外部測試的平均誤差再加以改進至 0.5 以下；相對來說，LMR_B 法之內部測試的平均誤差值 0.5038 已經很大，應不可能直接用 LMR_B 法去把外部測試的平均誤差值改進至 0.5 以下。

另外，為了和 GMM 為基礎的對映方法作比較，在此我們也使用相同的語者配對語料和相同維度的 DCC 頻譜係數，去訓練出傳統 GMM 對映模型[4]的參數，以及音段式 GMM 對映模型(Segmental GMM) [5]的參數，其中傳統 GMM 對映模型使用 128 個高斯分佈，而每一種音段的音段式 GMM 模型則使用 8 個高斯分佈。然後，在內部測試與外部測試兩種情況下，我們分別去量測四組語者配對各自的 GMM 對映模型的平均轉換誤差距離，然後再取四組語者配對之平均轉換誤差的平均值，結果得到如表二所列的數值，雖然從表二的轉換誤差平均值可發現，音段式 GMM 對映模型的轉換誤差，不論在內部或外部測試情況，都會比傳統 GMM 對映模型的小，但是，本論文研究的完整型

LMR 對映法(LMR_F)，則更進一步地讓轉換誤差平均值減小了，比較表一 LMR_F 法的誤差值和表二列出的誤差值，可知 LMR_F 法在內部測試情況，能夠將轉換誤差改進 7.1%(比傳統 GMM 法)、和 4.5%(比音段式 GMM 法)，而在外部測試情況，則能夠將轉換誤差改進 1.5%、和 0.7%。因此，對於分段後的語音音框，LMR 為基礎的對映方法，確實可用於改進語音轉換的誤差。

表一、三種 LMR 對映方法之平均轉換誤差

平均轉換誤差		LMR_B	LMR_F	LMR_FC
內部測試	M_1=> M_2	0.4890	0.4794	0.4475
	M_1=> F_1	0.4782	0.4705	0.4451
	F_1 => M_1	0.4967	0.4881	0.4612
	F_1 => F_2	0.5514	0.5443	0.5149
	平均	**0.5038**	**0.4956**	**0.4672**
外部測試	M_1=> M_2	0.5467	0.5331	0.5398
	M_1=> F_1	0.5174	0.5106	0.5188
	F_1 => M_1	0.5388	0.5307	0.5413
	F_1 => F_2	0.5867	0.5782	0.5973
	平均	**0.5474**	**0.5382**	**0.5493**

表二、兩種 GMM 對映模型之平均轉換誤差

平均轉換誤差		GMM (128 mix.)	Segmental GMM (8 mix.)
內部測試	M_1=> M_2	0.5058	0.5096
	M_1=> F_1	0.5012	0.4910
	F_1 => M_1	0.5412	0.5095
	F_1 => F_2	0.5853	0.5673
	平均	**0.5334**	**0.5194**
外部測試	M_1=> M_2	0.5346	0.5403
	M_1=> F_1	0.5147	0.5146
	F_1 => M_1	0.5551	0.5361
	F_1 => F_2	0.5806	0.5766
	平均	**0.5463**	**0.5419**

5.2 語音品質聽測

我們使用未參加模型訓練的來源語者語句，來準備 6 個作語音品質聽測的音檔，它們的代號分別是 X1、X2、Y1、Y2、Z1、Z2，在此 X1 與 X2 表示使用傳統 GMM 對映模型[4]所轉換出的音檔，Y1 與 Y2 表示使用 LMR_F 對映方法所轉換出的音檔，而 Z1 與 Z2 表示使用 LMR_FC 對映方法所轉換出的音檔；此外，代號 X1、Y1、Z1 中的 1 表示使用 M_1 至 M_2 之語者配對的語料去訓練模型參數，而代號 X2、Y2、Z2 中的 2 表示使用 M_1 至 F_1 之語者配對的語料去訓練模型參數。這 6 個音檔可從如下網頁去下載試聽: http://guhy.csie.ntust.edu.tw/VCLMR/LMR.html。

使用這 6 個音檔，我們編排成四次的聽測實驗，第一次實驗裡，隨機指派 X1、Y1 成為 A 與 B 音檔，然後依序播放 A、B 音檔給受測者聽，再要求受測者給一個評分，以顯示 B 音檔的語音品質比起 A 音檔的是好或壞；第二次實驗裡，隨機指派 Y1、Z1 成為 A 與 B 音檔，然後播放給受測者聽；第三次實驗裡，隨機指派 X2、Y2 成為 A 與 B 音檔，然後播放給受測者聽；第四次實驗裡，則隨機指派 Y2、Z2 成為 A 與 B 音檔，然後播放給受測者聽。在四次聽測實驗裡，受測者都是同樣的 15 位學生，他們大部分都不熟悉語音轉換之研究領域，至於評分的標準是，2 (-2)分表示 B (A)音檔的語音品質比 A (B)音檔的明顯地好，1 (-1)分表示 B (A)音檔的語音品質比 A (B)音檔的稍為好一點，0 分表示分辨不出 A、B 兩音檔的語音品質。

在四次聽測實驗之後，我們將受測者所給的評分作整理，結果得到如表三所示的平均評分。從表三第一欄的平均評分(即 0.867 與 0.467)可發現，和傳統 GMM 對映方法比起來，本論文研究的 LMR_F 對映方法能夠轉換出品質稍好一些的語音；另外，從表三第二欄的平均評分(即 0.267 與 0.000)可發現，LMR_F 對映法和 LMR_FC 對映法，兩者所轉換出語音的品質，不能被感覺出有差異，雖然我們自己聽音檔後覺得，LMR_FC 對映法所轉換出語音的品質要比 LMR_F 對映法的稍好一些。

表三、語音品質聽測之平均評分

平均評分		GMM (128mix.) vs LMR_F	LMR_F vs LMR_FC
M_1 => M_2	AVG (STD)	0.867 (0.640)	0.267 (0.915)
M_1 => F_1	AVG (STD)	0.467 (0.704)	0.000 (0.378)

對於前一段得到的語音品質聽測之結果，在此我們嘗試以聲譜圖(spectrogram)來解釋其原因。當使用傳統 GMM 對映法來對一個來源語句作轉換，語句內的四個字("解決方案")所轉換出語音的聲譜就如圖五(a)所顯示的；而當使用 LMR_FC 對映法來對相同的來源語句作轉換，則得到如圖五(b)所示的聲譜圖。比較圖五(a)和(b)可發現，圖五(b)裡的共振峰(formant)條紋比圖五(a)裡的清晰，例如第二個字"決"的共振峰條紋，在圖五(b)裡的峰、谷對比(即黑、白顏色的對比)顯得較強烈，而在圖五(a)裡的峰、谷對比，就相對地比較緩和，因此，圖五(b)對應的語音聽起來會比圖五(a)的清晰一些。

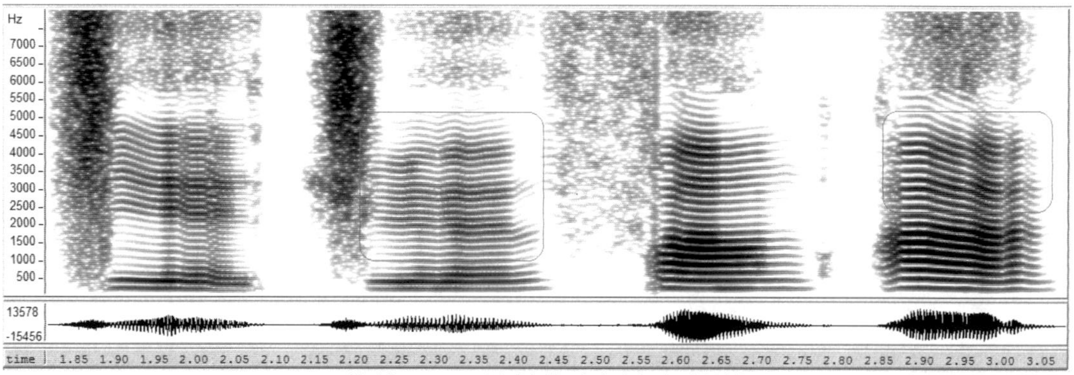

(a) 傳統 GMM 法轉換出語音之聲譜圖

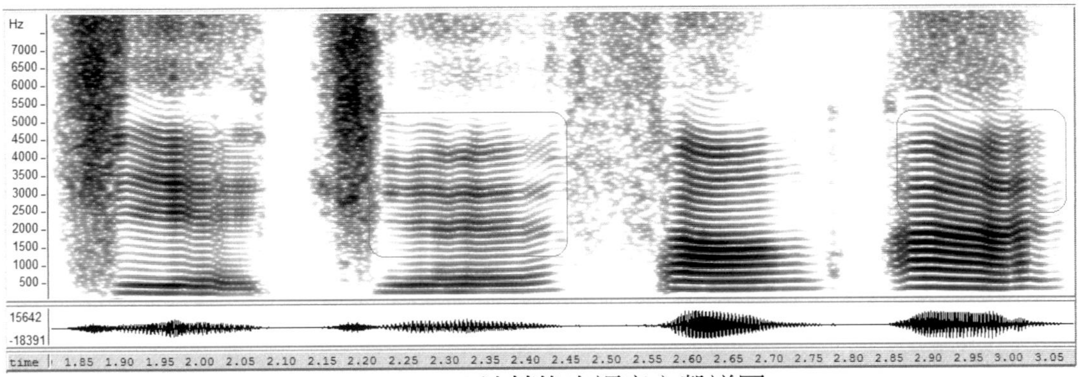

(b) LMR_FC 法轉換出語音之聲譜圖

圖五、兩種方法轉換/jie-3 jyei-2 fang-1 an-4/(“解決方案”)之聲譜圖

六、結論

本論文嘗試以線性多變量迴歸(LMR)作為頻譜對映之機制，去建構出一個語音轉換的系統，並且我們推導了 LMR 對映矩陣的解析求解公式。在使用平行語料、DCC 頻譜係數、和語音信號先分割成聲、韻母音段的情況下，我們經實驗測試發現，LMR_F 對映法進行語音轉換所導入的平均誤差距離值，不論在內部或外部測試之情況，都可以獲得比傳統 GMM 對映法更小的誤差距離值，內部測試時，平均的轉換誤差比起傳統 GMM 對映法的改進了 7.1%，而在外部測試時，平均的轉換誤差則比傳統 GMM 對映法的改進了 1.5%。此外，我們也進行了主觀的語音品質聽測之實驗，實驗的結果顯示，我們研究的 LMR_F 對映法，其轉換出的語音品值，可以比傳統 GMM 對映法的稍好一些。

另外，我們自己試聽轉換出的語音，發現 LMR_F 對映法轉換出的語音聽起來仍有一些模糊的感覺，我們認為這是因為轉換出的頻譜仍存在過平滑的現象，就像傳統 GMM 對映法所遇到的。不過，當使用 LMR_FC 對映法時，這樣的模糊感覺可以減少一些，LMR_FC 對映法能夠轉換出比較清晰的語音，我們覺得它的解釋是，LMR_FC 對映法裡要先作向量量化分群，而分群可以讓頻譜相近的音框聚集在一起，如此就可以減少發生頻譜過平滑的現象。LMR_FC 對映法導入的轉換誤差，內部測試時會比 LMR_F 對映法的小許多，但是外部測試時則比 LMR_F 對映法的大一些，因此，將來可再繼續研究對 LMR_FC 對映法作改進。

參考文獻

[1] M. Abe, S. Nakamura, K. Shikano, and H. Kuwabara, “Voice Conversion through Vector Quantization,” *Int. Conf. Acoustics, Speech, and Signal Processing*, New York, Vol. 1, pp. 655-658, 1988.

[2] H. Mizuno and M. Abe, “Voice Conversion Algorithm Based on Piecewise Linear Conversion Rules of Formant Frequency and Spectrum Tilt,” *Speech Communication*, Vol. 16, No. 2, pp. 153-164, 1995.

[3] 吳嘉彧、王小川，"不需平行語料而基於共振峰與線頻譜頻率映對之語者特質轉換系統"，*第二十一屆自然語言與語音處理研討會*(ROCLING 2009)，台中，第 319-332 頁，2009。

[4] Y. Stylianou, O. Cappe, and E. Moulines, "Continuous Probabilistic Transform for Voice Conversion," *IEEE Trans. Speech and Audio Processing*, Vol. 6, No. 2, pp.131-142, 1998.

[5] H. Y. Gu and S. F. Tsai, "An Improved Voice Conversion Method Using Segmental GMMs and Automatic GMM Selection", *Int. Congress on Image and Signal Processing*, pp. 2395-2399, Shanghai, China, 2011.

[6] S. Desaiy, E. V. Raghavendray, B. Yegnanarayanay, A. W Blackz, and K. Prahallad, "Voice Conversion Using Artificial Neural Networks," *Int. Conf. Acoustics, Speech, and Signal Processing*, Taipei, Taiwan, pp. 3893-3896, 2009.

[7] E. K. Kim, S. Lee, and Y. H. Oh, "Hidden Markov Model Based Voice Conversion Using Dynamic Characteristics of Speaker," *Proc. EuroSpeech*, Rhodes, Greece, Vol. 5, 1997.

[8] C. H. Wu, C. C. Hsia, T. H. Liu, and J. F. Wang, "Voice Conversion Using Duration-Embedded Bi-HMMs for Expressive Speech Synthesis," *IEEE Trans. Audio, Speech, and Language Processing*, Vol. 14, No. 4, pp. 1109-1116, 2006.

[9] H. Valbret, E. Moulines, J. P. Tubach, "Voice Transformation Using PSOLA Technique," *Speech Communication*, Vol. 11, No. 2-3, pp. 175-187, 1992.

[10] E. Godoy, O. Rosec, and T. Chonavel, "Alleviating the One-to-many Mapping Problem in Voice Conversion with Context-dependent Modeling", *Proc. INTERSPEECH*, pp. 1627-1630, Brighton, UK, 2009.

[11] O. Cappé and E. Moulines, "Regularization Techniques for Discrete Cepstrum Estimation," *IEEE Signal Processing Letters*, Vol. 3, No. 4, pp. 100-102, 1996.

[12] H. Y. Gu and S. F. Tsai, "A Discrete-cepstrum Based Spectrum-envelope Estimation Scheme and Its Example Application of Voice Transformation," *International Journal of Computational Linguistics and Chinese Language Processing*, Vol. 14, No. 4, pp. 363-382, 2009.

[13] Y. Stylianou, *Harmonic plus noise models for speech, combined with statistical methods, for speech and speaker modification*, Ph.D. thesis, Ecole Nationale Supèrieure des Télécommunications, Paris, France, 1996.

[14] H. Y. Kim, et al., "Pitch detection with average magnitude difference function using adaptive threshold algorithm for estimating shimmer and jitter," 20-th Annual *Int. Conf. of the IEEE Engineering in Medicine and Biology Society*, Hong Kong, China, 1998.

Acoustic variability in the speech of children with cerebral palsy

Li-mei Chen[+]
Han-chih Ni*
Tzu-Wen Kuo*
Kuei-Ling Hsu*
Department of Foreign Languages and Literature
National Cheng Kung University

[+] Associate Professor, leemay@mail.ncku.edu.tw
*Undergraduate students, mspasaya@gmail.com, sls15239@hotmail.com, ling1991411@hotmail.com

摘要

本研究檢視兩對四歲腦性麻痺孩童和正常孩童的構音聲學變異性，研究項目包含母音空間、聲調和語速。研究語料爲四位孩童的四卷錄音檔，內容爲孩童的圖卡唸名和與大人的自然對話。分析結果顯示：1) 母音空間：腦性麻痺孩童的母音空間比正常孩童小，且共振峰頻率分佈較爲散亂且不穩定；2) 音高：腦性麻痺孩童除了在發音上會花較多的時間外，其聲調也較正常孩童不穩定；3) 說話語速：腦性麻痺孩童的語速和清晰度皆較低。這些初步的研究結果可再進一步驗證，腦性麻痺孩童聲學變異性特徵可提供臨床語言治療及評估的方向參考。
關鍵字：華語幼童、腦性麻痺、母音空間、聲調、語速

Abstract

This study examines the acoustic variability in four 4-year-old children: two with cerebral palsy (CP) and two typically developing (TD). One recording from each child, collected from the picture-naming task and spontaneous interaction with adults was analyzed. Acoustic vowel space, pitch and speech rate in their production were investigated. Study findings indicated the following: 1) children with CP have a smaller vowel space than TD children, and there was a scattered distribution of the formant frequencies in CP; 2) children with CP tend to spend more time producing the utterances and their production of tones was unstable; and 3) both the speech rate and speech intelligibility in CP were lower. Future studies are needed to verify these preliminary findings. The variability features in the production of children with CP provide important references in speech therapy.
Keywords: Mandarin-speaking children, cerebral palsy, vowel space, fundamental frequency, speech rate

1. Introduction

Cerebral palsy is a common speech motor disability in children, and an umbrella term to indicate a neurologic developmental condition that affects individuals from early childhood throughout their lifespan [1]. Due to the neurologic factors, children with cerebral palsy tend to have several types of speech deficits. According to a previous study [2], 60% of children with CP have some type of speech deficits, among which dysarthria, the most common speech disorder found in individuals with CP, has received more attention. This study focuses on the acoustic aspects of dysarthria: vowel space, pitch, and speech rate. Vowel space is an acoustic measure that indicates the jaw's coordination and the tongue's controlling ability [3]. Because of poor muscle coordination, individuals with dysarthria tend to have a smaller vowel space, which influences the accuracy of articulation and reduces the intelligibility of their speech. Moreover, because dysarthric speakers have a hard time controlling their respiratory and the laryngeal mechanisms, it is difficult for them to produce correct tones, which plays an important role in the intelligibility of tonal languages ([2], [4], [5]). Furthermore, the stability of the speech rate affects listeners' intelligibility, but dysarthric speakers usually present a rate disturbance [6]. Therefore, these three acoustic measures are vital to the speech of the individual with dysarthria. By analyzing these three measures, this study provides a preliminary index of cerebral palsied speech and a direction for speech-language intervention.

2. Literature review

2.1 Acoustic vowel space

Many researchers have used vowel space as an index for the size of the vowel articulatory working space, the accuracy of vowel articulation, and the tongue's controlling ability ([3], [7]). Moreover, the influences of dysarthria and unclear speech on the sizes of vowel areas and the relationship between vowel space and speech intelligibility were investigated ([8], [9]). According to a previous study [3], vowel area formed by the 1st formant (F1) and the 2nd formant (F2) can reflect the control ability and mobility of the tongue. In other words, if the mobility of the tongue is abnormal, the F1-F2 area would be reduced. In Higgins and Hodge's [10] study with 12 participants, six children had been diagnosed with dysarthria, and six were controls. They compared the vowel spaces of the corner vowels /a/, /i/, /æ/ and /u/ produced by the two groups and found that the vowel space of children with dysarthria is smaller. Jeng [9] indicated that the vowel quadrilaterals of the controls are more uniform, while CP groups' vowel quadrilaterals are variable because of the non-uniform F1-F2 formant values. People with dysarthria tend to speak at a slower rate or at a louder volume to make their speech intelligible, which may expand the vowel space [11]. In clinical treatment, controlling the speech rate is widely employed by speech therapists, and the effects of slowing the speech rate on vowel space and speech intelligibility was discussed in the previous study ([5], [9], [11]). Therefore, it can be inferred that the abnormality of vowel space is a critical reason for the inaccurate articulation and the reduced speech intelligibility of people with CP.

2.2 Pitch

Dysprosody, where the control of prosodic variables such as fundamental frequency (Fo) or pitch is impaired, is a common feature of dysarthria [12]. According to Ciocca et al. [2], in tonal languages, such as Cantonese, tonal-level contrast was the second most problematic phonetic contrast that influenced speech intelligibility.

In Mandarin Chinese, there are four dominant tones: high-level (tone 1), high-rising (tone 2), low-falling-rising (tone 3), and high-falling (tone 4) [13]. According to Han et al. [14], tone or pitch of each monosyllable makes meaningful contrasts. For instance, changing the four tones of the same syllable, *ma*, will create meaningful contrasts: "mother" (tone 1), "hemp" (tone 2), "horse" (tone 3), and "scold" (tone4). Therefore, pitch is central to the intelligibility of tonal languages.

In order to produce different tones to make meaningful contrasts, speakers alter the tension of the vocal folds and the amount of air flowing from the lungs [2]. However, because dysarthric speakers have difficulty controlling the respiratory and the laryngeal mechanisms, they cannot always produce correct tones ([2], [4], [5]). Bunton et al. [12] found that English-speaking dysarthric adults tended to decrease the duration of their tone units, or produce fewer words in a tone unit. In addition, the range of Fo of dysarthric speakers is restricted. Furthermore, Cantonese dysarthric speakers showed errors in Fo level and/or Fo contour due to the lack of control of laryngeal mechanism [2].

2.3 Speech rate

Due to the neuromuscular factors, it is not surprising that individuals with dysarthria tend to have a slower and more unstable speech rate ([3], [6], [15], [16]). Many researchers have tried to associate speech rate and speech intelligibility to further discuss the complete index of one's speech performance [17]. The previous study [4] stated that slower speech rate of individuals with cerebral palsy may contribute to higher speech intelligibility, which also serves as an aid to their communication efficiency. In contrast, other studies have found no significant correlation. Turner, Tjaden, and Weismer [8], by having dysarthric subjects read the passages at habitual, fast, and slow speaking rate, concluded that there is no specific correlation between these two issues. Therefore, there is still no agreement on the relationship between speech rate and speech intelligibility. Whether the slower speech can be a compensatory strategy to increase intelligibility remains unknown. This study explores the relationship between speech rate and speech intelligibility in spontaneous speech production in 4-year-olds with cerebral palsy, and answers the following questions: (1) Is the speech rate of the children with dysarthria slower than that of typically developing children? (2) How is speech rate related to speech intelligibility?

3. Methodology

3.1 The participants

Four children participated in this study: two with cerebral palsy (CP1 and CP2, mean age 52.3 months) and two with no specific medical history (TD1 and TD2, mean age 54.8 months). The tables provide background information of CP1 and CP2.

Table 1. Descriptive data of the two CP subjects

Subject	Gender	Months	Classification	Type of CP	Severity of impairment
CP1	Male	48.3	Dyskinetic	Quadriplegia	Moderate
CP2	Male	56.3	Other	Quadriplegia	Severe

Table 2. Descriptive data of the two TD subjects

Subject	Gender	Months
TD 1	Male	54.5
TD 2	Male	55.1

All of the subjects are male, in order to avoid any potential gender differences in pitch, and are have normal hearing and intelligence. The two CP subjects were recruited from a hospital. CP1 has the medical diagnosis of dyskinetic quadriplegia with moderate CP. He has been diagnosed with borderline language delay on the basis of Preschool Language Scale-Chinese Version (PLS-C), and has received language therapy. CP2 has the medical diagnosis of quadriplegia with severe CP. He received education in a special education center, but he has never received language therapy. The data of TD subjects were taken from a large-scale study of longitudinal phonetic development.

3.2 Data collection

CP1's data were collected in lab with less noise disturbance, while the data of CP2 and the two TD children were collected in their homes. Although the locations were different, the same recording equipment was used. A SHURE Wireless microphone system was linked to TASCAM DR-100 recorders for the purpose of sound recording. During the 50-minute observation period, speech productions in picture naming task were recorded, and the Peabody Picture Vocabulary Test-Revised (PPVT-R) was used to provide a quick assessment of the speech and language ability.

3.3 Data analysis – acoustic vowel space

The first 50 utterances with clear quality were transcribed and analyzed with the time-frequency analysis software program, TF32. Vowel formant frequencies were determined with reference to spectrogram, LPC, and FFT with Hillenbrand, Getty, Clark, and Wheeler [18] as the range reference of formant frequencies. F1 and F2 values and bandwidth were measured. Vowels with unrecognized formant patterns or with large bandwidth (larger than 1000Hz) were discarded.

All F1 and F2 values of vowels were normalized. The procedure of normalization is intended to reduce the differences caused by extrinsic vowel formant values and remaining the phonological distinctions among different vowels ([19], [20]). The differences of vowel productions of CP and TD were analyzed in three aspects: the F1 and F2 values of individual vowels /i/, /a/, /u/, /ə/, /ɛ/, and /ɔ/, standard deviation of formant frequencies, and vowel space. Overall F1-F2 vowel spaces were calculated to examine the data diversity, and the vowel space formed by the three corner vowels /i/, /a/, and /u/ were captured to illustrate the mobility and control ability of tongue and jaw.

3.4 Data analysis - pitch

Pitch values of bi-syllabic or tri-syllabic words were analyzed based on four dominant tones in Mandarin Chinese: high-level (tone 1), high-rising (tone 2), low-falling-rising (tone 3), and high-falling (tone 4) [13]. However, in Mandarin spoken in Taiwan, the low-falling-rising tone or dipping tone (tone 3) is always replaced by low-falling tone. The first 50 intelligible and less disturbed utterances were selected for pitch analysis. The same procedure was administered to all four children.

TF32, an acoustic analysis program, was used to estimate fundamental frequency (Fo), mean standard deviation of Fo, mean tone duration (TU), mean slope (in Hz/ms), and the maximum and minimum values of Fo. In addition, the beginning point (BP) and the end point (EP) were measured for tone 1 and 4; the beginning point (BP), the inflectional point (IFP), and the end point (EP) were measured for tone 2 and tone 3.
For slope of tones, two functions were used to measure.

Function 1: SLP1 (Tone1 and 4) = (EP-BP)/ ($\overline{\text{EP} - \text{BP}}$)

Function 2: SLP2 (Tone2 and 3) = (IFP-BP)/ ($\overline{\text{IFP} - \text{BP}}$)

SLP3 (Tone2 and 3) = (EP-IFP)/ ($\overline{\text{EP} - \text{IFP}}$)

Note that in Slope Function 2, tone 3 was in fact the low-falling tone.

3.5 Data analysis – speech rate

In speech rate, the target data were the phrases and sentences produced by the four children in spontaneous interaction. To examine speech intelligibility, the target data were 50 randomly chosen words from the picture-naming task in the same recordings. The following principles are based on the data collection procedures in [4].

(1) Syllables per minute (SPM): one judge listened to the phrases and sentences, transcribed the content syllable by syllable, and counted the number of the syllables. SPM is obtained by calculating the total number of the syllables divided by the time duration, and multiplying the quotient by 60. In the case of spontaneous speech, the intra-sentence pauses were included, but the inter-sentences pauses were not.

(2) Intelligible syllables per minute (ISPM): ISPM is acquired by counting only the number of the intelligible syllables divided by the duration, and multiplying the quotient by 60. Ten

percent of the data were re-analyzed by the second judge. The inter-judge was allowed to listen to the data again, and to the relevant context but no more than twice. The result of inter-judge reliability is 86.2%, which exceeds the standard proposed by Kassarjian [21].
Speech intelligibility: Three judges were recruited to transcribe productions of 50 words of each child in the picture naming tasks. The judges could only listen once and then transcribed what they heard. All the judges worked alone, and at their own pace. The total number of correctly transcribed syllables was divided by the total number of the syllables of the 50-word list. Mean intelligibility from the three judges was calculated as speech intelligibility of each child.

4. Results and discussion

4.1 Acoustic vowel space

Frequency of occurrence

The following results compare CP and TD group in vowel accuracy and the occurrence of main vowels (/i/, /a/, /u/, /ə/, /ɛ/, and /ɔ/).

Table 3. The occurrence of main vowel in the four children

Vowels	CP1	CP2	TD1	TD2
/i/	21.33%	17.39%	22.95%	25.86%
/a/	22.67%	21.74%	22.95%	29.31%
/u/	10.67%	15.94%	21.31%	13.79%
/ə/	22.67%	24.64%	11.48%	8.62%
/ɛ/	14.67%	10.14%	11.48%	13.79%
/ɔ/	8%	10.14%	9.84%	8.62%

Table 3 shows that vowels /i/ and /a/ have a high frequency of occurrence, and vowel /ɔ/ shows a lowest frequency in both CP and TD children. Furthermore, both CP1 and CP2 show a high frequency of occurrence in vowel /ə/ during their picture naming task.

Table 4. The accuracy of each main vowel in the four subjects' vowel production

Vowels	CP1	CP2	TD1	TD2
/i/	100%	80%	100%	100%
/a/	100%	100%	100%	75%
/u/	100%	100%	100%	100%
/ə/	80%	25%	100%	50%

Table 4 indicates high accuracy in corner vowels (/i/, /a/, and /u/), while a respectively lower accuracy in vowel /ə/. Comparing to TD children, children with CP show a lower accuracy of vowel production.

Overall vowel spaces

Figure 1 and Figure 2 show the un-normalized and normalized F1 and F2 of the four children. The dots in the figure represent each individual vowel production. In the figure of normalized vowel formant values, the influences of extrinsic vowel formant values are reduced during the normalization procedure.

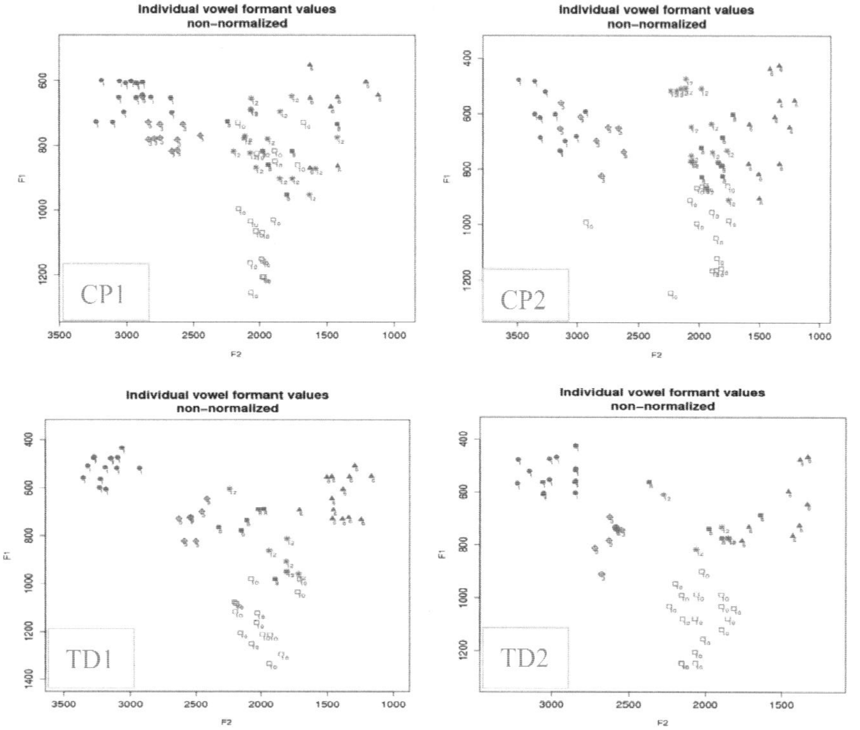

Figure 1. Vowel formant values of CPs and TDs.

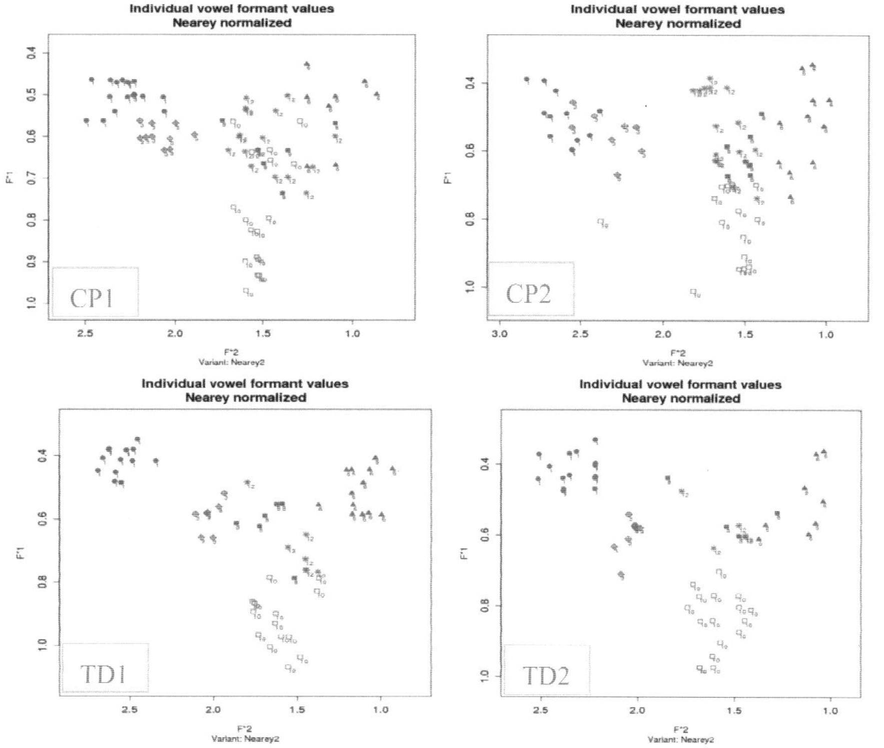

Figure 2. Normalized vowel formant values of CPs and TDs.

As Figure 1 and Figure 2 show, the distribution of CPs' individual vowel formant values is scattered, while that of TDs is more concentrated and more easily recognized. Moreover, the distinction of formant values distribution between central vowels and corner vowels was not clear in CPs.

Individual vowel spaces

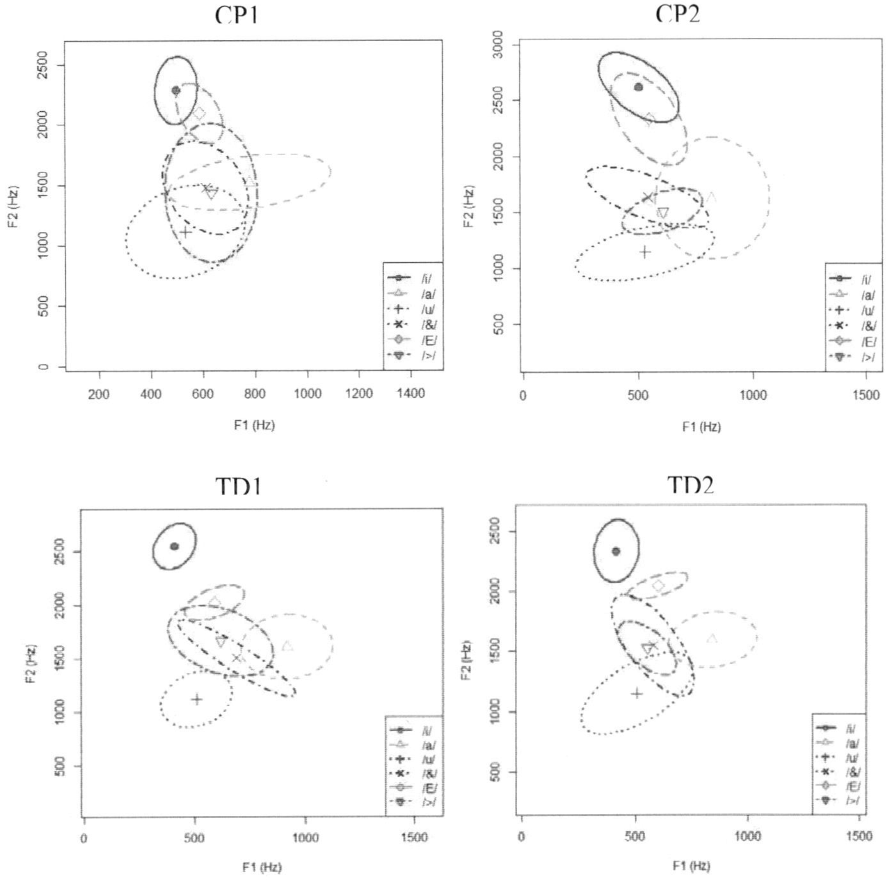

Figure 3. Individual vowel spaces of CP1, CP2, TD1, and TD2.

Figure 3 illustrates that almost all individual vowel spaces in CPs are larger than in TDs, especially in vowel /i/, /a/, and /ɛ/. That is, the deviations of the formant values of CPs are larger than those of TDs. Moreover, the overlapping of individual vowel categories looks more obvious in CP children. Almost all individual vowels overlap with each other, and the positions of vowel spaces gather to the central part, which reduces the distinction between formant values of different individual vowels in CPs.

Table 5. Mean and standard deviation of F1 and F2 values of individual vowels and vowel areas in 4 children

Vowels	**CP1**		**CP2**		**TD1**		**TD2**	
	F1	**F2**	**F1**	**F2**	**F1**	**F2**	**F1**	**F2**
/i/	497	2285	493	2623	406	2541	413	2333
	†(35.1)	(121.5)	(73.5)	(130.3)	(41)	(90.2)	(43)	(110.1)
/a/	778	1532	814	1618	917	1608	838	1598
	(134.8)	(100)	(106.7)	(233.7)	(88.4)	(128.3)	(84.9)	(100.9)
/u/	539	1112	514	1141	504	1127	491	1142
	(89.6)	(150.9)	(126.3)	(104.7)	(67.9)	(110.6)	(97.8)	(132.6)
/ə/	610	1477	539	1633	691	1503	578	1550

	(70.7)	(166.6)	(116)	(118.9)	(101.4)	(137)	(62.1)	(142.9)
/ɛ/	587 (36.9)	2095 (102.9)	546 (65.3)	2330 (162.2)	591 (51.1)	2023 (61.3)	599 (52.3)	2042 (43.5)
/ɔ/	632 (64.4)	1435 (209.3)	605 (66.4)	1504 (78.2)	619 (86.8)	1664 (120)	552 (43.7)	1525 (75.8)
Vowel area (Hz²)	152761		227608		315555		224572	

† Standard deviation reported in parentheses

Table 5 reveals the mean formant values of CP and TD groups. The CP group shows higher F1 values in high vowels (/i/ and /u/) and lower F1 values in low vowel /a/. There is no obvious difference between CP and TD group in F2 values. Moreover, the CP group shows a larger standard deviation of vowel formant frequencies, which indicates the instability of formant frequencies.

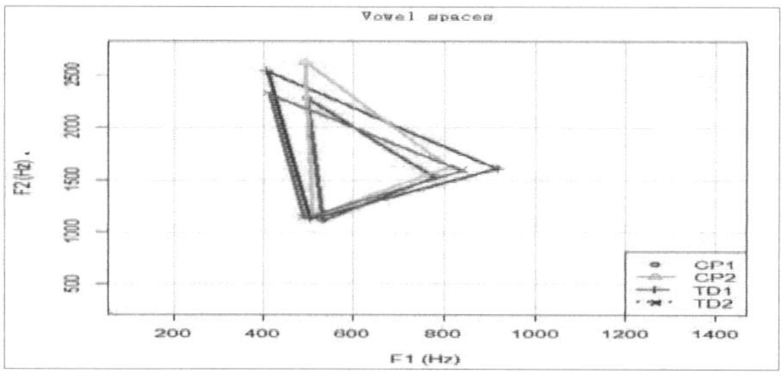

Figure 4. Overall vowel spaces of CP1, CP2, TD1, and TD2.

Compared with the TD group, the CP group shows a smaller overall vowel space. As illustrated in Figure 4, both CP1 and CP2 show a limited range in F1 values, while in F2 values there is no obvious difference between the CP2 and TD groups.

Discussion

The findings indicate that children with CP show a wide and variable range of distribution in individual vowel formant frequencies, while TD children's data of formant values are more concentrated and uniform. This is also found in previous study that the vowel quadrilaterals of controls are uniform, while those of CPs are relatively variable [9]. The deviation in vowel production might be attributable to CPs' abnormal control of the tongue. Moreover, the reduced distinction between corner vowels and other main vowels, and the obvious overlapping of different individual vowel spaces in CP1 and CP2 also indicate a reduced stability in vowel productions. Like what was found in the previous studies ([3], [7], [10]), CP children show a smaller overall vowel space area than TD children.

F1 and F2 values are related, respectively, to the height and advancement of the tongue. In this study, children with CP show a higher F1 in high vowel /i/ and /u/, while showing a lower F1 in mid vowel /ɛ/ and low vowel /a/. That is, they have limited mobility of tongue height. There is thus less of a distinction of F1 values between high and low vowels in children with CP than in TD children [9]. The difference in F2 is less obvious between CP and TD groups. Therefore, the limited F1 range contributes to the smaller vowel space in CP children. This finding is different from [10] which indicated that children with dysarthria used a lower tongue and jaw position to pronounce vowel/a/, and the dysarthric children's smaller vowel spaces were resulted from the reduction of F2 extent instead of F1.

4.2 Pitch

Figure 5 shows the frequency of occurrence of tones. Tone 3 appears to be the least in both groups. In addition, both TDs and CPs produced relatively more tone1 than others.

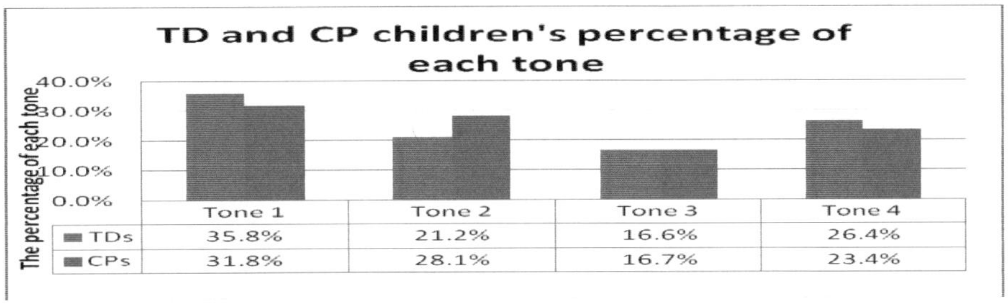

Figure 5. Frequency of occurrence of tones in TD and CP children

The accuracy and substitution patterns

As shown in Table 6, in TD 1, the accuracy rate of tone 1 is the highest among the four tones. The accuracy rate is 96.97% (32 words). The lowest accuracy rate was found in tone 3, which is 54.17% (13 words). TD 1 used tone 1, tone 2 and tone 4 to substitute for tone 3. Moreover, the accuracy rate of tone 4 is higher than tone 2. For TD2, his highest accuracy rate is tone 4 (96.65%; 22 words); while his lowest is tone 2 (70%; 14 words). Moreover, tone 1 appears to be more accurate than tone 3.

For CP1, tone 4 has the highest accuracy rate among the four tones (84.21%; 16 words). The lowest accuracy rate can be seen in tone 3, which is 61.11% (11 words). He used both tone 2 and tone 4 to replace tone 3. Moreover, the accuracy rate of tone 1 is higher than that of tone 2. For CP2, tone 1 has the highest accuracy rate, which is 81.82% (18 words.) The lowest accuracy rate is tone 3, which is 60% (9 words). He used tone 2 and tone 4 to replace tone 3. Moreover, the accuracy rate of tone 2 is higher than that of tone 4.

Table 6. The accuracy and substitution patterns in TD and CP children

Substitution	TD1	TD2	CP1	CP2
1→1*	32	30	27	18
1→2*	0	4	5	4
1→3*	0	0	1	0
1→4*	1	1	1	0
2→1*	2	0	0	4
2→2*	18	14	11	15
2→3*	4	6	2	0
2→4*	1	0	1	1
3→1*	3	0	0	0
3→2*	4	2	5	5
3→3*	13	8	11	9
3→4*	4	1	2	1
4→1*	2	0	0	6
4→2*	0	0	1	2
4→3*	2	1	2	1
4→4*	18	22	16	20

* one that substitute for the target tone

Mean duration

Figure 6 shows the mean duration of each tone of the four children. Both TD and CP children's tone 2 is the longest. For CP children, their tone 4 is the shortest; however, TD children's tone 3 is the shortest. Moreover, the mean duration of four tones in CP is about 1.3 to 1.8 times longer than in TD.

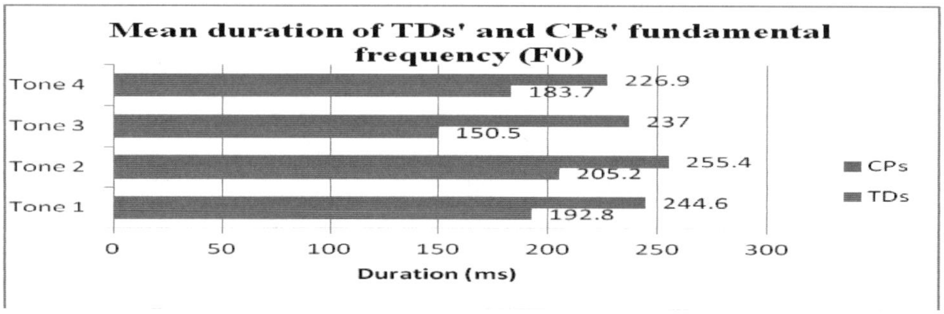

Figure 6. Mean duration of TDs' and CPs' fundamental frequency (Fo)

Mean standard deviation

Table 7 shows the mean standard deviation (SD) of pitch values in each individual tone category in the four children. The higher the SD is, the more unstable the pitch value. In general, the SDs of the pitch values of each tone in CPs are all higher than the SDs of TDs. CPs' SD is about 1.5-1.6 times larger than that of TDs. Therefore, the results indicated that CP children's pitch is indeed more unstable than TD children's, reflecting the lack of speech-motor control of children with cerebral palsy. In addition, for CP children, the SD of their tone 3 is the highest of all, 26.4 Hz, which implies that the pitch development of tone 3 is the most unstable among the four tones. The possible reason is that tone 3 is considered the most complicated in Chinese. According to a previous study [22], tone 3 has a tone notation of 214, which means that tone 3 initially falls from 2 to 1 and then rises from 1 to 4. Therefore, it takes CP children extra energy to produce tone 3, the most difficult one, under the condition that they lack mature speech-motor control. That is why CP children's tone 3 appears to be the most different from that of TD children.

Table 7. Mean standard deviation of fundamental frequency (Fo)

	Tone 1	Tone 2	Tone 3	Tone 4
TDs	13.8	14.6	20.8	20.9
CPs	16.2	22.2	26.4	24.5

Mean slope

In Table 8, we can see that the mean slope of tone 1 in TDs is -0.191 Hz/ms, while CPs' is -0.162 Hz/ms. Both TDs' and CPs' tone 1 tends to go below the level, causing a slight fall for this high-level tone. This lowering of high-level tone can also be found in dysarthric speakers of Cantonese [2] and in hearing-impaired Mandarin-speaking children ([13], [23]). Furthermore, CPs' tone 1 tends to approach the level more closely than that of TDs. The possible explanation is that tone 1 for CP children is actually not a difficult tone to master compared to the other tones. Tone 2 in Chinese has two segments of slope. Tone 2 is a high-rising tone [22]. Before raising the pitch, speakers must temporarily and quickly lower it. Therefore, there are two segments of slope of tone 2. CP children's pitch movement of tone 2 looks very similar to that of TD children. CP children, at first, lowered their tone 2 and then rose up just as TD children did when they produced tone 2. Like the pattern of tone 2, tone 3 has two segments of slope. The duration of the falling-down of tone 3 is longer than that of tone 2. CP children's tone 3 is more monotonous than that of TD children's because their slope, either from BP to IFP or from IFP to EP is closer to the level. The mean slope of TD and CP subjects' tone 4 (the high-falling tone) are negative. There is no obvious difference between TDs' and CPs' mean slope of tone 4. Compared to other tones, TDs' and CPs' tone 4 seem to be the most similar. Tone 4 for CP children is also a rather easy tone to master.

Table 8. Mean slope of fundamental frequency (Fo)

	Tone 1	Tone 2		Tone 3		Tone 4
TDs	-0.191	-0.710	0.308	-0.631	0.348	-0.388
CPs	-0.162	-0.795	0.262	-0.534	0.212	-0.348

Discussion

CP children's pitch differs from that of TD children in mean duration and in mean standard deviation. It was found that CP children tend to spend more time and make more efforts in speech production due to the disorder of speech-motor control. In addition, the results of SD indicated that pitch production of CP children is more unstable than TD children's, reflecting the lack of speech-motor control. As for the mean slope of each tone, there is no obvious difference between TD and CP children.

In general, for both TD and CP children, tone 1 and tone 4 are easier to handle than the other tones. Therefore, the accuracy rate of both tone 1 and tone 4 is the highest among the four tones for both TD and CP children. The tone values of tone 1 and tone 4 are 55 and 51, respectively [22]. The procedure involved in the production of these two tones is relatively easy. In contrast, tone 3 for TD1, CP1 and CP2 is considered the most difficult tone to produce because the accuracy rate is the lowest among the four tones. Although the most difficult tone for TD2 seems to be tone 2, the accuracy rate of TD2's tone 3 is also low (72.73%; 8 words). The tone value of tone 3 is 214 [22], which is difficult for both TD and CP children.

4.3 Speech rate

Speech rate: the results of both SPM and ISPM of four subjects are presented in figure 1. Both SPM and ISPM of CP1 and CP2 are slower than TD1 and TD2.

(1) SPM: although CP1 performed the slowest SPM among the four, the rates of the four subjects were actually close. If we take further examination of CP2, his rate of SPM was 239 SPM, which could almost compete with the typically developing children, which were 254 SPM and 272 SPM respectively.

(2) ISPM: the differences between the group of CP children and the group of TD children are extended. While the rates of typically developing children remain almost the same, the rates of the group with cerebral palsy dropped much more slowly, especially in CP2. CP2 produced the rapid speech rate with a lower intelligibility.

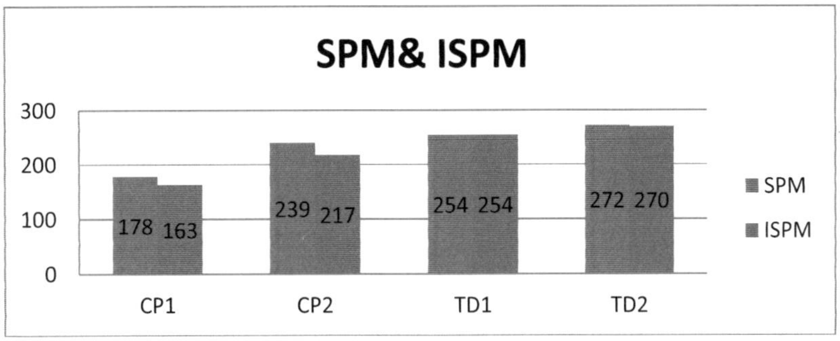

Figure 7. Speech rate in SPM (syllables per minute) and ISPM (intelligibles syllable per minute) of the four children

Speech intelligibility: in the part of speech intelligibility, the results in CP1 and CP2 were 76% and 63%, and in TD1 and TD2 were 98% and 92%, respectively. Compared with the speech rate, there is an obvious difference between CP children and TD children. Both CP1 and CP2 showed a lower intelligibility. Moreover, CP2's speech intelligibility was only 63%, which is the lowest of the four children. Compared to the group with cerebral palsy, TD1 and TD2 showed relatively high intelligibility, at 98% and 92% respectively. Furthermore, combined with the result of ISPM, although CP2 is the rapid speaker, his intelligibility has been affected by this rapidness and dropped more apparently than other three children. While CP1 produced the slower speech rate, his speech intelligibility was higher than CP2.

Discussion

Compared to that of typically developing children, the speech rate of the children with cerebral palsy group is slower. The findings in this paper that both SPM and ISPM of CP children are slower than TD children are consistent with the dysarthria literature ([3], [15], [16]). Moreover, group with cerebral palsy also demonstrated the lower speech intelligibility. Nevertheless, there were individual differences in CP children, especially in the case of CP2. CP2 showed similar speech rate as the TD group in SPM, which was much faster than CP1. This might be due to the different type of cerebral palsy. In this study, although CP1 is less severe than CP2 in cerebral palsy, CP1 is diagnosed with dyskinetic quadriplegia, and this type of cerebral palsy usually affects the speech production more obviously. Ingram and Barn [24] propose that the reason leading to dyskinetic dysarthria is generally because the motor control of the voluntary articulator in dyskinetic speakers has been aggravated by their involuntary movements, which leads to the disruption of the speech. Although there is disagreement in some of the latter findings [25], the influences of involuntary movements on the speech production of dyskinetic speakers merit investigation in future studies. As to CP2, his rapid speech may result from the repetition of the target items in picture naming. Through these repetitions, the duration of the repeated utterances became shorter. The repeated utterances take up 15% of the whole data, which might explain the fast speech rate of CP2. Furthermore, while examining the repeated utterances in CP2, it was found that even though children with cerebral palsy have some speech defects, they have the ability to adjust their speech rate at will. In the recording, when CP2 was mischievously playing with adults, he obviously slowed down or sped up the rate of the target utterances. This finding confirms previous literature that the dysarthric speakers can adjust their rate as needed, revealing that they are capable of planning speech production. From this rate flexibility in CP children, we can respond to the statement in LeDorze, Ouellet, and Ryalls [6] that the speech deficit in dysarthric speakers is a matter of performance, not of competence.

5. Summary and further studies

Due to the deficit of speech-motor control, children with cerebral palsy show substantial differences in speech production comparing with typically developing children. Regarding vowel space, CP children have scattered and non-uniform formant values of each vowel, which reflects that children with CP have a relative lack of ability to coordinate and control the movements of the tongue. Furthermore, the vowel space of CP children is smaller than that of TD children. This finding suggests that CP children have limited tongue mobility. As to pitch features of CP children, the mean duration of each tone in CP children is longer than that in TD children. This finding indicated that CP children tend to spend more time producing speech because of their impaired speech-motor control. In addition, pitch production in CP children tends to be more unstable than in TD children. With regard to speech rate, CP children have slower rate and reduced intelligibility than children who do not have CP. Moreover, a slower speech rate can improve the intelligibility of speech in children with CP.

The limitations in this preliminary study suggest directions for future research. First, the number of children included for analysis is limited. Future studies with more participants would yield more objective results, and the correlation of CP children's speech rate and their speech intelligibility could be verified. Second, the findings of this study were just based on the observation of 4-year-old children. Extended longitudinal observation can provide more complete data of the individual differences and the profile of the development in vowels, pitch patterns, speech rate, and other speech and language characteristics. Third, the background disturbance in the recording procedures compromised the quality of the recordings. The background noises made the measurement of vowel formant frequency and pitch values difficult.

Moreover, pitch production in CP children tends to be very inconsistent. Even within a monosyllabic utterance, CP children make constant changes in pitch. For instance, CP children pronounced "diàn" in "diànshì" (television) as "diàn én." The pitch movement of this utterance looked abnormal and changing (Figure 8). The change of pitch within one monosyllabic utterance is very common in the data of CP children. Therefore, this also created some difficulties in the transcription and later in pitch analysis.

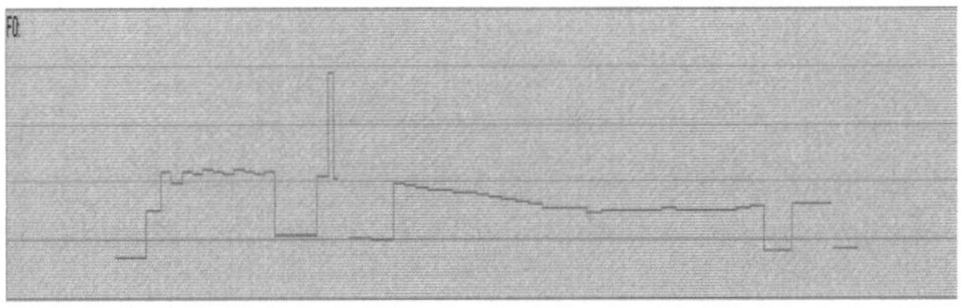

Figure 8. CP children's bumpy pitch movement due to pitch changes within one syllable

Furthermore, speech productions of CP children tend to be fractured and discontinuous, just like grow pulse in [26]. It seems that CP children press the muscles too strongly in their larynx while speaking. Thus, the pitch movement shown in Figure 9 appears to be unstable, bumpy, and usually broken. The bumpy and unstable pitch movement makes the measurement of fundamental frequency very difficult.

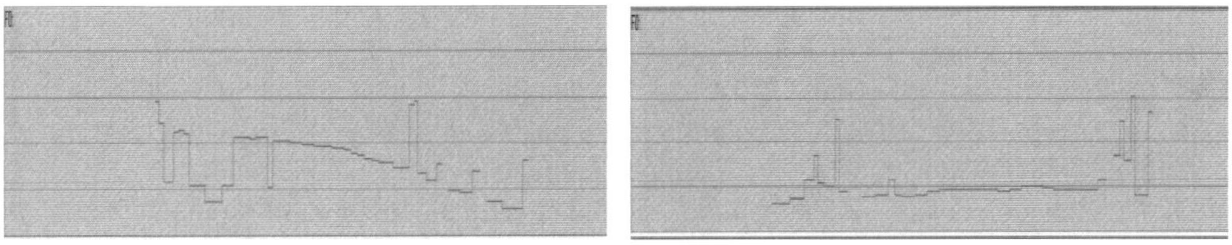

Figure 9. CP children's bumpy pitch movement due to growl pulse

Last, in this study, the spontaneous speech data used in speech rate analysis, inevitably introduces variables. During the recording procedures, when the children became bored about the tasks they had to perform, they would produce faster and more unintelligible speech because of their impatience. This affected the study results. Accordingly, if we could minimize or eliminate these limitations in future or extended studies, the findings would be valuable for clinical speech-language intervention.

References

[1] P. Rosenbaum, N. Paneth, A. Leviton, M. Goldstein, and M. Bax, "A report: The definition and classification of cerebral palsy April 2006," *Developmental Medicine and Child Neurology*, 2007, vol. 49, no. 2, pp. 8-14.

[2] V. Ciocca, T. L. Whitehill, and M. K. Y. Joan, "The Impact of Cerebral Palsy on the Intelligibility of Pitch-based Linguistic Contrasts," *Journal of Physiological Anthropology and Applied Human Science*, 2004, vol. 23, pp. 283-287.

[3] R. D. Kent and Y. -J. Kim, "Toward an acoustic typology of motor speech disorders," *Journal of Clinical Linguistics & Phonetics*, 2003, vol. 17, no. 6, pp. 427-445.

[4] K. C. Hustad, K.L. Gorton, and J. Lee, "Classification of speech and language profiles of 4-year old children with cerebral palsy: A prospective preliminary study," *Journal of Speech, Language, and Hearing Research*, 2010, vol. 53, pp. 1496-1513.

[5] H. -M. Liu, F. -M. Tsao, and P. K. Kuhl, "The Effect of Reduced Vowel Working Space on Speech Intelligibility in Mandarin-speaking Young Adults with Cerebral Palsy," *Journal of Acoustical Society of America*, 2005, vol. 117, no. 6, pp. 3879-3889.

[6] G. LeDorze, L. Ouellet, and J. Ryalls, "Intonation and speech rate in dysarthric speech," *Journal of Communication Disorders*, 1994, vol. 27, pp. 1–18.

[7] K. Tjaden, D. Rivera, G. Wilding, and G. S. Turner, "Characteristics of the lax vowel space in dysarthria," *Journal of Speech Language and Hearing Research*, 2005, vol. 48, no. 3, pp. 554-566.

[8] G. S. Turner, K. Tjaden, and G. Weismer, "The influence of speaking rate on vowel space and speech intelligibility for individuals with amyotrophic lateral sclerosis," *Journal of Speech and Hearing Research*, 1995, vol. 38, pp. 1001–1013.

[9] J. -Y. Jeng, "Intelligibility and acoustic characteristics of the dysarthria in mandarin speakers with cerebral palsy," Ph.D. dissertation, Univ. Wisconsin, Madison, USA, 2000.

[10] C. M. Higgins and M. M. Hodge, "Vowel area and intelligibility in children with and without dysarthria," *Journal of Medical Speech-Language Pathology*, 2002, vol. 10, no. 4, pp. 271–277.

[11] C. -Y. Yang and H. -M. Liu, "The impact of a speaking-rate training program on speech intelligibility in students with spastic cerebral palsy," *Bulletin of Special Education*, 2007, vol. 32, no. 4, pp. 65-83.

[12] K. Bunton, R. D. Kent, J. F. Kent, and J. C. Rosenbek, "Perceptuo-acoustic Assessment of prosodic Impairment in Dysarthria," *Clinical Linguistics & Phonetics*, 2000, vol. 14, no. 1, pp. 13- 24.

[13] T. -Y. Chen, "Tone Production in Mandarin-speaking Hearing-impaired Pre-school Children," M.A. thesis, National Cheng Kung University, Taiwan, 2007.

[14] D. Han, N. Zhou, Y. Li, X. Chen, X. Zhao, and L. Xu, "Tone production of Mandarin Chinese speaking children with cochlear implants," *International Journal of Pediatric Otorhinolaryngology*, 2007, vol. 71, no. 6, pp. 875-880.

[15] K. C. Hustad and K. Sassano, "Effects of rate reduction on severe spastic dysarthria in cerebral palsy," *Journal of Medical Speech-Language Pathology*, 2002, vol.10, pp. 287–292.

[16] G. Weismer, J. S. Laures, J. Jeng, and R. D. Kent, "Effect of speaking rate manipulations on acoustic and perceptual aspects of the dysarthria in amyotrophic lateral sclerosis," *Folia Phoniatrica et ogopaedica*, 2000, vol. 52, pp. 201–219.

[17] K. M. Yorkston and D. R. Beukelman, "Communication efficiency of dysarthric speakers as measured by sentence intelligibility and speaking rate," *Journal of Speech and Hearing Disorders*, 1981, vol. 46, pp. 296-301.

[18] J. Hillenbrand, A. L. Getty, M. J. Clark, and K. Wheeler, "Acoustic characteristics of American English vowels," *Journal of Acoustical Society of America*, 1995, vol. 97, no. 5, pp. 3103.

[19] E. R. Thomas and T. Kendall, NORM: The vowel normalization and plotting suite, 2011. [Web-based interface]. Available: ncslaap.lib.ncsu.edu/tools/norm/norm1.php

[20] J. Lee, G. Weismer, and K. C. Hustad, "Longitudinal changes of raw and normalized vowel space in children with cerebral palsy," presented at 161st meeting of Acoustical Society of America, Seattle, WA, 2011.

[21] H. H. Kassarjian, "Content analysis in consumer research," *Journal of Consumer Research*, 1977, vol.4, pp. 8-18.

[22] Y. R. Chao, A grammar of spoken Chinese, Berkeley: University of California Press. 1968.

[23] L. M. Chen and Y. W. Chen, "Mandarin tones in twins differ in auditory function: A longitudinal observation of 18-24 months of age," *Journal of the Acoustical Society of R.O.C.*, 2010, vol. 14, pp. 32-39.

[24] T. T .S. Ingram and J. Barn, "A description and classification of common speech disorders associated with cerebral palsy," *Developmental Medicine & Child Neurology*, 1961, vol. 3, pp. 57-69.
[25] P. D. Neilson and N. J. O'Dwyer, "Pathophysiology of dysarthria in cerebral palsy," *Journal of Neurology, Neurosurgery, and Psychiatry*, 1981, vol. 44, pp. 1013-1019.
[26] E. H. Buder, L. B. Chorna, K. Oller, and R. B. Robinson, "Vibratory Regime Classification of Infant Phonation," *Journal of Voice*, 2008, vol. 22, no. 5, pp. 553-564.

領域相關詞彙極性分析及文件情緒分類之研究

Domain Dependent Word Polarity Analysis for Sentiment Classification

游和正 Ho-Cheng Yu
國立臺灣大學資訊工程學系
Department of Computer Science and Information Engineering
National Taiwan University
p98922004@ntu.edu.tw

黃挺豪 Ting-Hao (Kenneth) Huang
國立臺灣大學資訊工程學系
Department of Computer Science and Information Engineering
National Taiwan University
r96944003@ntu.edu.tw

陳信希 Hsin-Hsi Chen
國立臺灣大學資訊工程學系
Department of Computer Science and Information Engineering
National Taiwan University
hhchen@ntu.edu.tw

摘要

情緒分析乃近年來發展迅速之一熱門研究領域[1,2]，旨在透過文本分析技術探討作者之意見傾向與情緒狀態。其中，以情緒詞與情緒詞典為基礎之各種方法尤為知名。然而，情緒詞之情感傾向及其行為於不同領域文本中之行為並不盡然相同。本研究聚焦於情緒詞彙於不同領域文本中之行為，對房地產、旅館、和餐廳等三種不同領域之文本進行分析，並發現部分情緒詞彙於不同領域文本中的情緒傾向非但有差異，甚至彼此衝突。此外，部分未收錄於情緒詞典中之「非情緒詞」，在特定領域中亦可能成為「領域相依」之詞彙，影響情緒分類。本研究繼而提出不同詞彙權重計算方式，將此資訊加入舊有情緒分類系統中。在使用 LIBSVM 的線性核函數方式，對房地產、旅館、和餐廳等三種語料使用 5 次交叉驗證方式進行分類。實驗結果顯示所提出之 TFSSIDF 分類方法，結合 TFIDF、臺灣大學情感詞典，及計算語料之領域極性情感傾向程度(SO)，強化領域相關及領域不相關之情緒詞之權重，通過 t 檢定有效提升各領域中文件分類之效能[3,4]。

Abstract

The researches of sentiment analysis aim at exploring the emotional state of writers. The analysis highly depends on the application domains. Analyzing sentiments of the articles in different domains may have different results. In this study, we focus on corpora from three different domains in Traditional and Simplified Chinese, then examine the polarity degrees of vocabularies in these three domains, and propose methods to capture sentiment differences. Finally, we apply the results to sentiment classification with supervised SVM learning. The experiments show that the proposed methods can effectively improve the sentiment classification performance.

關鍵詞：文件情緒分類、詞彙極性分析、機器學習

Keywords: Document Sentiment Classification, Word Polarity Analysis, Machine Learning

實驗結果

下表是採用單一詞彙不同詞彙權重、在三種不同領域文件的情緒分類結果，評估的標準是準確率。僅使用單一之 TFSO 或 TFIDF 的效果很接近，但是將 IDF 與 SO 相乘，也就是 TFSOIDF，其效果更好，TFSOIDF 優於其他兩種。若結合情感辭典，可將分類效果更進一步提昇。表中呈現 TFSSIDF 優於 TFSOIDF，TFSDIDF 優於 TFIDF。總結，Unigram 的結果以 TFSSIDF 為最佳，TFSOIDF 與 TFSDIDF 次之，接著是 TFIDF，與其他方法。(註：TF: 詞彙頻率，IDF: 逆向文件頻率，SO: 情感強烈程度，SD: 情緒詞典)

語料	TFIDF	TFRF	Delta	TFSO	**TFSOIDF**	TFSDIDF	**TFSSIDF**
房地產	0.848	0.849	0.853	0.847	0.854	0.852	**0.863**
旅館	0.916	0.906	0.914	0.915	**0.924**	0.918	0.923
餐廳	0.861	0.839	0.849	0.854	0.871	0.869	**0.875**

參考文獻

[1] Bo Pang and Lillian Lee, "Opinion Mining and Sentiment Analysis," *Foundations and Trends in Information Retrieval*, vol. 2, issue 1-2, pp. 1-135, 2008.

[2] Lun-Wei Ku and Hsin-Hsi Chen, "Mining Opinions from the Web: Beyond Relevance Retrieval," *Journal of American Society for Information Science and Technology*, vol. 58, no. 12, pp. 1838-1850, 2007.

[3] Man Lan, Sam-Yuan Sung, Hwee-Boon Low, and Chew-Lim Tan, "A Comparative Study on Term Weighting Schemes for Text Categorization," In *Proceedings of 2005 IEEE International Joint Conference on Neural Networks*, pp. 546-551, 2005.

[4] Justin Martineau and Tim Finin, "Delta TFIDF: An Improved Feature Space for Sentiment Analysis," In *Proceedings of the Third AAAI International Conference on Weblogs and Social Media*, pp. 258-261, 2009.

英文介系詞片語定位與英文介系詞推薦
Attachment of English Prepositional Phrases and Suggestions of English Prepositions

蔡家琦 劉昭麟
Chia-Chi Tsai Chao-Lin Liu

國立政治大學資訊科學系
National Chengchi University, Taipei, Taiwan
{g9906, chaolin}@cs.nccu.edu.tw

摘要

本研究專注於介系詞相關的二個議題：介系詞片語定位與介系詞推薦。我們將這二個議題抽象化為一個決策問題，並提出一個一般化的解決方法。這二個問題共通的部分在於動詞片語；一個簡單的動詞片語含有最重要的四個中心詞（headword）：動詞、名詞一、介系詞和名詞二。由這四個中心詞做為出發點，透過 WordNet 做階層式的選擇，在大量的案例中尋找語義上共通的部分，再利用機器學習的方法建構一般化的模型。此外，針對介系詞片語定位問題，我們挑選實驗具挑戰性的介系詞做實驗。藉由使用真實生活語料，我們的方法處理介系詞片語定位的問題，可以有不錯的表現；而對於介系詞推薦的問題，我們的方法難有全面比較的對象，但精準度可達到 47.76%。本研究發現，高層次的語義可以使分類器有不錯的分類效果，但透過階層式的語義選擇能使分類效果更佳。這顯示我們確實可以透過語義歸納一套準則，用於二個介系詞的議題。相信成果在未來會對機器翻譯與文本校對的相關研究有所價值。

關鍵字：語義分析、機器翻譯、文本校對

Abstract

This paper focuses on problems of attachment of prepositional phrases (PPs) and problems of prepositional suggestions. We transform the problems of PPs attachment and prepositional suggestions into an abstract model, and apply the same computational procedures to solve these two problems. The common model features four headwords, i.e., the verb, the first noun, the preposition, and the second noun in the prepositional phrases. Our methods consider the semantic features of the headwords in WordNet to train classification models, and apply the learned models for tackling the attachment and suggestion problems. This exploration of PP attachment problems is special in that only those PPs that are almost equally possible to attach to the verb and the first noun were used in the study. The proposed models consider only four headwords to achieve satisfactory performances. This study reconfirms that semantic information is instrument for both PP attachment and prepositional suggestions.

keyword : semantic analysis, machine translation, text proofreading

1 緒論

英文介系詞在句子裡所扮演的角色通常是用來使介系詞片語更精確的補述上下文，英文介系詞的使用對於英文母語的使用者而言是很直覺，即使英文母語的使用者不知道文法結構，仍然可以精確地表達語義。但對於電腦而言卻很難知道語義，因此不容易判斷正確的修飾對象。對於非英文母語的使用者，自然且正確地表達是有困難的。在現今資訊科技盛行爆炸的時代，我們期望透過大量資料以及資訊技術來輔助人類解決問題，並將我們研究應用於電腦自動化的流程。

介系詞一般出現在動詞片語裡，由動詞片語結構可以衍生出來的兩個有趣問題，也就是**介系詞片語定位**與**介系詞推薦**。

介系詞片語定位的問題是解決介系詞片語修飾對象是動詞或名詞片語，用一個具體的例子做說明，以句 1為例子。在我們主觀的認知中比較容易聯想的語境是：這群小孩用湯匙吃蛋糕。根據剛才想像的語境“with a spoon”這個介系詞片語修飾的應該是“ate”這個動詞。但是其實句 1也可以有另外一種想像的空間是這些小孩吃得是旁邊有放湯匙的蛋糕，這時“with a spoon”修飾的對象就是“the cake”這個名詞片語。

句 1. The children ate the cake with a spoon.[1]

介系詞推薦的問題是當動詞片語缺少介系詞時，應該要推薦何種適當的介系詞。對於非英文母語的使用者來說缺少了可以自然使用介系詞的直覺，只能透過介系詞的功能面決定它的用法。有些介系詞因為在功能面是類似的，例如 in、on、at 在時間的用途上是經常被混淆的。非英文母語的使用者只能透過大略的準則判斷介系詞的使用。

因為介系詞的使用是如此的廣泛，但是讓電腦瞭解語義和非英文母語的使用者來說都是有相當的門檻，所以我們對於介系詞的議題感到有興趣。為了可以更精確地使用介系詞，我們將深入探討這二種介系詞的議題。如果能夠解決這些議題，就可以將此應用做為機器翻譯基石和文本校對用途。

我們的研究嘗試找出上下文無關（context-free）的解決方案。這二個問題共通的部份是動詞片語，其結構是「動詞 -名詞片語一 -介系詞 -名詞片語二」的結構，簡化為四個中心詞「動詞 -名詞一 -介系詞 -名詞二（*V-N1-P-N2*）」。中心詞的定義為詞組中最核心被修飾的詞。我們直接探討動詞片語所抽出的四個主要中心詞並以此做為研究的出發點。再利用 WordNet 階層式的概念將中心詞提升到較抽象的語義層級，也就是找出上位詞，並利用資訊技術從大量的語料中找尋是否有一套準則能定位介系詞片語和推薦正確的介系詞。

在本研究，我們將介系詞片語定位問題與介系詞推薦問題分別做了一些假設與簡化。介系詞片語定位問題，在現實生活中，可能有的答案包含：修飾動詞、修飾名詞、二者皆可或其它。我們簡化為只有修飾動詞與修飾名詞二種可能。介系詞推薦的問題，在只提供動詞、名詞一和名詞二的資訊下，答案可能不只一個介系詞。因此我們將問題簡化成只有一個答案，只處理只有一個答案的案例。另外，只挑選數量較多的介系詞做實驗。

介系詞片語定位的問題依上述的假設是一個二分類的問題，介系詞推薦的問題則是一個多分類問題，所以，顯然地，我們可以看出推薦問題可能比定位問題的難度要高。

另外，針對介系詞片語定位的問題，許多學者大多希望能夠對所有介系詞找出一套一般化的通則。然而我們從 Ratnaparkhi 等人 [12] 所彙整的中心詞語料庫，也就是 RRR 語料庫[2]，統計各個介系詞數量分布的情況，結果如表 1所示，其中 NPP 為修飾名詞的介系詞片語，而 VPP 為修飾動詞的介系詞片語。可以發現每一個介系詞的定位情況都不相同，因此在我們的研究會針對各個介系詞歸納適用的準則。

表 1: RRR 語料庫，NPP 與 VPP 的數量

介系詞	NPP	VPP	總數	介系詞	NPP	VPP	總數	介系詞	NPP	VPP	總數
about	187	86	273	for	1342	1310	2652	of	6553	61	6614
as	123	497	620	from	360	716	1076	on	736	826	1562
at	166	594	760	in	1999	2061	4060	to	566	1486	2052
by	151	326	477	like	30	21	51	with	397	739	1136

研究成果裡，在介系詞片語定的問題中，本研究的效果比同樣考慮四個中心詞的最

[1]出自 Chris Manning 和 Hinrich Schütze，Foundations of statistical natural language prochessing 書中 8.3 節

[2]https://sites.google.com/site/adwaitratnaparkhi/publications/ppa.tar.gz?attredirects=0&d=1

大熵值法（Max Entropy）好，但與考慮上下文的 Stanford 剖析器結果是差不多。而在介系詞推薦的問題裡，我們的方法比起於目前方法的成果是有一小段差距。

介系詞的相關研究議題，一直是許多學者努力研究的目標，Baldwin 等人 [2] 於 2009 年時，回顧近十年各式各樣介系詞相關的議題，其中包含了本研究有興趣的二個介系詞議題。

從早期開始，有不少學者採用機率統計的方式試圖解決介系詞片語定位問題（如 Hindle 和 Rooth [8]、Liu 等人 [9] 和 Ratnaparkhi 等人）。經常使用得基本特徵資訊包含動詞片語的四個中心詞：動詞、名詞一、介系詞和名詞二。透過四個中心詞，再經由機率統計模型計算介系詞片語可能的定位。然而對假設已知四個中心詞，Atterer 和 Schütze [1] 指出這個假設不是憑空而來。但本研究依舊假設中心詞是已知條件，將中心詞的取得視為前處理的一部分，我們抽取中心詞的研究則是依靠 Stanford 剖析器[3]，而 Stanford 剖析則是建立在 Collins [3] 的研究之上。

在不少文獻中，可以看到每個介系詞均有自己的特色，如 Stetina 和 Nagao [13] 試圖為每一個介系詞製作合適的分類器。且大部分的介系詞更是有慣用方式，可參考表 1，例如介系詞“of”大多數的時候都是定位名詞。因此 Coppola 等人將語料中有“of”的案例去除。

推薦問題與定位問題的歷史相比較，是屬於比較年輕的問題。目前許多研究大多視為是語文學習應用，且視為是「介系詞校正」的問題，較早的相關研究有 De Felice 和 Pulman [5]、Gamon 等人 [7] 和 Tetreault 和 Chodorow [14]。

校正嚴格來說可以分成二階段：第一個階段是偵錯，第二個階段是更正。De Felice 和 Pulman [6]、Gamon 等人和 Helping Our Own 2012 Shared Task（Wu 等人 [16] 和 Quan 等人 [11]）都是二個階段皆著重。De Felice 和 Pulman [5] 是著重於後者。本研究也是著重於後者，廣義來說，我們將推薦視為是一種校正，但因為本研究不包含偵錯，所以我們強調是介系詞推薦。

De Felice 和 Pulman [5] 的研究與本研究的介系詞推薦是較相近，同樣是使用文法正確的語料庫訓練模型，且將實驗限縮在常用的介系詞。

2 語料介紹

2.1 語料庫

本研究使用 Peen Treebank 3（以下簡稱 PTB3）與 RRR 來作為介系詞片語定位問題的語料庫，而用自行蒐集的報導資料來當作介系詞推薦的語料庫。

RRR RRR 語料庫是由 Ratnaparkhi 等人 [12] 由 PTB0.5 匯整而成。其中每一筆資料都紀錄 PTB0.5 動詞片語中的四個中心詞與定位標記，我們將這種紀錄方式稱之為 RRR 格式。

PTB3 PTB3 是一個將自然語言結構化的資料庫，在許多自然語言處理的研究都被視為是黃金標準。本研究使用的版本是現行版本第三版，其中內容包含了三年份華爾街日報共 2499 篇報導，共有 98732 句結構化的句子，並且將這些句子分成 25 節。

華爾街日報與紐約時報 我們從華爾街日報[4]與紐約時報[5]的網站上蒐集了 2011 年部分報導內容，其中包含了華爾街日報的 68983 句和紐約時報的 55358 句。內容屬性上，華爾街日報是屬於財經類報導，而紐約時報是屬於綜合類的報導。這二類報導文章的句型句法都是屬於較現代的用法。

2.2 前處理

前處理的部分包含了句子的斷句與剖析、中心詞抽取、雜訊過濾以及挑選有挑戰性的介系詞等工作。流程圖可參考圖 1，圖中上半部是前處理的流程，下半部表示的是語料庫進入前處理的階段。使用華爾街日報與紐約時報需要從斷句與剖析句子的流程開始處理；使用 PTB3 語料庫，則是從結構樹中抽取中心詞的流程開始處理；使用 RRR 語料庫直接從雜訊過濾開始處理。最後所有語料彙整成 RRR 的資料格式，再統一處理

[3]Stanford Parser 2.0 版（2012 年 2 月 3 日），http://nlp.stanford.edu/software/lex-parser.shtml
[4]http://asia.wsj.com/home-page
[5]http://www.nytimes.com/

雜訊。雜訊過濾是一件重要的工作，雜訊包含了中心詞是定冠詞、代名詞等情況或是碰撞問題等情況。對於介系詞片語定位問題，挑選挑戰性介系詞是找出修飾動詞與修飾名詞機率相近的介系詞。每個語料庫介系詞分布情況大致上差不多，但仍有些許差異，因此我們以 RRR 語料庫為主。對於介系詞推薦的問題，則是找到數量較多或是差不多的介系詞。

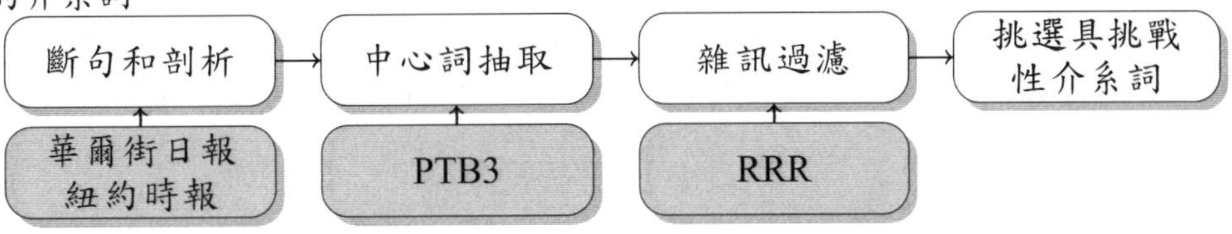

圖 1: 前處理流程圖

2.2.1 句子剖析與斷句

我們先利用 Stanford 剖析器與 Lingpipe[6]將所蒐集的語料斷句，接下來僅留下二者斷句有共識的句子。接著再利用 Stanford 剖析器剖析留下的句子，剖析後可得到結構樹。

2.2.2 中心詞抽取

當語料是結構樹時，才會需要中心詞抽取。我們的目標是從結構樹中比對修飾動詞或名詞的介系詞片語，如圖 2和圖 3分別表示修飾名詞與修飾動詞的介系詞片語結構，我們採用 Penn Treebank 的風格表示。這二個結構最大的不同點在於 PP 這個節點是掛在 NP 或是 VP 之下。二個圖中 VP 下方最左邊的節點表示是不同形態的動詞，如過去式、過去分詞等；IN 表示的是介系詞，“to” 這個介系詞會另外被表示成 TO。我們使用 Stanford Tregrex[7]比對圖 2和圖 3的樣式。

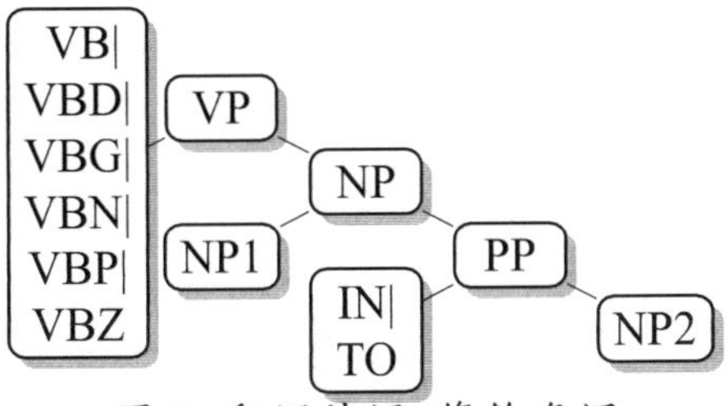

圖 2: 動詞片語: 修飾名詞

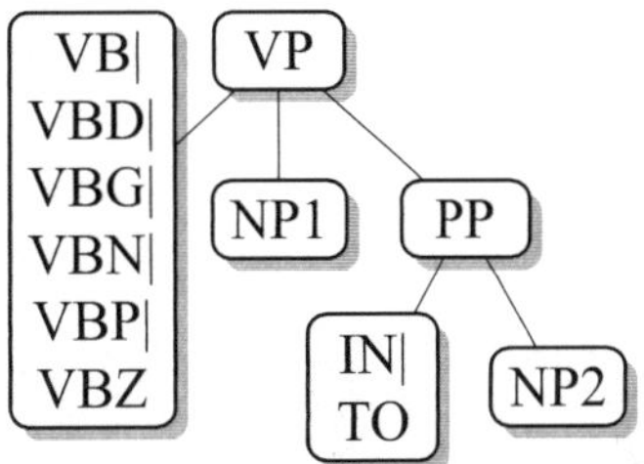

圖 3: 動詞片語: 修飾動詞

以句 2為例子，底線是我們要抽取的目標，它符合圖 3結構。比對出四個詞組如表 2片語一欄所示。最後利用 Stanford 剖析器的 SemanticHeadFinder[8]類別將的四個主要詞組的中心詞找出，得到的結果如表 2中心詞一欄所示。

句 2. ((S (NP-SBJ (DT The) (JJ Venezuelan) (JJ central) (NN bank))
(VP (VBD set) (NP (PP (NP (DT a)(ADJP (CD 30) (NN %))(NN floor))
(IN on)(NP (DT the) (NN bidding)))))(. .)))

表 2: 中心詞抽取

	片語	中心詞
動詞	(VBD set)	set
名詞片語一	(NP (NP (DT a) (ADJP (CD 30) (NN %)) (NN floor)))	floor
介系詞	(IN for)	for
名詞片語二	(NP (DT the) (NN bidding))	bidding

2.2.3 雜訊過濾

在我們的語料庫裡，也有不少句子因為語法上的關係，可能會有一些特殊的符號和數字被當成是中心詞，例如：“%”。然而這些符號和數字在我們的方法中是很難抽象化的，因此我們會事先將這些符號和數字過濾。

[6]http://alias-i.com/lingpipe/
[7]Stanford Tregrex 2.0.1 版（2012 年 1 月 6 日），http://nlp.stanford.edu/software/tregex.shtml
[8]http://nlp.stanford.edu/nlp/javadoc/javanlp/edu/stanford/nlp/trees/SemanticHeadFinder.html

除了上述情況之外，我們也發現雖然 RRR 的語料庫經由 Ratnaparkhi 等人整理過，但 Pantel 和 Lin [10] 在 RRR 語料庫裡找到 133 筆名詞一或名詞二為 “the”，PTB3 裡也有出現 “the” 的被當成是名詞的案例。另外在 RRR 與 PTB3 語料庫也均有一些名詞是 “a” 或 “an” 的情況。類似的情況，我們亦將之視為雜訊。

此外，我們會先利用 WordNet 做詞幹還原。接著，再給定還原後的詞彙和詞性，如果 WordNet 沒有查詢任何同義詞集（synset），那麼也會被過濾。

Coppola 等人 [4] 曾提到，如果名詞一是代名詞，則介系詞片語有較高的機率是定位於動詞。另一方面，代名詞不被收入於 WordNet 內，因此當名詞是代名詞的情況在我們的二個研究問題中也會過濾。

對於介系詞定位問題，碰撞是指當有二個以上的動詞片語具有四個相同的中心詞但介系詞定位卻不相同的情況。對於介系詞推薦問題，碰撞是指當動詞、名詞一和名詞二相同，但介系詞有二個以上的情況。上述這二類的案例，目前在本研究中暫不處理，因此也將之視為雜訊。

2.2.4 挑選具挑戰性的介系詞

在介系詞片語定位的問題中，我們將為每一個介系詞特製化分類器，並挑選修飾名詞與修飾動詞數量平衡的具挑戰性介系詞。這可以幫助我們去除掉幾乎有習慣用法的介系詞 “of”，使我們專注於幾個較難分類的介系詞。挑選具挑戰性介系詞時，因為後續使用機器學習演算法建構模型，所以不希望數量太少。因此我們採用 $Entropy$ 如式 (1) 和頻率這二個指標挑選介系詞，我們的目的是找平衡且數量多的介系詞。

$$Entropy = \sum_{d \in D} -Pr(d) \log_2 Pr(d) \tag{1}$$

式 (1) 中，以 “of” 為例，介系詞片語定位問題為 D，且只有二個分類因此 $D = \{VPP, NPP\}$，$Pr(d)$ 為修飾名詞與修飾動詞所佔的比例。因此，我們可以知道 $Pr(NPP) = 6553/6614$、$Pr(VPP) = 16/6614$，最後可以計算出 $Entropy$。$Entropy$ 數值越大表示偏好二個類別的數量越平衡越具挑戰性。

在介系詞推薦的問題中，我們會從語料庫挑選數量較多的介系詞。

2.3 目的語料

目的語料是我們經由 2.2節前處理的方法得到的結果。介系詞片語定位問題的語料，我們將以 RRR 所選到的介系詞為主，實際上，在我們的統計中，每個語料庫的介系詞分布幾乎都是差不多的。介系詞推薦問題則是依個別介系詞數量多寡不同而選擇的介系詞。對這二個問題我們設定了一個分布線（Distribution），分布線的意義是亂猜可以達到最佳的精準度。

介系詞片語定位問題，根據的介系詞數量分布的情況，分布線定義，如式 (2)。式 (2) 的 $Pr(VPP)$ 與 $Pr(NPP)$ 表示修飾動詞與修飾名詞在語料庫裡估得總量的比例。

$$Distribution = Max(Pr(V), Pr(N)) \tag{2}$$

介系詞推薦問題，我們比較著重於分析各個介系詞分類的情況，因此設定以介系詞在語料庫估得總量計算分布線，如式 (3)，其中 $|x|$ 表示 x 出現的頻率。而總體的分布線，則是以單獨分布線較高者為準。

$$Distribution = |Preposition|/|Total| \tag{3}$$

2.3.1 介系詞片語定位語料

表 3、表 4和表 5是 RRR 語料經由篩選過慮後的結果，我們選出 “for”、“on”、“in”、“with”、“from” 和 “to”，其中前三個介系詞都是數量多且較平衡的情況，而後三者則是數量多但較不平衡的情況，混合表示是將這六個介系詞一起做實驗。訓練語料、驗證語料和測試語料的分布大致上都是差不多。

表 6、表 7和表 8是 PTB3 過濾後的結果，分布的情況與 RRR 大致是相同的。為與 Stanford 剖析器做比較，我們選用 PTB3 的 02 到 21 節做測試語料，22 節做驗證語料，00、01、23 和 24 節做測試語料。

表 3: RRR 前處理結果: 訓練語料

介系詞	v	n	Entropy	分布線
for	829	869	0.9996	51.18%
on	512	485	0.9995	51.35%
in	1392	1314	0.9994	51.44%
with	454	268	0.9516	62.88%
from	451	237	0.9290	65.55%
to	1145	394	0.8207	74.40%
混合	4783	3567	0.9846	57.28%

表 4: RRR 前處理結果: 驗証語料

介系詞	v	n	Entropy	分布線
for	147	169	0.9965	53.48%
on	120	100	0.9940	54.55%
in	272	289	0.9993	51.52%
with	73	47	0.9659	60.83%
from	74	52	0.9779	58.73%
to	190	82	0.8831	69.85%
混合	876	739	0.9948	54.24%

表 5: RRR 前處理結果: 測試語料

介系詞	v	n	Entropy	分布線
for	111	148	0.9852	57.14%
on	66	93	0.9791	58.49%
in	156	200	0.9890	56.18%
with	55	35	0.9641	61.11%
from	60	32	0.9321	65.22%
to	135	76	0.9428	63.98%
混合	583	584	1.0000	50.04%

表 6: PTB3 前處理結果: 訓練語料

介系詞	v	n	Entropy	分布線
for	732	892	0.9930	54.93%
on	512	523	0.9999	50.53%
in	1531	1241	0.9921	55.23%
with	450	269	0.9538	62.59%
from	441	290	0.9690	60.33%
to	1064	335	0.7941	76.05%
混合	4730	3550	0.9853	57.13%

表 7: PTB3 前處理結果: 驗証語料

介系詞	v	n	Entropy	分布線
for	23	39	0.9514	62.90%
on	30	22	0.9829	57.69%
in	72	61	0.9951	54.14%
with	10	5	0.9183	66.67%
from	14	10	0.9799	58.33%
to	34	16	0.9044	68.00%
混合	183	153	0.9942	54.46%

表 8: PTB3 前處理結果: 測試語料

介系詞	v	n	Entropy	分布線
for	115	189	0.9568	62.17%
on	104	101	0.9998	50.73%
in	288	289	0.1000	50.09%
with	74	51	0.9754	59.20%
from	77	46	0.9537	62.60%
to	182	77	0.8780	70.27%
combine	840	753	0.9978	52.73%

表 9是表 8測試語料的原句總句數，我們會將這些原句讓 Stanford 剖析器剖器，再比對介系詞定位是否正確。

表 9: PTB3 前處理結果：測試語料原句句數

for	on	in	with	from	to
296	203	546	122	120	232

2.3.2 介系詞推薦語料

表 10是數量較大的語料庫，我們將處理後的語料切成訓練、測試資料，並從中選出數量較多的 11 個介系詞做實驗。

表 10: 華爾街日報與紐約時報前處理結果

	訓練資料		測試資料			訓練資料		測試資料	
	數量	分布線	數量	分布線		數量	分布線	數量	分布線
of	7341	28.36%	2390	27.71%	from	1300	5.02%	413	4.79%
in	5353	20.68%	1801	20.88%	at	1109	4.28%	359	4.16%
for	2892	11.17%	916	10.62%	as	694	2.68%	239	2.77%
to	2471	9.55%	892	10.34%	by	522	2.02%	162	1.88%
on	2248	8.68%	768	8.91%	about	329	1.27%	112	1.30%
with	1625	6.28%	572	6.63%	總數	25884	28.36%	8624	27.71%

3 研究方法

經過第2節語料處理後，可以得到動詞片語的四個中心詞：動詞、名詞一、介系詞和名詞二。在我們的研究裡，我們將這四個中心詞視為是已知條件，在這樣的條件下，對介系詞片語定位與介系詞推薦問題建構一般化的模型。

3.1 特徵處理

經過 WordNet 查詢而來的同義詞集被我們視為是特徵，然而這樣的特徵只是一個符號，但在現行許多機器學習的演算法，大多都是需要量化後的數值，因此如何將特徵量化是一個重要的議題。

本節特徵的處理包含了特徵量化與特徵加權，特徵加權可視為是廣義特徵量化的過程，因為加權本身也是將特徵數值化的一個過程。而本這節特徵量化特別強調如何表現特徵的存在，我們稱之為狹義特徵量化的定義。特徵加權主要是基於狹義特徵量化再給予不同的詮釋面向。

3.1.1 特徵量化

我們對於這三種量化的方式都有不同的詮釋：在一個透過 WordNet 查詢的詞彙中，從查詢到的第一個同義詞集到根節點所有的同義詞集，二元法考慮的面向是將所有節點都視為是均等的存在；平均法考慮的是每個節點平均負擔的語義；累計法考慮的是每一條至根節路徑中每一個節點被使用的頻率。下面我們將一一介紹每一種量化的方式：

二元法 二元法表示我們的特徵值只有 1 與 0，這代表所有同義詞集都視為是均等的存在。一個詞彙透過 WordNet 可以查詢的同義詞集以及至根節點間所有的同義詞集，凡是用到的同義詞集均以 1 表示，反之沒有用到以 0 表示。

平均法 二元法單純只考慮了同義詞集出現與否，然而一個同義詞集可能會有二個以上的上位詞，這使得一個同義詞集到根節點的路徑不只一條，因此我們認為這些分叉的路徑應該平均分擔這個詞彙的語義，這代表每個同義詞集在該詞彙裡平均負擔的語義。將原本是二元法的特徵值除以路徑數，若分叉的路徑有相同的同義詞集，那麼我們會再將該節點的特徵值合併，最後再將所有的路徑計算平均。藉此衡量同義詞集在一個詞彙中的重要性。

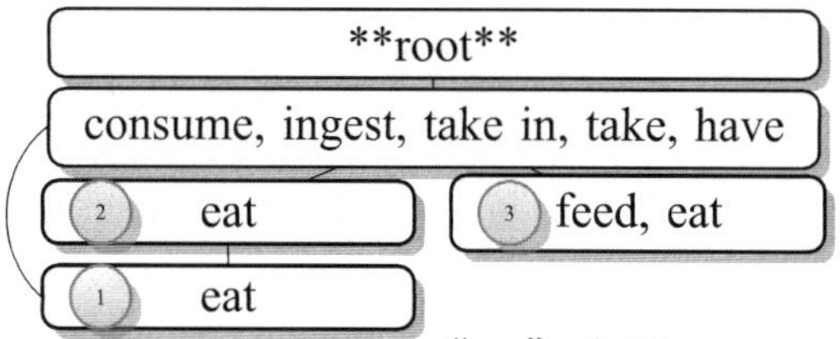

圖 4: 以動詞 "eat" 為例

圖 4表示動詞 "eat" 在 WordNet 的結構，每個節點都是上下位詞的關係，$\{**root**\}$ 是虛擬節點，在圖中的編號表示查詢 WordNet 得到的詞義（sense）編號，圖中僅列 3 個。以詞義編號 1 與詞義編號 2 作例子。路線量化的結果如表 11中間二欄，詞義編號 2 的路徑是 $\{eat\}-\{consume, ingest, takein, take, have\}-\{**root**\}$，因為詞義編號 2 ，只有走過這條路徑此，因此每個被走過的節點量化結果皆為 1。詞義編號 1 的路徑二條分別是 $\{eat\}-\{eat\}-\{consume, ingest, takein, take, have\}-\{**root**\}$ 和 $\{eat\}-\{consume, ingest, takein, take, have\}-\{**root**\}$，這時候我們會把 1 平均分擔於這二條路徑，因此這二條路徑上的每個量化的節點各是 0.5。接著我們合併同一個詞彙中相同的同義詞集，在詞義編號 1 的例子裡，二條路徑有 3 個同義詞集 $\{eat\}$、$\{consume, ingest, takein, take, have\}$ 和 $\{**root**\}$ 是重複的，因此我們把原本分擔於二條路徑上的 0.5 相加，使之成為 1，X 的部分視為 0，結果如表 11右邊二欄所示。最後，再計算每個同義詞集平均被經過的次數。以表 11詞義編號 1 與詞義編號 2 中的二個 $\{eat\}$ 為例，較抽象的 $\{eat\}$ 被經過次數只有一次，因此合併每個詞義量化後的結果再除以 1；較具體的 $\{eat\}$ 被經過的次數有二次，因此量化的結果相加後再除以 2。量化的結果如表 12所示。

表 11: 路線量化

	路線量化			加總合併	
詞義編號	1		2	1	2
路徑	1	2	1	1	1
$\{eat\}$	0.5	0.5	X	1	X
$\{eat\}$	0.5	X	1	0.5	1
$\{consume, ingest, takein, take, have\}$	0.5	0.5	1	1	1
$\{**root**\}$	0.5	0.5	1	1	1

表 12: 合併路徑量化

同義詞集	加總	平均法	累計法
$\{eat\}$	1	1	1
$\{eat\}$	1.5	0.75	1.5

累計法 與平均法相比較，累計法是比較重視上位詞，越是上位的同義詞集越是抽象，也表示被經過的次數會越多次，被我們視為是較具代表性的同義詞集。

同樣以"eat"為例，開始路線的標記同表 11。最後，將所有同義詞集加總的結果做正規化，正規化是將最後的量化的結果轉換到 0 到 1 之間，表 12的累計法未正規化。

3.1.2 特徵加權

我們也對二種不同的特徵加權的方法各有不同詮釋：同樣是考慮透過 WordNet 查詢的詞彙，從查詢到的同義詞集到根節點間所有的同義詞集，詞義頻率考慮的面向是找出較常被使用到的詞義，這可以幫助我們處理一些語義歧義的問題；語義深度考慮到 WordNet 是階層式的架構，在 3.1.1節是以類似詞袋（bag of word）概念量化的方式中，多加入了一些階層式的概念。底下我們分別介紹二種加權方式：

詞義頻率 頻率是取自於 WordNet 所記載的頻率，在 WordNet 所記載的頻率不僅是針對字面的頻率，而是有考慮詞義的頻率。雖然在我們的研究中不做語義歧義處理，但利用這點我們可以稍辨識常用詞義為何。通常頻率越高表示越常被用到。

以 $\{eat\} - \{consume, ingest, takein, take, have\} - \{**root**\}$ 這條路徑為例，透過 WordNet 我們可以查詢到 $\{eat\}$ 這個同義詞集在 WordNet 的頻率是 13，因此我們以 13 代表這條路徑在這個詞彙中的重要性。

語義深度 語義的深度取自於該節點到根節點所經過的節點數量，也就是樹的深度。當到根節點的路徑不只一條時，則會計算平均深度長。當語義的深度越深，則該同義詞集被我們視為越不重要，反之越淺則越重要。因此我們將語義深度以倒數表示，再乘上同義詞集在 3.1.1節中量化的結果。

同樣以 $\{eat\} - \{consume, ingest, takein, take, have\} - \{**root**\}$ 這條路徑為例，節點深度依序為 $3-2-1$。

3.2 特徵選擇

一個詞彙可能多義，但我們不做語義歧義處理，而是將所有可能的語義及其不同層次的抽象化語義均納入特徵池 (feature pool)，所以特徵池的特徵數量會非常的多，特徵池表示所有候選的同義詞集。由於特徵池非常龐大，而的特徵是從 WordNet 查詢來，所以這些特徵彼此存在著階層式的關係。因此我們設計了一套階層式特徵選擇的方法，而透過這樣階層式的選擇後，便可以找出具代表性的特徵，觀察與介系詞最相關連的語義層次為何，並瞭解我們研究的問題在何種語義層次上是可以被解決的。

3.2.1 階層式選擇

階層式選擇方法可參考演算法 1所示。首先，我們會將所有案例中的三個中心詞動詞、名詞一和名詞二（介系詞片語定位問題是給定已知的介系詞；介系詞推薦問題的介系詞則是答案）透過 WordNet 查詢同義詞集及到根節點間的所有同義詞集，並且將這些同義詞集都放到特徵池裡。首先，先從特徵池選出所有案例的最底層的同義詞集將之視為初始的特徵，利用 3.1節的方法將特徵數值化。再透過 3.2.2節篩選條件過濾不具代表性的同義詞集，被留下的同義詞集會繼續參選下一個世代的階層式選擇；被過濾掉的同義詞集則會被拋棄，在下個世代階層式選擇中，會以上位詞來取代。被保留下的特徵與被新選上的同義詞集也就是被拋棄的同義詞集的上位詞，會再被數值化，然後重做階層式選擇，如此反覆直到終止條件成立。這裡我們所設定的終止條件是當特徵量過少即會停止。另一方面，由於同義詞集在越高層次特徵量會越少，因此透過這樣階層式的選擇，可達到縮減特徵的目的。

我們將以圖 5為範例解釋階層式選擇流程。圖 5是一個簡化的 WordNet 結構，每一個節點都代表一個同義詞集，其中 S_i 代表同義詞集的編號。表 13是簡化的語料庫，假設我們只有三筆案例，將三個中心詞簡化成一個，每一個中心詞透過 WordNet 查詢後，都至少有一條從該節點到根節點 S_4 的路徑。同義詞集量化的過程，我們以二元法做為範例。

第 0 個世代被視為是初始的世代。首先我們會挑出所有案例最底層的同義詞集作為第 0 世代特徵，選上的同義詞集有 S_1、S_2 和 S_5，再以二元法量化，結果如表 14世代 0。透過 3.2.2節特徵篩選條件過濾後，假設 S_1 與 S_5 是這個世代被選出需要淘汰的特徵，那麼我們就會挑選 S_1 的上位詞 S_3 和 S_5 的上位詞 S_6 補上。此時 S_3 同時也是 S_2 的上位詞，因此對於 VP2 的案例而言，VP2 多出一個新的參選特徵，接著再重新量化新選出的特徵如表 14世代 1。接著在第二代參選中，如果我們淘汰 S_3，就會再以 S_4 補上如表 14世代 2 所示，那對於 VP2 這個案例 S_3 就會被視為是不存在。在第三代的參選中淘汰 S_2 則應補上 S_4，但 S_4 已經存在，所以這個世代特徵只會減少不會新增，如表 14世代 3。

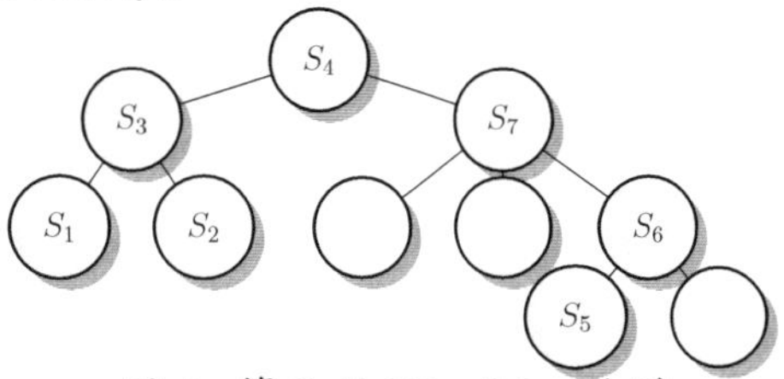

圖 5: 簡化的 WordNet 結構

表 13: 簡化語料庫案例

編號	同義詞集至根節點路徑
VP1	$\{S_1\} - \{S_3\} - \{S_4\}$
VP2	$\{S_2\} - \{S_3\} - \{S_4\}$
VP3	$\{S_5\} - \{S_5\} - \{S_7\} - \{S_4\}$

表 14: 階層式選擇範例: 世代

	世代 0			世代 1			世代 2			世代 3	
代號	S_1	S_2	S_5	S_3	S_2	S_6	S_4	S_2	S_6	S_4	S_6
VP1	1	0	0	1	0	0	1	0	0	1	0
VP2	0	1	0	1	1	0	1	1	0	1	0
VP3	0	0	1	0	0	1	1	0	1	1	1

3.2.2 篩選條件

篩選條件的方式可以分為三種：(一) 以計算該特徵使用的頻率並過濾低頻的部分，(二) 計算熵比例 (gain ratio) 並且過濾熵比例等於 0 的特徵，(三) 計算共現 (collocation) 同義詞集。被過濾的同義詞集表示其抽象化的程度不夠因此不具代表性，所以我們將其再度抽象化並以上位詞取代。

詞頻 在我們特徵選擇方法中，假設越抽象化的同義詞集應該是越重要且越常被使用。因此我們統計每個世代的特徵在案例中出現在的次數，將該回合的特徵的頻率依多寡排列並設二個門檻值，當特徵頻率低於 10 或門檻值時就會被過濾。

熵比例 熵比例是我們用來計算該特徵代表性的方法之一，以 $\{entity\}$ 為例子，$\{entity\}$ 這個特徵是名詞的同義詞集最抽象化的概念，所有的名詞的根節點一定是 $\{entity\}$，因此當這個同義詞集被選上做為特徵後，語料庫中的所有案例都會有 $\{entity\}$ 這個特徵，雖然它是詞頻最高的特徵，但因為它高到每個案例都有，因此這個特徵的重要性反而大大降低，所以我們透過熵比例把計算為 0 的特徵過濾。

共現同義詞集 除了單個同義詞集的頻率外，我們也統計了共現同義詞集頻率，也就是在這回合作為同義詞集的特徵中，每二個同義詞集一起出現的頻率。由於我們是將動詞、名詞一與名詞二的同義詞集混合在一起，所以再我們統計共現同義詞集後，我們也定了一些規則，將較不合理的狀況去除。不合理的組合包含：動詞 + 動詞、名詞一 + 名詞一、名詞二 + 名詞二組合。另外，我們大膽假設了一些情況，如果名詞二與

演算法 1 階層式特徵選擇

```
輸入： 語料庫
輸出： N 個世代具代表性特徵
find_representational_features_for_each_generation(Corpus)
  {將語料庫每個案例的動詞、名詞一和名詞二做特徵處理}
  for all  c ∈ Corpus  do
        fp_candidate ← feature_processing(c)
  end for
  i = 0 { 初始世代 }
  for all  c ∈ Corpus do
        g_i ← find_all_leaves_in_candidate_feature_pool(c)
  end for
  while (terminal_ conditions_ cannot_ be_satisfied) do
        ft = build_feature_vector(fp_candidate, g_i)
        fp_keeped, fp_abandoned = select_feature(ft)
        i = i + 1 { 進入下一個世代 }
        g_i ← fp_keeped
        for all f ∈ fp_abandoned do
              g_i ← find_hypenyms(f, fp_keeped, fp_abandoned)
        end for
  end while
  return  g
```

演算法 2 尋找上位詞

```
find_hypenyms(f, fp_keeped, fp_abandoned)
  ch = find_canditante_hynernyms(f)
  for all  h ∈ ch do
        if (h ∉ fp_keeped ∨ h ∉ fp_abandoned) then
              hypernyms ← h
        end if
  end for
  return  hypernyms
```

名詞一或名詞二與動詞的關聯性較強，那麼我們也把動詞 + 名詞一的組合刪除。透過上述的規則，我們希望可以再減少一些不具代性的特徵。

3.3 模型建構

特徵選擇後，下一步是使用機器學習的演算法建構模型，用以決策類別。

3.3.1 基準模型建構

我們針對介系詞片語定位問題設計了一套類似於 Naïve Bayes 的演算法，稱為基準模型，也就是模型決策的結果會被我們視為是基線。在特定的介系詞之下，我們考慮的不再是單一特徵而是動詞、名詞一與名詞二的同義詞集組合。在考慮同義詞集組合的情況下，我們有機會知道怎樣的組合是較有機會可以解決介系詞定位問題。

考慮動詞片語的四個中心詞，若限定在特定介系詞 P 的情況下，則以 $\vec{W} = (V, N1, N2)$ 表示一個動詞片語，其中 V、$N1$、$N2$ 分別表示動詞、名詞一以及名詞二。若我們想要解決的介系詞片語定位問題 D 是定位修飾動詞或修飾名詞一，則 $D = \{VPP, NPP\}$。更進一步，我們可計算修飾動詞的機率 $Pr = (D = VPP|\vec{W})$ 和修飾名詞的機率 $Pr = (D = NPP|\vec{W})$。透過 WordNet 查詢後，動詞的同義詞集表示為 $V = \{s_{v_1}, s_{v_2}, \cdots, s_{v_i}\}$，名詞一表示為 $N1 = \{s_{n1_1}, s_{n1_2}, \cdots, s_{n1_j}\}$，名詞二表示為 $N2 = \{s_{n2_1}, s_{n2_2}, \cdots, s_{n2_k}\}$。

以 $\vec{S} = \{s_{v_i}, s_{n1_j}, s_{n2_k}\}$ 代表 $\vec{W}$ 一個可能的詞義組合特徵，以 $R(\vec{S})$ 表示所有可能的詞義組合特徵。

因此我們可以將模型表示成式 (4)，式 (5) 我們假設 D 與 $\vec{W}$ 在已知 $\vec{S}$ 的情形下是條件獨立，$\vec{S}$ 展開後得到式 (6)，若再假設式 (6) 個別詞彙在語境中所負擔的詞義角色與其它詞彙無關，則最後可以得到式 (7)。

$$Pr(D|\vec{W}) = \sum_{\vec{S}\in R(\vec{S})} Pr(D, \vec{S}|\vec{W}) = \sum_{\vec{S}\in R(\vec{S})} Pr(\vec{S}|\vec{W}) \times Pr(\vec{D}|\vec{W}, \vec{S}) \tag{4}$$

$$= \sum_{\vec{S}\in R(\vec{S})} Pr(\vec{S}|\vec{W}) \times Pr(\vec{D}|\vec{S}) \tag{5}$$

$$= \sum_{\vec{S}\in R(\vec{S})} Pr(s_{v_i}, s_{n1_j}, s_{n2_k}|V, N1, N2) \times Pr(D|s_{v_i}, s_{n1_j}, s_{n2_k}) \tag{6}$$

$$= \sum_{\vec{S}\in R(\vec{S})} Pr(s_{v_i}|V) \times P(s_{n1_i}|N1) \times Pr(s_{n2_i}|N2) \times Pr(D|s_{vi}, s_{n1_j}, s_{n2_k}) \tag{7}$$

根據上述式子，最後推得的結果中 $Pr(s_{v_i}|V)$、$P(s_{n1_j}|N1)$ 和 $Pr(s_{n2_k}|N2)$ 項，以動詞為例，可經由式 (8) 而得，其中 $WN(S)$ 表示一個詞彙的其中一個同義詞集經由 WordNet 查詢得到的頻率。由於某些詞義詞頻可能為 0，因此我們使用 *Laplace estimator* 概念做平滑化（smooth），而式 (8) 中 $|V|$ 表示 V 的個數。

$$Pr(s_{v_i}|V) = (WN(s_{v_i}) + 1)/((\sum_{s_{vm}\in V} WN(S_{v_m})) + |V|) \tag{8}$$

$Pr(D|s_{v_i}, s_{n1_j}, s_{n2_k})$ 項，則是再訓練時，經由統計而得。

$$Pr(D|s_{v_i}, s_{n1_j}, s_{n2_k}) = |(s_{v_i}, s_{n1_j}, s_{n2_k}, D)|/|(s_{v_i}, s_{n1_j}, s_{n2_k})| \tag{9}$$

在只使用三個中心詞的情況，我們相信語義抽象化程高時，就可以使模型分類出大多數的案例。所以我們挑選代入名詞一與名詞二的同義詞集是從 WordNet 名詞根節點往下數第三層的同義詞集。動詞同義詞集與名詞較不同是它的樹狀結構深度淺，且虛擬根節點下一層的同義詞集非常多，因此我們挑選虛擬根節點下一層同義詞集的類別（lexicographer）代入。將這些選上的同義詞集經統計計算後代入式 (7)。

3.3.2 傳統模型建構

傳統模型表示我們使用的是現在常用的熱門演算法。我們共選了三種 SVM、C4.5 和 Naïve Bayes 演算法，其中 SVM 採用的是 Libsvm-3.11[9]版本，而後二者 C4.5 與 Naïve Bayes 使用的工具是 Weka3-6-6[10]版本。

SVM 我們選用的 kernel method 為 RBF，需要調整參數 γ 和 $cost$ 以使參數最佳化。我們使用 grid search 演算法調整參數，利用的工具是 libsvm 的 grid.py。將 x 軸對應到 $cost$ 參數範圍設為 -5 到 11，步數為 2。而 y 軸對映到 γ 參數範圍設為 -11 到 3，y 軸步數皆設為 2。再將 x 軸與 y 軸值代入涵數 $f(n) = 2^n$，並測試 $f(x)$ 與 $f(y)$ 分類的效果。

C4.5 的演算法需要調整二個參數：每個節點至少包含的案例數和 $confidencefactor$。將前者參數設為 x，範圍設為 5 到 50，步數為 5。後者參數設為 y，範圍設為 0.05 到 0.45，步數為 0.05。最後直接將 x 與 y 值代入演算法測試分類效果。

Naïve Bayes 則是無調整體的參數。

3.3.3 高階模型（meta learner）建構

現在許多成功的分類器背後都不單使用一個分類器，而是採用多個分類器整合而成。這類似於將每個模型都視為是一位專家，讓每位專家都發表自己的看法。

我們同樣使用第 3.3.2節所提到三種演算法：SVM、C4.5 和 Naïve Bayes 來建構高階模型。先利用訓練語料建立傳統模型，再決策驗證語料的答案，將決策的答案當作高

[9]http://www.csie.ntu.edu.tw/ cjlin/libsvm/

[10]http://www.cs.waikato.ac.nz/ml/weka/

階模型的訓練資料，用以訓練高階模型，最後把測試語料當作最終上線的測試資料並利用訓練好的高階模型來做最後決策。

我們設定了不同的條件，挑選品質較佳的傳統模型來建構高階的模型。條件 1，是將所有傳統模型結果都用來訓練高階模型；條件 2，表示會先計算所有模型的精準度，只挑選高於平均的模型來訓練高階模型；條件 3，同條件 2，但是我們只選擇傳統模型是由 SVM 演算法訓練而成的模型，事實上由 SVM 所訓練而成傳統模型表現是比較好的。

4 實驗評量與分析

本節將分析第 3 節建立模型的成效。

4.1 實驗評量

本研究中，評量方法最後會以百分比的方式呈現於實驗分析中。

我們以精準度（$Accuacy$）做為評量模型總體的方式。假設模型可以答對的案例數為 T，而語料庫的案例數為 N，則精準度如式 (10)。

$$Accuracy = T/N \tag{10}$$

另外，我們以準確率（$Precision$）、召回率（$Recall$）和綜合評量（F_1-$measure$）評量各個類別的決策效果。若是介系詞片語定位的問題，那麼決策的類別粗分為答對與答錯。若是評量介系詞校正問題，類別是各個介系詞。

精確率表示模型對於該類別分類的正確性。假設某一模型在語料庫中，決策某一類別數量為 E，而模型可以對該類別正確做決策的數量為 D，則準確率可以描述如式 (11)。

$$Precision = D/E \tag{11}$$

召回率表示的是我們的模型對於該類別的信心程度。假設某一類別有 G 個案例數，那麼召回率定義如式 (12)

$$Recall = D/G \tag{12}$$

實務上，我們希望精確率和召回率都很高。但往往結果是高精確率與低召回率或高召回率低精確率。在這樣的情況下，需要一個綜合評合的指標，因此我們採用綜合評量（F_1-$measure$），如式 (13)。

$$F_1\text{-}measure = (2 \times Precision \times Recall)/(Precision + Recall) \tag{13}$$

4.2 實驗分析：介系詞片語定位

本節將分析整體介系詞片語定位的實驗成果。我們根據 3.1.1節、3.1.2節和 3.2.2節設計 12 種不同的條件組合做實驗。實驗結果顯示不同量化和加權的方法對結果並沒有太大的差別，而篩選特徵的方式對於實驗結果是比較有影響。每個世代的特徵篩選結果，在精準度差不多的情況下，考慮共現義同義詞集相較於考慮詞頻是比較有用處。因為共現同義詞集是屬於較嚴苛的條件，以致在訓練時使用的特徵量是比較少。此外，詞頻與共現詞頻的門檻值不宜太高，若將每個世代使用的同義詞集照頻率高低排序，我們會發現與 Zipf's law 曲線是一樣的，這說明常用的同義詞集是有集中的現象，少用同義詞集數量較多，因此門檻值設太高容易在開始時就過濾掉大多數的同義詞集。另外，階層式選擇大約在 3 到 5 個世代就可以找到有用的特徵，之後的世代精準度就會開始明顯往下遞減。

我們從這些條件組合中，利用驗證語料選出表現最佳的模型，若有二個以上模型表現一樣好，則平均計算精準度。而選出最佳的模型幾乎都是以 SVM 演算法訓練而成。最後測試語料會用以衡量最終精準度。

在介系詞片語定位問題裡，我們將傳統模型再分為單一模型、混合資料模型。單一模型表示對每個介系詞特製化分類器，混合資料模型則是將我們挑選的 6 個介系詞混合訓練。

表 15是 RRR 語料的綜合結果，PTB3 語料庫我們也做了同樣的實驗，二者結果差不多。PTB3 語料庫比較著重於與 Stanford 剖析器做比較。表 15的 Max Enp 表示最大熵值法，最佳高階模型表示挑選每個介系詞最好的高階模型，高階混合資料 (3)SVM 表示混

合資料的高階模型是以 SVM 訓練且利用條件 3 選擇傳統模型。算數平均表示將所有介系詞都視為是一樣重要，因此所有介系詞的權重相同；而加權平均表示考慮到各個介系詞的數量，將數量視為是權重。

比較表 15的單一模型、混合資料模型與基線的精準度，單一模型與混合資料模型的精準度均較基準模型高。這表示透過階層式的特徵選擇比起只固定選擇較高層次的特徵有效。單一模型、混合資料模型精準，二者是差不多。但單一模型可以有效的針對特定介系詞找出具代表性的同義詞集做為特徵，這是混合資料模型無法做到。且混合資料模型的語料量遠較單一模型大，這可能也是無法突顯單一模型效果的原因之一。若能提升單一模型語料量，那麼單一模型應該還有進步的空間。最佳高階單一模型與單一模型，前者略勝一些；而高階混合資料與混合資料相比較，結果差不多，整體而言高階模型改善的幅度有限。最後比較我們的方法與最大熵值法，除表中基線精準度與最大熵值法差不多外，可以觀察我們每一組實驗的結果不僅較分布線佳而且也較最大熵值法好。

表 15: RRR 實驗結果

介系詞	個數	分布線 (%)	精準度 (%)					
			Max Enp	基線	單一	混合資料	最佳高階單一	高階混合資料 (3)SVM
for	259	60.86	62.55	67.57	74.13	73.75	74.13	71.81
on	159	63.90	67.92	67.30	69.81	72.96	73.58	74.84
in	356	64.64	75.56	72.47	79.21	79.78	79.21	80.34
with	90	64.80	60.00	63.33	66.67	67.78	72.22	68.89
from	92	66.67	69.57	75.00	79.35	78.26	82.61	76.09
to	211	66.80	72.51	70.62	85.31	83.89	88.15	83.89
算數平均		60.35	68.02	69.38	75.75	76.07	78.32	75.98
加權平均		59.21	69.41	69.67	76.95	77.21	78.66	77.12
混合資料	1167	50.04						

我們發現 Stanford 剖析器會將原本不是動詞片語的結構誤認為是動詞片語；反之也有可能原是動詞片語的結構，但 Stanford 剖析器無法辨識。我們將 PTB3 測試語料的原句讓 Stanford 剖析，並將答案粗分成二類答對與答錯，結果如表 16所示，P 表示精準率，R 是召回率，F 是綜合評量。如果將二種情況的案例去除，可得表 17。這時候比較我們的方法與 Stanford 剖析器的結果，可以看到二者的精準度差不多。

表 16: SP 答題狀況

介系詞	P(%)	R(%)	F(%)
for	87.26	74.90	80.61
on	89.73	75.72	82.13
in	88.39	79.53	83.73
with	91.01	72.97	81.00
from	88.17	78.10	82.83
to	87.82	79.72	83.57

表 17: PTB3 實驗結果

介系詞	個數	分布線 (%)	精準度 (%)		
			SP	單一	混合資料
for	247	63.97	74.90	77.63	77.63
on	173	50.29	75.72	75.28	79.02
in	469	50.32	79.53	77.47	78.68
with	111	56.76	72.97	67.20	75.20
from	105	62.86	78.10	76.15	79.67
to	217	70.51	79.72	83.59	81.47
算數平均		59.12	76.82	76.22	78.61
加權平均		57.72	77.53	77.25	78.77
混合資料	1322	52.27			

雖然我們的方法與 Stanford 剖析器差不多，但二種方法各有優缺點。在考慮語境資訊上，我們的方法考慮的語境資訊較少；但 Stanford 剖析器考慮的是全句，使用資訊較多。我們的方法需要事先給定四個中心詞；Stanford 剖析器只要有完整的句子便能夠剖析、定位修飾對象。

4.3 實驗分析：介系詞推薦

定位與推薦問題是用同樣的模型建構方式。除了華爾街日報與紐約時報外，我們也以 RRR 語料庫重複第 3節流程的實驗。不同組合的條件結果，影響較大的是考慮共現同義詞集的條件，不僅可以有效的大幅減少不必要的特徵且效果依舊不錯。三種傳統模型訓練結果仍舊是 SVM 勝過 C4.5 與 Naïve Bayes，後二者又以 C4.5 較佳。

數量大語料庫，在受限硬體環境的情況下，較沒有像辦法 RRR 語料庫將所有條件組合一一跑過一次，藉以挑選最好的模型條件。因此我們從 RRR 語料庫的結果中，挑選表現最佳的條件用於大語料庫上。介系詞推薦的分析主要會著重在華爾街日報與紐約時報組成的大語料庫上。

表 18: 大語料庫實驗結果

介系詞	分布線 (%)	P(%)	R (%)	F (%)
of	27.71	51.40	70.13	59.32
in	20.88	49.91	60.74	54.80
for	10.62	36.66	30.46	33.27
to	10.34	48.39	35.43	40.91
on	8.91	54.74	45.83	49.89
with	6.63	35.24	21.50	26.71
from	4.79	30.18	16.22	21.10
at	4.16	38.65	30.36	34.01
as	2.77	40.46	22.18	28.65
by	1.88	31.88	13.58	19.05
about	1.30	45.16	25.00	32.18
精準度		47.76%		

表 19: 對照組，原文僅表示到小數後第二位

介系詞	個數	分布線 (%)	P(%)	R(%)	F(%)
of	7485	38.18	88	78	83
to	4841	24.69	78	87	82
in	4278	21.82	75	78	77
on	1483	7.56	66	65	65
with	1520	7.75	73	69	70

表 20: 混淆矩陣: 華爾街日報與紐約時報

		決策答案										
		of	in	for	to	on	with	from	at	as	by	about
實際答案	of	**1801**	283	72	66	48	31	28	31	17	2	11
	in	421	**1101**	74	49	58	28	16	31	14	2	7
	for	**355**	188	243	42	26	26	6	21	4	1	4
	to	275	140	65	**283**	42	27	6	34	6	9	5
	on	216	124	36	24	**315**	13	12	14	7	0	7
	with	**267**	95	34	21	20	94	8	16	10	3	4
	from	**125**	117	37	28	20	7	56	17	1	4	1
	at	**111**	58	28	21	18	4	8	100	2	7	2
	as	**123**	30	10	6	7	7	2	7	45	2	0
	by	**71**	31	13	13	7	5	3	4	2	11	2
	about	**49**	14	5	7	3	5	0	0	1	0	28

表 18是實驗的結果。單獨看每個介系詞效果，"on" 的精確率最好的，"of" 的召回率和綜合評量是最好。與表 20混淆矩陣（confusion matrix）一起觀察，可以看到介系詞幾乎都偏好 "of"，第二名是 "in"。綜合在 RRR 語料庫所觀察的結果，我們發現模型的偏好可能與介系詞的特性關係較小，而與介系詞在語料庫裡分布的數量多寡比較有關，表中的召回率與分布線幾乎是呈現正相關，因此我們目前推測的模型效果與介系詞各類別語料的數量比較有關係。

在介系詞推薦實驗中，目前所回顧論文提及的語料取得較為困難，這使得我們難與其它方法比較。然而介系詞推薦只要能夠取得文章，就可以利用現有的工具，自動化的處理取得我們所需的部分。所以我們可以很容易大量取得語料完成實驗，因此在足夠大量的語料下，我們相信即使不能完全與其它方法相比較，但仍然可以參考語料庫介系詞的分部，以知道目前研究的成效。若與研究性質較近文獻比較，目前的成果與 De Felice 和 Pulman [5] 的成果是有一段差距，參考表 19。但本研究中所考慮的資訊的僅包三個中心詞，而 De Felice 和 Pulman 的研究則是考慮了上下文的語義而視窗大小

(window size) 設為 6，這也顯示我們的研究還有進步的空間。

5 結論

本研究以四個中心詞為出發，透過 WordNet 階層式的語義概念，建構一般化的模型，同時解決二個介系詞相關的議題。我們的實驗結果顯示，一般化的模型對介系詞片語定位問題能有不錯的表現，特別我們專注於幾個較具有挑戰性的介系詞。但對於介系詞推薦問題，與現行較好的成果是有一小段差，而目前的實驗成果只顯示混淆矩陣易偏好語料量較多的類別，那在未來我們希望能透過更多實驗探究可能的原因。我們發現透過 WordNet 發掘不同程度的抽象語義確實有助於改善分類效果，但 WordNet 對詞彙的描述分類過於細，因此希望未來能透過 SUMO[11] 再改善實驗成果。應用方面，希望介系詞片語定位與介系詞推薦在未來能對機器翻譯和文本校對有所幫助，並期望二者在未來可以輔助人類解決問題。其它限於篇幅因此不能在本文中全面交代相關細節，相關細節可參考 Tsai [15]。

致謝

本研究承蒙國科會研究計畫 NSC-100-2221-E-004-014-的部分補助，僅此致謝。我們感謝評審對於本文的各項指正與指導。

參考文獻

[1] M. Atterer and H. Schütze, "Prepositional Phrase Attachment without Oracles," *Computational Linguistics*, vol. 33, no. 4, pp. 469–476, 2007.

[2] T. Baldwin, V. Kordoni, and A. Villavicencio, "Prepositions in Applications: A Survey and Introduction to the Special Issue," *Computational Linguistics*, vol. 35, no. 2, pp. 119–149, 2009.

[3] M. J. Collins, "Head-driven Statistical Models for Natural Language Parsing," Ph.D. dissertation, University of Pennsylvania, 1999.

[4] G. F. Coppola, A. Birch, T. Deoskar, and M. Steedman, "Simple Semi-supervised Learning for Prepositional Phrase Attachment," in *Proceedings of the 12th International Conference on Parsing Technologies*, 2011, pp. 129–139.

[5] R. De Felice and S. G. Pulman, "Automatically Acquiring Models of Preposition Use," in *Proceedings of the Fourth ACL-SIGSEM Workshop on Prepositions*, 2007, pp. 45–50.

[6] ——, "A Classifier-based Approach to Preposition and Determiner Error Correction in L2 English," in *Proceedings of the 22nd International Conference on Computational Linguistics*, vol. 1, 2008, pp. 169–176.

[7] M. Gamon, J. Gao, C. Brockett, and R. Klementiev, "Using Contextual Speller Techniques and Language Modeling for ESL Error Correction," in *Proceedings of Joint Conference on Natural Language Processing 2008*, 2008, pp. 449–456.

[8] D. Hindle and M. Rooth, "Structural Ambiguity and Lexical Relations," *Computational Linguistics*, vol. 19, no. 1, pp. 103–120, 1993.

[9] C.-L. Liu, J.-S. Chang, and K.-Y. Su, "The Semantic Score Approach to the Disambiguation of PP Attachment Problem," in *Proceedings of the ROC Computational Linguistics Conference III*, 1990, pp. 253–270.

[10] P. Pantel and D. Lin, "An Unsupervised Approach to Prepositional Phrase Attachment Using Contextually Similar Words," in *Proceedings of the 38th Annual Meeting on Association for Computational Linguistics*, 2000, pp. 101–108.

[11] L. Quan, O. Kolomiyets, and M.-F. Moens, "KU Leuven at HOO-2012: A Hybrid Approach to Detection and Correction of Determiner and Preposition Errors in Non-native English Text," in *Proceedings of the Seventh Workshop on Building Educational Applications Using NLP*, 2012, pp. 263–271.

[12] A. Ratnaparkhi, J. Reynar, and S. Roukos, "A Maximum Entropy Model for Prepositional Phrase Attachment," in *Proceedings of the Workshop on Human Language Technology*, 1994, pp. 250–255.

[13] J. Stetina and M. Nagao, "Corpus Based PP Attachment Ambiguity Resolution with a Semantic Dictionary," in *Proceedings of the Fifth Workshop on Very Large Corpora*, 1997, pp. 66–80.

[14] J. R. Tetreault and M. Chodorow, "The Ups and Downs of Preposition Error Detection in ESL Writing," in *Proceedings of the 22nd International Conference on Computational Linguistics - Volume 1*, 2008, pp. 865–872.

[15] C.-C. Tsai, "Attachment of English Prepositional Phrases and Suggestions of English Prepositions," Master's thesis, National Chengchi University, 2012.

[16] J.-C. Wu, J. Chang, Y.-C. Chen, S.-T. Huang, M.-H. Chen, and J. S. Chang, "Helping Our Own: NTHU NLPLAB System Description," in *Proceedings of the Seventh Workshop on Building Educational Applications Using NLP*, 2012, pp. 295–301.

[11] http://www.ontologyportal.org/index.html

Associating Collocations with WordNet Senses Using Hybrid Models

陳奕均 Yi-Chun Chen

國立清華大學資訊工程學系

Department of Computer Science
National Tsing Hua University

jordanchengno1@hotmail.com

顏孜羲 Tzu-Xi Yen

國立清華大學資訊工程學系

Department of Computer Science

National Tsing Hua University

joseph.yen.@gmail.com

張俊盛 Jason S. CHang

國立清華大學資訊工程學系

Department of Computer Science

National Tsing Hua University

jason.jschang@gmail.com

Abstract

In this paper, we introduce a hybrid method to associate English collocations with sense class members chosen from WordNet. Our combinational approach includes a learning-based method, a paraphrase-based method and a sense frequency ranking method. At training time, a set of collocations with their tagged senses is prepared. We use the sentence information extracted from a large corpus and cross-lingual information to train a learning-based model. At run time, the corresponding senses of an input collocation will be decided via majority voting. The three outcomes participated in voting are as follows: 1. the result from a learning-based model; 2. the result from a paraphrase-based model; 3. the result from sense frequency ranking method. The sense with most votes will be associated with the input collocation. Evaluation shows that the hybrid model achieves significant improvement when comparing with the other method described in evaluation time. Our method provides more reliable result on associating collocations with senses that can help lexicographers in compilation of collocations dictionaries and assist learners to understand collocation usages.

關鍵詞：超語意標示，搭配詞分類，詞彙語意解歧，詞網、最佳熵值模型、重述

Keywords: supersense tagging, collocation classification, word sense disambiguation, WordNet, maximum entropy model, Paraphrase.

1 Introduction

A collocation is a pair of words that co-occur with more frequency than random. A collocation usually contains a base word (e.g., "*oil*" in *fuel oil*) and a collocate (e.g., "*fuel*" in *fuel oil*). In a collocations dictionary, we can find many collocates of a base word (e.g., *fuel oil*, *motor oil*, *peanut oil, salad oil*). Some collocations dictionaries show the collocates for all senses, while other collocations dictionaries present the collocates by senses of a base word so learners can better grasp the usage of a collocation.

Determining the set of broad senses to classify collocations is not an easy task. Researches have used thesaurus topics such as Roget's (Yarowsky, 1992) or arbitrarily top-level WordNet senses as classes. There are 44 semantic classes called lexicographer-files and each synset in WordNet is assigned to one lexicographer-file. There are 26 lexicographer-files (or *supersenses*), which can be used to tag common nouns. Consider the word "*oil*" which can be *used as fuel/to make machines work smoothly, or* as belonging to the *noun.substance* supersense and *used in cooking* could be seen as belonging to the *noun.food* supersense.

In this paper, we present a hybrid model that automatically associated a given collocation with the corresponding supersense. The hybrid model is composed of a learning-based method, a paraphrase-based method and a sense frequency ranking method. The output supersense of a collocation is decided via majority vote of the above three methods.

At training time, we need some collocations tagged with supersenses as seeds. There are a huge number of collocations in WordNet, so we can use those collocation and supersense pairs to train the model. Sentences containing the input collocations extracted from a large corpus and Chinese translation of the collocations are used as features of the model. We will descript the training process in more details in Chapter 3.

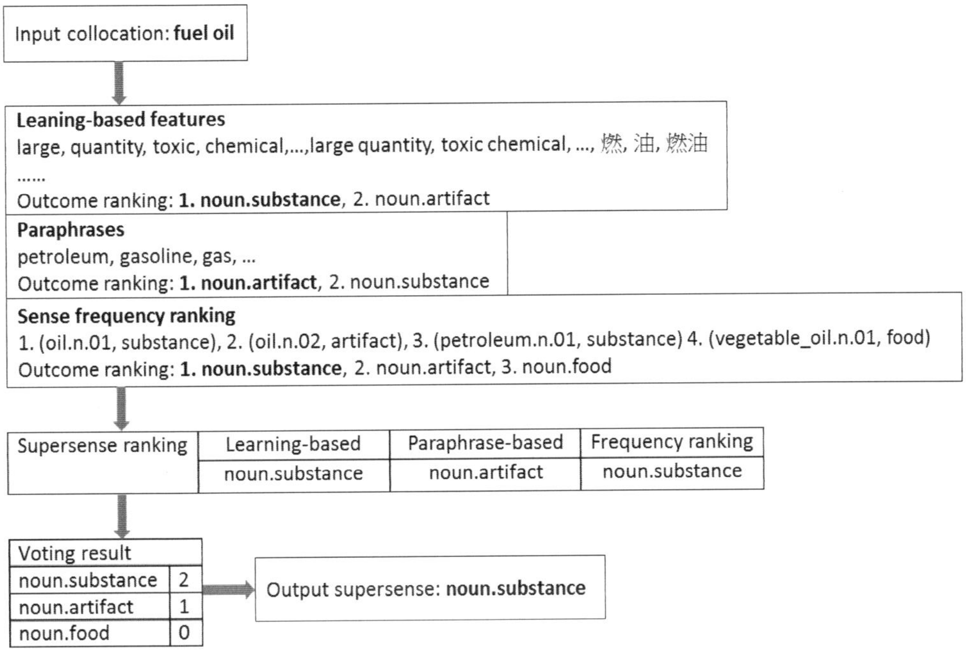

Figure 1. An example procedure for associating the collocation of fuel oil with a supersense *noun.substance*

An example procedure for associating the collocation of *fuel oil* with a supersense *noun.substance* is shown in Figure 1. We extract sentences containing the input collocation from a corpus and take the sentences and Chinese translation as features. Then, we use the pre-trained machine learning model to predict the supersense. Second, we use the words similarity and words dependency relations to paraphrase the base word. Then, we calculate the WordNet similarity of base word and the paraphrases to identify the supersense. Third, we simply list the lexicographer-files of the input collocation base word and choose the first one as the supersense since the order of the list corresponds to the sense frequency of that word. At last, a relative majority vote for the three results determines the final output.

The experimental results show that our hybrid method can automatically associate collocations with supersenses with a higher performance than the baseline method. The results can also be used to help lexicographers in compilation of a collocations dictionary. Furthermore, learners could understand the usage of collocations in a specific sense.

2 Related Work

Associating collocations with supersenses in WordNet is similar to Word Sense Disambiguation (WSD), the process of identifying the meaning of a specific word in a given context. In this paper, we address a special case of disambiguating the headword of a given collocation.

Previous work in WSD is mostly based on some kind of machine learning models. Hearst (1991) uses a set of orthographic, syntactic and lexical features to train large text corpora and disambiguates noun homographs. Yarowsky (1992) uses Naïve Bayesian model to train large corpora to disambiguate words to Roget's Thesaurus categories. Leacock, Towell and Voorhees (1993) bases on Bayesian decision theory, neural networks and content vectors to train the knowledge about patterns of words co-occurrences and disambiguates words to WordNet senses. The main disadvantage is that the demand of annotated training data which are time-consuming and labor intensive to obtain.

In a work more closely to our research, Inumella, Kilgarriff and Kovar (2009) try to assign the collocations for a word that automatically identified from a large corpus to its distinct senses. Their short term goal is to generate a new English collocations dictionary (Macmillan Collocation Dictionary). Most of the previous works focus on words level, while this research focuses on collocations. We describe two of their automatic approaches: Thesaurus method and Yarowsky's method (1995). The thesaurus method works on the promise that a sense shares its collocates with its thesaurus class members. For example, consider a thesaurus class with six members {cricket, butterfly, leech, worm, bee, queen}, they extract collocates such as young, fly, feed, breed that at least appear in two class members and insert them to that sense. Another method is Yarowsky's method, which relies on the heuristic of "one sense per collocation" (Yarowsky, 1993) and "one sense per discourse" (Gale, Church and Yarowsky, 1992). The algorithm first collects some seed collocations with senses by dictionary-parsing and uses supervised classification algorithms for training and labeling. Then they add new labeled collocations to training set and repeat labeling. Finally, they use a decision list algorithm to terminate.

In contrast to previous works in Word Sense Disambiguation and semantic classification, we present a hybrid system that automatically associates collocations to supersenses using a learning-based method, a paraphrase-based method and a sense frequency ranking method, with the goal to help lexicographers in compilation of collocation dictionaries and help learners to better grasp the usage of a collocation. We describe the method in more details in the next chapter.

3 Method

Associating collocations (e.g., required course) with dictionary senses often does not work very well. To obtain a better performance, we introduce a learning-based method using context and cross-lingual features, a paraphrase-based method using words similarity relation and dependency relation, and a sense frequency ranking method.

3.1 Problem Statement

We focus on automatically associating collocations with corresponding supersenses. The output senses could be used by lexicographers to save effort in compile collocations dictionaries and learners can better grasp the usage of a collocation. Supersenses are 26 lexicographer-files in WordNet noun hierarchy chosen by lexicographers and are believed to be general enough for sense allocation.

3.2 Training Sense Assignment Models

In this section, we explain our approaches to find the supersense including a learning-based method, a paraphrase-based method and a sense frequency ranking method. Figure 2 describes the processes of our methods.

(1) Generate collocation and supersense pairs from WordNet (Section 3.2.1)

(2) Train machine learning model from corpus for collocations (Section 3.2.2)

(3) Obtain supersense using machine learning model (Section 3.2.3)

(4) Obtain supersense using similarity and dependency information (Section 3.2.4)

(5) Obtain supersense using sense frequency ranking from WordNet (Section 3.2.5)

Figure 2. Outline of the process for obtaining supersense in different approaches

fuel oil	noun.substance
electrical discharge	noun.event
busy day	noun.time
required course	noun.act
fitted sheet	noun.artifact
bus driver	noun.person

Figure 3. Example of collocation and supersense pairs extracted from WordNet

3.2.1 Generating Collocation and Supersense Pairs

In the first stage (Step (1) in Figure 2), we attempt to find a set of collocations and their pre-tagged supersenses pairs

$$CSS = (< Col_1, S_1 >, < Col_2, S_2 >, < Col_3, S_3 >, \ldots, < Col_i, S_i >)$$

as seeds collocations to train a machine learning model M from WordNet. For example, the supersense for a collocation *fuel oil* is *noun.substance*. Examples of collocation and supersense pairs extracted from WordNet are shown in Figure 3.

We use two heuristics to achieve this goal. First, we go through each hyponyms of noun synsets and examine their lemma names to find collocations. For example, consider a synset *Synset('discharge.n.01')*, one of its lemma name is *discharge* and one of its hyponyms is *Synset('electrical_discharge.n.01')* with a lemma name *electrical_discharge*. Since the base word of *electrical_discharge* matches *Synset('discharge.n.01')*'s lemma name *discharge*, we can take *electrical discharge* as a collocation and the lexicographer-file of Synset('discharge.n.01') *noun.event* as a supersense to form the $< collocation, supersense >$ pair, (*electronic discharge, noun.event*).

Second, we search the collocations from definitions D_{wn} and example sentences E_{wn} of each noun synset. We utilize a parser to generate part-of-speech and lemma for D_{wn} and

E_{wn}. For a noun synset syn_i, one of its lemma name is lem_i, and the definition or example i as one of our selected $< collocation, supersense >$ pair. For example, a synset *Synset('day.n.05')* has one lemma name ***day*** and one example sentence "*it was a **busy day** on the stock exchange*". So we can take *busy day* as a collocation and the lexicographer-file *noun.time* as a supersense to form the $< collocation, supersense >$ pair, (*busy day, noun.time*).

3.2.2 Training Machine Learning Model

In the second stage (Step (2) in Figure 2), we use the collocation and supersense pairs obtained in section 3.2.1 to find sentences to train a sense classifier. First, a parser is used for generating part-of-speech tag and lemma form for all sentences in the monolingual corpus p and search from on-line machine translating system MT for Chinese collocation translation.

For example, consider the collocation required course and its supersense noun.act. We can find sentence such as "A required course for all students, to be completed before the end of the third year, and to be examined by individual colleges" from MC and its Chinese collocation translation "必修課" from on-line translation resource. The base word course has 6 different supersenses, but the words like students, third year, examined, colleges are highly related to the collocation required course and the supersense noun.act rather than other supersenses such as noun.food, noun.artifact or noun.object. The Chinese translation provides cross-lingual information like "課" to disambiguate the sense of course. The other translation for course like "路線" or "餐" would lead to different supersenses.

The input to this stage is a set of features. The above example *required course* showed that context words of a collocation may contain some words highly related to the corresponding supersense and cross-lingual information for a collocation also helps to disambiguate the supersense. So the features we use for one training event are

(1) unigram and bigram of a sentence extracted from MC_p containing the collocation

(2) Chinese translation of the collocation from MT

For each $< Col, S >$ pairs in CSS, we extract sentences containing Col from MC_p as $Sentences$ and obtain Chinese translation of Col from MT as $Trans$. Then, for each sentence $Sent$ in $Sentences$, we extract unigram Uni and bigram Bi from $Sent$. Note that stopwords are filtered for both Uni and Bi. The next step, we use Uni, Bi and $Trans$ as features and S as the standard output supersense to append machine learning event to $Features$. Note that $Trans$ actually transforms to a list of unigram and bigram of Chinese words while training. The output of this stage is a probability model M trained from a set of training events $Features$ for predicting the collocation supersenses using a machine learning tool ML.

3.2.3 Obtaining supersense using machine learning model

In the third stage (Step (3) in Figure 2), we attempt to predict the supersense for the input collocation $(C,\ B)$ using the machine learning model M described in Section 3.2.2. The runtime procedure is similar to the training algorithm.

First, we extract sentences containing $(C,\ B)$ from MC_p as $Sentences$ (Step(1a) in Figure 4) and use on-line machine translation system MT to obtain Chinese translation of $(C,\ B)$ as $Tran$ (Step(1b)). For associating $(C,\ B)$ with a supersense, we only consider i in $Sentences$, we extract unigram Uni (Step (2a)) and bigram Bi (Step (2b)) from $Sent$. Stopwords are filtered for both Uni and Bi similar to what is done at training time. Then, Uni, Bi and $Tran$ are combined together to predict the supersenses using M. The output of M is a supersense probability list $predictList$ that contains all supersenses and the probability for $(C,\ B)$ (Step 3)).

Algorithm 2. Obtaining supersense using machine learning model

PROCEDURE MachineLearningEvaluateSupersense($(C,\ B)$)

(1a) $Sentences$ = extractSentences($(C,\ B)$, MC_p)

(1b) $Trans$ = getTranslation($(C,\ B)$)

(1c) $Candidates$ = getLexFiles(B)

$topScore = \emptyset$, $topSense = \emptyset$, $freq = \emptyset$, $totalProb = \emptyset$, $avgProb = \emptyset$, $outcome = \emptyset$

for each $Sent_i$ in $Sentences$

(2a) Uni = extractUnigram($Sent_i$)

(2b) Bi = extractBigram($Sent_i$)

(3) $predictList$ = $M(Uni, Bi, Trans)$

for each ($sense_j$, $prob_j$) in $predictList$

if $sense_j$ in $Candidate$ and ($prob_j > numProb$)

(4a) $tmpScore_j = prob_j$

(4b) $tmpSense_j = sense_j$

(5a) $topScore_i$ = Max($tmpScore_j$)

(5b) $topSense_i = tmpSense_j$ that has Max($tmpScore_j$)

(5c) $totalProb[topSense_i]$ += $topScore_i$

(5d) $freq[topSense_i]$ += 1

for each $sense$ in $totalProb$

(6) $outcome[sense] = (freq[sense],\ totalProb[sense]/freq[sense])$

(7) $rankedSenses$ = Sort $outcome$ in decreasing order of $freq$, if more than 1 $sense$ share same frequency, sofrt those sense in decreasing order of average probability

(8) Return the top $rankedSenses$

Figure 4. Algorithm for obtaining supersense using machine learning model

We go through each ($sense_j$, $prob_j$) in $predictList$ and keep ($sense_j$, $prob_j$) as ($tmpSense_j$, $tmpScore_j$) if both $sense_j$ in $Candidate$ and $prob_j$ higher than a probability threshold $numProb$ (Step (4a and 4b)). Then we choose maximum $tmpScore_j$ as $topScore_j$, the corresponding $tmpSense_j$ as $topSense_j$ (Step (5a) and (5b)). A dictionary $totalProb$ is used to store the probability sum $topScore_j$ of each distinct $topSense_j$, and another dictionary $freq$ is used to store the frequency of each distinct $topSense_j$ (Step (5c) and (5d)). For each $sense$ in $totalProb$, we store the frequency $freq[sense]$ and the average sense probability $totalProb\ sense\ /freq[sense]$ to $outcome$ (Step (6)). Then, we sort $outcome$ in decreasing order of frequency as $rankedSenses$. If there is more than one sense in $outcome$ that have the same frequency, they would be sorted in decreasing order of the average sense probability. Finally, we output LB (Step (7)).

Corpus-based machine learning for associating collocations with supersenses can reduce the sense dominance problem, since context words of different supersenses are generally different and translations of a same base word in different senses tend to be different, too. With this in mind, we use sentences of a collocation extracted from a corpus and the collocation translation to disambiguate the supersenses of the base word of a given collocation.

3.2.4 Obtain supersense using similarity & dependency information

In the fourth stage (Step (4) in Figure 2), we use a paraphrase-based strategy to determine the supersense. A paraphrase is a restatement of the meaning of a text or passage using another form. By calculating the similarity between a collocation and its paraphrases, we can determine its supersense. This method is based on the assumption that original collocation shares the same supersense with its paraphrases.

For example, consider an input collocation *fitted sheet* using the paraphrase method. The word *sheet* has four supersenses: *noun.object, noun.communication, noun.artifacrt, noun.shape* in WordNet. Paraphrase candidates of *fitted sheet* are *coat, cloth, plate, pan, foil, plastic* identified base on similar words list of *sheet* and *coat,*

Table 1. Example similar words and dependent words of *required course*

Similar words of *sheet*	Dependency relation of *fitted*

('plate', 0.16), ('sheeting', 0.15)	('jacket', 9), ('suit', 5)
('pan', 0.14), ('steel', 0.14)	('bodice', 3), ('less', 3)
('coat', 0.13), ('tube', 0.12)	('gown', 2), ('Top', 2)
('metal', 0.12), ('paper', 0.12)	('carpet', 1), **('cloth', 1)**
('slab', 0.11), ('pipe', 0.11)	**('coat', 1)**, ('leader', 1)
('layer', 0.11), ('cold-rolled', 0.11)	('plaid', 1), ('topper', 1)
('stainless', 0.11), ('surface', 0.11)	('version', 1), ('a little', 1)
('glass', 0.11), ('tubing', 0.11)	('long', 1), ('uniquely', 1)
('booklet', 0.11), ('cut-sheet', 0.11)	('around', 1), ('than', 1)
('cloth', 0.11), …	

cloth, jacket, suit based on dependency relations list of *fitted*. The intersection of the two candidate list contains *coat* and *cloth*. It means that *coat* and *cloth* are paraphrases of *sheet* when collocating with *fitted*. The example similar words and dependency relations of *fitted sheet* is shown in Table 1.

Subsequently, we compare the synsets similarity for both *(coat, sheet)* and *(cloth, sheet)*. The top-ranked similarity of *(coat, sheet)* is *((Synset('coating.n.01'), Synset('sheet.n.06')), 0.769)* and the lexicographer-file of *Synset('sheet.n.06')* is *noun.artifact*; the top-ranked similarity of *(cloth, sheet)* is *((Synset('fabric.n.01'), Synset('sail.n.01')), 0.857)* and the lexicographer-file of *Synset('sail.n.01')* is *noun.artifact*. So the frequency of *noun.artifact* is 2, while other supersenses are all 0. We then output *noun.artifact* as the supersense of input collocation *fitted sheet*.

By using paraphrase-based method, words that related to the input collocation can be the extracted. The collocation could be disambiguated since most of the words with other senses tend not to share the paraphrases. So we can find the sense relation between input collocation and extracted words to obtain the supersense.

3.2.5 Obtaining supersense using sense frequency ranking

In the last stage (Step (5) in Figure 2), we use the sense frequency to identify the supersense. In many previous works on WSD, sense frequency plays an important role to indicate the sense. A word may have different senses, but most of time, it tends to associated with the dominant sense. So for disambiguating word senses, choosing the most frequent sense is often used as a baseline.

Many sense frequency methods are based on sense estimation in a corpus. But here we use the sense frequency information in WordNet. For any word in WordNet, there are one or more synsets and the synsets are listed in decreasing order of frequency. So we can simply return the first synset as the supersense. Sense frequency ranking method has the highest coverage, and that is important since our goal is to disambiguate all collocations. We also use this method as the baseline method to compare with our results. We will describe the details of evaluation in Chapter 4.

3.2.6 The Runtime Hybrid Process

Once the learning-based procedure, the paraphrase-based procedure and the sense frequency ranking procedure produce the supersenses, a relative majority vote is carried out to FR are the three predicted supersense described in sections 3.2.2 to 3.2.4. Each supersense has one vote and the supersense with the most votes is the final output S. As shown in Figure 2, after running the three procedures for collocation *fuel oil*, we obtain *noun.substance*, *noun.artifact* and *noun.substance*. The supersense *noun.substance* has 2 votes and *noun.artifact* has 1, so the final output S is *noun.substance*.

Sometimes the three procedures produce 3 different supersenses without an agreement. Moreover, the learning-based procedure or the paraphrase-based procedure produce no results, because either the sentences containing the input collocation cannot be found in corpus MC, or the paraphrases of the input collocation cannot be found and leads the voting has no agreement. In this case, we use back-off to find the supersense. When there is no agreement FR. As long as the base word of the input collocation exists in WordNet, we can produce an output.

4 Experimental Setting

We have proposed a hybrid model to associate collocations with broad sense classes, with the goal of helping lexicographers in compilation of collocation dictionaries. The evaluation focuses on the intended supersenses of a set of collocations produced by the proposed system. We extracted a set of collocation and supersense pairs from WordNet, so the evaluation could be done automatically.

4.1 Data set

In our experiment, we used WordNet, a large lexical database of English which contains approximately 117,000 synsets and 155,000 sense-disambiguated words and collocations, to generate the collocations for training, developing and testing. As we have described in Section 3.2.1, collocations are extracted from WordNet using two heuristics:

(1) extract collocations from hyponyms of noun synsets

(2) extract collocations from definitions and examples sentences of noun synsets

We extracted 18,586 collocation and supersense pairs from (1) and 1,784 pairs from (2). The extracted collocations were filtered through a collocation list. The collocation we used is a list of base word/collocates pairs for the top 60,000 lemmas from the Corpus of Contemporary American English (COCA) (Davies, 2008) which contains 4,200,000 collocations. After this step, the total number of collocations was reduced to 7,489. With heuristic (2), we used GENIA tagger (Tsuruoka, 2005) which analyzes English sentences and outputs the base forms, part-of-speech tags, chunk tags, and named entity tags to tag the definitions and example sentences.

We randomly selected 829 collocations as development set and 6,660 for training and testing from the collocation and supersense pairs. For training and testing, we split the 6,660 collocations into 10 parts that each part contains 666 collocations and we ran ten-fold validation to evaluate the performance of each part.

In learning-based procedure, we employed *Maximum Entropy* (*ME*) model to associate input collocations with supersenses. *ME* is a flexible statistical learning model that aims to maximize the entropy when characterizing some unknown events. The model estimates outcomes according to a set of features with least possible bias. The *ME* model we used for training and testing is Maximum Entropy Modeling Toolkit for Python and C++ (Zhang, 2004). The features we used for the *ME* model is extracted from *British National Corpus* (*BNC*), a 100 million word collection of samples of written and spoken language from a wide range of sources. We use *GENIA tagger* to tag the sentences in *BNC* and filtered the stopwords in the sentences using *Natural Language Tool Kit* (*NLTK*), a suite of open source program modules written in Python (Loper and Bird, 2002). More specifically, we used the *stopwords* in *nltk.corpus* and obtained the English stopwords list. Another feature, the Chinese translation of the collocations, was obtained from *Google Translate*.

In the paraphrase-based procedure, we use a set of words with similar words which contains 100,000 words and about 24,000,000 similar words and words with dependency relations which contains 20,000,000 dependency relations. The data is obtained using *MINIPAR* (Lin, 1993), a broad-coverage parser for the English language. The similarity comparison algorithm for words used in this stage is JCN similarity (Jiang and Conrath, 1997). JCN similarity bases on the information content (IC, a measure of the specific of a concept) of the Least Common Subsumer (LCS, most specific ancestor node). According to (Sinha and Mihalcea, 2007), JCN similarity tends to work best for nouns.

4.2 Methods compared

Our approach starts with an adjective-noun or noun-noun collocation given by a user, and determines the corresponding sense to the input collocation using external resources related to the input collocation. The output of our system is a supersense in WordNet associated with the input collocation that can be used to help lexicographers in compiling collocation dictionaries, or shown to English learners directly.

In this paper, we have proposed a hybrid model for associating collocations with supersenses, in which we used a learning-based model, a paraphrase-based similarity comparison, and a sense frequency ranking method. Therefore, we compare the results based on each method and combination of the above methods for evaluating the system performance in more details.

We compare different methods to associating the collocation with supersense using the test set described in Section 4.1. The methods evaluated for the comparison are listed as follows:

— **FR**: Sense frequency ranking method as we described in Section 3.2.5, using the sense frequency information to determine the supersense of a collocation. This method is also the baseline method in our experiment.

— **LB**: Learning-based method as we described in Section 3.2.3, using learning-based method to determine the supersense of a collocation.

— **LB+FR**: Combinational method of learning-based method and sense frequency ranking method, using **FR** as a back-off if **LB** cannot be applied.

— **PB**: Paraphrase-based method as we described in Section 3.2.4, using similarity and dependency relations of a collocation to determine the sense of that collocation.

— **PB+FR**: Combinational method of paraphrase-based method and sense frequency ranking method, using **FR** as a back-off if **PB** cannot be applied.

— **LB+PB**: Combinational method of learning-based method and paraphrase-based method, using **PB** as a back-off if **LB** cannot be applied.

— **LB+PB+FR**: Hybrid method of all methods we proposed. The running sequence is **LB→PB→FR** that **LB** determines all the test set, then **PB** determines those **LB** cannot solve, then **FR** determines those **PB** cannot solve.

— **MV+BO**: The most complete version of the system we proposed. First, we run the test set using all three methods **LB**, **PB** and **FR** and use relative majority vote to rank supersense results. The rest of collocations that cannot be determined run in the following sequence **LB→PB→FR**.

5 Evaluation Result and Discussion

In this chapter, we report the evaluation results of our experiments using methodologies and the settings we described in Chapter 4. We evaluated 8 different methods as described in Section 4.2. We ran ten-fold validation on 6,660 random selected collocations. We report the average performance of the 10 test results. For non-learning based method, we evaluated the whole 6,660 collocations. Table 2 shows the performance for development dataset and test dataset in 8 different methods based on *precision*, *recall* and *F-measure*.

Table 2. Performance for development dataset and test dataset in 8 different methods based on *precision*, *recall* and *F-measure*

strategy	Development Set			Test Set		
	Prec.	Rec.	F-m.	Prec.	Rec.	F-m.
FR (baseline)	.74	.74	.74	.75	.75	.75
LB	.80	.61	.69	.80	.62	.70
LB+FR	.78	.78	.78	.80	.80	.80
PB	.79	.57	.66	.76	.55	.63
PB+FR	.78	.78	.78	.76	.76	.76
LB+PB	.80	.72	.76	.80	.72	.75
LB+PB+FR	.80	.80	.80	.80	.80	.80
MV+BO	.81	.81	.81	**.81**	**.81**	**.81**

For comparison, we used the baseline of sense frequency ranking method **FR** with 75% precision, recall and F-measure. The learning-based method **LB** achieves the precision 80% and recall 62% with 5% increases in precision. But the recall decreases since no sentences containing the collocations are found in the corpus. Those collocations are not given a supersense. If we add **FR** to the system as **LB+FR**, the precision, recall and F-measure increases to 80%. The paraphrase-based method **PB** on development dataset has a 5% increase on precision comparing with baseline, but on test dataset, the precision decreases to 76% with a low recall of 55%. The low recall is due to the fact that many collocations paraphrases cannot be found. For this we also add **FR** to the system as a back-off and the precision, recall and F-measure of **PB+FR** increases to 76%. The experimental result on **LB+PB** shows that the precision maintains on 80%, and recall increases nearly 10% comparing with **LB** and achieves the highest recall in all the methods without **FR**.

The performance of **LB+PB+FR** reaches 80%, the same as **LB+FR** since the performance of **PB** is not good as **LB**. We believe that using a relative majority vote to determine the supersense would lead a better performance. **MV+BO** confirms our hypothesis and achieves the best performance of precision, recall and F-measure 81%. The precision of majority vote that has 3 votes is 95% with recall of 33% while the majority with 2 votes is precision 79% and recall 34%. So with more than 2 votes, the precision reaches 87% with a recall of 67% and F-measure of 76%.

Take a deeper look in the sense dominance problem we mentioned in Chapter 3. Previous work suffered from that the collocations are often associated with dominant senses. We show the performance of **MV+BO** when dealing with two different condition: (1) most frequent sense collocations, (2) non-most frequent sense collocations. We could see that when dealing with most frequent sense collocations, 93% of collocations can be correctly associated with supersenses. When dealing with non-most frequent sense collocations, we are still able to correctly associate 46% of collocations with supersenses. So we prove that the sense dominance problem can be reduced by using our hybrid algorithm.

6 Conclusion

Many avenues exist for future research and improvement of our system. For example, in the learning-based method, the recall could increase by using a larger corpus or the web data to extract more sentences as collocations' features. The cases where the sentences of the input collocation are not found in a corpus could be reduced. Additionally, we could improve the quality of collocation translations to improve the performance of the learning-based method. In the paraphrase-based method, both precision and recall are not satisfactory, but we still believe that the method has potential. By generating a new similar words list and dependency relations list using a large corpus could produce better paraphrases for associating collocations with supersenses and increasing the recall. Most of the 26 supersenses are natural and reasonable. However, we still find that some supersenses are not very intuitive and may cause problems in tagging. So finding more appropriate set of classes is worth further study.

In summary, we have introduced a hybrid method to automatically associate collocations with supersenses. Our goal is to help lexicographers in compilation of a collocation dictionary and help learners to better grasp the usage of a collocation. Our method is composed of a learning-based model, a paraphrase-based method, and a sense frequency ranking method. In our evaluation, we have shown that the hybrid method is significantly better compared with other methods described in this paper. And we also prove that our model can partially reduce the sense dominance problem.

References

[1] Baker L. D. and McCallum A. K., "Distributional clustering of words for text classification." Proceedings of the 21st annual international ACM SIGIR conference on research and development in information retrieval ACM, p. 96 , 1998.

[2] Curran J. R., "Supersense tagging of unknown nouns using semantic similarity." in proceedings of the 43rd annual meeting on association for computational linguistics Association for Computational Linguistics, 26 p., 2005

[3] Davies M. 2008. The corpus of contemporary american english (coca): 400 million

words, 1990-present. Available Online at http://www.Americancorpus.Org .

[4] Fellbaum C. "WordNet" in Theory and Applications of Ontology: Computer Applications, pp. 231-43, 2010.

[5] Gale W. A., Church K. W. and Yarowsky D., "One sense per discourse," in proceedings of the workshop on speech and natural language Association for Computational Linguistics, p. 233, 1992.

[6] Inumella A, Kilgarriff A, Kovar. Associating collocations with dictionary senses.

[7] Jiang JJ and Conrath DW., Semantic similarity based on corpus statistics and lexical taxonomy. Arxiv Preprint Cmp-lg/9709008, 1997

[8] Leacock C., Towell G. and Voorhees E., "Corpus-based statistical sense resolution." Proceedings of the ARPA workshop on human language technology. p. 260, 1993.

[9] Lin D., Dependency-based evaluation of MINIPAR. Treebanks, pp. 317-29, 2003.

[10] Miller GA. WordNet: A lexical database for English. Commun ACM 38(11):39-41., 1995.

[11] Pearce D., "Synonymy in collocation extraction." Proceedings of the workshop on WordNet and other lexical resources, second meeting of the north american chapter of the association for computational linguistics. 41 p., 2001.

[12] Tsuruoka Y, Tateishi Y, Kim JD, Ohta T, McNaught J, Ananiadou S, Tsujii J., "Developing a robust part-of-speech tagger for biomedical text." In Advances in Informatics, pp. 382-92, 2005.

[13] Yarowsky D. "Unsupervised word sense disambiguation rivaling supervised methods." Proceedings of the 33rd annual meeting on association for computational linguistics Association for Computational Linguistics. 189 p., 1995.

[14] Yarowsky D. "Word-sense disambiguation using statistical models of roget's categories trained on large corpora." Proceedings of the 14th conference on computational linguistics-volume 2 Association for Computational Linguistics. 454 p., 1992.

Measuring Individual Differences in Word Recognition: The Role of Individual Lexical Behaviors

林欣霓 Hsin-Ni Lin
國立臺灣師範大學英語所語言組
Department of English, Linguistics Division
National Taiwan Normal University
hnlin98@std.ntnu.edu.tw

謝舒凱 Shu-Kai Hsieh
國立臺灣大學語言所
Graduate Institute of Linguistics
National Taiwan University
shukaihsieh@ntu.edu.tw

詹曉蕙 Shiao-Hui Chan
國立臺灣師範大學英語所語言組
Department of English, Linguistics Division
National Taiwan Normal University
shiaohui@ntnu.edu.tw

Abstract

This study adopts a corpus-based computational linguistic approach to measure individual differences (IDs) in visual word recognition. Word recognition has been a cardinal issue in the field of psycholinguistics. Previous studies examined the IDs by resorting to test-based or questionnaire-based measures. Those measures, however, confined the research within the scope where they can evaluate. To extend the research to approximate to IDs in real life, the present study undertakes the issue from the observations of experiment participants' daily-life lexical behaviors. Based on participants' Facebook posts, two types of personal lexical behaviors are computed, including *the frequency index of personal word usage* and *personal word frequency*. It is investigated that to what extent each of them accounts for participants' variances in Chinese word recognition. The data analyses are carried out by mixed-effects models, which can precisely estimate by-subject differences. Results showed that the effects of personal word frequency reached significance; participants responded themselves more rapidly when encountering more frequently used words. People with lower frequency indices of personal word usage had a lower accuracy rates than others, which was contrary to our prediction. Comparison and discussion of the results also reveal methodology issues that can provide noteworthy suggestions for future research on measuring personal lexical behaviors.

Keywords: individual differences, lexical behaviors, word recognition, computational linguistic approach, naturalistic data

1. Introduction

In the field of psycholinguistics, a major research interest is to investigate how people recognize written words or access the corresponding word representations stored in their mental lexicon. Psycholinguists usually undertake the investigation starting from isolated words since less factors are involved, compared to words within sentences. Therefore, research on the isolated word recognition is fundamental for understanding how lexical access takes places. In general, the term 'visual word recognition' is used to simply address the recognition of isolated written words.

Research of word recognition traditionally have concentrated on how characteristics of words *per se* (e.g. word length, word frequency, or neighborhood size) affected the procedure of recognition [1] [2] [3] [4] [5], taking the discrepancies between participants' performance as merely statistical deviation. Recently, however, there has been a growing interest in the individual differences (IDs, henceforth) of experiment participants. Results of the ID studies showed that the issue was noteworthy because personal experiences and knowledge of words (e.g. print-exposure experience [6] [7], reading skills [8], or vocabulary knowledge [9] [10] [11]) accounted for systematic variances between participants in word recognition. Even when participants were homogeneous in their educational level, their IDs sufficiently resulted in distinct performance in word recognition. Furthermore, [8] provided compelling evidence that conflicting results of regularity effects[1] in the literature were attributable to lacking control over participants' IDs of reading skills.

To date, the studies of IDs, however, have focused on test-measured or self-rated ID variables. In such approaches, the observed IDs were confined in the boundary of a test or questionnaire design, and the uniqueness of each individual in real life was neglected. In an attempt to examine the approximate real-life IDs, this research measures and analyzes IDs based on each participant's own lexical behaviors. Lexical behaviors here refer to a person's word usage and preference in his/her daily life. Intuitively, language usage reveals one's vocabulary knowledge, such as the words the person knows and how to use those words within context. Vocabulary knowledge was proved relating to word recognition [9] [10] [11]; hence, it is highly possible that IDs of lexical behaviors can explain the disparity of participants' performance in word recognition. The lexical behaviors mainly have two merits over the measure of vocabulary tests. First, people's lexical knowledge will be evaluated not by a small set of vocabularies in a given test, but by the words used by themselves. In this case, a variable's value assigned to a given participant is personalized and not confined to the scale or the total score of a test. The other merit resides in that the data of language usage can provide a deeper insight into a person's lexical knowledge, compared with a vocabulary test. If a person is able to use or produce a given word naturally (and frequently), it suggests that the word's representation has been firmly established in his/her mental lexicon.

Besides, it is worth noting that the stance we take in measuring the 'individuality' is **naturalistic** rather than **natural**, in that the lexical behaviors we describe are assumedly anchored in the interaction as naturalistic situated interactions, rather than natural ones (like using camera to collect data). A pitfall of the natural ones is that when observers and/or cameras are present those interactions are not quite what they would be in our absence.

[1] Regularity denotes that the extent to which the spelling-to-sound correspondence in words are invariant. The effects of regularity are that a response is made slower to less 'regular' words (e.g. pint) than to 'regular' words (e.g. name).

Therefore, the present study begins with a preliminary survey on the lexical behaviors of participants' naturalistic data on Facebook[2] Walls (Figure 1).

Figure 1. A snapshot of Facebook Wall

Our attention for lexical behaviors computed from participants' Facebook data is fastened upon *the frequency index of personal word usage* and the *personal word frequency* calculated from participants' language data. Whether the two variables are associated with participant's performance in a lexical decision task[3] will be explored respectively in two experiments. More important, as a pioneer study on lexical behaviors and word recognition, the other main objective of this research is to preliminarily explore its computational methodology.

The rest of this paper is organized as follows: Section 2 presents the procedure of our data collection, including conducting a lexical decision experiment and extracting the experiment participants' language usage data from the Facebook. Section 3 demonstrates the methods and results of two experiments, each of which computed a lexical behavior variable and further examined the relationships between participants' IDs of lexical behaviors and lexical-decision responses. Section 4 concludes this study by giving a summary and contributions of the current study. Section 5 provides potential research directions for future work.

2. Data collection

2.1 Lexical decision task

2.1.1 Participants

Sixteen Chinese native speakers (10 females and 6 males; ages ranging from 21 to 29 years old) consented to participant in the task and were offered participant fees. For the purpose of augmenting the possibility of finding individual differences (IDs) of personal lexical behaviors, the participants were recruited from diverse backgrounds. They should be right-handed, which was examined via a self-report handedness inventory [12].

2.1.2 Materials

Experiment materials included 456 Chinese words and 456 non-words. The word stimuli

[2] http://www.facebook.com/

[3] The lexical decision task is an extensively-used experiment of visual word recognition.

were nouns selected from the Chinese Lexicon Profile (CLP) [4], comprising 152 high-frequency, 152 mid-frequency, and 152 low-frequency words. In addition to word frequency, the number of characters, the number of senses, and the neighborhood size of words were collected from the CLP and will be treated as covariates at the stage of statistical analysis because we intended to disentangle their impacts on the lexical-decision responses.

To equalize yes and no stimuli, 456 non-words were also subsumed into the stimuli. These non-words were randomly generated by using characters of existing nouns in Chinese. Take two-character non-words for example. The procedure of random generation is illustrated in Figure 2. The first and second characters of existing nominal words were separately stored into two vectors. Next, the first and second characters of a non-word were randomly selected from the two vectors respectively and then combined altogether. If an automatically generated non-word sounded like an existing word, it would be removed from the non-word list.

The task is a within-subjects design; that is, a participant saw all of the 912 stimuli. The non-words, high-, mid-, and low-frequency words were evenly divided into four blocks. The order of four blocks was counterbalanced across 16 participants. Within a block, experimental stimuli were administered in a random order.

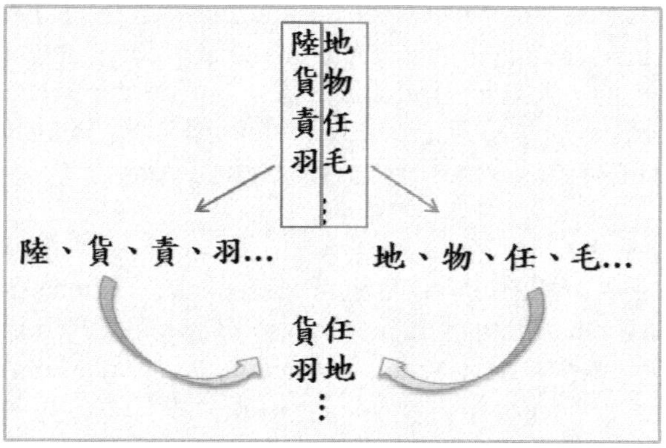

Figure 2. The procedure for random generation of two-character non-word stimuli in the visual lexical decision task

2.1.3 Procedure

Each participant was tested individually in a quiet room. The experiment was conducted and presented on a laptop via *E-prime 2.0 professional*. Participants were instructed to judge whether a visually presented stimulus was a meaningful word in Mandarin Chinese. They were required to respond as quickly as possible but without expense of accuracy, and their judgment were recorded as soon as they pressed the 'yes' or 'no' response button.

The procedure of a trial was initiated with a fixation sign (+) appearing in the center of the monitor for 1000 ms. Next, a stimulus was presented. The presentation would be terminated immediately when a participant responded. If no response was detected in 4000 ms, the given stimulus would be removed from the monitor. After termination of the stimulus

[4] The Chinese Lexicon Profile (CLP) is a research project launched at LOPE lab at National Taiwan University. The project purports to build up a large-scaled open lexical database platform for Chinese mono-syllabic to tri-syllabic words used in Taiwan. With its incorporation of behavioral and normative data in the long term, the CLP would allow researchers across various disciplines to explore different statistical models in search for the determinant variables that influence lexical processing tasks, as well as the training and verification of computational simulation studies. The number of Chinese words in CLP has been accumulated up to 204,922 so far.

presentation, a feedback was provided on the monitor for 750 ms, along with the participant's accumulated accuracy rate in a block.

The entire experiment included four blocks and lasted approximately one hour. Prior to the experiment, a practice session was given to familiarize participants with the experimental procedure. The session contained 4 words and 4 non-words, none of which appeared in the formal experiment.

2.2 Facebook data

The Facebook module in i-Corpus[5] was employed to gathering participants' data of language usage and preferences. The procedure is presented beneath. For the module was in its rudimentary stage of development, it was still semi-autonomous; more specifically, the initial steps in the procedure were manually accomplished.

[Step one] Log in an APP to get a user's access token to Facebook

[Step two] Paste the access token in the i-Corpus program

[Step three] Type in a participant's Facebook ID

[Step four] Save the data on the participant's Facebook Wall (JSON format)

[Step five] Extract each message in categories of post, photo, comment, and other users' walls (One message was saved as a text.) In this study, the quantification of participants' lexical behaviors is based on only the category of posts given that other categories of messages have context which is not shown in themselves.

[Step six] Pre-process the 'post' messages by the CKIP Chinese Word Segmentation System[6]. After the segmentation, we obtained the token number in each participant' data of language usage (see Table 1).

Table 1. The token numbers in participants' Facebook posts

Subject	Chinese Token Number	Subject	Chinese Token Number
Subject01	12506	Subject09	7487
Subject02	2765	Subject10	7690
Subject03	2144	Subject11	4727
Subject04	3590	Subject12	4389
Subject05	8251	Subject13	5908
Subject06	3442	Subject14	18636
Subject07	4293	Subject15	985
Subject08	2960	Subject16	2260

[5] i-Corpus is an on-going NSC-granted research project conducted at the LOPE lab, National Taiwan University. This project envisions an effort to construct i-corpora so as to obtain and analyze a wide spectrum of individual linguistic and extra-linguistic data. Considering the collected material is restricted by some copyright issues, a set of iCorpus toolkits is proposed which performs the tasks of autonomous corpus data collection and exploitation (by running an integrated software package) to extract, analyze huge volumes of individual language usage data, and automatically provide an idiolect sketch with quantitative information for the benefits of linguistic and above all, sociolinguistic studies.

[6] http://ckipsvr.iis.sinica.edu.tw/

Results of the automatic segmentation were not further checked and corrected by human labor because the present study purports to explore and develop a methodology that is not labor-consuming and rather feasible for future research to compute and control the IDs of lexical behaviors. The segmented words from participants' Facebook posts were prepared for the computation of personal lexical behaviors proposed in the subsequent section.

3. Experiments on the individual differences of lexical behaviors

3.1 Experiment 1: The role of the frequency index of personal word usage in visual word recognition

Word frequency in corpora was attested to have a high negative correlation with word difficulty [13]. In this experiment, the Academia Sinica Balanced Corpus[7] frequency of a word was analogously taken as the possibility that the word is generally acquired and used by native speakers, thus being referred to for computing *the frequency index of personal word usage*. A lower frequency index of word usage indicates that a person was apt to use low-frequency words, which was preliminarily assumed to imply a person's relatively broader vocabulary knowledge. It was concerned that whether IDs of the frequency indices across participants were capable of explaining their differences in response latencies and accuracies.

3.1.1 Method

There were four steps to compute the frequency index per person, as shown in the following.

[Step one] Produce a list per participant which contained all of the words he/she used and the occurrence frequency of those words in his/her segmented Facebook data. Examples are shown in the first and second columns of Table 2.

[Step two] Gather from the CLP the corresponding word frequency in Sinica Corpus of each word on the list, as exemplified in the third column of Table 2. Note that a few words were assigned a missing value "NA" in the column since they did not appear in the Sinica Corpus. Those words, which possessed no Sinica frequencies, would be excluded from the calculation of participants' frequency indices. Given that some of them were a string that was erroneously grouped as a word by the automatic segmentation program (e.g. *zai4 wuo3 nao3* (在我腦) 'in my brain'), the exclusion enabled this experiment to filter out the data noise procured by automatic segmentation, thus diminishing the impact of segmentation errors on the calculation of individual lexical behaviors.

[Step three] Compute the frequency index of personal word usage U_j of the participant j by (1), where P_{ij} was the participant's personal frequency of the ith word, and S_i was the word's frequency in the Sinica Corpus. In this equation, U_j can be interpreted as the mean Sinica frequency of words used by the participant j on the Facebook. The lower the index was, the more rarely-seen words used by the participant were, which assumedly meant the person had broader word knowledge.

[7] http://db1x.sinica.edu.tw/kiwi/mkiwi/

$$U_j = \frac{\sum_{i=1}^{n} P_{ij} S_i}{\sum_{i=1}^{n} P_{ij}} \tag{1}$$

[Step four] The U_j index of each participant was put along with his/her response latencies and accuracies in the lexical decision task for analysis.

The steps of computation introduced above applied to the complete word list of each participant (called as "the Intact word list" hereafter). In addition to the list, this experiment also made the other word list for each participant to calculate another index. This word list (called as "the NV word list" hereafter) comprised only multi-character words tagged as nouns and verbs by CKIP Segmentation System and was preliminarily considered to be less affected by segmentation errors, compared with the Intact list.

Table 2. An example of a portion of one participant's word list

Word	Personal word frequency	Sinica word frequency
就	12	48749
這樣	4	7582
完全	2	3280
桔茶	1	NA
咒怨	1	NA
在我腦	1	NA

3.1.2 Results and Discussion

The data analyses were conducted by mixed-effects models in the *lme4* package of *R*[8] since the models can precisely estimate by-subject differences. In both the latency and accuracy analyses, experiment stimuli and participants were treated as random factors in the models. Procedure variables (i.e. block number and trial number) as well as word variables including types of word frequency, sense number, character number, and neighborhood size were taken as covariates. The inclusion of covariates was intended to disentangle their independent influences on the reaction latencies and accuracies. Provided that any covariate did not reach significance, it would be dropped out of the analysis; afterwards, the other variables would refit the models.

Ahead of the analysis of response latencies, incorrect responses (2.57%) were discarded at first. Two frequency indices of personal word usage respectively fitted mixed-effects models together with the above-mentioned random factors and covariates. Besides, note that the response latencies put into statistical analyses were log-transformed so as to reduce skewed distribution of reaction time. Inspection of the residuals of the models found notable non-normality, as shown in the upper right panel of Figure 3[9]. To improve the goodness of fit, we removed outliers with standardized residuals outside the interval (-2.5, 2.5) [14, 15], which were 2.54% of the correct-response data set in models of the Intact list and the NV list. After the removal, the models were refitted; the residuals of the refitted models are displayed in the lower right panel in the figure. As can be seen, the non-normality of the residuals was

[8] http://www.r-project.org/

[9] Figure 3 displays the residuals of the model fitted by the values computed from the Intact word list. The plot of residuals in the NV list model is not demonstrated because it was the same as Figure 3.

attenuated. In the final models, statistical results showed that the frequency indices from the Intact list (p = .3638) and NV list (p = .4926) both did not significantly vary with participants' response.

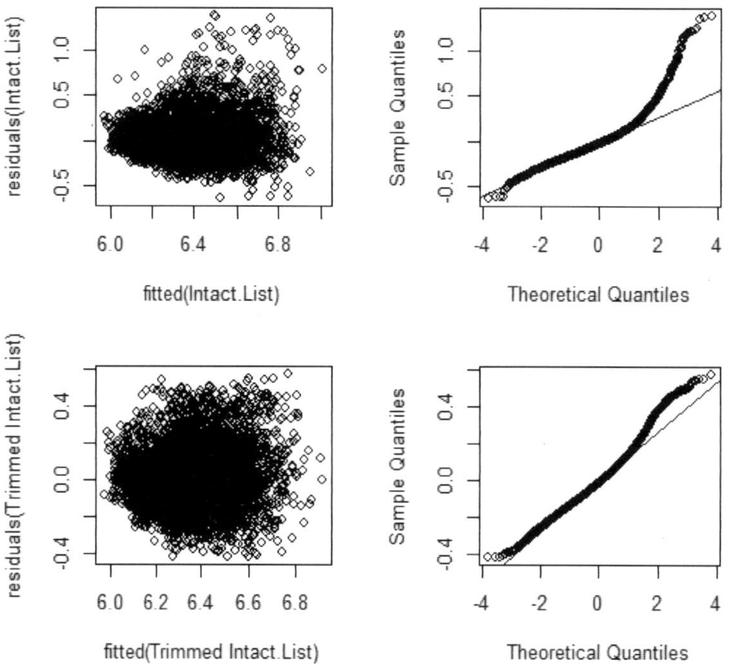

Figure 3. Residual diagnostics for the models of the Intact list before (upper panels) and after (lower panels) removal of outliers

Concerning the analysis of response accuracies, responses to all of the word stimuli in the task were taken into the analysis. Correct responses were coded as ones, and incorrect response as zeros. Seeing that the accuracy values were binomial, the analysis was carried out by the logistic mixed-effect models. Results suggested that the index computed from participants' NV lists was found to affect response accuracies ($p < .001$). Its effect on the accuracy, however, was opposite to our preliminary prediction that lower indices should suggest a person had broader lexical knowledge, thus relating to higher accuracy rates. Experimental results revealed that people with lower indices responded less accurately than those with higher indices. The counter-prediction may be ascribed to our methodology of computing the frequency index in two aspects.

The first aspect resides in that the personal indices were calculated by referring to an external lexical resource (i.e. the Academia Sinica Balance Corpus), where word frequency counts mainly came from written data rather than spoken data. When observing the calculation, we found that low-frequency words in the Sinica corpus encompassed not only rarely-used words but also words that were commonly used in daily-life conversation. Under the circumstances, a participant might receive a low frequency index from our computation because he/she utilized a number of 'low-frequency' words that are ubiquitous in spoken data, which are certainly not associated with broad lexical knowledge. This problem would become apparent when the frequency index was computed from the NV list of personal word usage. Unlike the NV list, the Intact list contained function words in addition to nouns and verbs. Function words, such as pronouns or conjunctions, are words that express grammatical relations between sentences and other words, so their occurrence in both written and spoken data must be high. With the involvement of function words, the Intact list could relieve the computation problem which was yielded by the huge discrepancy of word frequencies between written and spoken data. This is the possible reason why our results depending on the NV list showed that people with lower frequency indices had lower response accuracies but the results relying on the Intact list did not.

The second aspect is that participants posted messages on their own Facebook Wall for diverse main purposes. Facebook is a social network designed for users to convey themselves and communicate with friends. Users can freely post any kind of messages they would like to share on their own Facebook Walls. Some users favored confiding their feelings at one moment; some preferred sharing anecdotes they experienced on a day; others often made serious comments on news and social events to evoke friends' or even the public's awareness. A skim over the Facebook data we collected could detect that the phenomena happened to users participating in this study. Accordingly, modes of the collected personal language data varied over a continuum illustrated in Figure 4. For instance, participants who were used to casually express their feelings in the data would be closer to the "informal" and "spoken" end of the continuum. A concern is raised about those who tended to take the Facebook Wall as the space to share informal messages. Even if a person has broad vocabulary knowledge and would use rarely-seen words when writing formal messages or articles, the possibility that he/she uses those words in the informal/spoken mode might decrease. Furthermore, due to the inconsistent modes across participants' Facebook data, the seriousness of the problem caused by the Sinica Corpus word frequency might vary from person to person. As mentioned above, various commonly-used spoken or informal words were shown as low-frequency words in the Sinica corpus. Those spoken vocabularies were the sources from which our computed frequency indices were distorted. Consequently, if one's Facebook posts were generally close to the informal end of the mode continuum, his/her index would be largely affected by the problem originated from the Sinica word frequency.

Figure 4. Continuum of modes in Facebook posts

According to the two forgoing aspects, our counter-hypothesis findings were predominately accredited to the Sinica word frequencies. Thereupon, it is suggested that the computation of frequency indices in future research should take a spoken corpus as the reference of general word frequencies. With respect to the concern that people with broad lexical knowledge may use informal register and extensively-used vocabularies on the Facebook, it is a reflection we had when looking at the Facebook data. The extent to which it impacted on the index computation was unsure. A future research may probe into the extent by comparing the frequency indices calculated from people's Facebook posts with those form their compositions in an academic exam. The compositions in an exam would be scored. In that case, people must write in the formal mode to show their competence as they can as possible. Via a comparison with this formal data of language usage, the influence of the informal Facebook posts on the frequency index can be known.

3.2 Experiment 2: The role of personal word frequency in visual word recognition

This experiment investigates whether a subject's personal word frequency of a certain LDT[10] stimulus would influence his/her corresponding reaction latency. It was preliminarily hypothesized that if he/she used a word more frequently than other words, the response to the word would be more rapid. Besides, as shown in Table 1, each participant's data differ in length; to render frequency counts across the data sets comparable, two kinds of normalization were conducted. A comparison on the effectiveness of the normalization methods is also provided in the discussion on experiment results.

3.2.1 Method

The *personal word frequency* referred to the relative degrees to which a given LDT occurred in one's Facebook posts. Steps for its calculation are as follows:

[Step one] All of 16 participants' Facebook data were joined altogether into a file at first. If an LDT word stimulus appeared at least once in the file, it was chosen to be examined in this experiment. In total, there were 218 LDT stimuli conforming to the criterion, thus taken as the stimuli in this experiment.

[Step two] Personal word frequencies of the 218 stimuli were automatically counted.

[Step three] Two distinct methods were utilized to normalize the frequency counts. The first method was to divide the each subject's word frequencies by his/her own summed token numbers (see (2)). In the equation, F_{ij} was the participant *j*'s frequency count of the *i*th word; the *i* was limited between 1 to 218 since only 218 words were selected as stimuli in this experiment. However, note that the *i* in the denominator was not limited within the range, but by *n* instead. The *n* was the number of word types in a participant's Facebook data. In other words, the denominator added up word frequencies of all word types, thus representing the participant's total token number. Consequently, the output of the equation, R_{ij}, was the participant *j*'s frequency ratio of the *i*th stimulus.

$$R_{ij} = \frac{F_{ij}}{\sum_{i=1}^{n} F_{ij}} \qquad (2)$$

A potential problem of (2) was that the normalized figures were affected by each participant's token number. The token number was calculated according to the results of automatic segmentation, so it certainly would be contaminated by segmentation errors. Therefore, the other approach (i.e. the z-score approach) was also adopted. Like the previous equation, F_{ij} in (3) was the participant *j*'s frequency count of the *i*th word. $\overline{F_i}$ was the mean of the participant's 218 word frequency counts, and S_{F_i} was the standard deviation of those frequency counts.

$$Z_{ij} = \frac{F_{ij} - \overline{F_i}}{S_{F_i}} \qquad (3)$$

[10] LDT refers to the lexical decision task in this paper.

[Step four] The two types of personal word frequency were respectively put along with his/her response latencies in the lexical decision task for analysis.[11]

3.2.2 Results and Discussion

Response errors in the lexical decision task (approximately 0.06% of the data set) were first screened. Two types of normalized personal word frequencies (i.e. ratio and z-score) were analyzed by mixed-effects models. Like the analysis in Experiment 1, in both models, two random factors and six covariates were also included. Random factors encompassed experiment stimuli and participants. Covariates were procedure variables (i.e. block number and trial number) and word variables (i.e. types of word frequency, sense number, character number, and neighborhood size). The covariates were subsumed in order to avoid mis-attributing the variances caused by procedure and word variables to the effect of personal word frequency. If there was any covariate not reaching significance, which meant it statistically did not affect the lexical-decision responses, it would be removed from the analysis and the other variables refitted the mixed models.

The residuals of the two models, however, showed marked non-normality, especially at the end of long response latencies (see the upper right panel in Figure 5)[12]. To attenuate the unfitness, outliers with standardized residuals outside the interval (-2.5, 2.5) were removed. The removed data in both the ratio and z-score models were 2.48% of the data set. After trimming the outliers, we refitted the models. The residuals in the trimmed models were close to normality, as shown in the lower right panel of Figure 5.

Statistical results showed that personal word frequency significantly accounted for response latencies in both the analyses of frequency ratio ($p < .001$) and z-score ($p < .05$). The estimates of them were negative, which are visualized in Figure 6. According to the figures, the negative estimates indicated that participants responded faster to stimuli with higher personal word frequencies. The experimental results revealed that IDs of frequencies of stimuli could explain individual variances between participants in lexical decision.

Words that frequency occurred in one's Facebook data revealed the things or issues he/she paid closer attention, the words he/she got accustomed to use but was unaware of, or his/her daily-life surroundings. Therefore, the effect of personal word frequencies in this experiment was considered to result from people's conscious or subconscious familiarity with words or concepts. The familiarity with word form and meaning facilitated the access to corresponding underlying lexical representations in the participants' mental lexicon.

Another discussion brought up in this experiment is a methodological issue of computing personal lexical behaviors. Among two types of normalization of personal word frequency counts, the ratio method was assumed to be possibly problematic since segmentation errors were involved, and the z-score method was hypothesized to be a better one. Nevertheless, the analyses of word frequency ratio and z-score both reached significance. This indicated that normalizing frequency counts by the token number in each personal corpus is feasible even though there are segmentation errors and noise among the tokens. Evidence can be found when we compare each participant's total token number, which includes segmentation errors, with his token number summed from the 218 stimuli in Experiment 2, which includes no errors. The two categories of token numbers are highly correlated ($r = .95$). The correlation suggests that although segmentation errors make the total token numbers of Facebook data imprecise and inaccurate, the numbers still generally reflect

[11] Unlike Experiment 1, the response accuracies were not analyzed in this experiment. It was because the accuracy of the 218 stimuli here was extremely high (99.4%).

[12] Figure 5 is the residuals of the model fitted by the personal word frequency ratios. The residuals of the z-score model are the same as those of the ratio model, so its residual plot is not given here.

the comparative differences between participants' genuine token numbers.

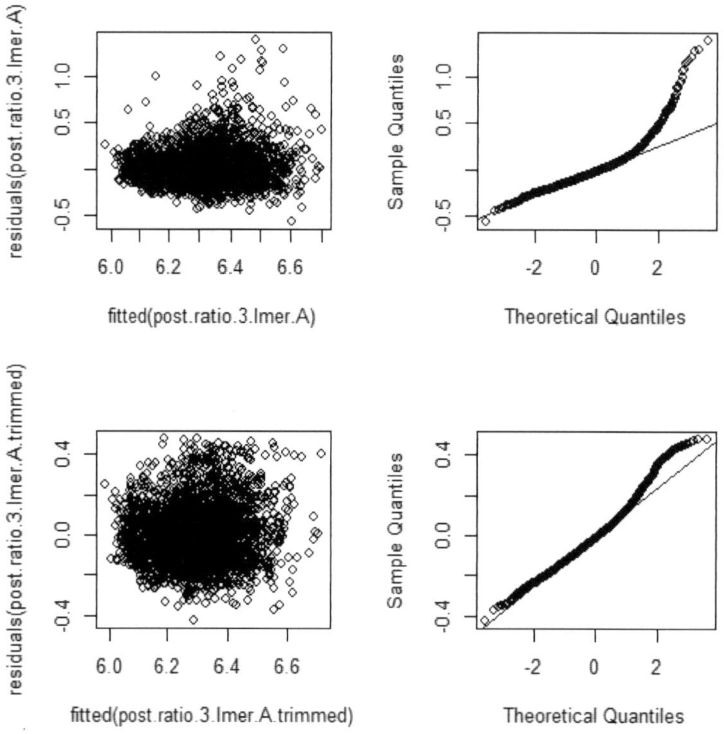

Figure 5. Residual diagnostics for the model of personal word frequency ratios before (upper panels) and after (lower panels) removal of outliers

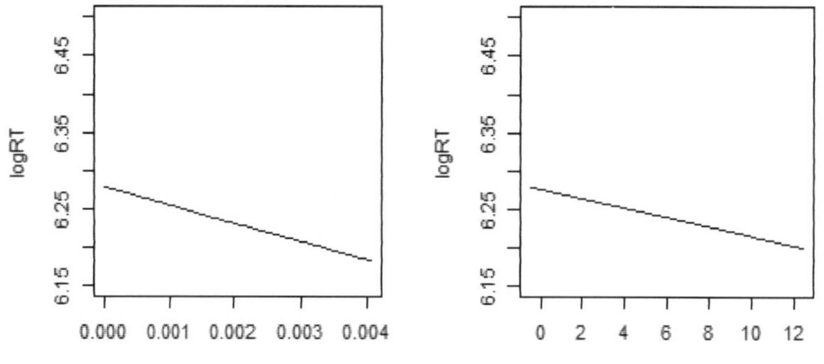

Figure 6. Partial effects of personal word frequency (ratio and z-score) in the analysis of Experiment 2

4. Conclusion

By integrating the approach of computational linguistics into a psycholinguistic experiment, the current study sheds a new light on methods of capturing the nature of IDs in word recognition. The interdisciplinary effort testified that the quantified personal lexical behaviors were associated with word recognition, thus uncovering a territory to be explored. One promising prospect of this study is that as the methodology of measuring lexical behaviors grows mature in the future, the readily available data of language usage, like Facebook posts, can function as convenient and valid resources for researchers to control the participant factors.

Furthermore, through the comparison of experimental results, the present study made a preliminary exploration on the methodology of measuring lexical behaviors and suggests the relatively appropriate methods. The counter-prediction finding in the *frequency index* experiment was possibly attributed to that the Sinica Corpus mainly consists of written data; therefore, it is suggested that similar experiments in future research resort to the frequency counts in a spoken corpus. Additionally, according to our examination, a person's total token number is feasible for normalizing his/her frequency counts even though word segmentation errors were contained within the tokens. Finally, when naturalistic data like the Facebook posts are utilized for the measurement, it is recommend basing the computation on personal preference or pattern of lexical usage (e.g. Experiment 2), instead of on every single word in one's language usage data (Experiment 1).

5. Future Work

The present study examines word recognition by only concentrating on the lexical decision task. To obtain a clearer picture of the IDs in recognition, the future work can collect converging evidence from other types of extensively-used tasks, such as the naming task [16, 17]. Besides, this preliminary research recruited 16 participants. It is expected that when the number of participants increases in future research, it might give us other or deeper insight into the issue of individual differences (IDs). Moreover, in the Chinese Lexicon Profile (CLP) corpus mentioned in Section 2.1.2, there provides a great number of characteristics of words *per se*. Researchers may try to compute and explore individual lexical behaviors from the available characteristics, aside from the word frequency which is utilized in this study. In the respect of personal language usage data, we are constructing i-Corpus, which will comprise individualized corpora. A corpus per person will include various types of his/her language usage data, which can be looked into in the future so as to uncover multiple facets of personal language usage.

References

[1] S. Andrews, "Frequency and neighborhood effects on lexical access: Activation or search?," *Journal of Experimental Psychology: Learning, Memory, and Cognition,* vol. 15, pp. 802-814, 1989.

[2] K. I. Forster and S. M. Chambers, "Lexical access and naming time," *Journal of Verbal Learning and Verbal Behavior,* vol. 12, pp. 627-635, 1973.

[3] J. Grainger, "Word frequency and neighborhood frequency effects in lexical decision and naming," *Journal of Memory and Language,* vol. 29, pp. 228-244, 1990.

[4] B. New, *et al.*, "Reexamining word length effects in visual word recognition: New evidence from the English Lexicon Project," *Psychonomic Bulletin & Review,* vol. 13, pp. 45-52, 2006.

[5] C. P. Whaley, "Word—nonword classification time," *Journal of Verbal Learning and*

Verbal Behavior, vol. 17, pp. 143-154, 1978.

[6] D. Chateau and D. Jared, "Exposure to print and word recognition processes," *Memory & Cognition,* vol. 28, pp. 143-153, 2000.

[7] C. Sears, *et al.*, "Is there an effect of print exposure on the word frequency effect and the neighborhood size effect?," *Journal of Psycholinguistic Research,* vol. 37, pp. 269-291, 2008.

[8] S. J. Unsworth and P. M. Pexman, "The impact of reader skill on phonological processing in visual word recognition," *Quarterly Journal of Experimental Psychology,* vol. 56A, pp. 63-81, 2003.

[9] M. J. Lewellen, *et al.*, "Lexical familiarity and processing efficiency: Individual differences in naming, lexical decision, and semantic categorization," *Journal of Experimental Psychology: General,* vol. 122, pp. 316-330, 1993.

[10] L. Katz, *et al.*, "What lexical decision and naming tell us about reading," *Reading and Writing,* in press.

[11] M. J. Yap, *et al.*, "Individual differences in visual word recognition: Insights from the English Lexicon Project," *Journal of Experimental Psychology: Human Perception and Performance,* vol. 38, pp. 53-79, 2012.

[12] R. C. Oldfield, "The assessment and analysis of handedness: The Edinburgh inventory," *Neuropsychologia,* vol. 9, pp. 97-113, 1971.

[13] H. M. Breland, "Word frequency and word difficulty: A comparison of counts in four corpora," *Psychological Science,* vol. 7, pp. 96-99, 1996.

[14] M. J. Crawley, *Statistical computing: An introdution to data analysis using S-plus.* Chichester: Wiley, 2002.

[15] R. H. Baayen, *Analyzing linguistic data : A practical introduction to statistics using R.* Cambridge: Cambridge University Press, 2008.

[16] D. A. Balota and J. I. Chumbley, "Are lexical decisions a good measure of lexical access? The role of word frequency in the neglected decision stage," *Journal of Experimental Psychology: Human Perception and Performance,* vol. 10, pp. 340-357, 1984.

[17] D. A. Balota and J. I. Chumbley, "The locus of word frequency effects in the pronunciation task: Lexical access and/or production?," *Journal of Memory and Language,* vol. 24, pp. 89-106, 1985.

遞迴式類神經網路語言模型應用額外資訊於語音辨識之研究

Recurrent Neural Network-based Language Modeling with Extra Information Cues for Speech Recognition

黃邦烜 Bang-Xuan Huang
國立臺灣師範大學資訊工程學系
699470204@ntnu.edu.tw

郝柏翰 Hank Hao
國立臺灣師範大學資訊工程學系
60047082s@ntnu.edu.tw

陳冠宇 Menphis Chen
中央研究院資訊科學研究所
kychen@iis.sinica.edu.tw

陳柏琳 Berlin Chen
國立臺灣師範大學資訊工程學系
berlin@ntnu.edu.tw

摘要

近年來類神經網路興起，其運用在語言模型領域有不錯的成效，如前饋式類神經網路語言模型。不同於傳統 N 連語言模型，前饋式類神經網路語言模型是將詞序列映射至連續空間來估測下一個詞出現的機率，以解決資料稀疏的問題。此外，更有學者使用遞迴式類神經網路來建構語言模型，期望藉由遞迴的方式將歷史資訊儲存起來，進而獲得長距離的資訊。

本論文根據遞迴式類神經網路的基礎，使用關聯資訊來捕捉長距離資訊；另外，也探討了根據語句的特性來動態地調整語言模型。實驗結果顯示，使用額外資訊於遞迴式類神經網路語言模型對於大詞彙連續語音辨識的效能有相當程度的提昇。

關鍵詞：語音辨識、語言模型、遞迴式類神經網路

一、緒論

語音是人與人溝通的基本媒介，如果無法透過語音來對話，便無法正確表達彼此的想法。在對話中，人們藉由語調和詞句，了解對方的情緒與想法等諸多細節，而聽懂對方想表達的資訊；這些人所擁有的天賦，是目前資訊科技所無法達到而需研究的；因此，自動語音辨識的研究也變得更加重要。在自動語音辨識的過程中，我們需先透過特徵擷

取(Feature Extraction)來處理語音訊號，得到可以代表此段語音訊號的特徵參數；接著，將所擷取的特徵參數轉換成語音特徵向量，以利語音辨識系統使用或分析。另一部分，則使用語音語料和文字語料分別建構出聲學模型(Acoustic Model)和語言模型(Language Model)，用以表示語音與文字之間的對應關係以及代表語言中各種詞彙的出現情形。再根據聲學模型、語言模型、詞典和特徵向量所提供的資訊以進行語言解碼(Linguistic Decoding)，獲得最後辨識結果。為了達到電腦能理解人類的語音的目標，本論文研究語音辨識中的語言模型，希望藉由語言模型能捕捉語言的規律性。*N* 連語言模型是較常見的語言模型之一，它易於產生且容易使用的特性引發許多學者研究與使用。但此語言模型有資料稀疏與缺乏長距離資訊等問題，因此有不同類型的語言模型被發展出並期望解決這些問題，前饋式類神經網路語言模型(Neural Network Language Models, NNLM)則是其中之一。它將歷史詞序列的資訊投影到連續空間，借以解決資料稀疏的問題，但對於長距離資訊的取得仍不盡理想。因此，為了獲得長距離的資訊，有所謂遞迴式類神經網路語言模型(Recurrent Neural Network Language Models, RNNLM)被提出。1994 年有研究[1]指出，遞迴式類神經網路較難取得更長距離的資訊，其理由是當句子越長時，越遠距離的資訊透過機率相乘所得到的值會趨近於零。本論文延續先前對於遞迴式類神經網路語言模型之研究，嘗試使用額外的資訊來增進遞模型的預測能力，期望在大詞彙連續語音辨識中有相當程度的改善。

本論文的安排如下：第二章簡介類神經網路語言模型；第三章介紹遞迴式類神經網路語言模型於自動語音辨識之使用，並且說明遞迴式類神經網路語言模型相關理論及架構；第四章探索遞迴式類神經網路語言模型之改進；第五章介紹實驗語料、實驗設定以及實驗結果分析；第六節則是結論及未來展望。

二、類神經網路語言模型於自動語音辨識之使用

(一)、 類神經網路簡介

類神經網路(Neural Networks)起源於人工智慧(Artificial Intelligence)，又可稱為人工類神經網路(Artificial Neural Networks, ANN)。自 1940 年開始科學家開始模仿神經元(Neuron)的運作模式，認為如果兩個神經元同時被觸發，則它們之間的連結就會獲得增強。直到近年來，類神經網路結合了各項領域，如資訊、金融甚至心理學等都有不錯的成效，其中；像是感知器演算法(Perceptron)是第一個實踐出類神經網路的創舉。

目前類神經網路主要被用於分類及預測上，在影像處理方面，如圖案的辨識或雜訊的處理等，而在語音處理中則有語言模型、語音合成與強健性語音辨識等；另外則是氣象預測、電腦輔助教學、手寫辨識以及超大積體電路的應用。本論文則是探討語音辨識裡的語言模型部份；以下介紹目前所發展出來各種常見的類神經網路語言模型。

(二)、 類神經網路語言模型

將類神經網路與語言模型結合則可表示成圖一，稱為前饋式類神經網路語言模型[2]。

其主要架構包括輸入層(Input Layer)、隱藏層(Hidden Layer)和輸出層(Output Layer)；有時會額外加入一層投影層(Projection Layer)，用來將歷史詞序列的資訊投影至此連續空間，並降低輸入層的維度。

不同於N連語言模型會有資料稀疏的問題，投影層可以接受所有可能的詞序列組合；並且，詞序列中的每個詞能各自貢獻出權重值來估測下一個詞出現的可能性。層跟層之間的神經元靠著突觸(Synapse)來傳遞訊息。各層可以向量表示，層之間的突觸則以矩陣表示。接下來先介紹各層所代表的意義：

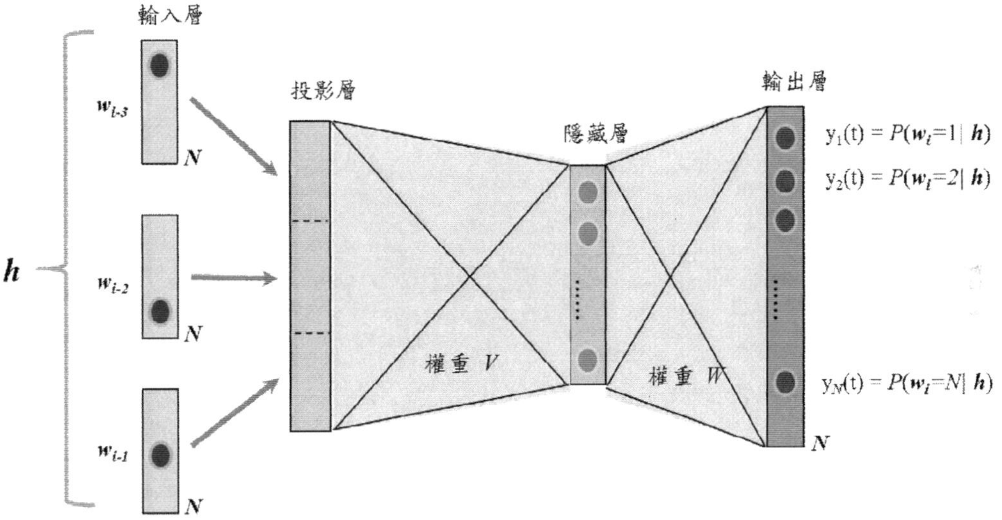

圖一、類神經網路語言模型架構

- 輸入層與隱藏層

輸入層為欲預測詞的歷史資訊，其中歷史資訊以 $\boldsymbol{h}$ 表示。每個詞使用 one-of-N 方式進行編碼，例如詞 w_i 為詞典中的第 l 個詞，在長度為 N 的向量中，詞 w_i 只有第 l 維是 1 其餘為 0。輸入層、隱藏層及輸出層中包含了許多節點，輸入層中的節點以變數 i 表示，隱藏層的節點以變數 j 表示，輸出層的節點則以變數 k 表示。各層的節點結合後可形成一個向量，式(1)為各節點在向量中的表示方式。$x_i(t)$表示輸入層中於 t 時間點第 i 個節點，其中 i 為 1 到 N 之間表示輸入層大小，N 為詞彙的數量。

$$x_i(t) = \begin{cases} 1 & \text{if } i \in \text{對應的詞} \\ 0 & \text{其他} \end{cases} \tag{1}$$

以圖一為例，$\boldsymbol{h}$ 代表了前三個詞(t=3)的歷史資訊，結合了三個歷史詞向量，成為另一個長度為 $3N$ 的輸入層向量 $\boldsymbol{x}$，可視為一個四連的類神經網路語言模型。在傳統前饋式類神經網路裡，向量 $\boldsymbol{x}$ 則會透過權重 V 來傳遞，而權重 V 會以矩陣的方式來表示，權重 V 中包含了許多輸入層節點和隱藏層節點間的鏈結權重值。式(2)為輸入層各節點傳遞至

隱藏層中的節點 j。v_{ji} 是第 j 個隱藏層節點對第 i 個輸入層節點的鏈結權重值，θ_j 為第 j 個隱藏層節點的偏權值，net_j(t)為第 j 個隱藏層節點淨輸入值，$y_j(t)$則為第 j 個隱藏層節點。

$$net_j(t) = \sum_i v_{ji} x_i(t) + \theta_j$$
$$y_j(t) = f(net_j) \tag{2}$$

其中， $f(net_j)$為網路的活化函數(Activation Function)。為了保證輸出值能介於 0 到 1 之間，本論文中所使用的是雙彎曲函數(Sigmoid Function)，如式(3)所表示：

$$f(x) = \frac{1}{1+e^{-x}} \tag{3}$$

- 隱藏層與輸出層

如同輸入層與隱藏層，隱藏層的各個節點會透過權重 W 傳遞給輸出層，可以透過式(4)來表示：

$$net_k(t) = \sum_j w_{kj} y_j(t) + \theta_k$$
$$y_k(t) = g(net_k) \tag{4}$$

其中，w_{kj} 是第 k 個隱藏層節點對第 j 個輸入層節點的鏈結權重值，θ_k 為第 k 個隱藏層節點的偏權值，$net_k(t)$為第 k 個隱藏層節點淨輸入值，$y_k(t)$為第 k 個輸出層節點。為了使輸出層各節點的值總和為 1，最後的 $g(net_k)$為軟化最大值活化函數(Softmax Activation Function)，也是轉移函數(Transfer Function)的一種。如式(5)來表示：

$$g(net_k) = \frac{e^{net_k}}{\sum_k e^{net_k}} \tag{5}$$

最後輸出層的結果可視為一個 N 維的向量，其第 l 維的意義是在歷史詞序列 $\boldsymbol{h}$ 發生的情況下，目前預測的詞 w_i 發生的機率，其數學表示式為 $P(w_i = l \mid h)$ 。

三、遞迴式類神經網路語言模型

有別於傳統類神經網路，遞迴式的類神經網路更能帶來較好的訓練能力，一般常見的是於 1990 年由 Elman 所發展的艾爾曼網路(Elman Networks)[3]。其概念是將隱藏層的輸出當作下一次時間點隱藏層的輸入，而根據不同的需求也有許多不同的網路形成，如喬丹網路(Jordan Networks)[4]是將輸出層的輸出再傳遞給下一時間點的隱藏層、雙向遞迴式類神經網路(Bi-directional RNN)[5]利用歷史資訊和未來資訊來做預測，使用的是兩個遞迴式類神經網路來做結合及階層遞迴式類神經網路(Hierarchical RNN)等。本論文則是以艾爾曼網路來進行探討。

遞迴式類神經網路語言模型和傳統類神經網路語言模型主要的差別除了少了投影層、增加了前一時間點的隱藏層外，另一個差別就是輸入層部分。在訓練過程時，輸入層是一次以一個詞來表示並訓練，每一個詞的表示方法則與傳統前饋式類神經網路語言模型相同。其網路的結構是把輸入層加大，將上一時間點的隱藏層預先儲存起來，若以時間方式來階層展開的話，將會更清楚看出其遞迴的概念，如圖二所示。由於遞迴式類神經網路具有時序處理(Temporal Processing)的能力，而一般來評估此類型的網路常會注意它們的穩定性(Stability)、可控性(Controllability)及可觀察性(Observability)。穩定性注重的是隨著時間改變，網路輸出結果需是受侷限的且輸出後的調整量不可過於劇烈，例如網路中輸出的部份或權重。可控性在意的是「是否能夠控制的動態行為」，如果在有限的步驟中，一個初始狀態是可控制至任何期望的狀態，則此遞迴式網路可被稱為具有可控性的。可觀察性關注的是「是否可觀察出控制應用的結果」，如果網路的狀態可以確定從一組有限的輸入或輸出測量，則稱做此網路有可觀察性。

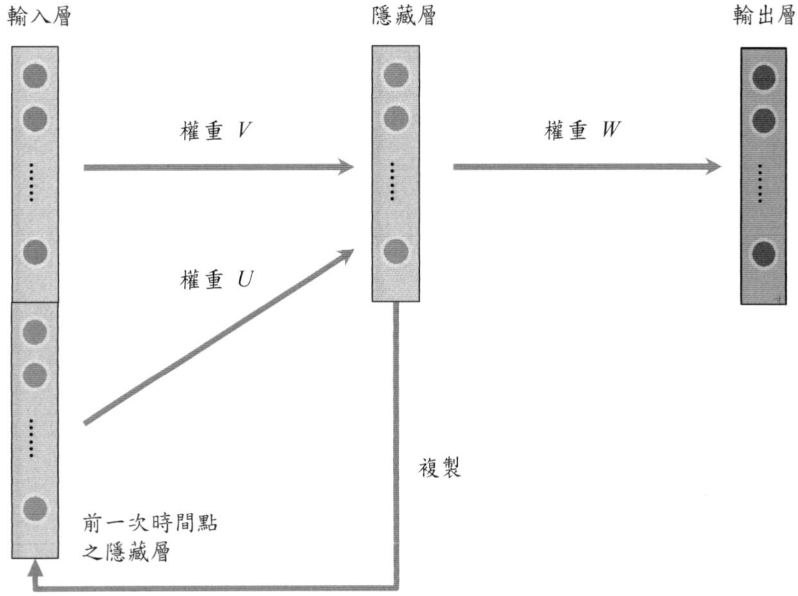

圖二、遞迴式類神經網路架構

但 Bengio 等學者[6]發現，利用梯度下降法(Gradient Descent Method)於遞迴式類神經網路中，對於學習長距離的資訊是十分困難的。而要獲得長距離資訊必須要具有任意時間學習並且擁有抵抗其它資訊干擾的能力。但因為隨著時間變化，距離較遠的資訊會被每一次時間點的輸入資訊所干擾，反而降低了遞迴式結構的好處。因此下一章將討論如何將遞迴式類神經網路語言模型做進一步的改進。

四、探索遞迴式類神經網路語言模型之改進

(一)、 結合關聯資訊於遞迴式類神經網路語言模型

傳統統計式 N 連語言模型是容易使用而且是目前常見的方法之一，但此模型仍有缺乏表示長距離資訊的能力與以及會有資料稀疏的問題。使用類神經網路語言模型能有效解決資料稀疏之問題，可惜在長距離資訊上仍稍嫌不足；因此，遞迴式類神經網路語言模型的發展是希望能取得更多長距離資訊。許多國外研究也顯示遞迴式類神經網路語言模型的確能比一般類神經網路語言模型帶來更好的成效，這也是本論文使用遞迴式類神經網路語言模型來探討之原因。遞迴式類神經網路語言模型中回饋的方式是使用時序性倒傳遞演算法；然而，此方法被證明出此模型無法有效獲得長距離的資訊。因此，本論文將探討透過加入關聯資訊(Relevance Information)來幫助預測下一個詞的可能性。

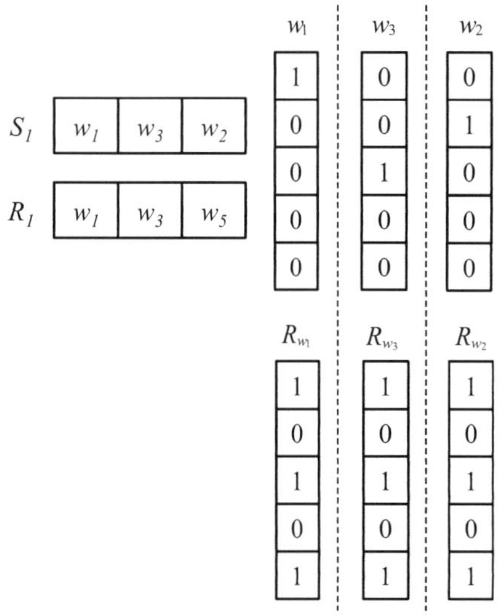

圖三、語句關聯資訊概念圖

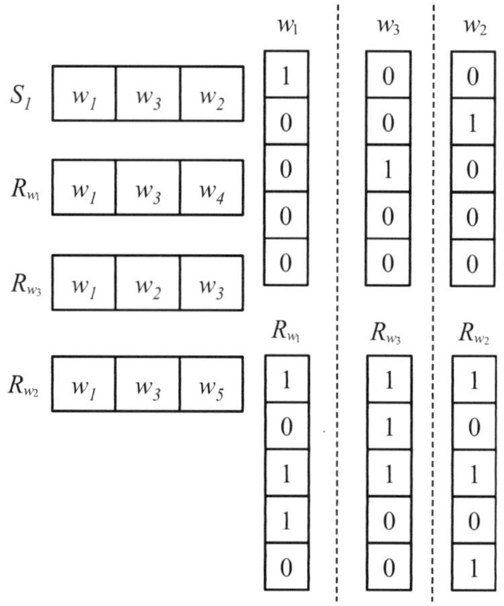

圖四、詞關聯資訊概念圖

關聯資訊則以向量來表示，大小如同原本的輸入層一樣，因此本論文將輸入層擴增為兩倍，前半段為原本訓練資料的資訊，後半段為對應訓練資料的關聯向量。關聯向量主要又分為兩種，一種為句子間的關聯，稱做語句關聯資訊(Sentence Relevance Information)，另一種為詞跟詞之間的關聯，稱為詞關聯資訊(Word Relevance Information)。語句關聯資訊的產生，是將欲檢索的句子放進訓練語料中進行一次檢索，檢索完可得知對所有訓練語句的關聯分數，根據此關聯分數我們可以決定要使用多少關聯語句來當作關聯向量。圖三為語句關聯資訊的概念圖，以句子 S_1 為例，S_1 中依序包含了詞 w_1 、w_3 和 w_2 ，R_1 則為對應 S_1 的語句關聯資訊。但在訓練模型時是以詞為單位進行訓練，因此賦予每個詞的關聯資訊皆為此句的語句關聯資訊。R_{w_1} 、R_{w_3} 和 R_{w_2} 則為詞 w_1 、w_3 和 w_2 所對應的關聯資訊。而詞關聯資訊則是避免使每個詞對應到相同的關聯資訊，其產生的方式是從訓練語料中收集每一個詞左右相鄰文段中，相隔一定距離內其它詞出現的頻率，結果會得知數個關聯的詞，每一個詞的關聯資訊長度也皆不同，其概念如圖四所示。

另外，本論文將關聯資訊以三種不同方式來表示，分別為詞頻數、正規化後及值設定為 1 或 0 來進行探討，觀察關聯資訊帶來之影響。以詞頻數表示則代表我們使用實際的次數來增加詞與詞之間的關聯性，具有較真實的資訊。以正規化表示使所有關聯資訊的總和為 1，此表示法以較公平的方式來給予值，貢獻大的，也就是次數較多的則值越高；反之，貢獻低的則值較低。而以設定為 1 或 0 來表示，則是將有次數出現的維度以 1 來表示；反之，沒有出現為 0，因此此種表示法代表詞與關聯詞之間，其關聯程度均相同。

除此之外，也發展了動態詞關聯的方式，由於每個詞所對應的關聯向量是固定的，因此我們將歷史資訊中的關聯資訊做結合，得到新的關聯資訊。其中，因為每個詞的歷史資訊大部分皆不同，所以結合出來的關聯向量也皆不同。而根據歷史資訊的遠近，分別使用不同權重來做結合，越遠的歷史資訊則隨著時間越來越小，我們可以用遞迴的方式以式(6)來表示。

$$\begin{cases} if \;\; \mathrm{t}=0, & R_t^{'}=R_0 \\ if \;\; 0<t\le L, & R_t^{'}=(1-\alpha)\cdot R_{t-1}+\alpha\cdot R_t \end{cases} \tag{6}$$

R_t 為在 t 時間點之原始關聯資訊，$R_t^{'}$ 為新獲得的關聯資訊，L 為在該語句所含詞的數目，α 則為可調控之參數。

一開始時，詞的關聯資訊為原始的關聯資訊；而當時間點大於 0 且小於等於句子長度時，會與所有歷史詞的關聯資訊做線性結合。因此距離越遠的詞，其關聯資訊的權重就越小，相反地，距離越近的詞，其關聯資訊的權重就越大，因而達到動態效果的詞關聯資訊。本論文的 α 值為 0.6。以圖五為例，句子 S_1 中含有五個詞，而圖中為詞 w_4 的關聯資訊。可看出其關聯資訊為所有歷史詞的加總，權重部份則取決於詞的距離。

S_1	w_1	w_2	w_3	w_4	w_5

$$R_{w4}^{'}=0.064R_{w1}+0.096R_{w2}+0.24R_{w3}+0.6R_{w4}$$

圖五、動態詞關聯資訊範例

(二)、 語句相關之遞迴式類神經網路語言模型

本節探討藉由動態語言模型調整方式來增進語言模型預測能力；因此，對於不同測試語句使用不同的遞迴式類神經網路語言模型或是結合不同群的遞迴式類神經網路語言模型。

不同於上述的方法裡，所有測試語句皆使用由相同訓練語料訓練出的遞迴式類神經網路語言模型，本論文希望針對各句測試語句，以線性組合的方式結合不同訓練語料所

訓練出的遞迴式類神經網路語言模型，期望找出較適合各句測試語句的遞迴式類神經網路語言模型。一開始，先將所有訓練語句的正確轉寫語句以單連詞向量(Unigram Word Vector)表示，並進行分群(Clustering)。本論文所使用的分群方法為 K 平均演算法(K-means)[7]，在透過分群過後，我們可用各群所分好的訓練語句來訓練各群的遞迴式類神經網路語言模型，假設所有訓練語句可分為 S 群。接著，對 S 群中每一群訓練語句分別算出各自的特徵權重向量，意即平均向量(Mean Vector)，此部分可由每一群中各句訓練語句的單連詞向量進行加總並取平均求得。

可以用式(7)來表示：

$$v_s = \frac{\sum_{k=1}^{L_s} v_{s,k}}{L_s} \tag{7}$$

其中 $v_{s,k}$ 為第 S 群中第 k 句訓練語句的單連詞向量，v_s 是第 S 群的平均向量，L_s 為 s 訓練語句群中所含訓練語句之句數。如此一來，當有一測試語句需要進行估測時，可以利用此測試語句之單連詞特徵向量和所算好的各群特徵權重向量來求取相似度(Similarity)，並選取欲使用的遞迴式類神經網路語言模型或結合不同群的遞迴式類神經網路語言模型。由於我們無法得知測試語句的正確轉寫語句。在此，測試語句之單連詞特徵向量皆以其 M 條最佳辨識結果中的第一名來表示。

本論文主要使用三種選取方式來選取，在計算相似度時，使用的是餘弦值來計算：

$$\cos(U_k, v_s) = \frac{u_k \cdot v_s}{\sqrt{u_k^{\ 2}}\sqrt{v_s^{\ 2}}} \tag{8}$$

其中 U_k 表示第 k 句測試語句，u_k 為測試語句第 k 句中 M 條最佳辨識結果第一名之單連詞向量，v_s 為使用第 s 群訓練語句的單連詞特徵向量。以下則介紹三種選取方式：

(1) 選取相似度最大權重法：此方法只選取和測試語句最相似的訓練語句群，也就是所謂相似度最大的。可用式(9)來表示：

$$RNNLM_{U_k} = \arg\max_s \cos(U_k, v_s) \tag{9}$$

其中，$RNNLM_{U_k}$ 代表所挑選出來的遞迴式類神經網路語言模型，因此式(9)則表示挑選 P 群中餘弦值最大之遞迴式類神經網路語言模型。

$$P(U_k) \approx P_{RNNLM_{U_K}}(U_k) \tag{10}$$

因此估測 U_k 的機率便可表示成式(10)。

(2) 相似度線性組合法：此方法之組合係數是經由計算測試語句與 S 群訓練語句間的相似度來求得，因此如果某測試語句和某群相似度較大則表示該群較符合測試語句之特性，也就是該群會有較大之貢獻。而測試語句與各訓練語句群的組合係數 $\gamma_{k,p}$ 為：

$$\gamma_{k,s} = \frac{\cos(u_k, v_s)}{\sum_{s'=1}^{S} \cos(u_k, v_{s'})} \tag{11}$$

接著將各群之模型分數用此係數線性組合以獲得新的語言模型機率：

$$P(U_k) = \sum_{s=1}^{S} \gamma_{k,s} \cdot P_{RNNLM_s}(U_k) \tag{12}$$

而 $P(U_k)$ 為測試語句經過線性結合之遞迴式類神經網路語言模型機率，$P_{RNNLMs}(U_k)$ 為第 s 群之遞迴式類神經網路語言模型機率。

(3) 相似度均勻組合法：
該方法類似相似度線性組合法，將原本組合係數調整成均勻(Uniform)組合係數，因此各群的貢獻度將會相同，則各群均勻組合係數 $\beta_{k,s}$ 為：

$$\beta_{k,s} = \frac{1}{S} \tag{13}$$

其中 S 為分群個數。所以最後結合完的分數可以用式(14)來表示：

$$P(U_k) = \sum_{s=1}^{S} \beta_{k,s} \cdot P_{\mathrm{rnnlm}_s}(U_k) \tag{14}$$

我們可以將算好的分數結合原本背景語言模型所預測的機率，以此來得到更好的結果。

五、實驗結果與分析

(一)、 實驗語料

本論文使用之實驗語料是來自於公視新聞(Mandarin Across Taiwan-Broadcast News, MATBN)[8]。公視新聞語料是 2001 年至 2003 年間由中研院資訊所口語小組(SLG)與公共電視(PTS)合作錄製，共計 197 個小時之語音資訊與其內容標記。

選自公視新聞 2001 年至 2002 年外場採訪記者，分別為訓練集語料 30,600 句(約 23 小時)、測試集語料 1,997 句(約 1.5 小時)及發展集語料 1,998 句(約 1.5 小時)。如表一所示。聲學模型訓練語料為公視新聞 2001 至 2002 年外場採訪記者語料，共 30,632 句(約 23 小時)，其中包含了實驗訓練語料 30,600 句。

另外背景語言模型使用的訓練語料是來自 2001 至 2002 年中央通訊社(Central News Agency, CNA)的文字新聞語料，內含有約一億五千萬個中文字，經由斷詞之後約有八千萬個詞。此語言模型是使用 SRI Language Modeling Toolkit (SRILM)[9]訓練而得，採用 Katz Back-off 平滑化方法[10]來解決資料稀疏的問題。

短句語料	句數	長度(小時)
訓練集語料	30,600	約 23
發展集語料	1,998	約 1.5
測試集語料	1,997	約 1.5

表一、實驗語料統計資訊

(二)、 基礎實驗結果

實驗的產生是從詞圖產生 100(M=100)句最佳候選詞序列，再經由訓練好的遞迴式類神經網路語言模型得到各句詞序列的分數，並加入聲學模型的資訊以此獲得語音辨識的總分數。透過所選出的第一名詞序列和正確答案去算出編輯距離(Edit distance)得到字正確率。遞迴式類神經網路語言模型則是使用 Mikolov 等學者[11]所發展的 Recurrent Neural Network Language Modeling Toolkit (RNNLM)訓練而得。本論文所提出的應用關聯資訊則是對其套件做修改，將關聯資訊加入於遞迴式類神經網路語言模型；語句相關之遞迴式類神經網路語言模型則是利用此套件來訓練遞迴式類神經網路語言模型。而實驗的目的，則是希望透過藉由遞迴式類神經網路語言模型來重新排序找出字正確率最高的詞序列。

語言模型設定方面，在訓練遞迴式類神經網路語言模型時隱藏層個數為 100、類別層個數也為 100 、遞迴的次數為 4 且訓練及辨識過程中，句子和句子之間是獨立的，也就是說上一句的句子和目前訓練的句子是不相關聯的。

	發展集語言複雜度	發展集語言複雜度	發展集語料字正確率 (%)	測試集語料字正確率 (%)	絕對提昇率 (%)	相對提昇率 (%)
背景三連語言模型 (BG)	450.93	459.06	84.73	83.61	-	-
RNN	607.07	623.50	82.31	82.41	-1.2	-7.32
RNN+BG	232.31	236.97	85.67	85.17	1.56	9.52
Oracle	-	-	93.22	92.66	-	-

表二、遞迴式類神經網路語言模型之基礎實驗結果

表二是關於遞迴式類神經網路語言模型的基礎實驗結果，從語言複雜度的角度來看，遞迴式類神經網路語言模型(RNN)的語言複雜度為 623.50，再看到背景三連語言模型(BG)的部份，由於訓練語料較多，因此其效果會比遞迴式類神經網路語言模型來的好。而根據文獻中所看到的，遞迴式類神經網路語言模型在獨自使用時效果較不明顯，必須和其它模型做結合，才會有更好的表現。實驗中也可看到背景語言模型結合遞迴式類神經網路語言模型(RNN+BG)效果會來得最好；可以見得，遞迴式類神經網路語言模

型仍然具有不錯的成效。

另一部分，我們可以看到 Oracle 部分(意即假使能正確選取到 100 句最佳詞序列中字錯誤率最低的詞序列)，字正確率可到達 93.22%，這意味著我們仍有很大的進步空間。而這部份的趨勢也和語言複雜度相同，單獨使用遞迴式類神經網路語言模型時，辨識率下降 1.2%，但透過與背景語言模型的結合，其絕對提昇率有 1.56%以及相對提昇率 9.52%。

在以下第(3)節和第(4)節的實驗中，我們將使用背景語言模型結合遞迴式類神經網路語言模型(RNN+BG)的語言複雜度 236.97 和辨識率 85.17%作為 RNN 的基礎辨識率，以此來和我們所提出的方法做比較。

(三)、 結合關聯資訊於遞迴式類神經網路語言模型之實驗結果

首先，我們使用語句關聯資訊來幫助遞迴式類神經網路語言模型做估測。在訓練模型時，語句關聯資訊是挑選最相關的訓練語句，由於挑選過多的關聯資訊會導致辨識率下降，因此只挑選最相關的部分。其中，因為遞迴式類神經網路語言模型是以詞為單位進行訓練，所以每個詞需要對應到一個關聯向量，此部分的詞的關聯向量為此句的關聯向量。而關聯向量的表示方式分別使用了句子中詞出現的次數、將詞出現的次數做正規化及出現該詞的維度設為 1。從表三中可看到語言複雜度部份，以句中詞出現的次數較好，而辨識率方面，則是使用正規化的表示較好，相較於基礎辨識率 85.17%小幅度的進步了 0.04%，而使用句中次數則下降了 0.08%，以及設定為 1 的方法也下降了 0.14%。

表三是在結合語句關聯資訊中，使用三種表示法的辨識率結果，可看出使用正規化值的表示法較好，其餘兩種的辨識率則較 RNN 基礎辨識率來得低。探究其辨識率進步不大的原因應為每一語句內，詞的關聯向量皆為此句的關聯向量，因此關聯向量的重複率就等同於語句中詞的數量。這也成為了辨識率降低的原因之一，另一個原因則是原本輸入的資訊可能被關聯資訊所干擾。因此我們嘗試將關聯資訊切得更細，使用詞關聯資訊來幫助估測。

關聯資訊表示方式	發展集語言複雜度	測試集語言複雜度	發展集語料字正確率 (%)	測試集語料字正確率 (%)	絕對提昇率 (%)	相對提昇率 (%)
RNN 基礎辨識率	232.31	236.97	85.67	85.17	-	-
句中詞出現的次數	223.63	229.01	85.63	85.09	-0.08	-0.56
正規化值	230.51	236.45	85.71	85.21	0.04	0.27
出現該詞則設為 1 否則為 0	226.04	231.19	85.56	85.03	-0.14	-0.95

表三、結合語句關聯資訊之實驗結果

詞關聯資訊不同於語句關聯資訊之處，就是每一語句中的詞有各自的關聯資訊。詞關聯資訊的產生，是將訓練語料中，詞出現的地方找其相鄰詞作為關聯資訊，出現相同的相鄰詞則會累加出現次數，本論文則是取左右距離為 3。

關聯資訊表示方式	發展集語言複雜度	測試集語言複雜度	發展集語料字正確率 (%)	測試集語料字正確率 (%)	絕對提昇率 (%)	相對提昇率 (%)
RNN 基礎辨識率	232.31	236.97	85.67	85.17	-	-
詞出現的次數	230.05	234.93	85.88	85.36	0.19	1.26
正規化值	230.13	234.75	85.83	85.34	0.17	1.16
出現該詞則設為 1 否則為 0	230.12	234.83	85.77	85.40	0.23	1.52

表四、結合詞關聯資訊之實驗結果

表四使用詞關聯資訊於遞迴式類神經網路語言模型的實驗結果，由於部分詞的詞關聯資訊相當多，包含了關聯詞和非關聯的詞，因此，我們試著去調整詞關聯資訊的使用程度，其中詞關聯資訊的長度是根據發展集中最好的結果來設定。語言複雜度方面，詞出現次數、正規化值及出現該詞則設為 1 否則為 0 也都有進步；而字正確率方面，詞出現次數、正規化值及出現該詞則設為 1 否則為 0 均有提昇，絕對提昇率分別為 0.19%、0.17%及 0.23%，相對提昇率則有 1.26%、1.16%及 1.52%的進步。比較三種表示法的辨識率，可看到出現該詞設為 1 否則為 0 的辨識結果較好，因為此方法對於每個關聯詞的關聯度較公平，大家皆設定為 1。而詞出現的次數和正規化值，因為每個關聯詞之間的歧異度較高，尤其是詞出現的次數，次數的差距很大，導致有些關聯詞的貢獻被埋沒。

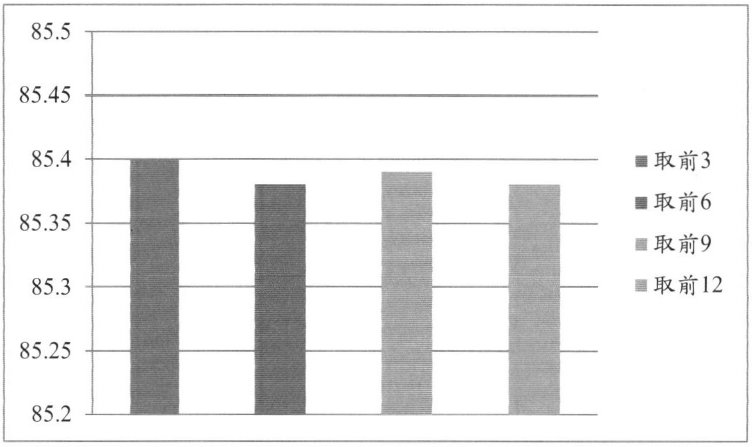

圖七、使用不同長度之詞關聯資訊辨識結果

另外，此部份實驗結果也顯示，使用出現該詞設為 1 且調整詞關聯資訊的長度較好；於是我們進一步去觀察使用此表示法在不同詞關聯資訊長度上的比較。圖七則是其辨識結果，可以看出使用過多的資訊反而會導致效果減弱。

雖然從實驗結果中得知，使用詞關聯資訊的確提升了辨識率，但我們仍希望可以突破目前的瓶頸。於是我們發現到，雖然詞關聯資訊解決了語句關聯資訊的問題，但是仍有類似語句關聯資訊的缺點存在，其缺點則是語料中的每個詞所對應到的詞關聯資訊仍然一樣，造成在訓練中重複使用同樣的詞關聯資訊。此作法的詞關聯資訊是比較屬於全域(Global)的，也就是是針對所有訓練語料中，獲得詞與詞的關聯度。而在訓練遞迴式類神經網路語言模型中，我們也需要區域性的資訊，因為相同的詞在不同的句子可能代表著不同的意思，所以我們希望藉由區域性的資訊來獲得上下文或句子中的資訊，使得在預測下一個詞時能夠符合句子中的意思。因此，我們希望詞的關聯資訊必須是會變動的或是動態的，如此一來才能包含全域性的資訊和區域性的資訊。為此，本論文提出了動態詞關聯資訊來做更進一步的改進，此部分是先將所有歷史詞的關聯資訊做結合，其結合依據遠近來給予權重。因此，歷史詞與目前的詞距離越遠，則該歷史詞的關聯資訊貢獻越小；反之，歷史詞與目前的詞距離越近，則該歷史詞的關聯資訊越大。表五則是使用動態詞關聯資訊的實驗結果，結果顯示使用動態詞關聯資訊效果與一般的詞關聯資訊較差一點，辨識率大約為 85.34%左右；而其語言複雜度表現則較詞關聯資訊好。探究其原因，應為關聯資訊中常包含關聯與非關聯的資訊，因此我們難以準確知道越近距離的詞關聯資訊有較相關的資訊，造成使用的關聯資訊無法正確代表與該詞相關。

根據本論文所提出的結合關聯資訊於遞迴式類神經網路語言模型的確有助於辨識率的提升，但是其效果仍有限且不是那麼的明顯，其原因大概歸類為三種，其一是關聯資訊可能會對輸入層所要傳遞的資訊造成干擾，使得輸入層所要傳遞的資訊減弱，而關聯資訊被成為主要傳遞的資訊；其二是關聯資訊結合輸入層，也可能只是將其表示方式做了延伸，而關聯資訊的表示法可能有更佳的表示方法；其三則是難以準確的決定關聯資訊，導致效果無法彰顯。

關聯資訊表示方式	發展集語言複雜度	測試集語言複雜度	發展集語料字正確率 (%)	測試集語料字正確率 (%)	絕對提昇率 (%)	相對提昇率 (%)
RNN 基礎辨識率	232.31	236.97	85.67	85.17	-	-
詞出現的次數	229.72	234.35	85.84	85.26	0.09	0.58
正規化值	231.42	236.19	85.83	85.34	0.17	1.14
出現該詞則設為 1 否則為 0	229.98	234.62	85.86	85.34	0.17	1.16

表五、結合動態詞關聯資訊之實驗結果

(四)、 語句相關之遞迴式類神經網路語言模型之實驗結果

本節主要探究利用語句相關之遞迴式類神經網路語言模型之實驗結果，以下表六是將訓練語料分為兩群用於發展集語料之結果，表七是將發展集語料的最佳設定用在測試語料的辨識結果；表八與表九，分別為將訓練語料分為四群的發展集語料與測試語料測試結果。

表七為分成兩群後的字正確率，分別為兩群使用選取相似度最大權重法、使用相似度線性組合法與使用相似度均勻組合法的字正確率。此部分我們會額外使用一個全部訓練語料所訓練出的遞迴式類神經網路語言模型來做輔助，稱為遞迴式類神經網路背景語言模型。首先利用三種權重組合方式將各群做結合，接著再將結合完的結果加入遞迴式類神經網路背景語言模型，最後才結合背景語言模型。比較表六可以看到利用選取相似度最大權重法會有較好的結果與基礎遞迴式類神經網路語言模型相比，絕對提昇率有 0.24% 的進步。

RNNLM 權重參數	選取相似度 最大權重法	相似度 線性組合法	相似度 均勻組合法
0	84.29	84.29	84.29
0.1	85.64	85.68	85.58
0.2	85.87	85.88	85.94
0.3	85.86	85.92	85.94
0.4	85.90	85.91	85.81
0.5	85.81	85.78	85.74
0.6	85.70	85.57	85.44
0.7	85.46	85.43	85.29
0.8	85.05	84.97	84.99
0.9	84.60	84.55	84.52
1	82.56	82.62	82.59

表六、發展集語料字正確率之兩群辨識結果

	字正確率(%)	絕對提昇率(%)	相對提昇率(%)
選取相似度最大權重法	85.41	0.24	1.60
相似度線性組合法	85.24	0.07	0.46
相似度均勻組合法	85.29	0.12	0.82

表七、測試語料字正確率之兩群辨識結果

而選取相似度均勻組合法與相似度線性組合法則略差於基礎辨識率，探究其原因應為資料較偏向某一群，因此使用相似度均勻組合法與相似度線性組合法則較差，只要使用相似度最大的那群就能有較好的效果。

表九則是分成四群。將訓練語料分四群來訓練的實驗中，也可得知使用相似度最大權重法是較佳的。但是跟兩群的實驗相比，雖然與基礎辨識率相比仍有進步，三種選取方法還是較差一點。探討其原因應為訓練語料不足的關係。由於分群數目提高，則每群中的訓練語料則隨之減少。因此無法訓練出學習能力較佳的遞迴式類神經網路語言模型，導致字正確率的下降。而實驗中也可看出，結合完各群結果後的辨識率仍不好，需要加入遞迴式類神經網路背景語言模型來輔助，以得到更好的辨識率。

RNNLM 權重參數	選取相似度 最大權重法	相似度線性組合法	相似度均勻組合法
0	84.29	84.29	84.29
0.1	85.65	85.55	85.59
0.2	85.73	85.73	85.71
0.3	85.86	85.86	85.78
0.4	85.87	85.81	85.69
0.5	85.79	85.77	85.60
0.6	85.61	85.50	85.52
0.7	85.39	85.35	85.35
0.8	85.15	85.13	85.05
0.9	84.71	84.66	84.63
1	82.75	83.39	83.31

表八、發展集語料字正確率之四群辨識結果

	字正確率(%)	絕對提昇率(%)	相對提昇率(%)
選取相似度最大權重法	85.33	0.16	1.06
相似度線性組合法	85.31	0.14	0.94
相似度均勻組合法	85.32	0.15	1.02

表九、測試語料字正確率之四群辨識結果

六、結論與未來展望

傳統 N 連語言模型是目前語言模型當中常見的方法之一，但是卻難以捕捉到長距離的語句資訊，加上擁有資料稀疏和維度的詛咒之特性，長期以來一直難以突破。近年國外學者的研究發現類神經網路語言模型有不錯的成效，不僅能擁有 N 連語言模型的特性也能解決資料稀疏缺點，為語音辨識與語言模型帶來嶄新的視野；然而類神經網路語言模型也仍存在一些缺點，例如外詞彙問題(out-of-vocabulary, OOV)、缺乏長距離資訊、運算的時間複雜度過高以及詞的表示方式缺少了詞的特性等問題。因此，也有學者針對類神經網路的變形，使用了具有遞迴能力的類神經網路來建構語言模型，而效果也比一般類神經網路語言模型好。

本論文針對遞迴式類神經網路語言模型做了更進一步的改善，期望使用關聯資訊和動態調整語言模型來輔助機率的估測。從實驗結果中可以看出使用關聯資訊的確能帶來幫助，但是效果仍不夠明顯，其原因應為輸入層或前一時間點的資訊被關聯資訊所干擾，導致成效有限。而實驗中也發現到減少部分關聯資訊能提升辨識率，因此關聯資訊或其他資訊的表示法在未來研究上也是值得注意的部分。另一部分，本論文藉由將訓練語料分群並訓練各群的遞迴式類神經網路語言模型，期望藉由動態的調整語言模型來達到更好的辨識率。此部分實驗結果也顯示分兩群時，使用相似度線性組合法有較佳的成效。但分成四群時，由於各群中的訓練語料不足，因此無法訓練出學習能力較佳的遞迴式類神經網路語言模型。

在未來的研究裡，可以根據遞迴式類神經網路語言模型無法有效學習長距離資訊之缺點來進行改善，如加入不同的特徵或其他資訊來幫助估測，抑或是針對時序性倒傳遞演算法的缺點進行結構上的改進。而隨著時代的變遷，語言也不斷地在進化，許多以前沒有的詞語也不停出現，因此用不同平滑化的方法來處理外詞彙問題也是相當重要的議題。另外，與現行的語言模型結合，如主題模型或鑑別式語言模型等，使語言模型更具有一般性能力、適應性能力，甚至鑑別性能力也是將來值得探討的部分。由於鑑別式語言模型的概念和類神經網路語言模型相當的像，差別在於前者是監督式的，後者是非監督式的。而倘若將類神經網路語言模型改良成監督式的方法，則辨識率應該會有更好的提升，期望在未來能將此兩種語言模型做結合，並進一步的獲得更好的辨識結果。

致謝

本論文之研究承蒙教育部－國立台灣師範大學邁向頂尖大學計畫（101J1A0900 和 101J1A0901）與行政院國家科學委員會研究計畫(NSC 101-2221-E-003 -024 -MY3 和 NSC 99-2221-E-003 -017 -MY3)之經費支持，謹此致謝。

參考文獻

[1] Y. Bengio, P. Frasconi, and P. Simard, "The problem of learning long-term dependencies in recurrent networks," in *Proc. IEEE International Conference on Neural Networks*, Vol. 3, pp. 1183-1188, 1993.

[2] Y. Bengio, R. Ducharme, P. Vincent, C. Jauvin, J. K, T. Hofmann, T. Poggio, and J. Shawetaylor. A neural probabilistic language model. In Journal of Machine Learning Research, 2003.

[3] J. L. Elman, "Finding structure in time," *Cognitive Science*, Vol. 14, No. 2, pp. 179-211, 1990.

[4] M. L. Jordan, "Attractor dynamics and parallelism in a connectionist sequential machine," in *Proc. the eighth annual conference of the cognitive science society*, pp.531-546, 1986

[5] M. Schuster and K. K. Paliwal, "Bidirectional recurrent neural networks," *IEEE Transactions on Signal Processing*, Vol. 45, No. 11, pp. 2673-2681, 1997.

[6] Y. Bengio, P. Simard, and P. Frasconi, "Learning long-term dependencies with gradient descent is difficult," *IEEE Transaction on Neural Networks*, Vol. 5, No. 2, pp. 157-166, 1994.

[7] J. B. MacQueen, "Some methods for classification and analysis of multivariate observations," in *Proc. 5th Berkeley Symposium on Mathematical Statistics and Probability*, pp. 281–297.

[8] H.-M. Wang, B. Chen, J.-W. Kuo and S.-S. Cheng, "MATBN: A Mandarin Chinese broadcast news corpus," *International Journal of Computational Linguistics & Chinese Language Processing*, Vol. 10, No. 2, pp. 219-236, 2005.

[9] Stolcke, Andreas. Srilm - an extensible language modeling toolkit. In Proceedings of the International Conference on Spoken Language Processing, Denver, Colorado, September 2002.

[10] S. M. Katz, "Estimation of probabilities from sparse data for the language model component of a speech recognizer," in *Proc. IEEE Transactions on Acoustics, Speech, and Signal Processing*, Vol. ASSP-35, No. 3, pp. 400, 1987.

[11] T. Mikolov, S. Kombrink, A. Deoras, L. Burget and J. Černocký, "RNNLM - Recurrent neural network language modeling toolkit," in *Proc. IEEE workshop on Automatic Speech Recognition and Understanding*, 2011

基於決策樹演算法之台語連音變調預估模組

A Prediction Module for Taiwanese Tone Sandhi Based on the Decision Tree Algorithm

潘能煌　Neng-Huang Pan
建國科技大學資訊管理系
Department of Information Management
Chienkuo Technology University
nhpan@cc.ctu.edu.tw

余明興　Ming-Shing Yu
國立中興大學資訊工程學系
Department of Computer Science and Engineering
National Chung-Hsing University
msyu@dragon.nchu.edu.tw

蔡珮均　Pei-Chun Tsai
國立中興大學資訊工程學系
Department of Computer Science and Engineering
National Chung-Hsing University
tippy7346@hotmail.com

摘要

台語連音變調問題為研究台語文轉音系統的重要問題之一。在詞的階層，大多數的詞都遵循詞尾本調，非詞尾變調的一般變調規則。在句子的階層，台語的連音變調問題會變得比較複雜，因為一般變調規則並不能完全適用在句中的每個詞上。在這篇論文中，我們提出了一套可用於中文文句轉台語語音系統的台語連音變調預估模組。我們以決策樹 C5.0 演算法搭配三種 Special Case 來對句子中的各個音節做連音變調預估，此預估模組在內部測試和外部測試的預估正確率分別為 93.42%和 91.13%。

Abstract

Taiwanese tone sandhi problem is one of the important research issues for Taiwanese Text-to-Speech systems. In word level, we can use the general tone sandhi rules to deal with the Taiwanese tone sandhi problem. The tone sandhi becomes more difficult in sentence level because of that the general tone sandhi rules for words may not apply at each word in a sentence. In this paper we proposed a module to deal with the Taiwanese tone sandhi problem for Chinese to Taiwanese Text-to-Speech systems. We adopt Decision tree C5.0 algorithm accompanied with three Special Cases generated from training data to predict the tone sandhi of each syllable. In this module, the accuracy of the inside test and outside test are 93.42%

and 91.13%, respectively.

關鍵詞：台語連音變調，文轉音系統，決策樹

Keywords: Taiwanese Tone Sandhi, Text-to-Speech System, Decision Tree.

一、緒論

在我國最常被使用的三大語言分別是國語、台語及客語，這三種語言都屬於聲調語言(Tonal Language)，也都存有連音變調(Tone Sandhi)的現象。所謂連音變調指的是在連續語音中，某些音節因受其前後音節的影響而不再保有原有調號的情形。例加：在中文裡，「老/ㄌㄠˇ/」和「虎/ㄏㄨˇ/」都是三聲字，而當這兩個字組成「老虎」這個詞的時候，「老」這個字的讀音會變成二聲的/ㄌㄠˊ/。「展/ㄓㄢˇ /」、「覽/ㄌㄢˇ/」、「館/ㄍㄨㄢˇ/」組成「展覽館」時「展」和「覽」的讀音都變成二聲。在台語中，「土」的讀音是/to2/，「地」的讀音是/de7/，而「土地」的讀音是/to1 de7/，我們可以發現「土」這個字的聲調由原本的二聲變成一聲。在客語中，「針」和「線」的讀音分別爲/ziim2/與/sien1/，當它們組成「針線」這個詞時，「針」的讀音要變成三聲的/ziim3/。

在台語中，所有單字詞的讀音聲調稱爲本調。大多數的文獻都認爲台語的聲調只有七種，分別爲： 東/dong1/、黨/dong2/、棟/dong3/、督/dok4/、同/dong5/、黨/dong6/、洞/dong7/、獨/dok8/，其中台語的二聲和六聲同調。可是我們發現若考慮連音變調和南腔北調的情形，台語的聲調變化高達十二種，詳見表一。舉例來說，台語三疊音中第一個字的聲調，不屬於常見聲調的任何一種，如：凍/dong0/凍凍以及入聲音的毒/dok0/毒毒。而聲調 9 和聲調 8 則爲南北腔調的不同。在詞的階層，只有少數的詞其所有的音節都讀本調，例如「頭痛/tau5 tiann3/」，而大多數的台語詞都遵循詞尾音節讀本調，非詞尾音節讀變調的台語一般變調規則。台語變調的情形可分成非入聲字與入聲字變調這兩個部分，詳細的變調規則可參考圖一。在入聲字的變調處理上，一般多認爲四聲和八聲互換，而我們認爲的入聲字變調處理應爲四聲轉爲二聲，而八聲和九聲變調後應爲三聲。台語詞內的變調範例可參考表二。台語拼音系統有很多，我們所採用的是台灣拼音系統[3]，因爲它能同時適用於國語、台語及客語等多種在台灣通行的語言，這有利於我們未來的發展。

在句子的階層，台語的連音變調情形就變得比較複雜了。有時候一個句子裏只有最後一個字讀本調，其餘的字都要變調。以句子「我買洗衣機」爲例，底下我們列出句中每個字的本調發音以及句子正確的台語讀音(經變調處理)。

例句：	我	買	洗	衣	機
本調：	ghua2	bhe2	se2	sann1	gi1
變調：	ghua1	bhe1	se1	sann7	gi1

另一種情形則是我們可以將一個句子視爲由數個語法段落組成，每個語法段落稱爲變調詞組[4]。變調詞組的最後一個字讀本調，其餘的字皆變調。請看以下的例子，(底線表變調詞組)：

例句：	運	動	是	一	個	好	習	慣
本調：	un7	dong7	si7	zit8	ei5	ho2	sip8	guan3
變調：	un3	dong7	si3	zit3	ei5	ho1	sip3	guan3

句子「運動是一個好習慣」，經過中研院詞庫小組的線上斷詞器處理後可分解成六個詞，分別是「運動」、「是」、「一」、「個」、「好」、「習慣」。若依照圖一的規則來處理連音變調，那麼其結果就不會正確。因爲變調詞組是由一個或多個詞所組合而成，所以圖一的規則運用到句子上時就顯得不夠完善。我們由訓練語料發現非詞尾的音節有 95%的機率讀變調，而詞尾的音節有 60%的機率讀本調，40%的機率讀變調。這表示句中的非詞尾音節大致遵循一般的台語連音變調規則，而詞尾音節則沒有這種傾向，因此在句子階層裡需要有更佳的方法來處理台語的連音變調問題。

表一、台語聲調說明例表

聲調	例字（台語發音）	聲調名稱與註解
dong0	凍（dong0）凍凍	高聲（三連音第一字）
dong1	東	高平
dong2 dong6	黨	高降
dong3	棟	低降
dong5	同	低緩上升
dong7	洞	中平
dok0	毒（dok0）毒毒	高入（入聲音）
dok2	剁（dok2）斷	中降（入聲音）
dok3	獨（dok3）立	低入（入聲音）
dok4	督	中入（入聲音）
dok8	獨	高入（入聲音南腔）
dok9	獨	高入（入聲音北調）

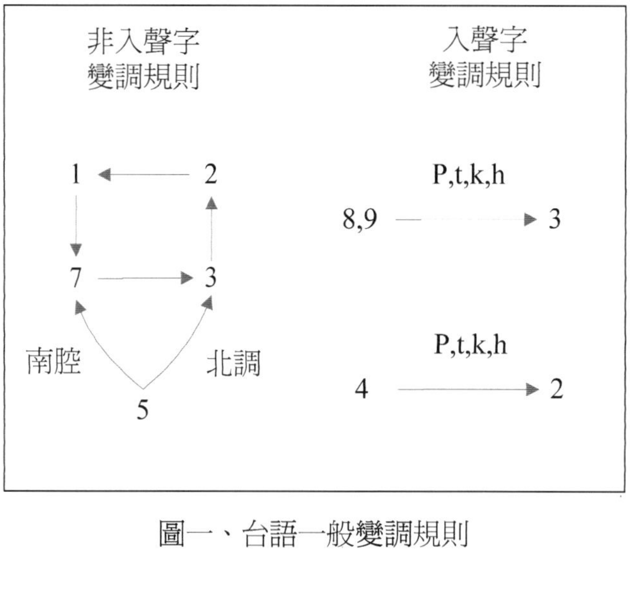

圖一、台語一般變調規則

表二、台語變調範例

本調(詞尾)	變調(非詞尾)
放心/sim1/	心/sim7/境
長久/gu2/	久/gu1/長
拖欠/kiam3/	欠/kiam2/人
委屈/kut4/	屈/kut2/服
同台/dai5/	台/dai3/北 (北調) 台/dai7/北 (南腔)
出外/ghua7/	外/ghua3/人
拘役/ik8/	役/ik3/男

目前台語連音變調問題的研究，大多數學者專家採用規則式方法來處理台語連音變調問題[1][4][8-10]。其中，Lin 與 Chen[1]利用四大規則(一般變調規則、「仔」前變調規則、輕聲變調規則、三疊形容詞變調規則)來實作連音變調模組，其測試語料的規模爲 5576 個音節，此系統的連音變調正確率爲 82.53%。楊允言等人[9]利用 20 條變調規則來處理台語的連音變調問題，在使用這些規則時會先將句中的每個音節都先設爲本調，然後再依後面的規則來修正其變調情形。原則上愈後面的規則的重要性愈強，所以後面的規則可以修正前面規則所產生的結果。此模組的測試語料規模比較小，只有 962 個音節，正確率爲 88.98%。梁敏雄[8]所發展出的文轉音系統也是採用規則式的方法來處理連音變調問題，其正確率爲 65%。洪俊詠[6]利用馬可夫語言模型來處理台語連音變調問題，其所採用的語料爲台語佛經，語料中有 6593 個句子內含 35543 個字，平均句長爲 5 個字。其預估正確率爲 84%。許書豪[7]先利用貝氏網路取得初步的連音變調預估結果，再用中文詞對應台語變調規則來修正這些結果的方式來處理台語連音變調問題。其訓練語料共有 583 句，內含 8138 個音節，外部測試正確率爲 85.84%。

在本論文中，我們提出了以決策樹 C5.0 演算法搭配三種 Special Case 來對句子中的各個音節做連音變調預估的方法。我們的模組可以應用在中文句轉台語語音系統中，用來提升文轉音系統在文句分析上的能力。本論文的章節安排如下:在第二節，我們將介紹我們的實驗方法。第三節主要介紹各種方法的實驗結果。結論在第四節。

二、實驗方法

(一)語料

我們從 Chinese Gigaword Third Edition 的繁體中文語料中隨機抽取 3672 個句子作爲實驗語料，並將語料分爲訓練語料(約佔 75.5%)和測試語料(約佔 24.5%)。並透過先前開發的中文文句轉台語語音系統[12]，取得中文文句所對應的台語拼音，最後再使用台語文句拼音校正工具[7]來做人工校正。表三為我們實驗語料的相關數據。Chinese Gigaword Third Edition 中的文章包含了斷詞結果與詞性標記，為了避免資料稀疏問題，我們透過中研院詞類標記表將所有的詞性標記改為精簡詞類。

表三、訓練語料與測試語料數據

	句子數	音節數
訓練語料	2772	38508
測試語料	900	12452
總數	3672	50960

(二)決策樹C5.0 演算法

台語連音變調問題可被視為一種分類問題，因為每個音節的讀音只有本調和變調這兩種可能。決策樹(Decision Tree)是使用樹狀分岔來產生分類規則，藉由一連串的問題和規則將資料做分類，藉由相似的形態來推測相同的結果。下列說明決策樹規則產生的過程[2]：

步驟1. 首先，將所有輸入資料母體作為根節點。

步驟2. 決策樹逐一掃描所有的輸入變數，以計算每個輸入變數對應預測變數的分岔準則，然後根據分岔準則挑出最佳分岔變數，用此分岔變數產生資料分割，以產生子節點。各個子節點根據案例的預測變數分布機率，指派分類結果以及產生分類機率。

步驟3. 將子節點視為新母體，透過同樣步驟持續讓決策樹生長，最後採用修剪技術(Pruning)修剪不必要的規則。

一般常用的決策樹演算法大致為 C5.0、CART、CHAID 與 QUEST 等四種方法。我們的研究使用決策樹 C5.0 演算法來處理台語的連音變調問題。C5.0 演算法屬於監督式學習演算法，也可稱為規則推理模型。它能夠對連續型變數及類別型變數做分析。C5.0 的每一個節點可以產生不同數量的分支，它會依最大資訊增益(Information Gain Value)的欄位切割樣本，重複切割直到樣本子集不能再被分割為止，且能依使用者需求產生決策樹及規則集兩種模型[11]。

我們利用詞性、詞長、前一詞詞性、前一詞詞長、前二詞詞性、前二詞詞長、後一詞性、後一詞詞長、後二詞性、後二詞詞長、是否為詞尾以及是否為句尾等十二項參數透過決策樹 C5.0 演算法產生台語連音變調分類規則。以下將利用一個例句來說明我們所使用的各項參數。

例句：可(ADV)作爲(Vt)人工(N)肝臟(N)的(T)生物(N)感應器(N)。

1. 詞性：音節所在詞的詞性。例句中的「可」所在詞爲一單字詞，其詞性爲 ADV。「作」這個音節所在詞「作爲」是一個二字詞，其詞性爲 Vt。

2. 詞長：音節所在詞的字數。「可」這個音節所在詞爲一單字詞，詞長爲 1。「作」這個音節所在詞爲一個二字詞，詞長爲 2。

3. 前一詞詞性：音節所在詞的前一詞詞性。「可」這個單字詞爲句子中的第一個詞，沒有前一詞，故標記爲 Null。「作」這個音節所在詞爲「作爲」，其前一詞「可」的詞性爲 ADV。

4. 前一詞詞長：音節所在詞的前一詞所含字數。單字詞「可」爲句子中的第一個詞，沒有前一詞，故前一詞詞長記爲 0。「作」這個音節所在詞的前一詞爲「可」，其詞長爲 1。

5. 前二詞詞性：音節所在詞的前面第二個詞的詞性。「可」爲句子的第一個詞，故此項參數標記爲 Null。「作」這音節所在詞，「作爲」，爲句子的第二個詞，無前二詞，故前二詞詞性標記爲 Null。「人」這個音節所在詞，「人工」，爲句子中的第三個詞，其前面第二個詞爲單字詞「可」，因此其前二詞詞性爲 ADV。

6. 前二詞詞長：音節所在詞的前面第二個詞所含字數。「可」這音節所在詞爲句子的第一個詞，無前二詞，故前二詞詞長記爲 0。「作」這音節所在詞爲句子的第二個詞，無前二詞，故前二詞詞長記爲 0。「人」這個音節所在詞爲句子中的第三個詞，前面第二個詞爲單字詞「可」，其前二詞詞長爲 1。

7. 後一詞性：音節所在詞的後一詞的詞性。單字詞「可」的後一詞爲「作爲」，其詞性爲 Vt。「工」這音節所在的詞爲「人工」，其後一詞爲「肝臟」詞性爲 N。「感」這音節所屬的詞爲「感應器」，爲句子中最後一詞，無後一詞因此標記爲 Null。

8. 後一詞詞長：音節所在詞的後一詞所含字數。「可」的後一詞爲「作爲」其詞長爲 2。「工」這音節所在的詞爲「人工」，其後一詞爲「肝臟」字數爲 2。「感」這音節所在的詞「感應器」爲句子中最後一詞，無後一詞故此項參數記爲 0。

9. 後二詞詞性：音節所在詞的後面第二個詞的詞性。單字詞「可」的後面第二個詞爲「人工」其詞性爲 N。「工」這音節屬於二字詞「人工」，其後面第二個詞爲「的」詞性爲 T。「感」這音節所在的詞爲「感應器」，是句子中最後一詞並無後二詞，故標記爲 Null。

10. 後二詞詞長：音節所在詞的後面第二個詞所含字數。「可」的後面第二個詞爲「人工」其詞長爲 2。「工」這音節所在的詞爲「人工」，其後第二個詞爲單字詞「的」，故「工」的後二詞詞長爲 1。「感」這音節所屬詞爲「感應器」是句子中最後一詞並無後二詞，故其後二詞詞長應記爲 0。

11. 是否為詞尾：音節是否為其所在詞的最後一字。「可」這音節所在詞為一單字詞，故「可」為詞尾。二字詞「作為」的第一個音節為「作」，故「作」屬非詞尾。而「為」是二字詞「作為」的第二個音節，故「為」為詞尾。

12. 是否為句尾：音節所在位置是否為句子的最後一音節。「可」這音節所在位置不為句子的最後一音節，故標記為非句尾。「感」這音節所在詞為句子的最後一個詞，但「感」這音節為「感應器」詞中的一個音節故仍為非句尾。「器」這音節為句子最後一個詞「感應器」中的最後一個音節，故標記為句尾。

(二)三種Special Case

我們從訓練語料中發現某些詞的變調情形在語料中是固定的，所以我們進一步分析詞的本身是否會影響連音變調的結果，以下是我們探討的三種 Special Case。

1. Word：在訓練語料中，若某個中文詞出現次數大於等於 2 次，且詞內各音節的本變調樣式在訓練語料中各音節本變調順序中所佔比例大於等於 94%，我們就將這樣的中文詞收錄當成規則，往後遇到完全一樣的中文詞時，可直接給定各音節本變調結果。例如，在我們的訓練語料中，「總統府」這個詞出現過 4 次且每次的讀音都是/zong1 tong1 hu2/，所以在「總統府」這個詞內的本變調樣式為(變調，變調，本調)的機率為 100%。往後只要遇見「總統府」這個詞，系統將會直接指定其連音變調結果為(變調，變調，本調)。

2. POS+Word$_R$：在訓練語料中，若某一詞 W 的詞性為 POS 且其下一個詞為某一特定中文詞時，這樣的“詞性”加上“中文詞”的組合，在訓練語料中出現次數大於等於 2 次且 W 的詞尾音節本變調在此種情形下出現比例大於等於 94% 時，我們就會將這種組合收錄成 Special Case。我們從語料中發現，若詞 W 的詞性為 DET 且其下一個詞為「國」這個單字詞時，W 的詞尾音節有明顯的變調傾向。在下面的兩個例句中，詞性為 DET 的兩個詞的詞尾都讀變調。

例句 1：分頭 拜會 各(DET)/gerh2/ 國 駐 聯合國 代表團。
例句 2：這 是 兩(DET)/nng3/ 國 政治 最 主要 的 分野。

3. Word$_L$+POS： 訓練語料中，若某一詞 W 的詞性為 POS 且其上一個詞為某一特定中文詞時，這樣的“中文詞”加上“詞性”的組合，在訓練語料中出現次數大於等於 2 次且 W 的詞尾音節本變調在此種情形下出現比例大於等於 94%，我們就會將這種組合收錄成 Special Case。我們從語料中發現，若詞 W 的詞性為為 ADV 且其前一個詞為二字詞「如果」時，W 的詞尾音節有明顯的變調傾向。在下面的兩個例句中，詞性為 ADV 的兩個詞的詞尾都讀變調。

例句 1：政府 如果 不(ADV)/m3/ 加強 保護 淡水魚 。
例句 2：大陸 各 地 民族 如果 都(ADV)/long1/ 使用 這 個 招數。

從訓練語料中抽出三種 Special Case 的相關規則之後，我們會把這些規則與前一小節所發展的 C5.0 連音變調預估模組結合在一起。以下我們將說明兩者結合的處理過程，假設輸入的文句為「台灣(N) 光復(Vt) 后(N) 土地(N) 改革(Vt) 研討會(N)。」

步驟1. 首先要檢查句子的內容有無符合三種 Special Case 的規則。

a、 Word 規則：

「台灣」在我們的 Word 規則中出現，有 98.62%的機率讀(變調，本調)。

「土地」在我們的 Word 規則中出現，有 94.74%的機率讀(變調，本調)。

b、 POS+$Word_R$ 規則：

在本例中找無符合條件的規則。

c、 $Word_L$+POS 規則：

找到(土地，Vt)的規則，即當詞性為 Vt 且前一詞為「土地」時，有 94.74%的機率使詞性 Vt 的詞尾讀本調。故在本例中，音節「革」應讀本調。

步驟2. 利用決策樹 C5.0 演算法預估剩餘音節的連音變調結果。

本說明例的最終結果如下，在此“本”表本調，“變”表變調。

音節	台	灣	光	復	后	土	地	改	革	研	討	會
預估結果	變	本	變	變	本	變	本	變	本	變	變	本

三、實驗結果

我們的語料共有 3672 個句子，內含 50960 個節，其中 2772 句，38508 個音節(約 75.5%)為訓練語料，其餘 900 句，12452 個音節(約 24.5%)為測試語料。表四為我們的實驗結果，決策樹 C5.0 演算法的內部測試與外部測試的正確率分別為 89.39%以及 88.84%，而決策樹 C5.0 演算法搭配三種 Special Case 方法的內部測試與外部測試的正確率分別為 93.42%及 91.13%。我們可以發現決策樹 C5.0 演算法在加入三種 Special Case 的相關規則後其預估正確率有顯著的提升。表五列出台語連音變調問題相關研究的實驗數據，雖然各研究所採用的語料都不同，所以無法做出完全客觀的比較，但仍有一定的參考價值。我們可以從中發現本論文所提出的方法具有較高的預估正確率，且測試語料的規模也比較大。

表四、實驗結果(預估正確率)

	內部測試	外部測試
決策樹 C5.0 演算法	89.39%	88.84%
決策樹 C5.0 演算法+Special Case	**93.42%**	**91.13%**

表五、台語連音變調問題相關研究實驗數據

相關研究	正確率	測試語料大小
Lin and Chen [1]	82.53%	5576 音節
洪俊詠[6]	84%	未知
楊允言等[9]	88.98%	962 音節
許書豪[7]	85.84%	159 句
本研究	**91.13%**	**12452 音節**

四、結論

國語、台語和客語為我國三大常用語言，這三種語言都是聲調語言，也都存有連音變調的現象。和另外兩種語言相比，台語的連音變調問題比較複雜，因此也成為發展高品質的台語文轉音系統的一大難題。本論文提出一個以決策樹 C5.0 演算法搭配三種 Special Case 的方法來處理台語的連音變調問題，我們的模組之內部測試和外部測試的預估正確率分別為 93.42%及 91.13%。我們的方法與其它台語連音變調問題相關研究相比，我們的模組具有較高的預估正確率。

參考文獻

[1] C. J. Lin and H. H. Chen,"A Mandarin to Taiwanese Min Nan Machine Translation System with Speech Synthesis of Taiwanese Min Nan," **Internal Journal of Computational Linguistic and Chinese Language Processing**, Vol. 4, No. 1, pp. 59-84, 1999.

[2] 尹相志，*SQL Server 2008 Data Mining 資料採礦*，悅知文化，2009。

[3] 中興大學資工系語音語言實驗室網站，2012，http://speechlab.cs.nchu.edu.tw/

[4] 李尚德，*台語辭典建構與台語變調探討*，碩士論文，資訊科學研究所，中興大學，2007。

[5] 邱玉雪，*台灣閩南語偏正結構詞組中的變調分界*，碩士論文，台灣語言與語文教育研究所，新竹師範學院，2004。

[6] 洪俊詠，*馬可夫語言模型應用 di 台語變調 gah 注音*，碩士論文，統計學研究所，清華大學，2005。

[7] 許書豪，*台語連音變調問題研究*，碩士論文，資訊網路與多媒體研究所，中興大學，2010。

[8] 梁敏雄，*台灣多語語音資料庫之建立及應用*，博士論文，電機工程學研究所，長庚大學，2008。

[9] 楊允言、李盛安、劉杰岳、高成炎，"台語變調系統實作研究，" *第十七屆自然*

語言與語音處理研討會論文集，台南，台灣， pp.293-304，2005。

[10] 鄭良偉，*台語的語音與詞法*，遠流出版公司，1997。

[11] 廖述賢、溫志皓，*資料探勘理論與應用-以 IBM SPSS Modeler 爲範例*，博碩文化，2012。

[12] 潘能煌、余明興、蔡宗謀，2008，"中文文句轉台語語音系統，" *第十三屆人工智慧與應用討論會論文集*，宜蘭，中華民國，pp. 1-5，2008。

台語文字與語音語料庫之建置

Development of a Taiwanese Speech and Text Corpus

廖子宇 Tzu-Yu Liao
中央研究院資訊科學所
Academia Sinica
Institute of Information Science
ziiyu@iis.sinica.edu.tw

呂仁園 Ren-yuan Lyu
長庚大學資訊工程學系
Department of Computer Science and Information Engineering
Chang Gung University
renyuan.lyu@gmail.com

高明達 Ming-Tat Ko
中央研究院資訊科學所
Academia Sinica
Institute of Information Science
mtko@iis.sinica.edu.tw

江永進 Yuang-chin Chiang
國立清華大學統計學系
Institute of Statistics
National Tsing Hua University
chiang@stat.nthu.edu.tw

張智星 Jyh-Shing Roger Jang
國立清華大學資訊工程學系
Department of Computer Science
National Tsing Hua University
jang@cs.nthu.edu.tw

摘要

台語在台灣是三大主要語言之一，台語的使用人口約為 70%的人口，可是，其台語方面的相關研究卻是很少、研究論文主要還是以華語為主。優質的計算語言學研究需要大規模的語料來支持，本計畫目的是建立大規模的台語語料庫，建立台語計算語言學研究發展的厚實基礎。同時希望以此經驗嘗試建立台灣弱勢語言的計算語言學研究發展模式。本計畫中，將建立一個台語語料，語料來源類型為台語朗讀、新聞、戲劇及談話。建立 200 個小時的台語文字與語音語料。

Abstract

The main goal of this paper is to develop a large scale Taiwanese corpus. In the mean time, we try to establish a successful model for the computational linguistic research on other minority Taiwanese languages such as Haka.In this paper, we will build a Taiwanese speech corpus. The source of speech corpus is Taiwanese dramas and news from TV stations. The goal of the corpus is 200 hours speech material with annotation.

關鍵詞：corpus, speech recognition, Taiwanese, transcription

一、緒論

根據 2005 年的統計[1]，台語的總人口數為四千五百萬人，台灣是其中台語使用人口較多的地區，約有一千五百萬人。由使用人口數而言，台語是個不可忽視的語言。台語在台灣是三大（華語、台語以及客語）主要語言之一。在台灣，大部份的人有能力說這兩種或三種語言，根據統計[2]，華語的使用人口約為 82%，而台語的使用人口約為 70%的人口，且台灣是目前唯一以台語為重要語言的國家。

然而，目前台灣對於台語方面的相關研究，如語言學、應用科學（語音辨識、語言辨識、網路資訊檢索，等等），其論文數量卻是很少、研究論文主要還是以華語為主。在台灣，台語是重要語言，使用人口眾多，使用環境相當好，不論在學術或社會應用而言，台語研究都應該受到重視。在台灣台語和華語的使用人口並沒相差多少，但研究台語的論文量和研究華語的論文量是相差非常多。其中一個原因是因為台語目前沒有統一的文字書寫系統，甚至大部分使用台語的人口並不會書寫台語。這一方面造成台語文字資訊來源貧乏，另一方面也造成自動化處理台語文字的困難。這兩者使得台語的研究發展產生了阻礙，而間接的影響到台語研究的數量。

現今優質的計算語言學研究都需要大規模的語料來支持。使用的語料規模越大通常代表其訓練出來的應用系統的準確率越高。本計畫的目的即是建立大規模的台語語料庫，以建立台語計算語言學研究發展的厚實基礎。同時希望以此經驗嘗試建立台灣弱勢語言的計算語言學研究的發展模式。

台語文字語料的收集因書寫系統的分歧與書寫人口的缺乏，有其困難。但台語的口語人口相當多，台語的語音資料非常豐富，加上大多數的台語人口都能使用華語，提供建置大量台語語料的可能性。

二、語料庫處理流程

以下，我們描述整個語料庫處理的流程，分成下列幾個步驟來敘述：

（一） 語音蒐集

我們先設法取得高品質之語料作為來源，首先對語音資料做些格式的正規化，指定取樣頻率、聲道數、以及取樣位元數分別為 16000Hz, 單聲道以及 16 bit/sample。

（二） 切音

依據語音串流中較長的靜音段，做為切音成段落的依據，再進一步根據所設定文句長度來切到句的層級。

（三） 聽打

將每一段經過切音的聲音段做聲音內容的聽打，使用的拼音系統為台語通用拼音。目前聽打工作只做聲音內容的音節聽打，並未做聲音內容的漢字聽打，若是語音蒐集時同時蒐集語音和文本內容時，會將文本內容保存下來並將音節聽打增加在文本內容之後。

聽打的儲存格式為 XML 檔案格式，副檔名為.trs，下面為經過聽打所儲存的 trs file 的儲存檔案內容範例。

```
<?xml version="1.0" encoding="UTF-8"?>

<Sync time="2.746"/>

001 牛墟 （hi）//de3-it1-pinn1-,qu3-hi1-

<Sync time="5.982"/>

紀傳洲（18/04/07thk 改寫）//zok1-zia4-,gi4-tuan2-ziu1-

<Sync time="8.821"/>

古早，//go1-za4-

….
```

此範例中，聽打的內容是用 UTF-8 編碼，同時記錄了每一句的時間、拼音以及蒐集取得的文字。

1. 聽打工具

使用 LDC(Linguistic Data Consortium)提供的 Transcriber[3]系統來聽打與標記節目錄音資料。

2. 聽打說明

（1） 聽打人員

以各地方教育單位之鄉土語言老師為主，每位老師從事鄉土教育工作皆有一定之年資。

（2） 拼音系統

本語料蒐集計畫使用台語通用拼音，並以自然調型的方式做聽打。

（3） 事件標記

聽打過程中所出現的非台語聲音會使用標記 Event 的方式作註記。紀錄聽打過程中出現的 Event 需紀錄三種資料分別是 Type、Description、Extent。

Type 是用來區分聲音的種類，Description 為說明，Extent 則是標記起始與終始點或該段時間。

3. 成果儲存格式

本計畫決定運用 xml 格式來做為資料聽打成果的儲存方式，其內記錄以下四個項目：

（1） 檔頭：記錄檔案建立時間及對應聲音檔

（2） 語者(Speakers)：記錄內容出現所有語者的名字以及 id 編號，id 編號於後續內容中使用。

（3） 主題(Topics)：記錄內容所有出現的主題段落名稱與 id 編號，id 編號於後續內容中使用。

（4） 內容(Episode)：記錄所有段落、語者、標音的時間位置。

（5） 段落標記(Section)

此標記包含於內容(Episode)之中，子項目分別為：Topic 標記主題的 id 編號，startTime 段落內容開始時間，endTime 段落內容結束時間。

（6） 語者標記(Turn)

此標記包含於內容(Episode)之中，Speaker 標記說話人的 id 編號，startTime 段落內容開始時間，endTime 段落內容結束時間。

（7） 標音標記(Sync)

此標記包含於內容(Episode)之中，主要記錄聽打內容與開始時間，子項目分別為：Time 標音開始時間。

（8） 事件標記(Event)

此標記包含於內容(Episode)之中，所有語音中出現的非台語聲音都會以此做標記，子項目分別為：type 事件種類，desc 事件內容，exten 事件位置。

（四） 校正

校正工作以聽打人員兩人為一組互相校正，兩人於聽打完成時交換檔案做校正，校正者於聽打內容中標記其認為聽打錯誤之內容並加註其認為正確之聽打內容，保留聽打者之聽打標音與校正者之校正標音，並於後續之二校中做選擇。二校由聽打者執行，搜尋校正者所做之校正標記並從原始聽打標音與校正標音中選擇其認為正確之標音。

以上流程我們以圖一綜合呈現之。

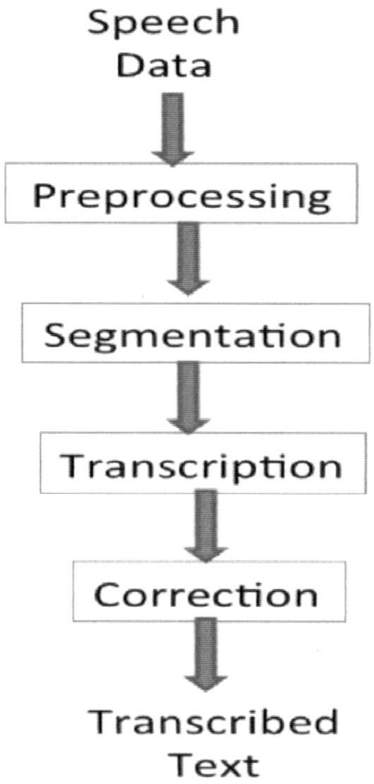

圖一、聽打工作流程

三、已建立之語料內容簡介及數量統計

本計畫準備以三年的時間蒐集及處理 200 小時的台語語音資料，語料類型分為朗讀、新聞、戲劇、以及談話。以下分別就各類型語料做些描述：

（一） 朗讀語料

所謂朗讀語料，在我們的研究中，指的是先有朗讀文稿，說話人完全照本宣科，完全不加入說話人的思考或情緒，是一種文字和語音完全相符的語音資料。目前，我們有 2 套朗讀語料，分別如下：

1. TW03-GS

這是長庚大學多媒體實驗室於 2003 年所錄製的錄音語料，由呂仁園教授主持的語料蒐集計畫，錄製文本內容以台語所有音節(約一千五百個)平均分布在各個句子當中，並邀請四位台語教學老師來錄製，所得到的語料庫。

2. TwEdu

由教育部邀請學者專家組成小組分組進行閩南語文章之選錄，並聘請專人將文章內容改寫成適合朗讀之文稿，名為「閩南語朗讀文章選輯」，也請國立教育廣播電台協助錄製聲音檔。「閩南語朗讀文章選輯」收錄文章 133 篇(含重複 7 篇共 140 篇)，其用字除依教育部公布之台語閩南語推薦用字外，部分不屬於前述用字者，為便利閱讀，依原著用字呈現。[4]

（二） 新聞語料

所謂新聞語料，在我們的研究中，指的是電視新聞記者在新聞節目中所報導之新聞內容，經過我們的蒐集以及人工聽打所製成的語料，原則上新聞主播有預先寫好的新聞稿來念，但是有些時候，新聞主播會自由發揮，加入個人臨場的反應，而且免不了有個人情緒參雜其中。典型的新聞語料，包括主播、記者、受訪者以及插播廣告，在我們蒐集的語料中，主播一定是用台語來播報，外場記者及受訪者不必然使用台語，我們的人工聽打，對於非台語的部分，不做音標轉寫，只標註該段聲音的語言屬性如英語、或華語。

目前，我們有 5 套新聞語料，其中 4 套來自民視台語新聞[5]簡稱 FTVN-1, FTVN-2, FTVN-3, FTVN-4，FTVN 為民視台語新聞的縮寫，後續編號則為不同時間所做的聽打工作時間順序，1 套來自公視台語新聞[6]，名稱為 PTSN-1，其內容詳情分別如下：

1. FTVN-1, FTVN-2

經過剪接後的新聞節目，只含主播以及台語記者，所以整個節目，幾乎都是以台語發音為主。

2. FTVN-3, FTVN-4

經過剪接後的新聞節目，只含主播以及台語記者，所以整個節目，幾乎都是以台語發音為主。

3. PTSN-1

同為完整的新聞節目，與前項 FTVN-1, FTVN-2 雷同。

（三） 戲劇語料

所謂戲劇語料，在我們的研究中，指的是電視台之台語戲劇節目，如民視的浪淘沙[7]或娘家[8]，我們取得該戲劇節目的現場錄音檔案，僅含演員的純語音，不含製成節目之後的混音，使得我們不必費神處理那些非語音的聲音。原則上戲劇演員應有劇本可供念誦，演員對劇本內容有一定的熟悉度，配合當下的情緒，說出含豐富情緒內容的對白。目前，我們有 2 套戲劇語料，都是來自民視，簡介如下：

1. 浪淘沙

   戲劇浪淘沙總集數為 30 集，從中挑選 10 集，挑選之集數為 3、6、9、12、15、18、21、24、27、30，完成語料時間約 8 小時。

2. 娘家

   戲劇娘家總集數為 415 集，從中挑選 16 集，挑選之集數為 3、13、23、33、43、53、203、223、243、253、263、333、363、383、393、413 集，完成之語料時間為 26.8 小時。

（四） 談話語料

所謂談話語料，在我們的研究中，指的是廣播節目中主持人與來賓之間，依固定主題做廣泛的交談，這種交談，通常沒有文稿，不做事先演練，幾乎完全是當場隨興的自由發揮，說話的形式無拘無束，語句也不見得很流暢或合乎文法規則。目前，我們有 1 套談話語料，是來自網路電台「夢中的國家」[9]，簡介如下：

1. 夢中的國家

   由張素華小姐所主持的台語談話性節目，談話主題遍佈生活、健康、教育、政治、財經等，內容非常多元。目前完成之語料有 29 集共 25.8 小時。

以上所描述的語料，以下表做一個綜合性的呈現：

表一、語料庫統計

類型	名稱	時間(分)	時間(小時)	檔案數	音節數	相異音節	音素數	相異音素	語者數
朗讀	TW03-GS	1421.53	23.69	14	312299	749	592616	139	4
朗讀	EUM	679.74	11.33	14	113838	681	219719	134	1
新聞	FTVN-1	332.34	5.54	6	102706	604	197191	130	484
新聞	FTVN-2	399.57	6.66	8					
新聞	FTVN-3	766.22	12.77	21	328995	712	643584	132	142
新聞	FTVN-4	716.74	11.95	25					86
新聞	PTSN	656.92	10.95	11	75004	577	145412	128	303
戲劇	LTS	474.86	7.91	9	38753	476	71672	125	85
戲劇	MH	1609.76	26.83	15	204194	656	374021	134	166
談話	DRM	1549.21	25.82	58	290524	684	547477	134	59
	total	8606.89	143.45	181	1472457	884	2804459	147	1252

同時將內容做統計與分析，統計所有音節數和音素數的出現次數並製作成統計圖如下：

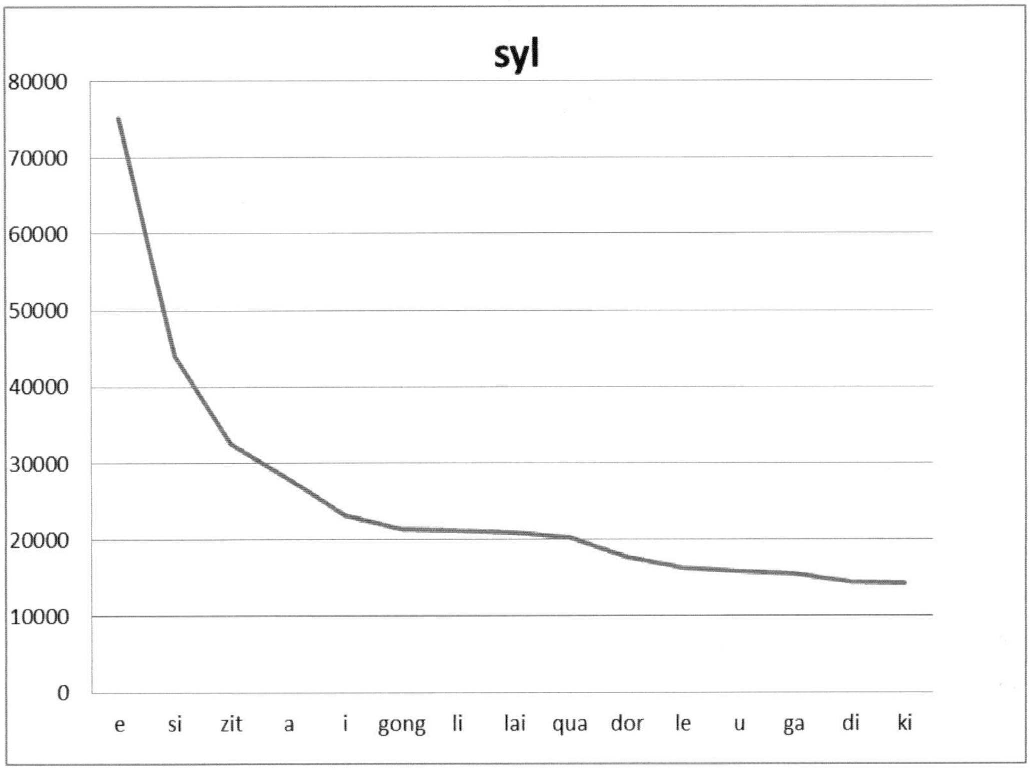

圖二 音節統計圖(1~15)

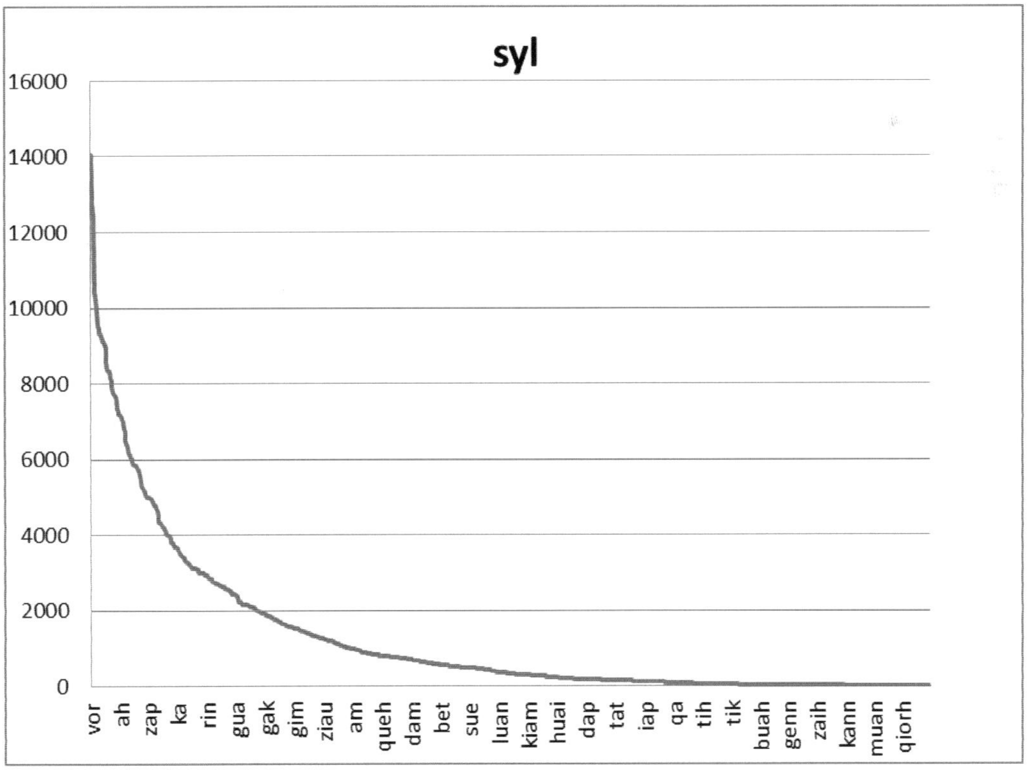

圖三 音節統計圖(16~885)

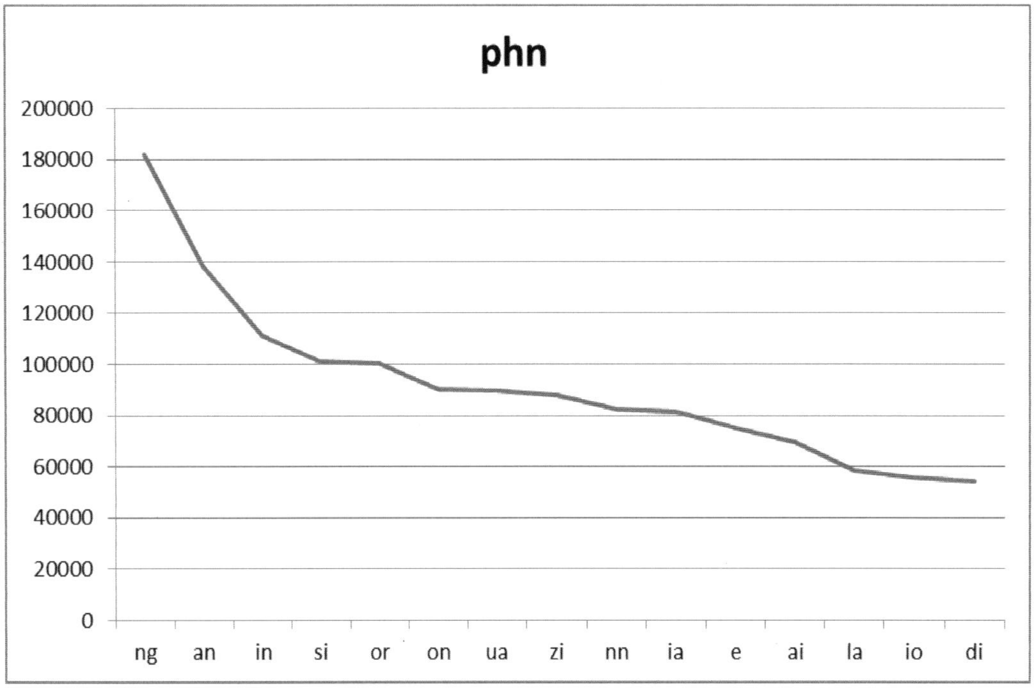

圖四 音素統計圖(1~15)

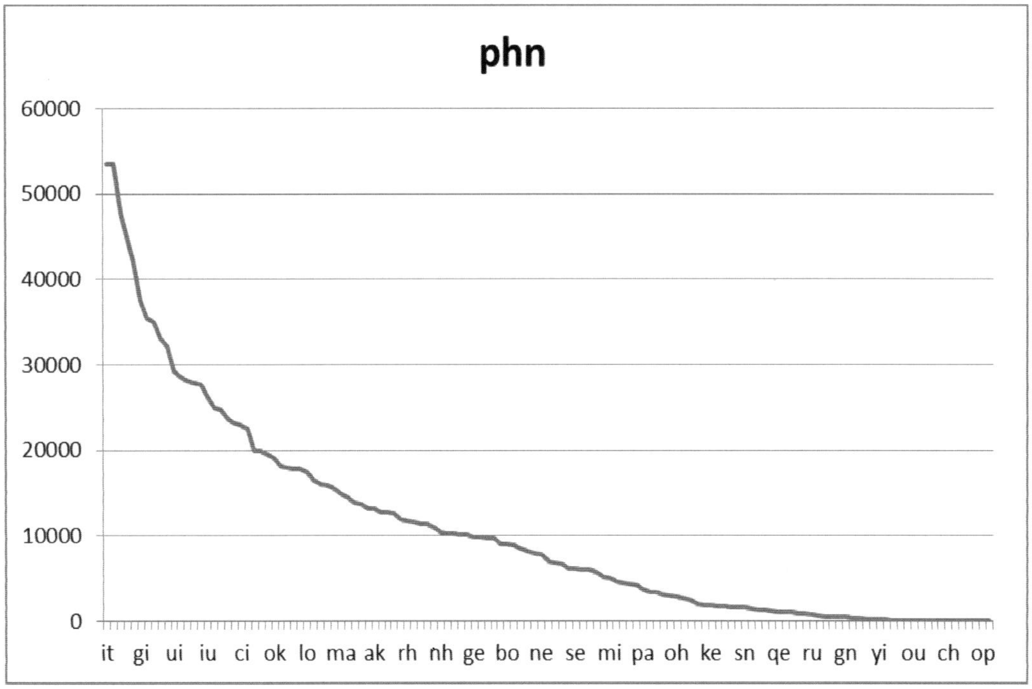

圖五 音素統計圖(16~148)

四、結論

目前語料庫蒐集進度尚未達到預期設定的數量，未來會加快腳步進行語料蒐集的工作，期望在計畫進行時間內完成。為使語料庫更方便使用，接下來會將語料庫整理成不同格式方便作使用與檢索以提供更簡單更大眾化的語料庫工具，讓語料庫不只能夠做語音相關研究也能夠作其他用途。目前計畫將所有聽打之內容與聲音製作為 EPUB 電子書並美化其排版與內容與建構語料庫檢索網頁提供線上檢索語料庫內容。

參考文獻

[1] http://www.ethnologue.com/14/show_language.asp?code=CFR

[2] Wikipedia. (2006). Available from http://en.wikipedia.org/wiki/Demographics_of_Taiwan

[3] Trainscribe http://www.seventhstring.com/

[4] 全國語文競賽台灣閩南語朗讀參考資料 http://140.111.34.54/MANDR/minna/first.html

[5] FTVN(民視新聞網)http://news.ftv.com.tw/

[6] PTSN 公視新聞網 http://news.pts.org.tw/

[7] LTS(浪淘沙)http://program.ftv.com.tw/Drama/TDoctress/

[8] MaternalHome(娘家)http://program.ftv.com.tw/Drama/Momshouse/

[8] Dream_State(夢中的國家)http://sowhuaa.ning.com/

以聲符部件為主之漢字學習系統設計研究

The Design of Chinese Character Learning System Based on Phonetic Components

張嘉惠 Chia-Hui Chang
國立中央大學資訊工程學系
Department of Computer Science and Information Engineering
National Central University
chia@csie.ncu.edu.tw

吳文斌 Wen-Pen Wu
國立中央大學資訊工程學系
Department of Computer Science and Information Engineering
National Central University
995202021@cc.ncu.edu.tw

摘要

有越來越多人把中文當作第二外語學習，本文目的是使其輕鬆識字。在常用字方面，形聲字約佔 60%，為此我們提出以聲符部件為主的漢字識字教學，再匹配適合的發音規則幫助漢字的學習。本系統類似於以字帶字識字教學，達到教導少量部件與少量部首，卻認識大量的字。最後與中文專家合作，從中研院漢字構形資料庫，分析出 1453 筆常用部件配合形音義及字詞教材，建立以聲符部件為主之漢字識字線上學習系統，並且由發音強度、筆畫數及其延伸字出現頻率作為教學順序。前 400 個部件與其延伸字時，對於一般文章，可達到 60%以上的識字率。前 800 個部件就可達到 9 成左右的識字率。

Abstract

An increasing number of people learn Chinese as second language in the world. About 60% of Chinese characters are picto-phonetic compounds which are composed of a phonetic component (PC) and semantic component. Therefore，one can make a guess at a character's pronunciation and meaning from its phonetic and semantic component for a new character. For this reason，we propose an order of phonetic components based on pronunciation strength，frequency and number of strokes for efficient learning with proper pronunciation rules and graph recognition. We adopt stem-deriving instructional method which extends each phonetic component with different radical component to derive new picto-phonetic compounds of similar pronunciation. Via simulation, the top 400 phonetic components and their picto-phonetic extensions are enough for the recognition of 60% characters in general articles; and top 800 phonetic components can help recognition of 90% characters of general news articles.

關鍵詞：形聲字，聲符部件，部件，以字帶字

Keywords: picto-phonetic compounds，phonetic component，component，stem-deriving instructional method.

一、緒論

這些年由於中國市場的崛起，加上華人第二代或第三代在海外的擴展，在台灣，由於外籍配偶人數的增加，使學習中文的人數增加。漢字的字形繁瑣，初學者難以掌握。其中最主要的原因在於漢字是圖形文字 (pictograph system)，圖形文字大部分為從字中表示出字的意思，若字本身形狀與音的連結度不高，就無法像英文等拼音文字(alphabet system)一樣，掌握了其拼音規則，就有基本能語文能力。再者，因為很難從一個漢字中得知其發音，通常我們還必須以漢語拼音(Hanyu pinyin)或是注音符號(Chinese phonetic symbols)等拼音輔助，才可知道每個漢字的發音。

以往中國有著相當比例的文盲，與現今對於海外人士的第二代、第三代，或是臺灣地區的新移民（新移民指的是外籍新娘或是外國人士），這些人由於平時都有機會接觸使用中文的人，自然有一定程度基本口語，卻可能因為不識字亦或是識字程度不高而無法閱讀。這些人在平常生活中，雖已有音跟義中間的連接關係，卻缺少與形之間的連接，因此還是看不懂中文字（圖一）。 以圖一來說，認識一個新的中文字，是需要形音義三者都結合，才等於認識了一個新的字。

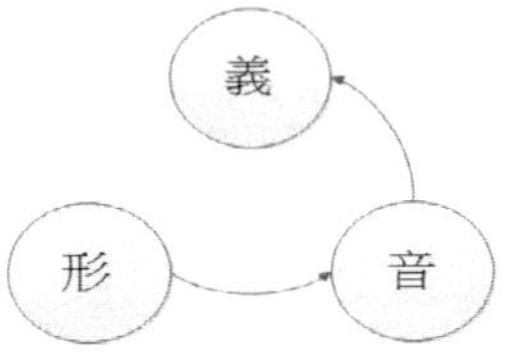

圖一: 語言學習形音義關係

另一方面，英文在認識一個新單字時，由於形與音之間有自然發音的連接，只需要記得其讀音與意思，即可學習新的語彙。相較於華語在學習一個新字時，首先要先建立形跟音中間的連結，再來要音跟義的連結，當形音義三者結合起來之後，才學習了一個新的字，可以說華語新字學習的成本，遠較英文單字的學習成本高。因而本篇論文主要目標是幫助漢字學習者強化形與音的連接關係，讓已經有基本口語能力的使用者可以輕鬆識字，讓人在念出字的讀音之後，透過其本身已有之音與義的連結，即可了解其詞句所包含的意思。

漢字分成六大類[1]據統計資料，教育部訂常用字4783個，其中形聲字佔3026個，佔總常用字中的六成以上。這麼多的形聲字在構字上，多採用[1+1]的方式，

也就是一個部首部件加上聲符部件，對於此種現象，我們可以從聲符部件出發，並擬定一套教學順序，並且建立以部件為主之漢字識字線上教學。

雖說部件教學意義重大，也可降低學習的成本，但卻未受到現有教學的重視，市面上部件介紹零散、不成系統；部件教學過於隨意、缺少完整計劃性[11]。因此本篇論文主要目標是希望用部件教學的角度，幫助漢字學習，並實際設計了一套以部件為主的漢字學系系統，更進一步的強化形與音的連接關係，讓已經有基本口語能力的使用者可以輕鬆識字。

本文第一部分著重於聲符部件的順序，總計 1453 個常用部件，與其延伸字即可涵蓋大部份教育部訂定的常用字，依照此種部件排序做為教學順序，在學習前面的字時，其涵蓋延伸字的學習曲線相對其他順序教學，有較高的投資報酬率。

第二部分在於強化形跟音中間的連結，並做成一套形音義三者結合，且以聲符部件為主的中文識字線上教學。在形的方面，我們提出了相似構字矩陣，可以一次教導多個相似構字的字或部件；在音的部分，我們對於每一個聲符部件針對聲母韻母呈現視覺化轉音規則，及匹配每個聲符部件的形聲字關聯規則；最後提供每個字基本屬性，並且參考邱博瑋 2012[8]論文裡繪製代表其字意義的圖形。

理想上，前 400 個部件之教學，其整體識字率已達到六成以上，對於市面上的一般文章，在學習了前面 800 個部件，整體識字率更高達九成以上，本文雖未能包含實地教學的實驗，但從模擬實驗中得到一些數據參考。

二、相關研究

中央研究院資訊科學研究所文獻處理實驗室從 1993 年開始，陸續建構古今文字的源流演變、字形結構及異體字表，做為記錄漢字形體知識的資料庫，也就是漢字構形資料庫[5]。

為了了解漢字中形聲字發音規則的轉變，我們必須知道每一個形聲字的聲符為何。為此在 2010 年張嘉惠教授與李淑瑩等人於 ROCLING 2010[3]，提出以最佳化及機率分佈法去判斷漢字聲符，他們應用中研院文獻處理實驗室所建立的「漢字構形資料庫」，建立形聲字標記系統，並由中央大學中文所研究生與教授，以人工標記漢字構形資料庫中 14598 有注音標示的漢字是否為形聲字以及其聲符部件。

在 ROCLING 2011[2]，張嘉惠教授與林書彥等人提出聲符部件排序與形聲字發音規則探勘，對於形聲字的發音規則，找出高支持度與高信賴度的規則。另外，依據部件發音強度、延伸字出現頻率與筆畫數三種因素，比較線性加總、幾何平均與調和級數三種排序方式，發現幾何平均的方法，其延伸字涵率相較其他兩種成長更快。幾何平均公式如下:

$$Score_1(PC) = \frac{\text{PC(延伸字出現頻率)} * \text{PC(發音強度)}}{\text{PC}(\sqrt{\text{筆劃數}})} \qquad (1)$$

主要支持我們使用以部件教學的研究為高嘉慧在2011年[4]，此論文比較了傳統分散式教學，與以部件為主的以字帶字識字教學。傳統分散式教學是以主題課文為主學習，學習的生字多為課文內所帶出的生字。而以部件為主的以字帶字識字教學，則是教導部件與部件組字規則的一種教學方法。經由教學實驗，得到一個重要結論，當使用以部件為主的以字帶字識字教學時，受試者在識字率方面會更有效率的成長，尤其是對低口語能力的人更是顯著。

三、問題描述

為驗證聲符部件對於漢字學習的幫助，本文實際設計一個以聲符部件為主的漢字識字線上教學平台，從聲符部件的教學順序，到聲符部件與其延伸字的組合關係、延伸形聲字的發音規則，加強形跟音中間的連接關係。

3.1 、部件排序

在 ROCLING2011 所提出的部件排序是依據發音強度、頻率、及筆劃三個因素來組合，存在的問題是筆畫數的權重太過於高，導致筆畫少的部件容易被排序在教學順序的前面。如 ㇒ 厶 乚 等部件。(實驗教學字[10]的一部分)，初學漢字的人可能會因為學習太細碎的部件，而喪失了字形的結構性，另外可能因為筆劃數目太少，會讓人覺得切割太細，同時也可能讓人覺得此類部件不應該為聲符部件進而誤導使用者，所以這類型的部件希望使用者有一定的口語能力之後，在去做學習。另一個問題則是延伸字的頻率同時包含許多的非常用字，學習此類部件，真正應用情形不高。對於這兩個方面，我們對原本所提出的方法。重新定義一個聲符重要性分數計算如下：

$$Score_2(PC) = \frac{PC(\text{常用延伸字出現頻率}) * PC(\text{發音強度})}{PC(\sqrt{\text{筆劃數}})} \quad (2)$$

對於公式(2)與公式(1)排序的差異，我們比較排名前一百的部件如圖二(表格橫著看，以公式(2)為例，第一名是「包」，第二名是「分」以此類推)，公式(2)新增及減少之部件如圖三所示。 我們可以發現，新增的部件多半是個體已有相當的結構性，而且都為一個完整的字，相反的減少的部件，大都是筆劃少並且結構性較低部件的部件，單獨難成為一個完整的字。

分	包	丁	古	方	令	非	巴	莫	各
尚	交	工	尚	台	亥	亡	可	寸	反
亢	屯	千	乍	比	加	它	由	刃	于
卑	牙	白	儿	俞	且	青	皮	艮	甬
文	正	二	者	皇	票	召	甲	圭	申
元	其	甫	辰	乃	十	弗	乚	少	登
半	旁	主	也	子	朱	今	斤	厶	共
采	倉	同	寺	章	卜	丿	里	氏	婁
至	句	易	每	占	巠	兆	支	辟	尞
旬	爭	侖	勺	果	耳	并	廷	夬	扁

包	分	非	古	莫	方	令	丁	巴	尚
各	尚	交	亥	台	可	俞	卑	票	乍
工	反	青	加	登	亢	皇	屯	者	甬
它	亡	比	由	寸	旁	艮	其	章	白
且	倉	千	皮	婁	甫	辰	辟	圭	牙
正	采	尞	龍	召	甲	刃	申	文	易
于	朱	賓	弗	里	共	同	寺	堯	元
半	粦	主	每	巠	爭	侖	扁	少	至
果	僉	氏	兆	區	今	斤	儿	奇	廷
旬	音	句	占	敫	咼	耳	宗	軍	并

圖二: 聲符排序公式(1)左與公式(2)右前 100 部件之比較

龍	賓	堯	粦	僉	區	奇	音	敫	咼	宗	軍

夬	勺	支	丿	卜	厶	子	也	乚	十	乃	二

圖三: 聲符排序公式(1)與公式(2)前 100 部件：新增（上）及減少（下）的部件

3.2、設計以部件為主的漢字識字學習

在這一節中，我們希望設計出一套有效率的以部件為主的漢字識字學習，形的方面使用相似複合字矩陣；音的方面為形聲字發音規則。

3.2.1、相似複合字矩陣

由於形聲字多為聲符與部首所組成的複合字，因此我們想要找尋相似複合字矩陣（如圖四），希望藉由此種矩陣，讓使用者了解形聲字由部首及聲符組字的大原則，藉由所教導的聲符部件與一些部首去做結合，而產生不一樣的複合形聲字，達到以字帶字的學習效果。

	手 shǒu	水 shŭei	火 hŭo
包 bāo	抱 bào (hold)	泡 pào (loose and soft)	炮 pào (a big gun)
喿 cāo	操 cāo (to grasp)	澡 zǎo (a bath)	燥 zào (dry)
堯 íao	撓 náo (to hinder)	澆 jīao (to pour)	燒 shāo (to burn)
齊 qí	擠 jì (to squeeze)	濟 jì (various)	

圖四: 相似構字矩陣

過去網路上也有類似的相似構字矩陣[4]，但是由專家標記產生的方式，很難對每一個聲符部件產生對應的矩陣。我們希望自動產生相似複合字矩陣。我們使用兩個步驟的 K-NN 演算法。

第一步為，找出與給定聲符的相似聲符，再由這些聲符的延伸字中找出共同的部首，建立而成矩陣，其相似複合字矩陣的建構方法，首先為找到 K 個相似的聲符部件，我們所使用的相似度公式 Jaccard，計算兩個聲符 x 與 y 延伸字的共同部首比例：

$$\text{Similarity}(x,y)=\text{Jaccard}(M_x，M_y)，$$

$$Jaccard(A,B)=\frac{A\cap B}{A\cup B}$$

$$M_x=\cup_{w\in W(x)}RC(w)$$

其中 W(x)是指聲符 x 的延伸字，而 RC(w)指的是形聲字 w 的部首。

	刀	口	手	人	食
包	刨	咆	抱		飽
喿		噪	操		
堯			撓	僥	饒

圖五：由 K-NN 演算法輸入聲符找出其相似聲符範例

我們以聲符「包」、「喿」及「堯」為例，三者之間的 Similarity 相似度計算分別為：

$$\text{Similarity}(包，喿) = \frac{口,手}{刀,口,手,食} = \frac{2}{4}$$

$$\text{Similarity}\ (包，堯) = \frac{口,手}{刀,口,手,人,食} = \frac{2}{5}$$

對於每一預備教導的聲符部件，我們先計算其與每個部件相似度，並且找出最相似的前三名部件，並只考慮構字方式相同的延伸字。當相似部件分數一樣，我們會採用之前經過排序的部件，把排名前面的部件做為我們所要使用的部件。

第二步我們給定聲符部件的延伸字部首，去除不能同時與前三名部件和預備教導的聲符部件構成形聲字的部首，構成所要的相似構字矩陣，以圖六為例。

	刀	口	手	人	食
包	刨	咆	抱		飽
喿		噪	操		
堯			撓	僥	饒

圖六：由 K-NN 演算法刪除不要的部首範例

3.2.2 聲符與形聲字之轉音機率

在 Chang 等人的論文中所探勘的形聲字發音規則中，找出來規則大多數屬於沒有轉音的發音規則，同時對於這些發音規則，我們很難對其做視覺化。針對於這個部分我們提出了視覺化聲符與其延伸字的轉音機率。

在這裡，我們目標是希望能輕易的觀察出，聲符與其延伸字中間的轉音機率。為此，我們先把所有聲符與其延伸字的關係統計出來，我們使用聲符「包」與聲符「巴」當我們的例子。我們把聲符的聲母為「ㄅ」與延伸字的聲母也都為「ㄅ」的字全部統計出來，相同的我們把聲符的聲母為「ㄅ」與延伸字聲母也都為「ㄆ」的字也全部統計出來。

我們使用 Graphviz 的 Api，將轉音機率大於 10%的聯結考慮進來，即可得到最接近平面圖的圖形。藉由此種圖，我們可以很輕易觀察到每個 Node 間的轉音關係。當把所有 Node 與 Node 間的轉音機率都輸入之後，則我們可以得到圖七一樣是以聲母為例，深色箭頭代表轉音機率 50%以上，白色箭頭代表轉音機率 50%以下。由圖七所示，這些轉音關係與小學注音歌謠教導之注音有相似之處，也有相異之處：如ㄅㄆㄈ、ㄉㄊ、ㄐㄑ、ㄍㄎㄏ、ㄓㄔㄕ、ㄗㄘ不僅是發音相近，也是轉音機率高的相似聲母；然ㄇ、ㄌ則自成一組，本身發音強度高，轉移至其他發音的機率相當低；而ㄙㄒ、ㄖㄋ則是在注音歌謠中未顯示出來的。

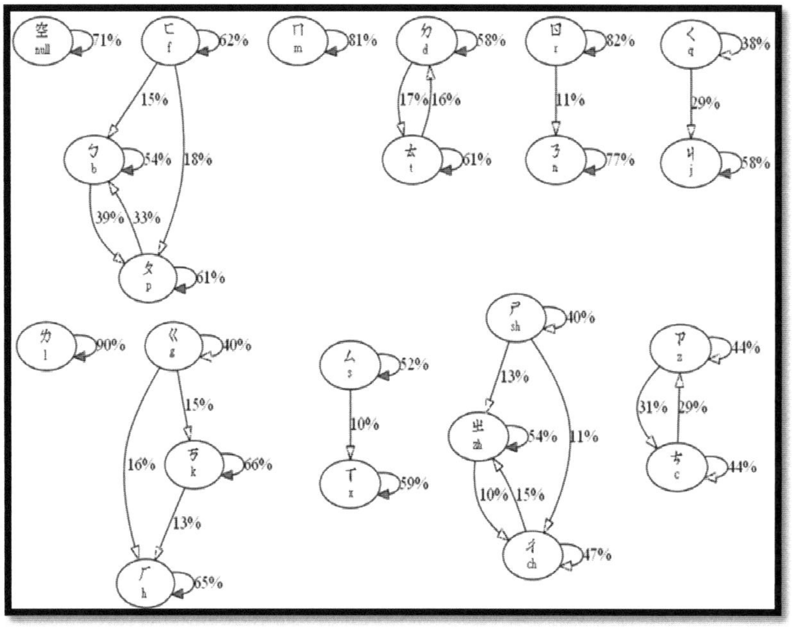

圖七：聲符聲母與其延伸字的聲母轉音機率圖

四、策略模擬驗證實驗

為了驗證我們所提出來的部件排序在學習上的助益，我們以學習曲線成長的情形來做為比較，學習曲線指的是累計與學習聲符部件有相似發音的延伸字數。在這裡我們用數種資料集來做評估，並用單字取向及文章取向兩種不同的方法，來計算識字率，識字率是學習曲線的數值除以資料集裡面的總字數。對於相同的單字我們只會計算一次的單字取向，與相同的單字會被重複計算的文章取向。

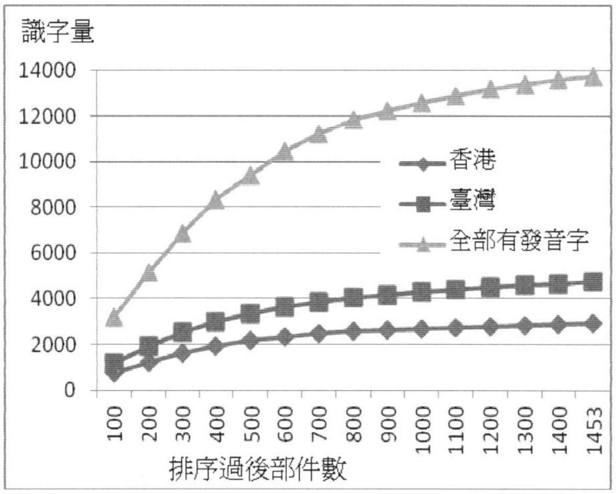

圖八：三種不同資料集以單字為主的學習曲線成長情形

在以單字取向的學習曲線中，我們使用三種資料集，第一種為香港地區在 1987 年[9]所訂定分成 6 個等級的常用 3000 字，第二種為中華民國教育部所制定的 4783 個常用字，最後一種為我們所使用的，漢字構形資料庫裡面所有有標記發音的字，總計 14598 個字。

圖八為三種資料集的學習曲線，X 軸為部件排序，Y 軸為累積的延伸字，我們可以發現，不管在哪個資料集裡面，其學習曲線一開始都成長得很快。我們對圖八做正規化，也就是將累計的延伸字數除上資料集裡的總字數，得到識字率，如圖九。經由圖九我們可以發現其識字率曲線對三個資料集的成長幅度是差不多的，並且大約 400 個部件(361、370 及 435)時可以達到識字率 60%以上。

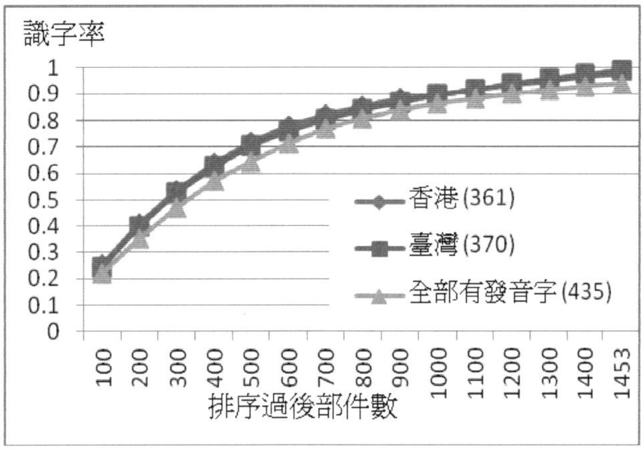

圖九：正規化以單字為主的學習曲線

深入分析聲符部件延伸字與傳統以主題為主的課文教學方法的差異，我們以柯華葳與吳敏而等人對香港常用字集所做的六個分級，在延伸字中的分佈情形，做成加強版的圖形，如圖十所示，右邊 level 的數字代表等級內有多少個字。我們發現同一聲符部件的延伸字，均勻地散佈在六個等級，這表示傳統上被視為較為困難的字，只要把其聲符部件拆解出來，其實可以降低這個字的困難度。某種程度上，這也解釋了『以字帶字』教學法對低口語者為什麼成效較佳。一般說來能力較佳的學習者，比較能自我發掘形聲字以部首及聲符部件構字的關係，並且簡化其發音的記誦，因此對於識字學習上有其優勢。而『以字帶字』教學將這層關係透明化，使得低口語者掌握識字的要訣，達到輔助教學的目的。

不過以聲符部件為主的教學策略，對於非形聲字仍有不足之處，對香港常用字集來說，有 26 個字是無法被我們的教學方法所涵蓋的，如表一所示，表二則是臺灣教育部所訂定常用字裡面不能被涵蓋的 40 個非形聲字。這些聲符部件所無法涵蓋的部分，在教學時是需要被特別拿出來教學的。

接著我們在以文章取向的學習曲線中，準備了市面上 200 字的小短文 7 篇，400 字的小短文 14 篇，500 字小短文 14 篇，600 字小短文 20 篇，皆為小學生優良作文，並從此種資料集中觀察其識字率的成長情形，並且與目前南一版國小課本前三個年級(共六冊)的教學順序所得之識字率作一個比較。

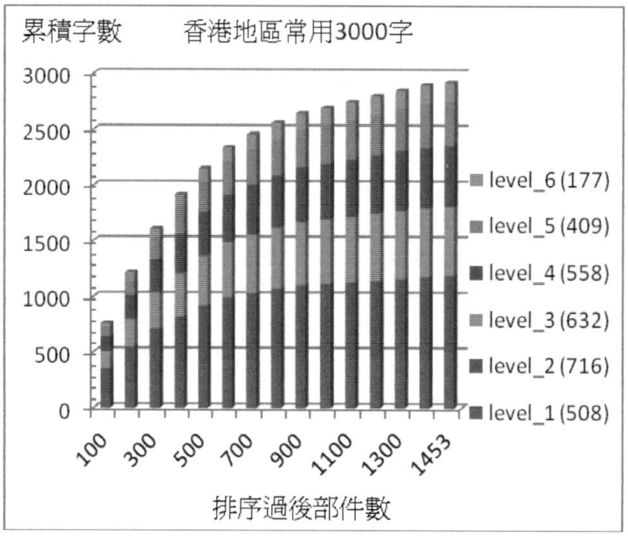

圖十：香港常用 3000 字以單字為主的學習曲線成長詳情

表一：1453 個聲符部件無法涵蓋的香港常用字

竹	已	年	事	飛	候	互	森	晶	囊
惱	傷	浸	畢	惰	龜	佩	承	絕	凸
秉	·侵	姦	喪	鼎	磊				

表二：1453 個聲符部件無法涵蓋的臺灣常用字

鼎	韭	龜	飛	沉	孑	孓	候	臯	森
潸	楞	絕	已	侵	佩	弔	姦	浸	傷
畢	喪	卅	承	囊	事	互	年	竹	晶
珮	丫	凸	甩	瑙	惱	愣	惰	磊	秉

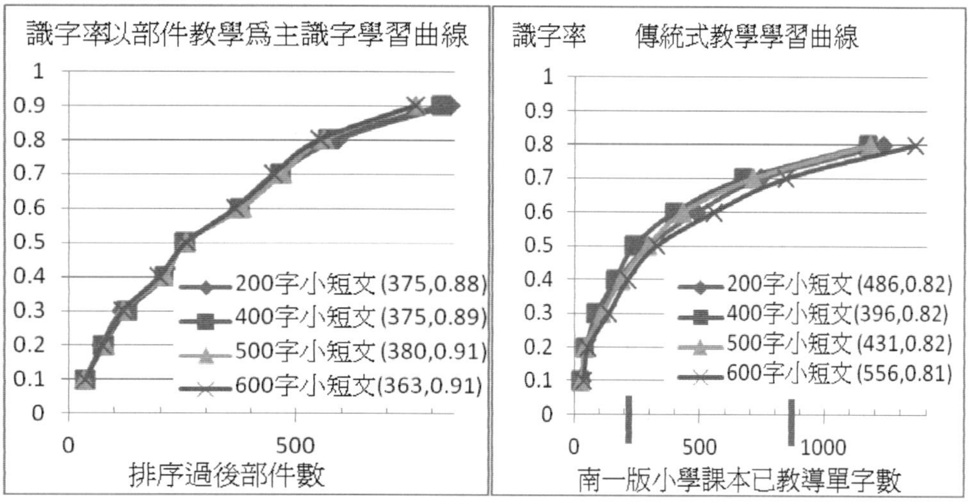

(a) 以部件教學為主　　　　(b) 以傳統教學為主

圖十一：市面上小短文學習曲線

圖十一(a)括弧內兩個數字一樣分別為識字率 60%時所需要教導聲符部件數，與教導了 800 個聲符部件時的識字率，會選用 800 個聲符部件是希望在三年內可以交導完畢。觀察圖十一我們可以發現不管文章字數多寡，識字率 60%所要需的聲符部件個數是差不多的(363~380)。而以南一版六冊 1400 個字的教學順序，也可計算相似的學習曲線。圖十一(b)中橫軸兩條紅線為年級的分界線，意思為學習超過了線之後就為下一個年級。經由觀察兩圖可發現，我們所採用的以部件為主的識字教學，其成長曲線優於傳統式的教學方法，並且我們提出來的方式其識字率可維持在九成左右的水準，高於南一版前六冊的八成二識字率。

最後我們對於市面上的新聞，也採用類似的方式去看其學習曲線成長為何，了解以聲符部件為主之華語教材的適用性。在這邊我們選用五個不同類型的新聞，如圖十二所示，並且圖中括弧內兩個數字分別為識字率 60%時所需要教導聲符部件數，與教導了 800 個部件時的識字率。經由觀察兩張圖之後，可以發現我們提出來的方式一樣優於傳統式的教學，並且很快速的就可達到 60%以上的識字率；傳統式的教學要在第三年之後才可達到相同的識字率水準，此外在 800 個部件與 1400 個單字，我們的識字率一樣可維持在 9 成左右，而傳統式的教學卻只能在 7 成左右。

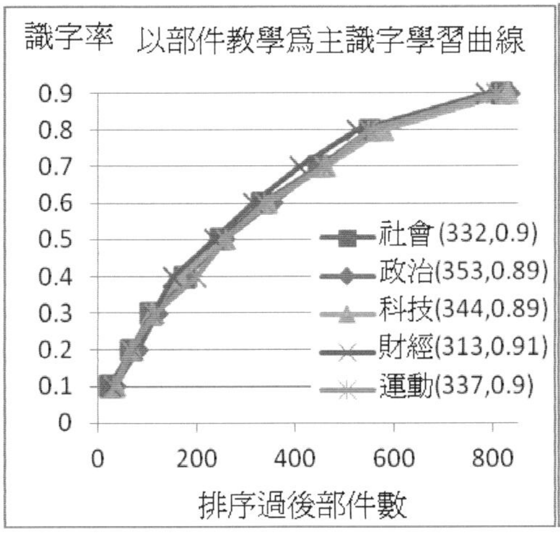

(a) 以部件教學為主

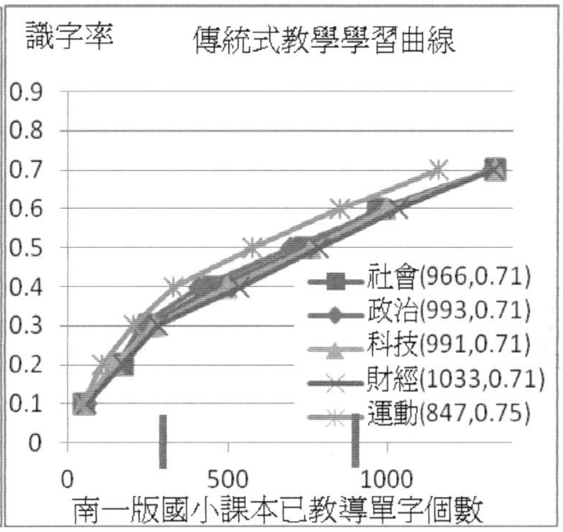

(b) 以傳統教學為主

圖十二: 新聞類學習曲線

五、線上學習介面

以聲符部件為主的漢字教學線上系統分成了形音義三大部分，形的方面為「組字練習」，音的部分有「轉音機率」和「發音規則」，義的部分是「基本屬性」。

5.1 形：組字練習

在介面設計上，雖可以直接呈現相似構字矩陣，但為避免過多資訊，我們以「組字練習」方式，讓使用思考漢字的構成。另外在這裡，我們希望與使用者有著一些互動，所以使用踩地雷的方式呈現給使用者，在點擊交織地方的同時，才呈現是否有構字，以「包」為例全部點擊完後如圖十三所示。

圖十三：組字練習介面

5.2 音：轉音機率、發音規則

在「轉音機率」的介面裡，我們對於每個所教導的部件或是字，把其聲母與韻母個別拆開，並個別繪製轉音機率圖，依照當前的聲母或韻母，對其延伸字呈現其轉音機率。以聲符「包」為例，在漢字學習系統中介面如圖十四。

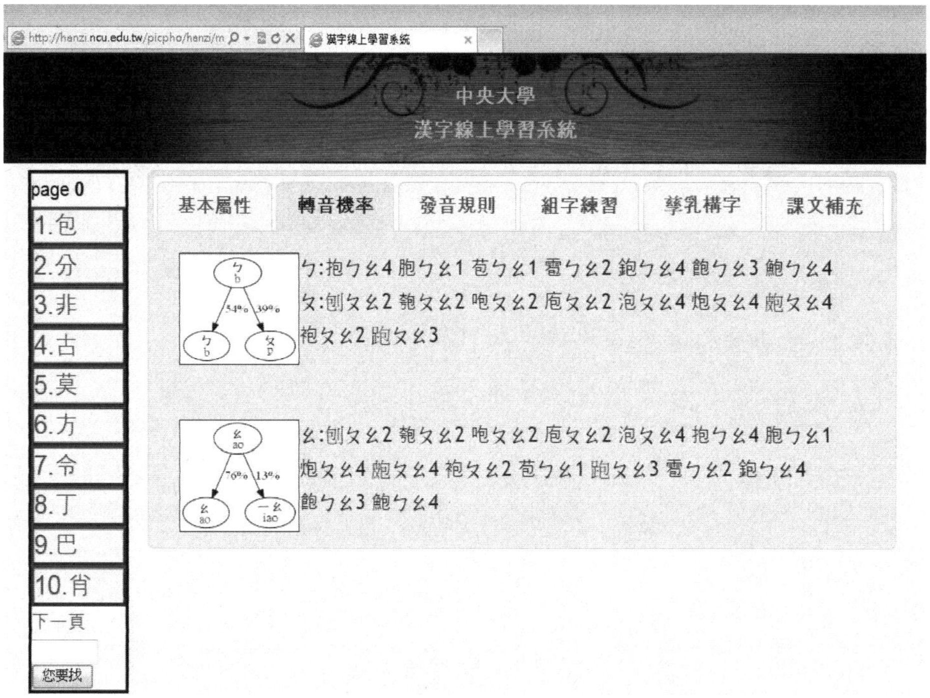

圖十四：聲符之聲母與韻母之轉音機率

圖十五：基本屬性介面

5.3 義：基本屬性

對於字義的部分，在「基本屬性」中的介面中，我們呈現的內容包括字義、字音、部件拆解、以及字形來源的圖解。以圖十五為例，圖解來源參考邱博瑋 2012 年[8]的論文裡繪製代表其字意義的圖形，使用者如果以象形圖示方式來記憶部件，鮮少出現錯誤或是想不起來的情形[10]。

六、結論與未來工作

本篇論文主要分成兩大部分，在第一部分我們重新定義了部件的排序，使得其更接近教學方向，經由與 ROCLING 2011[2]比較，可以發現延伸字在常用字方面，有很大的成長，並且降低了非常用延伸字的部分。在模擬實驗方面，選用不同資料集去做識字率的呈現，成長曲線遠大於一般傳統式教學，也發現在學習了前 400 個部件之後，已經有基本能力應付各種不同的資料集，並且識字率皆可達到了 6 成以上；在學習了前 800 個部件甚至達到 9 成的水準，幾乎可涵蓋整篇文章；另一部分，我們為使用者打造以部件為主之漢字線上學習系統，在形的方面我們提出相似複合字矩陣，可經由教導少數的部首與聲符達到大量識字的目的，在音的方面則有視覺化形聲字轉音機率，與匹配每個教導部件的形聲字發音規則，藉由選出高 support 與高 confidence 的發音規則，強化形跟音中間的連接關係，並且達到以字帶字的教學效果。

然而，仍然有許多地方尚待我們改進的，目前只有在針對單字的識字教學，還欠缺延伸詞的搭配，另外破音字沒有考慮。發音規則對形聲字的涵蓋可以轉成 set covering 的問題，希望可以找到少數的發音規則卻可以還蓋大量的形聲字，另外在本系統中，對每一個字拆解成部件之方式係依照漢字構形資料庫所提供之拆解方式，但有些部份會拆解的太過瑣碎，與一般使用者認知的拆解不同，也是可以改善之處。此外目前本系統尚屬測試階段，未來還需加強和字線上學習系統的介面，或是推廣到手機上面，使之變成有趣的 App 供使用者下載，才能進行實地測試，邀請受試者的參與。最終目的，是希望正在為學習中文字發音而苦的使用者，能更快掌握漢字的發音。

參考資料

[1] 許慎撰、段玉裁注《說文解字注》，台北藝文印書館，1988年。

[2] 張嘉惠、林書彥《聲符部件排序與形聲字發音規則探勘》，ROCLING 2011。

[3] 張嘉惠、李淑瑩、林書彥等《以最佳化及機率分佈判斷漢字聲符之研究》，ROCLING 2010。

[4] 高嘉慧《識字教學法與口語詞彙能力對新移民女性中文識字學習之影響》，2010 年，中央大學碩士論文。

[5] 中研院文獻處理實驗室「漢字構形資料庫」網站。

[6] 莊德明、謝清俊《漢字構形資料庫的建置與應用》，漢字與全球化國際學術研討會，台北，2005 年。

[7] 莊德明、鄧賢瑛《文字學入口網站的規畫》，第四屆中國文字學國際學術研討會，山東煙台，2008 年。

[8] 邱博瑋《說文解字數位編輯規劃研究—以繪圖、檢索與排版為探討對象》，2012 年，中央大學碩士論文。

[9] 柯華葳、吳敏而等《國民小學常用字及生字難度研究──六年級》。台北：台灣省國民學校教師研習會編印，1990。

[10] 賴富美《部件識字教學對國小學習障礙學生識字學習成效之研究》，2008，台東大學碩士論文。

[11] 盛繼豔《華文教學中漢語的部件教學》。

[12] 費錦昌《現代漢字部件探究與語言文字應用》，1996。
http://wuxizazhi.cnki.net/Article/YYYY602.004.html

字形相似別字之自動校正方法

Automatic Correction for Graphemic Chinese Misspelled Words

張道行　　Tao-Hsing Chang
蘇守彥　　Shou-Yen Su
國立高雄應用科技大學 資訊工程系
Department of Computer Science and Information Engineering
National Kaohsiung University of Applied Sciences
changth@kuas.edu.tw
shouyen@gmail.com

陳學志　　Hsueh-Chih Chen
國立台灣師範大學 教育心理與輔導學系
Department of Educational Psychology and Counseling
National Taiwan Normal University
chcjyh@ntnu.edu.tw

摘要

不論華語為母語或外語的學習，錯別字是相當重要的議題。許多研究對於正在求學階段的學生提出矯正錯別字的建議，以及對教師提出教學正字的策略建議。儘管學生在求學時對錯別字的產生作了許多的防範和矯正，但有時候在撰寫文件時，還是會有錯別字產生而不自覺，因此除了在教學上強調錯別字辨認外，如何在使用文字過程中提示錯別字發生成為重要的問題。利用部件組字與形構資料庫，可以得知字的形體結構和組成的部件元素，探討字形相似性的混淆，進而找出造成錯誤的別字。然而，如何由程式自動又正確地找出文件中的別字並不是容易的事情。現階段在字形的錯別字偵測皆有研究者在各領域進行研究和應用，然而正確率距離實際需要仍有一段距離。若是能仔細分析別字的型態、機率以及發生時的語境，應該能夠更精確且快速的偵測出別字並有效的更正。本文利用 bi-gram 字詞比值、bi-gram 詞性比值和候選詞相似度三種特徵，嘗試利用分類模型：SVM、Neural Network 和線性迴歸法對別字偵查與校正。

Abstract

No matter that learning Chinese as a first or second language, a quite important issue, misspelled words, needs to be addressed. Many studies proposed that there was a suggestion of correcting misspelled words for students who are still schooling as well as a suggestion of teaching and learning strategies of Chinese characters for teachers. Although in schooling, it does to prevent students who do lots of precautions and corrections from generating misspelled words; students sometimes are unconscious of their misspelled words while writing. As a result, in addition to emphasize the recognition of misspelled words in teaching, mentioning how to prevent from generating misspelled words during the process of using words becomes a critical issue. Nevertheless, it is not an easy matter to find misspelled words automatically and correctly within documents by using formula. Currently, there are researchers conducting research on graphemic misspelled words detection and applying it to different fields. But the accuracy is still far from the real demand. If it can analyze the model, probability and context of misspelled words in detail, it could be detecting the misspelled words more quickly and precisely as well as correcting those words effectively. We had been already accumulated quite research experiences on graphemic misspelled words. This project will combine with resources provided by the mainline project to process the problem of graphemic misspelled words. If it can achieve a breakthrough, it will not only offer a quite effective auxiliary tool for teaching Chinese misspelled words, but assist in establishing a learning tool of Chinese character errors corpus more quickly.

關鍵詞：別字偵測、別字校正、字形相似

Keywords: Misspelled Words Detection, Misspelled Words Correction, Graphemic Similarit

一、緒論

不論華語為母語或外語的學習，避免錯別字的發生都是相當重要的課題。中、小學甚至高中職課程中都會不斷的要求學生認識、更正錯別字，因為長期寫錯別字在一般人的既定印象中認為是語文水準低落，而實際上在國中基本學力測驗和高中學力測驗的中文作文寫作測驗，錯別字也一直是評分重點項目。而在工作文件中出現錯別字，可能會造成讀者對句子誤解，甚至不了解所要表達的意思，徒增事後再溝通的時間，影響整體的工作效率，甚至造成工作單位的損失。由於以上的問題皆是錯別字所引起，所以更需要正視這個問題。

錯別字分為字體不存在的錯字、以及字體本身為正字但使用錯誤的別字。在目前電腦如此普及和網路通訊發達的環境下，文件的產生多由鍵盤以輸入法輸入，因此只會有別字而不會有錯字產生。若系統可以在使用者書寫文章到一個段落後，自動偵測別字和校正，將可以提升文件的整體品質和效率，減少許多事後的訂正或誤會，也可以讓使用者察覺到別字的發生，進而減少再使用同樣別字的機會。然而，如何由程式自動又正確地找出文件中的別字並不是容易的事情。在英文句子中，字詞之間有空白間隔，因此很容易就可以檢測出是否有錯字和未知字；而中文句子是以連續的單字組成，而單字也可能是一個詞，當發生別字時很難確認是正確字或是別字。

早在 1995 年 Chang[1]已提出中文別字自動偵錯技術，雖然能夠自動找出別字，但還是存在需要改善的缺點。例如：False Alert 過多、偵錯時間過長或無法參考前後文…等。Ren 等人[4]使用規則式加上語言模型的混合方法偵測錯誤，雖然其效能並不理想，但也在此領域提出新概念。而 2002 年 Lin[6]針對倉頡輸入法造成別字的情況進行研究，並提出偵錯的系統。Huang 等人[2]對拼音錯誤的別字設計了一套檢測校正系統，對於每個字建立以拼音相似或相近的混淆字集，利用 bi-gram 語言模型找出別字的位置，並以可能性最高的字替代之。之後陸陸續續還有其他人針對不同情況提出偵錯方法，例如洪大弘等人[7]對國中生作文進行別字的偵查，提供了別字的更正建議，並說明別字與正字的資訊和其關係，用來提升學生的學習能力。而陳勇志等人[8]則以前者為基礎，改良了偵錯模板自動產生正反面知識語料庫，利用 Template 和 Translate 模組進行句子校正，最後以 POS Language Model 作最後校正，提升對別字校正的正確率。

一般而言別字類型分為字音相似與字形相似。現階段在字形的錯別字偵測皆有研究者在各領域作過研究和應用，然而正確率距離實際需要仍有一段距離。若是能仔細分析別字的型態、機率以及發生時的語境，計算出正字詞彙的判別參數，利用分類器訓練出高精確度的模型，或許能夠更精確且快速的偵查出別字並有效的更正。本文的目的是提出一套方法能自動且準確的識別句子中是否有別字，且能精準地偵測句子中別字的位置，並校正為正確字。我們利用字形部件資料庫以字形相似方法辨識疑似含有別字的詞彙，結合字形相似度、Bi-gram 字頻機率和 Bi-gram 詞性機率，將這三個判別特徵分別嘗試以三種分類器模型：SVM、Neural Network、Linear Regression 判別，進而找出正字，最後再提供正字與別字在字形的相似差異，以利使用者比較，避免再次犯錯。

二、方法架構與流程

本文利用詞彙集(Lexicon-based)斷詞法的特性偵測別字。假設句子中的詞彙沒有別字，理想的斷詞系統會將句子分割成正確的詞彙組合，若是詞彙中存在別字，系統則會將絕大部分含有別字的詞彙以單字詞的形式斷開。例如：句子「我們都喜歡學校」，經過斷詞方法處理後會被切割成「我們 都 喜歡 學校」四個詞彙；假設撰寫者寫成「我們都喜歡學佼」，經過斷詞方法處理則會被切割成「我們 都 喜歡 學 佼」，因為詞典無法找到「學佼」這個詞彙，所以會將「學」與「佼」分別斷開。利用此特性，可以假設在連續單字詞片段中可能存在含有別字的詞彙，因此對包含兩個以上單字詞的句子片段，可以對每個單字詞逐一從詞典中搜尋出所有含有該單字詞的詞彙，稱為「候選詞」。再利用預測模型判斷被找出的詞彙是否為原句子片段中的正確詞彙。而句子中疑似含有別字的原字串組合稱為「疑似字組」。

在辨識字形易混淆的單字時，可以利用部件組合判斷字體空間結構，找出字形相似度高的混淆字。並將字形所計算的相似度作為候選詞的參數之一。接著，利用候選詞和疑似字組在原本句中的前後字詞分別計算 bi-gram 字頻機率，再計算兩者的比值做為候選詞的第二個參數。最後，以候選詞和疑似字組分別在原句子中前後詞性文法組成的合理性做為候選詞的第三個參數。

訓練資料中每個候選詞的三個參數以及是否真的具有別字的結果，可以用以訓練預測模型。已訓練之模型可以藉由輸入的三個參數值，輸出該疑似字組是否有別字。若預測模型判斷候選詞為疑似字組的正字詞彙，則可對使用者發出警告和校正詞彙，否則就捨棄。若同時有多個候選詞皆被預測模型判斷為疑似字組的正字詞彙，則以候選詞衝突情形來判別兩候選詞的分數，以分數高者為最後校正對象，如圖一流程圖所示。

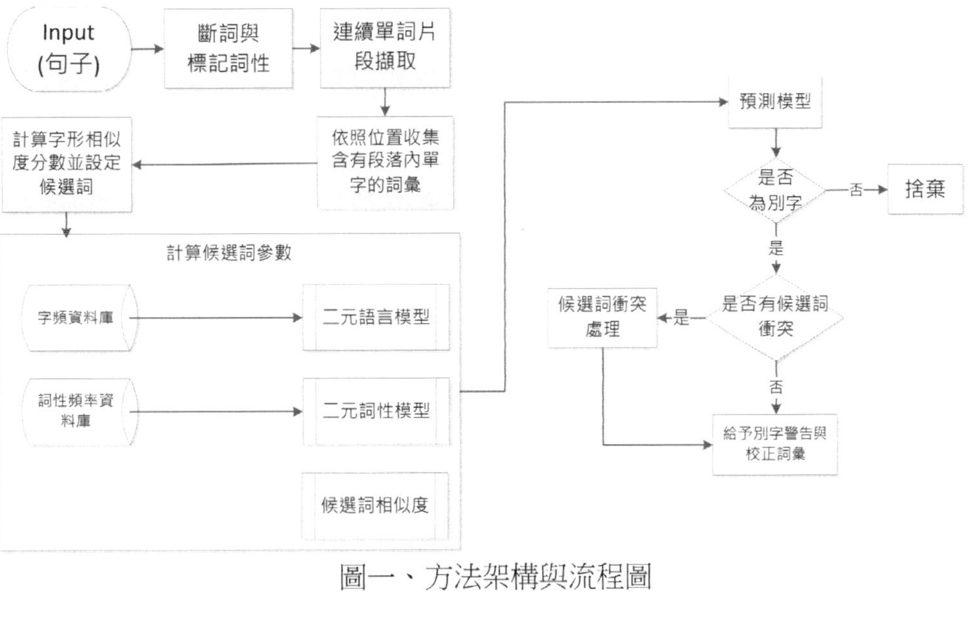

圖一、方法架構與流程圖

三、偵測與校正方法

（一） 偵測可能別字及產生候選詞

所有待處理句子首先經過斷詞及詞性標記處理。由於含有別字的詞彙會造成連續單字詞片段，因此從詞典中找出由片段中任一字所產生的所有詞彙。例如圖二所示，句子「我們的眼精看著前方」經過斷詞處理成「我們_的_眼_精_看著_前方」，其中句子裡「精」為「睛」的別字，因此「眼」和「精」被各自斷開。依照連續單字詞片段「的眼精」，從詞典中搜尋含有「的」為字首且詞彙長度小於等於三的詞彙，例如：「的話」、「的確」；以「眼」為第二字的詞彙且長度小於等於三的詞彙，例如：、「入眼」「心眼」…等，和以「眼」為第一個字且詞彙長度小於等於二的詞彙，例如：「眼力」、「眼睛」…等；以「精」為尾字且詞彙長度小於三的詞彙，例如：「狐狸精」、「綠油精」、「酒精」…等。這些詞彙即為「候選詞」。

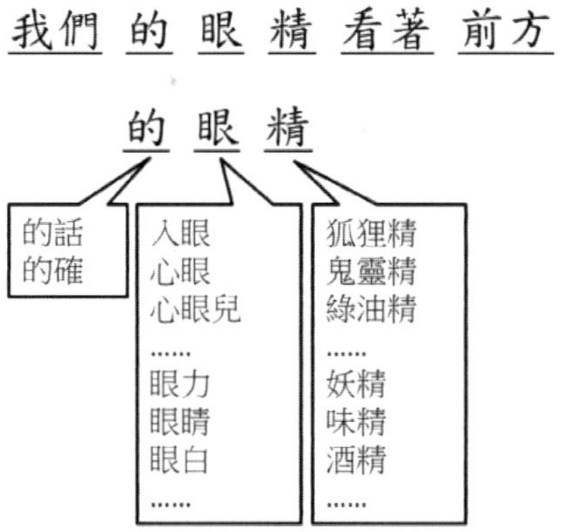

圖二、透過斷詞搜尋出可能含有別字的詞彙

（二） 字形相似度

對連續單字詞片段收集候選詞後，計算每一候選詞與所對應疑似字組的字形相似度，並做為後續判斷候選詞是否為正字詞彙的參數之一。

1. 部件和字形結構關係介紹

字形相似比較方法是使用陳學志等人[9]所提供的中文部件組字資料庫.i 拆解字進行比較。漢字的部件是漢字組成的基本單位。資料庫中有 439 個基礎中文部件，而部件的複雜程度也有所不同，筆劃數從 1 劃到最多 17 劃，例如：「一」、「丶」、「丨」「ノ」…「齒」、「龍」、「龜」、「龠」。字形的空間結構歸納出 11 個空間結構關係，例如：垂直組合、水平組合、封閉組合…等。本文比較兩字部件和字形結構的組合，累加其相同部件的筆劃數，計算出兩字之相似度。

部件分成兩大類，若部件本身是個字則稱為「成字部件」，例如：「女」、「火」；若不是成字則稱為「非成字部件」，例如：「丶」、「丨」。但有些非成字部件無法在 Windows 系統的 Unicode 呈現，所以需要配合結構關係符號，並以中括號 "[]"表示。例如：「即」的右邊非成字部件為「卩」；但左邊的非成字部件是無法呈現，所以以「[|即]」來表示左邊的非成字部件。在 439 個基礎中文部件中，包括 246 個成字部件和 193 個非成字部件。陳學志等人[9]歸納出 11 種不同的結構關係和符號表示，分別為：

(1) 單獨存在(X)：單獨的部件，為字組最基本的組成元素，不可再進行拆解。例如：「木」、「心」。
(2) 垂直組合(-)：其結構關係表示某字的組成型態為部件或部件組以上下垂直相鄰的方式組成。而部件組成順序從左至右，為由上至下的組成方式。例如：「員= -(口,貝)」、「豈= -(山,豆)」。
(3) 水平組合(|)：其結構關係表示某字的組成型態為部件或部件組以左右水平相鄰的方式組成。而部件組成順序從左至右，為由左至右的組成方式。例如：「明= |(日,月)」、「辦= |(辛,力,辛)」。
(4) 封閉組合(0)：其結構關係表示某字的組成型態為部件四面包圍其他部件或部件組的方式組成。其第一個部件表示為包圍的部件，其他為被包圍的部件或部件組。例如：「圍= 0(囗,韋)」、「困= 0(囗,木)」。
(5) 左上包圍(/)：其結構關係表示某字的組成型態為部件從左方和上方覆蓋其他部件或部件組的方式組成。其第一個部件表示為覆蓋的部件，其他為被覆蓋的部件或部件組。例如：「彥= /(-(文,厂),彡)」、「屏= /(尸,-(丷,一,廾))」。
(6) 右上包圍(\)：其結構關係表示某字的組成型態為部件從右方和上方覆蓋其他部件或部件組的方式組成。其第一個部件表示為覆蓋的部件，其他為被覆蓋的部件或部件組。例如：「或= /(戈,-(口,一))」、「氣= \(气,米)」。
(7) 左下包圍(L)：其結構關係表示某字的組成型態為部件從左方和下方包覆其他部件或部件組的方式組成。其第一個部件表示為包覆的部件，其他為被包覆的部件或部件組。例如：「超= L(走,-(刀,口))」、「近= L(辶,斤)」。
(8) 上方三面包圍( )：其結構關係表示某字的組成型態為部件從左方、右方和上方覆蓋其他部件或部件組的方式組成。其第一個部件表示為覆蓋的部件，其他為被覆蓋的部件或部件組。例如：「同= (冂,-(一,口))」、「咸= (戊,-(一,口))」。
(9) 下方三面包圍(V)：其結構關係表示某字的組成型態為部件從左方、右方和下方包覆其他部件或部件組的方式組成。其第一個部件表示為包覆的部件，其他為被包覆的部件或部件組。例如：「凶= V(凵,乂)」、「幽= V(山,幺,幺)」。
(10) 左方三面包圍(<)：其結構關係表示某字的組成型態為部件從左方、上方和下方包覆其他部件或部件組的方式組成。其第一個部件表示為包覆的部件，其他為被包覆的部件或部件組。例如：「匪= <(匚,非)」、「區= <(匚,-(口,|(口,口)))」。
(11) 左右夾擊(T)：其結構關係表示某字的組成型態為部件位局中央，兩旁為其他部件左右夾擊。其第一個部件表示為位居中央或被夾擊的部件，第二部件為左邊夾擊的部件、第三部件為右邊夾擊的部件。例如：「夾= T（大,人,人）」、「巫= T（工,人,人）」。另一種情況，若左右各有兩個夾擊部件時，其他第二至第五的部件分別表示左上、左下、右上、右下之夾擊部件。例如：「噩= T(王,口,口,口,口)」

2. 部件和字形結構關係介紹

字形可由一連串部件結構表達，每一個部件結構由若干個部件或部件子結構透過一個結構關係連結，而部件子結構也是一個部件結構，例如：「醫」的部件結構為「-(|(<(匚,矢),殳),酉)」，由部件子結構「|(<(匚,矢),殳)」和部件「酉」透過結構關係「-」所連結組成，因此可以將部件結構轉換成樹狀結構的形式進行討論。其中，部件結構的最外層結構關係可以視為樹狀結構的根節點(Root)，例如：「醫」部件結構中最外層的結構關係「-」可視為樹狀結構中的根節點，如圖三所示；部件結構內的部件則表示成樹狀結構的葉結點(Leaf Node)，在此稱為部件節點；部件子結構則視為樹狀結構的子樹(Subtree)，而部件子結構的結構關係則為分支節點(Branch Node)，依照部件和部件子結

構級數設定為樹狀結構中的階度(Level)，並將部件的筆劃視為葉的權重(Weight)，而分支節點的權重為其子節點向上累加的權重，所以根節點所表示的權重為整個字的筆劃數。例如：「醫」其部件結構為「-(|(<(匸,矢),殳),酉)」，可以發現「醫」是由「|(<(匸,矢),殳))」和 「酉」上下相鄰的的空間結構關係「-」所組成，依照由左至右的順序，以結構關係「-」為根部向下建構左子樹「|(<(匸,矢),殳))」和右子樹「酉」，左子樹以遞迴方式繼續向下建構，右子樹則為一個節點「酉」。部件「酉」在部件結構為第一級部件相對於樹狀結構的階度 1，「殳」第二級部件為樹狀結構的階度 2，「匸」和「矢」第三級部件為樹狀結構的階度 3，如圖三所示。

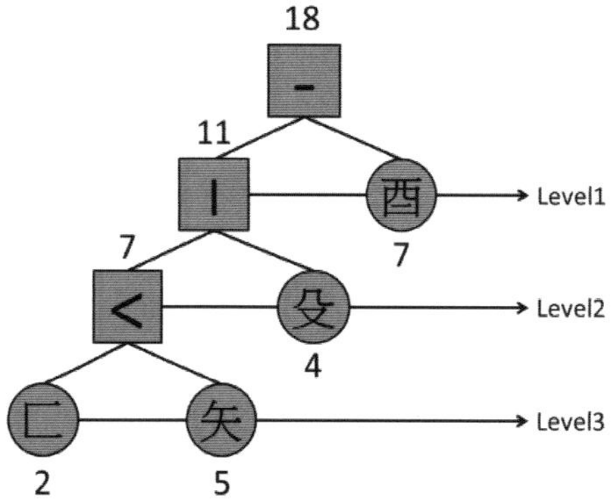

圖三、字形「醫」樹狀結構

藉由上述的樹狀結構，我們可以比較兩個字形的相似度。比較過程中會出現三種型態，分別是單節點和單節點、單節點和樹狀結構、樹狀結構和樹狀結構。第一種型態為單節點和單節點比較，單節點表示為一個部件，而部件為字組成的基本單位，因此兩個單節點比較相似度，若相同則相似度為 1，否則為 0，例如：「女」和「火」兩者皆為成字部件，其樹狀結構皆為單節點，而兩部件不同，因此直接給予相似度 0。

第二種型態為單節點和樹狀結構比較。此型態又分成兩種情形，第一種若單節點不屬於樹狀結構中的節點，則兩者的相似度為 0，例如：「火」和「努」比較，「火」的結構為單節點，而單節點「火」沒有出現在「努」的樹狀結構中，因此直接判別兩者相似度為 0。第二種情形為單節點為樹狀結構中的一個節點，則以單節點的權重值除以樹狀結構根節點的權重值，作為兩者的相似度，例如：「女」和「努」的比較，單節點「女」為「努」的樹狀結構中的一個節點，則以「女」的筆劃數除以「努」的筆劃數為兩者的相似度。但以字形結構觀察，階層值越大之部件，所占整個字體比例越小，例如圖四所示，「妨」和「努」兩者筆劃數相同且樹狀結構皆包含節點「女」，而節點「女」在兩樹狀結構的階層不同，因此在兩字字形上所佔的比例也明顯不同。因此將相似度再乘上一個階層權重值(1-(x-1)*0.05)，x 為單節點在樹狀結構中所在之階層，作為兩者的相似度。如圖五所示，「女」分別與「妨」和「努」比較相似度，「女」的筆劃數為 3，「妨」和「努」的筆劃數皆為 7，節點「女」為「努」的子節點且階層為 2，因此其相似度計算為 3/7*0.95=0.407；節點「女」為「妨」的子節點且階層為 1，因此其相似度計算為 3/7*1=0.429。

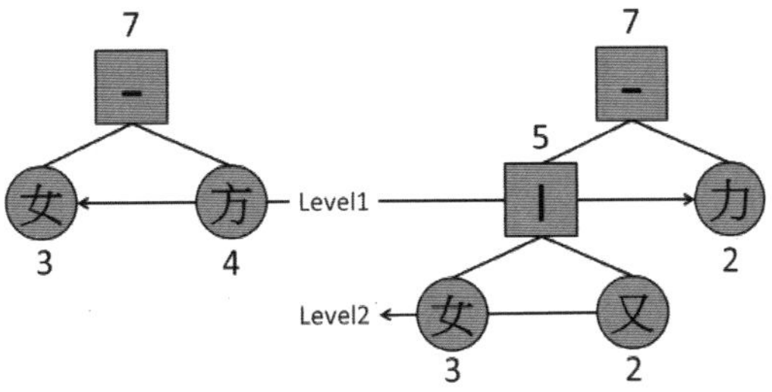

圖四、「妨」和「努」的樹狀結構

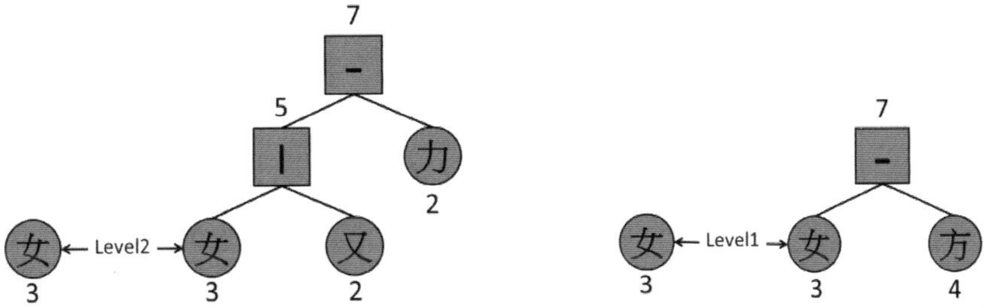

圖五、樹狀結構「努」和「妨」與部件「女」比較

第三種型態為樹狀結構和樹狀結構比較，共分下列 3 種情形。第一種情形為其中一方樹狀結構為另一方樹狀結構的子樹，則以子樹的根節點權重除以父樹的根節點權重，乘上階層權重值作為兩者的相似度。如圖六所示：「櫃」和「貴」比較，「貴」的筆劃數為 12，「櫃」的筆劃數為 18，而樹狀結構「貴」為樹狀結構「櫃」的子樹且階層為 2，因此其相似度計算為 12/18*0.95=0.666。

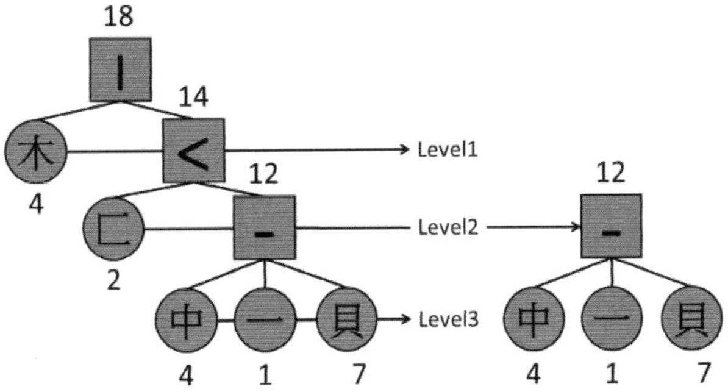

圖六、「櫃」與「貴」相似度比較

第二種情形為兩樹狀結構的根節點相同。兩個根節點相同表示兩字字形屬於相同的結構關係，因此以階層 1 的子樹交叉比較，累加相同部件節點的權重值，以累加的權重值分別除以兩樹根節點權重值並平均作為兩字的相似度。如表一所示，「噪」和「橾」的比較，「噪」階層 1 的子樹為「口」和「喿」；「橾」階層 1 的子樹為「木」和「喿」，交叉比較相同的部件並累加其部件節點權重，選取最大權重值的組合「木」跟「口」比和「喿」和「喿」比為，其累加樹重為 0+13=13，分別除上兩樹根節點的權重並平均為((13/16)+(13/16))/2=0.8125。

子樹在比對到相同的部件節點，若此部件節點的父節點不同，表示其部件的結構關係組成不同，則不累加其部件結點權重值。以表二為例，「估」和「伽」比較，「估」階

層 1 的子樹為「亻」和「古」，「伽」階層 1 的子樹為「亻」和「加」，其中子樹「古」和子樹「加」比較，發現有相的部件「口」，但其父節點不同，「加」的結構關係為「|」，「古」的結構關係「-」，因此不累加部件「口」的筆劃數，因此兩字相似度為((2/7)+(2/7))/2=0.2857。

表一、「橾」和「噪」階層 1 子樹比較表

噪 \ 橾	口	喿
木	0	4
喿	3	13

表二、「估」和「伽」階層 1 子樹比較表

估 \ 伽	亻	古
亻	2	0
加	0	0

我們發現筆劃數較少的字和筆劃數較多的字在比較時，相同部件權重值固定下，除以字筆劃數較少的筆劃數，分數會較高，平均後會影響整體相似度。如表三所示，「叭」和「嘿」比較，其相同部件權重值為 3，以原來的計算方式，其相似度為((3/5)+(3/15))/2=0.4。我們期望遇到此類形時，相似度不應該這麼高，因此則另外計算其相似度。以 6097 字的筆劃數由少至多排列，設定前 30%屬於筆畫數較少的一類，即筆劃數低於 10 的字。判斷兩樹狀結構中任一方的根節點權重小於 10，則以相同部件權重值除以兩者間較大的根節點權重值為相似度。如表 5 所示，「叭」和「嘿」比較，因為「叭」的筆劃數為 5，屬於筆劃數較少的一類，因此將原本相似度更改為 3/15=0.2。

表三、「叭」和「嘿」階層 1 子樹比較表

叭 \ 嘿	口	八
口	3	0
黑	0	0

第三種情形為兩樹狀結構的根節點不相同。從部件資料庫中 6097 字來看，可以觀察幾種結構關係是較特殊的字形所有，例如包圍字形結構(0)共 28 字，大部份以「囗」部件為包圍型態，例如：「國」、「圓」；下方三面包圍字形結構(V)共 4 字，分別為「凶」、「函」、「幽」、「豳」，其包圍部件為「凵」和「山」；左方三面包圍字形結構(<)共 15 字，階為「匚」部件所包圍；左右夾擊字形結構(T)共 35 字，例如：「衝」、「夾」。上述四種字形結構較為特殊，當兩樹比較相似度時，若其中一樹根節點為上述其中之一，則另一樹根節點必須是相同，才可利用第二情形進行比較，否則不比較並設定相似度為 0。

觀察垂直組合結構關係(-)和水平組合結構關係(|)，這兩種字形結構上較有衝突如圖七所示，「棍」和「查」兩字擁有相同部件「木」、「日」，且樹狀結構也相似，但觀察兩字的字形結構較不相似。

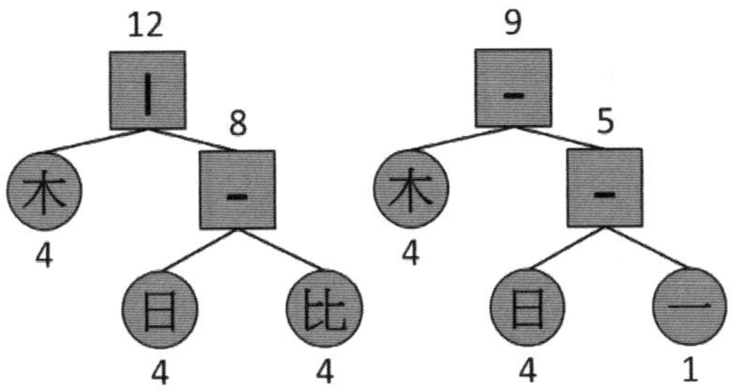

圖七、「棍」和「查」樹狀結構比較

因此兩字的字形結構為垂直組合和水平組合時，則利用第二種情形計算完相似度後再乘上 0.8 最為最後的相似度，如表四所示，「棍」和「查」比較，其相同部件相似度為 8，其中「查」的筆劃數為 9，屬於筆劃數較少的一類，而兩樹的根節點又分別屬於垂直組合和水平組合，因此相似度為(8/12)*0.8=0.5333。排除上述幾個例子，兩字根節點不相同的情況下，則以計算字形相似度後，乘上 0.9 作為最後的相似度。

表四、「棍」和「查」階層 1 子樹比較表

查 \ 棍	木	旦
木	4	0
昆	0	4

（三） bi-gram 字頻機率

在語料中可以觀察到某一些字會與另外特定的字頻繁的相鄰出現，稱為共現關係，而共現的次數稱為共現頻率，利用共現頻率計算出現機率稱為共現機率。若句子中含有別字，可以猜測別字與前後字的共現頻率低於正字與前後字的共現頻率，因為語料庫中所收集的資料為一般寫作常使用的正字組合。因此若候選詞的字與前後字的共現頻率比疑似字組高時，可以合理的懷疑句子中出現別字。本文利用 bi-gram 字頻機率計算字與字之間的共現機率，以候選詞的共現機率和疑似字組的共現機率比較，經過正規化計算，設定為候選詞的參數。本文整理聯合報 2003 全年度的報紙內容，分析後記錄 7205 個單字所出現的頻率和兩個單字相鄰出現的頻率。bi-gram 字頻機率為連續條件機率公式，計算字與字的共現機率。假設由 n 個字元組成字串 S: $X_1X_2X_3 \dots X_{n-1}X_n$，其 bi-gram 字頻機率值由公式(1)所示。

$$P(S) = \prod_{i}^{n} \frac{f(X_{i+1}|X_i)}{f(X_i)} \quad (1)$$

其中$P(S)$表示在字串中字元的連續機率；$f(X_{i+1}|X_i)$表示字元X_i、X_{i+1}連續出現的頻率；$f(X_i)$表示X_i單獨出現的頻率。分別計算完候選詞和疑似字組與句子中前後字的 bi-gram 字頻機率，將候選詞機率值除以兩者相加之值做為候選詞的第二個參數，稱為 bi-gram 字頻機率比值，。

（四） bi-gram 詞性機率

當別字取代正字時，句子中的詞性組合必會有所改變，因為正確句子其標記的詞性應該較合乎語法，因此正確句子的詞性組合的共現機率會比含有別字句子的詞性組合的共現機率來得高。因此本文利用 bi-gram 詞性機率來判別別字的依據之一。

將原句子和候選詞替換疑似字組的句子作斷詞處理和標記詞性，利用連續條件機率公式計算詞性與詞性間的共發機率，我們稱為 bi-gram 詞性機率。假設連續 n 個詞性組合 A:$Y_1Y_2Y_3\ \ldots Y_{n-1}Y_n$，bi-gram 詞性機率如公式 2 所示。

$$P(A)=\prod_{i=1}^{n}\frac{f(Y_{i+1}|Y_i)}{sqrt(f(Y_i)\times f(Y_{i+1}))} \tag{2}$$

其中$P(A)$表示連續 n 個詞性組合的機率；$f(Y_{i+1}|Y_i)$表示詞性Y_i、Y_{i+1}連續出現的頻率；$f(Y_i)$表示Y_i單獨出現的頻率。含有別字的句子會比正確句子多出一個以上的詞彙，因此詞性數量也會較正確句子多。以圖八為例，句子「晚上在工司吃」，經過斷詞和詞性標記處理為「晚上(Nd)_在(P)_工(Na)_司(Nb)_吃(Vc)」五個詞彙和詞性組合；而由候選詞「公司」替換疑似字組，經過斷詞和詞性標記處理為「晚上(Nd)_在(P)_公司(Nc)_吃(Vc)」四個詞彙及詞性。

<table>
<tr><td>詞彙</td><td>晚上</td><td>在</td><td colspan="2">公司</td><td>吃</td></tr>
<tr><td>詞性</td><td>Nd</td><td>P</td><td colspan="2">Nc</td><td>Vc</td></tr>
<tr><td></td><td colspan="5"></td></tr>
<tr><td>詞彙</td><td>晚上</td><td>在</td><td>工</td><td>司</td><td>吃</td></tr>
<tr><td>詞性</td><td>Nd</td><td>P</td><td>Na</td><td>Nb</td><td>Vc</td></tr>
</table>

圖八、正確句子和含有別字的句子其斷詞和詞性組合

因為兩句子的詞性數量不同，無法皆以公式 2 直接計算比較。我們對含有別字的句子其計算公式稍作修正，假設正確句子的詞性數為 n 個，而含有別字的句子詞性數為 n+k 個，k 為疑似字組比原來句子多出的詞性數量，而疑似字組拆解的位置為 x，將位置 x 之前的詞性組合設為 A1，位置 x+k 之後的詞性組合設為 A2，則含有疑似字組的句子其 bi-gram 詞性機率如公式 3 所示。

$$P(A1)P(A2)=\prod_{i=1}^{x}\frac{f(Y_{i+1}|Y_i)}{sqrt(f(Y_i)\times f(Y_{i+1}))}\times\prod_{i=x+k}^{n+k}\frac{f(Y_{i+1}|Y_i)}{sqrt(f(Y_i)\times f(Y_{i+1}))} \tag{3}$$

我們另外計算「詞性共現強度權重值」用以調整公式(3)。首先對於 36 個詞性共現機率作排序，可以發現以「Df-Vh」的共現機率為最高：P(Vh|Df)=0.721。在詞性共現機率排序中間的組合為「De-Ve」，其共現機率為 P(De|Ve)=0.01206。假設 P(X)為疑似字組內部的詞性共現機率，其權重值計算方式為公式 4 所示。

$$W = (1 + (\frac{P(X)}{(P(X) + 0.01206)}) \quad (4)$$

對一個疑似字組而言，其 bi-gram 詞性機率為公式(3)之值乘以公式(4)之值。將候選詞機率值除以兩者相加之值做為候選詞的第三個參數，稱為 bi-gram 詞性機率比值。

（五） 候選詞衝突

候選詞可以分成兩類，第一類為候選詞是疑似字組的替換對象，我們稱為應替換詞；另一類為候選詞不是疑似字組的替換對象，我們稱為不替換詞。有時一個疑似字組會同時出現多個候選詞都被視為應替換詞，因此我們以下列規則解決這個問題。當候選詞長度為相同時，則以三個參數總和比較；當候選詞長度為不同時，則比較候選詞與疑似字組的相同字數，若相同字數一樣則比較候選詞的相似度，若前兩者皆相同則比較兩者字數。

四、預測模型

將每個候選詞經過運算可以得到字形相似度、bi-gram 字頻機率比值和 bi-gram 詞性機率比值。當候選詞字形越像、字頻機率越高、詞性機率越高，則為應替換詞機率也越高。本文利用訓練資料中的三個參數訓練幾種監督式預測模型，並在第五節的實驗比較其預測應替換詞的正確性。

(一) 線性回歸法

候選詞的三個判別參數可以作為線性迴歸方程的三個參數項，利用已知的資料計算出迴歸系數β_i，如公式 5 所示。

$$y = \beta_1 X_1 + \beta_2 X_2 + \beta_3 X_3 \quad (5)$$

對一個測試資料，其 y 值越大越可能為應替換詞，因此我們對 y 須設一閥值，若 y 高於閥值則判別為應替換詞， 反之則判別為不替換詞。圖九為應替換與不替換資料各半組成之訓練資料對不同閥值的預測正確率。在閥值設定為 1 時，全部資料皆判別為不替換詞，因此正確率為 50%。隨著閥值向下調整，正確率會漸漸上升，達到一個高峰後，正確率就開始下降。因此可以利用閥值對正確率的變化，取正確率最高的閥值為設定值。

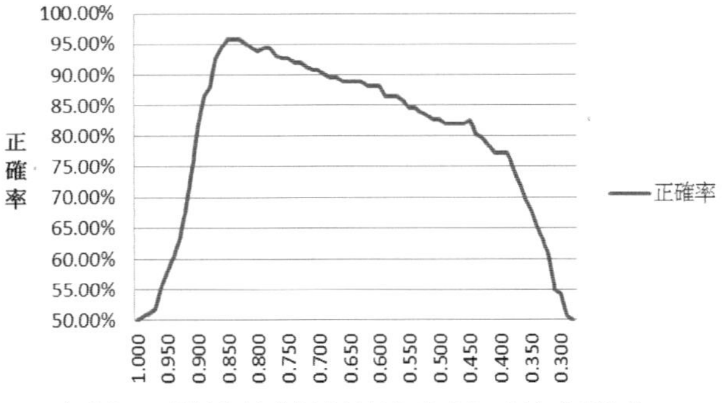

圖九、門檻值對於訓練資料正確率變化

(二) SVM 與 NN

本文也嘗試以支援向量機(Support Vector Machine)和類神經網路(Neural Network)模型預測應替換詞，以比較線性與非線性預測模型是否有差異。類神經網路使用倒傳遞類神經網路(Back Propagation Neural Network)演算法，而支援向量機所使用的核心函數為 RBF。

五、實驗

（一） 實驗環境

本實驗所採用訓練資料和測試資料是由「國立台灣師範大學心理與教育測驗研究發展中心」所提供九年級 1187 位學生根據題目為「用餐時刻」所撰寫之寫作所產生。每篇寫作經由二至三位受過訓練的閱卷者評分，評分等級為 1 至 6 分。因為分數較低的文章通常誤用別字的情形會比分數高的文章來得多，故選取 1 至 3 分共 258 篇文章，合計 6015 句，以人工檢查含有別字 81 個。產生應替換詞數量有 81 筆。由表五可知，字形相似度低於 0.625 即皆為不替換詞，故僅保留高於此值之不替換詞 647 筆。應替換詞與不替換詞比例約 1：8。

表五、各字形相似度區間之應替換詞和不替換詞數量

類別＼相似度	1~0.9	0.9~0.8	0.8~0.7	0.7~0.6	總數
應替換詞	10 (12.35%)	49 (60.49%)	20 (23.69%)	2 (2.47%)	81
不替換詞	1 (0.15%)	20 (3.09%)	106 (16.38%)	520 (80.37%)	647

由於本文在預測模型需要訓練資料，然資料內容中應替換詞和不替換詞的數量懸殊，可能導致訓練時產生過度學習的情形，因此不替換詞資料透過隨機的方式擷取與應替換詞相同數量作為訓練資料。

（二） 實驗結果與討論

本實驗以 4-fold cross validation 檢驗各模型的精確度。將不替換詞 81 筆與應替換詞 81 筆隨機分成 4 個資料集，其中，資料集二、資料集三、資料集四，兩類詞各為 20 筆，共 40 筆，資料集一兩類詞各為 21 筆，共 42 筆。

本文使用預測正確率、recall rate 和 precision rate 三個指標評估三種預測模型的效能。假設 *Tr* 為可能出現別字而確實有別字的句子數；*Tf* 為可能出現別字但沒有別字的句子數。三項評估指標計算公式如下:

$$\text{預測正確率} = \frac{Pr+Nr}{Pr+Pw+Nr+Nw}\ ;\ \text{Recall} = \frac{Pr}{Pr+Pw}\ ;\ \text{Precision} = \frac{Pr}{Pr+Nw}$$

其中 *Pr* 為 *Tr* 中被正確校正別字的句子數；*Pw* 為 *Tr* 中被預測不須校正的句子數；*Nr* 為 *Tf* 中被預測不須校正的句子數；*Nw* 為 *Tf* 中被錯誤校正的句子數。

1. 使用 SVM 預測

本實驗以 LibSVM[3]為本實驗的訓練和測試工具。依照 LibSVM 所預設的參數對訓練資料進行訓練，模型對於測試資料的判別正確率不高，因此必須找出最佳的參數重新訓練模型。因為無法直接得知最佳的參數值，只能以訓練的方式找出最佳參數設定。利用 LibSVM 裡的 grid 工具找出最佳參數值：kernel 為 RBF、cost 設定為 32、gamma 設定為 0.5，依此參數進行交叉驗證，如表六所示。由實驗結果可知，平均預測正確率為 95.63%、recall rate 平均為 97.50%、precision rate 平均為 94.10%。

表六、SVM 預測結果

訓練集	測試集	測試筆數	正確預測數	預測正確率	Recall Rate	Precision Rate
234	1	42	42	100%	100%	100%
134	2	40	37	92.50%	95.00%	90.48%
124	3	40	38	95.00%	100%	90.90%
123	4	40	38	95.00%	95.00%	95.00%
平均				95.63%	97.50%	94.10%

2. 使用 Neural Network 預測

本文使用 Qnet2000 設定 Neural Network 並運算結果。網路結構設定經最佳化測試為 3 層，包含輸入層 3 個運算元、隱藏層設定為 10 個運算元，最後的輸出層為 1 個運算元。轉換函數設定為一般倒傳遞網路所使用的雙曲函數(Sigmoid function)，學習率(Learn Rate)設定為 0.01，動量(Momentum)設定為 0.8，最大訓練次數(Max Iterations)設定為 10000 次。表七為 Neural Network 的預測結果。字形判別平均正確率為 96.25%、recall rate 平均為 96.25%、precision rate 平均為 96.37%。

表七、Neural Network 的預測結果

訓練集	測試集	測試筆數	正確預測數	預測正確率	Recall Rate	Precision Rate
234	1	42	42	100%	100%	100%
134	2	40	39	97.50%	95.00%	100%
124	3	40	37	92.50%	95.00%	90.48%
123	4	40	38	95.00%	95.00%	95.00%
平均				96.25%	96.25%	96.37%

3. 使用線性迴歸法預測

表八表示交叉驗證的各訓練資料集透過線性迴歸找出的參數權重值和閥值。表八顯示字形相似度和 bi-gram 字頻機率比值的權重值較高，bi-gram 詞性機率比值之權重值較低。表九表示以表八閥值進行預測之結果。平均預測正確率為 97.50%、recall rate 平均

為 96.25%、precision rate 平均為 98.75%。

表八、不同訓練資料集產生之迴歸參數權重值和閥值

訓練集	bi-gram 字頻機率比值權重值	bi-gram 詞性機率比值權重值	候選詞相似度權重值	最佳閥值
234	0.476108	0.047314	0.495112	0.82
134	0.533153	0.041051	0.426089	0.83
124	0.515488	0.065720	0.446411	0.85
123	0.527719	0.038126	0.446539	0.85

表九、線性迴歸法預測結果

訓練集	測試集	測試筆數	正確預測數	預測正確率	Recall Rate	Precision Rate
234	1	42	42	100%	100%	100%
134	2	40	39	97.50%	95.00%	100%
124	3	40	38	95.00%	95.00%	95.00%
123	4	40	39	97.50%	95.00%	100%
平均				97.50%	96.25%	98.75%

4. 結果討論

本實驗透過 SVM、Neural Network 和以線性迴歸三種預測方法，以交叉驗證的方式對資料集進行預測。透過 SVM 平均預測正確率為 95.63%，透過 Neural Network 平均預測正確率為 96.25%，透過線性迴歸法平均預測正確率為 97.5%，如表十所示。

表十、各模型的評估指標平均值

模型	預測正確率	Recall Rate	Precision Rate
SVM	95.63%	97.50%	94.10%
NN	96.25%	96.25%	96.37%
LR	97.50%	96.25%	98.75%

實驗結果顯示預測正確率和 precision rate 最高者為線性迴歸法，recall rate 最高者為 SVM。其中，線性迴歸法其 precision rate 較其他模型來得高，表示找到的候選詞較正確，不容易有錯誤警告產生。若在真實應用環境下，應替換詞和不替換詞的比例為 1:8，因此實驗 precision rate 的些微差異會使得在真實環境下使用者的感受有相當明顯的不同，因此線性迴歸法應較適合在真實環境下使用。

六、結論

本文提出一個偵測字形相似別字及校正的方法，透過陳學志等人[9]部件結構來計算字形間的相似度，利用相似度對別字搜尋候選詞，再計算候選詞的 bi-gram 字頻機率比值、bi-gram 詞性機率比值，最後利用預測模型判斷候選詞是否為應替換詞。在先前

研究中多依靠混淆字集所收集的資料，雖然多為相似度較高且易混淆的對應字，但若別字不屬於混淆字集，則無法偵測校正。本文所提方法能不被混淆字集侷限，此方法若遇到應替換詞相似度低時，可依靠其他參數得到正確預測。經由實驗結果顯示，線性迴歸法的正確率及 precision rate 較其他模型來得高，表示找到的別字較正確，產生錯誤警告的機率也相對較低，因此較符合真實環境下的使用需要。

本研究仍有許多限制待未來進一步研究。首先，本研究只針對二字詞以上的詞彙別字進行探討，對於單字詞的別字無法偵測與校正。第二、對於被偵測之別字是否可能為未知詞並未考慮，若語料中含有大量未知詞則可能造成未知詞的片段被誤認成詞彙，導致預測正確率降低。第三、本研究只針對字形部分探討，字音相似之別字是否可用本文所提架構與模型加以偵測與校正，值得進一步探討。

誌謝

本文作者感謝教育部及國立台灣師範大學「邁向頂尖大學計畫」編號 101J1A0301 以及編號 101J1A0701 計畫支持，同時感謝國立台灣師範大學心理與教育測驗研究發展中心提供語料。

參考文獻

[1] Chao-Huang Chang. A New Approach for Automatic Chinese Spelling Correction. In Proceedings of Natural Language Processing Pacific Rim Symposium'95, Seoul, Korea. pp: 278-283,1995.

[2] Chuen-Min Huang, Mei-Chen Wu, and Ching-Che Chang. Error Detection and Correction Based on Chinese Phonemic Alphabet in Chinese Text. World scientific publishing company, International Journal of Uncertainty, Fuzziness and Knowledge-Based Systems, Vol.16, Suppl. 1 pp.: 89-105, 2008.

[3] Chih-Jen Lin, Chih-Chung Chang. LIBSVM -- A Library for Support Vector Machines. Take from http://www.csie.ntu.edu.tw/~cjlin/libsvm/

[4] Fuji Ren, Hongchi Shi, and Qiang Zhou. A hybrid approach to automatic Chinese text checking and error correction, in Proceedings of 2001 IEEE International Conference on Systems, Man, and Cybernetics. pp: 1693-1698,2001.

[5] J.A.K. Suykens and J. Vandewalle. Least Squares Support Vector Machine Classifiers. Neural Processing Letters. Volume 9, Number 3 , 293-300, 1999.

[6] Yih-Jeng Lin, Feng-Long Huang and Ming-Shing Yu. A Chinese Spelling Error Correction System. Proceedings of the Seventh Conference on Artificial Intelligence and Applications, 2002.

[7] 洪大弘，2009，"基於語言模型及正反陳語料知識庫之中文錯別字自動偵錯系統"，朝陽科技大學，碩士論文。

[8] 陳勇志，2010，"利用雜訊通道模型與自動產生偵錯模板改良學生中文作文錯別字偵測與改正"，朝陽科技大學，碩士論文。

[9] 陳學志、張瓅勻、邱郁秀、宋曜廷、張國恩，2011，"中文部件組字與形構資料庫之建立及其在識字教學的應用"，教育心理學報。

利用機器學習於中文法律文件之標記、案件分類及量刑預測

Exploiting Machine Learning Models for Chinese Legal Documents Labeling, Case Classification, and Sentencing Prediction

林琬真 Wan-Chen Lin[1], 郭宗廷 Tsung-Ting Kuo[1], 張桐嘉 Tung-Jia Chang[2],

顏厥安 Chueh-An Yen[2], 陳昭如 Chao-Ju Chen[2], 林守德 Shou-de Lin[1]

[1] 國立台灣大學資訊工程系

[2] 國立台灣大學法律學院

[1]Department of Computer Science and Information Engineering, National Taiwan University

[2]College of Law, National Taiwan University

myownstuff@hotmail.com, d97944007@csie.ntu.edu.tw, d97a21003@ntu.edu.tw,

filawsof@ntu.edu.tw, tanchiauju@ntu.edu.tw, sdlin@csie.ntu.edu.tw

摘要

法律審判體系大致可分為成文法(civil law)與判例法(common law)。台灣的法律體系屬於成文法，其中刑法明訂屬於犯罪行為的不法行為，以及這些犯罪行為所對應的刑罰。

然而，儘管法律條文已明確列出各種犯罪行為，在於實際判斷上仍具有模糊地帶，例如刑法中「強盜罪」與「恐嚇取財罪」具有類似不法構成要素[1, 2]：刑法第 328 條第 1 項定義普通強盜罪：「意圖為自己或第三人不法之所有，以強暴、脅迫、藥劑、催眠術或他法，至使不能抗拒，而取他人之物或使其交付者，

為強盜罪，處五年以上有期徒刑」；刑法第 346 條第 1 項定義恐嚇取財罪：「意圖為自己或第三人不法之所有，以恐嚇使人將本人或第三人之物交付者，處六月以上五年以下有期徒刑，得併科一千元以下罰金」。兩者之最大差異[3]在於行為人的犯罪行為脅迫程度，是否足以使得被害人不能抗拒，若脅迫程度使被害人無法抗拒，則成立強盜罪，否則屬於恐嚇取財罪。

然而此差異在實際案例上，卻容易造成判斷混淆，而一旦誤判，對於嫌疑人所處之刑期影響甚鉅。例如「行為人持槍進入超商叫被害人把錢拿出來」以及「行為人持美工刀進入超商叫被害人把錢拿出來」，前者判屬強盜罪刑處五年以上有期徒刑而後者則屬恐嚇取財罪刑處五年以下有期徒刑。因此，一個能支援及協助法官判別「易有模糊地帶之相關罪行」，乃至進一步提供建議刑期的系統，便極為重要[4-6]。

要建置這樣的系統所面對的挑戰包含：首先，此系統需能自動標記法律要素標籤，以降低對人力、時間的花費；其次，此系統需根據法律要素標籤進行案件分類及量刑預測；最後，對於影響分類以及預測結果的因素亦需討論其可信度。為了解決上述的問題，本研究針對「強盜罪」與「恐嚇取財罪」定義 21 種法律要素標籤，並期望達成自動標記法律要素，接著利用法律要素資訊來分類「強盜罪」與「恐嚇取財罪」以及預測此兩種罪的判處刑期，最後討論「強盜罪」與「恐嚇取財罪」的分類特徵以及影響判刑的因素。

參考文獻

1. 林山田, *刑法通論*: 元照出版公司.
2. 林山田, *刑法各罪論*: 元照出版公司.
3. 鄭凱鴻, *「強盜」與「恐嚇取財」間*, 2003: 國防管理學院法律研究所.
4. 劉邦繡, *被告犯後態度在法院量刑上之評價—最高法院 95 年度臺上第 701 號、97 年度臺上字第 6725 號、98 年度臺上字第 5827 號判決探討*. 2011.
5. *坦白未必從寬，抗拒未必從嚴？！「竊盜罪」統計實證研究結果大公開！*. Available from: http://www.jrf.org.tw/newjrf/RTE/myform_detail2.asp?id=1289.
6. Maria Jean J. Hall, D.C., Tania Sourdin, Andrew Stranieri, and John Zeleznikow, *Supporting Discretionary Decision-Making with Information Technology: A Case Study in the Criminal Sentencing Jurisdiction*. University of Ottawa Law and Technology Journal, 2005. **2**(1).

Detecting and Correcting Syntactic Errors in Machine Translation Using Feature-Based Lexicalized Tree Adjoining Grammars

Wei-Yun Ma
Department of Computer Science
Columbia University
ma@cs.columbia.edu

Kathleen McKeown
Department of Computer Science
Columbia University
kathy@cs.columbia.edu

Abstract

Statistical machine translation has made tremendous progress over the past ten years. The output of even the best systems, however, is often ungrammatical because of the lack of sufficient linguistic knowledge. Even when systems incorporate syntax in the translation process, syntactic errors still result. To address this issue, we present a novel approach for detecting and correcting ungrammatical translations. In order to simultaneously detect multiple errors and their corresponding words in a formal framework, we use feature-based lexicalized tree adjoining grammars (FB-LTAG) [1]. In FB-LTAG, each lexical item is associated with a syntactic elementary tree, in which each node is associated with a set of feature-value pairs, called Attribute Value Matrices (AVMs). AVMs define the lexical item's syntactic usage. Our syntactic error detection works by checking the AVM values of all lexical items within a sentence using a unification framework. Thus, we use the feature structures in the AVMs to detect the error type and corresponding words. In order to simultaneously detect multiple error types and track their corresponding words, we propose a new unification method which allows the unification procedure to continue when unification fails and also to propagate the failure information to relevant words. We call the modified unification a fail propagation unification. Our approach features: 1) the use of XTAG grammar [2], a rule-based English grammar developed by linguists using the FB-LTAG formalism, 2) the ability to simultaneously detect multiple ungrammatical types and their corresponding words by using FB-LTAG's feature unifications, and 3) the ability to simultaneously correct multiple ungrammatical types based on the detection information.

Grammar checking methods are usually divided into three classes: statistic-based checking [3][4][5][6], rule-based checking [7][8][9] and syntax-based checking [10]. Our approach is a mix of rule-based checking and syntax-based checking: The XTAG English grammar is designed by linguists while the detecting procedure is based on syntactic operations which dynamically reference the grammar. In our procedure for syntactic error detection, we first decomposes each sentence hypothesis parse tree into elementary trees, followed by associating each elementary tree with AVMs through look-up in the XTAG grammar, and finally reconstruct the original parse tree out of the elementary trees using substitution and adjunction operations along with AVM unifications with fail propagation ability. Once error types and their corresponding words are detected, one is able to correct errors based on a unified consideration of all related words under the same error types. In this paper, we present some simple mechanism to handle part of the detected situations. We use our approach to detect and correct translations of six single statistical machine translation systems. The results show that most of the corrected translations are improved.

References

[1] K. Vijay-Shanker and Aravind K. Joshi. 1988. *Feature structure based tree adjoining grammar*. In Proceedings of COLING-88, pp. 714-719

[2] The XTAG-Group. 2001. *A Lexicalized Tree Adjoining Grammar for English*. Technical Report IRCS 01-03, University of Pennsylvania.

[3] Eric S. Atwell and Stephen Elliot. 1987. *Dealing with Ill-formed English Text*. The Computational Analysis of English, Longman.

[4] Md. Jahangir Alam, Naushad UzZaman, Mumit Khan. 2006. *N-gram based Statistical Grammar Checker for Bangla and English*. In Proceedings of ninth International Conference on Computer and Information Technology (ICCIT 2006), Dhaka, Bangladesh.

[5] Shih-Hung Wu, Chen-Yu Su, Tian-Jian Jiang, Wen-Lian Hsu. 2006. *An Evaluation of Adopting Language Model as the Checker of Preposition Usage*. In Proceedings of ROCLING.

[6] Anta Huang, Tsung-Ting Kuo, Ying-Chun Lai, Shou-De Lin. 2010. *Identifying Correction Rules for Auto Editing*. In Proceedings of ROCLING.

[7] Daniel Naber. 2003. *A Rule-Based Style and Grammar Checker*. Diploma Thesis. University of Bielefeld, Germany.

[8] George E. Heidorn. 2000. *Intelligent writing assistance*. A Handbook of Natural Language Processing: Techniques and Applications for the Processing of Language as Text. Marcel Dekker, New York. pp. 181-207.

[9] Sara Stymne and Lars Ahrenberg. 2010. *Using a Grammar Checker for Evaluation and Postprocessing of Statistical Machine Translation*. In LREC.

[10] Karen Jensen, George E. Heidorn, Stpehen D. Richardson (Eds.). 1993. *Natural language processing: the PLNLP approach*. Kluwer Academic Publishers

An Improvement in Cross-Language Document Retrieval Based on Statistical Models

Long-Yue WANG
Department of Computer and Information Science
University of Macau
vincentwang0229@hotmail.com

Derek F. WONG
Department of Computer and Information Science
University of Macau
derekfw@umac.mo

Lidia S. CHAO
Department of Computer and Information Science
University of Macau
lidiasc@umac.mo

Abstract

This paper presents a proposed method integrated with three statistical models including **T**ranslation model, **Q**uery generation model and **D**ocument retrieval model for cross-language document retrieval. Given a certain document in the source language, it will be translated into the target language of statistical machine translation model. The query generation model then selects the most relevant words in the translated version of the document as a query. Finally, all the documents in the target language are scored by the document searching model, which mainly computes the similarities between query and document. This method can efficiently solve the problem of translation ambiguity and query expansion for disambiguation, which are critical in Cross-Language Information Retrieval. In addition, the proposed model has been extensively evaluated to the retrieval of documents that: 1) texts are long which, as a result, may cause the model to over generate the queries; and 2) texts are of similar contents under the same topic which is hard to be distinguished by the retrieval model. After comparing different strategies, the experimental results show a significant performance of the method with the average precision close to 100%. It is of a great significance to both cross-language searching on the Internet and the parallel corpus producing for statistical machine translation systems.

Keywords: Cross-Language Document Retrieval, Statistical Machine Translation, TF-IDF, Document Translation-Based.

1. Introduction

With the flourishing development of the Internet, the amount of information from a variety of domains is rising dramatically. Although the researchers have done a lot to develop high performance and effective monolingual Information Retrieval (IR), the diversity of information source and the explosive growth of information in different languages drove a great need for IR systems that could cross language boundaries [1].

Cross-Language Information Retrieval (CLIR) has become more important for people to access the information resources written in various languages. Besides, it is of a great significance to alignment documents in multiple languages for Statistical Machine Translation (SMT) systems, of which quality is heavily dependent upon the amount of parallel sentences used in constructing the system.

In this paper, we focus on the problems of translation ambiguity, query generation and searching score which are keys to the retrieval performance. First of all, in order to increase the probability that the best translation can be selected from multiple ones, which occurs in the target documents, the context and the most likely probability of the whole sentence should be considered. So we apply document translation approach using SMT model instead of query translation, although the latter one may require fewer computational resources. After the source documents are translated into the target language, the problem is transformed from bilingual environment to monolingual one, where conventional IR techniques can be used for document retrieval. Secondly, some terms in a certain document will be selected as query, which can distinguish the document from others. However, some of the words occur too frequently to be useful, which cannot distinguish target documents. This mostly includes two types, one is that the word frequency is high both in the current and the whole document set, which is usually classified as stop word; the other is that the frequency is moderate in several documents (not the whole document set). This type of words gives low discrimination power to the document, and is known as low discrimination word. Thus, the query generation model should filter the words which are of these types and pick the words that occur more frequently in a certain document while less frequently in the whole document set. Finally, the document searching model scores each document according to the similarity between generated query and the document. This model should give a higher mark to the target document which covers the most relevant words in the given query.

There are two cases to be considered when we investigated the method. In one case, both the source and target documents are long text, which are hard to extract exact query from the large amounts of information. In the other case, the contents of the documents are very similar, which are not easy to distinguish for retrieval. The results of experiments reveal that the proposed model shows a very good performance in dealing with both cases.

The paper is organized as follows. The related works are reviewed and discussed in Section 2. The proposed CLIR approach based on statistical models is described in Section 3. The resources and configurations of experiments for evaluating the system are detailed in Section 4. Results, discussion and comparison between different strategies are given in Section 5 followed by a conclusion and future improvements to end the paper.

2. Related Work

CLIR is the circumstance in which a user tries to search a set of documents written in one language for a query in another language [2]. The issues of CLIR have been discussed from different perspectives for several decades. In this section, we briefly describe some related methods.

On the matching strategies for CLIR, query translation is most widely used method due to its tractability. However, it is relatively difficult to resolve the problem of term ambiguity because "queries are often short and short queries provide little context for disambiguation" [3]. Hence, some researchers have used document translation method as the opposite strategies to improve translation quality, since more varied context within each document is available for translation [4, 5].

However, another problem introduced based on this approach is word (term) disambiguation, because a word may have multiple possible translations [3]. Significant efforts have been devoted to this problem. Davis and Ogden [6] applied a part-of-speech (POS) method which requires POS tagging software for both languages. Marcello et al. presented a novel statistical method to score and rank the target documents by integrating probabilities computed by query-translation model and query-document model [7]. However, this approach cannot aim at describing how users actually create queries which have a key effect on the retrieval performance. Due to the availability of parallel corpora in multiple languages, some authors have tried to extract beneficial information for CLIR by using SMT techniques. Sánchez-Martínez et al. [8] applied SMT technology to generate and translate queries in order to retrieve long documents.

Some researchers like Marcello, Sánchez-Martínez et al. have attempted to estimate translation probability from a parallel corpus according to a well-known algorithm developed by IBM [9]. The algorithm can automatically generate a bilingual term list with a set of probabilities that a term is translated into equivalents in another language from a set of sentence alignments included in a parallel corpus. The IBM Model 1 is the simplest among the five models and often used for CLIR. The fundamental idea of the Model 1 is to estimate each translation probability so that the probability represented is maximized

$$P(t \mid s) = \frac{\varepsilon}{(l+1)^m} \prod_{j=1}^{m} \sum_{i=0}^{l} P(t_j \mid s_i) \tag{1}$$

where t is a sequence of terms $t_1, ..., t_m$ in the target language, s is a sequence of terms $s_1, ..., s_l$ in the source language, $P(t_j|s_i)$ is the translation probability, and $\mathcal{E}$ is a parameter ($\mathcal{E} = P(m|e)$), where e is target language and m is the length of source language). Eq. (1) tries to balance the probability of translation, and the query selection, in which problem still exists: it tends to select the terms consisting of more words as query because of its less frequency, while cutting the length of terms may affect the quality of translation. Besides, the IBM model 1 only proposes translations word-by-word and ignores the context words in the query. This observation suggests that a disambiguation process can be added to select the correct translation words [3]. However, in our method, the conflict can be resolved through contexts.

3. Proposed Model

The approach relies on three models: translation model which generates the most probable translation of source documents; query generation model which determines what words in a document might be more favorable to use in a query; and document searching model, which evaluates the similarity between a given query and each document in the target document set. The workflow of the approach for CLIR is shown in Fig. 1.

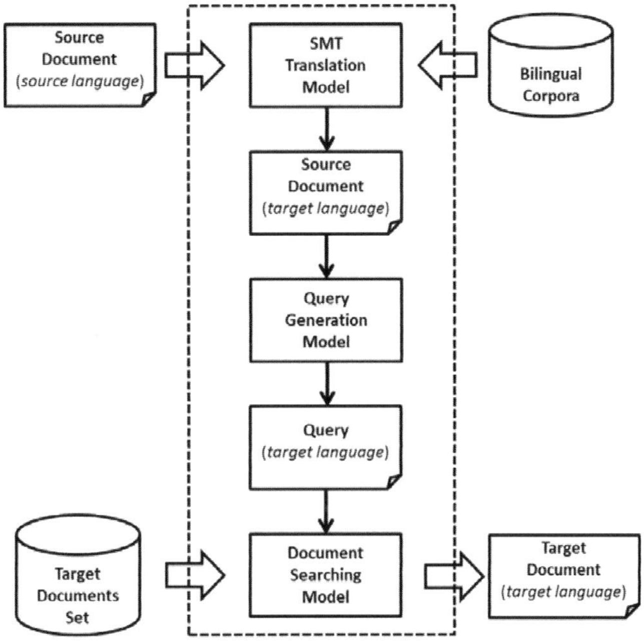

Figure 1. Approach for CLIR

3.1. Translation Model

Currently, the good performing statistical machine translation systems are based on phrase-based models which translate small word sequences at a time. Generally speaking, translation model is common for contiguous sequences of words to translate as a whole. Phrasal translation is certainly significant for CLIR [10], as stated in Section 1. It can do a good job in dealing with term disambiguation.

In this work, documents are translated using the translation model provided by Moses, where the log-linear model is considered for training the phrase-based system models [11], and is represented as:

$$p(e_1^I \mid f_1^J) = \frac{\exp(\sum_{m=1}^{M} \lambda_m h_m(e_1^I, f_1^J))}{\sum_{e'^I_1} \exp(\sum_{m=1}^{M} \lambda_m h_m(e'^I_1, f_1^J))} \tag{2}$$

where h_m indicates a set of different models, λ_m means the scaling factors, and the denominator can be ignored during the maximization process. The most important models in Eq. (2) normally are phrase-based models which are carried out in source to target and target to source directions. The source document will maximize the equation to generate the translation including the words most likely to occur in the target document set.

3.2. Query Generation Model

After translating the source document into the target language of the translation model, the system should select a certain amount of words as a query for searching instead of using the whole translated text. It is for two reasons, one is computational cost, and the other is that the unimportant words will degrade the similarity score. This is also the reason why it often responses nothing from the search engines on the Internet when we choose a whole text as a query.

In this paper, we apply a classical algorithm which is commonly used by the search engines as a central tool in scoring and ranking relevance of a document given a user query. Term Frequency–Inverse Document Frequency (TF-IDF) calculates the values for each word in a document through an inverse proportion of the frequency of the word in a particular document to the percentage of documents where the word appears [12]. Given a document collection *D*, a word *w*, and an individual document $d \in D$, we calculate

$$P(w,d) = f(w,d) \times \log \frac{|D|}{f(w,D)} \tag{3}$$

where $f(w, d)$ denotes the number of times *w* that appears in *d*, $|D|$ is the size of the corpus, and $f(w,D)$ indicates the number of documents in which *w* appears in *D* [13].

In implementation, if *w* is an Out-of-Vocabulary term (OOV), the denominator $f(w,D)$ becomes zero, and will be problematic (divided by zero). Thus, our model makes $log\ (|D|/ f(w,D))=1$ ($IDF=1$) when this situation occurs. Additionally, a list of stop-words in the target language are also used in query generation to remove the words which are high frequency but less discrimination power. Numbers are also treated as useful terms in our model, which also play an important role in distinguishing the documents. Finally, after evaluating and ranking all the words in a document by their scores, we take a portion of the (*n*-best) words for constructing the query and are guided by:

$$Size_q = [\lambda_{percent} \times Len_d] \tag{4}$$

$Size_q$ is the number of terms. $\lambda_{percent}$ is the percentage and is manually defined, which determines the $Size_q$ according to Len_d, the length of the document. The model uses the first $Size_q$-th words as the query. In another word, the larger document, the more words are selected as the query.

3.3. Document Retrieval Model

In order to use the generated query for retrieving documents, the core algorithm of the document retrieval model is derived from the Vector Space Model (VSM). Our system takes this model to calculate the similarity of each indexed document according to the input query. The final scoring formula is given by:

$$Score(q,d) = coord(q,d) \sum_{t_{in}q} tf(t,d) \times idf(t) \times bst \times norm(t,d) \tag{5}$$

where $tf(t,d)$ is the term frequency factor for term *t* in document *d*, $idf(t)$ is the inverse document frequency of term *t*, while $coord(q,d)$ is frequency of all the terms in query occur in a document. *bst* is a weight for each term in the query. $Norm(t,d)$ encapsulates a few (indexing time) boost and length factors, for instance, weights for each document and field.

As a summary, many factors that could affect the overall score are taken into account in this model.

4. Model Evaluation

4.1. Datasets

In order to evaluate the retrieval performance of the proposed model on text of cross languages, we use the Europarl corpus which is the collection of parallel texts in 11 languages from the proceedings of the European Parliament [13]. The corpus is commonly used for the construction and evaluation of statistical machine translation[1]. The corpus consists of spoken records held at the European Parliament and are labeled with corresponding IDs (e.g. <CHAPTER *id*>, <SPEAKER *id*>). The corpus is quite suitable for use in training the proposed probabilistic models between different language pairs (e.g. English-Spanish, English-French, English-German, etc.), as well as for evaluating retrieval performance of the system.

Among the existing CLIR approaches, the work of Sánchez-Martínez et al. [8] based on SMT techniques and IBM Model 1 is very closed to our approach proposed in this paper. We take it as the benchmark and compare our model against this standard. In order to be able to compare with their results, we used the same datasets (training and testing data) for this evaluation. The chapters from April 1998 to October 2006 were used as a training set for model construction, both for training the Language Model (LM) and Translation Model (TM). While the chapters from April 1996 to March 1998 were considered as the testing set for evaluating the performance of the model.

We split the test set into two parts: (1) TestSet1, where each chapter (split by <CHAPTER *id*> label) is treated as a document, for tackling the large amount of information in long texts. (2) TestSet2, where each paragraph (split by <SPEAKER *id*> label) is treated as a document, for dealing with the low discrimination power. The analytical data of the corpus are presented in Table 1. There are 1,022 documents in TestSet1, which is the number chapter that the data contains. The average document length of this dataset is 5,612 words. In TestSet2, after processing, the data contain 23,342 documents (<SPEAKER *id*> level) which are the splitting 1,022 chapters (<CHAPTER *id*> level) from TestSet1. 22 out of 100 documents are in the same topic (<CHAPTER *id*> level). Table 1 summarizes the number of documents, sentences, words and the average word number of each document.

Table 1. Analytical Data of Corpus

Dataset	Size of corpus			
	Documents	**Sentences**	**Words**	**Ave. words in document**
Training Set	2,900	1,902,050	23,411,545	50
TestSet1	1,022	80,000	5,735,464	6,612
TestSet2	23,342	80,000	7,217,827	309

4.2. Experimental Setup

In order to evaluate our proposed model, the following tools have been used.

[1] Available online at http://www.statmt.org/europarl/.

The probabilistic LMs are constructed on monolingual corpora by using the SRILM [15]. We use GIZA++ [16] to train the word alignment models for different pairs of languages of the Europarl corpus, and the phrase pairs that are consistent with the word alignment are extracted. For constructing the phrase-based statistical machine translation model, we use the open source Moses [17] toolkit, and the translation model is trained based on the log-linear model, as given in Eq. (2). The workflow of constructing the translation model is illustrated in Fig. 2 and it consists of the following main steps[2]:

(1) Preparation of aligned parallel corpus.

(2) Preprocessing of training data: tokenization, case conversion, and sentences filtering where sentences with length greater than fifty words are removed from the corpus in order to comply with the requirement of Moses.

(3) A 5-gram LM is trained on Spanish data with the SRILM toolkits.

(4) The phrased-based STM model is therefore trained on the prepared parallel corpus (English-Spanish) based on log-linear model of by using the nine-steps suggested in Moses.

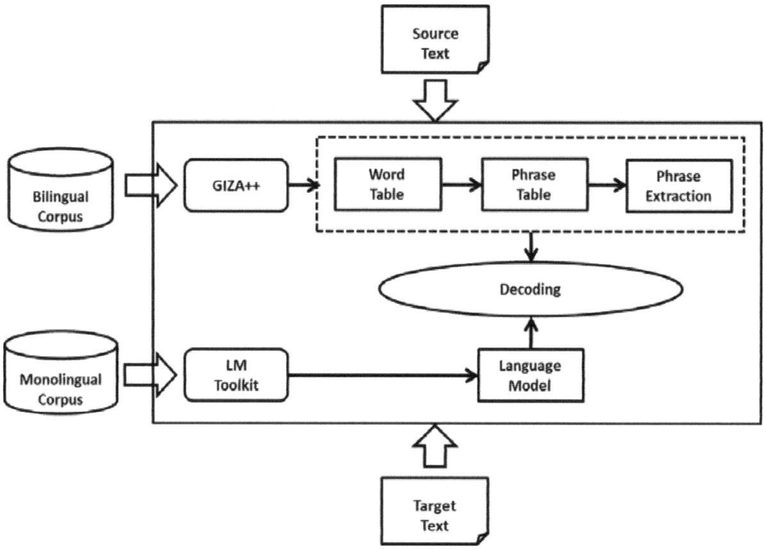

Figure 2. Main workflow of training phase

Once LM and TM have been obtained, we evaluate the proposed method with the following steps:

(1) The source documents are first translated into target language using the constructed translation model.

(2) The words candidates are computed and ranked based on a TF - IDF algorithm and the n-best words candidates then are selected to form the query based on Eq. (3) and (4).

[2] See http://www.statmt.org/wmt09/baseline.html for a detailed description of MOSES training options.

(3) All the target documents are stored and indexed using Apache Lucene[3] as our default search engine.

(4) In retrieval, target documents are scored and ranked by using the document retrieval model to return the list of most related documents with Eq. (5).

5. Results and Discussion

A number of experiments have been performed to investigate our proposed method on different settings. In order to evaluate the performance of the three independent models, we also conducted experiments to test them respectively before whole the CLIR experiment. The performance of the method is evaluated in terms of the average precision, that is, how often the target document is included within the first N-best candidate documents when retrieved.

Table 2. The average precision in Monolingual Environment

Retrieved Documents (*N*-Best)	**Query Size ($Size_q$ in %)**						
	2	**4**	**8**	**10**	**14**	**18**	**20**
1	0.794	0.910	0.993	0.989	0.986	1.000	0.989
5	0.921	0.964	1.000	1.000	1.000	1.000	0.996
10	0.942	0.971	1.000	1.000	1.000	1.000	0.996
20	0.946	0.978	1.000	1.000	1.000	1.000	0.996

5.1. Monolingual Environment Information Retrieval

In this experiment, we want to evaluate the performance of the proposed system to retrieve documents (monolingual environment) given the query. It supposes that the translations of source documents are available, and the step to obtain the translation for the input document can therefore be neglected. Under such assumptions, the CLIR problem can be treated as normal IR in monolingual environment. In conducting the experiment, we used all of the source documents of TestSet1. The steps are similar to that of the testing phase as described in Section 4.2, excluding the translation step. The empirical results based on different configurations are presented in Table 2, where the first column gives the number of documents returned against the number of words/terms used as the query.

The results show that the proposed method gives very high retrieval accuracy, with precision of 100%, when the top 18% of the words are used as the query. In case of taking the top 5 candidates of documents, the approach can always achieve a 100% of retrieval accuracy with query sizes between 8% and 18%. This fully illustrates the effectiveness of the retrieval model.

5.2. Translation Quality

The overall retrieval performance of the system will be affected by the quality of translation. In order to have an idea the performance of the translation model we built, we employ the commonly used evaluation metric, BLEU, for such measure. The BLEU (Bilingual Evaluation Understudy) is a classical automatic evaluation method for the translation quality of an MT system [18]. In this evaluation, the translation model is created using the parallel corpus, as described in Section 4. We use another 5,000 sentences from the TestSet1 for

[3] Available at http://lucene.apache.org.

evaluation[4].

The BLEU value, we obtained, is **32.08**. The result is higher than that of the results reported by Koehn in his work [14], of which the BLEU score is **30.1** for the same language pair we used in Europarl corpora. Although we did not use exactly the same data for constructing the translation model, the value of **30.1** was presented as a baseline of the English-Spanish translation quality in Europarl corpora.

The BLEU score shows that our translation model performs very well, due to the large number of the training data we used and the pre-processing tasks we designed for cleaning the data. On the other hand, it reveals that the translation quality of our model is good.

5.3. Evaluation of CLIR Model

In this section, the proposed CLIR model is compared against the approach proposed by Sánchez-Martínez et al. Table 3 presents the retrieval results given by his model. As illustrated, the best precision of the model can achieve up to 97% in precision, counting that the desired document is returned as the most relevant document among the candidates. In his method, both the probability of the translations and the relevance of the terms are taken into account in the retrieval model. The model is created based on IBM Model 1, Eq. (1), however, it still has a problem as we stated in Section 2.

Table 3. The average precision of Sánchez-Martínez et al.

Retrieved Documents (*N*-Best)	**Query size (Num. of word in query)**			
	1	**2**	**5**	**10**
1	0.32	0.51	0.84	**0.97**
2	0.43	0.63	0.90	0.98
5	0.51	0.73	**0.95**	0.99
10	0.55	0.77	0.97	1.00
20	0.56	0.80	0.98	1.00

Table 4. The retrieval results on TestSet1

Retrieved Documents (*N*-Best)	**Query Size ($Size_q$ in %)**						
	1.0	**1.4**	**1.8**	**2.0**	**3.0**	**6.0**	**10.0**
1	0.90	0.93	0.95	0.97	0.99	**1.00**	0.99
5	0.98	0.98	0.99	0.99	0.99	**1.00**	0.99
10	0.98	0.98	0.99	0.99	1.00	1.00	1.00
20	0.98	0.99	1.00	1.00	1.00	1.00	1.00

In order to obtain a higher retrieval precision, our model has been improved from different points. First, we only use individual words, instead of phrases, as well as numbers as query, which can alleviate the scarcity of tending to select long phrases that are less occurred in the training data. Secondly, our method can do better in dealing with the problem of term disambiguation because of the phrase-based SMT system, which takes a wider context of sentence in producing considers the translation. Last but not least, we did not use a fixed number of query words, instead portion of most relevant words is considered for different input of the document, Eq. (4). In other words, the longer the document, the more words will

[4] See http://www.statmt.org/wmt09/baseline.html for a detailed description of MOSES evaluation options.

be used for retrieval of the target documents. So the $Size_q$ is considered as a hidden variable in our document retrieval model.

What still needs to be explained is that the metrics in Table 3 and 4 are different. One experiment selected *static number* of words for a query, so all the queries have the same size; while the other one considers the *percentage* of the document length as its corresponding query size. Although it is hard to compare with their performances from corresponding columns, the improvements can be seen clearly when the desired document is among the first *N* (*N*=1, 2, 5, 10, 20) documents retrieved. Reviewing the experimental results presented in Tables 3 and 4, it shows that our model is able to give an improvement of 2% in precision and achieves 99% of success rate, in the case that the desired candidate is ranked in the first place. Moreover, the success rates achieved by our proposed model in different levels in all tests are above 90%.

As expected, the more the words we used to generate the query, the more the documents returned, and the higher the rate that the target document is retrieved within the candidates list.

However, the documents in TestSet1 are too large to align sentences from document level for further work, because a large document includes more sentences, which not only need more computational cost but also lead to higher error rate during sentence alignment. One way to solve this problem is to further split the large document and to retrieve it in a smaller document size. The problem in this case is that word overlap between a query and a wrong document is more probable when the document and the query are expressed in the same language. Furthermore, similar documents may include the same translation of words in the query, because the document retrieval model does not consider the weight of each word in the query which results in using more words to distinguish. This is the reason why different query size is used in Table 4 and 5, in order to guarantee the comparable retrieval performance on different types of documents.

Table 5. The retrieval results on TestSet2

Retrieved Documents (*N*-Best)	**Query Size ($Size_q$ in %)**						
	10	**15**	**20**	**25**	**30**	**35**	**40**
1	0.884	0.936	0.964	0.972	0.983	0.987	0.990
5	0.944	0.970	0.984	0.989	0.992	0.993	0.995
10	0.955	0.977	0.987	0.991	0.993	0.994	0.996
20	0.966	0.984	0.991	0.992	0.994	0.994	0.997

As we stated in Section 4.1, TestSet2 is another concern. The results obtained are presented in Table 5. On average, the success rate is normally above 90% (in precision) by using a larger query size. It can even achieve 99.5% when the 5-best candidates are considered in the retrieval results. This result indicates that the reliable estimation of the profanities is more important than the plausibility of the probabilistic models. This fully illustrates the discrimination power of the proposed method.

6. Conclusion

This article presents a TQD statistical approach for CLIR which has been explored for both large and similar documents retrieval. Different from the traditional parallel corpora-based model which relies on IBM algorithm, we divided our CLIR model into three independent parts but all work together to deal with the term disambiguation, query generation and document retrieval. The performances showed that this method can do a good job of CLIR for not only large documents but also the similar documents.

The speed efficiency may be another big issue in our approach as some researchers have stated[2]. However, with the increasing of computing ability in hardware and software, there will be no difference in speed efficiency between query and document translation-based CLIR. Besides, our system only translates a certain amount of the source document to be retrieved instead of all the indexed target documents.

Acknowledgement

This work was partially supported by the Research Committee of University of Macau under grant UL019B/09-Y3/EEE/LYP01/FST, and also supported by Science and Technology Development Fund of Macau under grant 057/2009/A2.

References

[1] L. Ballesteros and W. B. Croft, "Statistical methods for cross-language information retrieval," *Cross-language information retrieval*, pp. 23-40, 1998.

[2] K. Kishida, "Technical issues of cross-language information retrieval: a review," *Information Processing & Management*, pp. 433-455, 41, 3 2005.

[3] D. W. Oard and A. R. Diekema, "Cross-language information retrieval," *Annual review of Information science*, 33, pp. 223–256, 1998.

[4] M. Braschler and P. Schauble, "Experiments with the eurospider retrieval system for clef 2000," *Cross-Language Information Retrieval and Evaluation*, pp. 140-148, 2001.

[5] M. Franz et al, "Ad hoc, cross-language and spoken document information retrieval at IBM," NIST Special Publication: *The 8th Text Retrieval Conference,* TREC-8, 1999.

[6] M. W. Davis and W. C. Ogden, "Quilt: Implementing a large-scale cross-language text retrieval system," *ACM SIGIR Forum*, pp. 92-98, 31, SI 1997.

[7] M. Federico and N. Bertoldi, "Statistical cross-language information retrieval using n-best query translations," *Proceedings of the 25th annual international ACM SIGIR conference on Research and development in information retrieval*, pp. 167-174, 2002.

[8] F. Sanchez-Martinez and R. C. Carrasco, "Document translation retrieval based on statistical machine translation techniques," *Applied Artificial Intelligence*, pp. 329-340, 25, 5 2011.

[9] P. F. Brown et al, "The mathematics of statistical machine translation: Parameter estimation," *Computational linguistics*, pp. 263-311, 19, 2 1993.

[10] L. Ballesteros and W. B. Croft, "Phrasal translation and query expansion techniques for cross-language information retrieval," *ACM SIGIR Forum*, pp. 84-91. 31, SI 1997.

[11] F. J. Och, H. Ney, "Discriminative Training and Maximum Entropy Models for Statistical Machine Translation," In *Proceedings of the 40th Annual Meeting of the Association for Computational Linguistics (ACL)*, pp. 295–302, Philadelphia, PA, July

(2002)

[12]J. Ramos, "Using tf-idf to determine word relevance in document queries," *Proceedings of the First Instructional Conference on Machine Learning*, 2003.

[13]A. Berger et al, "Bridging the lexical chasm: statistical approaches to answer-finding," *Proceedings of the 23rd annual international ACM SIGIR conference on Research and development in information retrieval*, pp. 192-199, 2000.

[14]P. Koehn, "Europarl: A parallel corpus for statistical machine translation," *MT summit*, 5, 2005.

[15]A. Stolcke, "SRILM-an extensible language modeling toolkit," *Seventh International Conference on Spoken Language Processing*, 2002.

[16]F. J. Och and H. Ney, "A systematic comparison of various statistical alignment models," *Computational linguistics*. pp. 19-51, 29, 1 2003.

[17]P. Koehn et al, "Moses: Open source toolkit for statistical machine translation," *Proceedings of the 45th Annual Meeting of the ACL on Interactive Poster and Demonstration Sessions*, pp. 177-180, 2007.

[18]K. Papineni et al, "BLEU: a method for automatic evaluation of machine translation," *Proceedings of the 40th annual meeting on association for computational linguistics*, pp. 311-318, 2002.

English-to-Traditional Chinese Cross-lingual Link Discovery in Articles with Wikipedia Corpus

Liang-Pu Chen[†*], Yu-Lun Shih[‡], Chien-Ting Chen[♭], Tsun Ku[†], Wen-Tai Hsieh[†], Hung-Sheng Chiu[†], Ren-Dar, Yang[†]

[†]IDEAS, Institute for Information Industry, Taiwan
[‡]CSIE, National Taipei Univeristy of Technology, Taiwan
[♭]ISA, National Tsing Hua Univeristy, Taiwan

[*]corresponding author

eit@iii.org.tw, t100598029@ntut.org.tw, s961441@gmail.com, {cujing, wentai, bbchiu, rdyang}iii.org.tw

Abstract

In this paper, we design a processing flow to produce linked data in articles, providing anchor-based term's additional information and related terms in different languages (English to Chinese). Wikipedia has been a very important corpus and knowledge bank. Although Wikipedia describes itself not a dictionary or encyclopedia, it is if high potential values in applications and data mining researches. Link discovery is a useful IR application, based on Data Mining and NLP algorithms and has been used in several fields. According to the results of our experiment, this method does make the result has improved.

摘要

本篇論文中提出了一套自動化流程以發掘潛在的關鍵字連結，並且在找出文章關鍵字後能夠提供關鍵字於跨語言的相關資訊，而我們利用了Wikipedia做爲我們的知識庫，藉由Wikipedia的資料，系統能夠提供相關的關鍵字內容資訊，進而幫助使用者閱讀文章。論文中所提出的系統整合了相關的資訊檢索技術以及自然語言處理相關的演算法，以利於幫助我們進行關鍵字的識別以及相關的跨語言翻譯，同時系統整合了跨語連結發掘的技巧來幫助提供跨語言的關鍵字資訊。經過初步的實驗證實，相較於baseline方法，此方法確實能夠始數據有所提昇。

Keywords: Cross-lingual link discovery, Linked data, Wikipedia, Link Discovery
關鍵字: 跨語連結發掘, 資料連結, 維基百科, 連結發掘

1 Introduction

For our goal, we have to conquer some issues to find every potential linked data on articles. This paper focuses on Cross-lingual link discovery. Cross-lingual link discovery contains a lot of important tasks of NLP(Natural Language Processing) such as WSD(Word Sense Disambiguation) [1], NED(Named Entities Disambiguation) [2] or Machine Translation. The cross-lingual links in the Wikipedia[1] are established by the human contributors, and not all Wikipedia Pages have cross lingual links because no human editors established these links yet. Thus, when one visits English Wikipedia page which describes some special information, users cannot find any cross lingual link to visit the Wikipedia page whose language is the same as the user's mother tongue. This problem has been raised by many recent studies [3,4] , and recovering these missing links between two languages is the main goal of the CLLD (Cross-Lingual Link Discovery). In this paper, we propose a system which can automatically help users to tag potential links in

[1]http://wikipedia.org

their articles, and automatically find out the cross language link of the tag based on Wikipedia cross language links. As for cross lingual link discovery, our system is able to find the missing links between two related Wikipedia pages in two different language systems by exploiting and extracting data from Wikipedia dump files in two languages. In addition, we use two additional translation mechanisms to help find out the corresponding cross lingual translation , one is the *Pattern Translate* , the other one is *Google Translate*[2]. We further integrate the *Lucene*[3] software package to deal with the ambiguous phases in the articles. In order to find out the missing links between two pages, and automatically tagged this cross language link in users' articles.

The remainder of this paper is organized as follows: First, we described corresponding background of Wikipedia and cross-lingual link discovery in Section 2. In Section 3,The proposed WSD method and translation mechanism will be described in detail. Finally, the experiment and conclusion will be discussed in Section 4.

2 Background

2.1 Wikipedia

Wikipedia is a free, collaboratively edited, and multilingual Internet encyclopedia supported by the non-profit Wikimedia Foundation[4]. Recently, many researchers focus on developing data mining applications with Wikipedia's large-scale collaborative user data. Although Wikipedia describes itself not a dictionary, textbook or encyclopedia, exploiting its characteristics to develop new services is regarded as a promising method on auto text explanation.

One of the special feature of Wikipedia is that it contains many hypertext links to help users easily retrieve the information they need. These hypertext links might be embedded within the text content under the corresponding pages, and each of these links is linking to other pages related with different terms. Obviously, information flow is thus being traversed very easy and smoothing when the hypertext links are extensively tagged. Unfortunately, the hypertext links between different languages are mostly not being tagged because of the hypertext link is generated by human contributor, mostly monolingual ones. To solve this problem, we design a process flow trying to make it more completely.

2.2 Cross-lingual link discovery

The goal of cross-lingual link discovery(CLLD) is trying to find the potential links that are missing between the two different languages. There are three main challenges for the system to overcome. First, the system providing solution on CLLD can proactively recommends a set of words which called anchors. The set of words have higher chances to have their corresponding cross lingual links than other words in the same article. For example, considering different cases as following:

1. Let's go *dutch*.
2. A *Dutch* auction is a type of auction that starts with a high bid.

The system must determine the boundaries between anchor and rest of words, considering the first case above, the word "dutch" is meaning to share the money on something instead of meaning some behavior or something related to the country "Holland". In other words, the

[2]http://translate.google.com
[3]http://lucene.apache.org
[4]http://en.wikipedia.org/wiki/Wikipedia

word "dutch" should not be chosen as an anchor here and choosing the phase of "go dutch" is more significant. Considering the second case above, the word "Dutch auction" is an appropriate anchor rather than "Dutch".

After the system identifies these anchors, there must exist many highly ambiguous cases in these anchors and this is the second challenge of CLLD, for example, the anchor *Apple* can be refer to the link which is related with *Apple(Computer Manufacturer)*, or the link which is related to *Apple(Fruit)*. The system must be able to choosing the most related corresponding links and also ensure the correctness of link discovery.

Once the system can return the most related links of each anchor, there is only one more problem need to solve. In the end of the CLLD flow, the system have to automatically discover the cross-lingual link based on the anchors which generated from previous steps. The system can just use simple parser or crawler to check the content of corresponding wikipedia page or combines some different mechanism to increase the accuracy of link discovery. In this paper, we implement these CLLD steps to help us find the corresponding cross-lingual links and we focus on anchor disambiguation and cross-lingual link discovery, which are both described in Section 3.

3 Method and System Description

In English-to-Chinese cross-lingual link discovery, the goal is to find every potential links in documents. At first, the system searches out potential terms as candidate terms. Overlapping problem happens in this stage, and adequate candidate term selection is required. We propose an *similarity-scoring* formula to calculate score of relevance. When candidate terms are selected, relevant pages in Chinese Wikipedia need to be linked with these terms. There are some cross-lingual articles in Wikipedia; however, many more links are still missed. (eg. *"Hundred Schools of Thought" with "*諸子百家").

3.1 Candidates finding

To find cross-lingual links in a language, every potential term or phrase is to be listed in the beginning. Here we adopt n-gram tokenizer [5] and Maximum Matching algorithm [6] to segment. For example, assume a sentence "Magic Johnson is one of the best basketball player in NBA", in our method , our approach will take "Magic Johnson" as an anchor rather than "Magic" or "John". The system will first examine the longer term in the sentence and exploit the Wikipedia as a anchor look-up table to check whether this long term is meaningful or not.

3.2 Anchor decision

Many terms in Wikipedia have the same title but different meanings depending on their occurrences in contexts. To address this problem, Wikipedia has already define it as "Disambiguation". In our system, we use redirect page, providing disambiguation information and candidate terms, to analysis and select one from terms for users by this system. For instance, a term "Virus" is shown in "A virus is a parasitic agent that is smaller than a bacterium and that can only reproduce after infecting a host cell." and "Virus (clothing), an Israeli clothing brand"...etc. It indicates users may look out the clothing brand but Wikipedia gives him a virus' definition in biology domain.

$$SimilarityScore(D_i, D_j) = \frac{TermRecog(D_i) \bigcap TermRecog(D_j)}{TermRecog(D_i) \bigcup TermRecog(D_j)} \quad (1)$$

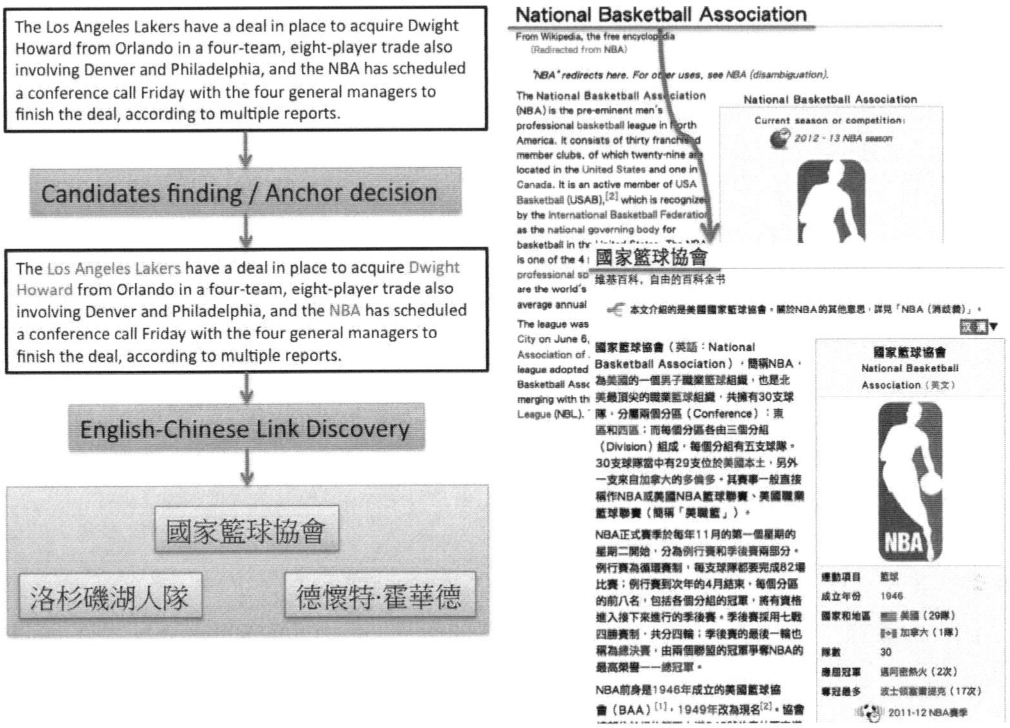

Figure 1: Processing flow of our system.

$$Anchor = max(SimilarityScore(D_{current}, D_i)), \forall i \in candidates \tag{2}$$

In our work, we design a content-aware approach to perform auto selection among disambiguation terms. Our design principle is to analyze the input article, especially the source of terms, and use full-featured text search engine with a prepared index file. If a term has the disambiguation property, the system will extract the features from article and search the existed index to decide which term is more likely to the source article.

3.3 English-Chinese Link Discovery

In this section, we describe how we translate the anchor first and than how we find the cross lingual Wikipedia link after the translation. There are two main approaches of the translation mechanism, namely ***Cross-Lingual Link Dictionary and Google Translate***. We first use a ***Cross-Lingual Link Dictionary*** as the translation scheme, once if ***Cross-Lingual Link Dictionary*** can not provide any corresponding translation, ***Google Translate*** is then used by the system to discover the corresponding translation from the online *Machine Translation mechanism*. Google Translate is a state-of-the-art online commercial machine translation scheme, and it is exploited by our system to trying find out some possible translation when there doesn't have any corresponding translation which can be provided by the ***Cross-Lingual Link Dictionary***. With the support by the Google Translate, the system can provide higher translation coverage compared to using Cross-Lingual Link Dictionary only. We will describe the detail about the two translation mechanisms below and will also discuss the missing link recovery approach in the end of this section.

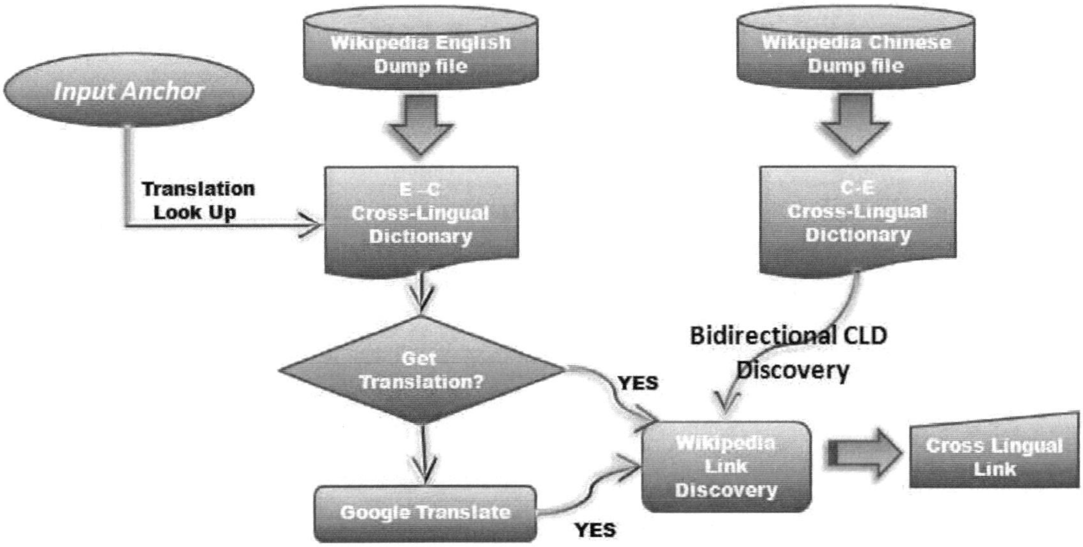

Figure 2: Flow of our English-Chinese Link Discovery system.

3.4 Anchor Translation Mechanisms and Missing Link Recovery

3.4.1 Google Translate

We first describe the Google Translate here because we are going to introduce the translation and missing link recovery within Cross-Lingual Dictionary in the end of this section together.

Google Translate has been a famous automatic translation mechanism, one distinguishing feature of this online translator is that it enables users to choose different languages that users want to translate. As for whole sentence translations, the users have a chance to modify the translation sentence once they find the output translation inadequate. As Google collects enough user data of modifying the translation sentence, Google Translator gets higher translation accuracy.

Although Google Translate has such special characteristic, it can not providing good accuracy at Anchor translation [7]. However, there is a special characteristic of Google Translate; that is, it can provide more possible translation candidates than previous methods such like Cross-Lingual Link Dictionary. The reason is that Google Translate is tends to adopt a best-effort approach, it aims to provide many translation candidates which enable users to understand what the untranslated sentence might be supposed to mean.

As a result, we put the lowest translation priority in Google Translate, namely, once the previous method(*Cross-Lingual Dictionary*) can not find out any possible translation candidates, we will try to get some translation suggested from Google Translate. The main reason is just what we describe above, we want to take a chance to find out the corresponding translation when we do not have any other translation candidate, only to use some anchor translation from Google Translate to find out the corresponding cross-language links.

For example, in our Cross-Lingual Link Dictionary, it does not contain the Chinese Translation of "***Freeway***". However, Google Translate can provide some useful Chinese translation like "高速公路", thus we can find the corresponding link of Chinese article page of Wikipedia page at "`http://zh.wikipedia.org/wiki/`".

3.4.2 Cross-Lingual Link Dictionary

Wikipedia provides a well formatted dump file for all languages. As a result, we can get the chinese translation from the english dump files and vise-versa. We exploit this property to construct both Chinese-English bilingual link dictionary and an English-Chinese bilingual link dictionary. Furthermore, once the translation in the dictionary has be found, there is a high probability that we can directly discover the link by adding the translated anchor after the specific wikipedia URL(e.g. `http://en.wikipedia.org/wiki/Computer_accessibility`), both in English and Chinese. We refer these two dictionaries as the translation dictionaries, one is the *English to Chinese (E-C) translation dictionary* and the other one is *Chinese to English (C-E) translation dictionary*. Once we use these two bilingual dictionaries as translation dictionaries, in our case, English-to-Chinese vise versa,we can have a chance to retrieve the link informations **bidirectional**. The reason is that we have noticed that links for Chinese-to-English are more than English-to-Chinese, because many Chinese editors will add English link for annotation or reference.

On link discovery part, we find out that some links may be missing in one translation dictionary, such as the term "Flag of Republic of China" is not able to found any corresponding Chinese translation in E-C translation dictionary. However, we can find the corresponding english translation of chinese term "諸子百家" in the C-E translation dictionary, which is the "*Hundred Schools of Thought*".

There is an additional problem about the English-Chinese dictionary with the Wikipedia disambiguation page. If the anchor which exist in the English-Chinese dictionary is a title of the Wikipedia disambiguation page, then we can not directly get the Chinese translation from the page content of disambiguation page. The reason is that a Wikipedia disambiguation page only contains the possible candidates that are referring to this title.

Fortunately, Wikipedia have a complete dump file format and it provide the *redirect information* of the disambiguation page. Therefore, we can using the redirect link information to find out the corresponding Chinese translation. The problem may also occur at Chinese Wikipedia disambiguation page, and it can be also solved by redirection information.

4 Results and Discussion

We use four articles as evaluation to see the performance of cross-lingual discovery, we first randomly choose four Bilingual news article from Yahoo! News, all terms in the Chinese articles are tagged by two human experts to generate correct answers. We apply two methods, the first method is tagging the English articles with English Wikipedia entries by means of long-term-first algorithm. Those tagged terms are then directly transformed into Chinese Wikipedia entries by original anchored links; the second method is to implement our proposed method, we then compare these two methods to see the coverage rates. As Figure 4 shows, the experiment result shows that our proposed method has 8% coverage rates higher than the that of direct anchor transformation method.

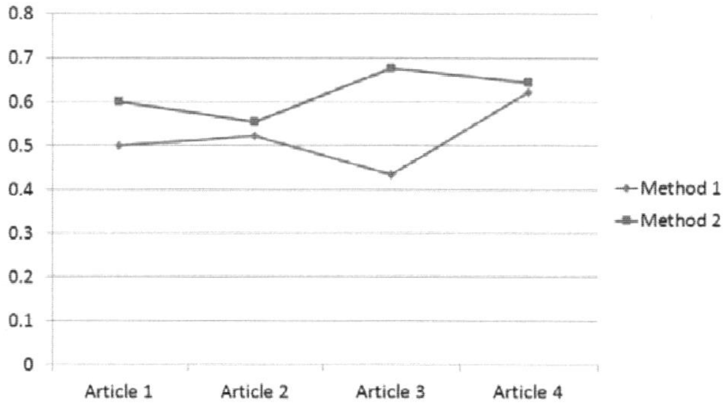

Figure 3: Results of English to Chinese link discovery.

5 Conclusion

In conclusion, we present a system to find potential cross-lingual linked data on articles, trying to discover miss cross-lingual links. The main contribution of our proposed method includes finding anchor and discovering missing cross-lingual links. We have successfully designed a practical system to perform tagging task on real-world articles. and proved that maximum match algorithm has a better performance than the original Wikipedia anchor links transformation. However, there are still issued to be improved for future work. First, the precision of WSD is still low, and second, we can apply machine learning approaches in our method, in which we are convinced that our proposed method might have higher performance in the future.

References

[1] Mihalcea and Csomai, "Wikify! linking documents to encyclopedic knowledge", in *sixteenth ACM conference*, 2007.

[2] Bunescu and Pasca, "Using encyclopedic knowledge for named entity disambiguation", in *EACL*, 2006.

[3] J. Kim and I. Gurevych, "Ukp at crosslink: Anchor text translation for cross-lingual link discovery", in *NTCIR-9*, 2011.

[4] A.F.V. Nastase and M. Strube, "Hits'graph-based system at the ntcir-9 cross-lingual link discovery task", in *NTCIR-9*, 2011.

[5] W. B. Cavnar and J. M. Trenkle., "N-gram based text categorization", in *Proceeding of the Symposium on Document Analysis and Information Retrieval*. University of Nevada, Las Vegas, 1994, pp. 161–175.

[6] Y. Shiloach Amos Israeli, "An improved parallel algorithm for maximal matching", in *Information Processing Letters*, 1986, vol. 22, pp. 57–60.

[7] Yu-Chun Wang Richard Tzong-Han Tsai Liang-Pu Chen, Chen-Ting Chen, "Exploit wikipedia and name-entity pattern as translation method on chinene-korean cross language multimedia information retrival", in *International Conference on Digital Contents*, 2009.

應用跳脫語言模型於同義詞取代之研究

Skip N-gram Modeling for Near-Synonym Choice

陳士婷 Shih-Ting Chen
元智大學資訊管理學系
Department of Information Management
Yuan Ze University
s996222@mail.yzu.edu.tw

何維晟 Wei-Cheng He
元智大學資訊管理學系
Department of Information Management
Yuan Ze University
s1006250@mail.yzu.edu.tw

關松堅 Philips Kokoh Prasetyo
Living Analytics Research Centre
Singapore Management University
philipskokoh@gmail.com

禹良治 Liang-Chih Yu
元智大學資訊管理學系
Department of Information Management
Yuan Ze University
lcyu@saturn.yzu.edu.tw

摘要

同義詞(Near-Synonym)不只在自然語言應用中是重要的一環，也是對第二語言學習者很重要的部分。同義詞雖然是一群意思相近的單字集合，但在特定的情況與特殊用法下，選擇錯誤的同義詞會造成句意上的誤解，甚至是整個文法錯誤，因此我們希望能夠藉由上下文的訊息，再利用系統分辨出正確的同義詞，來協助外語學習者做有效率的學習。目前為止已有許多同義詞的相關研究，這些研究的方法包含：點式交互資訊(Pointwise Mutual Information, PMI)與 N 連詞(N-gram)模型都是常用的方法，我們想使用與以往不同的方法來提升正確率，因此我們使用跳脫(Skip N-gram)語言模型的方法針對 SemEval-2007 資料進行實驗，結果顯示我們提出的方法是可行的，正確率也有明顯的提升。

關鍵字：同義詞、點式交互資訊、跳脫語言模型

一、緒論

詞彙語意在許多自然語言應用中扮演很重要的角色。像是”arm”這個英文單字，他就有武器(weapon)和手臂(bodypart)這兩個意思可供系統來作詞義消歧的動作。此外，同義詞在自然語言中的應用非常多。例如:arm 假設他意思等同於 weapon，與他同義的詞就包含 weapon 本身和 arsenal，在這個範例 arm 這個單字就可擴張成 weapon 和 arsenal 兩個單字，藉由這樣的性質應用在資訊檢索的詞彙擴張上，可增進其應用效益[1,2]。另外，也可利用同義詞於電腦輔助語言學習(Computer-Assisted Language Learning, CALL) [3,4]。

最近有許多關於同義詞的研究，表示有些同義詞因為他們的特殊用法與搭配上的限制，所以實際運用上是不可互換的，如以下所示：

(1) ____coffee [5]

Near-Synonym：{strong, powerful}

(2) ghastly____ [6]

Near-Synonym：{error, mistake}

(3) ____ under the bay [7]

Near-Synonym：{bridge, overpass, tunnel}

在上面的(1)和(2)兩個範例都是因上下文搭配限制的範例，範例(1)中兩個同義詞 strong, powerful 都有強大、強壯的意思，但是 strong 還有濃烈的意思，因此此句意思是濃咖啡時，正確答案應該是 strong coffee，而不可使用 powerful；範例(2)中 error, mistake 都有錯誤的意思，在這個範例中英語國家的人通常都是使用 ghastly mistake 因此應選擇 mistake，；範例(3)的同義詞集{bridge, overpass, tunnel}代表一個可以穿越障礙將分離的兩個地方連接起來的物理結構。假設在”under the bay”的上下文中，原本的單字為”tunnel”。”tunnel”這個單字無法被同義詞集裡的其他同義詞取代，因為其他同義詞的語意在這裡是不合乎情理的[7]。從上面三個範例就可知道同義詞雖是意義相近，但因為用法上的限制，所以無法完全取代與互相交換。有時以英文為母語的人都不一定能正確分辨，何況是一個學習第二語言的人在分辨上更是難上加難，所以我們希望可以藉由系統分析判斷同義詞之間的差異，來幫助語言學習者使他們能學習到正確的語言知識。

學習外語者最基本的就是從單字學起，在學習過程中，同義詞是必定會遇到的難題，原因在於同義詞反映出一個詞彙通常不只有一個意思；另一個原因是同義詞意思雖然相近，但是根據習慣以及特殊用法他們會選用特定詞彙，因此我們希望藉由上下文的訊息，讓系統能夠分辨出同義詞之間的細微差異，並選擇出正確的同義詞，以幫助第二語言學習者在學習上的效率。本研究的目的就是想使用新的研究方法來分析一個特定句子，使系統能夠自動選擇出正確的同義詞，避免選擇錯誤的同義詞造成整個句子語意上的錯誤，並讓語言學習者了解單一詞彙不只有一種意思，而是還含有其他意義，在遇到同義詞問題時可以確切明白他們之間的差異，來增加學習的效率及正確性，並且在寫作文章時也可以靈活運用同義詞，使文章更加豐富、多元。

本研究是使用跳脫語言模型(Skip N-gram)的方法對同義詞作選擇，跳脫語言模型就是將 N 連詞(N-gram)方法與跳脫式(Skip)方法做結合，N 連詞方法是利用目標詞周圍連續 N 個字詞在 Web 1T 5-gram corpus 出現的頻率去計算出 N 連詞的分數。跳脫式方法是以 N 連詞擷取出的詞組為基礎，將 N 連詞詞組中某些字詞可以為任何單字的情況下，他們在 Web 1T 5 gram corpus 中出現的次數加總，跳脫式方法是為了補強 N 連詞在 N 較大時出現頻率時常過低的缺陷，因此在 N 較大時我們使用跳脫式方法，這就是本論文提出的跳脫語言模型方法。

二、文獻探討

(一) Web 1T 5-gram

我們研究方法使用的是 Google Web 1T 5-gram corpus 做為系統消歧的語料庫，此語料庫是 Google 從 2006 年由網路上蒐集的，語料庫是由 1 到 5 連詞，以及這些連詞所出現的頻率組成，在學術上有很多研究也使用 Web 1T 5-gram 語料庫，有些學者使用 Google 語料庫來校正拼錯的英文單字[8]、有些學者利用 Google 語料庫來推斷名詞之間的語意關係[9]。表 1 為 Web 1T 5-gram 的相關資料。

表 1 Web 1T 5-gram

資料大小約 24GB	
Tokens	1,024,908,267,229
Sentences	95,119,665,584
Unigrams	13,588,391
Bigrams	314,843,401
Trigrams	977,069,902
Fourgrams	1,313,818,354
Fivegrams	1,176,470,663

(二) 詞彙選擇驗證

我們利用系統自動選擇出最適合的同義詞後，要如何驗證我們選出的同義詞是否適合上下文也是一個很重要的問題，因此有學者提出 FITB(fill-in-the-blank)任務來驗證，FITB(fill-in-the-blank)是較早的學者所研發的驗證方式，其任務內容是將句子中的目標詞去除，留下空格(gap)，將同義詞集裡的同義詞替換在空格上，然後根據各個研究學者使用不同研究方法計算出來的分數，選出最適當的同義詞後與原文做驗證，因為此方式是從原本完整的句子將正確的目標詞去除，因此在驗證時，只要將原本的目標詞和學者們選出來的同義詞作比對，就可明顯知道各個學者選取的同義詞是否適當[10,11]，圖 1 為 FITB 的中文和英文範例。

English Sentence: This will make the _____ message easier to interpret.
Original word: error
Near-synonym set: {error, mistake, oversight}

Chinese Sentence: 這 將 使 這 _____ 訊息 容易 解釋
Original word: 錯誤
Near-synonym set: {錯誤, 錯, 差錯, 失察, 過失}

圖 1 中文與英文的 FITB 驗證範例

(三) 同義詞研究

在自然語言處理的研究領域中，對於同義詞的研究非常多。Inkpen 早期研究是使用 PMI(Pointwise Mutual Information,點式交互資訊)方法[6]，PMI 就是比較兩個詞之間共同出現的機率，不同同義詞計算出不同的分數後，分數越高者就是研究者認為最適合的同義詞；Gardiner 和 Dras 也在同義詞研究上使用 PMI 的方式來判別[11]。另外也有人使用 N 連詞的方式來研究同義詞的詞意問題，Inkpen 也曾使用 N 連詞的方式做同義詞選擇的研究，N 連詞就是藉由目標字周圍連續 N 個字詞出現的頻率，計算出分數的高低，來選擇適當的同義詞[12]。除了 PMI 和 N 連詞方法外，WSD(Word sense disambiguation) 也是時常運用在同義詞選擇的方法，WSD 是藉由目標詞和同義詞是否為同義來判別[13]。Dagan 描述 WSD 是一個間接的方法，因為他需要有中間詞意確認的步驟，從而提出一個意義相配的技術來解決這項任務[14]。

三、研究方法

本章我們將先介紹資料前處理的部分，之後再介紹本論文研究方法所會運用到的觀念，最後在介紹本論文所提出的方法。

(一) 資料前處理

資料前處理的部分包含擷取同義詞、測試句以及測試句替換同義詞，因為我們處理的是英文語料，每個單字之間已有空白符號斷開，所以不用像中文語料必須經由斷詞程式將詞與詞之間斷開，以下介紹資料前處理的部分：

1. 擷取測試句:測試句中的原始資料檔為 XML 檔，並且是完整的句子，我們須將 XML 的標籤去除後，再從完整的句子中擷取出所有包含目標字的 5 連詞(5-gram)詞組，範例如表 2：

表 2 測試句擷取範例(句子來源：EIC)

範例:目標詞為 clean

原始資料:
<instance id="388"> <context>Grace has the money to <head>clean</head> up .</context> </instance>
結果:
has the money to clean the money to clean up money to clean up .

2. 擷取同義詞：同義詞的擷取方式是由同義詞檔中擷取出來，擷取範例如表 3：

表 3 同義詞擷取範例(句子來源：EIC)

原始資料:
clean.v 388 :: win 1;profit greatly 1;clear 1;prosper 1;accumulate 1;make a fortune 1;
結果:
同義詞集:{win, profit greatly, clear , prosper, accumulate, make a fortune}

3. 測試句替換同義詞：我們將擷取出來的測試句與同義詞作替換搭配，產生新測試句，如表 4：

表 4 測試句替換同義詞範例(句子來源：EIC)

原始測試句:(5 連詞擷取出的測試詞組有三組，我們以一組為範例做說明)
has the money to clean
替換結果:
has the money to win has the money to profit greatly has the money to clear has the money to prosper has the money to accumulate has the money to make a fortune

(二) 方法概念簡介

我們提出的方法跳脫語言模型是利用跳脫式方式來彌補 N 連詞的缺點，N 連詞主要概念就是給定一個詞，然後去預測出下一個詞，其參考的依據是利用字詞出現的頻率高低，當字詞頻率較高時，則此字詞的機率越大，但是使用 N 連詞有個缺陷，當 N 越大他的正確性越高，但是出現的頻率往往很低或是 0 的情況，因此我們使用準確性較高的 5 連詞再結合跳脫式方式來取代連詞頻率過低的情況，希望能夠因此提升準確率。本研究跳脫語言模型方法是以 Islam 和 Inkpen 提出的 5 連詞方法為基礎[12]，以下對 N 連詞和跳脫語言模型做詳細介紹。

(三) N 連詞(N-gram)

N 連詞是一種常用的語言模型，主要是將句子裡目標詞周圍 N 個字擷取出來成為詞組，依照需求不同所取的 N 也不同，取出詞組後再利用 Google Web 1T 5-grams 語料庫搜尋擷取出的詞組頻率，將頻率應用機率統計的概念算出分數，藉由得到的分數選取合適的單字，根據 N 的不同，又分為單連詞(Unigram)、2 連詞(Bigram)、3 連詞(Trigram)、4 連詞(Fourgram)、5 連詞(Fivegram)。

1. N 連詞模組建立:

句子以 $s = ...w_{i-4}w_{i-3}w_{i-2}w_{i-1}w_i w_{i+1}w_{i-2}w_{i-3}w_{i+4}...$ 表示，w_i 代表目標詞，也就是同義詞替換的位置。省略不包含目標字的 5 連詞，因為他們的值是相同的，所以只考慮 $P(w_i | w_{i-4}^{i-1})$，$P(w_{i+1} | w_{i-3}^{i})$、$P(w_{i+2} | w_{i-2}^{i+1})$、$P(w_{i+3} | w_{i-1}^{i+2})$ 與 $P(w_{i+4} | w_{i}^{i+3})$，以上五個項目，根據 5-gram 語言模型和平滑方式將公式定義為:

$$
\begin{aligned}
P(s) &= \prod_{i=0}^{5} P(w_i | w_{i-n+1}^{i-1}) \\
&= \prod_{i=0}^{5} \frac{C(w_{i-n+1}^{i}) + (1+\alpha_n) M(w_{i-n+1}^{i-1}) P(w_i | w_{i-n+2}^{i-1})}{C(w_{i-n+1}^{i-1}) + \alpha_n M(w_{i-n+1}^{i-1})}
\end{aligned} \tag{1}
$$

其中 $M(w_{i-n+1}^{i-1})$ 為 5 連詞頻率過少的部分以平滑方法取代，公式為

$$
M(w_{i-n+1}^{i-1}) = C(w_{i-n+1}^{i-1}) - \sum_{w_i} C(w_{i-n+1}^{i}) \tag{2}
$$

這裡 $C(\cdot)$代表 N 連詞從 Web 1T 5-gram 語料庫中搜尋的頻率。假如較高階的 N 連詞的頻率找不到，將會往下尋找較低階的 N 連詞頻率，如果較低階頻率也找不到時，則繼續往更低階 N 連詞尋找，依此類推；相反的較高階的 N 連詞頻率找的到時，則直接採用較高階 N 連詞，就不會往下考慮低階的 N 連詞頻率。

(四) 跳脫語言模型(Skip N-gram)

跳脫式方法是將 5 連詞的詞組中，保留 N 個字詞後其餘字詞設定成可以為任意詞，然後到 Web 1T 5-gram 語料庫中重新搜尋頻率，用以替代 N 連詞頻率過低的情況，依據 N 的不同，可分為 Skip4、Skip3、Skip2，表 6-8 分別為 Skip4、Skip3、Skip2 的範例:

表 6 Skip4 範例

5 連詞詞組: has the money to clean	
Skip4	
* the money to clean	243
has * money to clean	0
has the * to clean	1099
has the money * clean	0
has the money to *	0

表 7 Skip3 範例

5 連詞詞組: has the money to clean	
Skip3	
* * money to clean	1025
* the * to clean	51774
* the money * clean	652
* the money to *	243
has * * to clean	5999
has * money * clean	0

表 8 Skip2 範例

5 連詞詞組: has the money to clean	
Skip2	
has the * * *	1435
has * money * *	0
has * * to *	6071
has * * * clean	21113
* the money * *	652
* the * to *	53074
* the * * clean	311100

表 6-8 中*代表任何單字，我們以 has the money to *為例，他代表 has the money to clean、has the money to afford、 has the money to back 、has the money to cover...等所有五連詞中前四個單詞為 has the money to 的集合，將這些詞組所有頻率相加起來就是 has the money to *的頻率。

我們為了改善 N 連詞在 N 較大時的缺陷，所以利用跳脫式方法來改善，我們將測試句使用 N 連詞方法在 N=2，3，4，5 時的頻率句數統計資料如表 9：

表 9 N 連詞頻率句數統計

	頻率為 0 的句數	正確句數
5-gram	950	370
4-gram	404	596
3-gram	352	591
2-gram	158	329
總句數:1703		

根據表在 N=5、N=4 和 N=3 的情況下，他無法找到頻率的句數較多，N=5 雖然無法找到的句數最多，但是的它的正確率卻是相對最高的，因此我們保留 N=5 的部分，而將 N=4 與 N=3 時改用 Skip4 與 Skip3 來代替。

四、實驗與結果分析

我們的實驗資料是引用 SemEval-2007 所提供的資料，SemEval-2007 是第四屆國際語意評測研討會，他提供許多詞義消歧的任務，主要是為了提升我們對同義詞與一詞多義的現象更加了解。我們參與的是 SemEval-2007 第 10 項任務[15]，他提供任務所需的實驗資料，讓參與任務團隊針對相同的資料進行實驗，並訂定統一的評分方式，以下我們簡單介紹任務提供的實驗相關資料與評分方式，如需要更詳細的資料可參考 McCarthy 和 Navigli 發表的論文[15]。

(一) 實驗資料-資料來源

實驗資料來源是由 Sharoff 的 English Internet Corpus(EIC)所取得的，此語料庫是 Sharoff 撰寫的一支在網路上抓取語料的語料庫系統。實驗資料包含 201 個單字，單字詞性分別有名詞、動詞、形容詞、副詞，而每一個單字再挑選 10 個句子，總共 2010 句。在 2010 句中將其中 1710 句當作實驗的測試句，再扣除 7 句同義詞集為 0 的部分，實際測試資料為 1703 筆。表 10 為實驗資料整理表。

表 10 實驗資料資訊(資料來源:SemEval-2007[15])

PoS	#
Noun	497
Verb	440
Adjective	468
Adverb	298
All	1703

(二) 實驗資料-同義詞集

SemEval-2007 在這項任務[15]找來以英文為母語的 5 個人，針對測試的 1710 筆資料，在不限時間的情況下，填上每個人認為適合的同義詞，每個人不限定只能填一個，只要認為適合都可填寫，因此可提出三個以上的同義詞，表 11 為同義詞集資訊。範例: If this Government had been doing its **job** they would have total confidence.

表 11 同義詞集資訊(資料來源:SemEval-2007[15])

參與者	1	2	3	4	5
替代詞	duty function	bit	responsibility	duty task	role
job.n 433 :: duty 2;function 1;bit 1;responsibility 1;task 1;role 1;					

(三) 評分方法

此任務[15]的評分方式是將系統依據研究方法提出一個最佳的同義詞後，利用兩個計算方法來評分，一個是召回率(Recall)，一個是最多頻率召回率(Mode Recall)，兩者之間的主要差別在於召回率(Recall)將系統提出的所有同義詞根據 5 位註解人所註解的次數算出分數，而最多頻率召回率(Mode Recall)只考慮擁有最高註解次數的同義詞與系統所選擇的最佳同義詞是否相同來計算分數，以下介紹兩種評分公式，表 12 為召回率(Recall)的變數資料。

$$R = \frac{\sum_{a_i : i \in T} \frac{\sum_{res \in a_i} freq_{res}}{|a_i| \cdot |H_i|}}{|T|} \tag{3}$$

表 12 Recall 變數資料

變數	代表意義
T	至少有兩個同義詞的測試句個數
H_i	同義詞集裡的同義詞次數加總
$freq_{res}$	最佳同義詞於同義詞集裡的次數

$$Mode\ R = \frac{\sum_{bg_i \in T_m} 1 \text{ if } bg_i = m_i}{|T_m|} \tag{4}$$

表 13 Mode Recall 變數資料

變數	代表意義
T_m	同義詞集擁有最多次數的測試句個數
bg_i	最佳的同義詞
m_i	註解次數最多的同義詞

(四) 實驗結果與分析

1. N-gram 與 Skip 組合分析

我們決定 N-gram 與 Skip 的結合方式是先將所有可能的組合全部列出來實作後，將組合的結果與純 N-gram 方法相比選出結果最佳的組合，結果如表 14:

表 14 N-gram+Skip 結果數據

	Recall	Mode Recall
N-gram	30.31	39.84
N5S4N3N2N1	31.55	39.84
N5N4S3N2N1	31.54	39.67
N5N4N3S2N1	30.97	37.8
N5S4S3N2N1	**31.6**	**40.24**
N5N4S3S2N1	30.9	37.48
N5S4N3S2N1	31.08	38.13
N5S4S3S2N1	30.88	36.99

由表 14 可看出在所有 N-gram 與 Skip 組合中結果最好的是 N5S4S3N2N1，N5S4S3N2N1 的意思代表這是 5-gram、Skip4、Skip3、2-gram、ungram 的組合，將 N5S4S3N2N1 組合與純 N-gram 相比，有加入 Skip 的方法比純 N-gram 的結果好，而 Skip 與 N-gram 結合時，Skip 在 N=4 與 N=3 位置計算出來的數據最好，因此我們跳脫語言模型的組合是使用 N5S4S3N2N1 的結合方式。

2. 正確率(Accuracy)

$$Accuracy = \frac{\sum_{bg_i \in T_m} 1 \text{ if } bg_i = \text{original word}}{\text{All}} \quad (6)$$

其中 bg_i 代表我們提出的最佳同義詞，originalword 代表測試句中原本的目標字，All 代表測試句的總句數，根據以上計算方式計算出來的結果如下表 15：

表 15 正確率結果數據

System	Accuracy
N-gram	30.30%
N5S4N3N2N1	34.66%
N5N4S3N2N1	**39.16%**
N5N4N3S2N1	32.11%
N5S4S3N2N1	38.63%
N5N4S3S2N1	34.42%
N5S4N3S2N1	33.71%
N5S4S3S2N1	33.83%

表 15 中以 N5N4S3N2N1 的結果最好 39.16%，我們是和參與 SemEval-2007 任務的團隊比較，因此雖然 N5N4S3N2N1 在正確率這裡是最好的，但我們還是選擇在 SemEval-2007 任務評分標準中最好的結合結果 N5S4S3N2N1 作為我們跳脫語言模型的結合方式。我們將 N-gram 與 Skip 的所有組合與純 N-gram 相比之下，N-gram 結合 Skip 的數據都比純 N-gram 來的好，因此可以證明我們提出的跳脫語言模型確實可以改善 N-gram。

3. 結果範例討論

此節我們將利用結果範例來討論跳脫語言模型是否真能夠改善 N 連詞，表 16 與表 17 為我們自行使用的 N 連詞結果與跳脫語言模型的結果比較:

表 16 N-gram 與 Skip N-gram 比較結果範例一

測試句: I ____ over and made a U turn while Chris got out, ran over and took a picture. 原始目標字: pull				
同義詞	pull		stop	
N-gram	5-gram		5-gram	
	pull over and made a	0	stop over and made a	0
	4-gram		4-gram	
	pull over and made	0	stop over and made	0
	over and made a	0	over and made a	0
Skip	Skip4		Skip4	
	pull * and made a	0	stop * and made a	0
	pull over * made a	0	stop over * made a	0
	pull over and * a	1172	stop over and * a	171
	pull over and made *	0	stop over and made *	0

表 17 N-gram 與 Skip N-gram 比較結果範例二

測試句: Java so that all of the clone( ) methods catch the CloneNotSupportedException rather than ____ it to the caller. 原始目標字: pass				
同義詞	pass		hand	
N-gram	5-gram		5-gram	
	than pass it to the	0	than hand it to the	50
Skip	Skip 4		Skip 4	
	than pass * to the	0	than hand * to the	50
	than pass it * the	157	than hand it * the	50
	than pass it to *	0	than hand it to *	50

表 16 與表 17 因為資料過多，我們無法列出全部數據，所以僅列出代表性的數據，表 16 為 5 連詞與 4 連詞頻率為 0 的情況，範例一中使用 N 連詞方法選出的最佳同義詞為 stop，跳脫語言模型最佳同義詞為 pull，原因在於使用 N-gram 方法時 pull 和 stop 在 5-gram 與 4-gram 頻率都為 0 只能往下找 3-gram、2-gram 與 ungram，在 4-gram 以下的低階連詞 stop 的頻率高於 pull 因此 N-gram 的最佳同義詞就選擇 stop；跳脫語言模型方面，在 Skip4 時就可明顯看出 pull 的頻率高出 stop 許多，因此跳脫語言模型的最佳同義詞為 pull。表 17 為兩個同義詞裡其中一個 5 連詞頻率不為 0 的情況，範例二中 N 連詞方法選出的最佳同義詞為 hand，跳脫語言模型最佳同義詞為 pass，原因在於使用 N-gram 方法時，hand 在 5 連詞的頻率為 50，pass 卻為 0，所以 N 連詞最佳同義詞為 hand，但是在 Skip4 時頻率卻是 pass 多於 hand，所以跳脫語言模型最佳同義詞選擇 pass。由上面兩個例子，我們可以證明跳脫語言模型確實比純 N 連詞的方法好。

五、結論

本篇論文使用跳脫語言模型的方法，並針對對 SemEval-2007 的第 10 項任務[15]進行實驗。我們採用跳脫語言模型的主要原因在於 N 連詞的方法準確性很高，但是缺點就是當 N 越大的時候，往往在語料庫中的出現頻率都是非常低，甚至是 0 的情況，因此我們希望使用跳脫的方法來取代 N 連詞的缺點，我們將 N 較大時，以跳脫方法的頻率來取代 N 連詞的頻率，使正確性能提高，而我們將跳脫語言模型方法參與 SemEval-2007 做實驗的結果以及分析過後，我們提出的方法確實能夠提升同義詞選擇的正確率，和其他團隊以 N 連詞方式進行實驗的結果相比，也明顯提升，因此我們提出的跳脫語言模型確實能夠彌補 N 連詞的缺點。未來工作將進一步找出正確率過低的原因，修改方法的計算方式或是找出新方法，促使正確率能夠再提升，讓同義詞之間的差異可以更加明確。

誌謝

本研究感謝林志誠同學在先期工作上所做的努力。此外，本研究承蒙國科會 NSC 99-2221-E-155 -036 -MY3 費補助特此致謝。

參考文獻

[1] D. Moldovan and R. Mihalcea, "Using WordNet and Lexical Operators to Improve Internet Searches," *IEEE Internet Computing*, pp. 34-43, 2000.

[2] J. Bhogal, A. Macfarlane, and P. Smith, "A Review of Ontology based Query Expansion," *Information Processing & Management*, pp. 866-886, 2007.

[3] C. Cheng, "Word-Focused Extensive Reading with Guidance," In *Proc. of the 13th International Symposium on English Teaching*, pp. 24-32, 2004.

[4] S. Ouyang, H. H. Gao, and S. N. Koh, "Developing a Computer-Facilitated Tool for Acquiring Near-Synonyms in Chinese and English," In *Proc. of IWCS-09*, pp. 316-319, 2009.

[5] D. Pearce, "Synonymy in Collocation Extraction," In *Proc. of the Workshop on WordNet and Other Lexical Resources at NAACL-01*, 2001

[6] D. Inkpen, "A Statistical Model of Near Synonym Choice," *ACM Trans. Speech and Language Processing*, pp. 1-17, 2007.

[7] L. C. Yu, C. H. Wu, R. Y. Chang, C. H. Liu, and E. H. Hovy, "Annotation and verification of sense pools in OntoNotes," *Information Processing & Management 46(4)*, pp.436-447, 2010.

[8] A. Islam, D. Inkpen, "Real-word spelling correction using Google Web 1T 3-gram, " In *Proc. of EMNLP-09*, pp. 1241-1249, 2009.

[9] P. Nulty, F. Costello, "Using lexical patters in google Web 1T corpus to deduce semantic relation between nouns," In *Proc. of the NAACL/HLT Workshop on Semantic Evaluations: Recent Achievements and Future Directions,* pp. 58-63, 2009.

[10] P. Edmonds, "Choosing the Word Most Typical in Context Using a Lexical Co-occurrence Net Network," In *Proc. of ACL-97*, pp. 507-509, 1997.

[11] M. Gardiner and M. Dras, "Exploring Approaches to Discriminating among Near-Synonyms," In *Proc. of the Australasian Technology Workshop*, pp. 31-39, 2007.

[12] A. Islam, D. Inkpen, "Near-Synonym Choice using a 5-gram Language Model," In *proc. Research in Computing Science*, pp. 41-52, 2010.

[13] D. McCarthy, "Lexical Substitution as a Task for WSD Evaluation," In *Proc. of the SIGLEX/SENSEVAL Workshop on Word Sense Disambiguation at ACL-02*, pp. 109-115, 2002.

[14] I. Dagan, O. Glickman, A. Gliozzo, E. Marmorshtein, and C. Strapparava, "Direct Word Sense Matching for Lexical Substitution," In *Proc. of COLING/ACL-06*, pp. 449-456, 2006.

[15] D. McCarthy, R. Navigli, "The English lexical substitution task," In *Proceedings of the 4th International Workshop on Semantic Evaluations (SemEval-2007)*, pp. 48-53, 2009.

Metaphor and Metonymy in *Apple Daily*'s Headlines

莊智霖 Chih-lin Chuang
國立中山大學外國語文學所
Department of Foreign Languages and Literature
National Sun Yat-sen University
m001020003@student.nsysu.edu.tw

Abstract

The current study focuses on the similarities and differences of conceptual metaphor and metonymy between each genre in newspaper headlines. Headlines in news articles in *Apple Daily* from May 21st to May 27th were collected and analyzed. There are three basic findings. First, blocks for entertainment and sports used, in proportion, more metaphors and metonymies than any other blocks. Second, the idea of fighting was the most basic base for metaphors in *Apple Daily*. Third, TOPIC FOR SUBJECT was widely implemented to be economic in discourse. However, there may be more genres not included in *Apple Daily*. Also, the ways of categorization may not be specific enough for each block. Future studies are encouraged to further explore other genres excluded in the current study.

Key words: metaphor, metonymy, newspaper, headline

1. Introduction

Conceptual metaphor is the process of interpreting or understanding one domain which is relatively abstract by using another domain which is relatively concrete (Lakoff and Johnson, 2003). For example, TIME IS MONEY is a conceptual metaphor. The concrete domain "money" is used to understand abstract domain "time." We can both *spend* money and time. Also, we can both *waste* money and time.

Though most people are not aware of metaphors, they are everywhere (Lakoff and Johnson, 2003). In fat, since the rising of Conceptual Metaphor Theory, many scholars have been exploring examples of metaphors in specific contexts. For instance, Hsiao and Su (2010) have explored metaphors in discourse level. Even metaphors in pictorial representations are also the issues involving metaphors (Forceville, 1996).

Metonymy is, to some extent, similar to conceptual metaphor, differing in that metonymy uses one concept in one domain to "refer to" or "stand for" another concept within the same domain (Lakoff and Johnson, 2003; Kovecses 2010). Examples of metonymy include HAND FOR PERSON. In Chinese, *shou* ('hand'), which is part of body, is often referring to the whole person in example like *toushou* (pitch hand, 'the person who pitches the ball'). Though the definition of conceptual metaphor is different from that of metonymy, the two ideas are much related. In fact, metonymies serve as basis for, thus blend into, many conceptual metaphors (Kovecses, 2010).

Metaphors have been widely used in our daily lives. We can see it everywhere. In fact, abundant examples of conceptual metaphor or metonymy have been provided by Lakoff and Johnson (2003), Kovecses (2010), and Gibbs (1994). In addition to the examples provided by those scholars, a lot more evidence of conceptual metaphor and metonymy can be found in headlines in newspapers. A good news headline presents the main ideas of the text efficiently to the readers. Also, it has to be interesting to attract readers' attention. Metaphor no doubt plays an important role in the headlines. In other words, conceptual metaphors are implemented to present main ideas efficiently and attract readers' attention. Since metonymy is, in some degree, related to conceptual metaphor, the fact that metonymy can also be found in newspaper is not implausible.

In fact, Shie (2012) has discussed metaphors in headlines of news stories. Shie compared and analyzed the differences between headlines in *New York Times*, designed for English native speakers, and *Times Supplement*, designed for English as foreign language learners, in terms of language style, conventionality, and conceptual distance. Shie argued that metaphors in *New York Times* tend to be grand, unconventional, and long distance while those in *Times Supplement* prefer plain, conventional, and short distance (2012). Shie also discussed differences in metonymy in headlines in the two newspapers (2011). One of the main findings was that effect-for-cause metonymy was used to foreshadow the whole ideas and arouse reader's curiosity. Moreover, metonymy was often used to be economic in discourse.

Though Shie investigated much on differences of metaphors and metonymies in headlines in two newspapers, he did not pay any attention to the differences in headlines between each genre in one single newspaper. According to Devitt (1993), genre is patterns that writers would base on to categorize different writing tasks. Therefore, articles within one genre share similar features. Then, the application of metaphor and metonymy may be similar within one genre while different between different genres. Therefore, the current study will focus on the similarities and differences of conceptual metaphor and metonymy between each block in newspaper headlines in Chinese newspaper, *Apple Daily*, which is edited mainly for Chinese native speakers in Taiwan. The main goal is to investigate a) the overall tendency of usages of metaphors and metonymy, b) whether different blocks prefer different metaphors and metonymies, and c) the most basic metaphor and metonymy.

There are five sections in this study: Abstract, Introduction, Methodology, Results, Discussions, and Conclusion. Introduction deals with research questions and organization. Methodology will explain the data collection procedure and identification of metaphor and metonymy. Results will report main discoveries based on the analyses of data. Discussions will try to interpret the results. Conclusion will summarize the findings and suggests for future studies.

2. Methodology

A self-constructed corpus is the main source for the current study. The corpus consists of all the news articles in *Apple Daily* printed from May 21st to May 27th, 2012. Headlines were identified as metaphors when the intended meaning was inconsistent with the literal meaning, and they were in different domains. Headlines were identified as metonymy when the intended meaning was inconsistent with the literal meaning, but they were still in the same domain.

(1) 猿打小球踢鐵板

Yuan da xiao qiu ti tie ban

Monkey play small ball kick iron board

'Lamigo Monkeys played bunts but met obstacles.'

(Block D, May 27th, 2012)

The headline in (1) serves as an example for identification of metaphor and metonymy. The news story was about the basketball game between Uni Lions and Lamigo Monkeys. Lamigo Monkeys used bunts in order to score. However, this strategy did not work. Uni Lions still performed pretty well to prevent Lamigo Monkeys from scoring. In (1), the literal meaning of verb phrase *ti tie ban* was 'to kick iron board.' However, the intended meaning was 'to meet obstacles.' Since the literal meaning 'to kick iron board' and the intended meaning 'to meet obstacles' were different, and they belonged to two different domains, this expression was identified as an example of metaphor. Headline in (1) also included an example of metonymy. The literal meaning of *yuan* was 'monkey.' However, the intended meaning was the team 'Lamigo Monkeys.' Since the literal meaning 'monkey' and the intended meaning 'Lamigo Monkeys' were different, and they belonged to the same domain, this expression was identified as an example of metonymy.

Only non-lexicalized conceptual metaphors and metonymies, whose meanings could not be found in dictionaries, were selected into a sub-corpus. The dictionary the present author used was *Chongbian guoyu cidian xiuding ben* (Re-edited Chinese Dictionary-Revised Edition), an online dictionary edited by Ministry of Education in Taiwan. Therefore, the dictionary could be regarded as an authoritative dictionary. Therefore, only metaphors and metonymies whose meanings could not be found in *Chongbian guoyu cidian xiuding ben* were calculated and analyzed in this study.

The metaphors and metonymies were categorized based on the blocks they were in. There are six blocks in *Apple Daily*: A, B, C, D, E, and P. Block A deals with headlines, the big events happened recently. Block B deals with business and stocks. Block C deals with entertainment. Block D deals with sports. Block E deals with life. Block P deals with houses and furniture. (Note that Block P only appears on Fridays and Saturdays.)

In the following section, the basic descriptive statistics about the numbers of metaphor and metonymy discovered in each block will be presented. Second, one example of metaphor and one example of metonymy from each block will be given and analyzed.

3. Results

First, the basic descriptive statistics about the numbers of metaphor and metonymy discovered in each block were presented below.

Table 1 The number and percentage of news headlines with metaphor or metonymy in each block

	A	B	C	D	E	P
headlines with metaphor or metonymy	43	29	53	33	9	3
all headlines	306	165	229	128	74	23
percentage	14.05%	17.58%	23.14%	25.78%	12.16%	13.04%

Table 1 shows the number and percentage of news headlines with metaphor or metonymy in each block. As can be seen, Block C and D used more metaphors and metonymies than other blocks.

Table 2 The number of headlines with metaphor and metonymy in each block

	A	B	C	D	E	P
Metaphor	19	22	36	24	9	2
Metonymy	26	8	18	18	2	1
total	43	29	53	33	9	3

Table 2 shows the number of headlines with metaphor and metonymy in each block. (Note that a headline may use both metaphor and metonymy. Therefore, the total number may be less than the sum of the numbers of metaphor and metonymy.) As can be seen, most blocks had more headlines with metaphors than those with metonymies. However, Block A had more headlines with metonymies than those with metaphors.

After the descriptive statistics, one example of metaphor and one example of metonymy from each block will be given and analyzed. (Since that the examples of metaphor and metonymy in Block E and P were not many, they are excluded in the following discussion.)

3.1 Block A:

(2) 雨衣大盜月擲百萬

Yuyi dadao yue zhi bai wan

Rain coat robber month throw million

'The rain-coat robber spent million dollars in one month'

(Block A, May 26th, 2012)

The news story in (2) was about a robber who wore rain coat when he committed crimes. Since he had robbed for many times, and that the money he stole was very much, he often spent it casually. In (2), the metaphor TO SPEND CASUALLY IS TO THROW was used. *Zhi* is 'to throw'. However, the robber did not really throw the money. Instead, it meant 'to spent money without any worry or limitation.' Since 'to spend' and 'to throw' were not in the same domain, they were considered as one example of metaphor.

(3) 錢都涮涮鍋漲 7%

Qiandu shuanshuanguo zhang 7%

Cash City shabu shabu rise 7%

'The price of shabu shabu in Cash City rose 7%'

(Block A, May 22nd, 2012)

The news story in (3) was about the increase of the price of shabu shabu in Cash City. In (3), the metonymy WHOLE FOR PART was used. The original meaning of this headline was that shabu shabu rose 7%. However, shabu shabu did not really rise. In fact, it was "the price" of shabu shabu that rose 7%. Therefore, the topic 'shabu shabu' was used to stand for the subject 'the price.' Based on this explanation, it could be seen as an example of metonymy WHOLE FOR PART since that the subjects related to *shabu shabu* could include *price*, *ingredient*, or the *taste*. "Price" was only one of the subjects related to the topic *shabu shabu*.

3.2 Block B:

(4) 新幹線代理韓廠遊戲 搶攻下半年商機

Xinganxian daili han chang youxi, qianggong xia ban nian shangji

Xingganxian agent Korea factory game, rob attack down half year business chance

'The company Xinganxian acted as agent for Korean game company to seize the business chance for the other half year.'

(Block B, May 22nd, 2012)

The news story in (4) was about a company Xinganxian acting as agent for a Korean game "Heaven of Three Kingdoms." Since the game was very popular, it was very competitive to be the agent. In (4), the metaphor TO SEIZE CHANCES IS TO ATTACT was used. *Gong* is 'to attack'. However, the company was not really ready to attack the market. Instead, the company just 'seized the chance' and was ready to release the game to earn money. Since 'to attack' and 'to seize chances' belonged to different domains, they were considered as one example of metaphor.

(5) 鴻海聯手夏普 發揮 1+1=5

Honghai lianshou xiapu, fahui 1+1=5

Foxconn union hand Sharp, develop +1=5

'Foxconn worked with Sharp, hoping to have 1+1=5 effect.'

(Block B, May 22nd, 2012)

The news story in (5) was about the company Foxconn working with another company Sharp, hoping to bring their skills to their fullest. In (5), the metonymy BEING HAND-IN-HAND FOR BEING ALLIANCE was used. *Lianshou* was 'to be hand-in-hand.' However, Foxconn was not really hand-in-hand with Sharp. The two whole companies, instead of hands, would be together and work together. In other words, 'hand' stands for 'the whole company.' Based on this explanation, this headline can be taken as an example of the metonymy PART FOR WHOLE.

3.3 Block C:

(6) 美人撞臉陽剛 TOP

Meiren zhuanglian yanggang TOP

Beautiful woman collide face strong TOP

'The face of the beautiful woman is almost the same with strong TOP'

(Block C, May 26th, 2012)

The news story was about a Korean female artist Park Si Yeon, who looked like another Korean male artist TOP. In (6), the metaphor TO BE THE SAME IS TO COLLIDE was used. *Zhuang* meant 'to collide.' However, the two faces did not really collide. They just 'looked alike'. Since 'to look alike' and 'to collide' were in different domains, the headline could be seen as one example of metaphor.

(7) 吳辰君收 GUCCI 粉爽

Wuchenjun shou GUCCI fen shuang

Annie Wu accept GUCCI very happy

'Annie Wu is very happy to have the GUCCI bag.'

(Block C, May 26th, 2012)

The news story was about Annie Wu, who just received a GUCCI bag as a present from her fiancé. In (7), the metonymy WHOLE FOR PART was used. The original meaning of this headline was that Annie Wu accepted GUCCI very happily. However, GUCCI was a brand name. Annie Wu definitely did not receive the brand name. In fact, it was "the bag" of GUCCI that was sent as present to Annie Wu. Therefore, the topic 'GUCCI' was used to stand for the subject 'the bag.' Based on this explanation, it could be seen as an example of metonymy WHOLE FOR PART since that the subjects related to *GUCCI* could include *price*, *materials*, or the *places of origin*. "Bag" was only one of the subjects related to the topic *GUCCI*.

3.4 Block D:

(8) 阿格西都殺不死

Agexi dou sha bu si

Andre Agassi always kill not die

'Andre Agassi is hard to be defeated.'

(Block D, May 26th, 2012)

The news story was about Andre Agassi coming to Taiwan to have tennis competition with children. One of the girls who played with Agassi claimed that Agassi played so well that she could not find any way to defeat him. In (8), the metaphor TO DEFEAT IS TO KILL was used. *Sha* meant 'to kill'. However, it did not really mean to kill Agassi in this headline. Instead, it meant 'to defeat' him in the tennis competition. Since 'to defeat' and 'to kill' were in different domains, it could be considered as an example of metaphor.

(9) 金鶯連啄國民

Jinying lian zhuo guomin

Baltimore Orioles continue peck Washington Nationals

'Baltimore Orioles again defeat Washington Nationals.'

(Block D, May 21st, 2012)

This news story was about the basketball game between Baltimore Orioles and Washington Nationals. The literal meaning of *jinying* and *guomin* was 'a golden oriol' and 'national.' However, the intended meaning was the team 'Baltimore Orioles' and 'Washington Nationals.' Since the literal meaning 'oriol' and 'national' and the intended meaning 'Baltimore Orioles' and 'Washington Nationals' were different, and they belonged to the same domain, the two expressions were identified as examples of metonymy.

4. Discussions

The current study aimed to investigate the usages of metaphor and metonymy in news headlines. As shown above, Block C and D used more metaphors and metonymies than other blocks. It was not surprising that Block C used a number of metaphors and metonymies for the reason that *Apple Daily* is famous, or notorious, for articles that are full of "shan-se-xing" (陳培煌, 2008; 黃名芬, 2011). In other words, the news articles are often "sensational" in *Apple Daily* (Uribe and Gunter, 2007). Since *Apple Daily* often uses sensational articles to attract readers' attention, the usage of metaphors and metonymies were expected. With more metaphor and metonymies, the headlines would be more attracting to the readers, fulfilling the quality of sensation even before the texts are read.

The fact that Block D used the many metaphors and metonymies was quite surprising. This may due to the fact that articles in Block D were often made into "dongxinwen," which uses 3D animation to report the news. In fact, the third most used genre for dongxinwen is sports (黃名芬, 2011). Based on this fact, it is plausible to conclude that sports did not receive less attention. Therefore, sports may still use many metaphors and metonymies than other genres.

Though individual blocks seemed to use quite different metaphors, a general core metaphor for Block B, C, and D could still be found. In Block B, the metaphor TO SEIZE CHANCES IS TO ATTACT was used in (4). Actually, many other metaphors in Block B involved war. Those words like *explode*, *hack*, or *military* were common in Block B. Therefore, it could be generalized into a basic metaphor BUSINESS IS WAR. In Block C, the metaphor TO BE THE SAME IS TO COLLIDE was used in (6). Actually, many other metaphors in Block C involved fighting. Those words like *rob*, *fight*, or *bite* were common in Block C. Therefore, it could be generalized into a basic metaphor ENTERTAINMENT IS FIGHTING. In fact, this generalization is far from implausible. Since the news in Block C are often about the dark side of the artists, about how they compete each other, the fictitious fighting is represented by words that are related to physical fighting. Block D, with no exception, involved fighting, as well. Since sports are related to competition, the words related to fighting are expected in Block D.

From the above discussions of Block B, C, and D, it can be concluded that *Apple Daily* often uses metaphors related to "fighting" to attract readers. Therefore, "fighting" may be the most important usage of metaphors in *Apple Daily* to attract readers' attention.

In terms of metonymy, it was often found that TOPIC FOR SUBJECT was common in the data. (3) and (7) are examples of such metonymy. This discovery may due to the fact that Chinese is a null subject language (Fuller and Gundel, 1987; Jin, 1994). In other words, subjects are often omitted in Chinese. Chinese speakers often rely on topics to communicate. Therefore, the metonymy TOPIC FOR SUBJECT is expected. The other reason may be what Shie (2011) claimed that metonymy can promote economic in discourse. With metonymy, the words in headlines can be reduced. For example, without metonymy, headlines in (7) would be 吳辰君收 GUCCI 包粉爽(Annie Wu accept GUCCI bag very happy 'Annie Wu is very happy to have the GUCCI bag.'), which adds one more word than the original. If metonymy is used properly, the words that are reduced would be amazing.

5. Conclusion

The current study focused on the similarities and differences of conceptual metaphor and metonymy between each genre in newspaper headlines. Three general findings were concluded. First, blocks for entertainment and sports used more metaphors and metonymies than any other blocks. Second, "fighting" was the most basic metaphors in *Apple Daily* to attract readers' attention. Third, TOPIC FOR SUBJECT was widely implemented for the reason that Chinese is a null subject language, and that it would be economic in discourse.

However, there may be more genres not included in *Apple Daily*. For example, literature, architecture, or geography are not included in *Apple Daily*. Also, the ways of categorization may not be specific enough for each block. For example, Block A contains politics, economics, or international news. Future studies are encouraged to further explore other genres excluded in the current study.

References

[1] Devitt, A. J. (1993). Generalizing about genre: New conceptions of an old concept. *College Composition and Communication 44*(4): 573-586.

[2] Forceville, C. (1996). *Pictorial metaphor in advertising.* London: Routledge.

[3] Fuller, J., and Gundel, K. (1987). Topic-prominence in interlanguage. *Language Learning, 37*, 1-18.

[4] Gibbs, Raymond W. (1994). *The poetics of mind: Figurative thought, language, and understanding*. Cambridge University Press, New York.

[5] Hsiao, C. H., and Su, I. W. (2010). Metaphor and hyperbolic expressions of emotion in Mandarin Chinese conversation, *Journal of Pragmatics, 42*(5), 1380-1396.

[6] Jin, H. (1994). Topic-prominence and subject-prominence in L2 acquisition: Evidence of English-to-Chinese.. *Language Learning*, *44*(1), 101.

[7] Kovecses, Zoltán (2010). *Metaphor: A Practical Introduction*, 2nd edition. Oxford University Press, Oxford.

[8] Lakoff, George and Johnson, Mark (2003). *Metaphors We Live By*, revised edition, Chicago University Press, Chicago.

[9] Shie, Jian-Shiung (2011). Metaphors and metonymies in New York Times and *Times Supplement* news headlines. *Journal Of Pragmatics*, *43*(5), 1318-1334.

[10] Shie, Jian-Shiung (2012). Conceptual metaphor as a news-story promoter: The cases of ENL and EIL headlines. *Intercultural Pragmatics*.

[11] Tseng, Ming-Yu (2010). The performative potential of metaphor. *Semiotica*, 180: 115-145.

[12] 陳培煌 (2008). 台灣《蘋果日報》頭版新聞與其發行數據之關係探討. 國立臺灣師範大學大眾傳播研究所碩士論文。

[13] 黃名芬 (2011). 傳媒「腥」關係-蘋果動新聞閱聽內容接收研析. 崑山科技大學公共關係暨廣告系學士論文.

Phonetics of Speech Acts: A Pilot Study

莊智霖 Chih-lin Chuang
國立中山大學外國語文學所
Department of Foreign Languages and Literature
National Sun Yat-sen University
m001020003@student.nsysu.edu.tw

Abstract

This paper aims to investigate the effect of speech act and tone on rhythm. Participants were asked to produce four sets of words in five speech acts. PVI values of duration, pitch, and intensity were used to test the rhythm of vowels. Two main findings were concluded. First, speech act did not have any effect on rhythm, which may be caused by the fact that speech act were not performed on the controlled words in this study. Second, tone had an effect on rhythm in terms of pitch and intensity on some pairs. However, the comparison between the two pairs, tone1-tone2 and tone2-tone3, did not show any significant difference, which may be explained by the nature of phonetic features for tone1-tone2 pair while Chinese third tone sandhi for tone2-tone3 pair. However, this study only used the sets of words that had the same tone. Future studies can put more focus on different combinations of sets of words.

Key words: speech act, tone, rhythm

1. Introduction

The analysis of speech acts has been widely discussed since it was brought up by Austin (1962). A speech act consists of locutionary act, illocutionary act, and perlocutionary act (Austin, 1962). The main argument of speech acts have been focusing on semantic and syntactic domains. However, phonetic domain is little discussed. Though Searle (1965) further explored illocutionary act and proposed that the elements of function indicating device include stress and intonation contour, there was no further discussion related to phonetics. Therefore, in current study, it will examine speech acts in terms of phonetics.

Rhythm is one of the issues that are dealt with in the field of phonetics. Pike (1946) and Abercrombie (1965, 1967) could be seen as pioneers in investigating the rhythm of language. They claimed that isochronism existed in all languages, and languages could be divided into two categories: stress-timed and syllable-timed. There have been abundant studies on speech rhythm. Grabe and Low (2000) investigated and compared different speech rhythms in eighteen languages. Since then, many scholars have been studying further deep into certain languages. For example, Deterding (2011) investigated the speech rhythm of Malay. So far, the focuses have been mainly on the differences of speech rhythms between languages and the issue of second language acquisition. There are also many studies on the reasons for different speech rhythms within one language. Accents are believed to be one of the possible factors which may affect the speech rhythm (Rathcke and Smith, 2011). Nonetheless, many possible factors remain undiscovered. Therefore, the current study discusses the effects of two possible factors, tone and speech act, on speech rhythm in Chinese. The purpose of the current study is to locate whether tone or speech act have effects on speech rhythm of vowels in terms of duration, pitch, and intensity.

2. Method

Three male students and seven female students were invited in the study. All of them were students in National Sun Yat-sen University, and they were all Chinese native speakers. The age ranged from 19 to 30. In the experiment, the participants were required to produce four sets of sentences: *paobaobao* (to throw up the bags), *miaochaohao* (to depict the person, Chaohao), *paobaodao* (to run Formosa), and *qiaobaogao* (to skip the homework).With the same ending vowel / aʊ /, the effect of vowel quality was controlled. Also, the words in the same set had the same tone. Therefore, the effects of the tone are also under control. (Since the effect of tone sandhi on two tone 3 words is inevitable, it is not considered here.) In each set, there were five sentences corresponding to five different speech acts: command, warn, invite, refuse, and request. In other words, each participant produced 20 sentences in total. The subjects were asked to produce the sentence as if they were really performing the acts in the real context. They were free to add any words in the front or at the back of the sets of words to make the sentence sound more vivid and real. However, any changes to the sets of words were not allowed. All the sounds were recorded to be the data for current study. After the recording, pairwise variability index (PVI) of duration, pitch, and intensity of each vowel in the set of words was calculated. Analysis of variance (ANOVA) was used to detect if there is any significant difference of PVI values between different tones or different speech acts. Further, post hoc pairwise comparisons of the mean scores were performed using the Tukey HSD test if the result from ANOVA was significant. The significance level was set at .05 for all analyses.

3. Results

First, the results of the effects of speech acts on intensity, pitch, and duration are presented as follows, respectively.

Table 1 lays out the results of the one-way ANOVA comparing the mean difference between the PVI values for intensity of different speech acts. As shown, there was a non-significant difference in the PVI values for intensity of different speech acts [$F(4, 195) = .23$, $p = 0.92$].

Table 1 Results of the one-way ANOVA comparing the mean difference between the PVI values for intensity of different speech acts

Speech Acts	N	M	SD	Skewness	Kurtosis
Command	40	3.61	2.59	1.52	2.55
Warn	40	3.66	2.03	.99	.21
Invite	40	3.26	2.29	1.10	.97
Refuse	40	3.40	2.02	.97	.74
Request	40	3.60	2.37	1.20	2.36
Source of variation	SS	df	MS	F	Sig.
Between groups	4.64	4	1.16	.23	.92
Within groups	1004.00	195	5.15		
Total	1008.64	199			

*p< .05

Table 2 lays out the results of the one-way ANOVA comparing the mean difference between the PVI values for pitch of different speech acts. As shown, there was a non-significant difference in the PVI values for pitch of different speech acts [F (4, 195) = 1.61, p= 0.173].

Table 2 Results of the one-way ANOVA comparing the mean difference between the PVI values for pitch of different speech acts

Speech Acts	N	M	SD	Skewness	Kurtosis
Command	40	9.90	8.97	2.21	5.75
Warn	40	11.23	12.77	2.13	4.25
Invite	40	6.47	5.27	2.21	7.30
Refuse	40	12.59	15.99	3.53	14.78
Request	40	10.79	11.33	1.71	1.96
Source of variation	SS	df	MS	F	Sig.
Between groups	844.64	4	211.16	1.61	.173
Within groups	25560.27	195	131.08		
Total	26404.91	199			

*p< .05

Table 3 lays out the results of the one-way ANOVA comparing the mean difference between the PVI values for duration of different speech acts. As shown, there was a non-significant difference in the PVI values for duration of different speech acts [F (4, 195) = .55, p= 0.702].

Table 3 Results of the one-way ANOVA comparing the mean difference between the PVI values for duration of different speech acts

Speech Acts	N	M	SD	Skewness	Kurtosis
Command	40	36.94	14.76	.96	.87
Warn	40	34.66	17.04	.33	-.61
Invite	40	38.87	19.45	.45	.02
Refuse	40	38.42	19.15	.30	-1.06
Request	40	34.40	17.92	.43	-.56
Source of variation	SS	df	MS	F	Sig.
Between groups	688.49	4	172.12	.55	.702
Within groups	61387.18	195	314.81		
Total	62075.67	199			

*p< .05

Second, the results of the effects of tones on intensity, pitch, and duration are presented as follows, respectively.

Table 4 lays out the results of the one-way ANOVA comparing the mean difference between the PVI values for intensity of different tones. As shown, there was a significant difference in the PVI values for duration of different speech acts [F (3, 196) = 6.256, p< 0.01]. Tukey HSD test indicated that the mean difference between the PVI values for intensity of tone1-tone3 (p= .015), tone2 -tone4 (p= .024), and tone3-tone4 (p= .001) were significant.

Table 4 Results of the one-way ANOVA comparing the mean difference between the PVI values for intensity of different tones

Tone	N	M	SD	Skewness	Kurtosis
Tone 1	50	3.04	2.37	1.61	3.37
Tone 2	50	3.94	2.06	.73	.35
Tone 3	50	4.34	2.48	.97	.92
Tone 4	50	2.70	1.67	1.65	3.63
Source of variation	SS	df	MS	F	Sig.
Between groups	88.14	3	29.38	6.256	.000*
Within groups	920.50	196	4.70		
Total	1008.64	199			

*p< .05

Table 5 lays out the results of the one-way ANOVA comparing the mean difference between the PVI values for pitch of different tones. As shown, there was a significant difference in the PVI values for pitch of different tones [F (3, 196) = 4.513, p<0.01]. Tukey HSD test indicated that the mean difference between the PVI values for pitch of tone1-tone3 (p= .004) and tone1-tone4 (p= .022) were significant.

Table 5 Results of the one-way ANOVA comparing the mean difference between the PVI values for pitch of different tones

Tone	N	M	SD	Skewness	Kurtosis
Tone 1	50	5.44	5.91	3.41	14.88
Tone 2	50	10.31	8.70	2.49	7.40
Tone 3	50	13.10	12.26	1.88	3.33
Tone 4	50	11.93	15.59	3.22	12.94
Source of variation	SS	df	MS	F	Sig.
Between groups	1705.95	3	568.65	4.513	.004*
Within groups	24698.95	196	126.02		
Total	26404.91	199			

*p< .05

Table 6 lays out the results of the one-way ANOVA comparing the mean difference between the PVI values for duration of different tones. As shown, there was a non-significant difference in the PVI values for duration of different tones [F (3, 196) = 1.264, p= 0.288].

Table 6 Results of the one-way ANOVA comparing the mean difference between the PVI values for duration of different tones

Tone	N	M	SD	Skewness	Kurtosis
Tone 1	50	33.52	18.05	.62	-.14
Tone 2	50	40.25	16.97	.21	-.81
Tone 3	50	35.83	20.85	.92	-.38
Tone 4	50	37.03	13.95	-.26	.08
Source of variation	SS	df	MS	F	Sig.
Between groups	1178.06	3	392.69	1.264	.288
Within groups	60897.62	196	310.70		
Total	62075.67	199			

*p< .05

4. Discussion

The current study is dealing with the effects of tones and speech acts on the rhythm, which is analyzed in term of intensity, pitch, and duration. Based on the results of first part, the temporary conclusion is that speech acts dos not have any effect on rhythm. Some possible reasons may result in this conclusion. First, from the feedback of some participants, it is not really possible to ask subjects to perform the speech act without any situation given in advance. They often felt difficult to feel as if they were in the context. Therefore, it may be proper to collect the data from real contexts, or at least near-real contexts such as dramas or movies. Second, the phonetic cues performing speech acts often do not lie on the verb itself but other words not controlled in this study. For example, when we refuse to throw up the bags, we may say, "I do not want to throw up the bags." In this example, the words that perform the speech act "refuse" is "do not want to" rather than "throw up the bags." Therefore, future studies are encouraged to focus on the exact words that perform the speech act.

Based on the results of second part, the temporary conclusion is that tones have some effects on rhythm in terms of intensity and pitch. As Turkey HSD test had indicated, the differences of PVI values of either intensity or pitch between pairs tone1-tone3, tone1-tone4, tone2-tone4, and tone3-tone4 were significant. The only two pairs, tone1-tone2 and tone2-tone3 did not show any significant difference in rhythm. In terms of the pair tone2-tone3, Chinese third tone sandhi may play a role. Many scholars (Brotzman, 1964; Shih, 1986; Wang and Li, 1963) had done a large amount of research on Chinese third-tone sandhi and claimed that a third-tone word would become identical to tone2 when it is preceded by another third-tone word. Therefore, it is not surprising that tone2-tone3 did not show any significant difference in rhythm.

5. Conclusion

This study focused on the effects of speech acts and tones on rhythm in terms of duration, pitch, and intensity. The result showed that speech acts did not have any effect on rhythm while the result of tone showed quite the opposite. However, this paper only dealt with only Chinese. Other tone languages are worth further exploring on this issue.

References

[1] Abercrombie, D. (1965). *Studies in Phonetics and Linguistics.* London: Oxford University Press.

[2] Abercrombie, D. (1967). *Elements of General Phonetics.* Edinburgh: Edinburgh University Press.

[3] Austin, J. L. (1962). How to Do Things with Words, Oxford: Oxford University Press.

[4] Brotzman, R. (1964). Progress report on Mandarin tone study. *Project on Linguistic Analysis Report,* 8:1-35.

[5] Deterding, D. (2011). Measurements of the rhythm of Malay. In *Proceedings of the 17th International Congress of Phonetic Sciences, Hong Kong, 17–21 August 2011*, pp.

576–579.

[6] Grabe, E., and Low, E. L. (2002). Durational variability in speech and the rhythm class hypothesis. In N. Warner, and C. Gussenhoven (Eds.), *Papers in laboratory phonology 7* (pp. 515–546). Berlin: Mouton de Gruyter.

[7] Pike, K. (1946). *The Intonation of American English.* 2nd edition. Ann Arbor: University of Michigan Press.

[8] Rathcke, T., and Smith, R. (2011). Exploring timing in accents of British English. In *Proceedings of the 17th International Congress of Phonetic Sciences, Hong Kong, 17–21 August 2011*, pp. 1666–1669.

[9] Searle, John R. (1965). What is a speech act? In M. Black (Ed.), *Philosophy in America.*Allen and Unwin: New York. Reprinted in John Searle (Ed.), *The Philosophy of Language* (pp. 39-53). Oxford University Press.

[10] Shih, C.L. (1986). *The Prosodic Domain of Tone Sandhi in Chinese*. Ph.D. dissertation, University of California San Diego.

[11] Wang, S. Y. and Li, K. P. (1963). Research on Mandarin phonology. *Project on Linguistic Analysis, Ohio State University Research Foundation.* 6:1-63.

基於稀疏成份分析之旋積盲訊號源分離方法

Convolutive Blind Source Separation Based on Sparse Component Analysis

莊祥瓏 Hsiang-Lung Chuang
國立中央大學資訊工程學系
Department of Computer Science and Information Engineering
National Central University
pee0402@hotmail.com

謝宇勳 Yu-Shiun Shie
國立中央大學資訊工程學系
Department of Computer Science and Information Engineering
National Central University
e8010232002@gmail.com

林昶宏 Chang-Hong Lin
國立中央大學資訊工程學系
Department of Computer Science and Information Engineering
National Central University
fredlin1017@gmail.com

王家慶 Jia-Ching Wang
國立中央大學資訊工程學系
Department of Computer Science and Information Engineering
National Central University
jcw@csie.ncu.edu.tw

摘要

本論文針對的是在不知道源訊號個數的情況下，一個稀疏欠定的旋積盲訊號源分離。我們的演算法分爲兩個階段，先估計混合矩陣然後才利用此矩陣分離源訊號。在估計混合矩陣上，首先定義了兩個特徵參數，包括了 Level-Ratio 以及 Phase-Difference，我們藉由 KNN Graph 方式，去除資料中的離群樣本，並用 K-Means 分群演算法對其餘的資料分群，然後應用 DOA 解決不同頻率間的排列問題，以達到估計混合矩陣的目的。此外，我們對此混合矩陣進行相位之補償，以獲得更精確之混合矩陣估計。本方法是建立於最大後驗機率方法上，在求得混合矩陣之後，利用最小 L1 範數去解一個欠定的線性最佳化問題。此外，對於未知的源訊號個數，我們利用 K-Means 演算法和貝氏資訊準則作結合，並對所有頻帶的結果做整體考量，以達到估測源訊號個數的目的。在實驗模擬的部分，會將我們提出的方法與參考文獻作比較，也證實了此演算法在分離訊號效能之優越性。

關鍵詞: 盲訊號源分離，最大概似估計，稀疏成份分析，貝氏資訊準則

一、簡介

近年來盲訊號源分離蓬勃發展，相關的論文如雨後春筍般出現。如同前面所敘述，我們所面對的是一個「雞尾酒會問題」。換句話說，我們希望在源訊號以及混合過程的資訊未知的條件之下，單憑混合訊號就能達到重建源訊號的目的。可想而知，在前提和變數如此多的情況下，想得到源訊號並沒有這麼簡單。所以盲訊號源分離絕對是一個極富挑戰性的研究課題。

盲訊號源分離依混合模型的型態可分成兩類，一個是瞬時混合模型(Instantaneous Mixing Model)[1],[2]另一個則爲旋積混合模型(Convolution Mixing Mode)[3],[5]-[10]。令 X 是一個 $M \times T$ 的混合訊號矩陣，每一列向量都代表一個混合訊號；S 表一個 $N \times T$ 的源訊號矩陣，它的列向量分別代表著某一個源訊號；H 指的是混合矩陣，其中 M 是麥克風數，N 則爲語者個數，而 T 表示時間域上的樣本長度。依照上述代號，我們可將瞬時混合模型表示成：

$$X = H \times S \tag{1}$$

然而在這篇論文當中，我們所提出的方法是建構在旋積混合模型之上，接下來會在後面的章節詳細說明此模型以及運用和推導的過程。

盲訊號源分離問題可依麥克風和源訊號的個數區分爲兩種案例，分別爲 $M \geq N$ 的過定(Over-Determined)問題和 $M<N$ 的欠定(Under-Determined)問題[6]-[9]。典型的盲訊號源分離就被歸類爲過定的問題，而到目前爲止，最常被用來解決這類問題的方法就是獨立成份分析(Independent Component Analysis, ICA)[1]-[4]。但是在現實生活中，我們也經常會碰到麥克風數量少於語者的情形。在這種狀態下我們是無法藉由獨立成份分析解決問題的。原因在於獨立成份分析是以迭代的方式不斷對混合矩陣做更新，使得混合矩陣具有分離訊號的能力，所以在獨立成份分析底下，混合矩陣必需爲一個方陣(Square Matrix)，這與欠定盲訊號源方離背道而馳，因爲當我們的問題具備欠定的特質時，混合矩陣會是一個矩形矩陣(Rectangular Matrix)。基於這個原因，這幾年稀疏成份分析(Sparse Component Analysis, SCA)逐漸流行，這種分析方式大多建立在資料具備稀疏性的假設前提下，然後再利用一些統計方法達到目的。稀疏成份分析至今已在訊號分離領域中佔有很重要的地位[6]-[9]。

在許多文獻中，源訊號的個數往往被當成是已知。但實際上，在很多時候，語者的個數是無法預知的。所以如何得知或估測 N 就變得格外重要。通常是藉由判定資料分佈中群聚個數的方式來取得 N 值，目前有許多方法都已經有不錯的成效。而且不少學者都開始在他們所提出來的演算法中考量源訊號個數是未知的情形。

我們的目的就是利用盲訊號源分離有效的將涵蓋於觀察訊號中的語音給取出。除了準確的估測語者個數之外，也希望在欠定的限制下，當混合訊號中有其餘的干擾成份(噪音、殘響等等)時，仍然可以達到分離之效用。

本論文的組織如下：第 2 部分爲盲訊號源分離模型; 第 3 部分爲特徵參數選取以及源訊號數之估計；第 4 部分爲混合係數矩陣估測以及相位補償技術；第 5 部分爲實驗結果；最後，第 6 部分爲結論。

二、盲訊號源分離模型

這篇論文考量到一個旋積混合型態的模型。我們利用下面的數學表示方式來描述此模型。

$$x_q(t) = \sum_{k=1}^{N}\sum_{l=0}^{L-1} h_{qk}(l)s_k(t-l) \tag{2}$$

其中 x_q 是感測器 q 對應的麥克風混合訊號(Mixing Signal)，q=1,2,⋯,M，s_k 爲第 k 個語者的源訊號(Source Signal)，k=1,2,⋯,N， h_{qk} 則是語者 k 到麥克風 q 的脈衝響應，並且令這個濾波器(Filter)的型式爲一個 L 階(L – Tap)的有限脈衝響應(Finite Impulse Response, FIR)濾波器。由於語音在時間域上的稀疏特性並不明顯，所以我們採用短時傅利葉轉換(Short Time Fourier Transform, STFT)，以取樣頻率 f_s 將時間域上的混合訊號 $x_q(t)$ 轉換成頻率域上的時間序列 $x_q(f_i,\tau_j)$，並且在時頻域上做訊號的觀察和處理：

$$x_q(f_i,\tau_j) \leftarrow \sum_{t=-T/2}^{T/2} x_q(t+\tau_j S)win(t)e^{-j2\pi f_i t}$$
$$\text{, where } f_i \in \{0,(1/T)f_s,\cdots,((T-1)/T)f_s\} \tag{3}$$

其中 f_i 是某個頻帶，τ_j 爲短時傅利葉轉換音窗的指標(Frame Index)，S 爲窗的位移量。至於這篇論文，我們所使用的是一個漢寧窗(Hanning Window)。然而，在時頻域上執行盲訊號源分離的另一個好處是我們可以將旋積混合過程單純視爲各個頻帶的瞬時混合型式，即如同以下之敘述。

$$X(f_i,\tau_j) = H(f_i)S(f_i,\tau_j) = \sum_{k=1}^{N} H_k(f_i)S_k(f_i,\tau_j)$$
$$\text{, where } X(f_i,\tau_j)\in C^{M\times 1}, S(f_i,\tau_j)\in C^{N\times 1}, H(f_i)\in C^{M\times N} \tag{4}$$

其中 $X(f_i,\tau_j)$和 $S(f_i,\tau_j)$分別代表混合訊號以及源訊號在時頻域上的成份。$H(f_i)$則是某一個頻帶的混合矩陣。然而，假設在一個時頻點上，只有一個源訊號在活動，我們令 $H_k(f_i)$ 是 $H(f_i)$的第 k 個行向量，則可將式子(4)簡化爲：

$$X(f_i,\tau_j) = H_k(f_i)S_k(f_i,\tau_j) \quad ,k\in\{1,\cdots,N\} \tag{5}$$

所謂的波束形成(Beamforming)，即爲一種空間上之濾波器，它利用訊號的空間關係，希望能夠對不同方向的訊號做出不同的增益，以達到空間濾波的效果，藉以分離空間中不同方向聲源的訊號。依波束形成定理，我們靠著麥克風陣列的源訊號方向和時間延遲去近似混合過程。因此當頻率爲 f_i 時，語者 k 到麥克風 q 的混合係數可表示爲：

$$h_{qk}(f_i) = g_{qk} e^{j2\pi f_i c^{-1} d_q \cos\theta_k} \tag{6}$$

其中 g_{qk} 爲訊號 k 至麥克風 q 的增益值，d_q 表感測器 q 與麥克風陣列中心之間的距離，θ_k 是源訊號 k 對應到麥克風陣列的角度。我們可利用式子(6)，將混合矩陣表現成下面的形式，以下有關混合矩陣的推導過程，多數都是建立在這個預設形式之上。

$$H(f_i) = \begin{bmatrix} h_{11}(f_i) & \cdots & h_{1N}(f_i) \\ \vdots & \ddots & \vdots \\ h_{M1}(f_i) & \cdots & h_{MN}(f_i) \end{bmatrix} \tag{7}$$

三、特徵參數選取以及源訊號數之估計

(一) 樣本型態

我們定義了兩個混合訊號的特徵參數(Level-Ratio 和 Phase-Difference)[11]。利用觀察資料的二階範數對混合訊號的絕對值頻譜(Magnitude Spectrum)做正規化，我們稱之爲 Level-Ratio，我們這邊用$\psi_q^L(f_i,\tau_j)$表示；至於 Phase-Difference 被定義成與一個指定的混合訊號之間的相位角度差，以$\psi_q^P(f_i,\tau_j)$來表示。它們的表示式分別顯示如下：

$$\psi_q^L(f_i,\tau_j) = \frac{|x_q(f_i,\tau_j)|}{|X(f_i,\tau_j)|_2} \tag{8}$$

$$\psi_q^P(f_i,\tau_j) = \phi[x_q(f_i,\tau_j)] - \phi[x_1(f_i,\tau_j)] \tag{9}$$

其中ϕ爲相位的運算子。然後利用一個複數表示式(Complex Representation)來表現這兩個特徵參數。

$$\psi_q(f_i,\tau_j) = \psi_q^L(f_i,\tau_j) \times \exp[j\psi_q^P(f_i,\tau_j)] \tag{10}$$

於是我們得到了一個新的樣本型態(Sample Form)，由 M 個 Level-Ratio 和 Phase-Difference 組成的複數值所構成。將原先的觀察資料轉換成這樣的資料型式後，我們即可使用這些新建立的樣本，做後續的處理和訊號分析，包括估計源訊號個數以及混合矩陣。令 T 爲向量的轉置，則樣本型態表示如下：

$$\Psi(f_i,\tau_j)=\left[\psi_1(f_i,\tau_j)\ \cdots\ \psi_M(f_i,\tau_j)\right]^T \tag{11}$$

(二) 源訊號數之估計

我們是藉由 K-Means 分群演算法加上貝氏資訊準則，達到估測源訊號數（語者數）的目的。利用貝氏資訊準則判斷群聚個數 C 是 c 還是 c+1 時，執行 K-Means 分群法後所回傳的結果，何者較能描述資料模型。下面是我們用來選擇模型的貝氏資訊準則公式。

$$BIC=\sum_{u=1}^{c} n_u^c \times \log\left|\Sigma_u^c\right| - \sum_{u=1}^{c+1} n_u^{c+1} \times \log\left|\Sigma_u^{c+1}\right| - \lambda\left(M+\frac{M(M+1)}{2}\right)\times \log(n) \tag{12}$$

首先令 c=2，執行 c=2 和 3 的 K-Means 分群演算法，隨後拿這兩個分群結果去做貝氏資訊準則的判斷。若得到的值小於零，停止此程序，且把 c 值視爲我們偵測到的源訊號數；反之如果求得的值大於零，我們接著設 c=3，並執行重複的動作，也就是做 c=4 的 K-Means 演算法，然後伴隨著 c=3 的分群結果再做一次貝氏資訊準則的判斷。K-Means 演算法會因爲初始群中心設定的不同而產生明顯的誤差，造成不穩定的分群結果。有鑑於這個問題，我們經由多次執行 K-Means 演算法，並且從回傳的分群情形中選擇一個群聚變異數和(Sum of Cluster Variance）最小的當作最終決定的結果。

針對每個頻帶，我們會接收到一個 c 值，之後統計各個頻帶所回傳的 c 值，出現頻率最高的即爲最後決定的源訊號個數。

四、混合係數矩陣估測以及相位補償技術

我們將混合訊號的時頻點轉換成其對應的樣本型態，在這個樣本型態空間上，先將一些在資料分佈中的離群樣本捨去，使得之後在做估測時，能夠更爲準確。方法是參照 KNN 演算法中，搜尋最近鄰居的方式，對每一個資料點都找出與之距離最近的 K 個鄰居[12]。然而每筆資料都有一個 In-Degree 值，若有一個樣本被某筆資料視爲 K 個最近的鄰居之一的話，則該筆資料的 In-Degree 值會往上加一，示意圖如圖一所示。統計每筆資料所屬的 In-Degree 值，假使某一個資料的 In-Degree 值小於門檻值

(Threshold)V 時，我們就將此樣本當作離群樣本。相反地，如果 In-Degree 值大於 V，這個樣本就會被保留下來，為之後估計源訊號數和混合矩陣所用。

再利用著名且應用廣泛的分群方法 K-Means 演算法，將樣本型態分割到 N 個群聚 $C_k,\ldots,C_N$ 中，並且利用下面的式子獲得混合向量：

$$h_k = \frac{1}{|C_k|}\sum_{\Psi \in C_k} \Psi, \quad k \in \{1, \cdots, N\} \tag{13}$$

其中$|C_k|$代表第 k 個群聚擁有的樣本數。然而每個混合向量都會對應到一個源訊號。因為我們是根據每個頻帶上的時間序列去估測混合矩陣，所以各個頻帶執行過 K-Means 演算法後都會回傳 N 個群聚，並求出代表的 h_k。最後，如何確認 h_k 在矩陣中的位置也是一個很重要的問題。

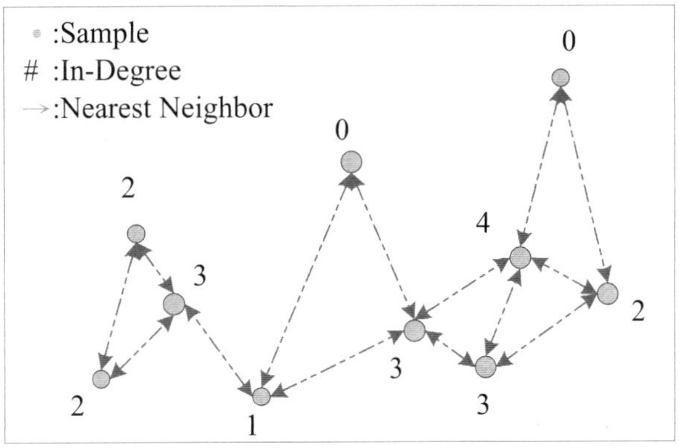

圖一、KNN Graph (c=2)。

根據式子(6)，可以得知

$$\frac{h_k(r)}{h_k(s)} = \frac{g_{rk}}{g_{sk}} e^{j2\pi f_i c^{-1}(d_r - d_s)\cos\theta_k} \tag{14}$$

所以經推導後，DOA 可以由下式獲得

$$\theta_k = \cos^{-1}\frac{\phi\left(h_k(r) \big/ h_k(s)\right)}{2\pi f_i c^{-1}(d_r - d_s)} \tag{15}$$

其中 r、s 是麥克風陣列中兩支距離最近的，它們在混合向量 h_k 中所對應到的指標，d_r、d_s 表示 r、s 兩支麥克風之間的距離。因為我們對所有 $h_k(k=1,\ldots,N)$都偵測 DOA，所以共得到了 N 個角度值。最後根據這個結果確定 h_k 在混合矩陣中所對應的行索引。

假設混合訊號的某個時頻點 $X(f_i,\tau_j)$，只有源訊號 k 為非零的值。透過式子(5)和式子(6)，可將 $X(f_i,\tau_j)$可表現為:

$$X(f_i,\tau_j)=\begin{bmatrix} g_{1k}e^{j2\pi f_i c^{-1}d_1\cos\theta_k} \\ \vdots \\ g_{Mk}e^{j2\pi f_i c^{-1}d_{M\cos\theta_k}} \end{bmatrix}\times g_{s_k(f_i,\tau_j)}e^{j\phi[s_k(f_i,\tau_j)]}$$
$$=\begin{bmatrix} g_{1k}g_{s_k(f_i,\tau_j)}\times e^{j(2\pi f_i c^{-1}d_1\cos\theta_k+\phi[s_k(f_i,\tau_j)])} \\ \vdots \\ g_{Mk}g_{s_k(f_i,\tau_j)}\times e^{j(2\pi f_i c^{-1}d_M\cos\theta_k+\phi[s_k(f_i,\tau_j)])} \end{bmatrix} \tag{16}$$

因為這篇論文要對由 Level-Ratio 以及 Phase-Difference 所組成的樣本作群聚分割。所以，得出了混合訊號樣本在極度稀疏的情形下表現的型式後，我們將式子(16)代入式子(8)和式子(9)，看看若利用這種形態的樣本去定義 Level-Ratio 和 Phase-Difference 這兩種特徵參數，$\psi_q^L(f_i,\tau_j)$和$\psi_q^P(f_i,\tau_j)$分別為：

$$\psi_q^L(f_i,\tau_j)=g_{qk}\big/norm([g_{1k}\cdots g_{Mk}]^T) \tag{17}$$

$$\begin{aligned}\psi_q^P(f_i,\tau_j)&=(2\pi f_i c^{-1}d_q\cos\theta_k+\phi[s_k(f_i,\tau_j)]) \\ &\quad-(2\pi f_i c^{-1}d_1\cos\theta_k+\phi[s_k(f_i,\tau_j)]) \\ &=2\pi f_i c^{-1}(d_q-d_1)\cos\theta_k\end{aligned} \tag{18}$$

然後，同樣的將上述兩個特徵參數用複數表示形態來敘述。最後，樣本$\Psi(f_i,\tau_j)$會以下面的樣子呈現。

$$\Psi(f_i,\tau_j)=\begin{bmatrix} \psi_1^L(f_i,\tau_j)\times e^{j2\pi f_i c^{-1}(d_1-d_1)\cos\theta_k} \\ \psi_2^L(f_i,\tau_j)\times e^{j2\pi f_i c^{-1}(d_2-d_1)\cos\theta_k} \\ \vdots \\ \psi_M^L(f_i,\tau_j)\times e^{j2\pi f_i c^{-1}(d_M-d_1)\cos\theta_k} \end{bmatrix} \tag{19}$$

其中，第一項爲一實數值。藉由上式，我們可以說，當語音具有極度稀疏的性質時，只會因爲主導的源訊號不同造成 θ_k 的改變而產生 N 種型式的 $\psi(f_i,\tau_j)$。所以當結束分群演算法估計混合矩陣之行向量的程序，並且解決了排列問題後，在最理想的情況下，也就是當極度稀疏的條件成立時，混合矩陣會成爲：

$$\begin{bmatrix} \psi_{11}^L & \cdots & \psi_{1N}^L \\ \psi_{21}^L e^{j2\pi f_i c^{-1}(d_2-d_1)\cos\theta_1} & \cdots & \psi_{2N}^L e^{j2\pi f_i c^{-1}(d_2-d_1)\cos\theta_N} \\ \vdots & \ddots & \vdots \\ \psi_{M1}^L e^{j2\pi f_i c^{-1}(d_M-d_1)\cos\theta_1} & \cdots & \psi_{MN}^L e^{j2\pi f_i c^{-1}(d_M-d_1)\cos\theta_N} \end{bmatrix} \tag{20}$$

當然，我們會希望被估計出的混合矩陣越逼近原始的形式越好。在經過估測各個頻帶的 DOA 後，就可以利用這些角度值對混合矩陣的頻率響應做補償，這裡是用 $\hat{\theta}_k^{f_i}$ 表示頻率爲 f_i 時源訊號 k 被估計出之 DOA。觀察式子(20)，可看出相位的地方都是利用到該行向量第一項的相位，採取相位差的表現方式。在我們估計出 $\hat{\theta}_k^{f_i}$ 之後，接著利用它去調整混合矩陣的相位部分，實際做法是對混合矩陣的第 k 個行向量乘上 $e^{j2\pi f_i c^{-1} d_1 \cos\hat{\theta}_k^i}$。所以修正後的混合矩陣結果爲：

$$\begin{bmatrix} \psi_{11}^L e^{j2\pi f_i c^{-1} d_1 \cos\hat{\theta}_1^{f_i}} & \cdots & \psi_{1N}^L e^{j2\pi f_i c^{-1} d_1 \cos\hat{\theta}_N^{f_i}} \\ \psi_{21}^L e^{j2\pi f_i c^{-1} R_{21}} & \cdots & \psi_{2N}^L e^{j2\pi f_i c^{-1} R_{2N}} \\ \vdots & \ddots & \vdots \\ \psi_{M1}^L e^{j2\pi f_i c^{-1} R_{M1}} & \cdots & \psi_{MN}^L e^{j2\pi f_i c^{-1} R_{MN}} \end{bmatrix} \tag{21}$$

$$R_{mn} = d_m \cos\theta_n + d_1(\cos\hat{\theta}_n^{f_i} - \cos\theta_n) \tag{22}$$

如果 DOA 的估測夠精準，也就是 $\hat{\theta}_n^{f_i}$ 等於 θ_n，或是說兩者的差距極小，則我們令

$$R_{mn} = d_m \cos\theta_n \tag{23}$$

最後，將式子(23)代入式子(21)，並且設 $\hat{\theta}_N^{f_i} = \theta_N$，我們可以得到下面這種形式的混合矩陣。

$$\begin{bmatrix} \psi_{11}^{L} e^{j2\pi f_i c^{-1} d_1 \cos\theta_1} & \cdots & \psi_{1N}^{L} e^{j2\pi f_i c^{-1} d_1 \cos\theta_N} \\ \psi_{21}^{L} e^{j2\pi f_i c^{-1} d_2 \cos\theta_1} & \cdots & \psi_{2N}^{L} e^{j2\pi f_i c^{-1} d_2 \cos\theta_N} \\ \vdots & \ddots & \vdots \\ \psi_{M1}^{L} e^{j2\pi f_i c^{-1} d_M \cos\theta_1} & \cdots & \psi_{MN}^{L} e^{j2\pi f_i c^{-1} d_M \cos\theta_N} \end{bmatrix} \tag{24}$$

盲訊號源分離在欠定的條件下，根據式子(4)，源訊號 S 可以有無限多個解，所以我們利用最小化 L1 範數之以及式子(1)作爲限制式，此最佳化問題的解即爲所求，如下列式子所示:

$$\min_{S} \sum_{k} |S_k|, \quad k = 1, \cdots, N, \quad s.t. \;\; HS = X \tag{25}$$

從這無限多組解中選取一個適當的答案。恢復源訊號的步驟就是依靠這個以 MAP 爲基礎的方法[6]。

五、實驗結果

(一) 實驗環境

環境架設的部分，示意圖如圖二所示，我們用四支麥克風(感測器)架設一個麥克風陣列。而這個麥克風陣列中，感測器與感測器之間的距離我們設爲 50 毫米。實驗情境中共存在六個源訊號，其中包含了三個男生以及三個女生的語音。並且以不同的入射角度圍繞在麥克風陣列的周圍。這些源訊號的取樣頻率(Sampling Rate)爲 8000 赫茲，訊號的時間長度爲 7 秒鐘。先前曾提到在執行盲訊號源分離前會利用短時傅立葉轉換將訊號轉至時頻域，而關於實驗，我們設短時傅立葉轉換裡的音框(Frame)大小爲 256 個樣本點，時間位移量爲 64 個樣本點，並採用漢寧窗爲訊號做加權的動作。

(二) 麥克風距離的影響

我們在測試時，發現到麥克風之間距離的長短與估計 DOA 的準確性有關連性。所以我們首先設計了一個實驗，模擬方式是固定 5 組源訊號，每一組包含了 3 個音源，然後取兩支麥克風，根據不同的麥克風距離去收錄源訊號，我們共有 22 種麥克風距離的設定，搭配 5 組源訊號，產生出了 110 種盲訊號源分離的案例。再來計算這 110 個案例中，被估計出之 DOA 與實際聲源角度的平均差距，得到的值越小，表示 DOA 估測的準確性越高。圖三即爲此實驗的結果。由此圖可看出，麥克風距離大約在超過 5 公分時，距離越大，準確性越差；然而距離並不是越小越好，當它小到某種程度，估計出的 DOA 與實際音源方位角的差距反而有些微的提高。從此實驗看來，我們理想的麥克風距離大概在 0.5 至 5 公分之間。

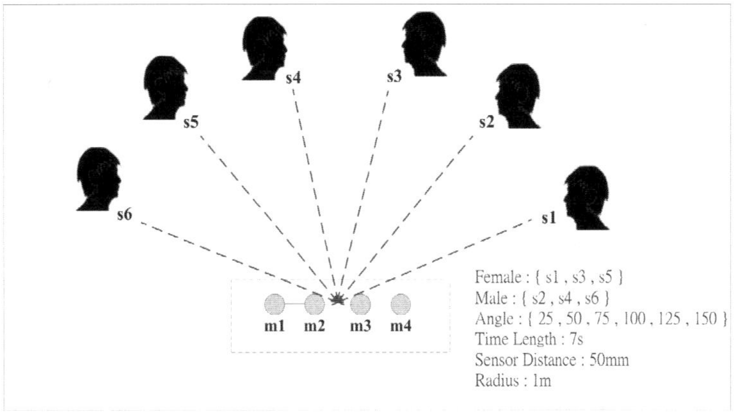

圖二、 模擬之實驗環境。{s1、s2、s3、s4、s5、s6}代表我們的 6 個聲源，{m1、m2、m3、m4}則爲麥克風陣列上的 4 個麥克風。

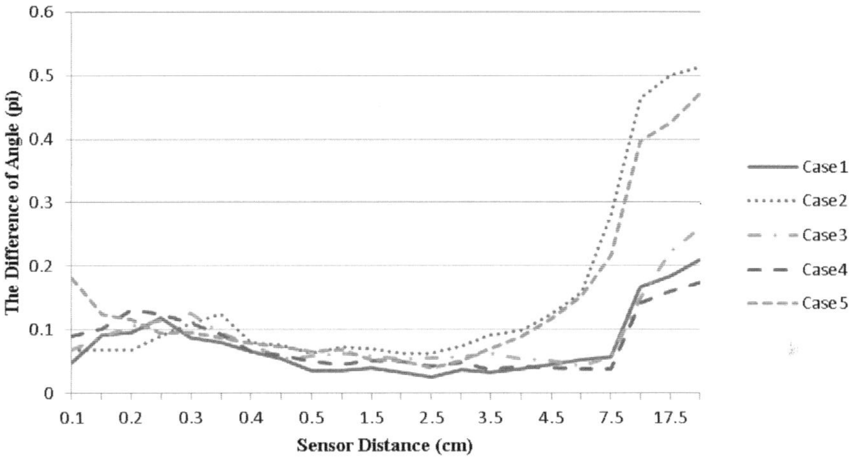

圖三、感測器距離與 DOA 估計之準確度的關聯性。

(三) 分離訊號效能之比較

本實驗用最大後驗機率的基礎方法和本論文所提出的演算法做比較。根據前面所形容的實驗環境，我們藉由各種可能的案例來評估效能，包括兩支麥克風三個源訊號(2m3n)、三支麥克風四個源訊號(3m4n)以及四支麥克風五個源訊號(4m5n)。針對這三種案例，我們各別選擇了十組、十組和五組測試音檔，然後比較了兩個演算法，我們將訊號干擾比(Signal To Interference, SIR)當作效能的評估準則，實驗數據如表一所示，公式如下所示：

$$SIR = 10\log_{10}\frac{\left\|y_{q_{target}}\right\|^2}{\left\|e_{q_{interf}}\right\|^2} \tag{26}$$

對於 2m3n 的盲訊號源分離情形，利用麥克風陣列中的 m2 和 m3 兩個感測器產生觀察訊號。在所有案例中，Baseline 方法與 Proposed 的 SIR 差距最大來到 4.89 分貝。以平均效能來講，Proposed 也高出 Baseline 方法 2.181 分貝。對於 3m4n 的盲訊號源分離情形，利用麥克風陣列中 m1、m2 和 m3 三個感測器產生觀察訊號。在所有案例中，Baseline 方法與 Proposed 的 SIR 差距最大來到 10.78 分貝。以平均效能來講，Proposed 也高出 Baseline 方法 7.321 分貝。對於 4m5n 的盲訊號源分離情形，Baseline 方法與 Proposed 的 SIR 差距最大來到 14.05 分貝。以平均效能來講，Proposed 也高出 Baseline 方法 7.27 分貝。

表一、兩支麥克風三個源訊號(2m3n)、三支麥克風四個源訊號(3m4n)以及四支麥克風五個源訊號(4m5n)實驗 SIR 比較。

Setting	Baseline [6]	Proposed
2m3n	10.705	12.886
3m4n	3.295	10.616
4m5n	-1.25	6.02

六、結論

本篇論文利用 KNN 的方法刪除離群資料，可以使較密集資料保留下來，以利混合矩陣之估測。此外，根據 DOA 的偵測結果，我們可以更進一步進行混和矩陣之相位補償，將其相位更精準的逼近混合矩陣的原貌，利用精準化後的混合矩陣來分離訊號，可獲得比原始方法(Baseline Method)更優異的效能。此外，K-Means 演算法和貝氏資訊準則作結合，並對所有頻帶的結果做整體考量，可達到估測源訊號個數的目的。實驗結果顯示，所有案例使用我們所提出的方法都比傳統最大後驗機率爲基礎的方法要出色。

參考文獻

[1] A. Hyvarinen, J. Karhunen, and E. Oja, *Independent component analysis*, New York, John Wiley and Sons, 2002.

[2] S. Roberts and R. Everson, *Independent component analysis: principles and practice*, Cambridge University Press, 2001.

[3] S. C. Douglas, M. Gupta, H. Sawada, and S. Makino, "Spatio – temporal FastICA algorithm for the blind separation of convolutive mixtures," *IEEE Trans. Audio, Speech, Lang. Process.*, vol. 15, pp. 1540 – 1550, Jul. 2007.

[4] H. Saruwatari, T. Kawamura, T. Nishikawa, A. Lee, and K. Shikano, "Blind source separation based on a fast-convergence algorithm combining ICA and beamforming," *IEEE Trans. Audio, Speech, Lang. Process.*, vol. 14, pp. 666-678, Mar. 2006.

[5] A. Belouchrani and M. G. Amin, "Blind source separation based on time-frequency signal representation," *IEEE Trans. Signal Processing*, vol. 46, pp. 2888-2898, Nov.

1998.
[6] S. Winter, W. Kellermann, H. Sawada, and S. Makino, "MAP-based underdetermined blind source separation of convolutive mixtures by hierarchical clustering and l_l-norm minimization," *EURASIP Journal on Advances in Signal Processing*, vol. 2007, Article ID 24717, 12 pages.
[7] P. Bofill, "Underdetermined blind separation of delayed sound sources in the frequency domain," *Neurocomputing*, vol. 55, no. 3-4, 99. 627-641, 2003.
[8] P. Bofill and M. Zibulevsky, "Underdetermined blind source separation using sparse representations," *Signal Processing*, vol. 81, pp. 2353-2362, Jun. 2001.
[9] Y. Li, S. I. Amari, A. Cichocki, D. W. C. Ho, and S. Xie, "Underdetermined blind source separation based on sparse representation," *IEEE Trans. Signal Processing*, vol. 54, pp. 423-437, Feb. 2006.
[10] A. Aissa-El-Bey, K. Abed-Mraim, and Y. Grenier, "Blind separation of underdetermined convolutive mixtures using their time-frequency Representation," *IEEE Trans. Audio, Speech, Lang. Process.*, vol. 15, pp. 1540-1550, Jul. 2007.
[11] S. Araki, H. Sawada, R. Mukai, and S. Makino, "Underdetermined blind sparse source separation for arbitrarily arranged multiple sensors," *Signal Processing*, vol. 87, pp. 1833-1847, Feb. 2007.
[12] V. Hautamaki, I. Karkkainen, and P. Franti, "Outlier detection using k-nearest neighbor graph," *IEEE International Conference, ICPR*, pp. 430 – 433, Aug. 2004.

Disambiguating Main POS tags for Turkish

Razieh Ehsani
Istanbul Technical University
Faculty of Computer and Informatics
Computer Engineering
rehsani@itu.edu.tr

Muzaffer Ege Alper
National University of Singapore
Faculty of Science
Department of Statistics and Applied Probability
m.ege85@nus.edu.sg

Gülşen Eryiğit
Istanbul Technical University
Faculty of Computer and Informatics
Computer Engineering
gulsenc@itu.edu.tr

Eşref Adalı
Istanbul Technical University
Faculty of Computer and Informatics
Computer Engineering
adali@itu.edu.tr

Abstract

This paper presents the results of main part-of-speech tagging of Turkish sentences using Conditional Random Fields (CRFs). Although CRFs are applied to many different languages for part-of-speech (POS) tagging, Turkish poses interesting challenges to be modeled with them. The challenges include issues related to the statistical model of the problem as well as issues related to computational complexity and scaling. In this paper, we propose a novel model for main-POS tagging in Turkish. Furthermore, we propose some approaches to reduce the computational complexity and allow better scaling characteristics or improve the performance without increased complexity. These approaches are discussed with respect to their advantages and disadvantages. We show that the best approach is competitive with the current state of the art in accuracy and also in training and test durations. The good results obtained imply a good first step towards full morphological disambiguation.

1 Introduction

The morphological disambiguation problem for morphologically rich languages differs significantly from the well known POS tagging problem. It is rather an automatic selection process from multiple legal analysis of a given word than the assignment of a POS tag from a predetermined tag set. The possible morphological analyses of a word (generally produced by a morphological analyzer) in such languages are very complex when compared to morphologically simple ones: They consist of the lemma, the main POS tags and the tags related to the inflectional and derivational affixes. The number of the set of possible morphological analyses may sometimes be infinite for some languages such as Turkish.

In this study, we focus on the determination of the main POS tags (which will be referred as "POS tagging" from now on) rather than the full disambiguation task. There are few methods for Turkish which directly tackle POS tagging problem. Instead many methods perform a full morphological disambiguation and the POS tags are obtained from the correct parses. In this work, we take a different approach and propose a model which directly tackles the POS tagging problem. While also being useful in its own right, this method is also a first step towards full morphological disambiguation through weighted opinion pooling approach [16].

To give a sense of the problem at hand and the general morphological disambiguation, we have measured the ambiguity corresponding to the POS tagging and Morphological Disambiguation problems. About 27% of the words in our corpus are ambiguous in terms of its POS tag and random guessing has an expected accuracy of 85%, on the other hand the ambiguity in terms of morphological disambiguation is about %50. The proposed approach in this paper improves the accuracy of POS tag to around 98.35%.

Our approach is based on the well known methodology of Conditional Random Fields, which is also applied to other languages with varying success. POS tagging problem was successfully tackled in languages with relatively simpler morphological properties (such as English) [16; 17; 6; 8]. On the other hand, other languages proved to be more problematic with lower tagging performance, [5; 15; 3] with accuracies ranging from %85 to %95. Smith et. al. [16] discusses the high computational burden of CRFs in both training and inference steps and argues that this is a major obstacle in its practical usage. In this work, we also discuss performance related issues and propose different approaches to lower the computational burden in inference step. The best approach among these approaches the state of the art [14] in performance, while being competitive in computational complexity. We also discuss the problem of feature selection in order to reduce training times and improve generalization capability. We employ the well known mRMR [13] method to this end. These efficiency improvements are important steps toward making CRFs more practical tools in NLP.

The paper is organized as follows, in Section 2 we discuss the properties of Turkish related to this paper. Next, a brief background on the statistical methodologies are given in Section 3. In Section 4, we introduce our approach to POS tagging together with a discussion of several methods to improve efficiency and performance of the basic method. Comparative results are given in the Experimental Results section and finally, we conclude in Section 6.

2 Turkish

Turkish is an agglunative language which has a complex morphological structure. This property of the Turkish language leads to vast amounts of different surface structures found in texts. In a corpus of ten million words, the number of distinct words exceeds four hundred thousand [10]. There are several suffixes, which may change the POS tags of the words from noun to verb or verb to adverb, etc. Thus, it is much harder to determine the final POS tag of a word using the root such as in English. Because of this, we can not resort to lexicons of words (roots) as in many studies on English. We must use the morphological analysis of the words to determine the tags. The context dependency of tags of words must also be taken into account.

There are several tags which determine respective properties of the associated words. These tags contain syntactic and semantic information and are called morphosyntactic or morphosemantic respectively. We use the same representation for the tags as [4]. Any words in Turkish can be represented by the chain of these tags. We call these chains of tags for words morphological analyses of these words.

Turkish morphological analysis considers 116 different tags. To better model these tags and circumvent the data sparseness problems, we have partitioned these into 9 disjoint groups, called slots. The slots are determined such that the semantic relation among the tags in a slot is maximum, while it is minimum for tags across slots. Also a word can not accept more than one tag from a single slot. Essentially transforming the problem into a multiple class classification problem. Such a construction of the problem, with this particular slot partitioning, is one of the contributions of the paper. The main properties of the words are expressed in the main POS category and the other slots serve to fill in the details such as plurality, tense, etc. In this paper, we are concerned with the correct disambiguation of the main POS tags, so we are interested in identifying the value of a single slot. However, the other slots serve as features in our models, which will be discussed in detail in later sections.

Many words in Turkish texts have more than one analysis. Sometimes the number of analyses reach 23. Because of the Turkish language derivative and inflective property, in theory, one word can use an infinite number of suffixes. Due to this, we are faced with immense vocabulary in Turkish. The large vocabulary size causes data sparseness problem. Some of these suffixes change the word meanings. In this case, these changes are expressed with inflectional groups (IGs) that are separated by *^DB* sign, where *^DB*'s mean derivation boundary (root+IG1+ ^DB+IG2+ ^DB+...+ ^DB+IGn). One Turkish word can have many IGs in its analyzes. These IGs and the related tags can also be represented as tags. The standard morphological tags, also used in this work, are shown in Table 1. The example below shows the analyses for the word "alındı" produced by a Turkish two-level morphological analyzer [11].

1. al+Verb^DB+Verb+Pass+Pos+Past+A3sg (It was taken)
2. al+Adj^DB+Noun+Zero+A3sg+P2sg+Nom^DB+Verb+Zero+Past+A3sg (It was your red)
3. al+Adj^DB+Noun+Zero+A3sg+Pnon+Gen^DB+Verb+Zero+Past+A3sg (It was the one of the red)
4. alındı+Noun+A3sg+Pnon+Nom (receipt)
5. alın+Verb+Pos+Past+A3sg (resent)
6. alın+Noun+A3sg+Pnon+Nom^DB+Verb+Zero+Past+A3sg (It was the forhead)

Slot Groups	Slot Values
Main POS	Adj, Adv, Conj, Det, Dup, Interj, Noun, Num, Postp, Pron, Punc, Verb
Minor POS	Able, Acquire, ActOf, Adamantly, AfterDoingSo, Agt, Almost, As, AsIf, AsLongAs, Become, ByDoingSo, Card, Caus, DemonsP, Dim, Distrib, EverSince, FeelLike, FitFor, FutPart, Hastily, InBetween, Inf, Inf1, Inf2, Inf3, JustLike, Ly, Ness, NotState, Ord, Pass, PastPart, PCAbl, PCAcc, PCDat, PCGen, PCIns, PCNom, Percent, PersP, PresPart, Prop, Quant, QuesP, Range, Ratio,Real, Recip, ReflexP, Rel, Related, Repeat, Since, SinceDoingSo, Start, Stay, Time, When, While, With, Without, Zero
Person Agreements	A1pl, A1sg, A2pl, A2sg, A3pl, A3sg
Possessive Agreements	P1pl, P1sg, P2pl, P2sg, P3pl, P3sg, Pnon
Case Markers	Abl, Acc, Dat, Equ, Gen, Ins, Loc, Nom
Polarity	Neg, Pos
Tense/Mood	Aor, Desr, Fut, Imp, Neces, Opt, Pres, Prog1, Prog2, Cop, Cond, Past, Narr
Compund Tense	Comp_Cond, Comp_Narr, Comp_Past
Cop	Cop

Table 1: Morphological Tags

3 Background

In this section, we shall introduce the basic statistical mechanisms employed in this work. Discussion on details will be given in Section 4.

3.1 Conditional Random Fields

Simply put, CRF is a conditional distribution $p(\mathbf{y}|\mathbf{x})$ in the form of a Gibbs distribution and with an associated graphical structure encoding conditional independence assumptions. Because the model is conditional, dependencies among the input variables x are not explicitly represented, enabling the use of rich and global features of the input (neighboring words, capitalization...). CRFs are undirected graphical models used to calculate conditional probability of realizations of random variables on designated output nodes given the values assigned to other designed input nodes. In the special case, where the output nodes of the graphical model are linked by edges in a linear chain, CRFs make a first-order Markov independence assumption and thus can also be understood as a conditionally-trained finite state machine (FSM).

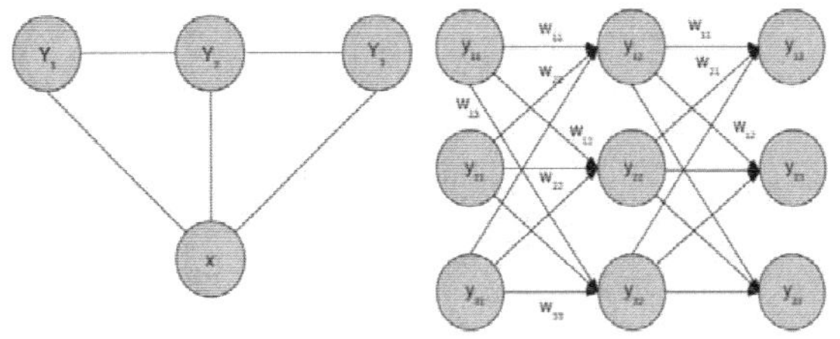

Figure 1: The equivalent expression of a linear chain CRF (on the left) as a FST (on the right)

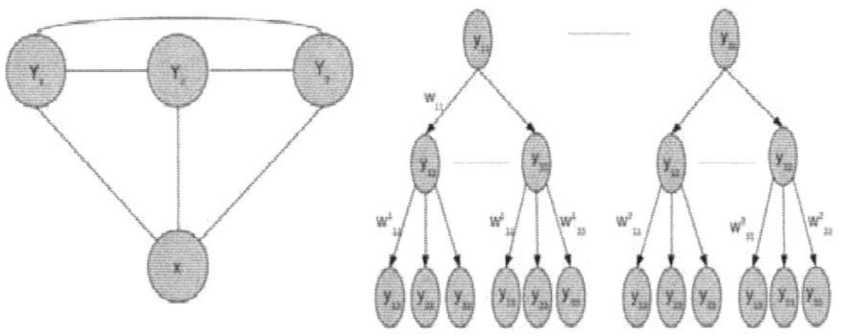

Figure 2: The equivalent expression of a 2nd order CRF (on the left) as a FST (on the right)

The distribution related to a given CRF is found using the normalized product of potential functions ($\Psi_C(\mathbf{y}_C)$) for each clique (C). The potential function itself can be, in principle, any non-negative function. Formally, the conditional probability $p(\mathbf{y}|\mathbf{x})$ can be expressed as

$$\begin{aligned} p(\mathbf{y}|\mathbf{x}) &= \frac{1}{Z(\mathbf{x})}\Pi_C \Psi_C(\mathbf{y}_C, \mathbf{x}) \\ &= \frac{1}{Z(\mathbf{x})} exp(-\sum_C H_C(\mathbf{y}_C, \mathbf{x})) \end{aligned} \quad (1)$$

On the above equations, $H_C(\mathbf{y}_C, \mathbf{x}) = \log(\Psi_C(\mathbf{y}_C, \mathbf{x}))$. A CRF can also be seen as a weighted finite state transducer [16]. For example, in Figures 1 and 2, we can see the equivalent expression of a linear chain (1st order) CRF and 2nd order CRF as finite state transducers. These figures clearly show the parameter explosion when the order is increased. Higher number of parameters denies us the possibility of accurate parameter explosion in finite data. Indeed, using CRFs with order greater than one, deteriorates the model performance. On the other hand, a CRF of order 0 discards all neighbourhood information, effectively eliminating the advantages of sequential modeling. Unlike MEMM (see [7]), the transition weights in CRF are unnormalized, the weight of the whole path is normalized instead, which alleviates the label-bias problem.

The associated undirected graph of a CRF also indicates the conditional independence assumptions of the models. In undirected graphs, independence can be established simply by graph separation: if every path from a node in X to a node in Z goes through a node in Y , we conclude that $X \perp Z|Y$. In other words, X and Z are independent given Y. Properly modeling conditional independencies is essential in any statistical machine learning application, as having too many parameters will most often result in degraded performance.

3.2 Automatic Feature Selection

One method to improve the performance of a machine learning method is to select a subset of informative features [2]. The minimum Redundancy Maximum Relevance (mRMR [13]) method relies on the intuitive criteria for feature selection which states that the best feature set should give as much information regarding the class variable as possible while at the same time minimize inter-variable dependency as much as possible (avoiding redundancy). The two concepts, relevancy and redundancy, can be naturally expressed using information theoretic concept of mutual information. However, real data observed in various problems are usually too sparse to correctly estimate the joint probability distribution and consequently the full mutual information function. The solution proposed in [13], employs two different measures for redundancy (Red) and relevance (Rel):

$$Red = 1/|S|^2 \sum_{F_i, F_j \in S} MI(F_i, F_j) Rel = 1/|S| \sum_{F_i \in S} MI(F_i, R) \tag{2}$$

In the expressions above, S is the set of features of interest, $MI(.,.)$ is the mutual information function, R is the class variable and F_i is the random variable corresponding to the ith feature. Then the goal of mRMR is to select a feature set S that is as relevant ($\max(Rel)$) and as non redundant ($\min(Red)$) as possible. In the original work [13], two criteria to combine Rel and Red were proposed. In this work, the criterion of Mutual Information Difference ($MID = Rel - Red$) is used, because it is known to be more stable than the other proposed criterion ($MIQ = Rel/Red$) [1].

As a side note, we have also considered the "feature induction" in [8]. However, we have observed a significant drop in accuracy and therefore will not discuss this approach in this paper.

4 Proposed Framework

In the proposed method, POS tagging of a sentence is performed in a series of steps. In the most basic form we begin by computing the features related to the sentence, later the conditional probabilities of possible tag assignments are computed and the most probable tag sequence are selected.

The proposed method makes use of the mallet library [9] and the mRMR source code found in [12].

4.1 Features

In a linear chain conditional random field, there are two types of features, edge features and node features. Edge features are functions of labels of consecutive words ($f_k(y_i, y_{i+1})$) and node features are functions of words in the sentence ($f_k(y_i, \mathbf{x})$, where **x** denotes words of the sentence). The probability of a sequence is determined by the feature values as well as the associated model parameters. Thus, determining good feature functions that describe the important characteristics of the words is crucial for a successful model. We employ several morphological/syntactical properties as features.

In our model, the feature functions f_k are determined using several tests such as capitalization, end of sentence, etc. Results of these tests together constitute the features vector $F = f_1, f_2, ..., f_k$ for a word.

To illustrate the two kinds of features, let's consider one feature for node and edge type features used in our model. The *Color* feature is an example for a node feature, it is a function that returns one if the word is among a set of words describing colors and zero otherwise. The indicator function $\Phi(y_i = Adj, y_{i+1} = Noun)$, which returns one if the expression is true and zero otherwise, is an example of an edge feature.

The edge functions in our proposed method consist of all possible slot value pairs. The node functions are given in Table 2. The features "Color Set Feature", "Digit Set Feature", "Pronoun Set Feature", "Transition Set Feature" and "Non-Restrictive Set Feature" indicate whether the word is a member of corresponding sets of special words. These sets correspond to specific linguistic classes in Turkish language. The "Noun Adj Feature" indicates whether the word has suffixes that are generally used to change a noun to an adjective. "Capital Feature" indicates whether the word starts with a capital letter. "Before amount feature" and "Before Ques Morpheme Feature" indicate whether the word is followed by a special word/class of words. As their names imply, "Beginning Sentence Feature" and "End Sentence Feature" indicate whether the word is at the beginning or the end of the sentence. Finally, "Equal Slot", "X2Y Before" and "X2Y After" feature

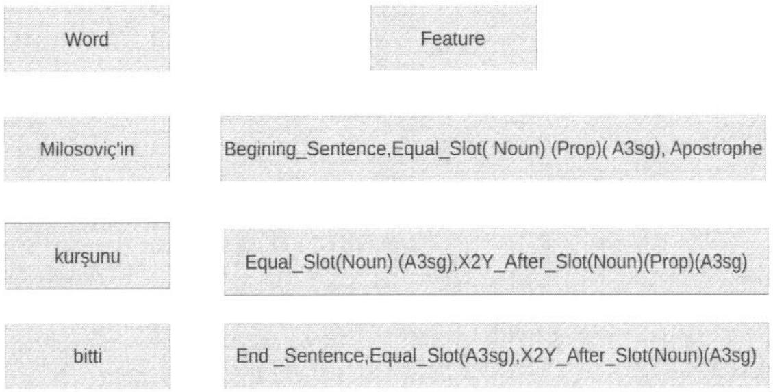

Figure 3: A sample sentence and the corresponding features

templates generate features based on whether respectively the word itself, the word before or after it has a particular slot value which is unambiguously known, i.e. these values are the same for all possible analyses of the word. These classes of features contain 363 feature functions. However, in application, some of these features were discarded using mRMR as explained in Section 3.2. Figure 3 shows a sample sentence and the corresponding features. In this Figure, we observe that the first word "Milosevic'in" gets the "Beginning" feature. Since the morphological analyzer states that the fact that this word is "A3sg", "Noun" and "Prop" unambigously, i.e. these tags showup in all of the possible parses, we also have the "Equal Slot" generated features of "A3sg", "Noun" and "Prop". Finally, we see the feature "X2Y Before A3sg" which means the word after this one is unambigously known to be "A3sg". We can confirm this by checking the next word "kursunu" where we can see the feature "A3sg" as expected. The features for the other words can be understood similarly.

Feature Templates	**Number of Corresponding Features**
Capital_Feature	1
End_Sentence_Feature	1
Begining_Sentence_Feature	1
Color_Set_Feature	1
Equal_Slot_Feature	116
Digit_Set_Feature	1
Before_Mi_Feature	1
Pronoun_Set_Feature	1
Transition_Set_Feature	1
Nonrestrictive_Set_Feature	1
Before_Amount_Feature	1
Noun_Adj_Feature	1
X2Y_Before_slot	116
X2Y_After_slot	116
After_Capital_Feature	1
Proper_Feature	1
PostP_Feature	1
Apostrophe_Feature	1
Total	363

Table 2: The features considered in this work

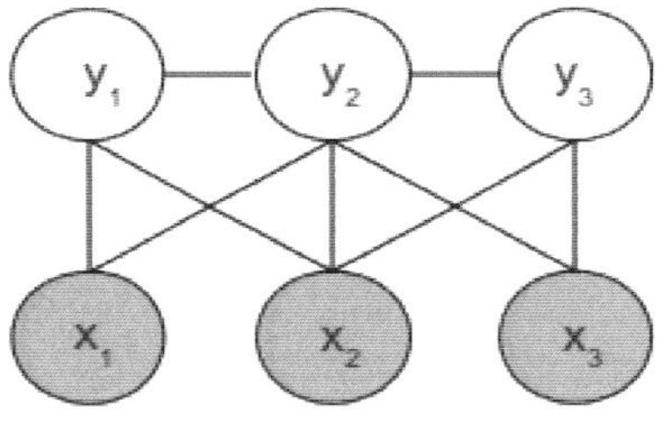

Figure 4: The graphical model of the proposed approach

4.2 Models

In this section, we explain our basic approach for POS tagging and introduce some slight variations which improve the efficiency and performance.

4.2.1 Basic Model

The CRF trained for POS tags are conditioned on the features of the sentence. However, during POS tagging, we also know a set of possible tags given by the morphological analyzer, which we call possible solution sequences ($\mathbf{S}_i$). Thus, we have a further conditioning.

$$p(\mathbf{S}_i|C) = \frac{p(\mathbf{S}_i|\mathcal{F}(C))}{\sum_j p(\mathbf{S}_j|\mathcal{F}(C))} \tag{3}$$

Where C is the sentence and $\mathcal{F}(C)$ is the corresponding feature representation of the sentence, given by the CRF. In other words, we do not assign the most probable tag sequence according to the conditional probability given by the CRF but select the most probable sequence ($\hat{\mathbf{t}}$) among possible sequences instead. This selection is performed by a constrained Viterbi approach, where the Viterbi is run on states that are deemed possible by the morphological analyser, instead of running Viterbi on the whole state space.

$$\hat{\mathbf{t}} = \arg\max_{S_i} p(\mathbf{S}_i|C) \tag{4}$$

The graphical model for the proposed method is shown in Figure 4.

Figure 5 shows a sample sentence and how our method chooses the POS tags. The top part of the figure shows the features for the respective words and the bottom part shows the possible POS tags as given by the analyzer. The values indicated above the arrows show transition weights. Note that in this example, any path from a tag of the initial word to a tag of the last word is a possible solution. In this figure, the weights of the transitions are the functions of the initial state, the final state and the features of the final word. The weight function is actually a factored expression, where $f(s_i, s_{i+1}, \mathcal{F}(w_{i+1})) = q(s_i, s_{i+1})q(s_{i+1}, \mathcal{F}(w_{i+1}))$, the first term corresponds to the edge features and the second term corresponds to node features.

4.2.2 Alternative Models

The basic approach of using CRF for POS tagging has an important disadvantage: high computational complexity. To remedy this issue, we propose these methods: dividing sentences into shorter sub-sentences and using marginal probabilities of tag assignments per word to eliminate the unlikely tags. In addition, we introduce a new approach to improve the performance of the basic method without significant overhead. In this section, we describe these methods and briefly comment on their performances. The quantitative results will be given in the Results Section.

Note that the complexity of the constrained Viterbi is $O(T \times |S|^2)$, where T is the length of the sequence and $|S|$ is the maximum number of possible states in any element of the sequence.

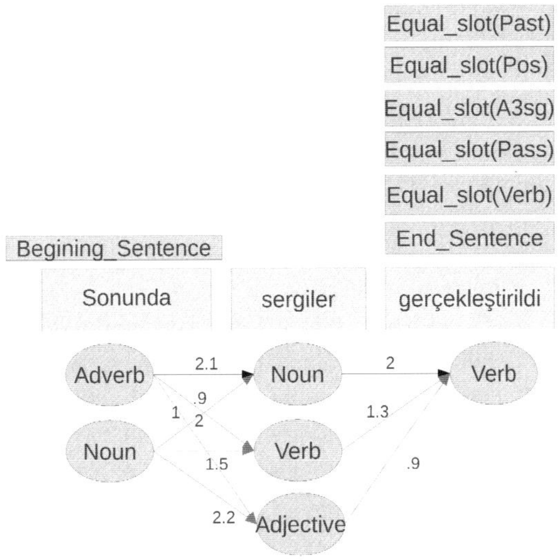

Figure 5: A sample sentence ("The exhibition has been finally realized.") with features and possible solutions. The tag chosen by our method is shown in bold arrows.

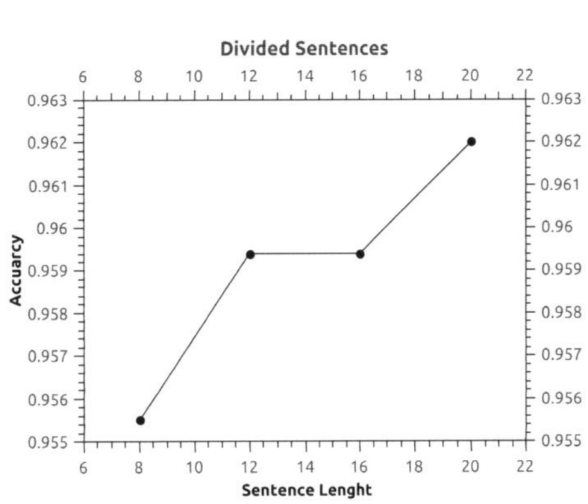

Figure 6: Accuracy vs. the length of the partial sentences

4.2.3 Model I: Splitting Sentences

This fast approximation method is conceptually the easiest one. The idea is to split a long sentence into multiple parts such that each part is shorter than a maximum length. Let's explain this method with an example sentence from our corpus. This sentence has 35389440 different possible morphological analysis sequences. The poor performance that would result from computing the probabilities of all of these possible solutions is obvious. Now suppose we divide the sentence into 4 parts of lengths 9,9,9,7. The corresponding number of possible solutions are 384, 960, 30 and 32 which sum up to 1406. The huge savings in the number of solutions to consider is apparent. However, despite these good reductions in the number of possible solutions to consider, this method results in the worst accuracy among the alternatives. This is due to the fact that splitting sentences this way enforces an independence assumption on the splitted sub-sentences, which reduces the performance especially in words that are closer to the cut-off boundaries. The Figure 6 shows the tradeoff between the performance and the length of the partial sentences.

Using this approach, the complexity of disambiguating a sentence is reduced to $O(T' \times |S|^2)$, where T'

is the maximum length of the sub-sentences, so the reduction is linear.

4.2.4 Model II: Trim Unlikely Tags

Notice that the compexity of the constrained Viterbi is linear on the length but quadratic on the maximum number of states for any element of the sequence. This observation becomes even more important when we note that the number of possible analysis of a word can reach up to 23 in our corpus and possibly more in general texts. Thus a reduction on the number of possible tag assigments of a word can have significant effects. Out of the many possible sequences for the sentence mentioned in Section 4.2.3, many include highly unlikely values for some words. The approach discussed in this section exploits this pattern by trimming out the highly unlikely tags for words but still allowing multiple possible POS tags. In our implementation, we select the words for which the number of possible tag assignments is greater than 6. For such words, we remove the least likely tag assignments using marginal probabilities until either this number is 6 or the number of eliminated tags is 5. We use such an upper limit in order not to remove too many such tags in order not to degrade accuracy. The additional complexity of this approach is obviously linear on the length of the sequence and the trimmed sequence can be disambiguated by constrained Viterbi in $O(T \times 6) = O(T)$. We can see that there can be huge savings in long sentences with compex morphological properties. The conservative approach outlined here means the accuracy is not effected at all, as shown in the next section.

4.2.5 Model III: Model Complexity of the Solutions

An interesting observation of morphological properties of words in Turkish is that the correct POS tags of the words tend to be the less morphologically complex ones. In other words, simpler interpretations of words tend to be used more often than the more complex ones of the same word. One way to operationalise this observation is to take the Bayesian stance and model a prior. However, correctly assigning numerical values for our prior knowledge is difficult and we take the other position, where the nature of this relation is learned from the data itself. In Turkish, the morphological complexity of a word can be modeled by the number of IGs of it. Thus we model this number with a 0-order CRF, since we do not expect the neighbouring IG counts to effect each other. This CRF is combined with the original one by multiplying the probabilities, i.e. we assume the number of IGs and the POS tags to be independent, which is reasonable. Since we use a 0-order CRF, the compexity of inference is only $O(T \times |S|)$. However, we do note increased performance as can be seen in the next section.

5 Experimental Results

In this section, we first show the effect of feature selection on the performance. We then show the performance of the proposed method on a common dataset and compare it with the method of [14], which is considered as the state of art. The results are obtained using default parameters of the mallet library. The Java source codes used in the experiments will be made available online.

5.1 POS tagging Results

The results for the proposed method, together with the results from [14] (Perceptron) are given in Table 3. We use the same training data (1 million words) that is used in these studies. The training data is a semi-automatically tagged data set which consists some erroneous analyses. In this study, we strived to correct as many errors as possible and trained our methods as well as the previous methods on this dataset. We have also accounted to the difference in tags employed in Hasim Sak's method and ours so we kept two separate training files, each having the same corrections but slightly different tags, so that Hasim Sak's method does not suffer from the changes in some of the tag names. Our test data (a manually disambiguated data consisting nearly 1K words) is again from [18]. Note that this set also contains errenous analyses, which we had to correct. All the results are reported using this corrected dataset, which will be made available to

Method	test set
Perc [14]	98.60
Basic Model	98.35
Model I	96.2
Model II	98.35
Model III	98.48
Model II + Model III	98.48

Table 3: Pos Tagging Performances

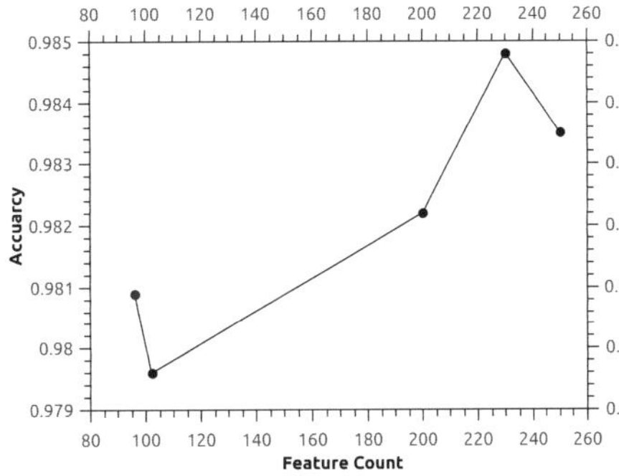

Figure 7: Accuracy vs. number of features selected by mRMR

researchers. These corrections are the reason why our results are slightly different than the ones reported in [14] The results are reported in Table 3.

The results in Table 3 exclude the punctuations in computing the accuracy. The results indicate the competitiveness of our approach. It is important to recognize that the POS tagging in Perceptron [14] method is performed by selecting the appropriate tags after a full morphological disambiguation. On the contrary, our method directly assigns a POS tag sequence to the sentence. The output of our method need not be a single assignment, instead we can output different "belief levels" for different tag assignments. If these POS tags are to be used in another procedure as an intermediate step, this will also be an advantage. Finally, the method in [14] contains a lot more number of features than our proposed approach, since our approach is flexible in the selection features, it can be extended using additional features from the Perceptron method.

5.2 Automatic Feature Selection Results

Feature selection is an important step in many machine learning tasks. The effect of feature selection is two-folds, the reduction of features may actually increase classification performance, since accidental correlations in the training data can mislead the classifier and generalization capability of classifiers is expected to be better for lower model complexity. Another effect is the improvement in training and classification efficiency, since inference in the model with a fewer number of features will be faster. For these reasons, we have dismissed the features that are not selected in the top 230 by mRMR.

Figure 7 shows the accuracy vs. the number of features. We can see that reducing the features below 230 degrades the performance significantly. Even though a significant increase in performance is not observed for the particular validation set, the reduction in features is still relevant to reduce computational complexity in test and training.

6 Conclusions

In this paper, we proposed a method using Conditional Random Fields to solve the problem of POS tagging in Turkish. We have shown that using several features derived from morphological and syntactic properties of words and feature selection, we were able to achieve a performance competitive to the state of art. Furthermore, the probabilistic nature of our method makes it possible for it to be utilized as an intermediate step in another NLP task, such that the belief distribution can be used as a whole instead of a single estimate. Note that our proposed method can also be employed to other languages, perhaps with the addition of language dependent features.

Another major contribution of this work is the discussion on several approaches to improve efficiency of POS tagging using CRFs. We believe this work constitutes a major step towards making CRF a more practical tool in NLP.

As part of our future work, we plan to investigate the addition of other features to improve the performance of the proposed method. One possibility is to incorporate features based on lemma. Eventually, we plan to combine several CRF models to solve the full disambiguation task, which poses several interesting challenges.

References

[1] Gokhan Gulgezen, Zehra Cataltepe, and Lei Yu. Stable and Accurate Feature Selection. In Wray Buntine, Marko Grobelnik, Dunja Mladenić, and John Shawe-Taylor, editors, *Machine Learning and Knowledge Discovery in Databases*, volume 5781, chapter 47, pages 455–468. Springer Berlin Heidelberg, Berlin, Heidelberg, 2009.

[2] Isabelle Guyon and André Elisseeff. An introduction to variable and feature selection. *J. Mach. Learn. Res.*, 3:1157–1182, March 2003.

[3] Nizar Habash and Owen Rambow. Arabic tokenization, part-of-speech tagging and morphological disambiguation in one fell swoop. In *Proceedings of the 43rd Annual Meeting on Association for Computational Linguistics*, ACL '05, pages 573–580, Stroudsburg, PA, USA, 2005. Association for Computational Linguistics.

[4] Dilek Hakkani-Tür, Kemal Oflazer, and Gökhan Tür. Statistical morphological disambiguation for agglutinative languages. *Computers and the Humanities*, 36(4):381–410, 2002.

[5] T. Kudo, K. Yamamoto, and Y. Matsumoto. Applying conditional random fields to japanese morphological analysis. In *Proc. of EMNLP*, volume 2004, 2004.

[6] J. Lafferty, A. McCallum, and F. C. N. Pereira. Conditional random fields: Probabilistic models for segmenting and labeling sequence data. 2001.

[7] Andrew McCallum, Dayne Freitag, and Fernando C. N. Pereira. Maximum entropy markov models for information extraction and segmentation. In *Proceedings of the Seventeenth International Conference on Machine Learning*, ICML '00, pages 591–598, San Francisco, CA, USA, 2000. Morgan Kaufmann Publishers Inc.

[8] Andrew McCallum and Wei Li. Early results for named entity recognition with conditional random fields, feature induction and web-enhanced lexicons. In *Proceedings of the seventh conference on Natural language learning at HLT-NAACL 2003 - Volume 4*, CONLL '03, pages 188–191, Stroudsburg, PA, USA, 2003. Association for Computational Linguistics.

[9] Andrew Kachites McCallum. Mallet: A machine learning for language toolkit. http://mallet.cs.umass.edu, 2002.

[10] Erhan Mengusoglu and Olivier Deroo. Turkish lvcsr: Database preparation and language modeling for an agglutinative language. In *in ICASSPâ2001, Student Forum, Salt-Lake City*, 2001.

[11] K. Oflazer. Two-level description of turkish morphology. *Literary and Linguistic Computing*, 9(2):137–148, April 1995.

[12] Hanchuan Peng. mrmr (minimum redundancy maximum relevance feature selection), 2012.

[13] Hanchuan Peng, Fuhui Long, and C. Ding. Feature selection based on mutual information criteria of max-dependency, max-relevance, and min-redundancy. *Pattern Analysis and Machine Intelligence, IEEE Transactions on*, 27(8):1226 –1238, aug. 2005.

[14] Hasim Sak, Tunga Gungor, and Murat Saraclar. Morphological disambiguation of turkish text with perceptron algorithm. In *Proceedings of the 8th International Conference on Computational Linguistics and Intelligent Text Processing*, CICLing '07, pages 107–118, Berlin, Heidelberg, 2007. Springer-Verlag.

[15] D. Shacham and S. Wintner. Morphological disambiguation of hebrew: A case study in classifier combination. In *Proceedings of EMNLP-CoNLL*, volume 7, pages 439–447, 2007.

[16] Noah A. Smith, David A. Smith, and Roy W. Tromble. Context-based morphological disambiguation with random fields. In *Proceedings of the conference on Human Language Technology and Empirical Methods in Natural Language Processing*, HLT '05, pages 475–482, Stroudsburg, PA, USA, 2005. Association for Computational Linguistics.

[17] C. Sutton and A. McCallum. An introduction to conditional random fields. *Arxiv preprint arXiv:1011.4088*, 2010.

[18] Deniz Yuret and Ferhan Töre. Learning morphological disambiguation rules for turkish. In *Proceedings of the main conference on Human Language Technology Conference of the North American Chapter of the Association of Computational Linguistics*, HLT-NAACL '06, pages 328–334, Stroudsburg, PA, USA, 2006. Association for Computational Linguistics.

台語朗讀資料庫之自動切音技術應用於音文同步有聲書之建立

Automatic Time Alignment for a Taiwanese Read Speech Corpus and its Application to Constructing Audiobooks with Text-Speech Synchronization

黃偉杰 Wei-jay Huang
長庚大學資訊工程研究所

林志柔 Jhih-rou Lin
長庚大學資訊工程研究所

呂仁園 Ren-yuan Lyu
長庚大學資訊工程研究所, CS Dept. Chang Gung University
renyuan.lyu@gmail.com

江永進 Yuang-chin Chiang
清華大學統計所, Institute of Statistics, Tsing Hua University

張智星 Jyh-Shing Roger Jang
清華大學資訊所, CS Dept., Tsing Hua University

高明達 Ming-Tat Ko
中研院資訊所, Institute of Information Science, Academia Sinica

摘要

本篇論文是運用語音辨識中的自動切音技術，來建立有聲書之音文同步的功能。目前我們使用台灣教育部網站公開的閩南語朗讀文章共 140 篇，處理了約 11 個小時的語音，將近有 83%的文字之對應語音的時間點可被切出。最後將這些帶有時間點的文字放到 Youtube 與自己架設的網站上來呈現音文同步的效果，以做為進階的語言訓練教材之應用。

關鍵詞：語音辨識，自動切音，有聲書，音文同步，音文對齊，強制對齊技術

一、緒論

台灣是多語的社會，其中華語、台語、客語、原住民語言、甚至日語以及英語皆有一定的族群使用之。在本論文中我們針對台語做為研究與應用的標的語言。近年來因本土化的影響，台語研究漸受到重視，台語的語音資料可以由網路上擷取或者由廣播電視之台語新聞以及戲劇節目取得，蒐集到的語音資料需要經過一番整理才能作為後續使用，近年來電腦有聲書逐漸流行，有了聲音和文字連結的輔助，應能讓學習台語的人有更好的學習效果，但是製作有聲書的過程中有一部分工作相當麻煩，亦即聲音與文字的連結。一般而言需要花費大量人工作切音以及音文對齊，由於成本考量，一般有聲書至多僅做到句子層級的音文同步，本論文嘗試運用語音辨識技術中強制對齊技術(force alignment)，來

令台語語音資料庫達到在字或音節層級的音文對齊，以做為進階的語言訓練教材之應用。

本論文語料蒐集為台語，我們所擷取的資料庫為「閩南語朗讀文章選輯」[3]，資料庫收錄文章 140 篇（含重複者 7 篇），資料庫的內容為教育部特別邀請學者專家選錄文章，並聘請專人將文章內容改寫成適合朗讀之文稿，名為「閩南語朗讀文章選輯」，以供各界學習參考，在文字標音方面則是依據臺灣閩南語羅馬字拼音方式標注，另外也請國立教育廣播電臺錄製聲音檔每一篇文章配置一個聲音檔，盼望藉此提升大眾學習母語的興趣，資料庫第一篇列在圖一以為參考。

001 牛墟（hi） //紀傳洲（18/04/07thk改寫）

古早，牛是台灣人上重要的作穡（tsoh-sit）伴，牛會犁田、拖車、駛石碾、挨塗礱（e-thôo-lâng）…便若較粗重的空課攏愛伊鬥做。伊攏是恬恬仔搰力（kut-la̍t）去做，予（hōo）人真感心。這種性癖真成（sîng）咱台灣人，毋才講咱是「台灣牛」。

圖一、「閩南語朗讀文章選輯」第一篇：「牛墟」部分內容

整個資料庫的資訊列表如表一。

表一、資料庫資訊

錄音人數	2 人
聲音檔 Wav 總容量	1.21G
聲音檔 Sample rate	16kHz
總時間	681.37 分鐘
總篇數	133 篇
總句數	15923 句
總字數	139271 字

由於文字格式的不同所以要經過格式的整理及編碼的轉換，後續才是拼音系統的轉換，本實驗都轉換為福爾摩莎 ForPA 拼音系統，傳統切音方式多為使用 Transcriber 軟體輔助以人工切割使得句子與聲音能夠做連結，然而人工切割不僅耗時且無法達到精細層面的切割。因此本論文提出一個精細層面的自動切音之機制以降低切割所需的時間與人力。此機制利用 HTK 訓練模型和辨識，使得電腦於音節(Syllable)的層次上自動找到最佳的切割時間點，接著再使用 Transcriber 呈現結果，經過效能分析的結果可知經過語音切割的方法錯誤平均值從 0.16 秒提升到 0.06 秒並且可知使用 HTK 切割效能比等切效能較佳。本論文採用 HTK 的音文對齊技術，針對台灣教育部出版的「閩南語朗讀文章選輯」之台語朗讀語料，做到聲音與文字在「音節」層級的對齊，音節對齊精確度可達 95%以上。這項技術應用於「音文同步有聲書」之建立，已將整套「閩南語朗讀文章選輯」建立成網頁應用程式，將在取得教育部授權後，開放給各界自由瀏覽聆聽。

二、台語文字處理

在「閩南語朗讀文章選輯」中出現的台語文字，是台語漢羅文，也就是漢字以及羅馬字並存的文字，其中羅馬字的部分採用教育部建議的「台羅拼音」。以下是一些典型的例句：

例 1.「牛是台灣人上重要的作穡（tsoh-sit）伴。」

例 2.「牛會犁田、拖車、駛石碾、挨塗礱（e-thôo-lâng）。」
例 3.「人來客去濟 kah 若鰗（but）仔魚。」
例 4.「規車疊 kah 滇洘洘（tīnn-khó-x）。」

在上述例句中，「作穡（tsoh-sit）」、「挨塗礱（e-thôo-lâng）」、「鰗（but）」、「滇洘洘（tīnn-khó-x）」等，即是漢字後面括弧加註「台羅拼音」式的「音標」，把音標移除並不影響文義的表達；而「濟 kah 若鰗仔魚」、「疊 kah 滇洘洘」之中的「kah」則本身是「文字」，是文句中不可或缺的一部份。由於台羅拼音包含字母修飾符，如上述例子中的「ô」、「â」、「ī」、「ó」等，用來做為台語的聲調記號，因此我們必須採用 Unicode 做為編碼集，不能沿用一般的 Ascii/Big5 編碼，否則會有資訊遺失及顯示出現亂碼的現象，此為台語文字處理必須特別留意之處。下圖為轉換流程圖。

將輸入文章分漢羅

分漢羅之後的每一個字串:

1. 檢查英文
2. 調形字母轉換成平常字母
3. TL 拼音轉換 ForPA 拼音

輸出轉換完成後的文章

圖二、轉換流程圖

1. 分漢羅：

所謂分漢羅，意思是將文句中的漢字與羅馬字分離出來。舉例來說，要將如下字串分成子字串序列：

```
'這種性嘛真成（sing5）咱台灣人。'
⇩
['這', '種', '性', '嘛', '真', '成', '（', 'sing5', '）', '咱', '台', '灣', '人', '。']
```

分成子字串之後，進一步的處理、轉換較容易進行。
分漢羅可以用“正規表示法”(regular expression)實現。較細節之處暫時不管，分漢羅的 python 表示可以是：

```
re.split('([一-鶴]|[a-zA-Z]+\d*)',漢羅字串)
```

re 是 Python 的 regularexpress 模組，詳細語法請見 Python 參考書。 其中漢字“一”的 unicode 編碼是\u4E00 漢字“鶴”的 unicode 編碼 是\uFA2D，中間包括大多數現在台灣使用的漢字。以前例而言，Python 執行結果如下：

```
>>> jj='這種性嘛真成（sing5）咱台灣人。'
>>> re.split('([一-鶴]|[a-zA-Z]+\d*)',jj)
['', '這', '', '種', '', '性', '', '嘛', '', '真', '', '成', '（', 'sing5', '）', '咱', '', '台', '', '灣', '', '人', '。']
```

(注意到分漢羅的子字串包括幾個空白字串，但那些不造成處理轉換的困難。)
不幸的，上述的分漢羅，對有調形的拼音字，會產生錯誤：

```
>>> ii='真成（sîng）咱台灣人。'
>>> re.split('([一-鶴]|[a-zA-Z]+\d*)',ii)
['', '真', '', '成', '（', 's', 'î', 'ng', '）', '咱', '', '台', '', '灣', '', '人', '。']
```

注意到 調形拼音字“sîng”， 沒有分正確。

“讓格書寫的 Python 工具箱(LGO.py)”中的 hunHL 函式[2]，正是基於類似的想法，考慮了更多的細節，正合乎我們的需要：

```
>>> ii='這種性嘛真成（sîng）咱台灣人。'
>>> hunHL(ii)
['這', '種', '性', '嘛', '真', '成', '（', 'sîng', '）', '咱', '台', '灣', '人', '。']
```

由上述的執行結果可看出，調形拼音字“sîng”，已正確完成分開。

2. 調形字母的轉換：

所謂調形字母的轉換，是將調形字母轉換成對應的數字加在字母後面做代表，譬如 e-thôo-lâng， 需要轉換成數字拼音字 e1-thoo5-lang5。台羅拼音所使用的調形字母，及其對應的拼音、調號，我們用三個字串表示，如下表二對應表。

表二、對應表

```
調形字 ='ô â a̍ ō î'
平常字 ='o a a o i'
聲調   ='5 5 8 7 7'
```

有了這三個字串，我們容易製作出調形字母的轉換函數，轉換需要想法是，針對每一字母，檢查是不是調形字母，若是，則轉換平常字母，並且記憶該聲調數字，最後才將數字串接在後。

```
>>> toBSR('siâ')
'sia5'
>>> toBSR('dâ')
'da5'
```

圖三、轉換例子

3. 轉換 ForPA 拼音：

將 TL 拼音字 替換成 ForPA 拼音字，至少要經過兩個步驟：

(1) 第一步是分聲韻(Python 函式 hunSU)

(2) 第二步是聲韻分別替換(使用 Python Dict 直接替換) 再串接

以 TL 拼音'thoo5'為例，轉換成 ForPA 拼音的過程主要如下。

```
>>> s,u,d = splitSUD('thoo5') #S,U,D 分別表 聲、韻、調
>>> [S2S.get(s,s), U2U.get(u,u), D2D.get(d,d)]
'to5'
```

其中 splitSUD 是 分聲韻調， S2S, U2U, D2D 分別是 執行聲韻調轉換的 Python 資料結構(Python 的 dict)。以下分為四個部分說明這個過程。

(2.1)分聲韻調：

對音節有母音時，如下方的正規表示法可拆開聲韻調，

re.split('([aeiou][a-zA-Z]*)(\d*)',syllable)

譬如：

syllable = song4 => ['s', 'ong', '4', '']

但台語還有無母音音素的音節，如下表三。

表三、ForPA 及 TL 的 子音音節

ForPA 子音音節				TL 子音音節			
m	ng			m	ng		
hm	bng	png	mng	hm	png	phng	mng
	dng	tng	nng		tng	thng	nng
	gng	kng	hng		kng	khng	hng
	zng	cng	sng		chng	chhng	sng

因為沒有母音，只好小步進行：
先拆音節後面的聲調 (若無則聲調設為空字串)，聲韻部份再試用母音拆開，若無母音則試拆(ng|m)，若再無，就整個字串當韻母。例子如下圖四。

>>> splitSUD('song4')	>>> splitSUD('oai')
['s', 'ong', '4']	['', 'oai', '']
>>> splitSUD('siong2')	>>> splitSUD('oe2')
['s', 'iong', '2']	['', 'oe', '2']
>>> splitSUD('sng5')	>>> splitSUD('dfgsfd3')
['s', 'ng', '5']	['', 'dfgsfd', '3']
>>> splitSUD('sng')	>>> splitSUD('字')
['s', 'ng', '']	['', '字', '']
>>> splitSUD('ng')	
['', 'ng', '']	

圖四、聲、韻、調例子

(2.2)聲韻分別轉換：

接著我們分別轉換聲韻調，從台羅拼音到 ForPA 拼音。下圖五分別是台羅拼音及 ForPA 拼音的聲、韻、調對照表。從這三組對應字串，Python 的 dict 很容易製作出需要的替換功能。

```
TLSVOR    ='p ph m b  t th n l  k kh ng g  ch chh s j h'.split()
ForPaSVOR ='b p  m bh d t  n l  g k  ng gh z  c   s r h'.split()
```

(a)、聲、韻、調例子

```
TLUVOR ="""
a  e  i  oo u  o
ai au   ia io iu iau    ua ue ui uai
am im om iam    an en in un uan ian    ang ing ong iang iong uang
ann enn inn onn unn
ainn aunn   iann iunn iaunn   uann uenn uinn uainn
m  ng
ah  eh  ih  ooh uh  oh
aih auh   iah ioh iuh iauh    uah ueh uih uaih
ap ip op iap    at et it ut uat iat    ak ik ok iak iok uak
annh ennh innh onnh unnh
ainnh aunnh   iannh iunnh iaunnh   uannh uennh uinnh uainnh
mh  ngh
""".split()
```

```
ForPaUVOR ="""
a  e  i   o  u   er
ai au   ia ior iu iau    ua ue ui uai
am im om iam    an en in un uan ian    ang ing ong iang iong uang
ann enn inn onn unn
ainn aunn   iann iunn iaunn   uann uenn uinn uainn
m  ng
ah  eh  ih  oh uh   erh
aih auh   iah iorh iuh iauh    uah ueh uih uaih
ap ip op iap    at et it ut uat iat    ak ik ok iak iok uak
annh ennh innh onnh unnh
ainnh aunnh   iannh iunnh iaunnh   uannh uennh uinnh uainnh
mh  ngh
""".split()
```

(b)、TL韻母 對應 ForPA韻母

```
TLDiau     = '1 7 3 2 5 8 4'.split()
ForPaDiau  = '1 2 3 4 5 6 7'.split()
```

(c)、TL對應ForPA聲調表

圖五、聲、韻、調例子

依據上圖使用 Python 容易製作出對照表，並且容易使用，程式碼如下圖六。

```
S2S = {k:v for k,v in zip(TLSVOR, ForPaSVOR)}
U2U = {k:v for k,v in zip(TLUVOR, ForPaUVOR)}
D2D = {k:v for k,v in zip(TLDiau, ForPaDiau)}
    #dict{...} will map from key to value
>>> [S2S.get(S,S), U2U.get(U,U), D2D.get(D,D)]
```

圖六、Python 容易製作出對照表

聲韻分別替換，輸入為['th', 'oo','5'] 使用 Python Dict 直接替換輸出為['to5']，如下圖七。

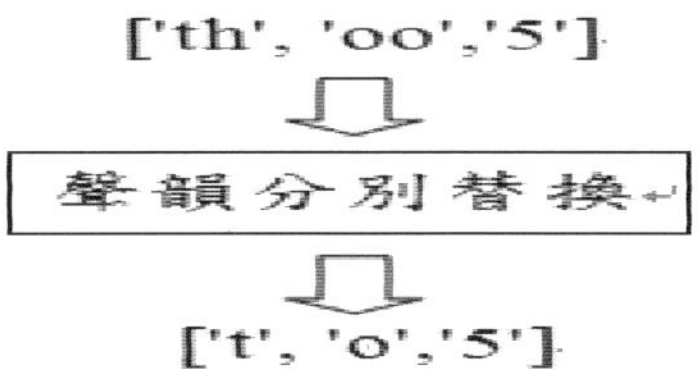

圖七、聲韻分別替換

但是，直接聲韻調替換，並沒有解決所有問題，因為台羅拼音還有“另類拼音”以及“條件變讀”問題。以下分(2.3)(2.4)進一步討論。

(2.3)台羅拼音的另類拼音法：

多少因為歷史原因，某些音素的台羅拼音，拼音法有變異，如下表另類拼音法幾個例子。

表四、另類拼音法幾個例子

TL 另類拼寫法	TL 拼音	ForPA 拼寫法
ts	ch	z
tsh	chh	c
oe	ue	ue
oa	ua	ua
oai	uai	uai

實作上， 如下圖，Python 字典可以輕易加入這些另類拼寫法：

```
S2S.update({'ts':'z','tsh':'c'})
U2U.update({'oe':'ue','oa':'ua','oai':'uai'})
```

加上這些另類拼寫，聲韻調轉換更加完整。

(2.4)台羅拼音的條件變讀問題：

台羅拼音(及教會拼音) 不幸的有條件變讀的問題，如下表：

表三、條件變讀的問題

台羅拼音		ForPA 拼音	
soo	oo 表ㄛ	so	o 表ㄛ
so	o 表ㄜ	ser	er 表ㄜ
mo	o 表ㄛ	mo	o 表
no	o 表ㄛ	no	o 表
ngo	o 表ㄛ	ngo	o 表

在此變讀是符號 o 在不同音節中代表不同的音素。所以，如果直接替換將 o 直接替換成 er，則 mo/no/ngo 換成 mer/ner/nger，將發生錯誤。因此聲韻調替代時，應考慮周遭音境，如下 Python 聲韻調替代程式。

```
S,U,D = splitSUD(syllable)
if S in {'m n ng'.split()} and U is 'o':
    rr = [S,U,D]
else :
    rr = [S2S.get(S,S), U2U.get(U,U), D2D.get(D,D)]
```

最後我們從教育部網站上取得「閩南語朗讀文章選輯」，再由台語的專業人士幫忙將漢字拼打成台語音標，接著我們依照上述的台語文字處理，將每句的漢字與台語音標使用 Transcriber 來表示如下圖八。

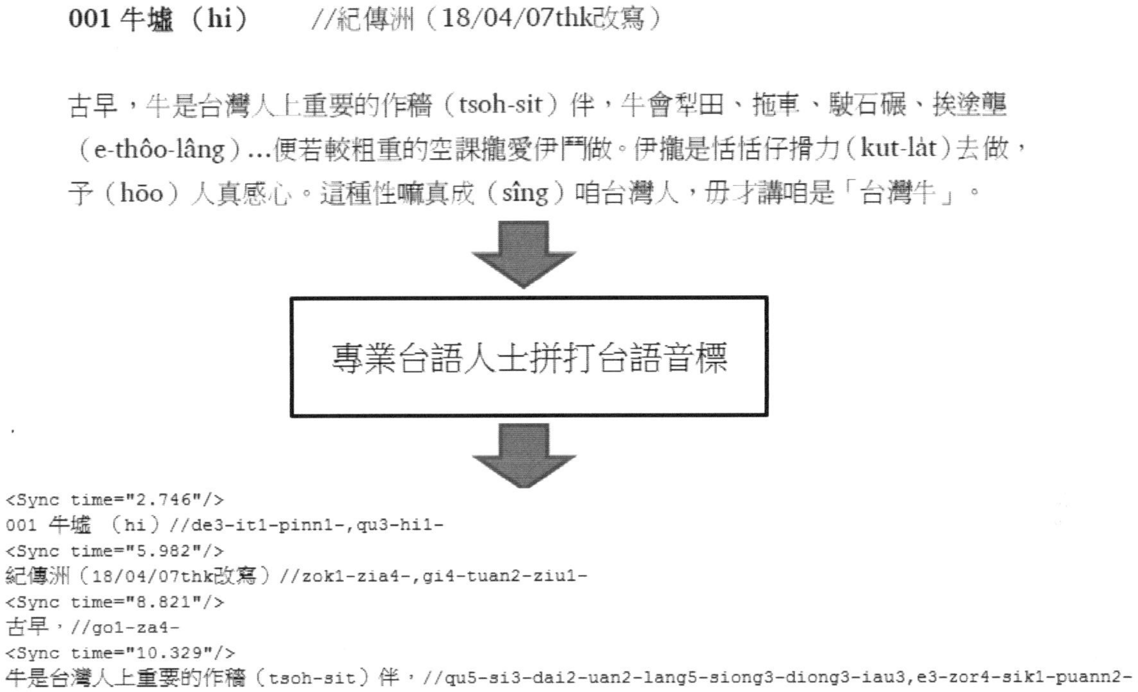

圖八、台語文字處理流程

三、台語語音處理

我們運用 HTK 以及 Python 程式語言寫成 CguAlign 程式，可以執行自動切音過程。
配合部分手動的處理，本篇論文以教育部閩南語朗讀 1~10 篇(Combine001)[3]為例，我們將整個手動的資料處理到自動切音的過程以下圖一來說明：

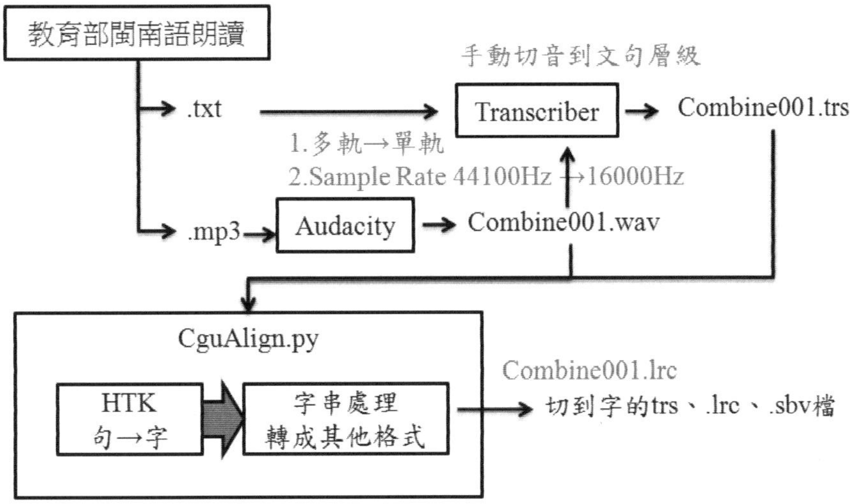

圖九、系統流程圖

手動的資料處理：

從教育部閩南語朗讀上取得 txt 文字檔以及對應的 mp3 語音檔，由於需要使用到 HTK 的幫助，而 HTK 在語音檔的部分只能處理 wav 的檔案，所以使用 Audacity[6]將原來 mp3 檔轉成 wav 檔，這裡需要將語音檔的 Sample rate 換成 16000Hz 以及雙軌變成單軌。接著將 txt 文字檔與轉好的 wav 語音檔傳入 Transcriber[5]中，以手動的方式將整段文章切到文句的層級，輸出一個 trs 檔。手動資料處理的部分告一段落，以下為 CguAlign 自動切音過程。

CguAlign 自動切音過程：

CguAlign 自動讀取一個切到文句的 trs 檔與一個 wav 語音檔，Output 出切到字層級的 trs 檔、lrc 檔與 sbv 檔。以下我們分為兩個部分來詳細介紹自動切音的過程。下圖二為 CguAlign 的主程式碼。

```
def CguAlign主程式():

    原文檔名集=['Combine001',#]
    '''
    '''

    建立資料夾()

    for x in 原文檔名集:

        trsFn = 'Input/切到句的trs檔/'+ x +'.trs'
        wavFn = 'Input/wav/'+ x +'.wav'

        語音總時間長度=將trs檔的時間與對應字串轉成多個lab檔(trsFn)

        將長語音檔依照lab檔所對應的時間來切割成多個短語音檔(wavFn)

        製造各個HtkTool所需的參數檔()

        處裡語音標籤及詞典()

        擷取語音特徵及訓練語音模型()

        將語音文字做對齊()

        轉成切到字的trs檔(trsFn,語音總時間長度)

        對齊原文格式並轉成切到字的lrc與sbv檔(x)

if __name__=='__main__':
    CguAlign主程式()
```

1.HTK 切音

2.字串處理
轉其他格式

圖十、CguAlign 主程式碼

1. 使用 HTK[1]來切音：

(1) 將 trs 檔的時間與對應字串轉成多個 lab 檔
抓取切到句層級 trs 中的時間與對應字串，在時間部分轉換時間的格式；在相同時間的字串部分，將字串頭尾加上 sil，並在字與字中間空白處替換成底線來連接成句。

(2) 將長語音檔依照 lab 檔所對應的時間來切割成多個短語音檔
將長語音檔依照 lab 檔中每行的時間進行切音，並轉存成多個短語音檔。

(3) 製造各個 HtkTool 所需的參數檔
這裡製造出 7 個參數檔，分別為 hLed.led、hLed00.led、hCopy.conf、hInit.conf、hRest.conf、hErest.conf、hVite.conf。

(4) 處裡語音標籤及詞典
主要在製作 mlf 檔。這裡開始介紹語音模型訓練及切割過程，使用 HTK 的 hled 程式，輸入為 scp 檔經過 hled 程式可以得到一個為 lst 檔另一個為 mlf 檔，這兩個檔案的差別在於 mlf 檔裡的每句話使用等切的方式記錄開始及結束的時間點。輸入為 scp 及 mlf 及 dic 檔 經過 hled 程式把 mlf 轉換成「雙音素」(Biphone)的格式，在 dic 檔中為音節對應「雙音素」的格式。

(5) 擷取語音特徵及訓練語音模型
這裡分為聲音處理與模型訓練兩個部分。
聲音處理：當我們把 lab 處理完後，下一步為自動電腦語音切音之訊號處理的層次，在訊號處理的層次來說語音辨識技術使用 mfc 可達到不錯語音辨識之效果，波型轉換到 mfc 過程中我們使用 HTK 工具，在 HTK 中要做特徵擷取的動作為 hcopy 這程式，主要觀念為輸入聲音檔經過 hopy 輸出為 mfc，在過程中需要提供 scp 檔案告訴 hcopy 什麼樣的 wav 對應到什麼樣的 mfc，另外 hcopy 本身也需要一些參數例如 windows 寬度及 windows shift 的長度…等等，hCopy.conf 檔案提供這些參數給 hcopy，執行這指令 os.system('hcopy -A -C hCopy.conf -S spWav2Mfc.scp') 來做上述的事情。
模型訓練：轉換成 mfc 後，接下來就是模型訓練因為在後續切割時需要用到，模型訓練使用 HMM 技術來製作，我們使用 HTK 的 HCompV 這程式執行以下指令為模型訓練的第一步 os.system('HCompV -A -C HCompV.conf -S spMfc.scp -m -I spLab_p.mlf -M hmms_p/ -o '+m+' myHmmPro') 。
輸入為 mfc 經過 HCompV 輸出為那些音標的 HMM 模型，並且為「雙音素」的模型，以細節來說在 spLab_p.mlf 檔案中如上圖語音標籤(lab)之處理過程為「雙音素」的型式儲存且切割的時間點為等切的時間點，spMfc.scp 檔案為在目錄下所蒐集的特徵檔列表，myHmmPro 檔案為未訓練之前先給定一個原型模型檔，內容為有幾個模型及 Mixture 及幾個 State，此檔案可以程式製作及手動製作，最後經過指令可得到初始的模型。
模型訓練的第二步讓模型更精緻化，在 HTK 中所使用的程式為 HERest，輸入為 mfc 檔經過 HERest 輸出為 HMM Phone 的模型，因為更精緻化的關係所以多提供了一個模型列表檔案，並且在跑了 5 次的迴圈，在我們程式中設定 N=5，經過更精緻化的訓練得到一組雙音素的模型，第一步及第二步做完後就把模型訓練完成，上述過程中把有加標籤的語音訊號已訓練成模型，下一步為語音切割。

(6) 將語音文字做對齊
主要為語音切割的部分。HTK 中使用語音切割的程式為 HVite，HVite 可以用在語音辨識，在賜此我們使用強制對齊(Forced alignment)這種功能，因為我們已知道音標但是不知道斷點，例如 SN0.mfc 的內容為 de_it_pinn_sil_qu_hi 對應到 lab 檔這是我們已知的語言標籤，這邊不使用。

spLab_p.mlf 檔是因為最後我們只需要切割至音節的層次不需要切割到雙音節的層次，最後在 HVite 中輸入為 mfc 及未切割時間點的 mlf 檔，經過 HVite 輸出為經過語音辨識切割出的時間點結果。請參考下圖十格式內容。

圖十一、Input、Output 格式內容

如下圖九為整個處理過程從所有語音檔及所有 lab 檔經過 hled、hcopy、HCompV、HERest、HVite 的指令，最後產生出切割好的時間點。

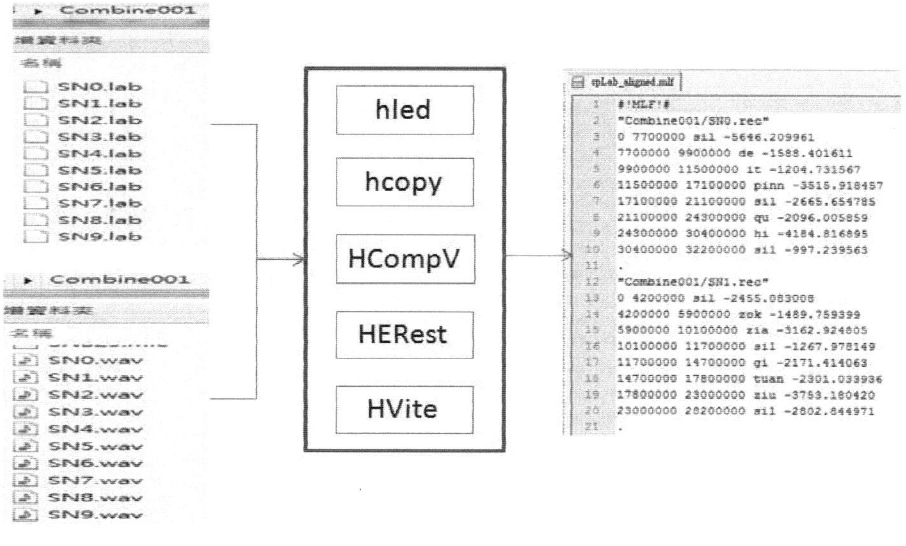

圖十二、整個處理過程

以上為 CguAlign.py 程式中的 HTK 自動切音的步驟，其中在製作聲學模型時，我們使用一個特別的方式，利用原文所出現的字當作字典，每個字一兩兩字母的方式連接做為此單字的音標，接著進行擷取語音特徵及訓練語音模型。

2. 字串處理轉其他格式：

在這部分主要將帶有切到字層級的音標與原文單字做對齊，以上述主程式碼中的 function(對齊原文格式並轉成切到字的 lrc 與 sbv 檔)來進行處理，以下圖十為此 function 的詳細說明。

```
def 對齊原文格式並轉成切到字的lrc與sbv檔(音標檔案名稱):

    音標檔內容 = 讀取檔案('Output/切到字的lab檔/'+音標檔案名稱+'_aligned.lab')

    (音標時間,音標字串,開始時間對應結束時間字典) = 將sil接到上一個音標(音標檔內容)

    (句子時間,句子字串) = 將trs檔時間與文字存成字典('Input/切到句的trs檔/'+音標檔案名稱+'.trs')

    (對齊後時間,對齊後字串) = 原文句字對齊音標(音標時間,音標字串,句子時間,句子字串,開始時間對應結束時間字典)

    轉成lrc檔(音標檔案名稱,對齊後時間,對齊後字串)

    轉成切到字的sbv檔(音標檔案名稱,對齊後時間,對齊後字串)
```

圖十三、對齊原文格式並轉成切到字的 lrc 與 sbv 檔

對齊原文格式並轉成切到字的 lrc 與 sbv 檔程式碼，將語音對齊文字 output 一個.lab 檔，其中.lab 為切到字的時間點，由於此 lab 檔所切出的字串為音標，所以將音標與原文做對齊，再轉成 lrc 與 sbv 檔以供音文同步效果之呈現，此音文同步效果可由以下網址來呈現 http://dl.dropbox.com/u/33089565/ryEx007_3.html。

四、台語切音實驗結果

（一)、切割效能分析

如下圖十一需把切音出來的結果轉回到 Transcriber 上面，因為 Transcriber 為圖型介面，很明顯的可以看出斷點，因此我們就利用人工根據主觀的判斷並且設定好螢幕解析度為 1280 x 800 一次大約可看 5 秒做調整，需要調整的地方為有明顯切割到別的音節地方才需做調整，經過人工修正我們稱為標準答案。

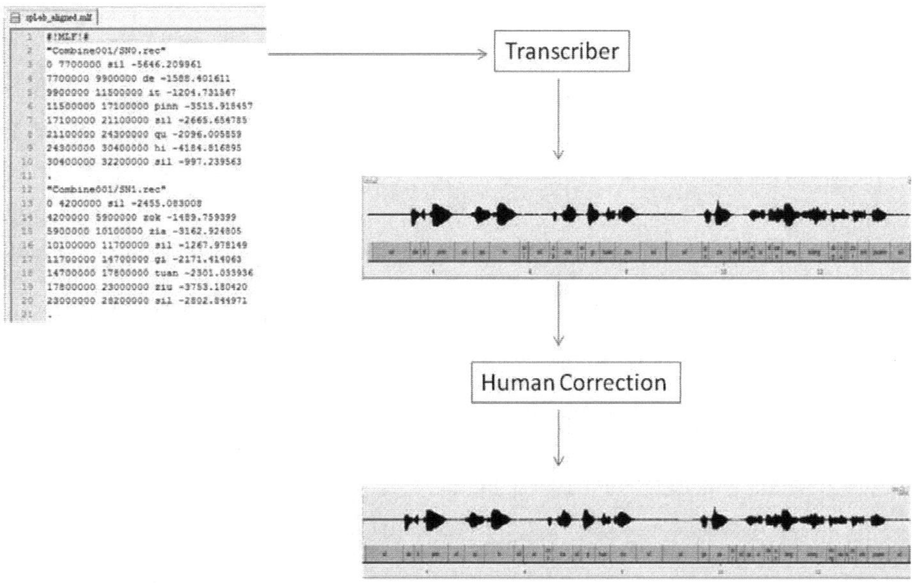

圖十四、轉回 Transcriber

有了標準答案分別再跟 HTK 切割和等切做比較，做為這邊的效能分析。如下圖十二，虛線為使用 HTK 切割出的結果，實線為標準答案，分別計算出互相對應之切割點之時間距離公式 $d_i = |r_i - t_i|$再依下式時間距離平均$\mu = \frac{\sum_{i=1}^{N-K} d_i}{(N-K)}$為錯誤平均值，其中$r_i$為 HTK 切割出的結果，為人工調整之結果即是標準答案，N 為時間點總數，K 為人工認定正確之切割點，所以不納入錯誤平均值之計算，而 N-K 為人工認定錯誤，有待調整之時間點。

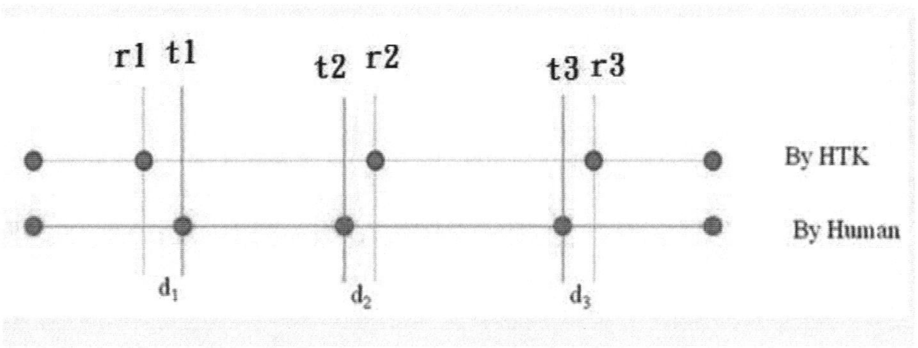

圖十五、效能分析

表四、效能分析比較

	HTK 切割	等切
錯誤平均值	0.06032 秒	0.164033 秒

此實驗的數據由第一篇文章總共 759 句產生，如上表一，以錯誤平均值來說 HTK 跟標準答案比相差 0.06 秒，等切跟標準答案比相差 0.16 秒由此可知經過語音切割的方法從 0.16 秒提升到 0.06 秒並且可知 HTK 切割其效能較佳。

（二）、切出率

我們使用切出率當做實驗結果的數據，所謂的切出率為一個時間單位只有一個單字，這裡我們分兩種方式來計算切出率，其方式一為以單字來計算切出率，方式二為以時間來計算切出率。切出率公式如下：

$$\text{切出率}(\%) = \frac{(1 - \text{未切出個數})}{\text{總數}} * 100$$

未切出個數：在方式一中代表未切出單字的數量；在方式二中代表未切出時間長度。

總數：在方式一中代表文章中全部單字的數量；在方式二中代表語音時間總長度。

表二為 CguAlign 計算教育部閩南語朗讀全集的切出率：

表五、CguAlign 計算教育部閩南語朗讀全集的切出率

	教育部閩南語朗讀全集
方式一(以單字來計算)	78.67%
方式二(以時間來計算)	82.93%

CguAlign 分析未切出之問題：語音中出現的字，文章中卻沒有出現此文字，如下圖十三教育部閩南與第一篇中在語音時間 5.176 到 5.962，出現作者但文章中卻未出現：

```
[3.506]0
[3.746]0
[3.896]1
[4.456]牛
[5.176]墟
[5.982]紀傳洲
```

圖十六、CguAlign 未切出之問題

五、音文同步有聲書系統

在音文同步效果呈現的部分，目前以兩種方式來進行，分別在 Youtube 上與我們自己所架設的網站 (CguTASync)，請連結此網址：https://dl.dropbox.com/u/36364100/wj.html ，以下為兩種方式的呈現說明：

（一）、Youtube[4]平台呈現：

我們將帶有時間點的文字放到 Youtube 平台上呈現，以 Combine001(教育部閩南語 1~10 篇)為例，下圖十四為音文同步效果的呈現，紅色框框中的牛為音文同步字幕效果呈現，點選下方紅色框框中的 CC 可以選擇你要呈現的字幕名稱，而我們就是在這裡提供帶有時間點的文字。

圖十七、Combine001 在 Youtube 平台上呈現音文同步效果

（二）、CguTASync(CguTextAudioSynchronization)呈現：

這是我們所架設的網頁，用多種方式來呈現音文同步的效果，因為某種套件的關係需由 Firefox 瀏覽器來開啟，以下圖十五為功能的介紹：

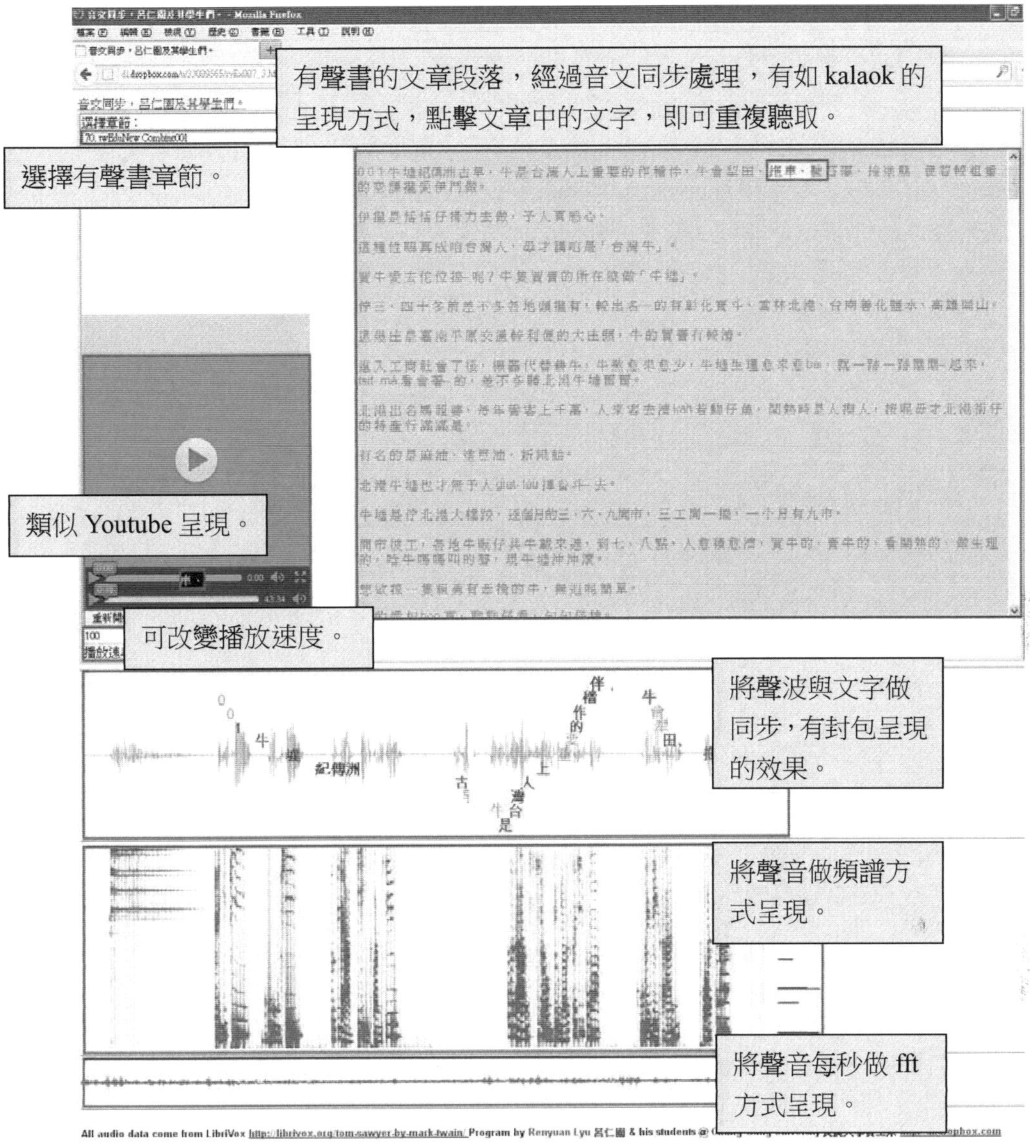

圖十八、CguTASync 音文同步效果呈現與功能說明

六、結論

台語文字在處理上較為複雜，蒐集語料庫時要注意格式、拼音的問題，蒐集的資料格式必須統一之後在進行統計，台語拼音中常使用特殊符號，所以就要使用 UTF8 來編碼，這裡特別要注意編碼的問題。把語料庫的聲音及文字利用 Transcriber 軟體做到以句子切割為時間點，以人工手動切割句子，一篇文章大約需要二十到三十分鐘總共有 140 篇文章如果要手動切割到音節的層次相對的需要花更多倍的時間，因此我們利用 HTK 工具幫我們找出音節的時間點在過程中需要訓練模型之後進行語音切割最後找出時間點並且轉回 Transcriber 格式，經過語音切割的方法從 0.16 秒提升到 0.06 秒並且可知 HTK 切割其效能較佳。在音文同步的部分，由於經過語音辨識音文對齊後，切出帶有時間的音標以與原來文章的文字不同，除之外還有失去標點符號原有的位置以及原文段落的格式，我們將這些帶有時間點的音標與原文做對齊，並還原原有文章的標點符號與段落格式。

目前我們處理了台灣教育部所提供的閩南語朗讀文章共 140 篇，處理了約 11 個小時的語音，將近有 83%的文字之對應語音的時間點可被切出。最後我們將教育部閩南語朗讀語料所處理完之帶有時間點的文字放到 YouTube 與自己架設的網站上來呈現音文同步的效果。

參考文獻

[1] S. Young, G. Evermann, D. Kershaw, G. Moore, J. Odell, D. Ollason,D. Povey, V. Valtchev, and P. Woodland, "The HTK book(for HTK version 3.4.1)," Cambridge University Engineering Department,Tech. Rep., March. 2009.

[2] 江永進(2011). 讓格書寫 Python 工具箱。 新竹：清華大學統計所。 (程式檔案 LGO.py)

[3] 全國語文競賽臺灣閩南語朗讀參考資料使用說明 http://140.111.34.54/MANDR/minna/first.html

[4] Youtube，http://www.youtube.com/

[5] Transcriber，http://trans.sourceforge.net/en/presentation.php

[6] Audacity，http://audacity.sourceforge.net/

以音韻屬性偵測擷取對話語音關鍵詞之研究

Study on Keyword Spotting using Prosodic Attribute Detection for Conversational Speech

黃昱睿 Yu-Jui Huang
國立嘉義大學資訊工程學系
Department of Computer Science and Information Engineering
National Chia-Yi University
s0990435@mail.ncyu.edu.tw

鐘尹蔚 Yin-Wei Chung
國立嘉義大學資訊工程學系
Department of Computer Science and Information Engineering
National Chia-Yi University
s0970421@mail.ncyu.edu.tw

葉瑞峰 Jui-Feng Yeh
國立嘉義大學資訊工程學系
Department of Computer Science and Information Engineering
National Chia-Yi University
ralph@mail.ncyu.edu.tw

摘要

在口語對話上，為了有效地理解使用者所要表達的資訊意義，擷取關鍵詞語是很重要的研究議題之一。本研究針對對話語音內容的關鍵詞，提出以音韻屬性來做為擷取關鍵詞的特徵。利用預先訓練的決策樹將語者語句分段成韻律詞，進一步使用支援向量機(SVM)來偵測韻律詞是否為關鍵詞。在此利用中研院語言研究所鄭秋豫所提出階層式多短語語流韻律架構與韻律詞邊界的偵測方法，而邊界偵測為利用其韻律特性建立的決策樹來偵測。最後，以音韻屬性為特徵來做為偵測的參數，藉由 SVM 分析各個韻律詞之特徵值找出焦點所在語音時間區段，藉由擷取此焦點作為關鍵詞。最後部分為針對錄製的對話語料進行實驗並分析，所得到的準確度與召回率比參照發音相似度或聲學特徵還要高，證實所提方法在關鍵詞擷取是可行的。

Abstract

It is one of most essential issues to extract the keywords from conversational speech for understanding the utterances from speakers. This thesis aims at keyword spotting from spontaneous speech for keyword detecting. We proposed prosodic features that are used for keyword detection. The prosody words are segmented from speaker's utterance according to the pre-training decision tree. The supported vector machine is further used as the classifier to judge the prosody word is keyword or not. The prosody word boundary segmentation algorithm based on decision tree is illustrated. Besides the data driven feature, the knowledge obtained from the corpus observation is integrated in the decision tree. Finally, the keyword in the focus part are extracted using prosody features by sported vector machine (SVM). According to the experimental results, we can find the proposed method outperform the phone verification approach especially in recall and accuracy. This shows the proposed approach is operative for keyword detecting.

關鍵詞：關鍵詞語、音韻屬性、韻律詞、口述語言。

Keywords: Keyword spotting, prosodic feature, prosody word, spoken language.

一、緒論

關鍵詞辨識(Keyword spotting)在近代語音研究與應用上為一項很重要的學問，其目的是讓電腦系統能夠從語音資料裡面，自動偵測出特定的關鍵詞彙。於應用上也包含了很多層面，例如語音資料檢索(新聞報導、影片資料、電視轉播等)、自動語音轉接總機系統、查詢服務等。在人機溝通方面，以自發性語音(Spontaneous speech)為主要輸入方式的對話系統(Dialogue system)裡，因為每個人的言談風格(Speaking style)都有所差異，很難以文法(Grammar)的角度來完整分析語者所要表達的涵義。在實際應用上，考量到對話系統之即時性(Real time)，如何讓系統對於使用者的語音資訊做充分的掌握，再再影響了對話系統之實用與否。Kawahara 等人就把關鍵詞語的擷取(Keyword extraction)與確認(Verification)結合剖析器應用於對話系統，其主要步驟分為關鍵片語偵測(Key-phrase detection)、關鍵片語驗證(Key-phrase verification)、句子剖析(Sentence parsing)以及句子驗證(sentence verification)四個部分。麻省理工學院則提出漸進式的對話理解架構(Incremental understanding)，有效擷取系統所需之資訊[1]，而這樣的理念最早是由心理學者 Charpter 等人根據人類口語對話之理解程序所提出的[2]。可以想見關鍵詞與漸進式理解方式在語音對話中是很關鍵的兩個部分。因此如何將語音的關鍵詞擷取出來加以確認，便是口述語言理解(Spoken Language Understanding, SLU)上一個重要的課題。另一方面，為了增加語音辨識的正確性，很多學者提出了不同的額外語音特性來幫助辨識，喬治亞理工李錦輝教授提出以知識為背景(Knowledge based)的方式[3]，導入了語音學上的音韻屬性(Prosodic attribute)作為額外的語音辨識輔助方式。為了有效地於系統上擷取關鍵詞，本研究提出音韻屬性之關鍵詞擷取方法，藉由中研院語言學研究所鄭秋豫提出的階層式多短語語流韻律(Hierarchical Prosodic Phrase Grouping, HPG)架構概念[4][5]，偵測語者的韻律詞(Prosodic word)，以偵測為基礎的方式，參照其各種特徵而辨別是否為關鍵詞。為了增加語音辨識的正確率，國外也有很多學者也借助於其他的知識背景方式。Ali 以聲學上的音韻特徵為基礎，針對每個音素不同的特徵來區別，利用這些特徵來以音素為單位進行連續語音辨識[1]。Wieland 則針對語言模型，提出以統計方式並結合考量語意的方式，建立 Bi-gram 模型，並且使用 Beam-search Viterbi 方式來搜尋最佳語句路徑。結合這兩點並應用於口述語言的辨識[6]。Bitar 提出探討結合知識背景，以這些特徵來作為辨識方法的各種參數，除了傳統 HMM，並結合專業知識再評估，結果在語音辨識上有不錯的成效[7]。Rabiner 在 1989 年，語音辨識還尚未很成熟時，提出了利用點。其一為隱藏式馬可夫模型方式來辨識語音的概念與針對其應用方式來討論，並且說明了其兩項擁有完整的數學理念與架構，並且可以廣泛應用在各種領域。第二點就是將其應用在語音辨識上確實有良好的效果[8]。Tatsuya Kawahara 與 Chin-Hui Lee 提到 Key-Phrase Detection 和 Verification 的結合，意即關鍵詞的擷取與組合，在對於針對富含文法結構鬆散且變化性大之特性的口述語言，系統理解其對話內容上有很重大的幫助[9]，也更加強化我們利用擷取關鍵詞來評估語言行為的重要性。

二、相關研究

在關鍵詞辨識的研究上，Rose[10]利用 HMM 建立了一個關鍵詞辨識系統，個別訓練關鍵詞與非關鍵詞部分，再利用為辨識關鍵詞的數個狀態，還有非關鍵詞的填詞器(filler)數個，架構整個辨識網絡來辨識整段語音的關鍵詞部分。Zhang[11]提出兩階段式的方法，第一階段辨識出可能性最高的音素序列，第二階段藉由混亂矩陣判斷其相似性，列出最有可能的序列，最後則擷取出信心度最高分的作為關鍵詞。Bahi[12]方法也是類似，將每個發音音節分開成字元列組合，先將可能性關鍵詞訓練好為字元列，同樣將辨識出來的各種可能字轉換成字元列，利用 HMM 方式去比對位置偵測出最有可能的關鍵詞並擷取出，此篇特點在於並沒有特意對非關鍵詞作模型。麻省理工學院的 Bazzi 研究在 HMM 辨識器下非關鍵詞的填詞器設計[13]，裡面提到關鍵詞辨識中，詞庫外字詞也是占很重要部分，分析了錯誤警報器的正確性跟整體辨識正確率相對關係與所占比例。Lee C.H.[14]在比對發聲相似性時，額外再參考相鄰的發音，利用貝氏理論中的貝氏因子計算方式，來計算出發音相似性。Kim[15]則以貝氏理論來作為評估辨識後的發音其信心度分數。另外幾種是以特徵參數作為偵測基礎訓練分類器[16][17]，利用訓練器來對要辨識的語音作分類，判定其是否為要關鍵詞。

Haizhou Li, Bin Ma, and Chin-Hui Lee 於期刊上發表的研究多語辨識[18]，提出了新的辨識單元構想，不再以音標為單元而是用實際人類發音來做為單位，並加以訓練模型。後端部分在各個語言特徵上建立了向量空間模型來儲存各種語言上每種發音的相對關係，並訓練出分類器來藉此分類辨識為何種語言，所呈現的辨識結果比用國際音標還要好上許多。

在音韻研究方面，近年以哥倫比亞大學發展出一個偵測重音部分的工具軟體 AuToBi，可以針對短語邊界偵測並且偵測發音重音部位[19]，其文章也提到這些年來各種不同的偵測重音方式，有利用聲學屬性、基頻、能量、POS 等，分析上也有 HMM、決策樹等方式。例如 Conkie 等人[20]，針對基頻與能量以及這些參數差值與差值之 delta，並結合 HMM 架構偵測重音部位。此外，也多加入了語者相關的聲學資料，在準確性上確實提升。Sridhar[21]在評估 HMM 中裡面的參數差值時，同時監督聲學屬性與句法屬性，並使用最大熵 HMM 模型來偵測重音部分所在位置。

研究對話心理學方面，我們參考了 Erteschik-shir 的著作[22]，裡面描述人類心理在對話行為上的各種情況與回應內容和情緒，語者和聽者會在對話的進行上不斷改變所掌握的不同資訊和心理所期望的內容。

長庚大學多年來一直從事於本土語音的研究，陳志宇[23]此篇論文探討同時對國台雙語的大詞彙連續語音辨識研究。早期國外已證實隱藏式馬可夫模型應用於語音辨識上的效果，楊永泰[24]將其應用於改善於中文的語音辨識，針對音素的替換改變將其用於中文系統上。余家興[25]所做之語音辨識的研究，是利用有限狀態機的方式來達到大詞彙連續語音辨識，將語音辨識上的三種主要模型，聲學模型、辭典、語言模型都建立成有限狀態機型式，這樣在擴充性上與結合上都更為容易。陳錫賢[26]研究偵測語音上的聲韻屬性偵測，包含一些鼻音、擦音、爆破音等。並結合聲韻屬性與 MFCC 來探討語音辨識的正確率。黃冠達[27]以音長、反模型距離、聲學分數等特徵，利用 SVM 分類器來對聲母驗證分類是否屬於關鍵詞，並另外在對核心函數修改來提升最佳效能。

國內中研院語言學研究所鄭秋豫針對漢語提出的 HPG 架構對中文韻律學研究影響很大，以 Fujisaki Model 計算分析並證實每一層韻律單位的相關性且互相影響，其他研究包括自動偵測韻律邊界，各地漢語在韻律上雖然存在差異卻本質相同等[4][5][28][29][30]，此 HPG 概念對語音學上有很多重要貢獻。

三、系統介紹

本研究的系統架構依其處理程序分為訓練階段與測試階段。訓練階段中，利用語料訓練出偵測關鍵詞模型，以及用來將語音分割成韻律詞語音段的決策樹模型。測試中，以此兩模型先後偵測韻律詞邊界與各韻律詞之特徵參數，最後偵測關鍵詞並擷取出。圖 1 為系統架構圖。

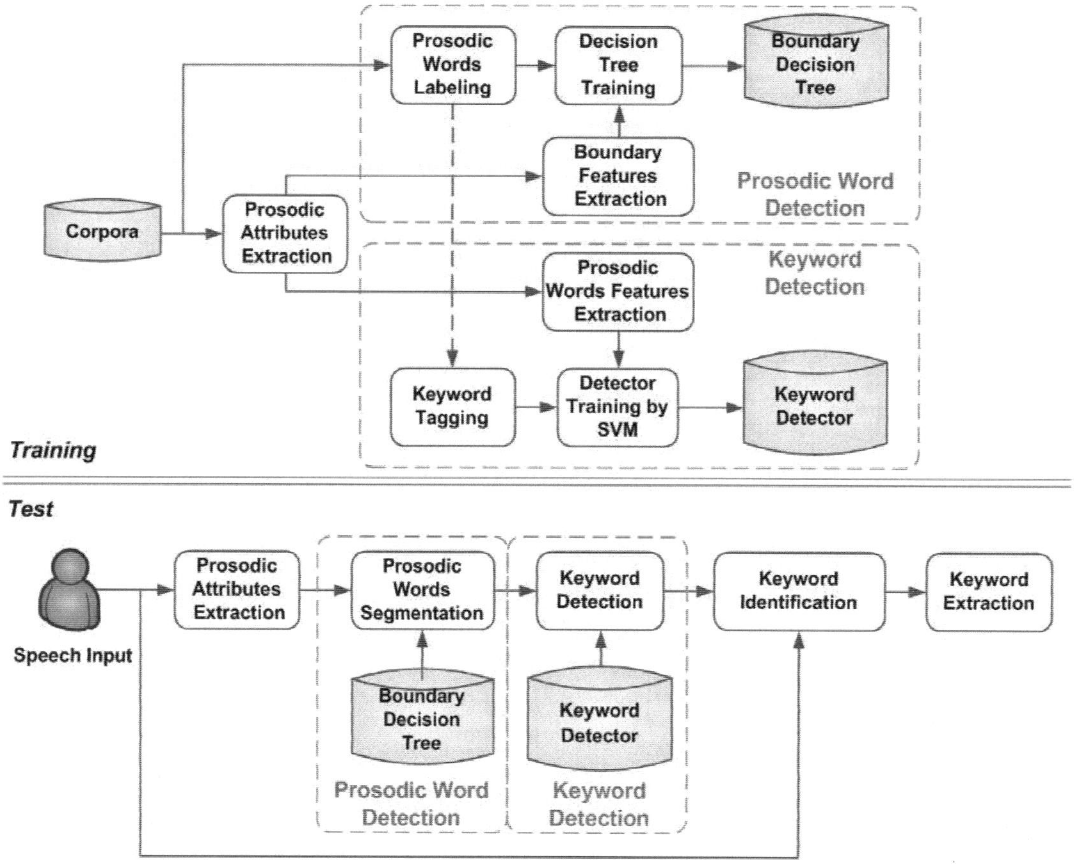

圖 1:系統架構圖

為了在實驗上偵測出韻律詞邊界用以偵測出關鍵詞，我們必須先訓練出所需要的模型。利用收集的語料庫，抽出各種音韻屬性參數(Prosodic Attributes Extraction)，包括了音高(Pitch)、音強(Intensity)、音長(Duration)。偵測韻律詞邊界模型利用階層式多短語韻律語流架構(HPG)知識，並統計分析從語料中所抽取的參數資料，最後訓練出韻律詞邊界(Prosodic Word Boundary)的決策樹(Boundary Decision Tree)，此為訓練韻律詞偵測模型部分。而另一方面，同樣由這些音韻屬性，統計分析找出各個語音事件物理現象與相對應的參數資料，利用 SVM 訓練出超平面模型以用來分辨關鍵詞與非關鍵詞，此亦即為各個的關鍵詞偵測器(Keyword Detector)，這部分便為關鍵詞偵測部分。

而測試部分中最重要的兩個部分即為韻律詞偵測(Prosodic Word Detection)與關鍵詞偵測(Keyword Detection)，偵測這兩部分都必須仰賴訓練階段所訓練出的模型。整個實驗首先從使用者輸入的語音訊號中，抽取出各個音韻屬性。利用這些訊號參數輔以邊界決策樹模型，找出韻律詞邊界，因而將整段音訊分割成若干個韻律詞組合。根據這些韻律詞的音韻屬性，逐一以各個語音事件偵測器分析鑑定其是否屬於關鍵詞或者為非關鍵詞，偵測出關鍵詞的時間區段並擷取出來。

較早之前對於語調的研究，國內一直並無專針對漢語來研究其單位組成，所訂定的韻律單位也是沿用於國外的，主要例如音節(syllable)、韻律詞(prosodic word)、語調短語(intonation phrase)等。近幾年來，中研院語言學研究所鄭秋豫研究漢語韻律結構，重新訂製韻律單位，此結構命名為「階層式多短語語流韻律」(Hierarchical Prosodic Phrase Grouping, HPG)[4][5]。

在其相關研究中證明了中文口語語流在基頻聲學上，各層級韻律單位與邊界效應有層級關係且互相影響。該架構層級由下而上，將韻律單位定為音節(syllable, Syl)、韻律詞(prosodic word, PW)、韻律短語(prosodic phrase, PPh)、呼吸組(breath-group) 及多短語韻律句群(prosodic phrase group, PG)，即語段，共五級的韻律單位。其邊界也分為五級，由下而上依序為 B1、B2、B3、B4 與 B5。其著作中所提出的架構圖，清楚分析出語篇的各個層級概念與關係，各層級標記順序由 B5 到 B1，可逐步將整個語篇分為各層及韻律單位，最後底層可以分成到最小韻律單位音節。

本研究參考此架構，汲取韻律詞概念作為定義各個關鍵詞之單位，因此只將邊界層級收斂到 B2 層級，使音段標記後即可視為由多個韻律詞所組合而成。並且針對各個韻律詞抽取音韻屬性特徵，利用這些特徵組合來判定其是否具備某些語音特性，最後才鑑定其是否為所需之關鍵詞。圖 2 為將一音段分成韻律詞示意圖。B 標示為其邊界，可看出整段語音分割成五個韻律詞。

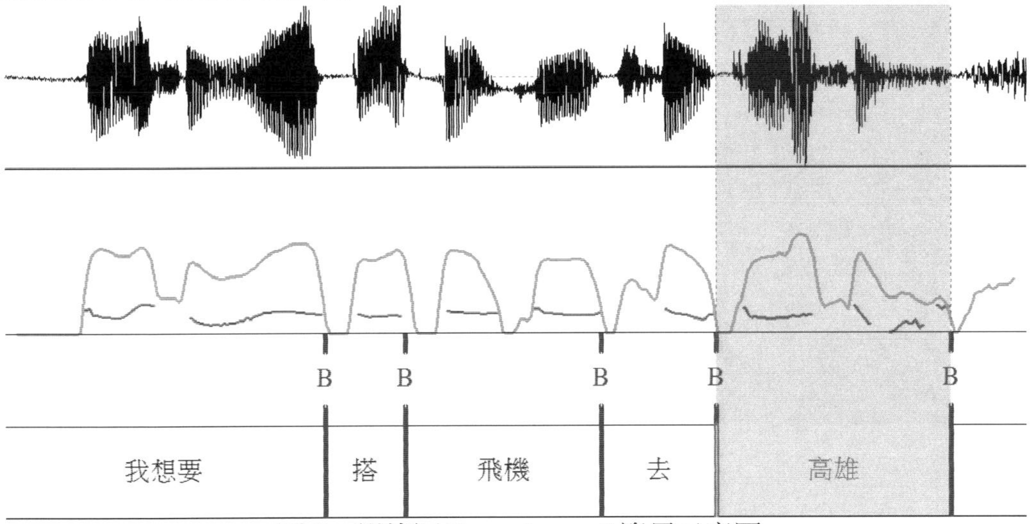

圖 2：韻律詞(Prosody word)邊界示意圖

在邊界偵測上，參考中研院語言學研究所鄭秋豫所提出的邊界特性定義[4][5]，並加入音強屬性來輔助偵測，以觀察其特性從語料庫中訓練出決策樹來作為邊界偵測法則。分析原則為在每個基頻段尾端分析其各項音韻屬性，涵蓋了此段之基頻屬性、音強屬性、以及與下一段的基頻調性。圖 3 為所訓練出決策樹原則，邊界判定上共分為 9 種類別，偵測位於哪種類別以判定是否為邊界。

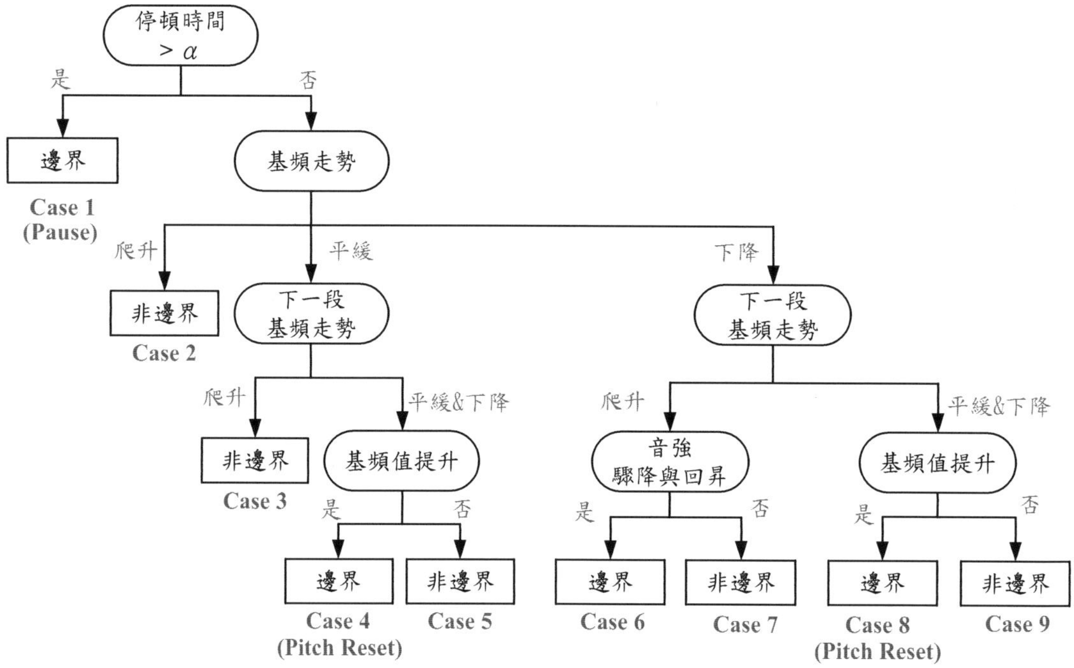

圖 3：HPG 邊界判斷決策樹

決策樹將每個基頻段的連接關係分為 9 個種類以判定是否為邊界，並且帶有不同的特徵現象，並同時表現出音韻屬性上的差異。基頻重設(Pitch reset)為邊界最重要之特徵，有此現象必為邊界處，其餘則必須比較各種基頻與音強來判定。表 1 即為各種不同類別的差異。

表 1：HPG 邊界判斷決策樹之分類

類別	特徵	音韻屬性
Case 1	韻律詞與韻律詞之間聲調轉換與停頓	停頓時間 $>\alpha$ 秒
Case 2	韻律詞的開始，並帶有上升發音必連接下個連續發音	韻律詞調性成上升走勢
Case 3	語調先平緩而後上升，必為連續語調	基頻平緩而後上升
Case 4	新的韻律詞開始之最主要特徵，即基頻重設(Pitch reset)，此為較不明顯的基頻重設	基頻值回到高點

Case 5	連貫語氣，語調大走勢呈現連貫性	基頻呈現大走勢向下或平緩
Case 6	韻律詞與韻律詞之間聲調明顯轉換	基頻下降而後上升，音強大幅度降下後提升
Case 7	韻律詞與韻律詞之間聲調轉換但調性連貫	基頻下降而後上升，音強呈現穩定走勢
Case 8	新的韻律詞開始之最主要特徵，即基頻重設 (Pitch reset)，此為明顯易見的基頻重設	基頻值回到高點
Case 9	連貫語氣，語調大走勢呈現連貫性	基頻呈現大走勢向下或平緩

以下列出決策樹上運用到的音韻屬性特徵之各項參數，並逐一介紹。

(1) 停頓時間 β=0.04 秒：

在訓練語料中統計的停頓時間於 0.03 到 0.05 之間總合佔了絕大多數，但部分時間極短的停頓容易與非停頓混淆，將明顯停頓的時間判定值定在 0.04 秒。

(2)基頻走勢判斷：

要判斷其走勢需運用到基頻段的回歸方程式(式 1)，並利用線性迴歸方式出計算出其斜率(slope)，即 βi。

$$P_i(t) = \alpha_i + \beta_i t \qquad \text{(式 1)}$$

式子中 $Pi(t)$表第 i 段基頻段於時間點 t 之基頻值，則 βi 為 i 段基頻段之斜率，bi 為此基頻段開始時間點，ei 為時間結束點。而 βi 其計算方法如式 2。

$$\beta_i = \frac{\sum_{t=b_i}^{e_i}(t-\overline{t})(P_i(t)-\overline{P}_i)}{\sum_{t=b_i}^{e_i}(t-\overline{t})^2}, \; t \in [b_i, e_i] \qquad \text{(式 2)}$$

$\overline{t}$ 為時間平均值，在時間軸上亦同於中間值，計算如式 3。$\overline{P}_i$ 為第 i 段基頻值平均值，計算如式 4。n 為此基頻音段取樣點數。

$$\overline{t} = \frac{1}{2}(e_i - b_i) \qquad \text{(式 3)}$$

$$\overline{P}_i = \frac{1}{n}\sum_{t=b_i}^{e_i} P_i(t) \qquad \text{(式 4)}$$

求得所需的β_i後，即可知道斜率並利用邊界條件上界 upper bound 與下界 lower bound 判定其走勢。假若$\beta_i \geq$upper bound，則其走勢為向上爬升；反之，$\beta_i \leq$lower bound，則為下降；而若 upper bound$>\beta_i>$lower bound，其走勢判定為平緩。此外，根據基頻走勢所產生的基頻重設也會有差異，case 4 的 pitch reset 值與 case 8 的 pitch reset 值也會有所差異。

本研究利用支援向量機，它為一監督式學習的二元分類器，其目的為尋找最佳化的向量分類，尤其運用在解決非線性化的問題。要訓練分類模型，必須給予標記好的語料作為訓練資料，另外需再準備一筆測試資料，SVM 利用已訓練好之模型作預測(predict)，將資料分類於相近的類別。在研究中，將測試資料分為兩類，標記為+1 的是關鍵詞，標記為-1 的是非關鍵詞，其數學式表示如式 5。

$$T_i = \begin{cases} +1, if\ \ T_i\ \ is\ semantic\ object \\ -1, \qquad\qquad otherwise \end{cases} \quad (式 5)$$

作為 SVM 分析中所要用到的特徵參數，我們利用音韻屬性來構成不同的特徵，組成一個向量空間，附表為我們研究中估計之各特徵參數與計算方式。包含了音長、停頓以及位置。

以下逐一列出評估之特徵參數：

(1) 音長：

此特徵考量所有韻律詞內與音長相關的特徵，考量了基頻音段數、基頻音長、音節數、發音音長以及各音節的音長，並將所有用來評估的特徵列於附表編號 01-10。n_i 表示為第 i 個韻律詞的基頻音段數。P_{ij} 為第 i 個韻律詞中第 j 段基頻段，且 $\{P_{i1}, P_{i2}, ... P_{in}\} \subseteq PW_i$。$P_{ij}^{Dur}$ 為第 i 個韻律詞中第 j 段基頻段的基頻音長。Bi 為此韻律詞開始時間點，Ei 為韻律詞時間結束點。Syl_N_i 表示為第 i 個韻律詞的音節數。Syl_{ij}_b 為第 i 個韻律詞的第 j 個音節之起始時間，Syl_{ij}_e 為第 i 個韻律詞的第 j 個音節之結束時間。

(2) 停頓：

語言行為上可能會為了表達重要字詞，會預先出現停頓現象再以加強語氣道出關鍵詞。評估此特性，計算韻律詞起頭的停頓時間作為特徵參數。bpause 停頓起始時間點，epause 停頓結束時間點。如附表編號 11。

(3) 位置：

在語言行為與文法上，或者語者的習慣性上，重要字詞容易出現在句尾與句首。因此我們評估每一個韻律詞的起始位置作為評估參數。計算方式以該韻律詞的起始時間除於語段結束時間。而第 13 個特徵則做為輔助用，計算整句話總共多少個韻律詞。如附表編號 12-13。

以上所提出之 13 個特徵將詳細表列於附表。

本研究所提之關鍵詞語辨識(Keyword spotting)乃是指系統根據語音動作(Speech act)所欲擷取之關鍵詞之可能內容值。因為關鍵詞的擷取或語意框架(Semantic slot)之填入關係到使用者端的輸入，而使用者端的輸入則與機器端的輸出息息相關，所以 DA pair 即是指相對應之機器端與使用者端的輸出入對應關係。參考 Erteschik-shir 著作[23]中，我們知道一段對話涵蓋著兩個意念，主旨(Topic)與焦點(Focus)。人在期望求得某項訊息時，在表達出所希望得到的訊息，這項渴望得到的大範圍目標內容即為主旨。而對於回話者的內容會以語用學(Pragmatics)的角度來指觀察談話的重點，此重點即為焦點，同時其他詞語與多餘的贅詞不在注意目標。而在描述這些對話中的重要資訊時，會不自覺的做出強調動作，根據上述的主旨與焦點的行為，可以觀察韻律詞訊號面發生的音韻特徵，用以偵測出對話中關鍵字。

如圖 4 和圖 5 所示，雖然使用者答句一樣，但因語意動作不同則關鍵詞語集合與關鍵詞位置亦為不同。圖 4 主旨在於詢問交通工具訊息，所以答句焦點部分所要得到的訊息內容是計程車。圖 5 主旨在於詢問地點訊息，所以答句焦點部分所要得到的訊息內容是於安平古堡。

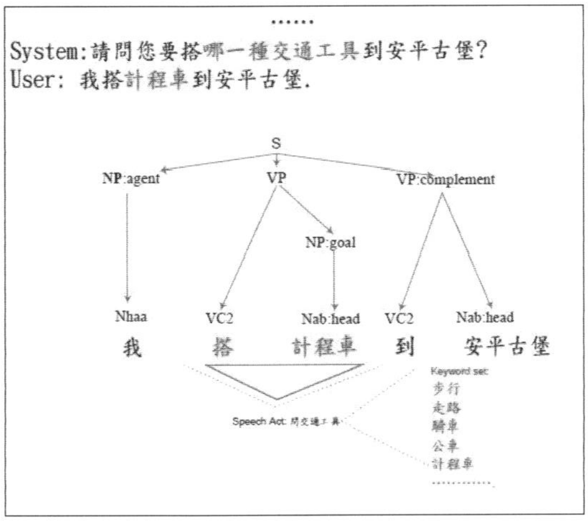

圖 4: DA pairs 動態定義關鍵詞

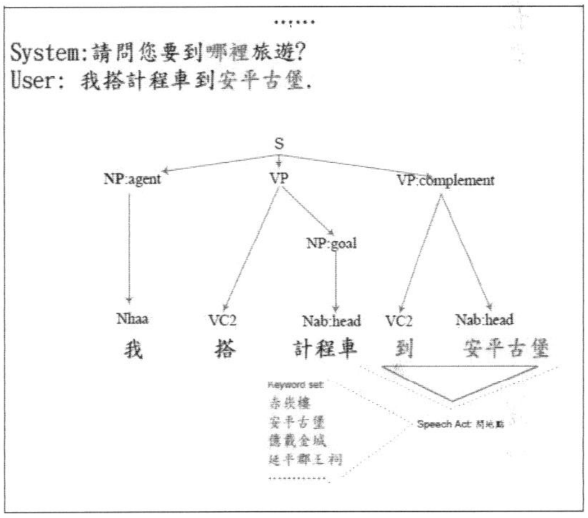

圖 5: DA pairs 動態定義關鍵詞

四、實驗結果與討論

實驗用語料使用國立教育廣播電臺線上廣播之錄音檔，並從中擷錄符合問答對話形式之語句，單元「好老師的 52 堂課」共截錄 247 句，單元「基測百分百」共 568 句。在「全球華文網，數位化出版品：快樂學華語」，從中的教學語音語料抽出 73 句。遠東圖書「旅遊中文開口說」共 173 句。語料總合共 1061 句。從中取 850 句作為訓練語料，剩下 211 為測試語料。所有語料檔皆標記韻律詞邊界，以及對各個韻律詞標註關鍵詞與非關鍵詞。訓練語料關鍵詞總量 850，非關鍵詞總量 2498。實驗語料關鍵詞總量 211，非關鍵詞總量 660。

本研究分析關鍵詞擷取的正確率，必須對訓練語料與測試語料皆標記上韻律詞邊界以及標註上是否為關鍵詞。如果經由系統分析出為關鍵詞，並且人工標記同為關鍵詞，則歸為正確的關鍵詞擷取，此為真陽性(True Positive, TP)。但是若標記為關鍵詞，分析出的為非關鍵詞，那麼即為錯誤，此為偽陰性(False Negative, FN)。反之，標記為非關鍵詞時，分析出為非關鍵詞，則為真陰性(True Negative, TN)。若分析出為關鍵詞，則為偽陽性(False Positive, FP)。如圖 6 所示，每個韻律詞分析結果為四種表示並作為分析的依據。

圖 6：分析結果示意表

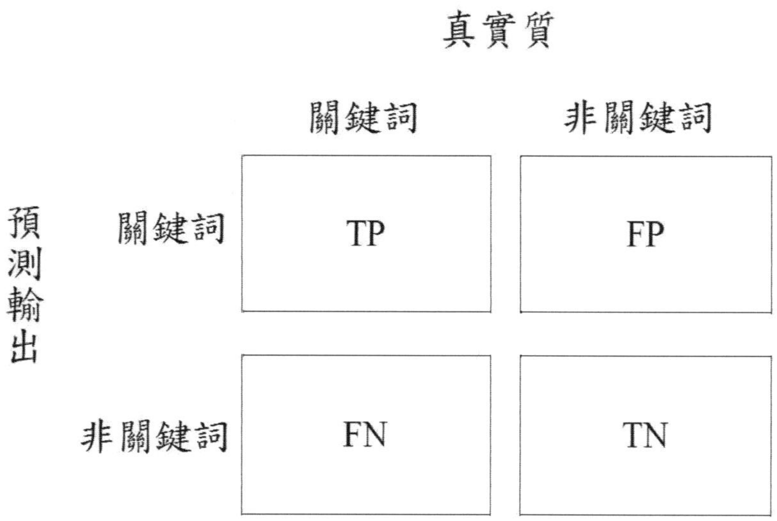

利用上述的結果來評估本系統的準確度(accuracy)、精確度(precision)、召回率(recall)。計算如式 6，7，8。

$$accuracy = \frac{TP + TN}{TP + FP + TN + FN} \qquad (式 6)$$

$$precision = \frac{TP}{TP + FP} \qquad (式 7)$$

$$recall = \frac{TP}{TP + FN} \qquad (式 8)$$

(1) 實驗一：人工標記邊界之 SVM 偵測關鍵詞

評估測試語料在人工標記邊界下，利用訓練好的 SVM 分類器來偵測關鍵詞，觀察其準確度，精準度與召回率，結果如表 2。實驗結果跟內部測試交叉驗證時相比，下降了約 3-5%的準確度，精準度最高的為 58%，召回率最高的是 80%。以召回率觀點評估，10 句話中約 8 句可以找到正確的關鍵詞，精準度上來說則是找到的關鍵詞，其真實值約有 58%。

表 2: 人工標記 SVM 分析結果

特徵組合	accuracy	precision	recall
4，5，12，13 (c=1，g=8)	77.16%	57.83%	68.25%

4，5，12，13 (c=10，g=16)	74.10%	52.90%	69.19%
4，5，11，12，13 (c=1，g=8)	**77.42%**	**58.17%**	69.19%
4，5，11，12，13 (c=10，g=16)	74.10%	52.94%	68.45%
3，5，6-9，12 (c=1，g=8)	75.83%	54.69%	**80.0%**
3，5，6-9，12 (c=10，g=16)	73.04%	51.25%	77.73%
4，5，6-8，12 (c=1，g=8)	74.90%	54.01%	70.14%
4，5，6-8，12 (c=10，g=16)	71.58%	49.5%	70.62%

(2) 實驗二：決策樹標記邊界之 SVM 偵測關鍵詞

評估測試語料在利用決策樹自動化偵測邊界下，利用訓練好的 SVM 分類器來偵測關鍵詞，觀察其準確度，精準度與召回率，結果如表 3。在自動化偵測邊界上，我們知道偵測邊界的精準度未滿 100%代表著會多切出更多韻律詞，也因此實驗中會將部分的關鍵詞韻律詞分為多個韻律詞，在 SVM 之判定上就會出現判斷為較多個關鍵詞，因此造成 TP 的計算量略為增加，自然伴隨著準確度、精準度、召回率的增長，所以我們在結果中可以發現數值反而比實驗一的結果提高。

表 3:決策樹標記邊界 SVM 分析結果

特徵組合	accuracy	precision	recall
4，5，12，13 (c=1，g=8)	83.38%	**70.95%**	75.33%
4，5，12，13 (c=10，g=16)	81.40%	65.41%	78.03%
4，5，11，12，13 (c=1，g=8)	**83.51%**	70.83%	75.56%
4，5，11，12，13 (c=10，g=16)	81.35%	64.91%	77.48%
3，5，6-9，12 (c=1，g=8)	82.45%	66.33%	**85.15%**
3，5，6-9，12 (c=10，g=16)	80.61%	63.00%	84.00%
4，5，6-8，12 (c=1，g=8)	80.47%	65.02%	75.33%
4，5，6-8，12 (c=10，g=16)	76.65%	58.42%	75.22%

比較對象為一個關鍵詞擷取方法[14]，其方式為利用 HTK 進行 forced alignment，針對關鍵詞進行編碼成各個相似序列，最後訓練 HMM 模型來辨識是否為關鍵詞或填充詞與(filler)。利用此方法應用於中文關鍵詞擷取，得到的結果如表 4，並與我們使用的方法做比較。參考論文的這類方式，如果出現發音類似於關鍵詞語的非關鍵詞，並無法有效的區分，因此造成正確率上比我們提出的方法低。精準度上則與我們差不多，而召回率上也少了 15%左右。

表 4：分析結果

比較對象	accuracy	precision	recall
Reference	68%	70.22%	68.45%
Label + SVM	77.42%	58.17%	80%
Decision Tree + SVM	83.51%	70.95%	85.15%

五、結論與未來研究方向

傳統的關鍵詞擷取方式，不外乎都藉著龐大關鍵詞訓練，使用聲學特徵或比對相似音來比照其相似性。本研究利用音韻屬性作為偵測特徵並結合中研院鄭秋豫所提出的 HPG 架構，以此方式偵測關鍵詞，證明其確實為一有效之方法。在 SVM 分類所應用的特徵上，對於鑑別關鍵詞與非關鍵詞有最大效果的多屬於音長類型的相關特徵，以及帶有部分文法性質意義的相對位置特徵，並實驗各種核心函數與參數以及利用這些的特徵組合測驗，訓練出最佳模型，以 SVM 去分類所獲得的結果。在人工標記邊界上的偵測，準確度約為 51%~58%上下，精準度有 68%~80%，召回率為 51%~59%。結合決策樹來偵測，會發生關鍵詞被切割為多個韻律詞之情形，被偵測出的情況而造成真陽性(True Positive, TP)上升，也造成各項評估值提高，其最後準確度約為 76%~83%上下，精準度有 58%~71%，召回率為 75%~85%。

致謝

本研究係國科會研究計劃「應用發音知識源於強健語者多樣性語音辨識之研究(NSC 99-2221-E-415-006-MY3)」之成果，承蒙. 國科會提供經費上的支援，特此申謝。

參考文獻

[1] Ali, J. Van der Spiegel, P. Mueller, G. Haentjens ,and J. Berman, “An Acoustic-Phonetic Feature-Based System for Automatic Phoneme Recognition in Continuous Speech,” ISCAS 1998.

[2] N. Chater, M. Pickering, and D. Milward. “What is incremental interpretation? ” Edinburgh Working Papers in Cognitive Science, 11:1–22, 1995.

[3] J. Li, Y. Tsao and C.H. Lee, "A Study on Knowledge Source Integration for Candidate Rescoring in Automatic Speech Recognition," ICASSP, IEEE International Conference, vol 1, pp837-840, 2005.

[4] 鄭秋豫, "語篇的基頻構組與語流韻律體現 ", 語言暨語言學 11(2):183-218, 2010.

[5] 鄭秋豫, "語篇韻律與上層訊息－兼論語音學研究方法與發現 ", 語言暨語言學 9.3:659-719, 2008.

[6] E. Wieland, F. Gallwitz, and H. Niemann. "Combining stochastic and linguistic language models for recognition of spontaneous speech." In Proceedings of the IEEE Conference on Acoustics, Speech, and Signal Processing, vol.1, Atlanta, May, pp 423–426, 1996.

[7] N. N. Bitar and C. Y. Espy-Wilson , "Knowledge-based Parameters for HMM Speech Recognition," ICASSP 1996.

[8] L. R. Rabiner, "A tutorial on hidden markov models and selected application in speech recognition," Proceedings of the IEEE, vol.77, no. 2, Feb. 1989.

[9] T. Kawahara, C.H. Lee, and B.H. Juang, "Flexible Speech Understanding Based on Combined Key-Phrase Detection and Verification", IEEE TRANSACTIONS ON SPEECH AND AUDIO PROCESSING, vol.6, NO. 6, pp.558-568, 1998.

[10] R. C. Rose, D. B. Paul, "A Hidden Markov Model Based Keyword Recognition System" Acoustics, Speech, and Signal Processing, ICASSP, vol.1, Page(s): 129 - 132, 1990.

[11] P. Zhang, J. Han, J. Shao, Y. Yan, "A New Keyword Spotting Approach for Spontaneous Mandarin Speech" Signal Processing, 8th International Conference on vol.1, 2006.

[12] H. Bahi, N. Benati, "A New Keyword Spotting Approach" Multimedia Computing and Systems, ICMCS, International Conference , pp.77–80, 2009.

[13] I. Bazzi and J. Glass, "Modeling out-of-vocabulary words for robust speech recognition," Proc. ICSLP, Beijing, 2000.

[14] H. Jiang, C.H. Lee, "A new approach to utterance verification based on neighborhood information in model space", IEEE Trans. Speech Audio Process. 11(5), pp. 425-434, 2003.

[15] T.-Y. Kim and H. Ko, "Bayesian Fusion of Confidence Measures for Speech Recognition", IEEE SIGNAL PROCESSING LETTERS, vol.12, NO. 12, Dec 2005.

[16] Y. BenAyed, D. Fohr, J. P. Haton, G. Chollet, "Improving the Performance of a Keyword Spotting System by Using Support Vector Machines", in IEEE Auto Speech Recogniton and Understanding Workshop ASRU, St, Thomas, U.S. Virgin islands, Dec 2003.

[17] R. Rose, "Confidence measures for the Switchboard database", Proc. of International Conference on Acoustics, Speech and Signal Processing, pp.511-514, 1996.

[18] H. Li, B. Ma, and C.H. Lee. "A Vector Space Modeling Approach to Spoken Language Identification", Audio, Speech, and Language Processing, IEEE Transactions on vol. 15,

NO. 1, JANUARY, pp 271-284, 2007.

[19] AuToBi. http://eniac.cs.qc.cuny.edu/andrew/autobi/index.html

[20] A. Conkie, G. Riccardi, and R. Rose. "Prosody recognition from speech utterances using acoustic and linguistic based models of prosodic events". In Eurospeech, 1999.

[21] V. R. Sridhar, S. Bangalore, and S. Narayanan. Exploiting acoustic and syntactic features for prosody labeling in a maximum entropy framework. IEEE Transactions on Audio, Speech & Language Processing, 16(4):797–811, 2008.

[22] N. Erteschik-shir, Information Structure: The Syntax-Discourse Interface, 2007.

[23] 陳志宇,"國台雙語大詞彙與連續語音辨認系統研究",長庚大學碩士論文,民國 89 年。

[24] 楊永泰,"隱藏式馬可夫模型應用於中文語音辨識之研究",中原大學碩士論文,民國 89 年。

[25] 余家興,"以有限狀態機辨認大字彙中文連續語音",台灣大學碩士論文,民國 93 年。

[26] 陳錫賢,"語音特定屬性之偵測與應用",國立清華大學碩士論文,民國 95 年。

[27] 黃冠達,"應用支撐向量機於中文關鍵詞驗證之研究",台灣科技大學碩士論文,民國 96 年。

[28] C.Y. Tseng, "Discourse Speech Tempo". JAIST Symposium on Modeling of Speech and Audiovisual Mechanism. Ishikawa, Japan. 2011.

[29] C.Y. Tseng, and C.H. Chang, 2007. "Pause or No Pause?—Phrase Boundaries Revisited". The 9th National Conference on Man-Machine Speech Communication (NCMMSC). 黃山,中國, 2007.

[30] 鄭秋豫、李岳凌、鄭雲卿兩岸口語語流韻律初探—以音強及音節時程分佈為例. 海峽兩岸語言與語言生活研究 280-312. 周薦、董琨(主編),上海商務印書館, 2008

附表

編號	符號	特徵	計算方式
01	$P^{Num}(PW_i)$	第 *i* 個韻律詞的基頻音段數	n_i
02	$P^{Dur}(PW_i)$	第 *i* 個韻律詞的基頻總音長	$\sum_{j=1}^{n_i} P_{ij}^{Dur}$
03	$P^{Dur\_Max}(PW_i)$	第 *i* 個韻律詞的基頻最大段音長	$Max\{P_{i1}^{Dur}, P_{i2}^{Dur}, ..., P_{in}^{Dur}\}$
04	$P^{Dur\_Min}(PW_i)$	第 i 個韻律詞的基頻最小段音長	$Min\{P_{i1}^{Dur}, P_{i2}^{Dur}, ..., P_{in}^{Dur}\}$
05	$Dur(PW_i)$	第 *i* 個韻律詞的音長	$B_i - E_i - Pause(PW_i)$
06	$Syl(PW_i)$	第 *i* 個韻律詞的音節數	Syl_N_i
07	$Dur(Syl_{i1})$	第 *i* 個韻律詞的第 1 個音節長	$Syl_{i1}\_e - Syl_{i1}\_b$
08	$Dur(Syl_{i2})$	第 *i* 個韻律詞的第 2 個音節長	$Syl_{i2}\_e - Syl_{i2}\_b$
09	$Dur(Syl_{i3})$	第 *i* 個韻律詞的第 3 個音節長	$Syl_{i3}\_e - Syl_{i3}\_b$
10	$Dur(Syl_{i4})$	第 *i* 個韻律詞的第 4 個音節長	$Syl_{i4}\_e - Syl_{i4}\_b$
11	$Pause(PW_i)$	第 *i* 個韻律詞的停頓音長	$e_{pause} - b_{pause}$
12	$pos(PW_i)$	第 *i* 個韻律詞位置係數	$\frac{B_i}{E}$
13	$N(Speech)$	韻律詞總數	N

Translating Collocation using Monolingual and Parallel Corpus

蔣明撰 Ming-Zhuan Jiang, 顏孜羲 Tzu-Xi Yen, 黃仲淇 Chung-Chi Huang,
陳玫樺 Mei-Hua Chen, 張俊盛 Jason S. Chang

國立清華大學資訊工程系
Dept of Computer Science
National Tsing Hua Univ.
{raconquer, joseph.yen, u901571, chen.meihua, jason.jschang}@gmail.com

Abstract

In this paper, we propose a method for translating a given verb-noun collocation based on a parallel corpus and an additional monolingual corpus. Our approach involves two models to generate collocation translations. The combination translation model generates combined translations of the collocate and the base word, and filters translations by a target language model from a monolingual corpus, and the bidirectional alignment translation model generates translations using bidirectional alignment information. At run time, each model generates a list of possible translation candidates, and translations in two candidate lists are re-ranked and returned as our system output. We describe the implementation of using method using Hong Kong Parallel Text. The experiment results show that our method improves the quality of top-ranked collocation translations, which could be used to assist ESL learners and bilingual dictionaries editors.

Keyword: collocation, statistical machine translation, computer-assisted translation

1 INTRODUCTION

A collocation is a recurrent combination of words that co-occur more frequently than expected by chance. Collocations can be classified into lexical and grammatical by the nature of their constituents. Another way of classifying collocations uses word positions to distinguish between rigid collocations and elastic collocations. Typically, a collocation consists of a base word and a collocate. Since collocations are used extensively, knowing the a right collocate for the base word plays an important role in second language learning as well as in machine translation. Translation of collocations is difficult for English as Second Language learners (ESL) because collocations are not always translated literally. For instance, the English collocation "delegate authority" can not be translated into "委託 機關".

Much previous work has been done on collocation translation by extracting bilingual collocations pairs from parallel corpora. Recently, researchers have also proposed methods for retrieve collocations and their translation based on parsers and bilingual dictionaries. However, previous works using parallel corpora are mostly heuristic and methods based on bilingual dictionaries may be limited by the availability of broad-coverage dictionaries.

More recently, the mainstream Statistical Machine Translation (SMT) system like Moses has been widely used in many translation tasks such as translating texts and sentences. Unfortunately, the traditional SMT system does not take into consideration of the structure of collocations including variable word forms and non-contiguous phrases. Little work has been done on improving the SMT system for finding flexible collocations translation as a tool to assist ESL learners or to help the task of compiling bilingual collocation dictionaries.

Consider the elastic collocation "delegate ~ authority" and its translations. The translations of "authority" can be "機關", "權力" and "管理局" which are found in parallel corpus. The traditional SMT system can find "delegate some authority" as "下放 一些 權力", but usually there is no continuous "delegate authority" phrase translation in the parallel corpus. The SMT system might translate the collocation word by word, resulting in a incorrect translation, such as "委託 機關" (Figure 2). Intuitively, a English collocation translation should be also a Chinese collocation, and using an appropriate Chinese collocation set might filter out the incorrect translations, and leads to better translations such as "下放 權力". As shown in Figure 1, Google Translate surely has a good translation in this example.

Figure 1. Submitting a English Collocation "delegate authority" to Google Translate

In this paper, we propose a method that automatically translates the given collocation, by a combination word-based translation model and a bidirectional alignment translation model relying on aligned parallel corpora. A sample process of translating the collocation "delegate authority" is shown in Figure 2. The output translation candidates are generated by these two models.

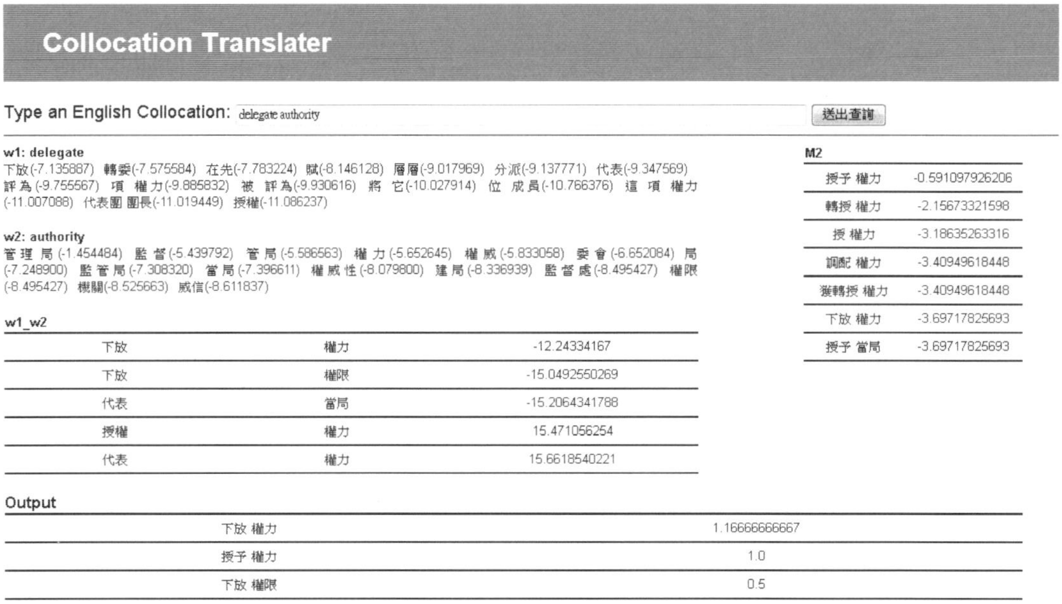

Figure 2. An example of translating "delegate authority"

At runtime, the given collocation is first decomposed into two parts as base words and collocates, in order to obtain a set of possible word translations. The combined translations of two words are then generated. The additional translations are also generated if available from the bidirectional alignment translation model. Finally, the top 3 Chinese translation candidates of these two models are combined, ranked and returned.

The rest of the paper is organized as follows. Chapter 2 reviews related works. Chapter 3 gives a formal statement of the problem that we attempt to resolve, and then present our method to extract translations from parallel corpus, involving generating translations by word alignment and filtering translation candidates using a dependency relation model. Chapter 4 describes the experimental settings and the data sets we utilize. In Chapter 5, we describe the evaluation results and present a further discussion. Finally, Chapter 6 gives the conclusion of this paper and points the future research direction.

2 RELATED WORK

Machine Translation (MT) has been an area of active research since 1950's.. In the early years, rule-based approach is the state of the art for Machine Translation. Brown et al. (1993) propose a series of statistical models for improving MT performance and create a new approach called Statistical Machine Translation (SMT). Recently, much previous work have been done on phrase-based SMT (Marcu and Wong, 2002; Koehn et al. 2003; Koehn et al. 2004). While the traditional phrase-based SMT system which translates a paragraph of texts or a complete sentence, there are much previous work that consider translation of phrases, such as technical term translation (Dagan and Church, 1994), noun phrase translation (Cao and Li, 2002; Koehn and Knight, 2003), or bilingual collocation translation (Smadja et al. 1996). These sub sentential translation tasks are helpful for assisting human translators or machine translation. In our work, we focus on retrieving bilingual collocations, similarly to what has been done by Smadja and McKeown 1996.

Acquisition of bilingual collocation translation has been an active research topic recently. However, most previous work address translation of rigid collocation, such as technical terms and noun phrases (Kupiec, 1993; Ohmori and Higashida, 1999; Dagan and Church, 1994; Fung and Mckeown, 1997). The traditional SMT and previous works also focus on translating continuous words in a sentence. Translating non-continuous words, such as elastic collocations, might result in an unseen phrase in training corpus and generate improper translations. In contrast, we focus on translating elastic collocations, which have intervening words between the base word and the collocate, such as verb-noun collocations.

Many previous researchers have used bilingual dictionaries to generate collocation translations. Lü and Zhou (2004) utilize bilingual dictionaries to generate collocation translation candidates and build a collocation translation triple model based on dependency parser using the EM algorithm. However, using bilingual dictionaries as the translation source might be limited by the coverage of dictionaries. In contrast, our method uses parallel corpora as source to generate collocation translations, in an attempt to avoid the problem of limited coverage of bilingual dictionaries.

Recently, retrieving collocation translation from sentence-aligned parallel corpora is a popular approach. Smadja et al. (1996) propose a statistical method based on DICE coefficient to measure the correlation of a collocation and its translations from sentence-aligned parallel corpus. However, using only statistical information, such as DICE, to translate collocations may generate translations which are not collocations in the target language. Intuitively, the translation of collocation is also a collocation in target language. For instance, the verb-noun collocation should have a translation which is also a verb-noun collocation in the target language. Zhou et al. (2001) found that about 70% of the Chinese translations have the same relation type with the source English collocations. Seretan and Wehrli (2007) introduce a similar method to identify verb-object collocation translation in sentence-aligned parallel corpus, using a parser to ensure that the both syntactical relations of the source collocation and the target translation are the same. Finally, an optional semantic filter using a bilingual dictionary can be used to validate the semantic head of collocations. Our approach, utilize a dependency parser, similar to Seretan and Wehrli' s (2007) method but with different experiment settings, to ensure that the target language translation has the same relation type as the source collocation using an additional monolingual corpus of the target language. The main difference between our work and previous works is that we extract word translations from a parallel corpus based on the word alignment information. More specifically, our method is based on statistical machine translation model, not statistical association measures such as DICE.

In contrast to previous works, we present a model that generating collocation to assist ESL learners or bilingual dictionaries editors. The process of extracting word translation extraction is based on word alignment from parallel corpus. The translation candidates are filtered and ranked based on dependency relations, generated from a monolingual corpus using a target language dependency parser.

3 Method

Submitting a collocation to the SMT system directly might not receive a correct or fluent translation. The traditional SMT system typically translates continuous phrases. Unfortunately, elastic collocations, such as verb-noun collocations, which contain intervening words, may be unseen phrases in the training corpus of an SMT system. The SMT system might translate unseen phrases word by word, and generates inappropriate translations. To generate a proper translation for elastic collocation, an effective approach is to consider the structure of collocations and various word forms.

3.1 Problem Statement

We focus on finding translation equivalents of verb-noun collocation in a parallel corpus. These translations then are ranked and returned as output. The returned translations can be examined by a human user directly, or passed to an SMT system to improve translation quality. Therefore, our goal is to return a set of ranked collocation translations. We now formally state the problem we are addressing.

Problem Statement: We are given a verb-noun collocation (V_c, N_c) and a word-aligned parallel corpus *PC*, and a phrase table *PT* from a SMT system (e.g., *Moses*). Our goal is to retrieve a set of combined translations of the base word and the collocate $CT_{combine} = \{(V_{t\_comb}, N_{t\_comb})_1, (V_{t\_comb}, N_{t\_comb})_2, \ldots, (V_{t\_comb}, N_{t\_comb})_m\}$ from *PT*, and another set of aligned collocation translations $CT_{align} = \{(V_{t\_align}, N_{t\_align})_1, (V_{t\_align}, N_{t\_align})_2, \ldots, (V_{t\_align}, N_{t\_align})_n\}$ from *PC*. These translations are finally ranked and returned as the system output.

In the rest of the paper, we describe the method for solving this problem in detail. First, we show the steps of extracting collocation translation from *PC* and building translation models (Section 3.2). Finally, we present how to generate collocation translations by these two models and ranks translation candidates at run time (Section 3.3).

3.2 Extracting Collocation Translation from Parallel Corpus

We attempt to find translations of verb-noun collocations from a parallel corpus, and filter translation candidates using a monolingual corpus. Our training process is showed in Figure 3.

(1) Generate word alignment from parallel corpus *PC*. (Section 3.2.1)
(2) Build the combination translation model. (Section 3.2.2)
(3) Build the alignment translation model from word alignment. (Section 3.2.3)

Figure 3. Outline of the training process

3.2.1 Generate word alignment from parallel corpus

In the first stage of the training process (Step (1) in Figure 3.), we generate word alignment data for each sentence pair in a parallel corpus using a alignment tool.

The input for this stage of training is a parallel corpus, as we will describe in Section 4.1. For each sentence pair in the parallel corpus, we use a word alignment tool to align a source word to the corresponding target words. The same procedure is performed in the inverse direction, from the target language to the source language. The output of this stage is the alignment information in both directions.

The alignment information in both directions is used to generate the phrase table (Section 3.2.2) and bidirectional alignment translation model (Section 3.2.3).

3.2.2 Build the combination translation model

In the second stage of the training process, we build a combination translation model based on a word translation model using a parallel corpus and a model based on a separate target language corpus.

The word translation model is used to generate translations of the base word and the collocate of a given collocation. To build this model, we need a phrase table *PT*, which is generated using an SMT tools, as our training data. A typical phrase table in the SMT system is usually contains the corresponding translation equivalents with direct and inverse translation probabilities for almost all the phrases up to a certain length in the training corpus. Figure 4 shows a sample part of the phrase table:

ePhrase	cPhrase	e_given_c	e_given_c_lexical	c_given_e	c_given_e_lexical	phrasePenalty
authority	管理局	5.78E-01	0.552336	0.404034	7.37E-04	2.72E+00
authority	事務 監督	0.755776	0.120515	3.12E-02	3.60E-05	2.72E+00
authority	管理局 共同	1	0.552336	6.54E-03	1.64E-04	2.72E+00
authority	監督	0.113352	0.221398	3.83E-02	3.87E-02	2.72E+00
authority	管局	0.329389	0.158094	1.14E-02	7.53E-03	2.72E+00
authority	權力	0.0603637	0.0872868	5.81E-02	3.72E-02	2.72E+00
authority	管理局 局長	0.515152	0.276991	5.79E-03	9.68E-04	2.72E+00
authority	權威	0.24152	0.191795	1.21E-02	6.73E-03	2.72E+00

Figure 4. An example of phrase table from English to Chinese

Take the phrase table in Figure 4 as an example, for each translation pair t_i in *PT*, the bidirectional translation probability $P_{i\_bidirect}$ is calculated:

$$P_{i\_bidirect} = \log(P_{i\_inverse}) + \log(P_{i\_direct})$$

where $P_{i\_inverse}$ (*e_given_c* in Figure 4.) is the inverse translation probability and P_{i_direct} (*c_given_e* in Figure 4.) is the direct translation probability. Then we build the word translation model, which consists of translation pairs and corresponding bidirectional translation probabilities. Table 1. shows an example of the word translation model.

Table 1. An example of the word translation model

Word	Translation	Bidirectional Probability
authority	管理局	-1.454484
	事務 監督	-3.747178
	管理局 共同	-5.029688
	監督	-5.439792
	管局	-5.586563
	權力	-5.652645
	管理局 局長	-5.814680
	權威	-5.833058

The target language model is also required to filter out inappropriate collocation translations. We build this model based on a target language monolingual corpus.

In the first step of the procedure, we parse a monolingual corpus of the target language using a dependency parser to generate *RelationPairs*. For each relation pair in *RelationPairs*, we only count the frequency of the verb-noun relation pairs <w1, w2, VN>, since we aim at translating verb-noun collocation. Next, we generate the target language model *VNPairsFrequency*, consisting of the frequency of each verb-noun relation pair. The combination translation model is then generated by combining the word translation model and the target language model. We will describe the run time process of combination translation in Section 3.3.

3.2.3 Build the bidirectional alignment translation model

In the third and final stage of training, we address building a bidirectional alignment translation model from word alignment for translating collocations. The input to this stage is the alignment information of both directions *Align_StoT* and *Align_TtoS*, generated in the previous section (Section 3.2.1). The algorithm is shown in Figure 5.

procedure BuildBidirectionalModel(*PC, Align_StoT, Align_TtoS*)	
(1)	*LemmatizePC* = Lemmatize(*PC*)
	for each $src\_sentence_i$, $tgt\_sentence_i$ in *fulfill their functions*
	for each src_word_j in $src\_sentece_i$
(2)	*SrcTrans* [*j*] = FindIntersection(src_word_j, *Align_StoT, Align_TtoS*)
	for each src_word_j in $src\_sentece_i$
(3a)	SkipBigramList = GenerateSkipBgram1toN (src_word_j, src_word_{j+N})
(3b)	TransList = TranslateSkipBigrams(SkipBigramList, SrcTrans)
(4)	BidirectionalTransFreq = CountFreq (TransList)
(5)	Return BidirectionalTransFreq

Figure 5. The algorithm of building bidirectional alignment translation model

In Step (1) of the algorithm, we first lemmatize all source sentences to generate the lemmatized parallel corpus *LemmatizePC*.

In Step (2) of the algorithm, we extract translations for each source word in each sentence pair. We first find target words aligned to the source word by the source to target alignment information. For each aligned target word, the target to source alignment information is then used to determine whether the source word is also aligned to this target word. We choose the target word as the translation of the source word if the source word is also aligned to it. The translations of each source word *SrcTrans* are generated.

In Step (3a), source skip bigrams are generated for each source sentence. A skip bigram is combined by the head word and the tail word of a phrase. In order to limit the amount of the data processed, we only consider phrases with the distance 1 to 4 words in generating skip bigram. Then, in Step (3b), we retrieve the corresponding translations for each skip bigram.

In Step (4), we count the frequency of each skip bigram translation pair. Since we focus on translating verb-noun collocation, we only deal with verb-noun bigram and translation pairs to reduce processing time. Table 1 shows examples related to the skip bigram "*play role*"

Finally, in Step (5), the frequency of skip bigram and translation pairs, *BidirectionalTransFreq*, is returned. Table 2 shows an example output of this stage.

Table 2. An example of bidirectional alignment translation model

Collocation	Translation	Frequency
play role	發揮 作用	1193
	扮演 角色	612
	擔當 角色	475
	擔任 角色	46
	發揮 功能	37

3.3 The Run Time Process

Once all collocation translation models are obtained, these models are combined and used to translate collocations. For a given collocation, we generate and evaluate translations using the procedure shown in Figure 6. In the following, we first present the translating process of the combination translation model, and then the bidirectional alignment model. Finally, we describe the ranking algorithm to output the collocation translations.

```
procedure  TranslatingCollocation ( C, CombTM, BiTM )
(1a) Base, Collocate = DecomposeCollocation(C)
(1b) BaseTransList = GenerateCombBaseTranslation(Base)
(1c) CollocateTransList = GenerateCombCollocateTranslation(Collocate)
(1d) CombTransList = ∅
        for each bTrans in BaseTransList,
            for each cTrans in CollocateTransList
(2a)            Score = CalculateCombTM_Score(cTrans, bTrans)
(2b)            CombTrans = (bTrans, cTrans)
(2c)            CombTransList += (CombTrans, Score)
(3)   Sort CombTransList in decreasing order
(4a) BiTransList = GenerateListOfBiTransWithScore( C )
(4b) Sort BiTransList in decreasing
(5)   RankedCandidates = Rank( CombTransList, BiTransList)
(6)   Return top N RankedCandidates
```

Figure 6. Generation and Ranking Procedure at run time

3.3.1 Combination Translation Model

In Step (1a), we first decompose the given collocation into the base word and the collocate. Consider the collocation "*delegate authority*" for example, "*authority*" is the base word and "*delegate*" is the collocate. A set of the base word translations is generated as *BaseTransList*, and translation list for the collocate *CollocateTransList* is also generated. We then generate possible collocation translations *CombTransList* using Cartesian product of each *bTrans* in *BaseTransList* and each *cTrans* in *CombTransList*. Each *CombTrans* (*bTrans*, cTrans) in *CombTransList* gets a word translation model score using the following formula:

$$Score_{WTM}(CombTrans) = Score_{WTM}(bTrans) + Score_{WTM}(cTrans)$$

and a target language model score as follows :

$$Score_{TLM}\ (CombTrans) = log\ (\lambda_s * P(CombTrans) + (1 - \lambda_s) * P(bTrans) * P(bTrans) * P(VN\_Collocation|AllCollocations))$$

where $\lambda_s = \frac{1}{1+Freq(CombTrans)}$ is the smoothing weight to cope with the data sparse problem, $0 \leq \lambda \leq 1$. We combine the $Score_{\mathrm{WTM}}$ and $Score_{TLM}$ by a weighting formula:

$$Score_{CombTM} = \lambda * Score_{WTM} + (1 - \lambda) * Score_{TLM}$$

where λ is the model weight and $0 \leq \lambda \leq 1$.

We retrieve the translations and rank translations in descending order of $Score_{CombTM}$. The N top-ranked translations of combination translation model are produced.

3.3.2 Bidirectional Alignment Model

In step (4a), we generate another set of translations using the bidirectional alignment model for the given collocation *C*. Translations of *C* are retrieved from the bidirectional alignment model, and each translation is scored as follows:

$$Score_{BiModel} = \frac{P(BiTrans)}{P(C)}$$

The generated translations are ranked in descending order of $Score_{BiModel}$, and N top-ranked translations of bidirectional alignment model are retrieved.

Once all translations of two models are generated, we merge the N top-ranked translations of two models and re-rank them. The ranking algorithm we use aims at retrieving the translations that two models have in common. The score of the top N translation of each model is re-calculated as the formula:

$$TransScore_N = \frac{1}{N}$$

where N means the output rank of a translation in a model. We then merge all translations, and if there is a translation that both in output of two models, we add two scores together. Finally, the merged translations are ranked with their merged score (Step 5), and the K top-ranked translations are returned as the final result produced by our method.

4 Experimental Setting and Results

We have proposed a new method to retrieve translations for a given collocation from parallel corpus that are likely to help ESL learners or bilingual collocation dictionary editors. As such, our method is trained and evaluated on top of word alignment information of parallel corpus and an additional monolingual corpus. Furthermore, since the goal of our model was to retrieve a set of good translations to assist bilingual collocation dictionary editors, we evaluated our method on a group of English collocations, which are selected from an English collocation dictionary. Finally, since we do not have reference answers for such translation advising task, we will use human judges to evaluate the quality of our generated collocation translations.

In this chapter, we first present the details of training our system for the evaluation (Section 4.1). Then, Section 4.2 describes the alternative methods that we used in our comparison. Section 4.3 introduces the datasets used in our experiments and the evaluation metrics for evaluating the performance of our system, and Section 4.4 describe the tuning process of our system module. Section 4.5 reports the results of our experiment evaluations. Finally, in Section 4.6, we analyze the experimental results in detail.

4.1 Experimental Settings

In our bidirectional alignment translation model, we used the Hong Kong Parallel Text (HKPT; LDC2004T08) as the training data, which contains approximately 222,000 sentence pairs,. English sentences of HKPT were lower-cased and performed lemmatization using Nature Language Toolkit (NLTK), a suite of open source modules written in Python. Chinese sentences of HKPT were word-segmented by the CKIP Chinese word segmentation system (Ma and Chen, 2003). To obtain word alignment information of English and Chinese sentences, we used GIZA++ (Och and Ney, 2003) as the word alignment tool.

For word translation model of our combination translation model, the phrase table of HKPT was built by the state-of-the-art phrase-based SMT system, Moses (Koehn et al., 2007). Common settings are used to run Moses: GIZA++ was used for word alignment, grow-diagonal-final (Koehn et al., 2005) heuristics were used to combine bi-direction word alignment, and extract bilingual phrase (Koehn et al., 2005).

For the target language model of our combination translation model, we used Central News Agency (CNA) as the monolingual corpus, by using the CKIP Chinese Parser to produce dependency relations.

Our system uses some parameters during training. The parameters were tested with different values and finally the values were set as shown in Table 3. We did not test these values exhaustively and further tuning may improve the performance of our system.

Table 3. Parameter used in training

Parameter	**Value**	**Description**
minBidiretionProb	**-15.0**	**Minimum bidirectional translation probability of the base word and the collocate translation.**
numWordTrans	**100**	**Number of the base word and the collocate translations used to generate collocation translations.**

4.2 Methods Compared

Recall that our method starts with an English verb-noun collocation given by a user, and find the Chinese translations of the collocation. The output of our system is a list of ranked translation candidates, which can either be shown to the user directly, or incorporated into the existing SMT systems.

In this paper, we have introduced a hybrid method for generating collocation translations from a parallel corpus and an additional target language monolingual corpus for a given collocation. Therefore, we compare the results of different translation retrieval methods from a parallel corpus.

We compared different methods for retrieving collocation translations from a parallel corpus, which are listed as follows:

— **MOSES**: The state-of-the-art SMT framework that are widely used recently. We build the Moses translating system using the same HKPT parallel corpus with default setting as our baseline system.

— **Combination Translation Model (CTM)**: The system based on translating the base word and the collocate separately and then combined them to generate candidates. The candidates are filtered by the target language model as output.

— **Bidirectional Alignment Translation Model (BTM)**: The system extracts translation based on the bidirectional alignment information of a word-aligned parallel corpus using GIZA++.

— **Hybrid Translation Model (HYBRID)**: Our system based on both CTM and BTM by combining the results of each model with the translation ranking scheme as described in Section 3.3.

4.3 Evaluation Data Sets and Metrics

The evaluation of the traditional SMT systems usually base on the quality of translated texts. Bilingual Evaluation Understudy (*BLEU*; Papineni et al, 2002) is a mainstream automatically scheme to evaluate quality of the MT translations. The translation of the input texts is compared the similarity with human-translated reference answers. However, since our system aims at assisting user to find appropriate translations for bilingual collocation dictionaries editors, the lack of reference translations results in a difficult situation of translation equivalents.

To evaluate our system, we randomly selected 55 English verb-noun collocations from the Oxford Collocations Dictionary (OCD; Oxford University Press, 2009), which collects about 25,000 common collocations. All nouns of collocations were chose from Academic Word List (*AWL*; Coxhead 2003). The testing data consisted of 80 collocations, which were selected in the same way.

We used two human judges to examine the generated translations for each collocation in the data sets for evaluation. The human judges were asked to examine retrieved collocation translation one at a time, and judge each translation candidate as "correct", "partial acceptable", or "unacceptable" for the collocations.

By using the judgments from two human judges, we evaluate the translations using the *Top-N accuracy*, and Mean Reciprocal Rank (MRR) metrics that describes in the next.

Definition 4.1. The *Top-N accuracy* of a translation model for *K* collocations in test data, in our definition, is the percentage of all collocations with translation results, where Top-N translations contain a correct translation.

Example 4.1. Consider top 3 translations returned by the system for 10 collocations in test data. If there are 3 collocations with correct translations at first place, 2 at second place, and 1 at third place, the Top-N accuracy of this system is (3+2+1)/10 = 60%.

We also compute Mean Reciprocal Rank (MRR), a measure of how much effort needed for a user to find a compatible translation in the returned order of collocation translations (Voorhees and Tice, 1999). The MRR value is a real number between 0 and 1, where 1 denotes the compatible translations always occur at first place. We report the MRR results to examine the effectiveness of our system being used to assist bilingual dictionaries editors.

Definition 4.2. The Reciprocal Rank for a system, for a input collocation *c* from the data set *D,* is defined as R_c^{-1}, where R_c is the first rank of a translation judged as a correct translation for *c*. The Mean Reciprocal Rank (MRR) of the system is the average of the Reciprocal Rank values over all evaluated collocations in *D*.

Example 4.2. Consider a collocation *c* and the system outputs 5 translations for *c*. If three translations are judged correct and ranked at 2, 3, 5. The *Reciprocal Rank* for *c* is 2^{-1} = 0.5.

We also calculate *Kappa statistics* (Cohen, 1960) to evaluate the agreement between two human judges. Cohen's Kappa coefficient κ is a statistical measure of the inter-judge agreement, which consider the agreement occurring by chance and the agreement of observed judgment result. If the judges are in complete agreement with each other for the classification totally, then $\kappa = 1$. If there is no agreement between the judges, then $\kappa \leq 0$.

Definition 4.3. The Cohen's Kappa coefficient κ is calculated as the equation:

$$\kappa = \frac{\Pr(a) - \Pr(e)}{1 - \Pr(e)}$$

where *Pr*(*a*) is relative observed agreement between judges, and *Pr*(*e*) is the hypothetical probability of agreement by chance, which is calculated by using the observed judgments by each human judge.

4.4 Tuning Parameters

In this section, we describe the process of tuning the parameter λ (weight of word translation model in the combination translation model (*CTM*)) by using the development data. Recall that the score of *CTM* is calculated as the following:

$$Score_{CombTM} = \lambda * \text{Score}_{\text{WTM}} + (1 - \lambda) * \text{Score}_{TLM}$$

The different weights of λ determine whether the word translation model (*WTM*) or the target language model (*TLM*) has more influence on the collocation translations score $Score_{CombTM}$. A higher value of λ means that $Score_{CombTM}$ relies more on *WTM* than *TLM.* In contrast, *TLM* has more influence for a lower λ.

To select a suitable weight λ, we choose a set values in the division between 0 and 1 to find the best *MRR* values by using development data. As the result. We make $\lambda = 0.4$ as our model weight.

4.5 Evaluation Results

In this section, we evaluate the performance of various systems in Section 4.2 using the testing data set and different metrics we described in Section 4.3.

For each compared system, we generated top 3 ranked translations for each collocation in the testing data. Samples of the system output for collocations in the testing data are listed in Appendix A. We first calculate the Kappa value to acquire the agreement between two judges. In order to calculate the Kappa value, we mixed all top 3 translations from various systems and generated a translation pool, which contains all generated translations from different systems for each collocation in test data. The human judges then evaluated on all 1451 translations in the translation pool, and we got the Kappa value $\kappa = 0.61$, which indicates that the human judges have substantial agreement while judging translation results

Table 4. Top-N precision of different systems

	Top-1	*Top-2*	*Top-3*	*Top-4*	*Top-5*
Moses (baseline)	.55	.73	.77	.78	.82
BTM	.49	.56	.59	.59	.60
CTM	**.67**	.75	.80	.82	.83
Hybrid (CTM+BTM)	.65	**.81**	**.85**	**.88**	**.89**

Table 5. MRR value for all translations for collocations in test data by seeing "correct

System	***MRR***
Moses (baseline)	.72
BTM	.55
CTM	.76
Hybrid (CTM+BTM)	**.78**

We report the top-N accuracies from top-1 to top-5 in Table 4. The results indicate that, except the top-1 accuracy, our **Hybrid** method has significantly better accuracy improvement than other three methods from top-2 to top-5. Compared with the baseline, our system improves 7% ~ 10% more accuracies. **Hybrid**, combined **CTM** and **BTM**, improves about more 6% accuracy than only **CTM**. This result indicates that although top-N accuracies of **BTM** is the lowest since it suffers from low translation coverage, **BTM** still improves

Table 4 reports the *MRR* value for all compared methods. The reported *MRR* is an average value of the judgment by two judges. **Hybrid** has the best *MRR* 0.78 of all methods , which means that a correct answer can be found at the first 2 translations in ranked translation list by a human user. Also our **HYBRID** method, compared to the traditional SMT system **MOSES**, improves 0.06 *MRR* score.

5 Conclusion and Future Work

In this paper, we have introduced a new method for translating verb-noun collocations by using a parallel corpus and an additional monolingual corpus. The generated collocation translations can be used to assist ESL learners and bilingual collocation dictionaries editors with the choice of proper translations. Our method is based on a parallel corpus to extract collocation translations, and a monolingual corpus of the target language to filter out inappropriate translations. Evaluations of our experiments have shown that our method produce better translations for a given collocation than the traditional SMT system.

Many avenues exist for future research and improvement of our system. For example, we could extend the parallel corpus by using more general corpora to increase the quality of collocation translations. The ranking algorithm to combine and rank outputs of two models could be used a better existing algorithm. Also, dealing with different types of collocation, such as Adjective-Noun and Phrasal Verb-Noun, could be considered to translate more collocations in our system. Additionally, an interesting direction to explore is to use more semantic information to improve translations. If example sentences of a collocation are available, we could use the word sense disambiguation technique to help us choose a precise translation.

References

[1] Cao Y. and Li H. 2002. Base noun phrase translation using web data and the EM algorithm. In Proceedings of the 19th international conference on computational linguistics-volume 1, Association for Computational Linguistics. 1 p.

[2] Cohen J. 1960. A coefficient of agreement for nominal scales. Educational and Psychological Measurement 20(1):37-46.

[3] Dagan I. and Church K. 1994. Termight: Identifying and translating technical terminology. In Proceedings of the fourth conference on applied natural language processing, Association for Computational Linguistics. 34 p.

[4] Fung P and McKeown K. 1997. A technical word-and term-translation aid using noisy parallel corpora across language groups. Machine Translation 12(1):53-87.

[5] Koehn P. 2004. Pharaoh: A beam search decoder for phrase-based statistical machine translation models. Machine Translation: From Real Users to Research :115-24.

[6] Koehn P. and Knight K. 2003. Feature-rich statistical translation of noun phrases. Proceedings of the 41st annual meeting on association for computational linguistics-volume 1Association for Computational Linguistics. 311 p.

[7] Koehn P., Och F. J. and Marcu D. 2003. Statistical phrase-based translation. Proceedings of the 2003 conference of the north american chapter of the association for computational linguistics on human language technology-volume 1Association for Computational Linguistics. 48 p.

[8] Koehn P., Hoang H., Birch A., Callison-Burch C., Federico M., Bertoldi N., Cowan B., Shen W., Moran C. and Zens R. 2007. Moses: Open source toolkit for statistical machine translation. Proceedings of the 45th annual meeting of the ACL on interactive poster and demonstration sessionsAssociation for Computational Linguistics. 177 p.

[9] Kupiec J. 1993. An algorithm for finding noun phrase correspondences in bilingual

corpora. Proceedings of the 31st annual meeting on association for computational linguisticsAssociation for Computational Linguistics. 17 p.

[10] Loper E. and Bird S. 2002. NLTK: The natural language toolkit. Proceedings of the ACL-02 workshop on effective tools and methodologies for teaching natural language processing and computational linguistics-volume 1Association for Computational Linguistics. 63 p.

[11] Lü Y. and Zhou M. 2004. Collocation translation acquisition using monolingual corpora. Proceedings of the 42nd annual meeting on association for computational linguisticsAssociation for Computational Linguistics. 167 p.

[12] Marcu D. and Wong W. 2002. A phrase-based, joint probability model for statistical machine translation. In Proceedings of the ACL-02 conference on empirical methods in natural language processing-volume 10. Association for Computational Linguistics. 133 p.

[13] Ohmori K. and Higashida M. 1999. Extracting bilingual collocations from non-aligned parallel corpora. In Proeeding. of the 8th international conference on theoretical and methodological issues in machine translation (TMI99). Citeseer. 88 p.

[14] Oxford University Press. 2009. Oxford collocations dictionary 2nd . USA: Oxford University Press.

[15] Papineni K., Roukos S., Ward T. and Zhu W. J. 2002. BLEU: A method for automatic evaluation of machine translation. In Proceedings of the 40th annual meeting on association for computational linguistics, Association for Computational Linguistics. 311 p.

[16] J. Richard Landis and Gary G. Koch. 1977. The Measurement of Observer Agreement for Categorical Data. Biometrics, 33(1):159-174. International Biometric Society

[17] Seretan V. and Wehrli E. 2007. Collocation translation based on sentence alignment and parsing. Actes de la 14e conférence sur le traitement automatique des langues naturelles (TALN 2007). Citeseer. 401 p.

[18] Smadja F, McKeown KR, Hatzivassiloglou V. 1996. Translating collocations for bilingual lexicons: A statistical approach. Computational Linguistics 22(1):1-38.

[19] Zhou M, Ding Y, Huang C. 2001. Improving translation selection with a new translation model trained by independent monolingual corpora. Computational Linguistics and Chinese Language Processing 6(1):1-26.

A possibilistic approach for automatic word sense disambiguation

Oussama Ben Khiroun[1], Bilel Elayeb[1,2], Ibrahim Bounhas[3], Fabrice Evrard[2], and Narjès Bellamine Ben Saoud[1]

[1]RIADI Research Laboratory, ENSI Manouba University, 2010 Tunisia.
oussama.ben.khiroun@gmail.com, Bilel.Elayeb@riadi.rnu.tn, Narjes.Bellamine@ensi.rnu.tn
[2]IRIT-ENSEEIHT, 02 Rue Camichel, 31071 Toulouse Cedex 7, France.
Fabrice.Evrard@enseeiht.fr
[3]Department of Computer Science, Faculty of Sciences of Tunis, 1060 Tunis, Tunisia
Bounhas.Ibrahim@yahoo.fr

Abstract

This paper presents and experiments a new approach for automatic word sense disambiguation (WSD) applied for French texts. First, we are inspired from possibility theory by taking advantage of a double relevance measure (possibility and necessity) between words and their contexts. Second, we propose, analyze and compare two different training methods: judgment and dictionary based training. Third, we summarize and discuss the overall performance of the various performed tests in a global analysis way. In order to assess and compare our approach with similar WSD systems we performed experiments on the standard ROMANSEVAL test collection.

Keywords: Word Sense Disambiguation, Semantic Dictionary of Contexts, Possibility Theory.

1. Introduction

Word Sense Disambiguation (WSD) is the ability to identify the meaning of a word in its context in a computational manner. A lexical semantic disambiguation allows to select in a predefined list the significance of a word given its context. In fact, the task of semantic disambiguation requires enormous resources such as labeled corpora, dictionaries, semantic networks or ontologies. This task is important in many fields such as optical character recognition, lexicography, speech recognition, natural language comprehension, accent restoration, content analysis, content categorization, information retrieval and computer aided translation [13] [14].

The problem of WSD has been considered as a difficult task in the field of Natural Language Processing. In fact, a reader is frequently faced to problems of ambiguity in information retrieval or automatic translation tasks. Indeed, the main idea on which were based many researches in this field is to find relations between an occurrence of a word and its context which will help identify the most probable sense of this occurrence [1][2].

We discuss in this paper the contribution of a new approach for WSD. We presuppose that combining knowledge extracted from corpora and traditional dictionaries will improve disambiguation rates. We also show that this approach may perform satisfactory results even without using manually labeled corpora for training. We also propose to apply possibility theory as an efficient framework to solve the WSD problem seen as a case of imprecision. Indeed, WSD approaches need training and matching models which compute the similarities (or the relevance) between senses and contexts. Existing models for WSD are based on poor, uncertain and imprecise data. Whereas, possibility theory is naturally designed to this kind of applications; because it makes it possible to express ignorance and to take account of the imprecision and uncertainty at the same time. For example a recent work of Ayed et al. (2012) [23][24] which have proposed possibilistic approach for the morphological disambiguation of arabic texts showed the contribution of possibilistic models compared to probabilistic ones. That is, we evaluate the relevance of a word sense given a polysemous sentence proposing two types of relevance: plausible relevance and necessary relevance.

This paper is structured as follows. First, we give an overview of the main existing WSD approaches in section 2. Section 3 briefly recalls possibility theory. Our approach is detailed in section 4. Subsequently, a set of experimentations and comparison results are discussed in section 5. Finally, we summarize our findings in the conclusion and propose some directions for future research.

2. Related Works

In this literature review, we briefly cite the most important methods which allowed to clarify the main issues in WSD. We mainly focus on the limits of traditional dictionaries in WSD process. In fact, the most popular WSD approaches are based on traditional dictionaries or thesauruses (such as WordNet), which are quite similar in terms of sense organization. Indeed, dictionaries were made for a human use and are not suitable for automatic treatments, thus missing accurate information useful for WSD. This fact is confirmed by Véronis [16][17] who argues that it is not possible to progress in WSD while dictionaries do not include in their definitions distributional criteria or surface indices (syntax, collocations, etc). In addition, the inconsistency of the dictionaries is well-known for lexicographers.

For these multiple reasons, many researchers proposed to build new types of dictionaries or to restructure traditional dictionaries. For example, Reymond [22] proposed to build a "distributional" dictionary based on differential criteria. The idea is to organize words in lexical items having coherent distributional properties. This dictionary contained initially the detailed description of 20 common nouns, 20 verbs and 20 adjectives. It enabled him to manually label each of the 53000 occurrences of these 60 terms in the corpus of the project SyntSem (Corpus of approximately 5.5 million words, composed of texts of various kinds). This corpus is a starting resource to study the criteria of automatic semantic disambiguation since it helps implement and evaluate algorithms of WSD.

Audibert [15] worked on Reymond's dictionary to study different criteria of disambiguation (co-occurrence, domain information, synonyms of co-occurring words and so on). In the same perspective, Véronis, [17] used a graph of co-occurrence to automatically determine the various usages of a word in a textual base. His algorithm searches high density zones in the graph of co-occurrence and allows to isolate non frequent usages. Thus, Véronis applied the advice of Wittgenstein: "Don't look for the meaning, but for the use". In fact, co-occurrence-based approaches generate much noise since unrelated words may occur in the same sentence. We also find that none of these methods treated in a sufficient manner the problem of lexicon organization. Even the methods based on computing the similarities do not seek to represent the semantic distances between senses and do not manage to correctly organize the obtained senses. However, several research works tried to resolve the problem of polysemia on the level of dictionary. Gaume et al. (2004) [18] used a dictionary as information source to discover relations between lexical items. His work is based on an algorithm which computes the semantic distance between the words of the dictionary by taking into account the complete topology of the dictionary, which gives him a greater robustness. This algorithm makes it possible to solve the problem of polysemia which exists in the definitions of the dictionary. He started to test this approach on the disambiguation of the definitions of the dictionaries themselves. But this work is limited to disambiguate nouns, using only nouns or nouns and verbs.

Our approach is supported by a semantic space where the various senses of a word are organized and exploited. Indeed, computing the sense of a sentence is a dynamic process during which the senses of the various words are mutually influenced and which leads simultaneously to the determination of the sense of each word and the global sense of the sentence. A distance between contexts and word senses is used to find the correct sense in a given sentence. Our work uses possibilistic networks to compute a preliminary rate of ambiguity of each sentence and to match senses to contexts. That is, we start by recalling principles of possibility theory in the following section.

3. Possibility Theory

The possibility theory introduced by Zadeh (1978) [10] and developed by several authors, handles uncertainty in the interval [0,1] called the possibility scale, in a qualitative or quantitative way. This section briefly reviews basic elements of possibility theory, for more details see [3][4][21].

3.1 Possibility distribution

Possibility theory is based on possibility distributions. The latter, denoted by π, are mappings from Ω (the universe of discourse) to the scale [0,1] encoding partial knowledge on the world. The possibility scale is interpreted in two ways. In the ordinal case, possibility values only reflect an ordering between possible states; in the numerical scale, possibility values often account for upper probability bounds [3][4][21].

Probability distribution mainly differs from possibility distribution because it requires that the probability sum of elements in the universe of discourse is equal to 1, but this restriction is not necessary in the case of possibility theory. Besides, the probability of the complement of a given event is relevant to provide the probability of this event in probability theory. But, it is not the same thing in possibility theory, which involves non-additive measures. When we use probabilities in uncertainty representation, it is required to list an exhaustive set of mutually exclusive alternatives. This is the fundamental difficulty to use probabilities in this case. In reality, an expert cannot provide events that are exhaustive and mutually exclusive due to the increasing of his/her knowledge along time, and so uncertainty about the situation decreases.

Furthermore possibility distributions may be more expressive in some situations and is able to distinguish between problems, *ambiguity* and *ignorance* whereas probability distributions can only represent *ambiguity*. In particular, the distribution $\pi(\omega) = 1$; $\forall\ \omega \in \Omega$ express a total ignorance which reflects the absence of any relevant information. However in probability theory, complete ignorance is modeled by a uniform distribution which results in assigning *equal* weights $p(\omega) = 1/n$; $\forall\ \omega \in \Omega$ for each event although no justification can explain this arbitrary assignment. For more reading, we can refer to [3][4].

3.2 Possibility and necessity measures

While other approaches provide a unique relevance value, the possibility theory defines two measures. A possibility distribution π on Ω enables events to be qualified in terms of their plausibility and their certainty, in terms of possibility and necessity measures respectively. In our context of WSD, the possible relevance allows rejecting non relevant senses. The necessary relevance permits to reinforce possibly relevant senses.

- The possibility of an event *A* relies on the most normal situation in which *A* is true.

$$\Pi(A) = \max_{x \in A} \pi(x) \tag{1}$$

- The necessity of an event *A* reflects the most normal situation in which *A* is false.

$$N(A) = \min_{x \notin A} (1 - \pi(x)) = 1 - \Pi(\neg A) \tag{2}$$

The width of the gap between $N(A)$ and $\Pi(A)$ evaluates the amount of ignorance about *A*. Note that $N(A) > 0$ implies $\Pi(A) = 1$. When *A* is a fuzzy set this property no longer holds but the inequality $N(A) \leq \Pi(A)$ remains valid [3][4][21].

3.3 Possibilistic Networks

A directed possibilistic network (PN) on a variable set *V* is characterized by a graphical and a numeric component. The first one is a directed acyclic graph. The graph structure encodes independence relation sets just like Bayesian nets [19][20]. The second component quantifies distinct links of the graph and consists of the conditional possibility matrix of each node in the context of its parents. These possibility distributions should respect normalization. For each variable *V*:

- If *V* is a root node and *dom*(*V*) the domain of *V*, the prior possibility of *V* should satisfy: $\max_{v \in dom(V)} \Pi(v) = 1$; (3)
- If *V* is not a root node, the conditional distribution of *V* in the context of its parents context satisfy: $\max_{v \in dom(V)} \Pi(v|Par_V) = 1; \quad Par_V \in dom(Par_V)$ (4)

Where: *dom*(*V*): domain of *V*; Par_V : value of parents of *V*; *dom*(Par_V): domain of parent set of *V*.
In this paper, possibilistic networks are exploited to compute relevance of a correct sense of a polysemous word given the context.

4. The Proposed approach

Our approach tries to avoid the limits of traditional dictionaries by combining them with knowledge extracted from corpora and organized as a Semantic Dictionary of Contexts (SDC). Thus, the richness of traditional dictionaries is improved by contextual knowledge linking words to their contexts. WSD is also seen as a classification task where we have training and testing steps. In the training step, we need to learn dependencies between senses of words and contexts. This may be performed in labeled corpora (Judgment-based training) leading to a semi-automatic approach. We may also weight these dependencies directly from a traditional dictionary (Dictionary-based training), what may be considered as an automatic approach. In this case, we need to organize all the instances in such a way that improves classification rates. In this paper, we propose to sort the instances by computing an ambiguity rate (sf. section 4.2). In the testing step, the distance between the context of an occurrence of a word and its senses is computed in order to select the best sense.
We present in the next sections the formulae for computing the DPR and the ambiguity rate.

4.1 The Degree of Possibilistic Relevance (DPR)

Supposing that we have only one polysemous word in a sentence *ph*, let us note $DPR(S_i|ph)$ the Degree of Possibilistic Relevance of a word sense S_i given *ph*. Let us consider that *ph* is composed of *T* words: $ph = (t_1, t_2, ..., t_T)$. We evaluate the relevance of a word sense S_i given a sentence *ph* by a possibilistic matching model of Information Retrieval (IR) used in [5][21]. In this case, the goal is to compute a matching score between a query and a document. In the case of WSD, the relevance of a sense given a polysemous sentence is modeled by a double measurement. The possible relevance makes it possible to reject the irrelevant senses. But, the necessary relevance makes it possible to reinforce relevance of the restored word senses, which have not been rejected by the possibility.
In our case, possibilistic network links the word sense (S_i) to the words of a given a polysemous sentence ($ph_i = (t_1, t_2, ..., t_T)$) as presented in figure 1.

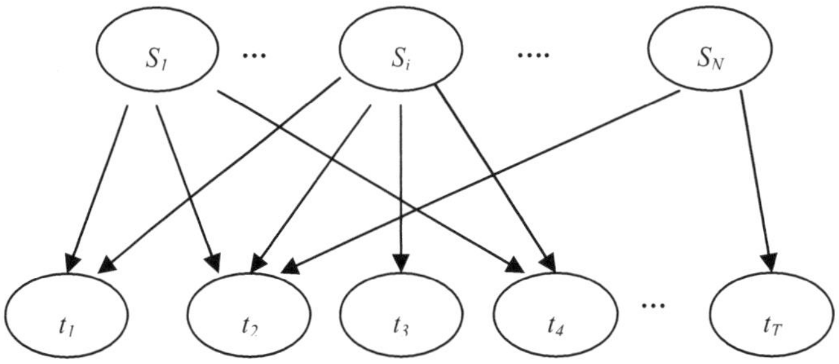

Figure 1. Possibilistic network of WSD approach

The relevance of each word sense (S_j), giving the polysemous sentence (ph_i) is calculated as follows:

According to Elayeb et al. (2009) [5], the possibility $\Pi(S_j|ph)$ is proportional to:

$$\Pi'(S_j|ph) = \Pi(t_1|\ S_j)*...*\ \Pi(t_T|\ S_j) = nft_{1j} *...*\ nft_{Tj} \quad (5)$$

With $nft_{ij} = tf_{ij}/\max(tf_{kj})$: the normalized frequency of the term t_i in the sense S_j

And tf_{ij} = (number of occurrence of the term t_i in S_j/number of terms in S_j)

The necessity to restore a relevant sense S_j for the sentence ph, denoted $N(S_j|ph)$, calculated as the following:

$$N(S_j|\ ph) = 1- \Pi\ (\neg S_j|\ ph) \quad (6)$$

Where: $\Pi(\neg S_j|\ ph) = (\Pi(ph|\ \neg S_j)*\ \Pi(\neg S_j))/\Pi(ph)$ (7)

At the same way $\Pi(\neg S_j|\ ph)$ is proportional to:

$$\Pi'(\neg S_j|\ ph) = \Pi(t_1|\ \neg S_j)*\ ...*\Pi(t_T|\ \neg S_j) \quad (8)$$

This numerator can be expressed by:

$$\Pi'(\neg S_j|\ ph) = (1- \phi S_{1j})*...*\ (1- \phi S_{Tj}) \quad (9)$$

Where: $\phi S_{ij}= \text{Log}_{10}(nCS/nS_i)*(nft_{ij})$ (10)

With: nCS = Number of senses of the word in the dictionary.

nS_i = Number of senses of the word containing the term t_j. This includes only senses which are in the SDC and does not cover all the senses of t_i which are in the traditional dictionary.

We define the Degree of Possibilistic Relevance (*DPR*) of each word sense S_j, giving a polysemous sentence ph by the following formula:

$$DPR(S_j|\ ph) = \Pi(\ S_j|\ ph) + N(S_j|\ ph) \quad (11)$$

The preferred senses are those which have a high value of $DPR(S_j|\ ph)$.

4.2 The Ambiguity rate of a polysemous sentence

We compute the ambiguity rate of a polysemous sentence ph using the possibility and necessity values as follow: (i) We index the definitions of all the possible senses of the ambiguous word; (ii) We use the index of each sense as a query; (iii) We evaluate relevance of the sentence given this query using a possibilistic matching model; and (iv) A sentence is considered as very ambiguous if it is relevant for many senses or if it is not relevant for any one. In other words, the relevance degrees of the sentence for all the senses are almost equal. Therefore, the ambiguity rate is inversely proportional to standard deviation value:

$$\text{Ambiguity\_rate}(ph) = 1 - \sigma(ph) \quad (12)$$

Where $\sigma(ph)$: standard deviation of DPR($S_i|ph$) values corresponding to each sense of ambiguous word contained in the polysemous sentence *ph*.

$$\sigma(ph) = \sqrt{1/N * \sum_i (\text{DPR}(S_i \mid ph) - S)^2} \quad (13)$$

Where S is the average of DPR(S_i|ph) and N is the number of possible senses in the dictionary.

4.3 Illustrative example

Let us consider the polysemous word M, which has two senses S_1 and S_2 such as:
S_1 is indexed by the three terms $\{t_1, t_2, t_3\}$ and S_2 is indexed by $\{t_1, t_4, t_5\}$.
Let us consider also the polysemous sentence ph = (M, t_2, t_4, t_5), which contains only one polysemous word (M) in order to simplify the calculus.
We have : $\Pi(S_1|ph) = nf_{(M, S1)} * nf_{(t2, S1)} * nf_{(t4, S1)} * nf_{(t5, S1)} = 0*(1/3)*0*0 = 0$
With: $nf_{(M, S1)}$ is the normalized frequency of M in the first sense S_1.
$\Pi(S_2|ph) = nf_{(M, S2)} * nf_{(t2, S2)} * nf_{(t4, S2)} * nf_{(t5, S2)} = 0*(1/3)*0*0 = 0$
We have frequently $\Pi(S_j|ph) = 0$, except if all the words of the sentence exist in the index of the sense.
On the other hand, we have a not null values of $N(S_j|ph)$:
$N(S_1|ph) = 1- [(1-\phi(S_1, M))* (1-\phi(S_1, t_2))* (1-\phi(S_1, t_4))* (1-\phi(S_1, t_5))]$
$nf(S_1, M) = 0$, so $\phi(S_1, M) = 0$; $\phi(S_1, t_2) = \log_{10}(2/1)*1/3 = 0,1$; $\phi(S_1, t_4) = \log_{10}(2/1)*0 = 0$; $\phi(S_1, t_5) = 0$
So: $N(S_1|ph) = 1- [(1-0)* (1-0,1)* (1-0)* (1-0)] = 1- [1* 0,9* 1* 1] = 0,1$.
And $DPR(S_1|ph) = 0,1$
$N(S_2|ph) = 1-[(1-\phi(S_2, M))* (1-\phi(S_2, t_2))* (1-\phi(S_2, t_4))* (1-\phi(S_2, t_5))]$
With: $\phi(S_2, M) = 0$ because $nf_{(S2, M)} = 0$; $\phi(S_2, t_2) = 0$; $\phi(S_2, t_4) = \log_{10}(2/1)*1/3 = 0,1$; $\phi(S_2, t_5) = 0,1$.
So: $N(S_2|ph) = 1- [(1-0)* (1-0)* (1-0,1)* (1-0,1)] = 1- [1* 0,9* 0,9* 1] = 0,19$.
$DPR(S_2|ph) = 0,19 > DPR(S_1|ph)$
We remark that the polysemous sentence *ph* is more relevant for S_2 than S_1 because it contains two terms of the second sense S_2 (t_4, t_5) and only one term of the sense S_1 (t_2).
The average is $S = (0,1 + 0,19)/2 = 0,145$. The Standard Deviation $= (1/2 *((0,1 - 0,145)^2 + (0,19 - 0,145)^2))^{1/2} = 0,045$ and the Ambiguity Rate = (1- Standard Deviation) = 0,955.

Let us notice in this example that the polysemous sentence *ph* is very ambiguous because two values 0,1 and 0,19 are very close.

5. Experimentation and results

This section introduces the test collection used in our experiments (cf. section 5.1). To improve our assessment, we performed two types of evaluation in the training step: the judgment-based training and the dictionary-based training (cf. sections 5.3 and 5.4 respectively). We analyze and interpret our results in section 5.5.

5.1 ROMANSEVAL test collection

We used in our experiments the ROMANSEVAL standard test collection which provides necessary tools for WSD including: (1) a set of documents (issued from the Official Journal of the European Commission); and (2) a list of test sentences including ambiguous words. The set of documents consists of parallel texts in 9 languages part of the Official Journal of the European Commission (Series C, 1993). Texts (numbering several thousand) consist of written questions on a wide range of topics and corresponding responses from the European Commission. The total size of the corpus is approximately 10.2 million words (about 1.1 million words per language), which were collected and prepared within MULTEXT-MLCC projects [6].
These texts were prepared in order to obtain a standard test collection. The corpus was split into words labeled with, in particular, categorical labels to distinguish the names N, adjectives A and verbs V. Then the 600 most frequent words (200 N, 200 A, 200 V) were extracted, and their contexts of occurrence. These words were annotated in parallel by 6 students in Linguistics, in accordance with the sense of the French dictionary "Le Petit Larousse", each occurrence of a word that can receive a label of a sense, several or none. After this first step, the 60 most polysemous words have been preserved (20 N, 20 A, 20 V). The body offered to participants for the experiment was therefore made up of 60 words and 3624 contexts in which they appear each with about 60 word occurrences.

5.2 Experimental scenarios

We performed three stages of tests as explained below. For each test, we prepared an XML Semantic Dictionary of Contexts (SDC). It is used as a training subset from the sentences to be evaluated in ROMANSEVAL corpus. For each parsed sentence *S* and given a polysemous word *W*, we link words of *S* with the correct sense of *W*. The "correct sense" may be identified from the tags of the corpus or using context-independent knowledge from the traditional dictionary. Thus, two subset selection methods for building the SDC are described in the following (cf. section 5.3 and section 5.4). To assess our system, we compute the accuracy rate for each word be using the *agree* and *kappa* [11][12] metrics which are computed as follows:

$$Agree = \frac{|\{S_i \in \Delta,\ where S_i^{system} = S_i^{judges}\}|}{|\{S_i \in \Delta\}|} \quad (14)$$

Where: Δ : The set of judged senses corresponding to test sentences. S_i^{system} : The selected sense by DPR measure (computed by the system). S_i^{judges} : Sense attributed by judges.

The *Kappa* measure is based on the difference between how much agreement is actually present ("observed" agreement) compared to how much agreement would be expected to be present by chance alone ("expected" agreement) as follow [7]:

$$k = \frac{Pobserved - Pexpected}{1 - Pexpected} \quad (15)$$

Kappa measure takes into account the agreement occurring by chance and is considered as a refined value. According to Landis and Koch [8], *Kappa* values between 0–0.2 are considered slight, 0.21–0.40 as fair, 0.41–0.60 as moderate, 0.61–0.80 as substantial, and 0.81–1 as almost perfect agreement.

5.3 Judgment-based training

To fill the XML SDC, we have applied the cross validation method. In each test case of the 10 iterations, we select 90% of sentences randomly and enlarge the training semantic dictionary by voted contexts. The 10% remaining ones are used in test by searching the most suitable context from the trained data. We applied there the DPR measure described in section 4.1. Averages agree values are presented in the following figures 2, 3 and 4.

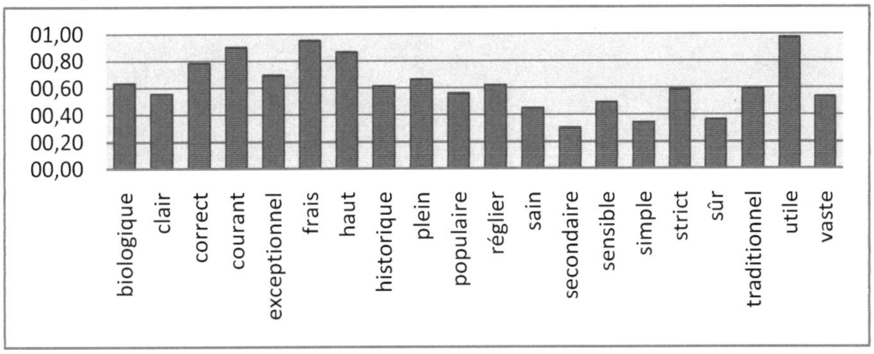

Figure 2. Adjectives mean agrees for judgment-based training WSD method

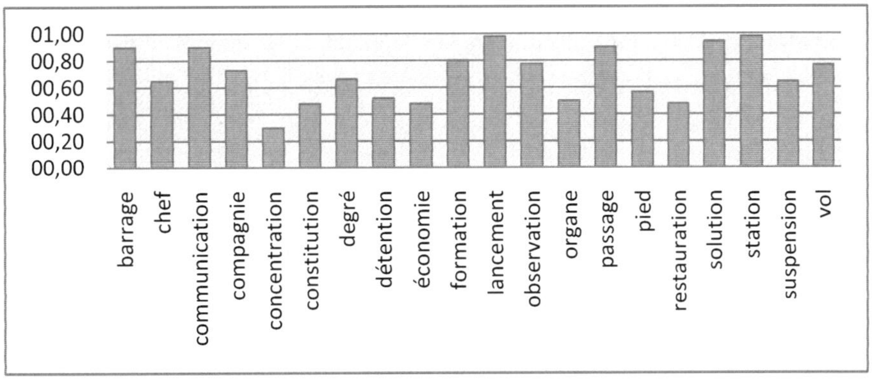

Figure 3. Nouns mean agrees for judgment-based training WSD method

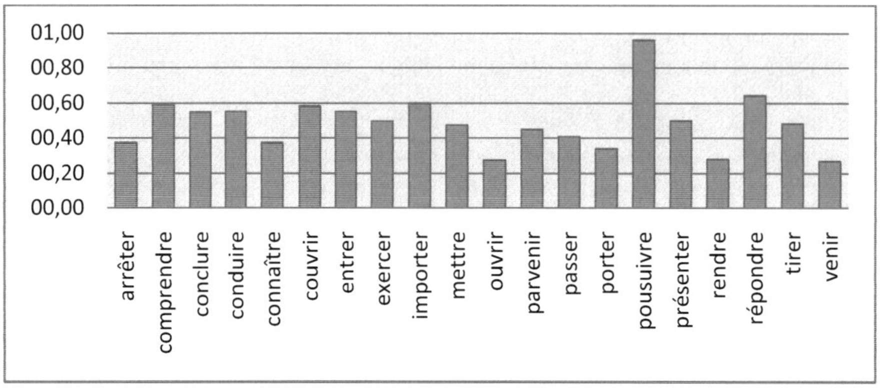

Figure 4. Verbs mean agrees for judgment-based training WSD method

As a first interpretation of these histograms, we conclude that more a word is frequent in the corpus and has few senses, the more is its accuracy rate. Thus, verbs represent the most ambiguous words, because they have fewer occurrences in the corpus. On the other hand, nouns (except for some ones) are less ambiguous, because they are more frequent. The accuracy rate depends also on the characteristics of the corpus. For example, we discuss the case of "constitution" which has a weak accuracy rate compared to other nouns. This word has many meanings ("constitution" has 6 different meanings: (1) constitution (constitution), (2) mise en place (establishment), (3) incorporation (incorporation), (4) règle (rule), (5) habitude (habit) and (6) code (code)). The legal discussion subjects in ROMANSEVAL articles contribute in increasing ambiguity of such words (the same interpretation is applied on "économie" word (meaning: économie (economy), finances (economics), épargne (saving), élevage (thrift or husbandry)).

5.4 Dictionary-based training

In this training method, senses are associated by the system (no more default judgments as the previous method). For each sentence, to be evaluated that contains an ambiguous word; one sense is attributed after computing the DPR values of each definition entry in the dictionary "Le Petit Larousse". Sense having the greatest DPR is considered as the best one to fit the sentence.

Sentences are therefore sorted in descendant (resp. ascendant) order by ambiguity rate (cf. section 4.2). Having the sorted list of sentences in descendent (resp. ascendant) order, the 80% most (resp. less) ambiguous sentences were used to build the SDC; the 20% remaining ones were used for test purpose.

Figures 5, 6 and 7 present the mean agrees for dictionary-based training WSD methods (descendant and ascendant sentences ambiguity rate) for respectively adjectives, nouns and verbs.

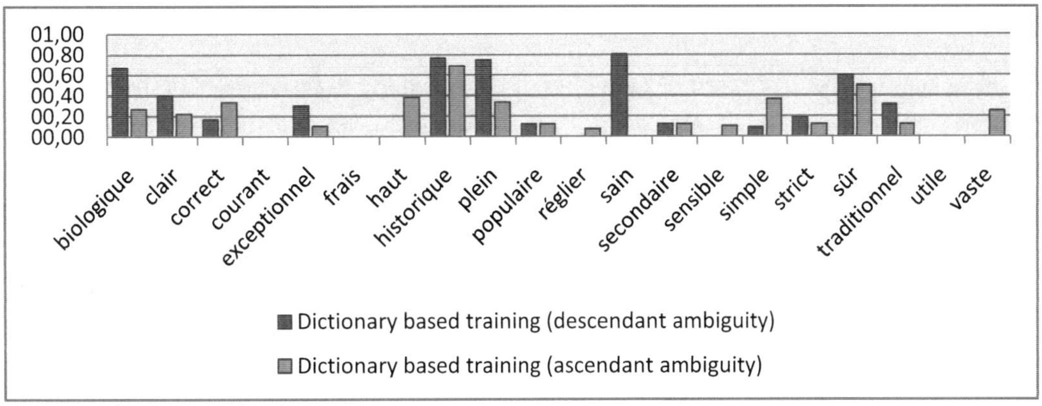

Figure 5. Adjectives mean agrees for dictionary based training WSD methods (descendant and ascendant sentences ambiguity)

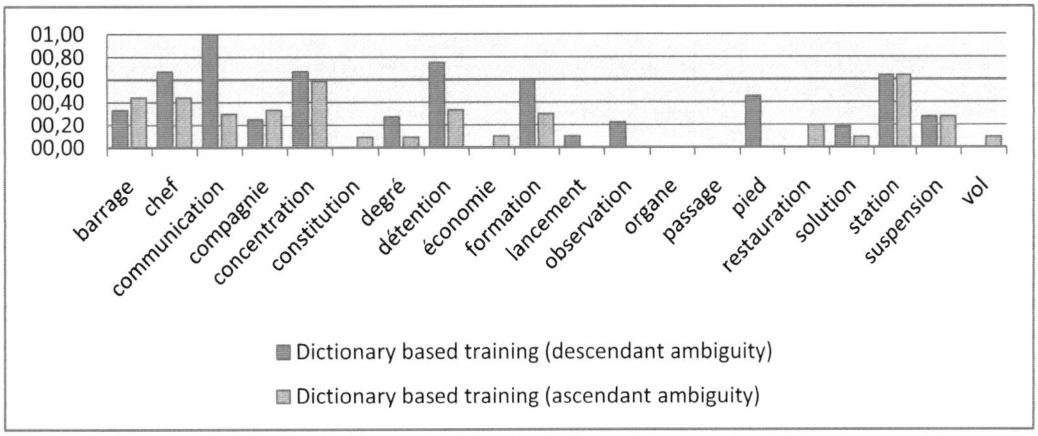

Figure 6. Nouns mean agrees for dictionary based training WSD methods (descendant and ascendant sentences ambiguity)

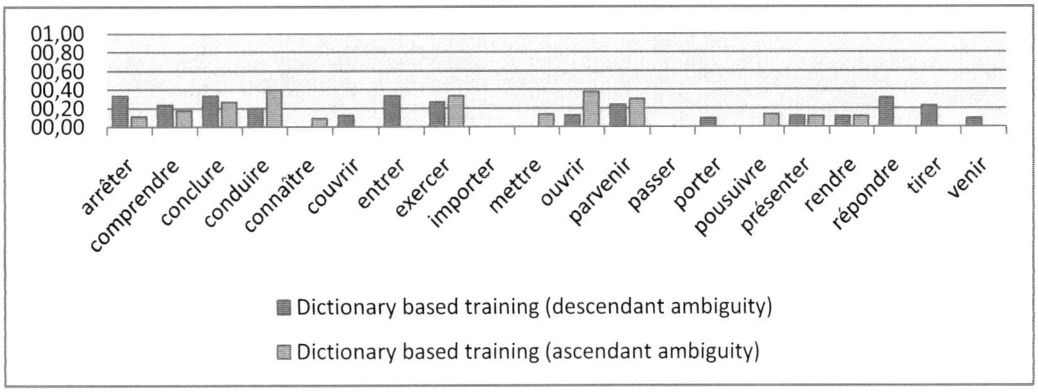

Figure 7. Verbs mean agrees for dictionary-based training WSD methods (descendant and ascendant sentences ambiguity)

These experiments confirm that training data should start from the most ambiguous sentences to the less ones (descendent ambiguity rate order). We should notice that the small accuracy rates are caused by the system selection of senses while building the SDC in the training step. However, this constitutes a first attempt for full automatic WSD.

5.5 Discussion and interpretation

This section summarizes and discusses the overall performance of the various performed tests. Figure 8 shows the mean agree rates over the three methods by Part-Of-Speech.

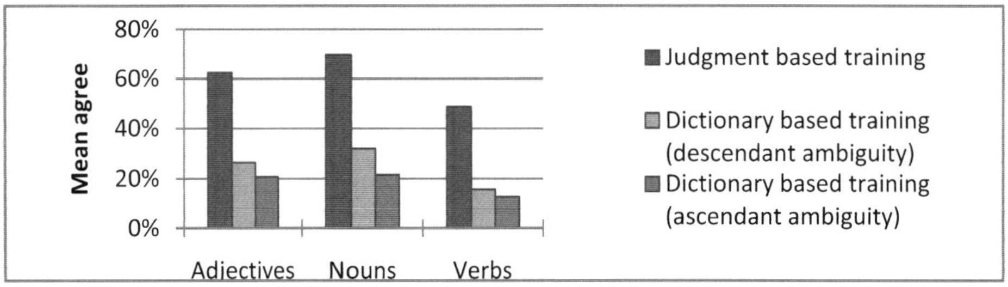

Figure 8. Mean agree rates over the three possibilistic WSD methods by Part-Of-Speech

We remark that the judgment-based approach performed better than dictionary-based approaches because it exploits human knowledge to build the SDC. However dictionary-based is a full automatic approach which may be used when labeled corpora are unavailable. In this case, it is more suitable to start from the most ambiguous sentences.

Then, we compare the performance of the best possibilistic method (judgment-based training) with five other WSD systems participating in the French exercise [6]. These systems are developed respectively by **EPFL** (Ecole Polytechnique Fédérale de Lausanne), **IRISA** (Institut de recherche en informatique et Systèmes Aléatoire, Rennes), **LIA-BERTIN** (Laboratoire d'informatique, Université d'Avignon, and BERTIN, Paris), and **XRCE** (Xerox Research Centre Europe, Grenoble). A comparative study between these systems is available at [6]. Figure 9 shows the values of *agree* and *Kappa* metrics (often used to evaluate WSD approaches) for these five systems and our approach (POSS).

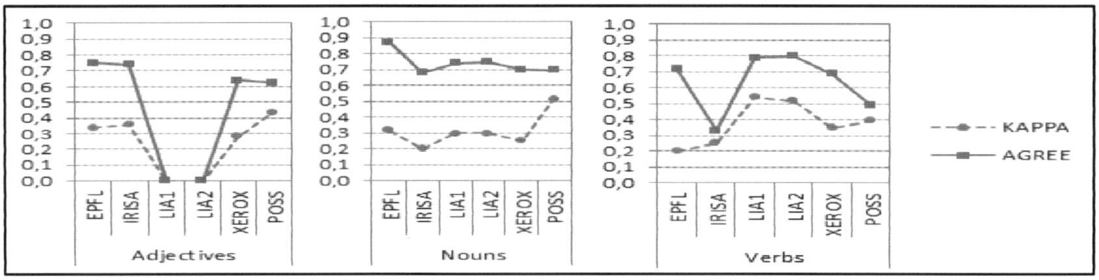

Figure 9. Mean *agree* and *Kappa* results by Part-Of-Speech

According to figure 9, the agree performance using POSS (especially for verbs) is worse than the other systems. We should also recognize that the *agree* metric does not provide alone accurate evaluation of WSD systems. Studying the agreement between two or more observers should include a statistic that takes into account the fact that observers will sometimes agree or disagree simply by chance [12]. The kappa statistic is the most commonly used statistic for this purpose. When focusing on the results over all Part-Of-Speech (cf. Figure 10), our system is distinguished from other systems for the *Kappa* value: in spite of having a medium agree mean in comparison with other systems, agreement between our system and other judges is not a stroke of chance according to a moderate *Kappa* value (0.45).

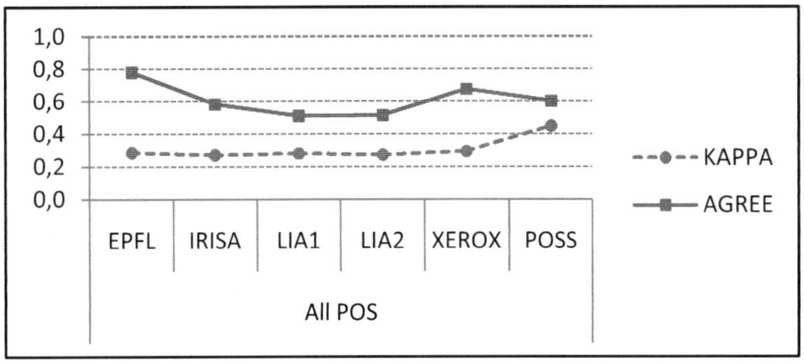

Figure 10. Mean *agree* and *Kappa* results for all Part-Of-Speech

According to *Kappa* results, the good agreement performance of the probabilistic WSD is by chance in many words: for example mean agree of the word "*pied*" (foot) is about 0.68 while *Kappa* measure is under 0.2. Thus, we notice that the possibilistic approach is finer than the probabilistic state-of-the-art systems. This explained by the fact possibility and necessity measures increase the relevance of correct senses and penalize the scores the remaining ones.

We should here notice that disagreement among the human judges who prepared sense tagging of the ROMANSEVAL benchmark is so important according to [9]: *Kappa* ranges between 0.92 (noun "detention") and 0.007 (adjective "correct"). In other terms, there is no more agreement than chance for some words. If human annotators do not agree much more than chance on many words, it seems that systems that produce random sense tags for these words should be considered as satisfactory.

5. Conclusion and future works

In this paper, we proposed and evaluated a new possibilistic approach for word sense disambiguation. In fact, in spite of their advantages, the traditional dictionaries suffer from a lack of accurate information useful for WSD. Moreover, there exists a lack of semantically labeled corpora on which methods of learning could be trained. For these multiple reasons, it became important to use a semantic dictionary of contexts ensuring the machine learning in a semantic platform of WSD. Our approach combines traditional dictionaries and labeled corpora to build a semantic dictionary and identifies the sense of a word by using a possibilistic matching model.

To evaluate our approach, we used the ROMANSEVAL collection and we compared our results to some existing systems. Experiments showed an encouraging improvement in terms of disambiguation rates of French words. This disambiguation performed better on nouns as they are most frequent among the existing words in the context. These results reveal the contribution of possibilistic theory, as it provided good accuracy rates in this first experiment. However, our WSD approach needs to be investigated in a practical case of application.

Indeed, the long term goal of our work is to improve the performance of a cross-lingual information retrieval system by introducing a step of queries and documents disambiguation in a multilingual context. Thus, this work will be wide towards other languages such as English and Arabic. Moreover, our tools and data structures are reusable components that may be integrated in other fields such as information extraction, machine translation, content analysis, word processing, lexicography and the semantic Web applications.

References

[1] X. Zhou and H. Han, "Survey of word sense disambiguation approaches," in *Proceedings of the 18th International Florida AI Research Society Conference*, Clearwater Beach, Florida, USA, pp. 307-313, 2005.

[2] R. Navigli, "Word sense disambiguation: A survey," *ACM Computing Surveys (CSUR)*, vol. 41, no. 2, p. 10, 2009.

[3] D. Dubois and H. Prade, *Théorie des Possibilités : Application à la Représentation des Connaissances en Informatique*. Paris: MASSON, 1987.

[4] D. Dubois and H. Prade, *Possibility Theory: An Approach to computerized Processing*. New York, USA: Plenum Press, 2004.

[5] B. Elayeb, F. Evrard, M. Zaghdoud, and M. Ben Ahmed, "Towards An Intelligent Possibilistic Web Information Retrieval using Multiagent System," *International Journal of Interactive Technology and Smart Education*, vol. 6, no. 1, pp. 40-59, 2009.

[6] F. Segond, "Framework and Results for French," *Computers and the Humanities*, vol. 34, no. 1, pp. 49-60, 2000.

[7] A.J. Viera and J.M. Garrett, "Understanding interobserver agreement: the kappa statistic" *Family Medecine*, vol. 37, no. 5, pp. 360-363, 2005.

[8] J.R. Landis and G.G. Koch, "The measurement of observer agreement for categorical data," *Biometrics*, vol. 33, no. 1, pp. 159-174, 1977.

[9] J. Véronis, "A study of polysemy judgements and inter-annotator agreement," in *Programme and advanced papers of the Senseval workshop,* Sussex, England, pp. 2-4, 1998.

[10] L. A. Zadeh, "Fuzzy Sets as a basis for a theory of Possibility", *Fuzzy Sets and Systems*, vol. 1, no. 1, pp. 3-28, 1978.

[11] J. Cohen, "Weighted kappa: Nominal scale agreement provision for scaled disagreement or partial credit", *Psychological Bulletin*, vol. 70, no. 4, pp. 213-220, 1968.

[12] B. Di Eugenio, "On the usage of Kappa to evaluate agreement on coding tasks", In *Proceedings of LREC,* Athens, Greece, pp. 441-444, 2000.

[13] D. Yarowsky, "Decision lists for lexical ambiguity resolution: Application to accent restoration in Spanish and French". In *The 32nd Annual Meeting of the Association for*

Computational Linguistics, New Mexico, USA, pp. 88–95, 1994.

[14] N. Ide, and J. Véronis, "Word sense disambiguation: The state of the art", *Computational Linguistics: Special Issue on Word Sense Disambiguation*, vol. 24 , no. 1, pp. 1-40, 1998.

[15] L. Audibert, "Outils d'exploration de corpus et désambiguïsation lexicale automatique", Ph.D. Thesis, Université d'Aix-Marseille I – Université de Provence, 2003.

[16] J. Véronis, "Sense tagging : Does it makes sense", Corpus Linguistics, Lancaster, United Kingdom, p. 599, 2001.

[17] J. Véronis, "Les dictionnaires traditionnels sont-ils adaptés au traitement du sens en T.A.L. ? ", *Journée d'étude de l'ATALA, Les dictionnaires électroniques*, Paris, 2002.

[18] B. Gaume, N. Hathout and P. Muller, P. "Word sense disambiguation using a dictionary for sens similarity measure", In *The 20th International Conference on Computational Linguistics*, Stroudsburg, PA, USA, pp. 1194-1200, 2004.

[19] S. Benferhat, D. Dubois, L. Garcia, and H. Prade, "Possibilistic logic bases and possibilistic graphs", In t*he 15th Conference on Uncertainty in Artificial Intelligence*, Stockholm, Sweden, pp. 57–64, 1999.

[20] C. Borgelt, J. Gebhardt and R. Kruse, "Possibilistic Graphical Models" Computational Intelligence in Data Mining (Proceedings of the 3rd International Workshop, Udine, Italy 1998) CISM Courses and Lectures 408, Springer, Wien, Austria, pp. 51-68, 2000.

[21] A. Brini, M. Boughanem, and D. Dubois, "Towards a Possibilistic Approach for Information Retrieval", In *Data and Knowledge Engineering Proceedings EUROFUSE*, Warszawa, Poland, pp. 92-102, 2004.

[22] D. Reymond, " Méthodologie pour la création d'un dictionnaire distributionnel dans une perspective d'étiquetage lexical semi-automatique", In *6ème Rencontre des étudiants Chercheurs en Informatique pour le Traitement Automatique des Langues*, vol. 1, pp. 405–414, 2002.

[23] R. Ayed, I. Bounhas, B. Elayeb, F. Evrard, and N. Bellamine Ben Saoud, "Arabic Morphological Analysis and Disambiguation Using a Possibilistic Classifier", In *The 8th International Conference on Intelligent Computing*, Huangshan, China, Springer-Verlag Berlin Heidelberg, LNAI 7390, pp. 274–279, 2012.

[24] R. Ayed, I. Bounhas, B. Elayeb, F. Evrard, and N. Bellamine Ben Saoud, "A Possibilistic Approach for the Automatic Morphological Disambiguation of Arabic Texts", In *The 13th International Conference on Software Engineering, Artificial Intelligence, Networking and Parallel/Distributed Computing*, August 08-10, 2012, Kyoto, Japan, IEEE Computer Society, 2012 (to appear).

利用關聯式規則解決台語文轉音系統中一詞多音之歧異

Applying Association Rules in Solving the Polysemy Problem in a Chinese to Taiwanese TTS System

林義証 Yih-Jeng Lin
建國科技大學資訊管理系
Department of Information Management
Chien-Kuo Technology University
yclin@ctu.edu.tw

余明興 Ming-Shing Yu
國立中興大學資訊科學與工程學系
Department of Computer Science and Engineering
National Chung-Hsing University
msyu@nchu.edu.tw

李尉綸 Wei-Lun Li
國立中興大學資訊科學與工程學系
Department of Computer Science and Engineering
National Chung-Hsing University
ww90053@hotmail.com

摘要

本論文提出一個利用關聯式規則解決台語文轉音系統中的一詞多音問題，台語中的一詞多音指的是一個詞在不同的場合會有不同的發音，如果不做適當處理，會造成合成之台語語音發音的錯誤，導致合成語音之瞭解度下降。有別於既有之解決一詞多音方法，關聯式規則具有推衍出較具物理意義之規則，可以模擬人們在語言使用的習慣，對於解決一詞多音有相當的助益，本文除了利用關聯式規則外，也使用了 E-Hownet 來解決訓練語料稀疏的問題。我們針對六種常見的多音詞進行實驗，分別為『上』、『下』、『不』、『你』、『我』、『他』等詞。分別得到正確率為 93.99%、94.44%、77.82%、95.11%、96.35%、95.99%。實驗結果顯示，相較於現有的實驗方法，本論文提出的方法對於上述六個多音詞皆達到更高的正確率。

Abstract

This paper proposed an approach that apply association rules to solve the polysemy problem in a Chinese to Taiwanese TTS system. In Taiwanese, one word possibly has several pronunciations. It leads to that Taiwanese TTS System can't work well if wrong pronunciation is synthesized. Thus, we need to decide which pronunciation is proper under some condition in order to enhance the performance of a Taiwanese TTS System. The approach of association rules has the advantage of similate the usage of language by human beings. We also use the information in E-Hownet to overcome the problem of data sparsity.The experiments focus on six common used words, they are “上”(up), ”下”(down), ”不”(no), “你”, “我”, and “他”(he). Experiment results show that the proposed approach can achieve higher accuracies than the existing methods.

關鍵詞：關聯式規則、知網、一詞多音、台語文轉音系統。

Keywords: Association rules, E-Hownet, Polysemy, and Taiwanese TTS system.

一、緒論

台語，是指具有臺灣地方特色的閩南語，為臺灣第一大母語，同時在台灣也是使用人數第二多的語言。根據統計[12]，約有 73%的臺灣民眾會使用台語。隨著近年來教育部對於母語教育的倡導，台語教學也逐漸受到國人重視，因此針對於台語文轉音系統之研究也開始成為一項重要課題。

然而台語並不像中文一樣擁有正式且統一的書寫文字。因此國內台語文轉音系統的研究主要以中文文句作為輸入，之後再將中文文句轉成台語語音輸出，即中文轉台語語音合成系統(Chinese to Taiwanese TTS system) [3][6][10][11][20]。

對於一套文轉音系統來說，能合成出正確的發音是相當重要的。然而，在中文轉台語文轉音系統中存在著一詞多音現象。所謂一詞多音現象，顧名思義就是：同一個中文詞，在不同的場合中有兩種以上不同的發音。如果沒有針對一詞多音現象提供適當的辨識機制，將會造成文轉音系統誤判多音詞的正確發音，進而影響到語音合成的正確性。

一個可能的中文轉台語文轉音系統架構包含(1) 文句分析模組、(2) 音的韻律訊息處理模組、和(3) 語音處理及輸出模組等。這三個模組的功能大致如下：

1. 文句分析：

　將文字對應的拼音找出來，其作法是將輸入的文字經過分析斷詞後（word segmentation)[4][7][9][11][20]，再找出中文詞對應到的台語發音並依台語的連音變調[3][6]方式決定每個音節的正確聲調。有的還有特殊符號的口語表示法或者是韻律段。

2. 音的韻律訊息：

　決定每個音在發音時的參數，有音調、音量、音長、音與音之間的停頓時間、音與音之間相連音的程度等。

3. 語音的處理：

　依照所給的韻律訊息，將每個音和連音做適當的處理，以得到所需要的語音。

以『我們真希望科學家能發明打下去不會痛的針』為例子，在中文轉台語語音時的文句處理過程如下：

【原始中文文句】：

<u>我們</u>真希望科學家能發明<u>打</u>下去<u>不</u>會痛的<u>針</u>。

【經過中文文句的斷詞後】:

我們/真/希望/科學家/能/發明/打/下去/不會/痛/的/針。

【轉換成台文語句後】:

阮(ghun2)/真/希望/科學家/能夠(e3-dang3)/發明/注/下去/不(bhe7)/痛/的/射。

在這個例子中，能夠發現一些文句分析模組中需要處理的多音歧異現象。首先是語意上多音歧異的問題：在原本的中文文句中的「我們」，對應到台語詞典中會發現有兩種結果，分別為「阮（ghun2）」和「咱（lan2）」。「阮（ghun2）」在語意上是不包含聽者的「我們」，相對地，「咱（lan2）」在語意上則是包含聽者的「我們」。

再來是一詞多音問題：輸入的中文文句中出現了一字詞「不」。然而，「不」的台語發音存在著/bhuaih4/、/bhe7/、/bho5/、/m7/、/but4/和/mai3/等六種。這種現象同時也會出現在其他詞上面，例如「你」、「上」、「下」和「會」等，這一類的多音歧義現象，我們稱為一詞多音。

除此之外，還有詞被分開的現象：如例句中「打下去不會痛的針」，原本中文詞「打針」對照到台語發音為「注射（/cu2 sia7/）」。但是像例句中的情況，「打針」這個詞卻被分開為「打」和「針」。如果單純地使用雙語詞典來進行中文轉台語對照的話，將會誤判為「打（/pah4/）」和「針（/ziam1/）」，而得到錯誤的台語標音。

本文將針對中文轉台語文轉音系統中的一詞多音問題進行探討，並且利用關聯式規則(Association Rules) [1][5][8]來進行多音詞讀音預測，以期提昇對於台語一詞多音辨識的正確率。

本論文中的第一章我們會先介紹台語文轉音系統；第二章說明台語一詞多音的問題及文獻探討；第三章則是研究的方法；第四章為實驗和實驗結果；第五章為結論及未來工作。

二、台語一詞多音現象及文獻探討

2.1 台語的一詞多音

台語的一詞多音是指同一個詞在不同的場合會有不同的發音。以『我們』這個詞為例。在一篇文章中，可能會代表二種意義，一個是文章中的『我們』包含了語者和聽者;另一個是文章中的『我們』不包含聽者。而前者的『我們』在台語中的唸法為『lan2(咱)』;後者的『我們』在台語中的唸法為『ghun2(阮)』。在台語語音合成系統中一詞多音的現象很常見，也比中文更多更複雜。例如:『行』在台語語音中就有八種發音，『不』也有六種發音。如果一個台語的文轉音系統無法正確決定發音，那會導致聽者誤解語意，嚴重影響到台語語音合成的品質。『不』在台語中有六種不同的發音[11][13][15][16]，如Ex1~Ex6 所示。而這些不同的發音通常會對應的不同的意義：

(Ex1)『但是社會上的一般人並不/bo5/容易看出它的重要性。』

(Ex2)『不/m7/知浪費了多少國家資源。』

(Ex3)『讓人一時聯想不/bhe3/到他與機械的關係。』
(Ex4)『我不/but4/忍心傷害她。』
(Ex5)『不/bhuaih4/作正面肯定答覆，』
(Ex6)『我希望不/mai3/傷她的心。』
Ex7-Ex9 說明了『上』的三種發音，其中 Ex7 的『上』表示前一個(previous)的意義；Ex8 的『上』表示在上面(above)的意義；而 Ex9 的『上』則表示搭乘(take)的意義。
(Ex7) 『我**上/ding2/**半月花了好多錢去買有關台語的教科書。』
(Ex8) 『我是在這地圖**上/siang7/**的哪裡？』
(Ex9) 『我**上/jiunn7/**了公車後才發現我搭錯車了。』

表一是我們列出了一些在台語中具有一詞多音現象的詞。

表一、 台語一詞多音詞

多音字	台語發音	範　例
你	/li2/	你是誰
	/lin2/	你媽媽、你家
我	/ghua2/	我知道
	/ghun2/	我爸、我家
他	/yi7/	給他機會
	/yin7/	他老婆、他家
上	/ziunn7/	電梯上樓
	/siong7/	社會上、歷史上
	/ding2/	車上
下	/e7/	下面
	/ha7/	在下、狀況下
	/au7/	下一次
	/loh8/	下雨
大	/dua7/	下大雨
	/dai7/	大人、大學
不	/bhe7/	不會、想不到
	/bho5/	不容易
	/m7/	不知道
	/mai3/	不去
	/but4/	不歸
	/bhuaih4/	不要去
長	/diunn2/	站長、市長、學長
	/dng5/	長工、長江
	/diong2/	專長、兄長
	/ciang5/	粗長、高長(高大)
	/senn1/	長的很像
生	/cen1/	生啤酒、生魚片（不熟的意思）
	/senn1/	滋生、怕生（有生長的意思）

	/sing1/	微生物、謀生（指物品或人）
香	/hiang1/	香油、香料
	/hiong1/	香港腳、香港人、香片
	/hiunn1/	蚊香、進香、香煙
	/pang1/	香味
少	/ziou2/	不少、少不了、至少
	/ziau2/	減了什麼東西
	/siau3/	少年、少女、少林寺
天	/ten1/	天上人間
	/tinn1/	天公
	/gang1/	一天、兩天
放	/hong3/	放心、放大
	/bang3/	放走、放棄
	/kng3/	放在

2.2 文獻探討

目前針對台語一詞多音問題的相關研究中，主要以監督式學習法來達成。在監督式學習法中，訓練語料需要事先進行人工標記，其優點是擁有較高的正確率。其中較佳的研究方法包括了組合式策略（結合語言模型和決策樹）[15]、階層式方法[13]以及規則轉換學習法[16]等。

組合式策略[15]是由林金玉等人提出，組合式策略主要將單詞語言模型（Word-base Uni-gram Language Model,簡稱 WU）和決策樹中的 CHAID 演算法 (CHi-squared Automatic Interaction Detector，卡方自動互助檢視法)兩者作一個結合的組合式策略。WU 以相鄰詞為特徵判斷發音，而 CHAID 則以詞性為主要的判斷依據，也就是當訓練資料較稀疏時，組合式中的 CHAID 演算法可以決定一些正確的發音。

階層式方法[13]的概念是考慮詞的相鄰位置關係，從而統計出目標多音詞在哪種發音下比較會常出現。階層式分成四層，由條件較嚴苛的第四層(需比對一詞多音詞前後各二個詞相同)先比較，若滿足則輸出預測相對應發音，否則進入第三層(需比對詞的 trigram 相同)，若滿足則輸出預測相對應發音，不滿足則繼續往下一層比對，若都無法找到相對應的比對，則輸出訓練語料比例最高的發音。

楊文德[16]利用規則轉換學習法(Transformation based learning, TBL)解決台語的一詞多音問題，規則轉換學習法的原理則是利用以人工標記過的標準文字檔(Standard Text)和經由模型標注的答案文字檔(Answer Text)互相比對後，找出錯誤的地方，再經由轉換規則樣版(Transformation Templates)，找出轉換規則。規則轉換學習法從所有的標準文字檔與答案文字檔不同的地方，套用轉換規則樣版，取出轉換規則，接著逐一代入所有規則，記住錯誤數最少的一條，作為第一輪學習的結果，然後在引入第一條規則後，重複代入、記住最少錯誤的規則、應用規則，直到整體錯誤率不再改變為止，學習才結束。接下來，就能將測試語料套用轉換規則樣版，以進行分類作業。

這三種方法對於判斷一詞多音，各有千秋，如表二所示，階層式方法對於『下』有很好的正確率；組合式策略則適用於『你』和『我』；TBL 對於『上』、『不』和『他』則表現較佳。

表二、階層式、組合式、TBL 正確率之比較

目目標詞 / 實驗方法	上	下	不	你	我	他
階層式方法[13]	90.42%	94.30%	74.47%	92.12%	89.23%	92.54%
組合式策略[15]	83.88%	88.43%	69.29%	94.20%	90.59%	93.29%
TBL[16]	90.98%	90.79%	73.25%	93.78%	88.17%	94.48%
TBL（規則有排序）[16]	90.51%	91.81%	76.84%	93.78%	89.39%	94.19%

三、研究方法

3.1 關聯式規則

關聯式規則(Association Rules)，是資料探勘中的一項技術，最早是由 Agrawal & Srikant 所提出的觀念[1][5]。關聯式規則可以幫助我們瞭解資料之間所存在的相互關係。透過關聯式規則，使用者便能夠分析資料中項目與項目之間的關係，並且以容易理解的蘊涵式表達出來。

舉個較為實際的用途，像是藉由關聯式規則來分析交易記錄的資料，藉此瞭解消費者的購買行為模式[5]，例如：「如果今天一個消費者購買了『牛奶』，那麼他有多大的機率也會一起購買『麵包』？」又或者「如果消費者買了『啤酒』，那麼他還有可能順便一起買什麼商品？」。藉此掌握消費者的購買習慣，賣場就能夠制定更有效的促銷方案。

如美國著名的超級市場沃爾瑪(Wal-Mart)，他們透過多年來所記錄的商品銷售資料來進行關聯式規則分析，結果從分析出來的規則中發現兩種看似毫不相干的商品：啤酒和尿布，在星期四同時會被購買的頻率相當地高。由於從關聯式規則中發現了這個特別的現象，沃爾瑪超市嘗試著將啤酒和尿布兩種商品放置在臨近的區域，以便消費者能夠拿取。最後成功地將兩種商品的銷售量都提升上去。

關聯式規則通常以「X⇒Y」的蘊涵式來表達，其記錄著項目集之間所存在的關係。這意味者在資料庫中，若 X 項目集出現，則 Y 項目集也出現的可能性。例如當 X={Milk, Diaper}而 Y={Beer}，此時{Milk, Diaper}⇒ {Beer}表達著：若顧客買了牛奶(Milk)和尿布(Diaper)，而他們同時也會購買啤酒(Beer)的可能性。

關聯式規則在生成的同時也會一併記錄兩個參數：支持度(support)和信心度(confidence)。當規則為 X⇒Y 時，其**支持度(support)**和**信心度(confidence)**的公式分別為：

$$\text{support}(X \Rightarrow Y) = P(X \cap Y) \quad \cdots\cdots(1)$$

$$\text{confidence}(X \Rightarrow Y) = P(Y|X) \quad \cdots\cdots(2)$$

支持度代表在資料庫所有交易記錄中，項目集 X 和 Y 同時出現的機率。信心度代表著在 X 出現的前提下，Y 也出現的條件機率。利用關聯式規則來對資料進行分類預測，稱之為關聯式分類（Associative Classification，AC）[1] [5]，為監督式學習法。

在使用關聯式規則進行分類作業的時候，需要事先將關聯式規則設定排序的機制。當我們要判斷一筆資料應該屬於哪種類別的同時，往往會出現多筆規則符合這筆資料。一般

在利用關聯式規則進行關聯式分類的時候，首先以信心度高的規則優先採用，當規則之間的信心度相等的情況下，才以支持度較高的規則優先採用[5]。

3.2 利用關聯式規則解決台語一詞多音問題

圖一是本文利用關聯式規則的實驗流程，我們將語料分成訓練語料和測試語料，前者用於找出關聯式規則及相關參數；後者則用於求得外部測試之正確率。

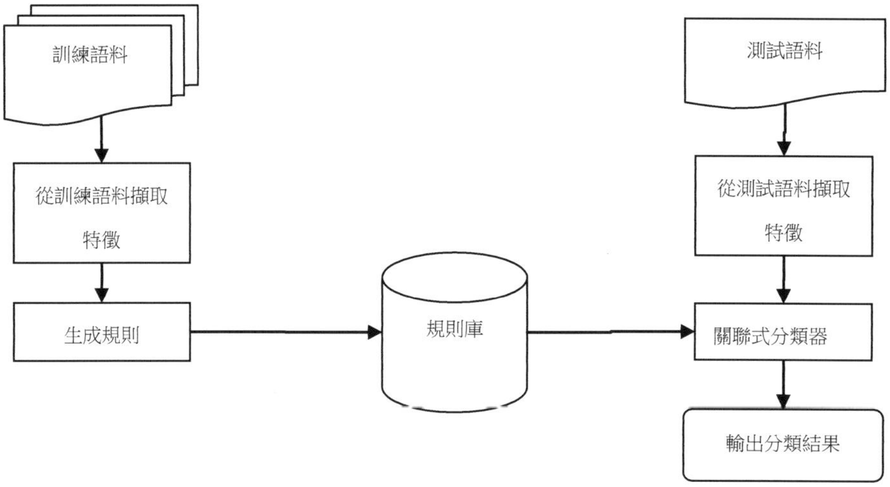

圖一、實驗流程

3.2.1 特徵擷取

判斷一詞多音問題時，首先第一步是從語料中進行特徵擷取。在台語文轉音系統中的文句分析模組裡面，會先將中文文句作斷詞的動作。例如一段中文句子經過斷詞與詞性標記之後，從結果我們可以發現，這段中文文句中出現了三個多音詞「上」：：

「我(Nh) 現在(Nd) 上(VCL) 了(Di) 公車(Na) ， 在(P) 車(Na) 上(Ncd) 發現(VE) 身(Na) 上(Ng) 沒有(VJ) 零錢(Na) 。」

一般在處理一詞多音問題時，是根據多音詞「上」前後所出現的詞、詞性以及「上」本身的詞性，作為判斷一詞多音問題用的特徵。如表三所示，多音詞「上」的樣本經過台語讀音的標記之後，即可作為生成關聯式規則時的實驗語料。

表三、 多音詞的特徵擷取（以「上」為例）

編號	讀音	特徵	前二	前一	目標詞	後一	後二	讀音
語料 1	/ziuun7/	詞	我	現在	上	了	公車	/ziuun7/
		詞性	Nh	Nd	VCL	Di	Na	
語料 2	/ding2/	詞	在	車	上	發現	身	/ding2/
		詞性	P	Na	Ncd	VE	Na	
語料 3	/siong7/	詞	發現	身	上	沒有	零錢	/siong7/
		詞性	VE	Na	Ng	VJ	Na	

3.2.2 規則生成

我們採用 Apriori 演算法來生成規則[8]。Apriori 演算法是關聯式規則探勘方法中較為著名的演算法之一，透過逐步刪除掉支持度過低的項目集作為生成規則的機制。首先在生成規則之前，需要事先設定好最低支持度(min-support) 和最低信心度(min-confidence)。定義一個包含了 k 個項目的項目集合稱為 k-項目集(k-itemset)，並且定義符號L_k為所有高於最低支持度這個門檻值的集合，稱為大型 k-項目集(large k-itemset)，定義為L_k。Apriori 的作法是先由資料庫找出 1-itemset(僅僅包含單一項目的項目集)，再從 1-itemset 之中剔除掉支持度過低的項目集，儲存為 L_1 (large 1-itemset) 。因為 1-itemset 之中被剔除掉的項目集無法成為L_2中任何一個項目集的子集，所以接下來只需要根據L_1中記錄的項目集來生成下一階段的 2-itemset(一次記錄兩個項目的項目集)。同樣再從 2-itemset 中剔除掉支持度過低的項目集，儲存為L_2。依此類推，直到最後 n-itemset 中所有的項目集皆低於最低支持度(即代表L_n無法生成)為止。接著再根據L_1至L_{n-1}來生成規則，並且計算每條規則的信心度，保留高於或等於最低信心度參數的規則。

針對生成規則方面，我們在參數設定上作了一點修正，以便在實作上能更加適用於預測一詞多音問題。

(1) 修正支持度的計算方法：一般在生成規則時必須連帶計算出規則本身的支持度，若規則本身的支持度低於事先設定好的最低支持度，那麼這條規則將不會被採用。原本的支持度公式為：

$$\text{support}（X\Rightarrow Y）=P(X\cap Y)=\frac{|X\cap Y|}{|D|} \quad \cdots\cdots(3)$$

在解決一詞多音的實驗中，X 記錄著出現的特徵項目集，Y 記錄著預測的讀音。|X ∩ Y|代表在訓練語料中對應的特徵和讀音同時出現的次數，|D|則代表生成規則時的訓練語料筆數。以目標詞「上」的實驗語料為例子。我們從 10648 筆訓練語料中生成關聯式規則，其中一條規則為：

『業務（前一詞）⇒ /siong7/（讀音）』

根據這 10648 筆訓練語料中的統計，「上」的前一詞為『業務』且讀音為『/siong7/』的組合共出現了 5 次。如此一來，換算成支持度為： 5/10648=0.00046957。從這個例子可以發現，若依照原本的方式來計算支持度，會得到一個極小的小數。在後續的實驗中，若我們想要針對最低支持度這項參數進行更動的時候，會變得難以調整。由於我們一詞多音的實驗中採用了中文詞作為特徵，而中文詞本身容易產生資料稀疏的問題(例如出現較少見的專有名詞)。解決的方法是改回原本的出現頻率代替原本的支持度參數，出現頻率的公式如下：

$$\text{Freq}（X\Rightarrow Y）=|X\cap Y| \quad \cdots\cdots(4)$$

例如上述例子中，前一詞為『業務』且讀音為『/siong7/』的組合共出現了 5 次，則將該條規則的出現頻率記錄為 5 次，如此一來就能夠以正整數的形式進行參數設定。

(2) 規則長度的上限：規則長度，即關聯式分類中規則的基數(rule cardinality) [7]，代表著規則左式記錄的項目數量。例如一字詞「上」的實驗中，某一規則為：

「Ncd(目標詞的詞性) 社會(前一詞) => /siong7/(讀音)」

這條規則的左式是由 2 個項目所組合在一起的項目集，即規則長度為 2，同時也代表這條規則是參考了兩種特徵來判斷讀音。原本在生成規則的演算法中並沒有特別限定規則長度，雖然長度較長的規則將會蘊藏更多的資訊量，但相對地也會拖慢生成規則和關聯式分類的整體速度。我們在實驗中加入了規則長度上限的設定，希望能夠藉此過濾掉因為長度過長而對分類沒有幫助的規則。表四為以「上」為例的生成的關聯式規則範例。

表四、 生成的關聯式規則範例（以「上」為例）

前二詞/詞性	前一詞/詞性	目標詞『上』詞性	後一詞/詞性	後二詞/詞性	讀音	信心度	頻率	支持度
-	身	-	-	Na	/siong7/	100.00%	99	0.93%
VE	-	Ng	-	-	/siong7/	100.00%	46	0.43%
Na	VH	-	-	-	/siong7/	100.00%	39	0.37%
-	車	-	-	Na	/ding2/	100.00%	21	0.20%
-	現在	-	-	-	/ziuun7/	100.00%	3	0.03%
-	身	-	-	-	/siong7/	99.35%	616	5.79%
-	車	-	-	-	/ding2/	93.98%	78	0.73%
Nd	-	-	-	-	/siong7/	90.09%	200	1.88%
在	-	-	-	-	/siong7/	80.09%	2586	24.29%
-	-	-	-	Na	/siong7/	77.95%	2574	24.17%
-	-	VCL	-	-	/ziuun7/	66.29%	474	4.45%

四、實驗結果

4.1 實驗設定

4.1.1 實驗語料描述

我們採用中央研究院平衡語料庫 3.0（簡稱 ASBC 3.0）[14]作為實驗語料的來源。中研院平衡語料庫是世界上第一個擁有完整詞類標記的漢語平衡語料庫，裡面收錄的文句包含了斷詞以及詞性標記，很適合作為我們一詞多音研究中的實驗語料。我們抽取出一些常見的多音詞作為實驗語料，並經由人工方式將正確發音標出，其中包括『上』、『下』、『不』、『你』、『我』、『他』等六個多音詞。表五為每種多音詞的語料筆數和可能會出現的讀音標記。

表五、 語料筆數和各種讀音標記

多音詞	台語讀音標記種類	讀音種類數	總筆數
上	/siong7/、/ding2/、/ziuun7/	3	21,294
下	/ha7/、/au7/、/loh8/、/e7/	4	6,840
不	/bho5/、/bhuaih4/、/bhe7/、/m7/、/but4/、/mai3/	6	38,688
你	/li2/、/lin2/	2	2,229
我	/ghua2/、/ghun2/	2	5,627
他	/yi1/、/yin1/	2	3,708

4.1.2 訓練與測試語料分配比例

我們採用的訓練、測試語料的分配比例如圖二的說明。一開始，先從實驗語料中隨機選取出 50%的實驗語料作為初始訓練語料。剩餘的 50%實驗語料再平均分成五等份作為測試語料，分別給予編號為測試語料 1 號至 5 號。

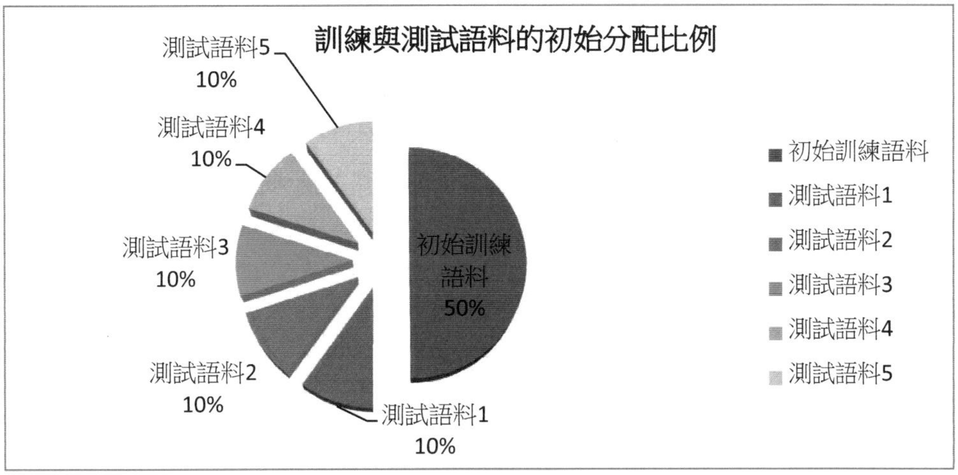

圖二、實驗語料切割

圖三則說明了每份訓練與測試語料的使用時機。在最初的實驗中，我們會先利用初始訓練語料生成關聯式規則，並且使用 1 號測試語料來評估實驗的效能。而後續的第二個實驗中，再將 1 號測試語料併入原本的訓練語料中，成為新的訓練語料（初始訓練語料加上 1 號測試語料），並且使用 2 號測試語料來評估實驗的效能，以此類推。而最後的外部測試實驗中，將會使用 5 號測試語料來評估實驗效能。

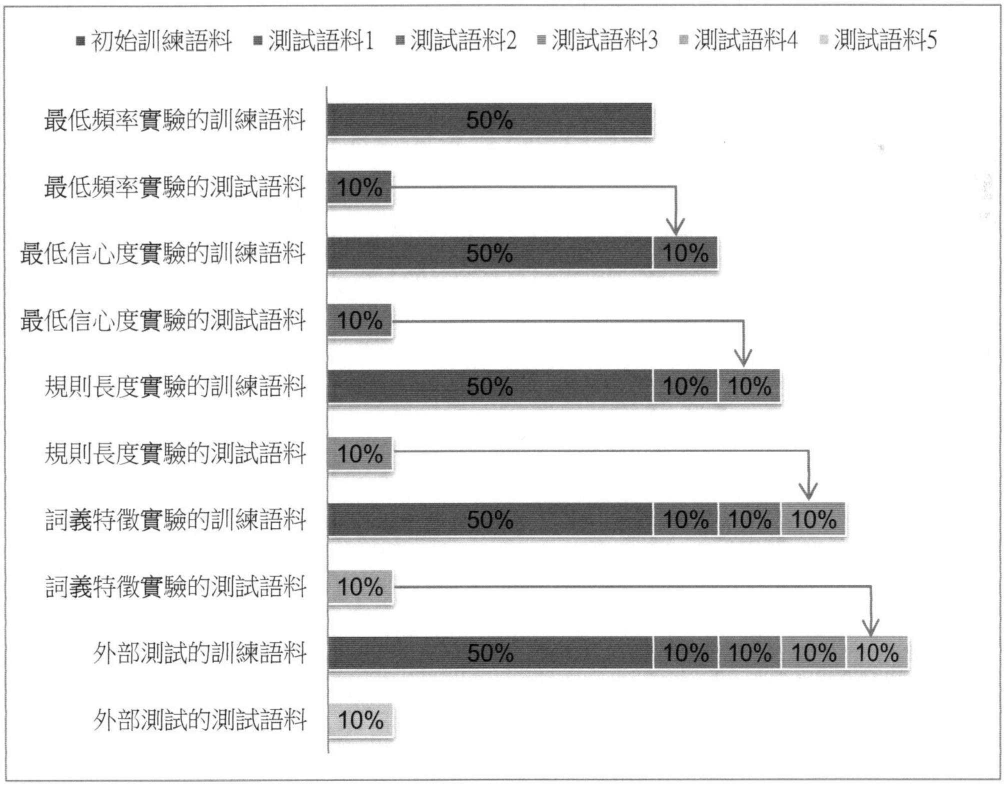

圖三、實驗語料分配比例

4.2 參數設定之實驗

在生成關聯式規則之前需要事先設定最低支持度和最低信心度兩種相關的參數。除此之外，我們在實驗中加入了規則長度上限的設定，希望能夠藉此過濾掉因為長度雖長但對於分類卻沒有幫助的規則。當一條規則低於設定的最低支持度或最低信心度，或者規則長度超過了設定的上限，這條規則將不會被記錄到規則庫中。理論上，即使沒有刻意設定上述參數，仍然有可能生成出關聯式規則來進行分類作業。但是這麼作會直接導致生成出來的規則數量過於龐大，進而拖慢分類的速度，而且不見得能夠達到最佳的預測正確率。

反過來說，若參數設定太過於嚴格（例如：最低支持度或最低信心度的設定過高、又或者規則長度上限設定過短），如此一來可以提供資訊的規則又會減少，進而造成分類的正確率下降。

接下來的實驗中，我們將逐步探討最低支持度、最低信心度和規則的長度上限應該設定為多少較佳。此外，為了因應台語一詞多音問題中使用了中文詞作為特徵的情況，最低支持度在計算方式上面需要額外作修正，以下章節將會特別說明。

4.2.2 最低出現頻率的設定實驗

我們分別將每個多音詞透過內部測試來探討規則的最低出現頻率應該為多少較佳。我們分別將最低出現頻率設定從 1 次到 10 次進行分類作業。在這個實驗中，我們採用初始訓練語料(佔整體實驗語料的 50%)來生成規則，並且採用 1 號測試語料來評估分類的正確率。

表六、 最低出現頻率參數的實驗結果

最低出現頻率 \ 多音詞	上	下	不	你	我	他
1	91.88%	92.55%	76.69%	94.25%	92.36%	94.13%
2	92.25%	92.70%	77.80%	94.69%	92.71%	94.67%
3	92.35%	92.26%	77.15%	95.13%	93.58%	94.93%
4	92.21%	92.26%	76.51%	93.81%	93.40%	94.67%
5	92.21%	91.82%	76.17%	93.36%	92.71%	94.67%
6	92.02%	91.68%	76.01%	93.36%	92.88%	94.67%
7	91.69%	91.53%	75.76%	93.36%	92.88%	94.67%
8	91.55%	91.24%	75.39%	93.36%	92.88%	94.67%
9	91.55%	90.95%	75.21%	93.36%	92.88%	93.07%
10	91.55%	90.80%	75.08%	93.36%	92.88%	93.07%
最低出現頻率的最佳設定	3	2	2	3	3	3
訓練語料筆數	10648	3420	19344	1114	2813	1854
最低支持度	0.028%	0.058%	0.010%	0.269%	0.107%	0.162%

從表六的實驗結果可以發現，當每個多音詞的最低出現頻率設定在 2~3 之間時，能夠讓

得到較佳的正確率。值得一提的是，實驗中的訓練語料筆數在不同多音詞之間存在著一定的差距。

4.2.3 最低信心度設定實驗

接下來的實驗裡面，我們分別將每個目標詞透過內部測試來探討規則的最小信心度的設定為多少最為適合。我們將最低信心度設定從 0%到 95%，每次提昇 5%，分別各作一次分類作業。我們將初始訓練語料和 1 號測試語料合併成為新的訓練語料(佔整體實驗語料的 60%)，作為這次實驗的訓練語料。在這個實驗中，採用 2 號測試語料來評估分類的正確率。我們從實驗結果中挑選出較佳的最低信心度設定，以正確率較高者優先，若相同則取設定值較高者，如此一來能夠再減少一部分不必要的規則。結果如表七。

表七、最低信心度參數的實驗結果

目標詞 / 最低信心度	上	下	不	你	我	他
0%~45%	92.11%	93.27%	77.62%	94.25%	94.44%	94.13%
50%	92.11%	93.27%	77.64%	94.25%	94.44%	94.13%
55%	92.11%	93.27%	77.64%	94.25%	94.44%	94.13%
60%	92.11%	93.27%	77.64%	94.25%	94.44%	94.13%
65%	92.11%	93.27%	77.64%	94.25%	94.44%	94.13%
70%	92.11%	93.42%	77.54%	94.25%	94.44%	94.13%
75%	92.11%	93.42%	77.28%	94.25%	94.44%	94.13%
80%	92.11%	93.42%	76.97%	94.25%	94.44%	94.13%
85%	92.11%	93.42%	76.14%	94.25%	94.44%	94.13%
90%	92.11%	93.27%	75.14%	94.25%	94.44%	94.13%
95%	91.97%	93.13%	73.84%	94.25%	94.44%	94.13%
最佳的最低信心度設定	90%	85%	65%	95%	95%	95%
多音詞的門檻值	81.28%	69.56%	41.37%	87.80%	80.15%	87.85%

4.2.4 規則長度上限設定之實驗結果

當我們在生成規則時，可以選擇只將指定長度以下的規則記錄到規則庫中。例如當我們設定長度上限為 2 時，生成的規則最多只能一次參考兩個特徵來判斷讀音。如果生成的規則長度越長，所能夠提供的資訊量會越多，但相對也會導致生成的規則數量劇增。我們將初始訓練語料、1 號測試語料、2 號測試語料合併成為新的訓練語料(佔整體實驗語料的 70%)，作為這次實驗的訓練語料。在這個實驗中，採用 3 號測試語料來評估分類的正確率。表八是長度上限最佳設定的實驗結果。

表八、規則長度上限的實驗結果

目標詞 / 長度上限	上	下	不	你	我	他
1	91.27%	93.57%	76.73%	92.44%	94.79%	93.87%
2	92.49%	95.47%	77.07%	92.44%	94.62%	93.60%
3	92.30%	94.88%	76.68%	93.78%	94.27%	93.60%
4	92.30%	94.88%	76.65%	93.78%	94.27%	93.60%
5 以上	92.30%	94.88%	76.65%	93.78%	94.27%	93.60%
長度上限的最佳設定	2	2	2	3	1	1

4.3 追加詞義特徵

由於中文詞的數量龐大，會有資料稀疏導致有些情形無法被訓練到的問題，例如『上』的一字詞多音實驗語料中，其中一句經過斷詞與詞性標記後的語料為：

廟(Na)/裡(Ncd)/供桌(Na)/上(Ncd)/的(DE)/水果(Na)/容易(VH)/順手牽羊(VA)

原本『上』的台語讀音應該為/ding2/，分類器卻誤將這筆語料分類為/siong7/。這是由於『上』的前一詞出現『供桌』的情況，在訓練語料中相當罕見，這將會導致沒有規則支持『上』應該念/ding2/。在人工標記的時候，標記者之所以能夠判斷此時的『上』應該念/ding2/，是因為標記者知道『供桌』其實意義上接近『桌子』。當『桌子』或『桌』等詞彙出現在『上』的前一詞時，『上』的讀音應該標記成/ding2/。為了解決這個問題，我們將使用廣義知網中文詞知識庫(E-HowNet) [17] [18] [19]來查詢對應的詞義，並且追加至特徵中。

我們根據輸入的中文詞和詞性，透過中文詞庫中的八萬目詞來查詢其對應到的詞義。如此一來，原本詞頻較低的中文詞將有機會被納入一個出現頻率較高的新特徵裡面。如果仍然因為詞義的頻率過低而導致規則庫中找不到對應的詞義，能夠再根據 E- HowNet 的樹狀結構來取得上一層的詞義，如圖四所示。

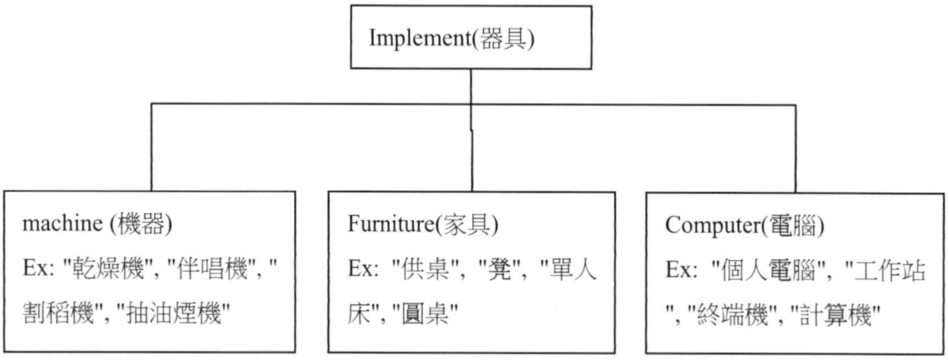

圖四、 E-Hownet 詞義樹範例（以『furniture|家具』為例子）

以上述『而且廟裡供桌上的水果容易順手牽羊』句子為例，我們將追加詞義作為新的特徵如表九所示：

表九、追加詞義作為新特徵的範例

特徵位置	前二詞	前一詞	目標詞	後一詞	後二詞
詞(WORD)	裡	供桌	上	的	水果
詞性(POS)	Ncd	Na	Ncd	DE	Na
詞義(Word Sense)	Internal	Furniture	Upper	Relation	Fruit

原本『供桌』等詞彙存在著出現頻率過低的問題，但是透過詞義 Furniture（家具）作為參考之後，就能夠得知『供桌』在詞義上也是一種家具。同樣地，當我們要判斷『供桌/上』、『凳/上』、『單人床/上』等情況的時候，分類器也能根據 Furniture（家具）這個特徵來判斷『上』的讀音。

我們將初始訓練語料、1 號至 3 號測試語料合併成為新的訓練語料(佔整體實驗語料的 80%)，作為這次實驗的訓練語料。在這個實驗中，採用 4 號測試語料來評估分類的正確率。從表十的實驗結果顯示，當我們添加詞義作為特徵之後，能夠再提升所有多音詞的分類正確率。

表十、追加詞義作為特徵的實驗結果

目標詞 / 使用特徵	上	下	不	你	我	他
詞&詞性	93.14%	93.42%	77.23%	93.33%	95.13%	94.12%
詞&詞性&詞義	93.38%	94.30%	77.33%	95.11%	95.83%	94.65%

4.4 外部測試與各種實驗方法比較

我們將上述實驗中所得到的最佳參數設定套用到最後的外部測試實驗中，並且以中文詞、詞性、詞義作為特徵來生成關聯式規則。我們將初始訓練語料、1 號至 4 號測試語料合併成為新的訓練語料(佔整體實驗語料的 90%)，作為外部測試的訓練語料。在最後的外部測試實驗中，採用 5 號測試語料來評估分類的正確率。表十一為本文提出之方法及參數設定和文獻上之方法正確率的比較，實驗結果顯示利用關聯式規則搭配多種參數之設定及加入詞義資訊，有助於大大提升一詞多音的預測正確率，表十一也說明本文提出的方法優於其他文獻上的方法。

表十一、各種方法外部測試正確率之比較

目目標詞 / 實驗方法	上	下	不	你	我	他
階層式方法[13]	90.42%	94.30%	74.47%	92.12%	89.23%	92.54%
組合式策略[15]	83.88%	88.43%	69.29%	94.20%	90.59%	93.29%
TBL[16]	90.98%	90.79%	73.25%	93.78%	88.17%	94.48%
TBL（規則有排序）[16]	90.51%	91.81%	76.84%	93.78%	89.39%	94.19%
本論文方法	93.99%	94.44%	77.82%	95.11%	96.35%	95.99%

五、結論

本論文利用關聯式規則來預測台語文轉音系統中一詞多音現象，並針對關聯式分類實驗進行參數上的調整，同時藉由 E-Hownet 來追加詞義特徵，以避免中文詞作為特徵時容易出現的資料稀疏問題。

從實驗結果能夠說明，在常見的『上』、『下』、『不』、『你』、『我』、『他』等多音詞，我們提出的方法擁有更好的預測正確率。儘管如此，將關聯式規則應用在一詞多音預測上仍然有許多進步的空間。尤其是面對一個多音詞能夠通用於兩種讀音的情況，在現有的實驗結果中，依然容易出現誤判的情況。未來能夠針對現有的台語一詞多音預測模組的系統架構作出這方面的修正，使訓練模型能夠處理讀音通用的情況。

參考文獻

[1] B. Liu, W. Hsu and Y. Ma, "Integrating classification and association rule mining",

Knowledge Discovery and Data Mining, pp. 86, 80, 1998.

[2] Brill, E. "Automatic grammar induction and parsing free text: A transformation-based approach." *In Proceedings of the 31st Meeting of the Association for Computational Linguistics.* Columbus, Ohio, USA, pp. 259-265, 1993.

[3] C. H. Hwang, "Text to Pronunciation Conversion in Taiwanese", *Master thesis, Institute of Statistics, National Tsing Hua University*, 1996.

[4] C. Shih and R. Sproat, "Issues in Text-to-Speech Conversion for Mandarin", *Computational Linguistics and Chinese Language Processing*, Vol., 1, No. 1, pp. 37-86, 1996.

[5] Fadi Thabtah, "A review of associative classification mining." , *Knowledge Engineering Review*, Vol. 22, pp. 37-65, 2007.

[6] J. Y. Huang, "Implementation of Tone Sandhi Rules and Tagger for Taiwanese TTS", *Master thesis, Department of Communication Engineering, National Chiao Tung University*, 2001.

[7] M. S. Yu, T. Y. Chang, T. H. Hsu, and Y. H. Tsai, "A Mandarin Text-to-Speech System Using Prosodic Hierarchy and a Large Number of Words", *Proceedings of the 17th Conference on Computational Linguistics and Speech Processing, (ROCLING XVII)*, pp. 183-202, 2005.

[8] R. Agrawal and R. Srikant. "Fast algorithms for mining association rules." Presented at *Proc. 20th Int. Conf. Very Large Data Bases*, VLDB, 1994.

[9] S. H. Chen, S. H. Hwang, and Y. R. Wang, "A Mandarin Text-to-Speech System", *Computational Linguistics and Chinese Language Processing*, Vol. 1, No. 1, pp. 87-100, 1996.

[10] Y. J. Lin, M. S. Yu, and C. J. Huang, "The Polysemy Problems, An Important Issue in a Chinese to Taiwanese TTS System", *Proceedings of the 2008 International Congress on Image and Signal Processing*, Paper number P1234, May 28-30, Sanya, China, 2008.

[11] Y. J. Lin, M. S. Yu, and C. Y. Lin, "Using Chi-Square Automatic Interaction Detector to Solve the Polysemy Problems in a Chinese to Taiwanese TTS System" , in *Proceeding of The 8th International Conference on Intelligent Systems Design and Applications* (*ISDA* 2008), pp.362-367, 2008.

[12] Y. J. Lin, W. S. Ji, M. S. Yu, and S. D. Lee, "Some Important Issues on Text Analysis in a Chinese to Taiwanese TTS System", *Proceedings of the 9th IEEE International Workshop on Cellular Neural Networks and their Applications*, 2005.

[13] Y. J. Lin, M. S. Yu, C. Y. Lin, and Y. C. Lin, "A Layered Approach to the Polysemy Problem in a Chinese to Taiwanese TTS System, " *Journal of Information Science and Engineering*, Vol. 26, No. 5, 2010.

[14] 中央研究院平衡語料庫 http://db1x.sinica.edu.tw/cgi-bin/kiwi/mkiwi/mkiwi.sh

[15] 林金玉，"中文轉台語文轉音系統中一詞多音之預測"，國立中興大學資訊科學與工

程學系碩士論文，2008。

[16]楊文德，” 利用規則轉換學習方法解決台語一詞多音之歧義” ，國立中興大學資訊科學與工程學系，2012。

[17]董振東、董強，知網(HowNet)，http://www.keenage.com/

[18]廣 義 知 網 知 識 本 體 架 構 (Extended-HowNet Ontology) http://ckip.iis.sinica.edu.tw/taxonomy/

[19]廣義知網知識本體架構線上瀏覽系統 http://ehownet.iis.sinica.edu.tw/

[20]鍾祥睿，”台語 TTS 系統之改進”，國立交通大學電信工程系所碩士論文，2002。

Context-Aware In-Page Search

林昱豪 Yu-Hao Lin, 劉郁蘭 Yu-Lan Liu, 顏孜羲 Tzu-Xi Yen, 張俊盛 Jason S. Chang

國立清華大學資訊工程學系
Department of Computer Science
National Tsing Hua University
{ catonmars.lin, ikulan12, joseph.yen, jason.jschang}@gmail.com

Abstract

In this paper we introduce a method for searching appropriate articles from knowledge bases (e.g. Wikipedia) for a given query and its context. In our approach, this problem is transformed into a multi-class classification of candidate articles. The method involves automatically augmenting smaller knowledge bases using larger ones and learning to choose adequate articles based on hyperlink similarity between article and context. At run-time, keyphrases in given context are extracted and the sense ambiguity of query term is resolved by computing similarity of keyphrases between context and candidate articles. Evaluation shows that the method significantly outperforms the strong baseline of assigning most frequent articles to the query terms. Our method effectively determines adequate articles for given query-context pairs, suggesting the possibility of using our methods in context-aware search engines.

Keywords: entity linking, word sense disambiguation, Wikipedia, support vector machine, search engine

1 Introduction

Today we surf the Internet through search engines most of the time. With the explosive growth of web pages, the accuracy and relevancy of search results have become ever more important. Traditional search engines accept keywords, and return a page full of possible relevant results. Then users can click one of the results to visit the sites they are interested in. We call this type of search "keyword-search". Today, almost all search engines are keyword-based.

However, various classes of results mixed in the search results. For example, when a user query the search engine with the keyword "apple", the search results comprise of two major class, "Apple Inc.", the computer company, and "apple", a kind of fruit. With only one keyword, even state-of-the-art keyword-based search engines could not distinguish between different search intents. Unlike keyword search, context-aware search assume each query is associated with a context.

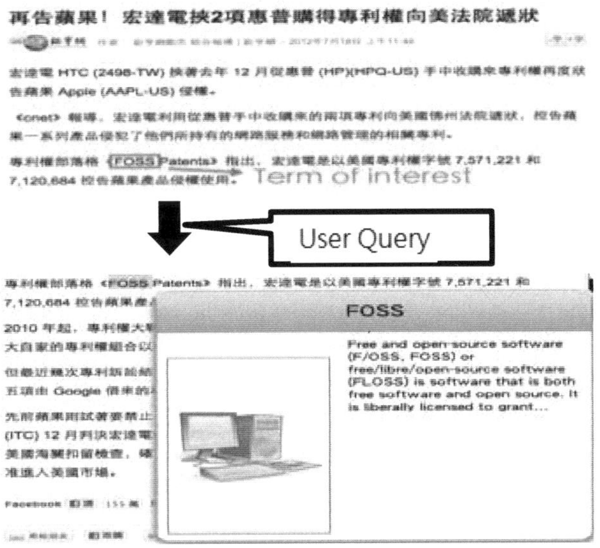

Figure 1. An example of context-aware search

John McCarthy (September 4, 1927 - October 24, 2011)[1][2][3][4][5][6] was an American computer scientist and cognitive scientist. He invented the term "artificial intelligence" (AI), developed the Lisp programming language family, significantly influenced the design of the ALGOL programming language, popularized timesharing, and was very influential in the early development of AI.

McCarthy received many accolades and honors, including the Turing Award for his contributions to the topic of AI, the United States National Medal of Science, and the Kyoto Prize.

Figure 2. The mention "John McCarthy" and its context.

In this paper, we present a prototypical system, In-Page Search, that automatically extract context information and use them to disambiguate ambiguous queries. Users could select the terms they are interested in, and then with a click of the mouse, the In-Page Search system shows a pop-up window with the most relevant results for the given context.(See Figure 1.) In-Page Search is similar to the "entity-linking problem", which has long been an active research topic in IR and Database community. Entity-linking problem could be informally described as follows: given a knowledge base, in which every entry is an entity and its associated information. Given a mention and the context with the mention, determine the correct entity that the given mention really links to. For example, Figure 2 shows the mention "John McCarthy" and it's context, in a knowledge base, there are more than 10 entities which may be linked to "John McCarthy". The problem is determining the correct entity to link to. Intuitively, entity-linking could be considered a Named-Entity Disambiguation problem or more generally, a word sense disambiguation problem.

In our approach, we also exploit the cross-language features in multi-language knowledge bases. This method augments information in one language with other languages in the same knowledge base to cope with the data sparseness problem which may be a problem for a language with less data. We discuss this multi-language model and the definitions of various link-based similarity measures in Chapter 3.

At run-time, In-Page Search starts with a query together with its context page submitted by the user. The system then extracts context terms and transforms them into machine-readable features. Finally, the system uses a *SVM* model (Chang and Lin, 2011) trained on a knowledge base to determine which entity in the knowledge base should be linked to the current query, and output a summarized abstract of this entity to the user. The results could be further augmented for other purposes. For example, for the input links to a geographic entity, we could show the location using a map application.

The rest of this thesis is organized as follows. We review the related work in the following chapter. Then we describe our preprocessing and runtime algorithm in Chapter 3. We then report on the experimental setup and compare our results to various baselines in Chapter 4. Conclusions are provided in Chapter 5 along with the directions of future work.

2 Related Work

Search engines and related technology has long been an active research topic in information retrieval and natural language processing. Most modern search engines (e.g. *Google, Bing*, and *Yahoo!*) accept keyword or keyphrase as input. Today keyword search engines have excellent performance in terms of both results relevancy and response time. However, keyword search engines do not consider a query may come with a context, so they could not distinguish between different search intents. With the rise of the mobile web, some search engines have evolved to provide better user experience. One reprehensive example is the *Google Now* feature of mobile edition of *Google*. While accepting user's voice input, it extracts user's context information such as GPS location, user's schedule recorded on calendar application, and the contact information on user's cell phone. Thus, *Google Now* can analyze user's search intent and provide the most relevant information using these contexts.

Previously, much effort has been made in research on word sense disambiguation based on machine learning (Black, 1988; Hearst, 1991; Leacock, Towell, and Voorhees, 1993; Bruce and Wiebe, 1994). Yarowsky (Yarowsky, 1992) uses a Naïve Bayesian classifier trained on Roget's thesaurus to classify words with given context into its sense category. They use class-based salient words list provided by Roget's thesaurus as features and tuning weight by counting the frequencies of surrounding salient words in context. While achieving high accuracy, this research can be viewed as prototypical framework of most machine learning WSD systems. These approaches often rely on sense-labeled corpus. Although supervised machine learning WSD algorithms frequently gives high performance, however, sense-labeled corpus is not always available. Compared to our approach, we use Wikipedia as our corpus, its cross-lingual nature enables us to augment smaller knowledge base with other languages.

An important branch of WSD is entity-linking. While WSD focuses on linking word to its correct sense given context, entity-linking systems focus on linking mentions of entities (often named-entities) to its correct entry in a given knowledge base. "Wikify" (Mihalcea and Csomai, 2007; Milne and Witten, 2008) is an example of entity-linking systems. These systems automatically augment user's input texts with hyperlinks to Wikipedia entries. For example, imagine Figure 2 with links removed, these systems will automatically detect them with anchors links to proper Wikipedia articles (e.g. John McCarthy in Figure 2 links to John McCarthy (computer scientist) in Wikipedia.). Mihalcea's system decomposes these task into two procedural: keyphrase extraction and word sense disambiguation. They achieve WSD by computing various linguistic features except the "Keyphraseness": how frequently one phrase in Wikipedia being hyperlinks.

Milne and Witten's system disambiguates mentions by incorporating more link-based measures. They apply normalized Google Distance (Cilibrasi and Vitanyi, 2007) to compute relatedness between two Wikipedia articles, and training machine learning models. Unlike Mihalcea's system, they first disambiguate possible candidates in input document, and then use information from this pass of disambiguation to aid keyphrase extraction. Their system has good performance both on Wikipedia articles and wild-life news pages.

Compared to our system, most entity-linking system developed their method on English, so they could not directly apply to languages that need segmentation pre-processing. To apply our method to CJK languages, we use a scheme similar in (Milne and Witten, 2008) to transform context page into vector of context entities. In addition, we extend traditional link-based measure to a cross-lingual augmented knowledge base. To the best of our knowledge, such technique hasn't been shown in previous systems.

3 Method

Understanding a user's search intent basing solely on query term (e.g., 蘋果) is a challenging task. Short query terms typically have more than one sense which leading to multiple entities in the knowledge base that could be linked to. To assign adequate entity for a given query, a promising method is to compute the similarity between a query's context and candidate entities' description, and returning the most similar entity (e.g. 蘋果公司 for 蘋果) in the context of a computer-related Chinese article.

3.1 Problem Statement

We focus on the essential step of determining user's search intent: choosing the appropriate entity in the knowledge base for the given query. Once the entity has determined, the system returns information of this entity in various ways (e.g. text description, image, audio, video). In a *Wikipedia-like* knowledge base, we treat each document as an entity, its description page as the context, and hyperlinks in this page as query terms. With the hyperlinked nature of such a knowledge base, we train a classifier which estimate the similarity of link structure between each query term's context, and determine whether a query term and an entity (i.e. the article titles) should be linked together. Thus, the problem of context-aware search is transformed to an entity-linking problem. We now formally state the problem we are addressing by first giving a definition of *Wikipedia-like* knowledge base.

A *Wikipedia-like* knowledge base is a collection of documents, each document should describe an unique concept with hyperlinks, *inter-wiki links* and *disambiguation pages* which list possible sense of an ambiguous term.

Problem Statement: We are given a set of Wikipedia-like knowledge bases $\boldsymbol{KB}=\{ \boldsymbol{kb}_1 ,\ldots, \boldsymbol{kb}_n | \; n \geq 1 \}$ (e.g., {Chinese Wikipedia, English Wikipedia}), a query term $\boldsymbol{q}$, a context document $\boldsymbol{c}$ of $\boldsymbol{q}$, and a knowledge base $\boldsymbol{kb}_j \in \boldsymbol{KB}$, where $\boldsymbol{q}$ should be searched. Our goal is to assign an adequate document $\boldsymbol{e}_i$, where $\boldsymbol{e}_i \in \boldsymbol{kb}_j = \{\boldsymbol{e}_1,\ldots, \boldsymbol{e}_j\}$ and $\boldsymbol{e}_1,\ldots, \boldsymbol{e}_j$ are candidate senses. For this, we compute the link structure similarity between each document pair $(\boldsymbol{c}, \boldsymbol{e})$, where $\boldsymbol{e}$ is in $\boldsymbol{kb}_j$, and then train a classifier to determine which $(\boldsymbol{c}, \boldsymbol{e})$ pair should be linked together.

3.2 Learning to Link with Wikipedia-like Databases

We attempt to resolve the sense ambiguity of a given query term by learning link structure characteristics from a collection of <Term, Entity> pairs in a Wikipedia-like knowledge base. Our learning process is shown in Figure 3.

```
(1)    Generate  Candidate Term-Entity Pairs From Knowledge Base (Section 3.2.1)
(2)    Augment Knowledge Bases by Inter-Wiki Links (Section 3.2.2)
(3)    Train Binary SVM Classification Model (Section 3.2.3)
```

Figure 3 Outline of the training process.

3.2.1 Generate Candidate Term-Entity Pairs From Knowledge Base

In the first stage of the learning process (Step (1) in Figure 3), we generate candidate <Term, Entity> pairs from ***KB***. Once the candidate pairs have been computed and stored, the *In-Page Search* system could use them to efficiently retrieve possible entities of a given query, instead of comparing every ***e*** in ***KB***. For example, given the query "蘋果", we retrieve { <"蘋果", "蘋果公司">, <"蘋果", "麥金塔電腦">, <"蘋果", "蘋果(水果)">, <"蘋果","蘋果日報">}, and then, these four entities will be disambiguated. We compute these pairs from ***KB*** using a hyperlink's anchor text and its destination entity. The rationale behind computing <Term, Entity> pairs using anchor texts is that anchor texts reflect how people mentioning entities in written articles.

The input to this stage is a set of *Wikipedia-like* knowledge base ***KB***. With their hyperlinked nature, we could compute <Term, Entities> pairs easily. To provide broader coverage of query, we also take into account the redirect links and disambiguation pages.

蘋果公司

維基百科，自由的百科全书

蘋果股份有限公司（Apple Inc.，NASDAQ：AAPL，LSE：ACP），原稱蘋果電腦公司（Apple Computer, Inc.）總部位於美國加利福尼亞的庫比蒂諾，核心業務是電子科技產品，目前全球電腦市場佔有率為7.96%。蘋果的Apple II於1970年代助長了個人電腦革命，其後的Macintosh接力於1980年代持續發展。最知名的產品是其出品的Apple II、Macintosh電腦、iPod音樂播放器、iTunes商店、iPhone手機和iPad平板電腦等。它在高科技企業中以創新而聞名。

蘋果公司原稱蘋果電腦公司，於2007年1月9日舊金山的Macworld Expo上宣佈改為現名。

2010年9月23日，據CNN報導，蘋果公司曾短暫成為第二市值的上市公司，僅次於美國的石油業巨擘埃克森美孚，超過位於第三的中石油[1]。2011年8月9日周二紐約股市盤中，蘋果公司市值曾短暫超越美國石油巨頭埃克森美孚，成為世界市值第一的上市公司[2]，次日周三收盤時蘋果公司再一次超過埃克森美孚，直到該周四埃克森美孚才重新奪回市值第一的名號[3]。

Figure 4. An input document from an Wikipedia-like knowledge base

Term	Entity	Term	Entity
NASDAQ	那斯達克	中石油	中國石油
LSE	倫敦證券交易所	加利福尼亞	加利福尼亞州
CNN	有線電視新聞網	蘋果電腦公司	蘋果公司

Table 1. Samples of <Term, Entity> pairs constructed from Figure 4.

The output of this stage is a collection of <Term, Entity> pairs of a certain knowledge base. Some <Term, Entity> pairs, automatically constructed, are shown in Table 1. Figure 5 shows the algorithm for computing <Term, Entity> pairs from a *Wikipedia*-like database.

```
procedure GenerateTermEntityPairs(kb)
(1)        docs = GetDocuments(kb)
(2)        list = emptyList
(3)        for each ei in docs
(4)             links = GetLinks(ei)
(5)             title = GetTitle(ei)
(6)             if ei is Disambiguation Page
(7)                   for each target in links
(8)                        list += <title,target>
(9)             else
(10)             for each <anchor,target> in links
(11)                  list += <anchor,target>
(12)       hist=Histogram(list)
(13)       return hist
```

Figure 5. Generating <Term, Entity> pairs.

In Step (1) of the algorithm we retrieve the list of all articles in ***kb***. Then we iterate through all articles. For each article, we first identify all hyperlinks and title of article (Steps (4), (5)). If this document is a *disambiguation page*, for each hyperlinks in this page, we add <document

title, link target> to a temp list. Otherwise we add <anchor text, link target> to the temp list (Steps (6)~(11)). Finally, we compute the histogram of the temp list, where every entry is a <Term, Entity> pair and its frequency (Steps (12)). An example of results is shown in Table 2.

Table 2. <Term, Entity> pairs of '蘋果'

Term	Entity	Frequency
蘋果	蘋果(植物)	149
蘋果	蘋果公司	23
蘋果	蘋果(電影)	1
蘋果	麥金塔電腦	1

3.2.2 Augmenting Knowledge Base using Inter-Wiki Links

In the second stage of the learning algorithm (Step (2) in Figure 3), we augment each *Wikipedia*-like knowledge base in ***KB*** using *inter-wiki* links. Consider *Chinese Wikipedia* and *English Wikipedia*, *language links* among them link two document describe the same entity together. For example, "*麥金塔電腦*" in *Chinese Wikipedia* and "*Macintosh*" in *English Wikipedia*. By linking one entity to its corresponding entity in other knowledge base, we could combine the knowledge to obtain a richer representation of information of each entity. For two imbalanced knowledge bases (e.g. *Chinese Wikipedia* and *English Wikipedia*), our algorithm could augment the one with less information using the one with more information.

In a *Wikipedia*-like knowledge base, each article can be viewed as a concept (i.e. entity). From hyperlinks in documents, we could build a directed graph of the entire knowledge base, in which nodes denote articles, the edge indicate an article mentions another via hyperlinks. Thus, out-going edges of a node point to other articles mentioned in the article represented by the node, while in-coming edges of a node indicate other articles mentioning the node. We call these two edges *out-links* and *in-links* respectively (See Figure 6.).

Figure 6. A link graph. Blue edges denote outlinks, green edges denote inlinks, orange edges denote both inlinks and outlinks.

The input of this stage is two *Wikipedia*-like knowledge bases (e.g. <*Chinese Wikipedia*, *English Wikipedia*>, we augment the first knowledge base using the second one. The output of this stage is an augmented knowledge base, in which each document is augmented.

```
procedure AugmentKB(kb_c, kb_e)
(1)         docs = GetDocuments(kb_c)
(2)         for each e_cn in docs
(3)             <olinks_cn,ilinks_cn> = <GetOLinks(e_cn),GetILinks(e_cn)>
(4)              if InterlinkOf(e_cn) exists:
(5)                  e_en=GetDocument(kb_e,InterlinkOf(e_cn))
(6)                  <olinks_en,ilinks_en> = <GetOLinks(e_en),GetILinks(e_en)>
(7)                  CombineLinks(olinks_cn,olinks_en)
(8)                  CombineLinks(ilinks_cn,ilinks_en)
```

```
procedure CombineLinks(link_cn,link_en)
(9)          for each lk_en in link_en:
(10)         if InterlinkOf(lk_en) exists:
(11)              lk_cn=translate(lk_en,InterlinkOf(lk_en))
(12)              link_cn+=lk_cn
(13)              link_en-=lk_en
(14)     AddToKB(<link_cn, link_en>)
```

Figure 7. The augmentation process.

Figure 7. shows the knowledge base augmenting process. In Step (1) of the algorithm, we retrieve the list of all articles in kb_c. For each article, we first examine whether it has an *inter-link* points to its corresponding entity in kb_e. If the result is negative, we leave the current article unchanged without augmentation. In Step (5), we identify the corresponding article in kb_e by looking at the target, e_{en} of *inter-wiki* link of e_{cn}. Then, we retrieve all *out-links* and *in-links* of e_{en} and carry out the *CombineLinks* procedure with both kinds of links (Step (6), (7), (8)). In the *CombineLinks* procedure, we iterate through all links in $link_{en}$, and then determine if the link (i.e. lk_{en}) has an *inter-link* (Step (10)). If such an *inter-link* exists, we "translate" the link by replacing lk_{en} with lk_{cn}, a hyperlink point to destination of the *inter-link* and has anchor text of destination title. Finally we add the translated link to the original set of link (i.e. $link_{cn}$), and store them in database. Note that the $link_{en}$ is also stored in kb_c (Step (14)). We do that to support cross-lingual entity-linking. Once the augmentation has been done, each article in kb_c has two link sets from each knowledge base. For articles with *inter-links*, the performance of entity-linking could be improved from the augmentation algorithm.

3.2.3 Training the Binary SVM Model

In the third and final stage of the learning process, we train a Link Similarity Model based on the link graph of *Wikipedia*-like knowledge base articles. To determine which entity to be linked given query term q, we compute link graph similarity between context c of q and candidate entities' articles, and transform them to feature vectors to train a binary SVM classifier. In the rest of this section, we first explain the Link Similarity Model, which is used to estimate the similarity between two entities, and show how we incorporate the Link Similarity Model with SVM.

Consider link graphs in Figure 6. We compute similarity between two link graphs which has vertices v_a, v_b as central node respectively using following equations:

$$Sim(v_a, v_b) = \frac{|E_a \cap E_b|}{\min(\|E_a\|, \|E_b\|)} \qquad (1)$$

In Eq. (1) $\boldsymbol{E_a}$, $\boldsymbol{E_b}$ denote the edges of $\boldsymbol{v_a}$, $\boldsymbol{v_b}$ respectively. The interpretation of Eq. (1) is that we compute the number of edges in common with both vertices respectively, and normalize it using edges of smaller graph constructed from v_a and v_b. In order to make range of Eq. (1) lies in [0, 1], we choose to normalize by smaller graph. Thus, bigger value means bigger similarity between two vertices.

Given training data, we use Eq. (1) to compute features from training data and use them to train a binary SVM classifier. The procedure is shown in Figure 8.

```
procedure GenerateSVMInput(kb)
(1)     <Terms, Articles>= RandomTermArticles(kb)
(2)     for each <term, article> in <Terms, Articles>
(3)         candidates = GetTermEntity(term)
(4)         for each <term, entity> in candidates
(5)             <lp, olinkSim, ilinkSim> =  extractFeatures(article, entity)
(6)             if entity==TargetOf(term)
(7)                 AddToOutput(<1, lp, olinkSim, ilink>)
(8)             else
(9)                 AddToOutput(<0, lp, olinkSim, ilink>)
```

Figure 8. Training SVM Classifier.

In Step (1) we retrieve a list of <Term, Article> pairs in which Term is an anchor text of randomly chosen hyperlink in Article, a randomly chosen article from ***kb***. We treat Terms as query terms, and Articles as their contexts. Using <Term, Entity> pairs computed in 3.2.1, we can get candidates <Term, Entity> pairs (Step (3)). Then we iterate through them (Step (4)). In Step (5), for each <Term, Entity> pairs, we extract three features from them:

lp: The link probability defined as P(Entity|Term), which could be easily computed since we have stored the histograms in 3.2.1.

olinkSim: The link similarity considering only *outlinks*, i.e. $\boldsymbol{Sim_l}$(article, entity).

ilinkSim: Likewise, the link similarity by considering only *inlinks*.

In the computation of link similarity, notice that since the knowledge base has been augmented in 3.2.2, each articles has two link sets. We utilize a set of constant coefficient <α_1, α_2, α_3> to interpolate between similarity computed from <$\boldsymbol{link_{en}}$, $\boldsymbol{link_{cn}}$, $\boldsymbol{link_{cn0}}$>, where $\boldsymbol{link_{cn0}}$ is the unaugmented link set of $\boldsymbol{kb_{cn}}$. Finally we examine whether the target of term's hyperlink equals entity, if the result is positive, we add the current feature vector to the input of SVM with positive example, otherwise with negative example (Steps (6)~(9)).

3.3 Run-Time Entity Linking

Once the SVM model is constructed, we are ready to classify or disambiguate query terms to corresponding entities in ***KB***. We associate adequate entities with given query terms and context using the procedures in Figure 9.

```
procedure ClassifyTerm(q, context, kb)
(1)     ctxEntity = transformContext(context, kb)
(2)     candidates = GetCandidateEntities(q)
(3)     for each entity in candidates
(4)          feature = <LinkProb(entity), olinkSim(entity,
        ctxEntity), ilinkSim(entity, ctxEntity)>
(5)          if SVMPredict(feature) is positive
(6)               AddToResultCandidate(entity)
(7)          else
(8)               continue
(9)     if ResultCandidate is empty
(10)          return "No entity could be linked"
(11)    else
(12)          return MaxLinkProb(ResultCandidate)

Procedure TransformContext(context, kb)
(1)     terms = LongestPossibleMostFrequentMatch(context, kb)
(2)     for each terms in terms:
(3)          entity = GetEntity(term)
(4)          CombineToCtxEntity(<olinks(entity), ilinks(entity)>)
(5)     return ctxEntity
```

Figure 9. Classification algorithm at run-time.

In Step (1) of ClassifyTerm procedure, we transform given context into an entity containing *out-link* set and *in-link* set, thus the link similarity measure could be applied. In TransformContext procedure, we first split the context into N-grams, and then do a longest possible match with the <Terms, Entity> pairs of ***kb*** computed in 3.2.1. For every N-gram there may be more than one matching <Term, Entity> pairs, we choose the one with highest frequency. Then we iterate through the matched terms (Step (2)), and then retrieve the corresponding entity (Step(3)), finally in Step (4) we make a union on the entity's link sets with the output, ctxEntity's link set, which is initialize as empty set.

We now return to the ClassifyTerm procedure. Once we get the transformed context entity, in Step (2) we retrieve the candidates <Term, Entity> pairs where "Term" equals the query term ***q***. For each entities in the candidate list, we compute feature vectors, where the first element is the link probability of current entity, the second and third elements are computed using eq. (1) with entity and context entity as input (Step (4)). After that we run the SVM model trained in 3.2.3 to predict the results, if it is positive, we add this entity to the result candidates list, otherwise we continue the iteration. After the end of the iteration, we select the one with highest link probability as the result entity to be linked (Steps (9)~(12)).

4 Experimental Setting

The proposed *Link Similarity Model* and knowledge base augmentation method was designed to resolve the sense ambiguity of given query terms and to leverage broader information from larger knowledge base. As such, our models will be trained on query terms and their target entities. In this thesis we treat hyperlinks and their destination in *Wikipedia* as query terms and target entities. Using such data, we compiled datasets from Chinese Wikipedia for training and evaluation. In this chapter, we first present the training and test data for the evaluation (Section 4.1). Then, Section 4.2 lists the methods we use in comparison. Section 4.3 introduces the evaluation metrics. Finally, we report the settings of the parameters in Section 4.4.

4.1 Data Set

In this thesis we focus on linking Chinese query terms to articles in Chinese *Wikipedia*. We used the Chinese *Wikipedia XML* file dumped at 20120503 as our main knowledge base. For the augmentation algorithm, we used 20120502 version of English Wikipedia to augment Chinese Wikipedia. Some statistics are shown in Table 3. Currently English *Wikipedia* is far more larger than Chinese *Wikipedia*, no matter in numbers of articles, numbers of language-links or average sense ambiguity. Notice that the sense ambiguity is lower in Chinese. To better investigate our algorithms, we compiled a collection of <hyperlink, article> pairs from Chinese *Wikipedia* with two criteria:

1. The sense ambiguity of hyperlink's anchor text (i.e. query terms) should not be too low or high. Lower ambiguity leads to easier datasets for our classifier, while extremely high value makes running time exponential longer, which is unacceptable for a real-time system. We set this value to lie in [2,7] in our experiment.

2. The contexts (i.e. articles) where each hyperlink appeared should not be too lengthy. Our *Link Similarity Model* uses hyperlinks information in context. In Wikipedia some special pages such as Lists pages, which lists instances of entities, contain extremely many hyperlinks that introduce too much noise to our model. In our implementation we make a threshold on number of hyperlinks per article to lower than 50.

Table 3. Statistics of Wikipedia

	Chinese Wikipedia	English Wikipedia
Number of articles	482,095	4,485,110
Percentage of language links	67%	9%
Average sense ambiguity	3.1	6.7

Using these criteria we randomly chosen 501 distinct <hyperlink, article> pairs from Chinese Wikipedia as our training data, and another distinct 2965 <hyperlink, article> pairs as testing data.

4.2 Methods Compared

The proposed method starts with a query term and its textual context, and determines a suitable entity (i.e. article) for the query term in Chinese *Wikipedia*. The output of our system is the linked article from Chinese *Wikipedia*.

In this thesis, we proposed a method for augmenting the smaller *Wikipedia*-like knowledge base (**CN**) using larger knowledge base (**EN**). In addition, we propose a model for computing link structure similarity between two hyperlinked articles, and then use it to train a *SVM* classifier, in which we use *out-links* (**OL**) and *in-links* (**IL**) as features. Further, the link probability (**LP**) is used as a feature to balance the system performance between rare and common entities. To inspect the effectiveness of the augmentation method and these modules in more detail, the baseline and the combinations of the three main modules, **OL**, **IL**, and **LP**, evaluated in our experiments are described as follows:

— **LP**: We train the *SVM* model using only link probability, and we use this model as baseline.

— **OL+IL+LP (CN)**: The full model trained using *out-links*, *in-links*, and link probability without augmentation.

— **OL+IL+LP (CN+EN)**: The most complete version of proposed system, using all features and augmentation process.

— **-LP (CN+EN)**: The full model with augmentation minus the link probability feature.

— **-OL (CN+EN)**: The full model with augmentation minus the *out-links* feature.

— **-IL (CN+EN):** The full model with augmentation minus the *in-links* feature.

4.3 Evaluation Results

In this section, we report the evaluation results of the experiments on the methodology described in the previous chapter. Table 4. shows the results evaluated on the testing data consist of 2965 <*query term*, *context*>.

Table 4. The evaluation results of different systems

System	*Classifier accuracy*	*Entity accuracy*
LP (Baseline)	95.87	90.54
OL+IL+LP(CN)	97.49	92.81
OL+IL+LP(CN+EN)	**97.61**	**93.02**
-LP (CN+EN)	90.38	71.38
-OL (CN+EN)	97.46	92.69
-IL (CN+EN)	95.94	88.81

As we can see, the full model (i.e. OL+IL+LP (CN+EN)) outperformed the strong baseline LP either on classifier accuracy or entity accuracy, which indicates that our classification strategy can effectively return the most compatible entity to a given query term. As identified in previous related research (Milhacea et al., 2007; Milne et al., 2008), the baseline LP is extremely effective for determining suitable English *Wikipedia* articles for ambiguous query terms, in our experiment performed using Chinese *Wikipedia*, this is also the case.

Comparing the two full models (i.e. OL+IL+LP), the results on CN and CN+EN indicate that our augmentation process provides a small performance improvement. Although the augmentation process does not greatly improve the performance, we perform 10-fold cross validation on another test set consisting of 3001 *<hyperlink*, *article>* pairs and found that the performance gain is statistically significant.

In general, there is no significant difference between average number of *in-links* and *out-links*, so the number of links does not explain this phenomena. We suggest that in Wikipedia, *in-links* reflect topics that mention an entity, while *out-links* reflect context terms of a certain entity. Since topics are more stable than context term, the performance influenced by *in-links* are stronger.

In sum, our model achieved impressive performance for linking query terms to articles in Chinese *Wikipedia.* The augmentation process further significantly improve performance.

5 Conclusion and Future Works

Many avenues exist for future research and improvement of our system. For example, more features used in training the classification models could be added to boost system performance. To improve our system, language features such as collocations, *N*-gram counts, or part-of-speech could be added. Additionally, an interesting direction to explore is to apply our model to cross-language entity-linking. To support cross-language entity-linking, we could also augment the *<Term*, *Entity>* pairs described in 3.2.1 using similar augmentation process. Once the augmentation has been done, we could cross-link a term to other knowledge base. For example, "*蘋果*" in *Chinese Wikipedia* may be linked to "*Big Apple*", the nickname of New York city, in *English Wikipedia.*

In summary, we have introduced a method for linking a *<query term*, *context>* pair to an appropriate article in Chinese *Wikipedia*. Our goal is to improve user experience so that the underlying search system could distinguish between different search intents based on the context. The method involves possible candidates construction, knowledge base augmentation via inter-links, computation of various link similarity measures, and multi-class classification using binary *SVM* classifier. We have implemented and thoroughly evaluated the method as applied to linking query terms to Chinese *Wikipedia* articles. In our evaluation, we have shown that the augmentation process slightly improved system performance. In addition, our full model significantly outperforms the strong baseline in terms of *entity accuracy*.

References

[1] Agirre, E., and Rigau, G. (1996). Word Sense Disambiguation using Conceptual Density. *16th Conference on Computational Linguistics*, (pp. 16-22). Copenhagen.

[2] Banerjee, S., and Pedersen, T. (2002). An Adapted Lesk Algorithm for Word Sense Disambiguation Using WordNet. *the Third International Conference on Intelligent Text Processing and Computational Linguistics.* Mexico City.

[3] Black, E. W. (1988). An Experiment in Computational Discrimination of English Word Senses. *IBM Journal of Research and Development* , 185-194.

[4] Bruce, R., and Wiebe, J. (1994). Word-Sense Disambiguation Using Decomposable Models. *32nd Annual Meeting of the Association for Computational Linguistics* (pp. 139-146). Las Cruces: Association for Computational Linguistics.

[5] Carpaut, M., and Wu, D. (2007). Improving Statistical Machine Translation using Word Sense Disambiguation. *2007 Joint Conference on Empirical Methods in Natural Language Processing and Computational Natural Language Learning* (pp. 61-72). Prague: Association for Computational Linguistics.

[6] Chan, Y. S., Ng, H. T., and Chiang, D. (2007). Word Sense Disambiguation Improves Statistical Machine Translation. *the Association for Computational Linguistics (ACL)*, (pp. 33-40).

[7] Chang, J. S., Lin, T., You, G.-N., Chuang, T. C., and Hsieh, C.-T. (2003). Building a Chinese WordNet via Class-based Translation Model. *Computational Linguistics and Chinese Language Processing* , 61-76.

[8] Chang CC and Lin CJ. 2011. LIBSVM: A library for support vector machines. *ACM Transactions on Intelligent Systems and Technology (TIST)* 2(3):27.

[9] Cilibrasi RL and Vitanyi PMB. 2007. The google similarity distance. *Knowledge and Data Engineering, IEEE Transactions on* 19(3):370-83.

[10] Diab, M., and Resnik, P. (2002). An Unsupervised Method for Word Sense Tagging using Parallel Corpora. *the 40th Annual Meeting of the Association for Computational Linguistics (ACL)*, (pp. 255-262). Philadelphia.

[11] Gale, W. A., Church, K. W., and Yarowsky, D. (1992). Using Bilingual Materials to Develop Word Sense Disambiguation Methods. *the International Conference on Theoretical and Methodological Issues in Machine Translation*, (pp. 101-112).

[12] Galley, M., and McKeown, K. (2003). ImprovingWord Sense Disambiguation in Lexical Chaining. *18th International Joint Conference on Artificial Intelligence (IJCAI 2003).* Acapulco.

[13] Hamp, B., and Feldweg, H. (1997). GermaNet - a Lexical-Semantic Net for German. ACL workshop Automatic Information Extraction and Building of Lexical Semantic Resources for NLP Applications, (pp. 9-15). Madrid.

[14] Hearst, M. A. (1991). Noun Homograph Disambiguation using Local Context in Large Corpora. *7th Annual Conference of the University of Waterloo Centre for the New OED*

and Text Research, (pp. 1-15).

[15] Hsieh, C.-T. (2000). Semi-Automatic Construction of Chinese WordNet - Using Class-based Translation Model.

[16] Huang, C.-C., Tseng, C.-H., Kao, K. H., and Chang, J. S. (2008). A Thesaurus-based Semantic Classification of English Collocations. *ROCLING 2008*, (pp. 38-52). Taipei.

[17] Huang, C.-R., Chang, R.-Y., and Lee, H.-P. (2004). Sinica BOW (Bilingual Ontological Wordnet): Integration of Bilingual WordNet and SUMO. *4th International Conference on Language Resources and Evaluation (LREC2004)*, (pp. 1553-1556). Lisbon.

[18] Leacock, C., Towell, G., and Voorhees, E. (1993). Corpus-based Statistical Sense Resolution. *ARPA Human Language Technology Workshop*, (pp. 260-265).

[19] Lesk, M. (1986). Automatic Sense Disambiguation using Machine Readable Dictionaries: How to Tell a Pine Cone from an Ice Cream Cone. *5th Annual International Conference on Systems Documentation* (pp. 24-26). Toronto: Association for Computing Machinery.

[20] Longman Group. (1992). *Longman English-Chinese Dictionary of Contemporary English*. Hong Kong: Longman Group (Far East) Ltd.

[21] Mihalcea, R., and Moldovan, D. I. (1999). A Method for Word Sense Disambiguation of Unrestricted Text. *the 37th annual meeting of the Association for Computational Linguistics on Computational Linguistics* (pp. 152-158). College Park: Association for Computational Linguistics.

[22] Miller, G. A., Beckwith, R., Fellbaum, C., Gross, D., and Miller, K. J. (1990). Introduction to WordNet: An On-line Lexical Database. *International Journal of Lexicography* , pp. 235-244.

[23] Medelyan O., Witten I. H. and Milne D. 2008. Topic indexing with wikipedia. Proceedings of the AAAI WikiAI workshop, AAAI Press. 19 p.

[24] Mihalcea R. and Csomai A. 2007. Wikify!: Linking documents to encyclopedic knowledge. Proceedings of the sixteenth ACM conference on conference on information and knowledge management. 233 p.

[25] Milne D. 2007. Computing semantic relatedness using wikipedia link structure. Proceedings of the new zealand computer science research student conference.

[26] Milne D. and Witten I. H. 2008. Learning to link with wikipedia. Proceedings of the 17th ACM conference on information and knowledge management, ACM. 509 p.

[27] Pasca, M., and Harabagiu, S. M. (2001). The Informative Role of WordNet in Open-Domain Question Answering. *NAACL 2001 Workshop on WordNet and Other Lexical Resources: Applications, Extensions, and Customizations*, (pp. 138-143). Pittsburgh.

[28] Towell, G., and Voorhees, E. M. (1998). Disambiguating Highly Ambiguous Words. *Computational Linguistics* , 125-145.

[29] Voorhees, E. M., and Tice, D. M. (1999). The TREC-8 Question Answering Track Evaluation. *TREC-8*, (pp. 84-106).

[30] Vossen, P. (1998). Introduction to EuroWordNet. *Computers and the Humanities* , 73-89.

[31] Wible, D., and Kuo, C.-H. (2001). A Syntax-Lexical Semantics Interface Analysis of Collocation Errors. *Pacific Second Language Research Forum.*

Implementation of Malayalam Morphological Analyzer Based on Hybrid Approach

Vinod P M, Jayan V, Bhadran V K
Language Technology Centre
CDAC Thiruvananthapuram
{vinodpm, jayan, bhadran}@cdac.in

Abstract

The Malayalam Morphological analyzer, which described in this paper, is developed based on the hybrid approach, i.e. combining methodologies of both paradigm and suffix stripping approaches. Lttoolbox, an important module in the Apertium package, acts as the back bone of this system. The analyzer program in Lttoolbox tokenizes the text in surface forms (lexical units as they appear in texts) and delivers, for each surface form, one or more lexical forms consisting of lemma, lexical category and morphological inflection information. This system also borrows the concepts of suffix stripping approach that would help a lot to improve the accuracy. The main objective of this system is to help the language students as well as common people.

Keywords: Apertium, Lttoolbox, paradigm approach, suffix stripping, hybrid approach.

1. Introduction

Malayalam language is one among the four major Dravidian languages in south India and also one among the 22 scheduled languages in India. It is mainly spoken by the people of Kerala state and the union territories of Lakshadweep and Mahe. Around 35.9 million people are using this language.

Developing a full fledged Morphological analyzer is very difficult due to the rich morphology and agglutinative nature of Malayalam language. The major problems of Malayalam morphology are wide range of inflections, multiple suffixes and tendency of adjacent words to concatenate etc. The multiple inflections can be solved by following the paradigm approach and Lttoolbox helps to implement the paradigm approach. In order to handle other problems we need a powerful suffix stripping module. The proposed system [1] follows a hybrid approach for developing the morphological analyzer, i.e., the combination of paradigm and suffix stripping approaches.

Lttoolbox is available with the Apertium toolkit, which is an open source shallow-transfer machine translation system originated within the project "Open-Source Machine Translation for the Languages of Spain" [2]. Lttoolbox can be customized to any language by including the required lexical dictionary. Agglutinative languages require some additional modules for better and accurate word processing.

2. Related Works

There are many works carried out in the field of Malayalam Morphological Analyzer, but no complete system is available for common people. References [3], [4] and [5] are some important works related to Malayalam Morphological Analyzer. Two common approaches identified towards the development of Morphological analyzer are suffix stripping and paradigm approaches. Reference [6] mentioned about a hybrid approach for developing the Malayalam Morphological Analyzer and its comparison with the above mentioned approaches.

3. Hybrid approach architecture

Lttoolbox plays an important role in our system. The lt-proc program processes the surface form in single pass. Multiple suffix words can be processed on iterative basis. So we added post processing and suffix stripping modules to handle multiple suffix problems.

As an example consider the case of a pronoun concatenate with a post position and it seems like a single word unit. In this situation the lt-proc cannot recognize the surface form even though both of these words are present in the dictionary. The post processing and suffix stripping modules help us to handle this situation by identifying the post position and provides a space between them. Then once again process them with the help of lt-proc program. Whenever the same surface form comes twice as the input of the post processing module, then it is considered as unknown.

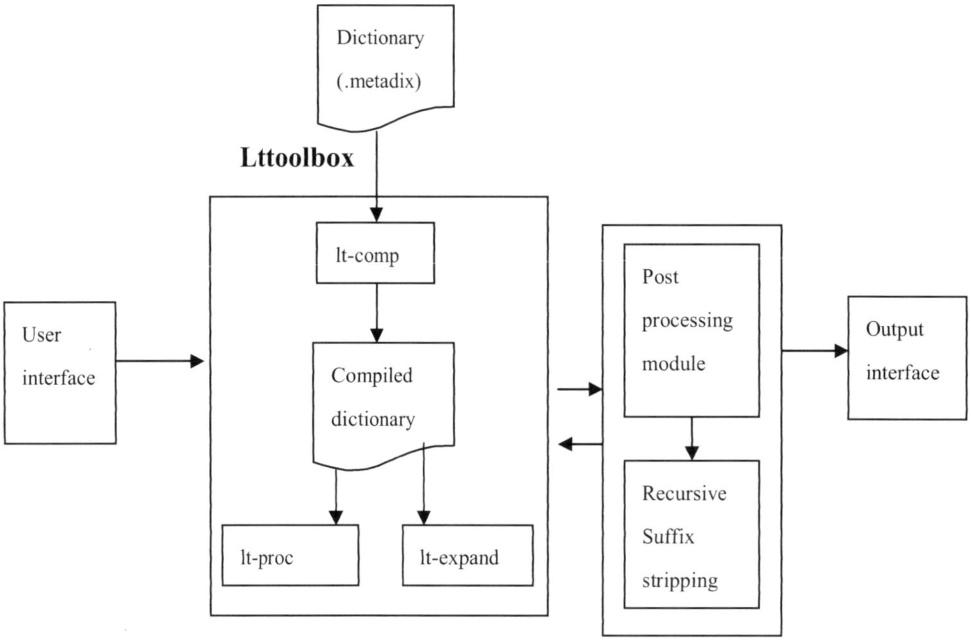

Figure 1. Architecture of Malayalam Morphological Analyzer.

4. Lttoolbox

Lttoolbox [1]can be used for lexical processing, morphological analysis and generation etc. Here we are using Lttoolbox for morphological analysis. Splitting the surface form into its lemma and the grammatical information is known as analysis process. For example the word 'cats' splits into its lemma 'cat' and grammatical information <noun><plural>. The reverse process is the generation process. The Lttoolbox doing this processing with the help of provided lexical dictionary.

Ltoolbox makes use of the finite state transducer (FST) approach for doing lexical processing. The class of FST used in Lttoolbox is 'letter transducer'. Lt-comp, lt-proc and lt-expand are the three programs provided by the Lttoolbox package. These programs are used for compiling, morphological analyzing/generating and expanding the dictionary respectively.

The first part of developing a morphological analyzer is the creation of lexical dictionary which is also called morphological analyzer specification file. Monolingual dictionary, bi-lingual dictionary and post generation dictionary are the three types of dictionaries used in the Lttoolbox. The dictionary files providing a facility to define and use paradigms which helps to share the same inflection pattern. The dictionary files are mainly found with ".dix" or ".metadix" extensions. We are using monolingual metadictionary [2] ('.metadix') since it provides some extra features like handling variable lemma and argument passing etc. Dictionary files for some languages are available from the Apertium incubator. [3]

4.1 Dictionary structure

The dictionary format is XML, which become very powerful in linguistic data representation and exchange. The dictionaries follow a typical block structure and the important blocks in the dictionary structure are,

- An alphabet definition: The list of alphabets used in the dictionary file.
- Definition of symbols: It contains the grammatical symbols that are present in the file.
- Definition of paradigms: Paradigm definitions to be used in the dictionary sections or in other paradigms.
- One or more sections with conditional tokenization.
- One or more sections with unconditional tokenization.

4.2 Paradigm Approach

A paradigm definition defines an inflection paradigm in the dictionary file. It groups the words which are having similar inflection pattern. The paradigm can be viewed as small dictionaries which specify regularities in the lexical processing of the dictionary entries. To specify these regularities, each paradigm has lists of entries <e> like the ones in the dictionary, that is, it has the same structure as a dictionary section <section>; therefore, paradigm entries consist of a pair (<p>) with left side (<l>) and right side (<r>). These elements can contain text or grammatical symbols <s>. Some times a paradigm definition contains entries of

---

[1] http://wiki.Apertium.org/wiki/Lttoolbox

[2] http://wiki.Apertium.org/wiki/Metadix

[3] http://wiki.Apertium.org/wiki/Incubator

another paradigm. An example of paradigm definition is shown below.

```
<pardef n="walk/ed__verb">
    <e><p>
          <l>ed</l>
          <r>ed<s n="verb"/><s n="past"/></r>
       </p></e>
  <e> <p>
          <l></l>
          <r><s n="verb"/><s n="present"/></r>
      </p></e>
</pardef>
```

5. Malayalam Morphological Dictionary

The main part in the development of a morphological analyzer using Lttoolbox is creating the morphological dictionary. Since Malayalam is morphologically rich with wide range of inflections [7] and [8], lot of attention is needed in creating the dictionary. We choose metadictionary in order to make use of its additional features over the normal dictionary.

The paradigm facility helps a lot to handle the inflections of the words. In order to cover all cases we created 24 noun paradigms, 56 verb paradigms, 12 adjective paradigms etc [9], [10], [11] and [12]. The alphabets used in the dictionary are in wx notation.[4]

5.1 Noun Paradigm

To understand the paradigm design the surface form of a word can be considered as two parts such as root and suffix. By examining the suffix portion of the noun word the grammatical information like case, gender and number can be obtained. The main task is identifying the suffix and root of the particular surface form. With the help of the compiled dictionary file the Lttoolbox will perform the morphological analysis provided the particular noun entry (consists of the word and the paradigm number) is present in the dictionary. While examining the noun suffixes we identify some common properties like plural markers, case markers etc. For example consider the noun 'മരം' (maraM) and 7 case markers comes in the suffix part are,

മരം Nominative case (maraM -> no suffix)

മരത്തെ Accusative case (marawwe -> -e)

മരത്തിന് Dative case (marawwin ->-in)

മരത്തോട് Sociative case (marawwOt ->-Ot)

[4] Phonetic Notations for Malayalam alphabets and which is used for the linguistic processing.

ı രത്തിൽ Locative case (marawwil_ ->-il_)

ı രത്താൽ Instrumental case (marawwAl_ ->-Al_)

ı രത്തിന്റെ Genitive case (marawwinZe ->-inZe)

Similarly the plural marker comes with the word ‘maraM’ is ‘kaL_’. The variant form of plural markers comes in the Malayalam morphology are ‘kaL_’, ‘mAZ_’ and ‘aZ_’. Examples for them are ‘ı രങ്ങൾ’ (maraffaL_), ‘രാജാക്കൻ്ı ാർ’ (rAjAkkan_mAZ_) and ‘ı നു ്യർ’ (manuRyaZ_) respectively.

```
<pardef n="mara/M__n">

<e><p>
    <l/>
    <r>M<s n="N_NOUN"/><s n="SG"/><sa/></r>
  </p></e>
<e><p>
    <l>ffaL_</l>
    <r>M<s n="N_NOUN"/><s n="PL"/><sa/> + <s n="kaL_"/></r>
 </p></e>
:
:
</pardef>
```

The tags used in the paradigm definition are given in Table 1. The ‘sa’ tag is used for passing some arguments while adding an entry of that particular paradigm. The name of the paradigm is "mara/M__n" (where n denotes noun) and which is specified in the ‘pardef’ tag. We can give name according to our convenience. The possible inflections of the word ‘maraM’ are maraM, maraffal_, marawwe, maraffaLe, marawwin, maraffaLkk, marawwOt, maraffaLOt, marawwil_, maraffaLil_, marawwAl_, maraffaLAl_, marawwinZe and maraffaLute.

This paradigm "mara/M__n" can be used for the words which have the same inflection pattern. The paradigm entries are mentioned in the main section in the dictionary. One entry for this paradigm is,

```
<e lm="vanaM">
        <i>vana </i>
             <par n="mara/M__n" sa="NTR"/> </e>
```

Table 1. List of some noun tags.

Tag	Description
N_NOUN	Nominative noun
SG	Singular
PL	Plural

MF	Masculine/Feminine
NTR	Neuter
M	Masculine
F	Feminine

While specifying the entries the attribute 'lm' (lemma name) contains the surface form of the word. The '<i>' element contains the root of the particular word and which may or may not be the actual root word according to the Malayalam language. The actual root word will be obtained after the processing. The next tag contains the paradigm name and the additional information that we are passing to the paradigm definition. With the help of the specified paradigm name the particular surface form is processed. When we give a word to the 'lt-proc' program it will check whether that word starts with any of the '<i>' element in the paradigm entries. If a match occurs the corresponding paradigm is used for processing that word. If the particular inflection is present in the paradigm the program will give a result.

5.2 Verb Paradigm

"The morphology of the verb in Malayalam is somewhat complex, and more research is needed before a definitive statement can be made about, firstly, what different aspectual values can be combined, and, secondly, what restrictions there are on the combination of different aspectual values with different modal forms. A hypothesis one might put forward for testing is that all morphological combinations are possible that are semantically interpretable and compatible." [13]. Malayalam verbs always have complex and multiple suffixes. Much of the complexity is resolved in the 53 verb classifications done for computational purpose by R Ravindra Kumar [9]. With the help of this classification we have created 56 verb paradigms. In order to know the paradigm classifications consider the first verb paradigm which groups the root words that are ends in "Y"(ഴ്). In this class "unnu", "uM" and "wu" are the present future and past tense marker respectively. The present and future suffixes are concatenated with out any addition and deletion from the root. To add the past tense suffix "wu" a "u" should be added to the root word and then the tense suffix will be added.

E.g.

Present (pr)	"unnu"	uYunnu	ഉഴുന്നു
Future (fu)	"uM"	uYuM	ഉഴും
Past (pa)	"wu"	uYuwu	ഉഴുതു

To get a causative form, causative suffix "kk" will be added to the root word except in past. In past the causative suffix will be "cc" and past tense suffix is "u". While adding "kk" or "cc" the link morph "uvi" will be added to the root.

E.g. uYuvikkunnu, uYuvikkuM, uYuviccu. (ഉഴുവിക്കുന്നു , ഉഴുവിക്കും , ഉഴുവിച്ചു)

The double causative forms can be generated by adding the causative marker "ppi" and "kk". The link morph 'uvi" will be added at the end of root verb before adding the double causative suffixes.

E.g. uYuvippikkunnu, uYuvippikkuM, uYuvippiccu.

(ഉഴു ി ിക്കുന്നു, ഉഴു ി ിക്കും, ഉഴു ി ി ു)

A noun form can be derived from the root word by adding the suffix “al_” at the end of root word.

E.g. uYal_ (ഉഴൽ)

Analogously paradigms are created for adjectives and pronouns also. But post positions and adverbs have no paradigm classes and they are specified in the main section of the dictionary file. Examples for adverb entries are,

```
<e> <p>
      <l>ennAl_</l>
      <r>ennAl_<s n="ADV"/> </r>
   </p></e>
<e> <p>
      <l>ivite</l>
      <r>ivite<s n="ADV"/> </r>
   </p></e>
```

6. Post Processing and Suffix Stripping Modules

The main problem associated with the Malayalam morphological analyzer is the identification of words which are formed by combining multiple words. These kinds of words are commonly called the complex words. The Lttoolbox cannot handle the complex words in Malayalam. So the presence of complex words and wide range of inflections makes our task very difficult. In order to overcome this situation we introduced the post processing module and the suffix stripping module. The task of post processing module is to identify and extract the words which are not accepted or unidentified by the processing module in Lttoolbox. And the suffix stripping module has a good collection of commonly used link morphs, post positions and suffixes. With the help of this collection the suffix stripping module can separate the word and its suffixes from the surface form. Recursive suffix stripping method is using for Malayalam. The sandhi rules are also taken into consideration during the splitting process.

6.1 Recursive Suffix Stripping Algorithm

We have been using a good collection of suffixes, postpositions and link morphs to perform the suffix stripping. The accuracy of splitting is very much depending up on these collections as well as the word splitting. A good sandhi splitter will improve the performance to a great extend.

1) Check for any link morphs present in the surface form. If no go to step 3
2) Split the word based on the information obtained from the previous step and check the prefix part for validity using lt-proc. If valid remove the prefix part from the word and stores in a word list. Then consider the remaining portion for further processing. If not valid go to step 3.
3) Check for a highest matching suffix. If not found any match then add the word to the word list. If found go to step 2.
4) Word list gives the splitted form of the complex word.

For example consider the complex word “ഓടിക്കൊണ്ടിരിക്കുകയായിരുന്നു”

(OtikkoNtirikkukayAyirunnu). This verb form contain the link morph 'കൊണ്ട് ' (koNt). The suffix stripping module processes this word in a step by step fashion as follows.

Step 1: [ഓടിക്കൊണ്ടിരിക്കുകയായിരുന്നു]

Step 2: ഓടി (കൊണ്ട്) ! രിക്കുകയായിരുന്നു

Step 3: ഓടി + കൊണ്ട് +[! രിക്കുകയായിരുന്നു]

Step 4: ഓടി + കൊണ്ട് + ! രിക്കുക (ആയിരുന്നു)

Step 5: ഓടി + കൊണ്ട് + ! രിക്കുക + ആയിരുന്നു

Here the word within the square bracket denotes the unknown word obtained from Lttoolbox. And the simple bracketed portion denotes the link morph of suffix which is identified by the suffix stripping module. The splitting is done based on the words shown with in the simple brackets. In each step the unknown word (if present) is processed with the suffix stripping module. The decomposed form of the complex word is generated in the fourth step. This outcome is given to the output interface. One important thing is that the tense of the complex word is identified from the last portion (here it is ആയിരുന്നു (Ayirunnu) which denotes past tense).

7. Evaluation and Results

Table 2. Dictionary entries.

Category	Number of Paradigms	Number of entries
Noun	24	25267
Adjectives	12	17213
Verb	56	9070
Pronoun	-	150
Adverb	-	2423
Postpositions	-	120

The important functions of the morphological analyzer are finding the exact lemma, segmenting the suffix part and identifying the POS tags. The evaluation is done based on the above 3 criteria's [14]. Since it is very hard to evaluate the accuracy of the system automatically, we compare the results with human intuitions and Malayalam lexicon books. The dictionary contains around 54,240 entries we randomly take 10000 words for the evaluation purpose. Each result is evaluated with respect to the 3 functionalities of the morphological analyzer. The average of 3 cases is considered as the total accuracy of the system.

Root identification accuracy	**94%**
POS identification accuracy	**85%**
Suffix segmentation accuracy	**72%**
Accuracy of MA (average of above 3)	**83.67%**

Output for the word "ഓടിക്കൊണ്ടിരിക്കുകയായിരുന്നു" (OtikkoNtirikkukayAyirunnu.) is given below.

ഓടി

Root: ഓട്
Verb Mun_Vineyaccam
Suffix: (!)

Root: ഓട്
Verb Past Transitive
Suffix: (!)

Root: ഓട്
Verb Past Intransitive
Suffix: (!)

ക്കൊണ്ട്

Postposition (കൊണ്ട്)

! രിക്കുക

Present (! രിക്കുക)

Root: ! ര്
Verb Nat_Vineyaccam
Suffix: (!) (! ക്ക്) (!_ക)

യായിരുന്നു

Past (ആയിരുന്നു)

8. Conclusion and Future Work

Malayalam is a morphologically rich and agglutinative Indian language. So it is very difficult to develop a computer system for Malayalam. The major problems which we have to face during the initial stages are multiple suffixes, high inflections, tendency of adjacent words to join together etc. But the hybrid approach is very effective for developing a morphological analyzer for Malayalam language. The accuracy of the system is mainly depends on the morphological dictionary and the suffix list used. The efficient handling of unknown words also improves the quality.

Morphological analyzer is a main and important module of the Parsing system. This work can be extended to develop a Malayalam parser.

References

[1] Vinod P M, Jayan V, Sulochana K G, "Malayalam Morphological Analyzer: A Hybrid Approach with Apertium Lttoolbox," *Proceedings of ICON-2011: 9th International Conference on Natural Language Processing*, Macmillan Publishers, India, Page: 219-224, 2011.

[2] Mikel L. Forcada, Boyan Ivanov Bonev, Sergio Ortiz Rojas, Juan Antonio Pérez Ortiz, Gema Ramírez Sánchez, Felipe Sánchez Martínez, Carme Armentano-Oller, Marco A. Montava, Francis M. Tyers. "Documentation of the Open-Source Shallow-Transfer Machine Translation Platform Apertium", 2010.

[3] Rajeev. R. R, Elizabeth Sherly, "Morph Analyser for Malayalam Language: A suffix stripping approach," *Proceedings of 20th Kerala Science Congress,* Thiruvananthapuram, 2008

[4] Jisha P. Jayan, Rajeev R.R, Dr. S Rajendran, "Morphological Analyser and Morphological Generator for Malayalam-Tamil Machine Translation," *International Journal of Compter Applications*, Volume 13, No.8, 2011.

[5] Saranya S. K, "Morphological analyzer for Malayalam Verbs," unpublished, 2008.

[6] Jisha P. Jayan, Rajeev R. R., S. Rajendran. "Morphological Analyzer for Malayalam-A comparison of Different Approaches", *IJCSIT*, Vol. 2: 155-160, 2009.

[7] A.R.Raja Raja Varma. 2000. "Keralapaanineeyam", D. C Books Kottayam-12.

[8] Suranad Kunjan Pillai, "Malayalam Lexicon", The University of Kerala, 2000.

[9] R. Ravindra Kumar, K. G. Sulochana , V. Jayan. "Computational Aspect of Verb Classification in Malayalam", *Information Systems for Indian Languages Communications in Computer and Information Science*, Volume 139, Part 1, 15-22, 2011.

[10] Sunil R, Nimtha Manohar, V. Jayan, K. G. Sulochana, "Morphological Analysis and Synthesis of Verbs in Malayalam", *ICTAM,* 2012

[11] Sunil R, Nimtha Manohar, V. Jayan, K. G. Sulochana, "Noun Classification in Malayalam for Natural Language Computing Applications", *NCILC*,2012.

[12] Nimtha Manohar , Sunil R, V. Jayan, K. G. Sulochana, "Malayalam Adjective and Pronoun classification for Computational Applications", *NCILC,* 2012.

[13] R.E. Asher, T.C. Kumari. "Malayalam", Routledge London and New York, 1997.

[14] Huihsin Tseng, Keh-Jiann Chen. "Design of Chinese morphological analyzer", *Proceedings of the first SIGHAN workshop on Chinese language processing* - Volume 18, 1-7, 2002.

A Light Weight Stemmer in Kokborok

Braja Gopal Patra, Khumbar Debbarma, Swapan Debbarma
Department of Computer Science and Engineering
NIT Agartala, India
brajagopal.cse@gmail.com, khum_10jan@yahoo.co.in, swapanxavier@gmail.com

Dipankar Das, Amitava Das, Sivaji Bandyopadhyay
Department of Computer Science and Engineering
Jadavpur University, Kolkata, India
dipankar.dipnil2005@gmail.com, amitava.santu@gmail.com, sivaji_cse_ju@yahoo.com

Abstract

Started from the very beginning, Stemming has been playing significant roles in several Natural Language Processing Applications such as information retrieval (IR), machine translation (MT), morph analysis and deciding the part of speech (POS). Several stemmers have been developed for a large number of languages including Indian languages; however no work has been done in Kokborok, a native language of Tripura. In this paper, we have designed a simple rule based stemmer for Kokborok using an affix stripping algorithm. The reduction of inflected words to the stem or root form is performed in the stemmer by stripping the affixes and applying boundary rules where needed. The stemming algorithm has been tested using a corpus of 32578 words and out of which 13044 were uniquely found to have an overall accuracy of 80.02% for minimum suffix stripping algorithm and 85.13% for maximum suffix stripping algorithm.

Keywords: Stemming, part of speech (POS), Kokborok, suffix, prefix.

[1. Introduction]

Kokborok, an Indian language is spoken mainly in the states of Tripura, Assam, Manipur and Mizoram in India and in the neighbouring countries of Myanmar and Bangladesh by more than 2.5 million speakers[1]. Kokborok belongs to the Tibeto-Burman (TB) language family. Kokborok shares the genetic features of TB languages that include phonemic tone, widespread stem homophony, subject-object-verb (SOV) word order, agglutinative verb morphology, verb derivational suffixes originating from the semantic bleaching of verbs, duplication or elaboration, evidentiality and emotional attitudes signalled through sentence final particles, aspect rather than tense marking, lack of gender marking and tendency to reduce disyllabic forms to monosyllabic ones. Very specifically, Kokborok has extensive list of suffixes with more limited number of prefixes and different word classes that are formed by affixation of the respective markers. Kokborok is represented either in Roman script or in Bengali script however Bengali script is less preferred as it is difficult to project the actual

[1] http://tripura.nic.in

tonal effect appropriately. The affixes play the most important role in the structure of the language. In Kokborok, the words are formed in three processes called affixation, derivation and compounding .The majority of the roots found in the language are bound and the affixes are the determining factor of the class of the words in the language.

Stemming is the process of splitting the stem or root part of the word with its affixes without doing any morphological analysis [6]. Stemming is generally used for Information Retrieval, but is also applied for other Natural Language Processing Applications (NLP) such as Machine Translation (MT), Morph Analysis and Part of Speech (POS) Tagging etc. To the best of our knowledge, at present, there is no such available stemmer in Kokborok language. Thus, the developed stemmer can also be used for the development of a root dictionary Kokborok.

An affix stripping algorithm is developed for reducing agglutinated Kokborok words to its stem or root. Maximum root words are bound roots. Affixes are attached to the root words to form a complete word. This algorithm strips affixes and check with the stored affixes for a match, if found then strip the affixes.

The paper is organized in the following manner. Section 2 gives a brief discussion about related works, Section 3 details about Kokborok word formation , Section 4 gives the list of prefixes, suffixes and an example of highly agglutinative word, Section 5 gives the idea about how words are stemmed, Section 6 which includes the experiments and evaluation while the conclusion is drawn in Section 7.

[2. Related Work]

Stemming is required for Information Retrieval, Part of Speech Tagging (POS) and Multiword Expression (MWE) etc. Porter stemmer is one of the famous stemmer for English [9]. Porter came up with the idea of forming root words through manipulation of suffixes. So many other stemmers are also present in English [2], [8]. Stemmer is used in Information Retrieval systems [5] to improve the performance. Recent study shows that non-native English speakers support the growing use of the Internet[2]. This raises the demand of linguistic resources for languages other than English.

In case of Indian languages, the related works are found in Hindi [10]; in which suffixes are striped off on a longest match basis. Another work in Carlos et al., 2009 [1] can be seen where stemmer is used in extraction of lexicon of stems and root word-forms from raw text corpus. On the other hand, a stemming work has been carried out for Bengali [11]. Among all other languages, Manipuri is quite similar to Kokborok as both of the languages fall under the Sino Tibetan language family. A Manipuri stemmer was developed by K. Nongmeikapam et al., 2011 [7]. In Manipuri, both suffixes and prefixes were stripped out in two separate experiments but without applying any rule. They have achieved 81.50%, precision of 91.36% and f-measure of 86.15% for suffixes and for prefixes 70.10%, precision of 76.99% and f-measure of 73.38%.

Even though works on other languages are reported, so far no work has done on Kokborok language as per authors' knowledge. Kokborok is a highly inflected language, thus needed a new approach for stemming.

[2] http://www.internetworldstats.com/stats.htm

[3. Word structure and construction in Kokborok]

In Kokborok, the words are formed by combining a single root word or multiple root words to which single or multiple affixes are attached. Words in Kokborok are basically constructed by *affixation* and *compounding* as shown in Table. 1. The **root word** is the primary lexical unit of a word, and of a word family (root is then called base word), which carries the most significant aspects of semantic content and cannot be reduced into smaller constituents[3]. Content words in nearly all languages contain, and may consist only of root morphemes. However, the term "root" is also used to describe the word without its inflectional endings, but with its lexical endings in place. For example, '*chatters*' has the inflectional root or lemma '*chatter*', but the lexical root '*chat*'. Inflectional roots are often called stems, and a root in the stricter sense may be thought of as a mono morphemic stem. The traditional definition allows the roots to be either in the form of free morphemes or bound morphemes. In Kokborok generally roots are of two types, *free* and *bound* root. From a statistics we have seen that, out of 32578 words 20289 much of words are bound, 5026 much words are free and rest few compound and others named entity.

Free Roots

The free roots are pure nouns, pronouns, adjectives, and some numerals for example aming (cat), bwrwi (girl). Sometimes, the suffixes are attached to the free root words to signify the number, case, locative, for example amingni (cat's), bwrwirok (girls), kamio (to village) where suffixes 'ni', 'rok', 'o' are used for case, number, location respectively.

[Table 1. Examples of word formed by single or multiple affixation and compounding]

Prefix	Root word	Suffix	Word as written
Bu	Pha (father)		Bupha
	Khai (to do)	di	khaidi
Ma	Thang (to go)	nai	mathangnai
ma+se+ma	Thang	lai+nai	masemathanglainai

[Table 2. Example of word formed by compounding]

Rootword1	Rootword2	Word formed
Ah(fish)	Suri(sword)	Ahsuri(swordfish)
Ma(mother)	Pha(father)	Mapha(mother and father)

Bound roots

[3] http://en.wikipedia.org/wiki/Root_(linguistics)

The Bound root only appears as part of a lengthy word. Verbs in Kokborok always appear in bound form with affixes to give the tense and other information. These are further subdivided as *nominal* and *verbal.*

Nominal bound roots: Nominal bound roots include kinship for example 'ma' (mother), 'pha' (father) to which prefixes 'a' (my), 'bu' (his/her).

Verbal bound roots: Kokborok verbs always occur in bound form to which multiple affixes are added to give the tense, manner of action, for example the word chahdi (eat), chahkha (ate), chahrere (about to eat) has bound root 'Chah' and suffixes 'di', 'kha', 'rere' respectively.

In Kokborok many compound words are found. Compound words are those words which contain more than one root word. Different types of compound words are shown in Table 2. Some compound words are form root word with the addition of prefixes. And the prefix changes according to the person. For example

Achwi-achu (my grandmother and my grandfather) = Ani(my)+ chwi-chu (Grandmother and Grandfather).

Affixes in Kokborok

Kokborok is highly agglutinative and has words which may have more than one affixes attached to the root word or stem. For example

Mathangliyanata(not been able to go) =ma(pref) + thang(RW) + liya(suf) + na(suf) + ta(suf)

Where 'thang' means to go.

Altogether, 91 affixes are there out of which 72 are suffixes and 19 are prefixes. Prefixes are less frequently used as compared to suffixes.

Frequent prefixes that used in Kokborok are bu, bw, ko, kw, ku, jwk, jwla, iri, ki, ke, ka, ma etc.

On the other hand, the frequent suffixes that are used in Kokborok are de, di, drop, bo, ya, na, nai, ni, lai, le, kha, o, khai, rokni, anw, bai etc.

[4. System Design]

The algorithm is designed to remove both multiple suffixes as well as prefixes from the inflected words. It has been observed that the boundary of root words in Kokborok change after addition of suffixes. These boundary changes are dependent on the boundary character and POS of the word to which affixation is taking place. Thus we have added some rules in the algorithm as boundary changes after addition of suffixes.

i.e. kogo = kok(root word)+o(suffix)

rwchabo = rwchap(root word)+o(suffix)

rwchabdi = rwchap(root word)+di(suffix)

kogwi= kok(root word)+ wi (suffix)

The stemming of such words, without applying rules led to meaningless word.

i.e. kogkha→kog + kha

Here "kog" is meaningless word. To avoid this meaningless output after stemming the boundary rules are applied to the boundary character of stemmed word that satisfies the condition. Since not many words exhibit such changes and limitations or constraints of rule less defined the result of stemmer was not very much improved by the incorporation of rules. In a particular word exhibiting boundary changes, it has been observed that only single rule is applicable at a time, simultaneous application of more than one rule is not approved.

In Kokborok, a new approach for stemming is required and several rules are needed to be implemented. In Kokborok the minimum length of root word is two and maximum length of root word is two and maximum length of suffix is ten. Thus, we maintained two separate dictionaries namely prefix and suffix containing the list of prefixes and suffixes. We took a text file containing 32578 numbers of words.

Algorithm:

Stripping -prefixes ()

1. Repeat the step 2 until all the prefixes are removed
2. Read the prefix, if matched then store it in array and decrease the length of string else read another prefix.
3. If length of string >2 then go for suffix stripping, else exit.

Stripping -suffixes ()

1. Repeat the step 2 until all the suffixes are removed
2. Read the largest suffix, if matched then check for rules, then store it in array and decrease the length of string else read another suffix.
3. Exit.

Example: Token=chahnairokno (len=12)

Checking for 0 to 10 from left for prefix i.e. chahnairok no. If prefix found from prefix dictionary strip prefix.

Checking for 0 to 10 from right i.e. ch ahnairokno. If suffix found from suffix dictionary then strip suffix.

Apply rule (replace the last character of stem word to k or p if it is g or b in case the suffix is 'o' or 'wi').

Output: stem+ suffix

Chah+nai+rok+no.

[5. Experiment and Result Evaluation]

The Indian languages are very resource constrained and less computerized to English. A very limited corpus was available as no work has been earlier carried out in Kokborok. The experiments of the systems have been conducted on the corpus collected from Kokborok story books and the holy Bible. The accuracy has been checked manually after applying the algorithm on the corpus that consists of total 32578 words out of which 13044 words are unique.

[Table 3. Result of Kokborok stemmer]

	minimum suffix first		maximum suffix first	
	Unique words	Whole words	Unique words	Whole words
Applying rule(accuracy)	82.9%	78.56%	85.5%	82.78%
With rule(error)	17.1%	21.44%	14.5%	17.22%
Without rule(accuracy)	80.4%	82.2%	87.9%	84.32%
Without rule(error)	19.6%	17.8%	12.1%	15.68%

We have calculated the accuracy by applying different approaches such as minimum suffix first and then maximum suffix striping. Table. 3 contains the result for minimum suffix stripping first. i.e. suffix stripping from right side of the word. We also applied these both of the algorithms to the whole corpus as well as for the unique words. In Evaluation of the result, the system for affix stripping (minimum suffix) gives an overall accuracy of 80.02%. In our case the mis-stemming, over-stemming and under-stemming leads to low accuracy of the system. For example,

Mis-stemming: tongo= tonk +o (output)

Desired output: tong+o

Under-stemming: brajno=brajn + o (output)

Desired output: braj+no

Over- stemming: bini(input)=bi+ni(output)

Desired output: bini

Out of the total error, there are 45.2% cases of mis-stemming, 31.42% over-stemming and 23.38% under-stemming. In case of Kokborok we have observed that stripping order affect the result. On stripping the suffix with smallest length first the word is under-stemmed when the minimum suffix is a part of the maximum suffix.

Example: buphangno →buphangn+o (under stemmed)

Here the suffix is 'no' but also 'o' is a suffix that's why 'o' is stripped first, though it's not a suffix here leading to under-stemmed output.

Table. 3 contains the result for affix stripping (maximum suffix) gives an overall accuracy of 85.13%. There is no case of under stemming seen as we striped largest suffix first. In this case out of the total error, there are 69.3% mis-stemming and 30.7% over-stemming. For example,

Over- stemming: sumano(input)=suma+no(output)

Desired output: suman+o

Mis-stemming cases are same as above.

[6. Conclusion and Future work]

The experiment results of the designed stemmer was found to be promising, however the stemmer can be made stronger by using larger corpus. This stemmer can be implemented for POS tagger, root word collection from corpus, Machine Translation etc. A better approach can be tried to reduce the case of miss stemming, under stemming and over stemming. More rules can be added to the stemmer, which will improve the accuracy but will substantially increase the computational cost. A mixed approach i.e. combination of minimum suffix and maximum suffix first can be tried later. Further unsupervised learning based on statistical machine translation may be applied to improve the accuracy of the current stemmer.

Most of the North-East Indian languages are similar. It will be interesting applying this stemming algorithm upon those languages or similar technique may be used to develop stemmer for these languages.

[7. Acknowledgements]

We would like to thank Dr Binoy Debbarma of Language Wing, Education Dept., TTAADC, Khumulwng, for the assistance in the creation of rules and finding the affixes.

[References]

[1]. Carlos, C. S., Choudhury, M., Dandapat, S., Large-Coverage Root Lexicon Extraction for Hindi. In Proceedings of the 12th Conference of the European Chapter of the ACL, pp. 121--129. Athens, Greece, 2009.

[2]. Dawson, J., Suffix removal and word conflation. ALL Cbulletin 2(3), pp. 33-46, 1974.

[3]. Debbarma, K., Patra, B.G., Debbarma, S., Kumari, L., Purkayastha, B. S., Morphological Analysis of Kokborok for Universal Networking Language Dictionary.In Proceedings of First International Conference on Recent Advances in Information Technology. Dhanbad, India, 2012.

[4]. Debbarma, B., Debbarma, B., Kokborok Terminology P-I, II, III, English-Kokborok-Bengali.Language Wing, Education Dept., TTAADC, Khumulwng, Tripura

[5]. Frakes, W., Baeva-Tates, R., Information Retrieval, Data Structures and Algorithm (eds). Prentice-Hall, Englewood Cliffs, New Jersey, USA, 1992.

[6]. Islam, Md. Z., Uddin, Md. N., Khan, M., A Light Weight Stemmer for Bengali and Its Use in Spelling Checker. In the Proceedings of First International Conference on Digital Communications and Computer Applications, Irbid, Jordan, 2008.

[7]. Kishorjit, Ng., Salam, B., Romania, M., Chanu, Ng. M., Bandyopadhyay, S.: A Light Weight Manipuri Stemmer. In Proceedings of National Conference on Indian Language, Computing (NCILC). Cochin, India, 2011.

[8]. Krovetz, R., Viewing morphology as an inference process. In 16th Annual International ACM SIGIR Conference on Research and Development in Information Retrieval, pp. 191-202, 1993.

[9]. Porter, M. F., An Algorithm for Suffix Stripping. Program, 14(3):130-137, 1980.

[10].Ramanathan, A., Rao, D. D., A Lightweight Stemmer for Hindi. In Proceedings Workshop of Computational Linguistics for South Asian Languages- Expanding Synergies with Europe, EACL: pp. 42-48. Budapest, Hungary, 2003.

[11].Sarkar, S., Bandyopadhyay, S., Design of a Rule-Based Stemmer for Natural Language Text in Bengali. In Proceeding of the IJCNLP-08 Workshop on NLP for Less Privileged Languages, pages 65-72. Hyderabad, India, 2008.

台語關鍵詞辨識之實作與比較

Implementation and Comparison of Keyword Spotting for Taiwanese

王崇喆 Chung-Che Wang
國立清華大學資訊工程學系
Department of Computer Science
National Tsing Hua University
geniusturtle@mirlab.org

周哲玄 Che-Hsuan Chou
國立清華大學資訊工程學系
Department of Computer Science
National Tsing Hua University
stephen.chou@mirlab.org

陳亮宇 Liang-Yu Chen
國立清華大學資訊系統與應用研究所
Institute of Information Systems and Applications
National Tsing Hua University
davidson833@mirlab.org

李毓哲 Yu-Jhe Li
國立清華大學資訊工程學系
Department of Computer Science
National Tsing Hua University
liyujhe@mirlab.org

張智星 Jyh-Shing Roger Jang
國立臺灣大學資訊工程學系
Department of Computer Science and Information Engineering
National Taiwan University
jang@mirlab.org

胡訓誠 Hsun-Cheng Hu，林世鵬 Shih-Peng Lin，黃友鍊 You-Lian Huang
財團法人資訊工業策進會 智慧網通系統研究所
{johnhu, shihpeng, uln}@iii.org.tw

摘要

本論文主要探討結合語音評分與音高走勢分類器辨識，來實做台語關鍵詞辨識系統，以改進其辨識率。第一階段先分別利用了不同方法來實做台語關鍵詞辨識系統，第二階段使用語音評分與音高走勢分類器進行驗證以改善辨識效能。首先，在第一階段使用了隱藏式馬可夫模型（hidden Markov model），以及音素匹配法（phone mismatch）。而第二階段則是將此兩種方法辨識出來的候選關鍵詞，進行語音評分和音高走勢分類器驗證，將此兩種方法分別設立門檻值，利用決策樹法進行驗證。實驗結果顯示，在兩種基礎方法後，加入語音評分做為驗證的相等錯誤率（equal error rate, EER），分別約可下降 20% 和 5%；進一步加入音高走勢分類器驗證後，約可再下降 1%，因此語音評分和音高走勢分類器對於台語關鍵詞系統的驗證是很有幫助的。

Abstract

This paper focuses on improving in the performance of a Taiwanese keyword spotting system by integrating speech assessment and pitch contour classification. In the first part of this research, we use different methods to implement a Taiwanese keyword spotting system. In second part, we improve the system by validation using speech assessment and pitch contour classification. Two methods are adopted in the first part to implement the keyword spotting system: hidden Markov model and phone mismatching method. We then perform speech assessment and pitch contour classification to validate the candidate keywords selected by these two methods to refine the results. A threshold is used for a decision tree to make the final decision. Experimental results shows that the equal error rates (ERRs) reduce about 20% and 5% after being incorporated speech assessment validation. After being incorporated with pitch contour classification, ERRs further reduce about 1%. This concludes that the validation technique using speech assessment and pitch contour classification can improve the performance of Taiwanese keyword spotting.

關鍵詞：關鍵詞辨識、隱藏式馬可夫模型、懲罰矩陣

Keywords: Keywords spotting, hidden Markov model, penalty matrix

一、緒論

本論文主要利用隱藏式馬可夫模型法與音素匹配法，實做台語關鍵詞辨識系統，再利用音高特徵與語音評分，以提升系統的辨識率。使用情境方面，我們針對 3C 產品的控制，而控制這些 3C 產品時，都是短短的指令，例如：開冷氣，開冰箱等等，故本論文針對短字詞的關鍵詞進行探討。

本論文的研究方向為實做不同方式的台語的關鍵詞辨識系統，並比較其優劣，再和語音評分和『音高走勢分類器』合併。在第一階段時我們實做的系統為一個移植性高，且可自由變換關鍵詞庫之系統，然而缺點是會犧牲辨識率，故在第二階段加入了關鍵詞的驗證來達到較好的成效。在第二階段我們以一種信心測量的方法(confidence measure, CM)進行語音評分，評判所擷取的關鍵詞語音是否足夠接近標準關鍵詞語音。而加入『音高走勢分類器』之主要原因為，使用一般關鍵字辨識系統較少使用到之語音特徵，例如音高和音量，來針對聲調做進一步的確認。經由這兩項改進，輔助原本的關鍵詞辨識系統達到較好的辨識效果。

本論文其餘部分之概要如下：第二章為相關研究；第三章為論文方法；第四章為實驗結果；第五章為結論與未來展望。

二、相關研究

（一） 關鍵詞辨識技術

使用隱藏式馬可夫模型來做關鍵詞辨識，傳統上為針對每一個關鍵詞都個別訓練一個關鍵詞的模型。其優點為辨識率較高，但缺點為移植性不高，並且不易更換關鍵詞，一旦遇到這種情況，必須重新搜集語料和訓練關鍵詞辨識模型，故本論文所採用的方法為使用右相關雙連音素的串接形成關鍵詞模型，這樣不論在更換領域或是增加關鍵詞上面會變的較有彈性，但其缺點為辨識率較低，故必須經由更進一步的關鍵詞驗證來提升整個關鍵詞辨識系統的效果。而在做關鍵詞辨識系統時，除了關鍵詞的模型外，我們必須建立一個非關鍵詞的模型來辨識非關鍵詞的部分，我們稱之為填充模型（filler-model），本論文所採用的方法為使用聲韻母模型來當做填充模型。而在辨識過程中，通常會針對聲韻母模型加入若干的懲罰值，其原因是避免在關鍵詞辨識中其進入聲韻母的機率太高，導致關鍵詞辨識容易產生錯誤，故在實驗中我們會針對聲韻母模型做些許的調整。

（二） 填充模型選取與訓練

在本論文中我們所採用的填充模型為聲母 18 個、韻母 61 個，在進行訓練之前會先把聲母標為 fi_init，韻母標為 fi_final，之後再進行訓練程序。

（三） 利用音素匹配法實做兩階段關鍵詞辨識

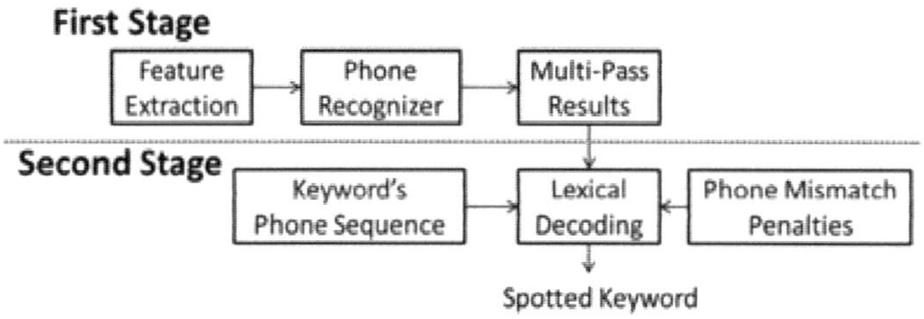

圖一、音素匹配懲罰矩陣法方塊圖

利用音素匹配法實做兩階段關鍵詞辨識[1]過程如下，其第一階段仍為訓練一個基礎模型，之後將測試語料進行自由音素的解碼，其結果可以採取最佳的數個。第二階段則將這些音素序列，與關鍵詞的音素序列，利用動態規劃進行比對，其比對的方法為經由音素匹配懲罰矩陣與關鍵詞辨識，制定門檻值來找出是否含有關鍵詞。音素匹配懲罰矩陣（Phone Mismatch Penalty Matrix）主要為利用訓練語料中之發展語料（development）做為內部測試，得到一種音素與音素之間相對關係的矩陣，而音素匹配懲罰矩陣主要是利用三種會產生的錯誤進行分析，分別是替換（substitution）、插入（insertion）、刪除（deletion），對於每組音素間分別對於這三種錯誤給予不同的懲罰，乃為此矩陣之精神所在，細節可參考[1]。

1. 懲罰矩陣法

替換的懲罰矩陣公式如下，其中$\emptyset_i$，$\emptyset_j$代表不同音素，Pr〔·〕代表事件的機率，而$\mathrm{II}[\alpha]$為一個 indicator 方程式，α_{sub}則是根據實驗與經驗而調整。取 log 原因是為了將懲罰值正規化至一個合理的數值。關於插入與刪除的懲罰矩陣公式與實做，可參考[17]。

$$PM_{sub}\ (\emptyset_i,\ \emptyset_j)=\begin{cases}-\log \Pr\left[P\left(x_k|\emptyset_j\right) < P(x_k|\emptyset_i)|p_k=\emptyset_j\right]+\alpha_{sub}\ , & \emptyset_i \neq \emptyset_j \\ 0\ , & \emptyset_i=\emptyset_j\end{cases}$$

$$\Pr\ \left[P\left(x_k|\emptyset_j\right) < P(x_k|\emptyset_i)|p_k=\emptyset_j\right] \cong \frac{\sum_{k=1}^{Np} \mathrm{II}[p_k=\emptyset_j, P(x_k|\emptyset_j)<P(x_k|\emptyset_i)]}{\sum_{k=1}^{Np} \mathrm{II}[p_k=\emptyset_j]}$$

2. 混淆矩陣法

混淆矩陣為發展語料經由自由音素解碼後的結果，在[2]中三種懲罰矩陣分別定義如下：

$$CM_{sub}\left(\emptyset_i,\emptyset_j\right)=log\{S(i,i)/S(i,j)\}\quad,\quad CM_{ins}\left(\emptyset_i,\emptyset_j\right)=I\quad,\quad CM_{del}\left(\emptyset_i,\emptyset_j\right)=D$$

概念上為利用辨識對的音素數目，除以辨識錯誤的音素數目來做為懲罰基準，$\emptyset_i$代表字典中第 i 個音素，I 和 D 為常數，可利用實驗調整。細節可參考[2]。

3. 距離矩陣法

在距離矩陣法中三種懲罰矩陣分別定義如下：

$$LD_{sub}\left(\emptyset_i,\emptyset_j\right)=\begin{cases}1, & \emptyset_i \neq \emptyset_j \\ 0, & \emptyset_i=\emptyset_j\end{cases}\quad,\quad LD_{ins}\left(\emptyset_i,\emptyset_j\right)=1\quad,\quad LD_{del}\left(\emptyset_i,\emptyset_j\right)=1$$

此方法為音素與音素間最基本的相互關係，而利用這種方法可以得知關鍵詞語句與測試語句的最小距離。

4. 音素匹配實做關鍵詞辨識系統

當得到三種不同的懲罰矩陣後，我們可以經由動態規劃，來得知測試音檔是否含有關鍵詞。假設$Q^{(n)}=(q_1^{(n)},q_2^{(n)},\cdots,q_{N_Q^{(n)}}^{(n)})$為一句測試音檔經由自由音素解碼的輸出結果，$\mathrm{P}=(p_1\ ,\ p_2\ ,\ \cdots\ ,\ p_{Np})$為關鍵詞的單音素序列，$C_{i,j}^{(n)}$為從 $\left(q_i^{(n)},p_j\right)$開始計算每個點的最佳距離，而下面為關鍵詞系統的 DP 遞迴式：

$$C_{i,j}^{(n)} = \begin{cases} PM_{sub}\left(q_i^{(n)}, p_j\right), & i = j = 1 \\ C_{i,j-1}^{(n)} + PM_{del}\left(p_{j-1}, p_j\right), & i = 1, j \neq 1 \\ \min[PM_{sub}\left(p_{j-1}, p_j\right), C_{i-1,j}^{(n)} + PM_{ins}(q_i^{(n)}, p_j)], & i \neq 1, j = 1 \\ \min[C_{i-1,j-1}^{(n)} + PM_{sub}\left(q_i^{(n)}, p_j\right), \\ \quad C_{i-1,j}^{(n)} + PM_{ins}(q_i^{(n)}, p_j) \\ \quad C_{i,j-1}^{(n)} + PM_{del}\left(p_{i-1}, p_j\right)], & otherwise \end{cases}$$

其中 $1 \leq i \leq N_Q^{(n)}$ and $1 \leq j \leq N_p$。我們可用以下範例圖來表示上述的方法：

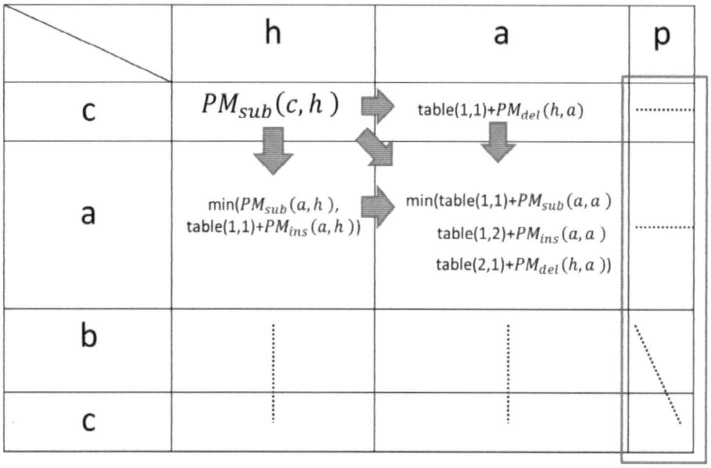

圖二、音素匹配法示意圖

由於我們不知道測試音檔中關鍵詞開始的位置，故在 $i \neq 1, j = 1$ 時我們使用 $\min[PM_{sub}\left(p_{j-1}, p_j\right), C_{i-1,j}^{(n)} + PM_{ins}(q_i^{(n)}, p_j)]$ 而非 $C_{i-1,j}^{(n)} + PM_{ins}(q_i^{(n)}, p_j)$，來猜測關鍵詞可能的起始位置，最後我們將選取最後一行中，正規化後的最小值，做為一個測試音檔對於一個關鍵詞的懲罰值，其公式如下：

$$D(P, Q^{(n)}) = \min_{1 \leq i \leq N_Q^{(n)}} (C_{i,N_p}^{(n)} / l_{i,N_p}^{(n)})$$

其中各個小標意義如下：

P：關鍵詞音素字串　　　　Q：測試音檔音素字串

(n)：測試音檔經由自由音素解碼後第 n 名結果

C：動態規劃所填之表格　　　　i：第 i 個 row

N_P：最後一個 column　　　　l_{i,N_p}：關鍵詞音素字串長度

而當得到此懲罰值和位置後，我們利用回溯法（backtracking），找出測試音檔所對應到關鍵詞的位置。最後辨認是否有關鍵詞定義如下：

$$\min_{1 \le n \le N} D(P, Q^{(n)}) \le \Upsilon$$

其中Υ為門檻值，若經由辨識得到小於或等於Υ，則表示有關鍵詞。

三、論文方法

（一） 關鍵詞驗證技術

在實做關鍵詞系統時，會分成關鍵詞的擷取和關鍵詞的驗證，以下為示意圖：

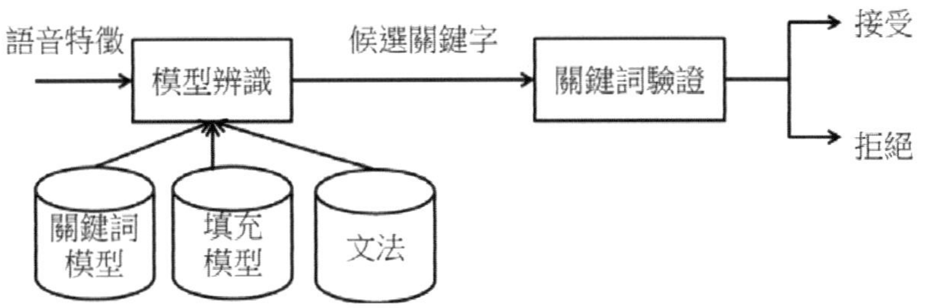

圖三、關鍵詞系統與驗證方塊圖

在實做關鍵詞辨識系統時，常常會因為模型的訓練較為簡單普遍，或是強制對位不準確的問題等等，導致關鍵詞系統辨識率不夠好，故會在第一階段關鍵詞擷取過後，加入關鍵詞驗證，來增加整個關鍵詞系統的辨識率，下面將介紹本論文所使用的驗證技術與如何結合原有的關鍵詞辨識系統。

（二） 排名評分 （rank ratio score）

排名評分(rank ratio score)[12][13]為一種對於關鍵詞的信心測量(confidence measure)，此評分方式將會定義一正確音素與其競爭音素，藉由維特比解碼計算出對數似然率進行排名，再使用此排名計算出排名分數，音素排名流程如下圖所示

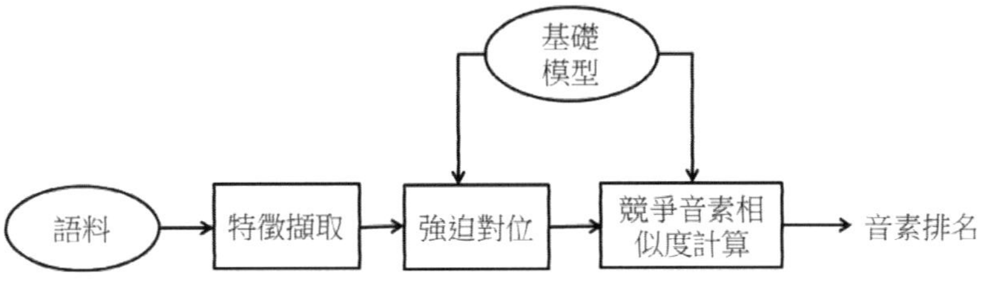

圖四、語音評分計算流程

我們將待評分音素的右相關雙連音素，做為其競爭音素。接著將待評分音素與競爭音素，依據對數似然率排名，再由公式 (2)、 (3)計算出排名評分。

$$Rank\ Ratio = \frac{\text{rank}-1}{\text{p}} \tag{2}$$

$$\text{Rank Ratio Score} = \frac{100}{1+\left(\frac{Rank\ Ratio}{a}\right)^{b}} \tag{3}$$

其中 rank 代表排名，對數似然率最高者為第一名，依此類推；p 代表競爭因素個數；而利用排名比所產生的分數是經由 a 和 b 進行調整，a 和 b 對於每一個右相關雙連音素模型會有不同的值，其主因為針對每個模型產生一個最佳的評分系統。

（三） 音高走勢分類器

音高與音量相較於梅爾倒頻係數而言，是較少被選為語音特徵的，而近年來在中文關鍵詞系統中，已有人加入聲調結合關鍵詞辨識系統來改進辨識率[11]，而在台語方面則無此方面的嘗試，故本論文多加入了音高與音量兩種特徵，來輔助原本的關鍵詞辨識系統。在台語聲調[14]方面，基本分為七種，為調 1～調 7。調 1～調 5 為非入聲字調，調 6、調 7 為入聲字調（即音節結尾為-p -t -k -h），而額外的兩種為調 8 和調 9，為變調而來的，並非單獨的字調。以下表說明台語聲調：

表一、台語聲調說明表

漢字	衫	鼻	褲	黨	人	直	血
基本頻率							
調號	1	2	3	4	5	6	7
調值	55	33	21	51	24	32	44
ForPA 拼音	sann1	pinn2	ko3	dong4	lang5	dit6	hueh7

經由上表，我們可以將台語聲調分為四個特性，平緩、上升、下降及短促急停（入聲字），本論文將針對這四種類別分別訓練一種模型，並且輔助關鍵詞系統的驗證。

1. 特徵擷取與分類器訓練

對於音高追蹤，我們採用了 UPDUDP[9]的方法。UPDUDP[9]是利用動態規劃（Dynamic programming, DP）方式，找出整句不中斷音高追蹤方法。作法是首先找出整句音檔的 AMDF[10] (average magnitude difference function)矩陣，並基於該矩陣進行 DP 之演算，取出連續不中斷的基頻軌跡曲線，使原本跳動幅度大的聲母位置的音高資訊更加完整。

音量特徵主要是作為發出不同聲調時，其音量相對大小的參考指標，而在利用時會減去平均值，觀察每個音框間的相對性。計算公式上，採用音框的每個取樣點其絕對值總和。

經由上述計算取得該音節的音高與音量向量之後，我們參考[8]的方法，取出代表該音節的特徵向量，以進行分類器的訓練。本論文利用高斯混合模型（Gaussian mixture model, GMM）來實作『音高走勢分類器』[15]。

2. 音高走勢分類器驗證方法

假設我們的關鍵詞為流血（ForPA 拼音為 lau2_heh7），發音為類別 1 與類別 4，而測試音檔經由第一階段的關鍵詞辨識可以得到候選關鍵詞，我們再將候選關鍵詞經由 GMM 得到每一個音節對於四個類別的 log-likelihood 值，之後再選取其類別 1 和類別 4 的組合相加並正規化至一個音節，此為候選關鍵詞經過『音高走勢分類器』後的分數，我們之後將利用此分數做為關鍵詞驗證的方法之一。

（四） 決策樹法結合語音評分與音高走勢分類器之關鍵詞辨識系統

當我們得到關鍵詞的語音評分與『音高走勢分類器』的分數後，我們將用決策樹(decision tree)決定測試音檔中是否含有關鍵詞，而因為在驗證關鍵詞時，使用語音評分比使用『音高走勢分類器』效果較佳，故在使用決策樹時採信語音評分較多，『音高走勢分類器』做為輔助來建立決策樹，以下為使用決策樹的示意圖：

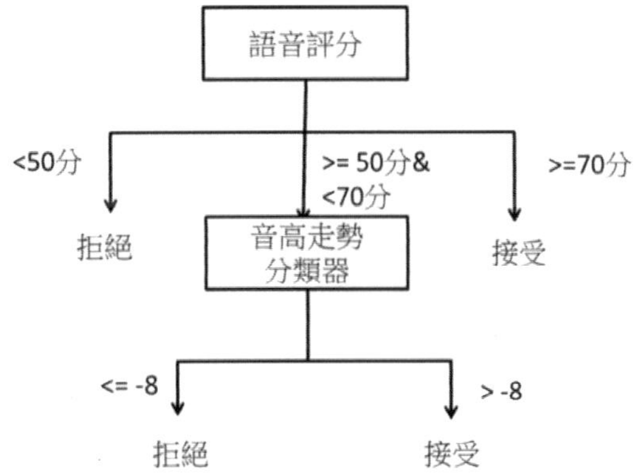

圖五、關鍵詞驗證之決策樹示意圖

第一個選定的問題為「關鍵詞的語音評分是否大於等於 70 分或小於 50 分？」，若滿足前者則我們將接受此關鍵詞，否則拒絕此關鍵詞，而第二個問題為「『音高走勢分類器』的 log-likelihood 值是否大於-8？」。而結合前面兩種關鍵詞辨識系統——隱藏式馬可夫模型法和懲罰矩陣法，其示意圖如下：

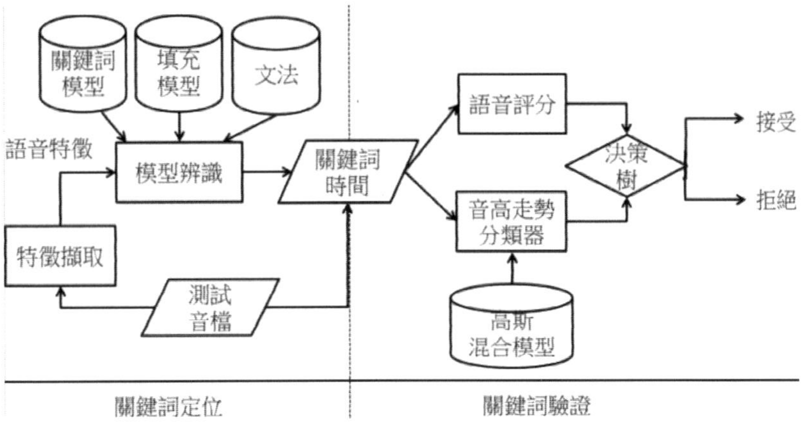

圖六、HMM 加入關鍵詞驗證之系統方塊圖

首先我們先將第一階段關鍵詞辨識所辨識出的可能關鍵詞進行切音，得到候選關鍵詞的音節切音，之後進行語音評分和『音高走勢分類器』辨識，我們可以發現大部分的候選

關鍵詞不會高於 70 分，而正確的關鍵詞往往會高於 70 分，但仍然有可能會有例外，故又多加入『音高走勢分類器』進行驗證。

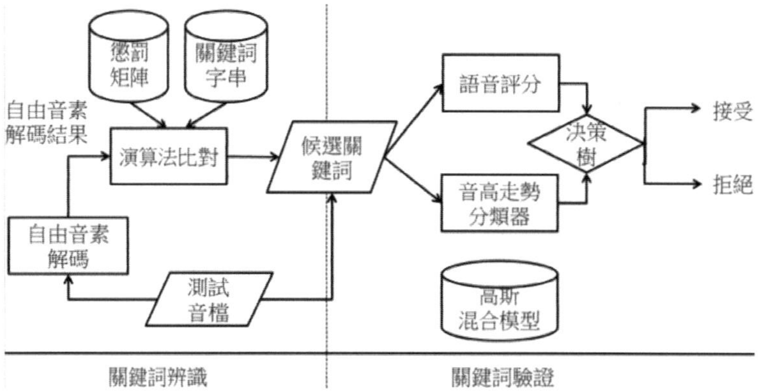

圖七、音素匹配法加入關鍵詞驗證之系統方塊圖

利用音素匹配法進行關鍵詞辨識，和隱藏式馬可夫模型大致相同，不同地方為第一階段音素匹配法是利用測試檔案的音素序列，與關鍵詞的音素序列進行比對而得，之後再利用回溯法得知關鍵詞的位置。得知候選關鍵詞的位置後我們一樣利用語音評分與『音高走勢分類器』來做關鍵詞的驗證，之後的方法與上一小節相同。

四、實驗結果與分析

（一） 訓練語料簡介

語料來源為論文[7]所蒐集的訓練語料，並把訓練語料分成訓練與發展（development）語料，分為兩種主要為實做不同的關鍵詞系統所需，下面為訓練語料數據，由數據可以知道男女生人數比例相當，並且在句數方面也相當平衡，而語料的標註是採用台語的ForPA 拼音。

表二、訓練語料資訊

	訓練語料	發展語料	測試語料
語料名稱	TW01 和 TW02 訓練語料	TW01 和 TW02 發展語料	TW02 測試語料
錄音格式	單聲道、16kHz、16bits		
錄音者	479 人，男 253、女 226	121 人，男 64、女 57	16 人，男 8、女 8
錄音句數	93638 句	23410 句	2080 句 男 1028 句、女 1052 句
錄音時間	26 小時	6.5 小時	0.7 小時

前面有介紹到本測試語料為短字詞(一個字代表在ForPA 標音的一個音節)的測試語料，

包含一字詞到五字詞，個數分別為 97、539、692、533、2 個。而實驗中的關鍵詞列表，及其在測試語料中的出現次數如下：

表三、關鍵詞列表

Keyword	出現次數	Keyword	出現次數	Keyword	出現次數	Keyword	出現次數
電話	15	語音	4	事件	7	單位	7
三更半瞑	8	合理	4	可惡	5	政府	7
活動	8	太太	4	流血	5	運動	4
朋友	8	社會	4	程度	4	臭屁	4
台灣	7	酒醉	4	分鐘	4	火車	4

（二） 效能評估方法

本論文所採用的評估方法為錯誤拒絕率（false rejection rate ,FRR）[16]與錯誤接受率（false acceptance rate , FAR）[16]兩種，但通常一邊的錯誤率降低，另一邊的錯誤率會隨之升高，所以我們採用的為相等錯誤率（equal error rate, EER）[16]來評估關鍵詞辨識系統。

（三） 辨識網路介紹

在使用隱藏式馬可夫模型實做關鍵詞辨識系統時，所採用的辨識網路為用來分辨關鍵詞與非關鍵詞，其中關鍵詞為右相關雙連音素串接而成，如下圖所示：

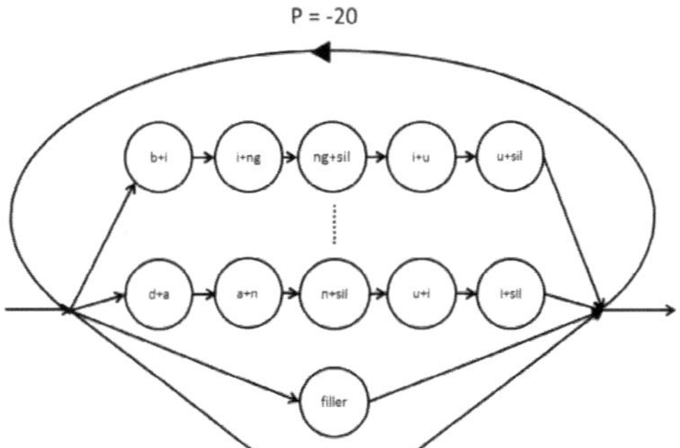

圖八、關鍵詞辨識網路示意圖

另一方面，在利用音素匹配法實做關鍵詞辨識系統時，在第一階段時則使用一般的自由音素解碼。

（四） 未加入關鍵詞驗證之系統比對

1. 實驗目的

本實驗目的為找出未加入關鍵詞驗證時其兩種實做關鍵詞系統方法最佳的辨識率，利用兩種系統最佳辨識率的方法之後再進行改進，期望能得到一個最好的關鍵詞辨識系統。

2. 實驗流程與設定

在隱藏式馬可夫模型實做關鍵詞辨識系統中採取調整填充模型的懲罰值和關鍵詞模型的機率值，期望能達到一個可以接受的效果。在測試音素匹配法前，先測試自由音素解碼的準確率，之後進行音素匹配－混淆矩陣法中其插入和刪除矩陣的常數值，並測試三種不同的音素匹配法，期望得到一個最佳結果再予以改進。

3. 實驗結果：音素匹配－混淆矩陣法中不同常數之測試

在此實驗結果中我們得知音素匹配－混淆矩陣法來實做關鍵詞辨識系統其在插入與刪除矩陣常數值分別設為 3.5、4、4.5 和 5 時，以 4.5 最好，故之後我們用其與另外兩種懲罰矩陣之方法比較。

4. 實驗結果：音素匹配法與隱藏式馬可夫模型法比較

表四、HMM 與音素匹配法結果比較(未加入關鍵詞驗證)

代稱	關鍵詞系統使用方法	EER
PM	音素匹配－懲罰矩陣法	39.4%
CM	音素匹配－混淆矩陣法	34.0%
LD	音素匹配－距離矩陣法	42.2%
HMM	隱藏式馬可夫模型法	46.5%

自由因素解碼在 penalty 為-20 時結果最好，準確率為 50.32%，之後我們皆用此結果做為音素匹配法中第一階段的輸出。在單純比較利用音素匹配法實做關鍵詞辨識系統時，其音素匹配－混淆矩陣法可以得到最好的效果，其原因可能為因為在利用發展語料(development)時所建立的混淆矩陣有把音素與音素之間的關係成功的表現出來，故即使在自由音素解碼效果沒有很顯著的情況下，關鍵詞辨識系統仍有一定的效果（相等錯誤率 34%），而音素匹配－懲罰矩陣法效果較音素匹配－混淆矩陣法略為遜色一點，可能原因為雖然在製作此懲罰矩陣利用 HTK 下了許多功夫，但在音素與音素之間可能會有切音不準確之問題，導致有時 log-likelihood 值或許沒有正確的表示出音素與音素間真正的關係，所以間接的導致了關鍵詞辨識系統的正確率，最後利用距離矩陣只有單純以 0、1 來表示音素間的關係，故用其在進行關鍵詞辨識時，其效果非常不好。最後為 HMM 實做關鍵詞辨識系統時，因為填充模型較為簡單且關鍵詞模型僅為右相關雙連連音素模型串接而成，故無法達到較佳的效果是可以預期的。

（五） 加入關鍵詞驗證後系統之比對

1. 實驗目的

經由上一節實驗的測試，我們得到了兩種實做關鍵詞辨識的基準，我們取一些較佳的效果來做驗證(音素匹配法取混淆矩陣法與懲罰矩陣法)，期望可以達到最佳的關鍵詞辨識系統。

2. 實驗流程與設定

一開始我們會先觀察『音高走勢分類器』的效果，得知音高分類的辨識率，之後我們先將兩種系統只加入語音評分來驗證，期望達到一個不錯的效果，之後再加入『音高走勢分類器』進行雙重驗證，觀察加入『音高走勢分類器』後是否與原本系統有互補的效果。

3. 實驗結果一：音高走勢分類器辨識結果

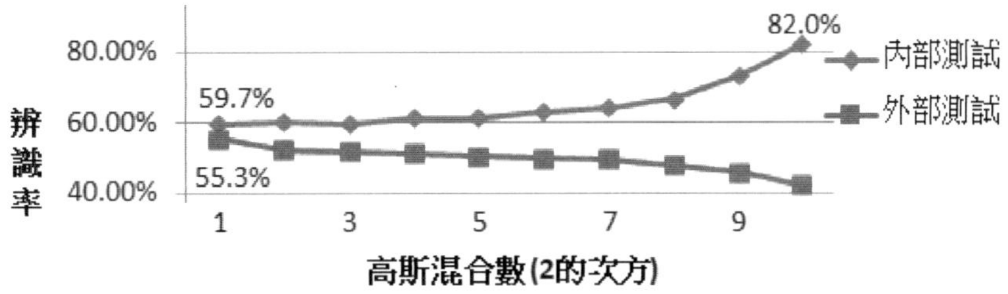

圖九、音高走勢分類器辨識結果

上圖為音高走勢分類器結果，可以得知當高斯混合數提升時，雖然內部測試的辨識率變高了，但對外部測試卻無法有幫助，故在此實驗中高斯混合數為 1 時有最好的效果，另一方面台語的入聲字（分類為 4，短促急停）辨識率大約只有 20%左右，因此大大的降低了整個音高走勢分類器其效果。

4. 實驗結果二：加入關鍵詞驗證之系統比較

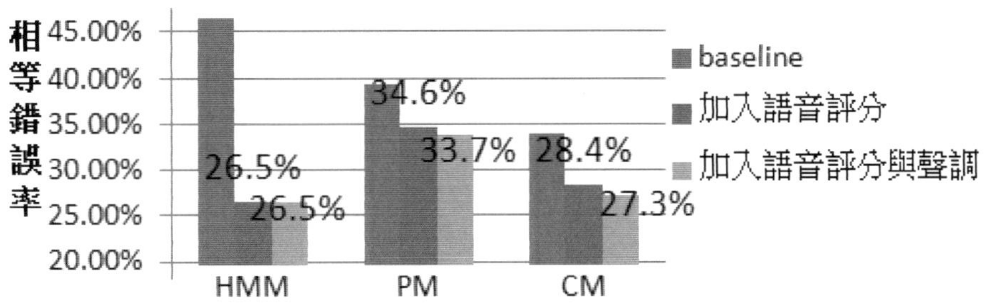

圖十、三種關鍵詞辨識系統加入關鍵詞驗證後之結果

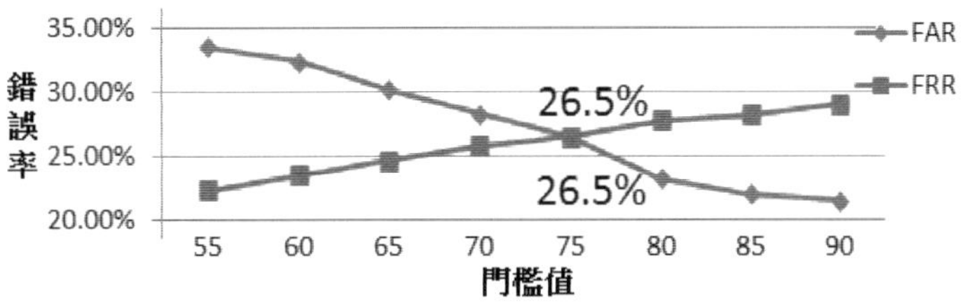

圖十一、HMM 加入語音評分之折線圖分析

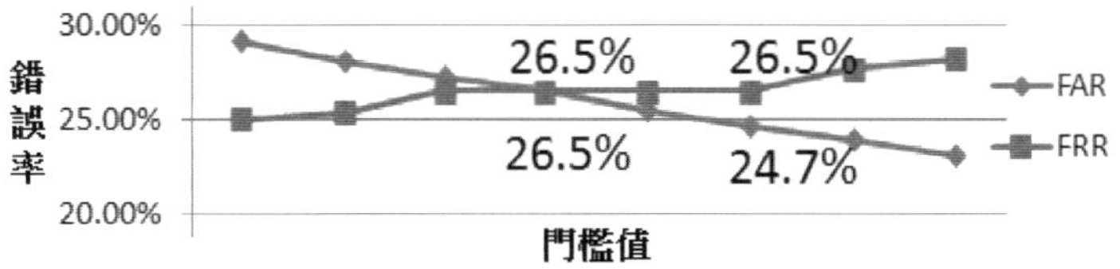

圖十二、HMM 加入語音評分和音高分類之折線圖分析

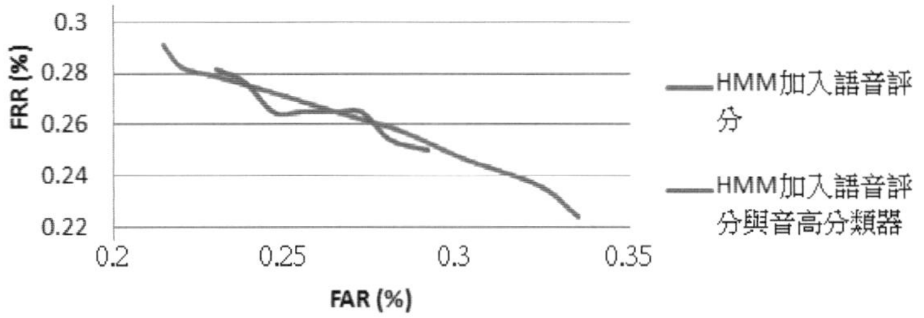

圖十三、HMM 加入語音評分與音高分類後 DET 曲線比較

經由結果我們可以知道利用語音評分來做為關鍵詞系統的驗證可以得到不錯的效果，其中隱藏式馬可夫模型法錯誤率下降了 20%，音素匹配法中之混淆矩陣法錯誤率下降了 5.6%、懲罰矩陣法下降了 4.8%，比較不符合預期的為其隱藏式馬可夫模型法其基準（baseline）較低，而音素匹配法其基準（baseline）較高，但經由語音評分後雖都有改進，但是原本效果較差的隱藏式馬可夫模型法錯誤率卻大為降低，推估原因為在進行隱藏式馬可夫模型時，其在第一階段關鍵詞辨識時是有進行切音與模型比對，此時雖然會有很高的錯誤接受率，但對於正確的關鍵詞並不會放過，而在實做語音評分時也是根據我們所建立的馬可夫模型做信心度的測量，兩階段都與我們所建立的馬可夫模型相關，故可以有較好的效果。而在使用音素匹配法時，雖然第一階段仍有使用自由音素解碼，並且利用發展語料調整音素與音素之間的相互關係並進行修正，但其內部的辨識核心仍與辨識網路無關，因此在關鍵詞驗證時無法達到我們所預期的效果。而另一方面我們加入了『音高走勢分類器』來跟語音評分做雙重的關鍵詞驗證，利用此方法在隱藏式馬可夫模型法中雖然相等錯誤率並沒有下降，但我們觀察到在相同的 FRR 中，其 FAR 降低了 1.8%，推測原因可能為因為關鍵詞的數量較少，在 FRR 中很容易達到一個飽和的情況，其錯誤率不容易在降低，但因為非關鍵詞的音檔較多，所以 FAR 的變動相對會比較大，所以在『音高走勢分類器』的部分是有助於改進 FAR。而在音素匹配法中混淆矩陣錯誤率下降了 1.1%、懲罰矩陣法下降了 0.9%，由此可以得知『音高走勢分類器』對於關鍵詞辨識系統是有幫助的。

五、結論

本論文提出了結合語音評分與音高走勢分類器的台語關鍵詞辨識系統，分別先實做了傳統實做關鍵詞系統的方法和另一種較新的方法，之後再利用語音評分做為信心度測量與『音高走勢分類器』，進行關鍵詞的驗證。而在本論文的實驗中，不論是使用隱藏式馬可夫模型法或是音素匹配法，其關鍵詞字典的擴充都很方便，前者只要更改關鍵詞的串

接模型，後者則只要更改關鍵詞的音素序列（phone sequence），故此為一個移植性高、關鍵詞擴充度高之系統，因此對於應用上可以有不錯的幫助。在隱藏式馬可夫模型法中，相等錯誤率從原本 46.5%，經由語音評分後下降至 26.5%，之後加入『音高走勢分類器』FAR 下降了 1.8%，一方面說明了利用語音評分來做為台語關鍵詞辨識系統的驗證是很有幫助的，另一方面也得知在之前未考慮到之語音的音高與音量特徵在與關鍵詞驗證做結合後是有達到互補的效果。在音素匹配法中，其混淆矩陣法與懲罰矩陣法也從相等錯誤率 34%、39.4%，經由語音評分後相等錯誤率下降為 28.4%、34.6%，而加入『音高走勢分類器』後相等錯誤率則下降到 27.3%、33.7%，音高走勢分類器辨識的改善效果也略為提高，其結果可以說是如我們預期。

六、未來研究方向

關鍵詞辨識部分，在隱藏式馬可夫模型方面，可以朝向訓練更為完善的填充模型[4]，使得關鍵詞模型與填充模型更加容易區分，讓關鍵詞驗證部分可以較為簡單。在音素匹配法部分，如何改善自由音素解碼的準確率算是首要課題，雖然可以利用發展語料調整懲罰矩陣的懲罰值，但若辨識正確而不用有懲罰值將會是最理想的。

關鍵詞驗證部分，可以試著採用其他不同的信心度測試方式來加強驗證效果，例如 LRT（likelihood ratio testing）的改良，而在『音高走勢分類器』部分可以使用 HMM 來訓練，使其達到更佳的辨識效果，或是增加像是時間長度（time duration）、停頓長度（pause duration）等來更精確的分類出入聲，或是其他聲調特徵，皆為可行之做法。

致謝

本論文經費來源由國科會計畫 NSC 99-2221-E-007 -049 -MY3 所提供

參考文獻

[1] C. W. Han, S. J. Kang, and N. S. Kim, "Estimation of phone mismatch penalty matrices for two-stage keyword spotting," IEICE TRANSACTIONS on Information and Systems Vol.E93-D No.8 pp.2331-2335

[2] K. Audhkhasi and A. Verma, "Keyword search using modified minimum edit distance measure," Proc. ICASSP, pp. 929-932,Apr. 2007.

[3] M. S. Barakat, C. H. Ritz, D. A. Stirling, "Keyword Spotting based on the Analysis of Template Matching Distances," 5th International Conference on Signal Processing and Communication Systems ICSPCS,2011

[4] S.L. Zhang, Z.W. Shuang, Q. Shi, and Y. Qin, "Improved mandarin keyword spotting using confusion garbage model", in Proc. ICPR, pp. 3700-3703, Istanbul, Turkey, 2010

[5] L.R. Rabiner, “A Tutorial on Hidden Markov Models and Selected Applications in Speech Recognition”, Proc. Of the IEEE, Vol.77, No.2, pp. 257-286, Feb, 1989.

[6] Huang, X., Acero, A., and Hon, H.W., “Spoken Language Processing”, New Jersey, Prentice Hall, 2001

[7] R.-Y. Lyu, M.-S. Liang, Y.-C. Chiang, Toward Constructing A Multilingual Speech Corpus for Taiwanese (Min-nan), Hakka, and Mandarin Chinese, International Journal of Computational Linguistics & Chinese Language Processing, 2004

[8] Liao, H.-C., Chen, J.-C. , Chang, S.-C., Guan, Y.-H., Lee, C.-H., “Decision tree based tone modeling with corrective feedbacks for automatic Mandarin tone assessment”, In INTERSPEECH 2010.

[9] Chen, J.-C., Jang, J.S. R., “TRUES: Tone Recognition Using Extended Segment”, ACM Trans. Asian Lang. Inform. Process. 7, 3, Article 10, 2008.

[10] Ross, M.Shaffer, H. Cohen, A. Freudberg, R., and Manley, H., “Average Magnitude Difference Function Pitch Extractor,” IEEE Transactions on Acoustics, Speech, and Signal Processing, Vol. 22,No. 5,353-362, 1974

[11] 鐘進竹，結合聲調辨認之中文關鍵詞辨認系統，國立交通大學碩士論文，民國 100 年

[12] 李俊毅，語音評分，清華大學碩士論文，民國 91 年

[13] 陳宏瑞，使用多重聲學模型以改良台語語音評分，清華大學碩士論文，民國 100 年

[14] 傅振宏，基於自動產生合成單元之台語語音合成系統，長庚大學碩士論文，民國 89 年

[15] 黃士旗，中文語音聲調辨識的改良與錯誤分析，清大碩士論文，民國 95 年。

[16] 黃冠達，應用支撐向量機於中文關鍵詞驗證之研究，國立臺灣科技大學碩士論文，民國 96 年

[17] 周哲玄，台語關鍵詞辨識之實作與比較，清大碩士論文，民國 101 年。

應用平行語料建構中文斷詞組件

Applications of Parallel Corpora for Chinese Segmentation

王瑞平 劉昭麟
Jui-Ping Wang Chao-Lin Liu

國立政治大學資訊科學系
Department of Computer Science, National Chengchi University
{g9916, chaolin}@cs.nccu.edu.tw

摘要

不同於直接提供中文斷詞服務，網路上的開放軟體讓人們可以利用自有的訓練語料來訓練中文的斷詞模型，藉以實踐自己的斷詞功能。如若可以全人工方式建構斷詞訓練語料，則以目前的機器學習技術所訓練出來的模型，常常可以達到相當好的斷詞效果。然而，實務上全人工的標記工作常常是難以提供足夠多的訓練語料。本文利用中英平行語料與各類辭典，搭配中文未知詞和近義詞的偵測，先建構一個粗略的斷詞器，藉以產生訓練語料，最後再利用網路上的開放軟體來建構中文斷詞服務。在目前的實驗中，雖然依照我們的程序所得的斷詞服務未能立即獲得優於知名的中文斷詞服務的成效，但是表現卻相去不遠；我們所提出的訓練語料產生程序提供了一個一般人可以考慮的選擇。

Abstract

Instead of directly providing the service of Chinese segmentation, some open-source software allows us to train segmentation models with segmented text. The resulting models can perform quite well, if training data of high quality are available. In reality, it is not easy to obtain sufficient and excellent training data, unfortunately. We report an exploration of using parallel corpora and various lexicons with techniques of identifying unknown words and near synonyms to automatically generate training data for such open-source software. We achieved promising results of segmentation in current experiments. Although the results fell short of outperforming the well-known Chinese segmenters, we believe that the proposed approach offers a viable alternative for users of the open-source software to generate their own training data.

關鍵詞：機器學習，語料標記，機器翻譯

1. 緒論

對於中文自然語言處理，中文斷詞是一項非常重要且基礎的工作。中文斷詞技術大致可分為法則式斷詞法[10]及統計式斷詞法[5][16][26]。統計式斷詞法在訓練斷詞模型時若以大量高品質的訓練語料進行訓練，則通常可有好的斷詞效能，但因為通常透過人工斷詞所得的訓練語料才能有較高的品質，所以高品質的訓練語料往往不易取得。因此我們建立一個透過以下程序來提供中文斷詞服務的系統：首先透過查詢各類辭典的方式來產生中英平行語料之所有中文句的各種斷詞組合，並將錯誤斷詞組合去除，藉以產生訓練語料；然後再將所產生的訓練語料提供給網路上的開放軟體去訓練斷詞模型，以建構中文斷詞服務。

在本論文後續內容，我們將所建立的提供中文斷詞服務的系統[1]簡稱為我們的系統。而當使用者提供未斷詞語料給我們的系統時，系統會以訓練好的斷詞模型對未斷詞語料斷詞。

中文斷詞存在兩個重要問題：斷詞歧異性問題、未知詞問題。斷詞歧異性問題是指當一個中文字串可以被斷成數種斷詞組合時，則包含該字串的句子在斷詞後可能會被斷成不符合句意的錯誤斷詞結果，進而影響斷詞效能。斷詞歧異性問題包含組合型歧異(combination ambiguity)和交集型歧異(overlapping ambiguity)，在本研究中我們只著重處理交集型歧異。交集型歧異是當一個中文字串「ABC」可以被斷成「AB/C」及「A/BC」時（A、B、C 皆為單一中文字，斜線代表詞彙間的斷詞點），則「AB」、「BC」會有共同的交集「B」，如此就會形成交集型歧異，而我們稱「ABC」為交集型歧異字串。Li[17]等利用非監督式（unsupervised）訓練的方法處理交集型歧異，本研究則透過英漢翻譯的資訊去處理交集型歧異。

未知詞指的是未收錄於辭典中的詞彙，例如人名、地名、組織名等。在日常生活中人們會不斷創造出新的詞彙，故未知詞經常會出現在文章中。斷詞系統在對未知詞斷詞時通常會出現錯誤斷詞的情形，所以如果想要提升斷詞效能，則處理未知詞問題會是必要的工作。在處理未知詞問題相關研究方面，Chen 等[11]利用以語料庫為基的學習法(corpus-based learning approach)去產生規則以進行未知詞偵測。擷取未知詞時，Chen 等[12]針對屬於未知詞一部份的單字詞，會判斷該單字詞是否可以和相鄰的詞彙進行合併。

我們從中英平行語料中擷取未知詞、新的中英詞對，藉此處理未知詞問題與提升利用英漢翻譯資訊去處理交集型歧異的效果。擷取中英詞對與未知詞之大略流程如下：首先從中英平行語料中擷取候選中英遺留詞對、候選中文遺留字詞。之後利用可能性比例(likelihood ratios)與共現頻率對候選中英遺留詞對進行篩選，將通過篩選的候選中英遺留詞對視為正確詞對，加入至英漢辭典模組；利用詞性序列規則對候選中文遺留字詞進行篩選，將通過篩選的候選中文遺留字詞視為未知詞，加入至中文辭典模組。

2. 系統架構

2.1 系統流程與架構

我們的系統之流程與整體架構如圖一所示，而流程中各步驟的詳細方法會在後續章節詳加說明；首先，將從中英平行語料中所篩選出的候選中英遺留詞對擴充至英漢辭典模組，將從中英平行語料中所篩選出

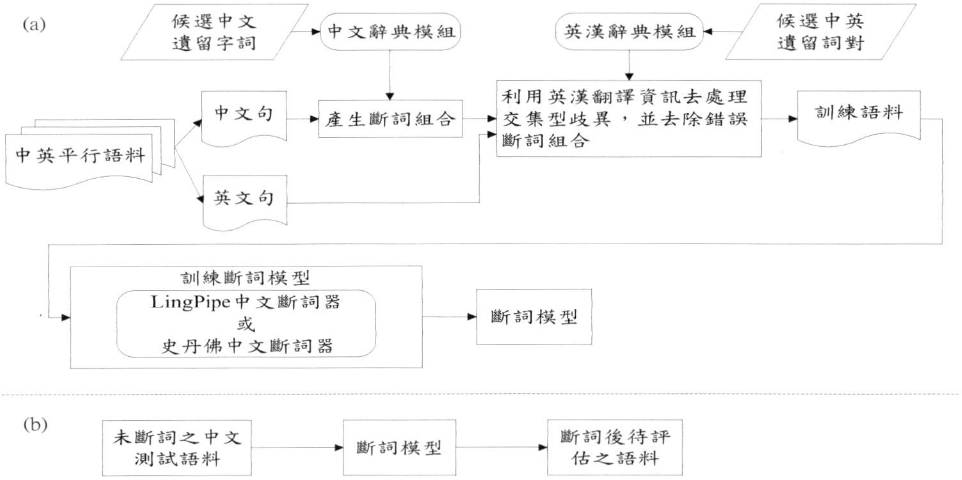

圖一、系統的流程與架構

[1] 因工作時程等因素，我們所建立的提供中文斷詞服務的系統目前並沒有線上版本。

的候選中文遺留字詞擴充至中文辭典模組。在提供我們的系統中英平行語料後，我們透過查詢中文辭典模組中的辭典之方式，對語料中的每一句中文句產生該句的各種斷詞組合。而為了得到較少錯誤的訓練語料，我們藉由查詢英漢辭典模組中的辭典之方式來利用英漢翻譯的資訊去處理交集型歧異，並將錯誤斷詞組合去除。得到訓練語料後，我們利用 LingPipe 中文斷詞器[18]及史丹佛中文斷詞器[23]訓練斷詞模型；透過上述兩種工具去訓練斷詞模型時，除了提供這兩種工具訓練語料之外，也可以加入外部辭典一起訓練。最後利用所得到的斷詞模型將未斷詞測試語料進行斷詞，得到已斷詞之語料。

3. 辭典模組介紹

我們的系統之辭典模組包含英漢辭典模組與中文辭典模組，而在這兩個模組中都包含一般辭典與專業辭典這兩種類別。中文與英漢辭典模組的各辭典之列表、辭典詞彙數統計如表一、表二所示。關於「英漢技術名詞辭典」與「中文技術名詞辭典」及「加入近義詞之英漢合併辭典」的建置會在後續內容中說明。

本研究從國家教育研究院學術名詞資訊網[8]下載了 138 個技術名詞檔案，並將其整合成「英漢技術名詞辭典」。「英漢技術名詞辭典」的內容格式為一個英文技術名詞對應一個中文技術名詞的形式，而「中文技術名詞辭典」是只取「英漢技術名詞辭典」中的中文技術名詞整合而成。

當中文句出現交集型歧異時，我們會利用英漢辭典中的英文詞彙之中文翻譯去進行比對，所以為了提高利用英漢翻譯的資訊去處理交集型歧異的效果，會須要增加英文詞彙的中文翻譯詞彙數目；我們參考[6]的作法將牛津現代英漢雙解詞典[1]和 Dr.eye 譯典通線上字典[13]合併成「英漢合併辭典」，以增加英文詞彙的中文翻譯數目。我們針對「英漢合併辭典」中的各個英文詞彙，從中央研究院現代漢語一詞泛讀系統[7]（以下簡稱一詞泛讀）及 E-HowNet[14]取得該詞彙的中文翻譯近義詞集後，把從一詞泛讀及 E-HowNet 得到的中文翻譯近義詞集與「英漢合併辭典」中的英文詞彙之中文翻譯進行整合，就完成「加入近義詞之英漢合併辭典」的建置。

4. 產生訓練語料

4.1 產生各種斷詞組合

我們針對未斷詞語料中的每句中文句，透過查詢中文辭典的方式，產生由不同的詞彙所組成的句子之各種斷詞組合，藉此得到訓練語料。我們產生各種斷詞組合的目的為希望在訓練斷詞模型的過程中，透過大量語料的統計現象，來得到較佳的斷詞模型。我們將句子表示成字串$C_{1:n}$（$C_{1:n}$ = $C_1\ C_{2...}C_n$），並依照下頁圖二的步驟來產生句子的各種斷詞組合。以下為圖二中V_i與$Cand_i$（i=1 to n）的定義。V_i為詞彙集合，在V_i內會存放句子中所有以C_i開頭的詞彙。$Cand_i$為候

表一、中文辭典模組之辭典列表、辭典詞彙數統計

中文辭典模組		
辭典類別	辭典名稱	中文詞彙數
一般辭典	教育部國語辭典	157704
一般辭典	成語詞典	13947
一般辭典	高級漢語大詞典	54467
專業辭典	中文技術名詞辭典	804053
專業辭典	世界人名翻譯大辭典	648612

表二、英漢辭典模組之辭典列表、辭典詞彙數統計

英漢辭典模組			
辭典類別	辭典名稱	英文詞彙數	中文詞彙數
一般辭典	加入近義詞之英漢合併辭典	99805	3729292
一般辭典	懶蟲簡明英漢詞典	121525	323766
專業辭典	英漢技術名詞辭典	586075	804053

1. 針對句子中的每一個字 C_i（i=1 to n）查詢中文辭典模組的辭典中是否包含句子中以該字開頭的不同長度之字串（字串的長度為 1 to n-i+1），若包含則將該字串加入 V_i 。
2. 將 i 的初始值設為 1。
3. (a).如果 V_1 中的某一詞彙等同於 $C_{1:i}$，則把該詞彙加入至 $Cand_i$。
   (b). for j =1 to i-1, i > 1
   如果 $Cand_j$ 中的某一斷詞組合加上 V_{j+1} 中的另一詞彙後，不含有「包含單字詞的詞彙組合」，並且等同於 $C_{1:i}$，則把該斷詞組合加入至 $Cand_i$。
4. 如果 i 不等於 n，則把 i 遞增 1，並重回到步驟 3。如果 i 等於 n，則 $Cand_i$ 內的所有斷詞組合即為該句子的各種斷詞組合。

圖二、產生句子的各種斷詞組合的步驟

選集合，在$Cand_i$內會存放字串$C_{1:i}$的各種斷詞組合。

在圖二步驟 3(b)中之「包含單字詞的詞彙組合」的定義為：當某詞彙組合包含單字詞，且該詞彙組合可以結合成一個詞彙時，則該詞彙組合為「包含單字詞的詞彙組合」。我們發現若句子內含有許多「包含單字詞的詞彙組合」時會產生大量的斷詞組合。若語料中的許多中文句都產生大量的斷詞組合，會使訓練語料過於龐大，造成訓練斷詞模型時消耗大量時間、資源。因此在步驟 3(b)我們不將含有「包含單字詞的詞彙組合」的斷詞組合加入$Cand_i$，藉此去除含有「包含單字詞的詞彙組合」之斷詞組合。

以下我們以「貼近市場需求，」這一句子為例，對產生句子的各種斷詞組合的步驟進行說明。在圖二步驟 1，會針對「貼」、「近」、「市」...「，」一一去查詢中文辭典模組的辭典中是否包含句子中以該字開頭的不同長度之字串。若以「貼」為例，會查詢辭典中是否包含「貼」、「貼近」、「貼近市」等字串，若辭典中有包含，則表示該字串為一詞彙，所以該字串會被加入至V_1；此外若C_i為標點符號，我們則把它視為存在於辭典中的單字詞，將其加入至V_i。最終的V_i如圖三所示。

在圖二步驟 3 中的i代表不同的階段，而在各個階段會產生字串$C_{1:i}$之各種斷詞組合。i等於 1 時，在步驟 3(a)會檢查V_1中是否有詞彙等同於$C_{1:1}$，而因為V_1中的「貼」等同於$C_{1:1}$，所以會被加入至$Cand_1$。i等於 2 時，在步驟 3(a)，因V_1中的「貼近」等同於$C_{1:2}$，所以會被加入至$Cand_2$；在步驟 3(b)，「貼」加上「近」後會形成「貼 近」，為含有「包含單字詞的詞彙組合」的斷詞組合，所以「貼 近」不會被加入至$Cand_2$。重複執行步驟 3、4 到i等於 6 時，在步驟 3(b)，$Cand_5$中的「貼近 市場 需」加上「求」後

字串 $C_{1:i}$						
C_1:貼	C_2:近	C_3:市	C_4:場	C_5:需	C_6:求	C_7:，

↓

查詢中文辭典中是否包含句子中以 C_i 開頭的不同長度之字串，若包含則將該字串加入 V_i

↓

詞彙集合 V_i						
V_1	V_2	V_3	V_4	V_5	V_6	V_7
貼	近	市	場	需	求	，
貼近		市場		需求		
		市場需求				

圖三、產生「貼近市場需求，」之 V_i

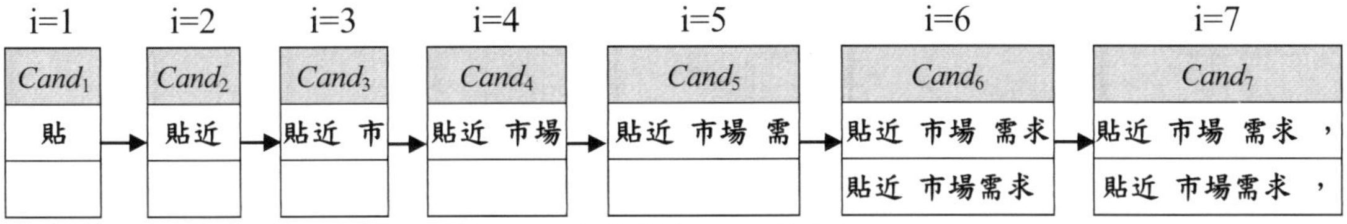

圖四、各階段的 $Cand_i$ 的內容

含有「需 求」這個「包含單字詞的詞彙組合」，所以不會被加入至$Cand_6$；而$Cand_4$中的「貼近 市場」加上V_5中的「需求」後等同於$C_{1:6}$，所以會被加入至$Cand_6$；$Cand_2$中的「貼近」加上V_3中的「市場需求」後等同於$C_{1:6}$，所以也會被加入至$Cand_6$。執行步驟 3、4 到i等於 7，則$Cand_7$內的所有斷詞組合就是句子之各種斷詞組合。圖四則是各階段的$Cand_i$的內容。

4.2 利用英漢翻譯的資訊處理交集型歧異

在產生句子的各種斷詞組合後，本研究利用英漢翻譯的資訊去處理交集型歧異。我們利用英漢翻譯的資訊去處理交集型歧異的原因為：當一個句子有交集型歧異時，透過英文詞彙的中文翻譯，可以挑選出符合英文陳述的正確斷詞組合。例如有交集型歧異的句子「一旦有機會」可以被斷成「一旦/有機/會」、「一旦/有/機會」，而透過英文詞彙 “chance” 的中文翻譯「機會」可以挑選出正確的斷詞組合「一旦/有/機會」。挑選出正確的斷詞組合之後，我們會去除錯誤的斷詞組合，以得到較少錯誤的訓練語料。

以下介紹處理交集型歧異的方法。給定含有交集型歧異字串「ABC」(A、B、C 皆為單一中文字，而「ABC」可以被斷成「A/BC」或「AB/C」) 的中文句之各個斷詞組合與該中文句所對應的英文句，我們利用英文句中各詞彙之中文翻譯集合中的中文翻譯去對應斷詞組合中的中文詞彙；如果某英文詞彙的中文翻譯集合中之中文翻譯對應到斷詞組合中的詞彙 AB，則將包含「AB/C」的斷詞組合視為正確斷詞組合，而包含「A/BC」的斷詞組合則是錯誤斷詞組合，所以我們會去除包含「A/BC」的錯誤斷詞組合。

以下藉下頁圖五說明處理交集型歧異的整體流程。中文句「即便是這類工程都可能引發地震，不過大半規模不大。」包含了交集型歧異字串「即便是」(「即便是」可被斷成「即便/是」及「即/便是」)，而圖五中的斷詞組合 1、斷詞組合 2 為該中文句的各個斷詞組合。經過步驟 1、 2 後，我們取得了英文句中各詞彙的中文翻譯集合，如“even” 的中文翻譯集合包含「縱使」、「縱然」、「即便」等詞彙。在步驟 3 正確斷詞組合的部分，我們標記<詞幹還原後的英文詞彙/中文詞彙>的意思是利用左側的詞幹還原後的英文詞彙之中文翻譯集合中的中文翻譯，可以對應到右側的中文詞彙，例如< even/即便>的意思是 “even”是經過詞幹還原後的詞彙，而“even”的中文翻譯集合中的中文翻譯會對應到斷詞組合 1 中的「即便」，所以在步驟 3 我們將包含「即便/是」的斷詞組合視為正確斷詞組合，並去除包含「即/便是」的錯誤斷詞組合。

4.3 擷取中英詞對與未知詞

本研究從中英平行語料中擷取新的中英詞對、未知詞，藉此提高利用英漢翻譯資訊處理訓練語料中的交集型歧異之效果與處理訓練語料中的未知詞問題。在擷取中英詞對與未知詞時，首先我們會從語料中擷取「候選中英遺留詞對」、「候選中文遺留字詞」。之後我們利用可能性比例與詞對之共現頻率對「候選中英遺留詞對」進行篩選，利用詞性序列規則對「候選中文遺留字詞」進行篩選。

4.3.1 擷取「候選中英遺留詞對」與「候選中文遺留字詞」

我們首先藉由查詢英漢辭典模組的方式來取得英文句的各個詞彙之中文翻譯集合，之後再利用英文句各詞彙之中文翻譯集合中的中文翻譯對中文句進行斷詞。在斷詞後，中文句會有未被斷詞的「中文遺留字

輸入

英文句：Even those projects can induce earthquakes, although most are small.
斷詞組合 1：即便/是/這/類/工程/都/可能/引發/地震/，/不過/大半/規模/不大/。
斷詞組合 2：即/便是/這/類/工程/都/可能/引發/地震/，/不過/大半/規模/不大/。

↓

步驟 1：利用史丹佛剖析器對英文句中之各詞彙進行詞幹還原

even、those、project、can、induce、earthquake、although、most、be、small

↓

步驟 2：至英漢辭典模組中的一般與專業辭典類型的辭典中查詢英文句中各詞彙的中文翻譯，取各辭典中查詢到的中文翻譯的聯集，作為該詞彙的中文翻譯集合

even：縱使、縱然、即便…	those：那些、那	project：計劃、方案、事業…
can：可能、會、可以…	induce：勸誘、促使、導致…	earthquake：地震、大動盪、天搖地動…
although：雖然、儘管、即使…	most：至多、頂多、最…	be：位於、身處、是…
small：小的、少的、小型的…		

↓

步驟 3：利用英文句中各詞彙之中文翻譯集合中的中文翻譯去對應斷詞組合中的詞彙，將錯誤斷詞組合去除

正確斷詞組合：<even/即便>即便/是/這/類/工程/都/可能/引發/地震/，/不過/大半/規模/不大/。
錯誤斷詞組合：~~即/便是/這/類/工程/都/可能/引發/地震/，/不過/大半/規模/不大/。~~

↓

輸出

即便/是/這/類/工程/都/可能/引發/地震/，/不過/大半/規模/不大/。

圖五、處理交集型歧異的整體流程

詞」，英文句會有無法在中文句中找到對應詞彙的「英文遺留字詞」。對於所有「中文遺留字詞」，我們使用 PAT-tree 抽詞程式**[21]**進行初步的詞彙擷取。我們發現利用 PAT-tree 抽詞程式所擷取出的結果中，許多錯誤的結果都含有停用詞，如「會不」、「確的」；因此對於以 PAT-tree 抽詞程式所擷取出的各結果，我們藉由停用詞列表將其中包含停用詞的結果去除後，其餘的結果即為「候選中文遺留字詞」。由同一平行句對的「候選中文遺留字詞」及「英文遺留字詞」所產生的詞對則稱為「候選中英遺留詞對」。

4.3.2 利用可能性比例與共現頻率進行篩選

因為可能性比例可用於分析兩個詞的關連度[20]，而由較有關連的「候選中文遺留字詞」與「英文遺留字詞」所形成的「候選中英遺留詞對」有較大的機會為正確的中英詞對，所以本研究利用可能性比例對「候選中英遺留詞對」進行篩選。可能性比例的公式如下：

$$\text{Likelihood ratio (c, e)} = \log\lambda = \log\frac{\mathrm{b}(Fce, Fc, p)\mathrm{b}(Fe - Fce, N - Fc, p)}{\mathrm{b}(Fce, Fc, p_1)\mathrm{b}(Fe - Fce, N - Fc, p_2)} \quad (1)$$

Fe為在所有英文句中「英文遺留字詞」出現的句數，Fc為在所有中文句中「候選中文遺留字詞」出現的句數，Fce為「候選中英遺留詞對」的共現頻率（共現頻率代表候選中英遺留詞對中的中文詞、英文詞共同出現之句對數），N為中英平行語料的總句數。我們將信心水準(confidence level)訂為 99.5%，則臨界值(critical value)為 7.88。當$-2\log\lambda$超過 7.88 時，代表「候選中文遺留字詞」與「英文遺留字詞」是有關連的。

以下透過表三說明如何利用可能性比例與共現頻率進行篩選，而表三中的候選中英遺留詞對已依照共現頻率大小由大到小進行排序（當共現頻率相等時再依照$-2\log\lambda$大小由大到小進行排序）。假設共現頻率的門檻值為 3，則雖然詞對「越高 increase」之共現頻率大於或等於 3，但因進行可能性比例檢測後其$-2\log\lambda$小於 7.88，所以該詞對會被視為錯誤的詞對。而「石墨薄膜 graphene」、「奈米碳管 nanotube」、「線寬 feature」、「波束 beams」之共現頻率皆大於或等於 3 且進行可能性比例檢測後其$-2\log\lambda$大於 7.88，所以這 4 個詞對會被視為新的中英詞對並加入至英漢辭典模組中。

4.3.3 利用詞性序列規則進行篩選

表三、候選中英遺留詞對之共現頻率與$-2\log\lambda$對應表

排名	候選中英遺留詞對	共現頻率	$-2\log\lambda$
1	石墨薄膜 graphene	11	65.154
2	奈米碳管 nanotube	10	55.323
3	線寬 feature	7	27.043
4	波束 beams	7	24.219
5	越高 increase	3	6.230
6	損失 major	1	1.152

我們發現「候選中文遺留字詞」可分成三大類：第一類為「已知詞」，第二類為「未知詞」，第三類為「不是詞彙的中文字串」，例如「我搶」。中文詞彙通常會擁有特定之構詞結構（如並列式、偏正式等結構[9]），而不是任意地由幾個中文字進行組合就可構成；我們稱由不同詞性之詞素所組成的規則為詞性序列規則，而詞彙之構詞結構可由不同詞性序列規則所構成。本研究設計了一套流程去取得構成辭典詞彙之構詞結構的各個詞性序列規則，之後利用所取得的詞性序列規則去對「候選中文遺留字詞」進行篩選。利用詞性序列規則篩選「候選中文遺留字詞」的原因是：當構成「候選中文遺留字詞」的構詞結構之詞性序列規則符合構成辭典詞彙之構詞結構的詞性序列規則時，表示「候選中文遺留字詞」所擁有的構詞結構符合辭典詞彙之構詞結構，因此我們認為該「候選中文遺留字詞」較可能為未知詞，而非「不是詞彙的中文字串」。

為了利用詞性序列規則去篩選「候選中文遺留字詞」，首先需建立詞性序列規則表。建立詞性序列規則表後，我們利用詞性序列規則的出現次數作為門檻值，並利用通過門檻值的詞性序列規則對「候選中文遺留字詞」進行篩選。

斷詞系統遇到未知詞時會將未知詞斷成幾個較小的單位。我們藉由去除辭典的部分詞彙的方式，將這些詞彙當作未知詞，所以這些詞彙經過斷詞處理後會被斷成幾個較小的單位。本研究把由這幾個較小的單位所構成的詞彙組合稱為「未知詞候選詞彙組合」。比方說我們將「房地產」由辭典中去除，使其成為未知詞。而「房地產」經過斷詞後被斷成「房地」、「產」兩個小單位，由「房地」、「產」所構成的詞彙組合「房地　產」即為「未知詞候選詞彙組合」。

我們透過下頁圖六之各個步驟來建立詞性序列規則表。在圖六中步驟 1，我們將 N 取 10，把辭典切割成十等份。以下我們對步驟 3 到 6 進行說明：在第 k 回合，我們將原始中文辭典的第 k 份去除，所以在辭典之第 k 份中的詞彙會被當成未知詞；對語料斷詞後，出現在語料中之第 k 份中的詞彙會被斷成「未知詞候選詞彙組合」。在步驟 5，本研究利用史丹佛剖析器[4]對語料標注詞性，而標注時所使用的字典模型為 xinhuaFactored.ser.gz。在標注詞性後，語料中的「未知詞候選詞彙組合」之詞性序列規則即為該詞彙之詞性序列規則。例如「房地　產」經過詞性標注後變為「房地/NN　產/NN」，則「房地產」之詞性序列規則為“NN　NN”。不過史丹佛剖析器在不同的語境下，對相同的「未知詞候選詞彙組合」可能會標注不同的詞性，如「房地　產」也可能被標注為「房地/NN　產/VV」，所以一個詞彙的詞性序列規則可能不只一種。在步驟 6 我們對各個經過詞性標注後的未知詞候選詞彙組合（如「房地/NN　產/NN」）

1. 將原始中文辭典切割成 N 等份
2. for k =1 to N
3. 　將原始中文辭典中的第 k 份去除
4. 　利用去除掉第 k 份的中文辭典對語料進行斷詞
5. 　利用史丹佛剖析器對已斷詞的語料標注詞性
6. 　從標注詞性後的語料中取得各詞彙之詞性序列規則，統計各個詞性序列規則的出現次數並記錄於R_k中
7. 合併上述$R_1, R_2, \ldots, R_N$的結果

圖六、建立詞性序列規則表的步驟

進行擷取，就取得各個詞彙之詞性序列規則；而在統計詞性序列規則時，我們將詞彙之可能的各種詞性序列規則都納入統計。最後我們將R_1到R_{10}的結果進行合併，就完成詞性序列規則表的建置。

以下我們藉圖七說明利用詞性序列規則篩選候選中文遺留字詞的整體流程。首先以長詞優先方式對候選中文遺留字詞進行斷詞，再利用史丹佛剖析器標注詞性，就可取得各個候選中文遺留字詞之詞性序列規則；若以「前鋒報」為例，因為「前鋒報」經過斷詞、標注詞性後變成「前鋒/NN　報/NN」，所以「前鋒報」之詞性序列規則為「NN　NN」。之後我們透過詞性序列規則表中大於或等於門檻值（詞性序列規則的出現次數）的各個詞性序列規則（圖中紅色斜體標示的規則）進行篩選，將詞性標記、空白去除就得到通過篩選之候選中文遺留字詞；例如透過詞性序列規則表中的詞性序列規則「VV　NN　NN」篩選出「淘/VV　寶/NN　網/NN」、「治/VV　區/NN　主席/NN」之後，將詞性標記、空白去除就會得到「淘寶網」、「治區主席」這兩個候選中文遺留字詞。最後我們將通過篩選之候選中文遺留字詞視為未知詞，將其加入至中文辭典模組。

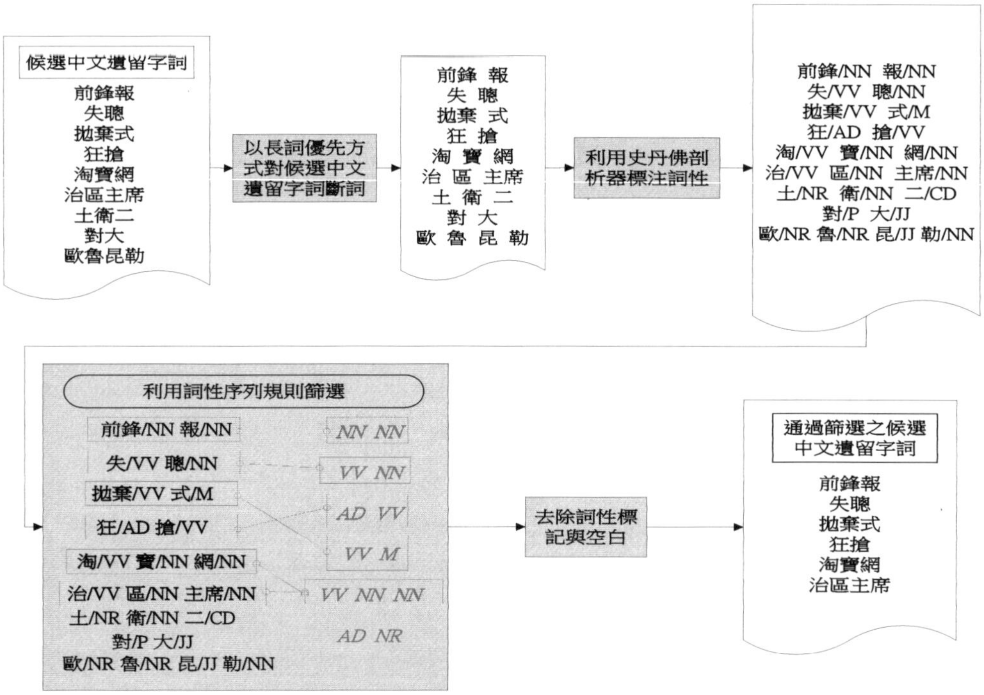

圖七、利用詞性序列規則篩選候選中文遺留字詞之範例

5. 實驗結果與分析

5.1 實驗語料來源

本研究使用的實驗語料皆為中英平行語料，而我們根據中英平行語料之中文語料是繁體或簡體中文將語料分為兩大類；繁體中文的部分有科學人雜誌中英對照電子書（以下簡稱科學人）以及新聞語料，簡體中文的部分則是有 C300、C220 與廣播會話(BroadCast Conversation)語料，實驗語料句數統計如表四所示，而以下將對上述提到的語料的來源及我們對語料所做的處理進行說明。

表四、實驗語料句數統計

語料	句數
科學人	63256
新聞語料	54002
C300	296748
C220	222250
廣播會話語料	24351

田侃文[3]使用英漢文句對列技術，將科學人之 1745 篇文章轉換成 63256 句中英平行句對，而我們沿用這 63256 句句對進行實驗。我們將自由時報中英對照讀新聞、雙語網站知識管理平台新聞、美國之音雙語新聞及聯合新聞網中英對照新聞這四種英漢雙語語料，利用英漢文句對列技術[3]轉換成中英平行句對後進行合併，就得到新聞語料。

Tseng等人[25]於Patent Machine Translation Task at the NTCIR-9[22]（以下簡稱NTCIR-9 PatentMT）時對 100 萬句專利平行語料進行前處理後得到了兩種英漢雙語訓練語料C300[2]、C220，而我們直接沿用這兩種語料進行實驗。我們從所購買的Linguistic Data Consortium之GALE Phase 1 Chinese Broadcast Conversation Parallel Text - Part 1 語料、Part 2 語料的檔案中擷取中英平行句對，並將短句(長度小於 6 之句子)、重複的句對及句中特殊符號去除。最後將GALE Phase 1 Chinese Broadcast Conversation Parallel Text - Part 1 、Part 2 語料之中英平行句對（已去除重複句對、短句）進行合併後就得到廣播會話語料。

5.2 擷取中英詞對與未知詞之實驗

在本實驗中我們從科學人、新聞語料、廣播會話語料、C300、C220 這五種語料中擷取中英詞對、未知詞，並評估其效果。首先我們從各語料中擷取候選中英遺留詞對、候選中文遺留字詞，而所擷取出的候選中英遺留詞對、候選中文遺留字詞之數量如表五所示。

我們透過可能性比例與共現頻率對候選中英遺留詞對進行篩選，並利用人工的方式去檢測以不同的共現頻率作為門檻值所篩選出的結果：在科學人、新聞語料、廣播會話語料的部分，我們對篩選出的所有候選中英遺留詞對都進行人工檢測，但在 C300、C220 的部分，因為篩選出的共現頻率為 2、共現頻率為 1 的詞對數量皆在數千以上，所以對於共現頻率為 2、共現頻率為 1 的候選中英遺留詞對，我們從每 100 名中取前 50 名進行檢測。我們以詞性序列規則的出現次數作為門檻值來取得不同的詞性序列規則，再透過所取得之各個詞性序列規則對候選中文遺留字詞進行篩選。之後對於所有被篩選出的候選中文遺留字詞，我們以人工的方式檢測其是否為未知詞。在結果評估上，則使用標準定義的

表五、候選中文遺留字詞、候選中英遺留詞對數量統計

語料名稱	候選中英遺留詞對數量	候選中文遺留字詞數量
科學人	5410	2484
新聞語料	3502	2475
廣播會話語料	831	356
C300	9326	4619
C220	7798	3469

[2] 雖然在[25]中並沒有記錄對 C1140 的進一步處理，但 Tseng 等人得到 C1140 後還有對 C1140 進行篩選，再利用篩選完的語料進行實驗。而 C1140 經篩選後約剩 30 萬句，故本研究以 C300 代替 C1140。

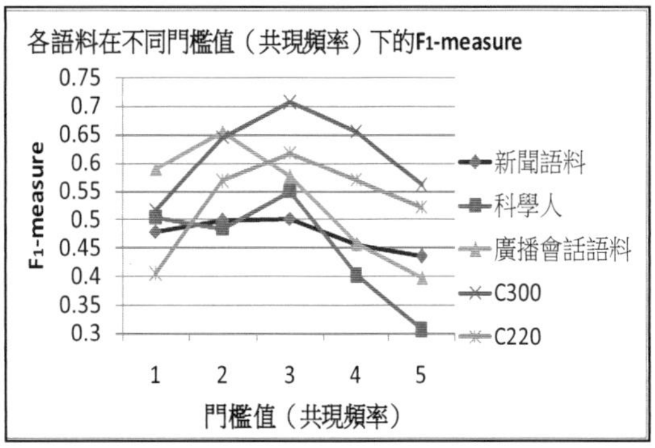

圖八、不同門檻值(共現頻率)下所得的 F_1-measure

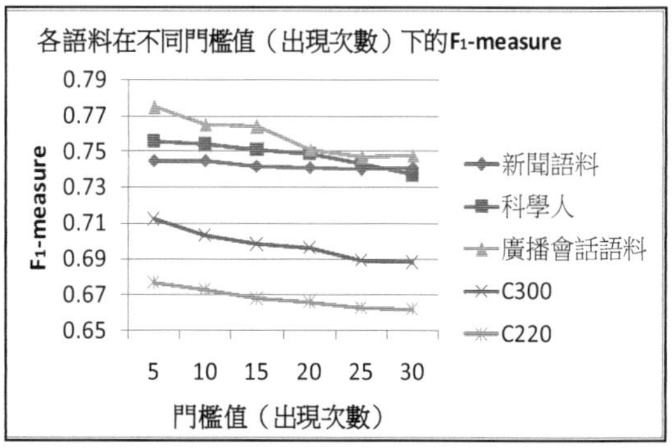

圖九、不同門檻值(出現次數)下所得的 F_1-measure

精確率（Precision）、召回率（Recall）、F_1-measure 這三個指標進行評估。

圖八是以不同門檻值去對各實驗語料之候選中英遺留詞對進行篩選所得的 F_1-measure。如圖八所示，在新聞語料、科學人、C300、C220 部分，F_1-measure 最高的都是門檻值為 3 之結果，故我們分別把這四種語料之以門檻值為 3 所篩選出的結果加入至英漢辭典模組。在廣播會話語料部分，F_1-measure 最高的是門檻值為 2 之結果，所以我們把以門檻值為 2 所篩選出的結果加入至英漢辭典模組。

圖九是以不同門檻值去對各實驗語料之候選中文遺留字詞進行篩選所得的 F_1-measure。如圖九所示，在新聞語料的部分，門檻值為 5 或 10 時有相同的F_1-measure。而門檻值為 5 之結果的召回率為 0.915，門檻值為 10 之結果的召回率為 0.907。因為我們希望取得較多正確候選中文遺留字詞，所以我們取召回率較高的門檻值為 5 之結果，並把以門檻值為 5 所篩選出的結果加入至中文辭典模組。在科學人、廣播會話語料、C300、C220 部分，F_1-measure 最高的是門檻值為 5 之結果，故我們分別把這四種語料之以門檻值為 5 所篩選出的結果加入至中文辭典模組。

5.3 以人工斷詞測試語料評估斷詞效能之實驗

5.3.1 實驗流程設計

我們將於本實驗中使用科學文章類型的科學人、新聞文章類型的新聞語料、會話文章類型的廣播會話語料這三種不同領域的實驗語料。在本實驗，我們從實驗語料中抽取出兩百句當作測試語料，實驗語料的其餘部分提供給我們的系統去產生訓練語料。由於科學人、新聞語料、廣播會話語料的測試語料都是直接由中英平行語料中切割而來，所以我們並沒有測試語料之斷詞標準答案。因此我們對兩百句測試語料進行人工斷詞，並以人工斷詞的結果當作斷詞標準答案，以進行斷詞效能的評估。

我們不以一些網路上開放使用的有斷詞標準答案之測試語料（如由中央研究院、香港城市大學等所提供的測試語料[24]）去評估我們的系統的斷詞效能之原因是：若將科學人等實驗語料提供給我們的系統，再以所得的各個斷詞模型對網路上開放使用的測試語料進行斷詞並評估斷詞效能，則可能因為實驗語料與測試語料並非是相同領域的語料，導致得到不精確的評估結果；此外一些網路上開放使用的訓練語料（與網路上開放使用的測試語料同領域）並非是中英平行語料，故無法提供給我們的系統去得到斷詞模型。因此我們不使用網路上開放使用的有斷詞標準答案之測試語料進行斷詞效能評估。

本實驗之產生訓練語料的方式由有或沒有利用英漢翻譯的資訊去處理交集型歧異之兩種情況去與有或沒有加入未知詞及中英詞對之兩種情況進行組合，故最後有 4 種產生訓練語料的方式。訓練斷詞模型的工具則是有 LingPipe 中文斷詞器(以下簡稱為 LPS)以及史丹佛中文斷詞器(以下簡稱為 SCS)。

為了比較我們的系統與其他斷詞系統或斷詞模型間的斷詞效能差異，我們將中研院斷詞系統[2]與斷章取義斷詞系統[27]、SCS 之 Pku 及 Ctb 斷詞模型、ICTCLAS 漢語分詞系統[15]（以下簡稱 ICTCLAS）作為我們的系統之比較的對象。而除了評估我們的系統之斷詞效能外，我們在 5.3.2 節分析透過本研究提出的加入未知詞及中英詞對或利用英漢翻譯的資訊去處理交集型歧異的方法能否提升斷詞效能。此外為了評估訓練斷詞模型時加入外部辭典對斷詞效能的影響，我們將分別就訓練斷詞模型時加入辭典與未加入辭典這兩種類型去進行實驗，而在訓練斷詞模型時所加入的辭典包含了中文辭典模組中的所有辭典。

$$\text{精確率} = \frac{\text{系統斷出的正確詞數}}{\text{系統斷出的詞數}} \quad (2)$$

$$\text{召回率} = \frac{\text{系統斷出的正確詞數}}{\text{參考答案中的所有詞數}} \quad (3)$$

$$F_1\text{-measure} = \frac{2 \times \text{Precision} \times \text{Recall}}{\text{Precision} + \text{Recall}} \quad (4)$$

我們使用精確率(Precision)、召回率(Recall)、F_1-measure 這三個評估指標去評估斷詞效能，公式(2)-(4)為各指標的個別定義；而在下頁表六中的 P 代表精確率，R 代表召回率，F_1 代表 F_1-measure。

5.3.2 實驗結果與分析

下頁表六為我們的系統對不同領域語料之斷詞效能。在表六各個實驗語料的實驗數據中，我們將我們的系統之最高 F_1-measure 與其他的斷詞系統或斷詞模型中的最高 F_1-measure 用紅色粗體加斜體標示。因為從 LDC 購買的廣播會話語料有版權問題，所以我們並沒有利用中研院斷詞系統、斷章取義斷詞系統對其進行斷詞，而在表六廣播會話語料之中研院斷詞系統、斷章取義斷詞系統的結果部分我們則將其標示為「-」。

以下為我們的系統與其他斷詞系統或斷詞模型之斷詞效能比較。在表六科學人部分，我們的系統的最高 F_1-measure 為 0.855，高於 SCS 之 Pku、Ctb 斷詞模型、ICTCLAS、斷章取義斷詞系統之 F_1-measure，比斷詞效能最佳的中研院斷詞系統之 F_1-measure 低了 0.049。在新聞語料部分，我們系統的最高 F_1-measure 為 0.787，比起斷詞效能最佳的中研院斷詞系統之 F_1-measure 低了 0.1，但高於斷章取義斷詞系統之 F_1-measure。在廣播會話語料的部分，我們的系統的最高 F_1-measure 為 0.837，低於 SCS 之 Pku、Ctb 斷詞模型、ICTCLAS 之 F_1-measure，但與 Pku、Ctb 斷詞模型、ICTCLAS 的 F_1-measure 之差距皆在 0.04 以內。

由以上分析可看出，在三種實驗語料的結果中，我們的系統之最佳斷詞效能都無法優於所有的其他斷詞系統或斷詞模型之斷詞效能。但在科學人、廣播會話語料部分，我們的系統之最高 F_1-measure 與斷詞效能最佳的其他斷詞系統或斷詞模型之 F_1-measure 的差距都在 0.05 以內，且我們的系統之最高 F_1-measure 都在 0.835 以上，因此我們覺得這顯示了我們的系統能夠有一定的斷詞效能。

在表六的結果中，不論訓練斷詞模型時加入辭典或未加入辭典，在科學人、新聞語料、廣播會話語料的部分，比起沒有利用英漢翻譯資訊處理交集型歧異的結果之 F_1-measure，有利用英漢翻譯資訊處理交集型歧異的結果之 F_1-measure 皆能提升，而其中 F_1-measure 提升最多的為訓練斷詞模型時未加入辭典的情況下，新聞語料部分之利用 SCS 訓練斷詞模型，且有加入未知詞及中英詞對的結果（由 0.762 提升至 0.787）。因此我們覺得這顯示了與沒有利用英漢翻譯資訊處理交集型歧異相比，有利用英漢翻譯資訊處理交集型歧異應能夠使斷詞效能提升。

由表六數據可看出，在訓練斷詞模型時未加入辭典的情況下，在所有實驗語料的部分，比起沒有加入未知詞與中英詞對的結果之 F_1-measure，有加入未知詞與中英詞對的結果之 F_1-measure 皆能提升，其中 F_1-measure 提升最多的為新聞語料部分之利用 SCS 訓練斷詞模型，且有利用英漢翻譯資訊處理交集型歧

表六、不同領域語料之斷詞效能

訓練斷詞模型時未加入辭典											
訓練工具	加入未知詞與中英詞對	利用英漢翻譯資訊處理交集型歧異	廣播會話語料			科學人			新聞語料		
			P	R	F_1	P	R	F_1	P	R	F_1
LPS	沒有	沒有	0.776	0.809	0.792	0.793	0.834	0.813	0.724	0.801	0.761
		有	0.788	0.818	0.803	0.806	0.843	0.824	0.727	0.803	0.763
	有	沒有	0.778	0.810	0.794	0.797	0.834	0.815	0.732	0.801	0.765
		有	0.792	0.820	0.806	0.815	0.847	0.831	0.737	0.803	0.769
SCS	沒有	沒有	0.792	0.827	0.809	0.762	0.897	0.824	0.679	0.863	0.760
		有	0.808	0.842	0.825	0.781	0.909	0.840	0.689	0.871	0.769
	有	沒有	0.801	0.832	0.816	0.778	0.906	0.837	0.681	0.864	0.762
		有	0.812	0.843	0.827	0.799	0.919	*0.855*	0.710	0.883	*0.787*
訓練斷詞模型時加入辭典											
訓練工具	加入未知詞與中英詞對	利用英漢翻譯資訊處理交集型歧異	廣播會話語料			科學人			新聞語料		
			P	R	F_1	P	R	F_1	P	R	F_1
LPS	沒有	沒有	0.819	0.791	0.805	0.792	0.805	0.798	0.742	0.786	0.764
		有	0.834	0.805	0.820	0.820	0.828	0.824	0.749	0.793	0.770
	有	沒有	0.818	0.790	0.804	0.797	0.805	0.801	0.753	0.784	0.768
		有	0.836	0.806	0.821	0.819	0.822	0.820	0.762	0.794	0.778
SCS	沒有	沒有	0.802	0.832	0.817	0.772	0.818	0.794	0.681	0.863	0.762
		有	0.823	0.851	*0.837*	0.792	0.834	0.812	0.688	0.870	0.768
	有	沒有	0.796	0.826	0.811	0.784	0.822	0.802	0.682	0.864	0.763
		有	0.819	0.845	0.832	0.790	0.830	0.810	0.705	0.880	0.783
其他斷詞系統或斷詞模型			廣播會話語料			科學人			新聞語料		
			P	R	F_1	P	R	F_1	P	R	F_1
中研院斷詞系統			–	–	–	0.878	0.932	*0.904*	0.854	0.923	*0.887*
斷章取義斷詞系統			–	–	–	0.754	0.739	0.746	0.743	0.753	0.748
SCS 之 Pku 斷詞模型			0.870	0.884	*0.877*	0.839	0.867	0.852	0.815	0.853	0.834
SCS 之 Ctb 斷詞模型			0.846	0.869	0.857	0.827	0.868	0.847	0.832	0.878	0.855
ICTCLAS			0.849	0.887	0.868	0.785	0.841	0.812	0.758	0.848	0.801

異的結果（由 0.769 提升至 0.787）。因此我們覺得這顯示了在訓練斷詞模型時未加入辭典的情況下，有加入未知詞與中英詞對應可提升斷詞效能。但在訓練斷詞模型時加入辭典的情況下，並不是所有的有加入未知詞與中英詞對的結果之 F_1-measure 皆高於沒有加入未知詞與中英詞對的結果之 F_1-measure。

以下藉由表六數據來比較訓練斷詞模型時加入辭典與未加入辭典的情況下，我們的系統對不同領域語料進行斷詞之斷詞效能。在新聞語料、廣播會話語料的部分，並不是所有訓練斷詞模型時加入辭典的結果之 F_1-measure 都可優於未加入辭典的結果之 F_1-measure。而在科學人的部分，則是所有訓練斷詞模型時加入辭典的結果之 F_1-measure 皆無法優於未加入辭典的結果之 F_1-measure。綜合以上可看出，訓練斷詞模型時加入辭典的結果不一定能夠比未加入辭典的結果有更好的斷詞效能。

5.4 以漢英翻譯的翻譯品質評估斷詞效能之實驗

在進行漢英機器翻譯時，需要先對中文語料進行斷詞才能進行後續處理，所以中文斷詞效能的好壞可能會影響到最後的翻譯品質。因此我們假設在大多數的情形下利用斷詞效能較佳的系統所斷出的中文訓練語料進行翻譯模型訓練，能夠有較好的漢英翻譯之翻譯品質，以利用漢英翻譯之翻譯品質的好壞去間接地評估我們的系統的斷詞效能。

5.4.1 實驗流程設計

我們於本實驗中使用不同領域之中英平行語料進行實驗，而所使用的實驗語料有：科學文章類型的 C220、C300、科學人與新聞文章類型的新聞語料以及會話文章類型的廣播會話語料。由於 NTCIR-9 PatentMT 並未提供測試語料的正確答案，所以我們以 NTCIR-9 PatentMT 提供的有正確答案之 2000 句優化資料（tuning data）作為 C300、C220 之測試語料。對科學人、新聞語料、廣播會話語料這三種語料，我們從語料中切割出 2000 句作為測試語料，其餘的部分則作為訓練翻譯模型之訓練語料。

本研究透過統計式機器翻譯系統「Moses」[19]去進行實驗。我們將用來訓練翻譯模型之中英平行語料稱為英漢訓練語料，以跟我們的系統所產生的中文訓練語料作區別。而實驗的流程大略為：首先我們將英漢訓練語料提供給我們的系統來得到各個斷詞模型；之後，我們使用所得到的各個斷詞模型對測試語料、英漢訓練語料之中文句進行斷詞。最後將英漢訓練語料之英文句、英漢訓練語料之已斷詞中文句提供給 Moses 進行翻譯模型訓練，將測試語料之已斷詞中文句提供給所得到的翻譯模型進行翻譯。

在 5.4.2 節我們將 SCS 之 Pku 斷詞模型、Ctb 斷詞模型及 ICTCLAS 作為我們的系統之斷詞效能比較對象。在 C300、 C220 的部分，我們另外將 Tseng 等在 NTCIR-9 PatentMT 利用優化資料進行評估所得之 BLEU 分數最高的結果（在 C300 的部分 BLEU 分數最高的為 Z16，在 C220 的部分 BLEU 分數最高的為 Z18*）作為我們的系統之比較對象。在翻譯結果的評估上，則使用 BLEU 和 NIST 這兩個指標進行評估。

5.4.2 實驗結果與分析

表七、下頁表八分別為 C300、C220 與科學人、新聞語料、廣播會話語料之漢英翻譯實驗結果；在表七，我們將我們的系統之最高 BLEU 分數與 Z16、Z18*的 BLEU 分數用紅色粗體加斜體標示；在表八，則將我們的系統之最高 BLEU 分數與其他斷詞系統或斷詞模型中的最高 BLEU 分數用紅色粗體加斜體標示。

以下我們透過漢英翻譯的品質去間接地評估我們的系統之斷詞效能。在表七中 C300 的實驗結果部分，我們的系統之最高 BLEU 分數，高於 ICTCLAS 之 BLEU 分數，但比同樣是利用 C300 作為訓練語料

表七、C300、C220 之漢英翻譯實驗結果

訓練斷詞模型時未加入辭典						
訓練工具	加入未知詞與中英詞對	利用英漢翻譯資訊處理交集型歧異	C300		C220	
			NIST	BLEU	NIST	BLEU
LPS	沒有	沒有	7.3614	0.2371	7.5545	0.2521
		有	7.4188	***0.2398***	7.5927	0.2541
	有	沒有	7.3496	0.2375	7.5195	0.2498
		有	7.3985	0.2393	7.5962	***0.2541***
SCS	沒有	沒有	7.1789	0.2310	7.4979	0.2496
		有	7.2094	0.2304	7.4834	0.2486
	有	沒有	7.3080	0.2357	7.4267	0.2455
		有	7.1315	0.2289	7.4922	0.2498
其他斷詞系統、Z18*、Z16			C300		C220	
			NIST	BLEU	NIST	BLEU
ICTCLAS			7.3104	0.2350	7.5012	0.2527
Z18*			—	—	7.6120	***0.2604***
Z16			7.3778	***0.2407***	—	—

表八、科學人、新聞語料、廣播會話語料之漢英翻譯實驗結果

訓練斷詞模型時未加入辭典								
訓練工具	加入未知詞與中英詞對	利用英漢翻譯資訊處理交集型歧異	科學人		新聞語料		廣播會話語料	
			NIST	BLEU	NIST	BLEU	NIST	BLEU
LPS	沒有	沒有	4.1036	0.0746	3.9775	0.0717	3.7987	0.0994
		有	4.1178	0.0770	3.9836	*0.0719*	3.8622	0.1024
	有	沒有	4.0959	0.0764	3.9385	0.0697	3.7938	0.1002
		有	4.1494	0.0778	3.9588	0.0695	3.8495	0.1014
SCS	沒有	沒有	3.8661	0.0692	3.8752	0.0685	3.8250	0.1020
		有	4.1493	*0.0793*	3.9331	0.0704	3.8611	*0.1035*
	有	沒有	4.1230	0.0775	3.8653	0.0672	3.8012	0.1017
		有	4.1582	0.0772	3.9689	0.0695	3.8306	0.1025
其他斷詞系統或斷詞模型			科學人		新聞語料		廣播會話語料	
			NIST	BLEU	NIST	BLEU	NIST	BLEU
SCS 之 Pku 斷詞模型			4.2462	0.0806	4.1131	0.0720	3.9019	0.1001
SCS 之 Ctb 斷詞模型			3.8329	0.0651	4.1411	*0.0738*	3.9263	0.1005
ICTCLAS			4.1883	*0.0813*	4.0367	0.0733	3.9316	*0.1067*

的 Z16 之 BLEU 分數低了 0.0009；在 C220 的實驗結果部分，我們的系統之最高 BLEU 分數，高於 ICTCLAS 之 BLEU 分數，但比同樣是利用 C220 作為訓練語料的 Z18*之 BLEU 分數低了 0.0063。由表八的數據可看出，在科學人的部分，我們的系統之最高 BLEU 分數，比 ICTCLAS 的 BLEU 分數低了 0.002，但比 SCS 之 Ctb 斷詞模型的 BLEU 分數高了 0.0142。在新聞語料的部分，我們的系統之最高 BLEU 分數，比起 SCS 之 Ctb 斷詞模型的 BLEU 分數低了 0.0019。在廣播會話語料的部分，我們的系統之最高 BLEU 分數，比 ICTCLAS 斷詞器之 BLEU 分數低了 0.0032，但比 SCS 之各個斷詞模型之 BLEU 分數皆高出 0.003 左右。

由以上分析可看出，在科學文章類型之科學人、C300 與新聞文章類型之新聞語料與會話文章類型之廣播會話語料的部分，我們的系統之最佳翻譯品質都略差於其他斷詞系統或斷詞模型中的最佳翻譯品質，而在 C300 的部分，我們的系統之最高 BLEU 分數跟其他斷詞系統或斷詞模型中的最高 BLEU 分數之差距只有 0.0009。所以我們覺得這間接顯示了我們的系統可以有一定的斷詞效能。

6. 結論

在本篇論文中，我們建立一個透過以下程序來提供中文斷詞服務的系統：首先透過查詢中文辭典的方式來產生中英平行語料之所有中文句的各種斷詞組合，並利用英漢翻譯的資訊將錯誤斷詞組合去除，藉以產生訓練語料；最後再將所產生的訓練語料提供給開放軟體去訓練斷詞模型，以建構中文斷詞服務。

在以人工斷詞測試語料評估斷詞效能之實驗中，本研究針對科學文章類型之科學人、新聞文章類型之新聞語料、會話文章類型之廣播會話語料這三種不同領域之語料進行實驗。在科學人、廣播會話語料部分，我們的系統之最高 F_1-measure 與斷詞效能最佳的其他斷詞系統或斷詞模型之 F_1-measure 的差距都在 0.05 以內，且我們的系統之最高的 F_1-measure 都在 0.835 以上。因此我們覺得這顯示了我們的系統能夠有一定的斷詞效能。另外由實驗結果可發現，訓練斷詞模型時未加入辭典的情況下，有利用英漢翻譯資訊處理交集型歧異或有加入未知詞與中英詞對的結果之斷詞效能都能提升。而在訓練斷詞模型時加入辭典的情況下，加入未知詞與中英詞對的結果之斷詞效能並沒有都優於未加入未知詞與中英詞對的結果之斷詞效能。此外實驗結果顯示訓練斷詞模型時加入辭典不一定能夠提升斷詞效能。

本研究另外進行了以漢英翻譯的翻譯品質評估斷詞效能之實驗，藉由翻譯品質去間接地評估我們的系統的斷詞效能。由實驗結果可看出，在四種實驗語料的結果中，我們的系統之最佳翻譯品質都略差於其他斷詞系統或斷詞模型中的最佳翻譯品質，我們覺得這間接顯示了我們的系統可有一定的斷詞效能。

致謝

本研究承蒙國科會研究計畫 NSC-100-2221-E-004-014 的部份補助，謹此致謝。我們感謝評審對於本文的各項指正與指導，限於篇幅因此不能在本文中全面交代相關細節。

參考文獻

[1] 牛津現代英漢雙解詞典，http://startdict.sourceforge.net/Dictionaries_zh_TW.php [連結已失效]。

[2] 中央研究院中文斷詞系統，http://ckipsvr.iis.sinica.edu.tw/ [2011/11/2]。

[3] 田侃文，*英漢專利文書文句對列與應用*，國立政治大學資訊科學所，碩士論文，2009。

[4] 史丹佛剖析器，http://nlp.stanford.edu/software/lex-parser.shtml [2012/2/26]。

[5] 林筱晴，*語料庫統計值與網際網路統計值在自然語言處理上之應用：以中文斷詞為例*，國立臺灣大學資訊工程學研究所，碩士論文，2004。

[6] 莊怡軒，*英文技術文獻中動詞與其受詞之中文翻譯的語境效用*，國立政治大學資訊科學所，碩士論文，2011。

[7] 現代漢語一詞泛讀，http://elearning.ling.sinica.edu.tw/introduction.html [2011/8/26]。

[8] 國家教育研究院學術名詞資訊網，http://terms.nict.gov.tw/download_main.php [2011/8/26]。

[9] 構詞篇（下），http://chcs-opencourse.org/chcs/full_content/A21/pdf/03.pdf [2012/2/27]。

[10] Keh-Jiann Chen and Shing-Huan Liu, Word Identification for Mandarin Chinese Sentences, *Proceedings of the 15th International Conference on Computational Linguistics*, 101-107, 1992.

[11] Keh-Jiann Chen and Ming-Hong Bai, Unknown Word Detection for Chinese by a Corpus-based Learning Method, *International Journal of Computational linguistics and Chinese Language Processing*, Vol. 3, Num. 1, 27-44, 1998.

[12] Keh-Jiann Chen and Wei-Yun Ma, Unknown Word Extraction for Chinese Documents, *Proceedings of the 19th International Conference on Computational Linguistics*, 169-175, 2002.

[13] Dr.eye譯典通字典, http://www.dreye.com/ [2011/8/26].

[14] E-HowNet, http://ckip.iis.sinica.edu.tw/taxonomy/taxonomy-doc.htm [2011/8/26].

[15] ICTCLAS漢語分詞系統, http://ictclas.org/ [2012/7/1].

[16] Wenbin Jiang, Liang Huang, Qun Liu, and Yajuan Lü, A Cascaded Linear Model for Joint Chinese Word Segmentation and Part-of-Speech Tagging, *Proceedings of 46th Annual Meeting on Association for Computational Linguistics: HLT*, 897-904, 2008.

[17] Mu Li, Jianfeng Gao, Changning Huang, and Jianfeng Li, Unsupervised Training for Overlapping Ambiguity Resolution in Chinese Word Segmentation, *Proceedings of the 2nd SIGHAN Workshop on Chinese Language Processing*, 1-7, 2003.

[18] LingPipe, http://alias-i.com/lingpipe/ [2011/8/26].

[19] Moses, http://www.statmt.org/moses/ [2011/12/22].

[20] C. D. Manning and Hinrich Schütze, *Foundations of Statistical Natural Language Processing*, 1999, MIT Press.

[21] PatTree 中文抽詞程式, http://www.openfoundry.org/of/projects/367/ [2012/3/16].

[22] Patent Machine Translation Task at the NTCIR-9, http://ntcir.nii.ac.jp/PatentMT/ [2012/3/11].

[23] Stanford Chinese Segmenter, http://nlp.stanford.edu/software/segmenter.shtml [2011/8/26].

[24] SIGHAN Bakeoff 2, www.sighan.org/bakeoff2005/ [2011/12/22].

[25] Yuen-Hsien Tseng, Chao-Lin Liu, Chia-Chi Tsai, Jui-Ping Wang, Yi-Hsuan Chuang, and James Jeng, Statistical approaches to patent translation - Experiments with various settings of training data, *Proceedings of the 9th NTCIR Workshop Meeting on Evaluation of Information Access Technologies: Information Retrieval, Question Answering and Cross-Lingual Information Access - PatentMT*, 661-665, 2011.

[26] Kun Wang, Chengqing Zong, and Keh-Yih Su, A Character-Based Joint Model for Chinese Word Segmentation, *Proceedings of the 23th International Conference on Computational Linguistics*, 1173-1181, 2010.

[27] Yahoo!斷章取義API, http://tw.developer.yahoo.com/cas/ [2011/11/2].

應用串接方法於連續變化轉速之四行程引擎聲音合成

Concatenation-based Method for the Synthesis of Engine Noise with Continuously Varying Speed

吳銘冠 Ming-Kuan Wu　　陳嘉平 Chia-Ping Chen
國立中山大學資訊工程系
Department of Computer Science and Engineering
National Sun Yat-Sen University
M003040056@student.nsysu.edu.tw,　cpchen@cse.nsysu.edu.tw

摘要

在本研究中，我們提出並實做一個串接式聲音合成系統，合成的標的物件是連續變化轉速之引擎聲音。我們提供一個繪圖的介面讓使用者畫出連續變化的引擎轉速曲線作為系統的輸入，然後輸出對應的引擎噪音。採用繪圖的方式，不僅能讓輸入更有彈性，也能減少輸入所需要的時間。主觀測試的實驗結果顯示，合成出來的聲音在自然度的測試上以及和原始引擎聲的相似度比較上有良好的表現。本論文所提出的方法，可以推廣到其他物理產生過程機制清楚簡單的聲音物件。此外，也可以應用到虛擬實境訓練或遊戲等等。

關鍵詞： 聲音物件合成、串接合成方法、引擎噪音合成、虛擬實境

Abstract

In this study, we propose and implement a concatenation-based audio signal synthesis system for the engine noises of continuously varying speed. A user simply draws the engine speed curve through an interface, and the corresponding audio signal is synthesized as output. This drawable interface makes the input function flexible and reduces the input time. The implemented system was evaluated with subjective tests. Overall, the performance was good regarding quality and similarity. The proposed method can be feasibly applied to the synthesis of any sound objects which are produced with a clear and simple physical process. Furthermore, the technology can be integrated to virtual reality, such as in training and gaming applications.

keywords: audio object synthesis, concatenation synthesis method, engine noise synthesis, virtual reality

一、緒論

(一)、研究背景、動機

聲音合成技術在人機介面裡扮演著重要的角色，目的是將聲音用人為的方式產生，其中串接式合成方式為主要的合成技術之一。此合成方法是從錄製的聲音中找出所需的合成單元，接著再做一些韻律方面的處理，之後將聲音單元串接。通常使用此方法得到的聲音自然度和品質都相當不錯。在虛擬實境(Virtual Reality, VR)的機車引擎聲或是坊間的賽車遊戲，往往用到的引擎聲都是預先錄製好的 [1]，這些錄製好的音檔，雖然品質較佳，但在錄製時往往需要大量的時間和人力，且缺乏彈性。因此在這裡提出一個手動繪圖的合成方式，來簡化輸入合成資訊的步驟，以四行程檔車的引擎聲為例，利用最短時間和最少資源，來合成上述應用程式所需要的音檔。

(二)、相關研究

1、聲音合成

在聲音合成技術裡，基週同步疊加法(Pitch Synchronous Overlap Add, PSOLA) [2]為串接式合成常用的調整動作。此方法先將波形分解成許多的基本波形，再將基本波形疊加以得到合成的聲音波形。關於基本頻率和音長的調整，可利用基本波形的重疊間隔和數目來達到，為現在常見的合成方法之一。但此方法的缺點為，在相鄰的合成單元的串接邊界上，若建立合成單元庫時採用自動作切割的話，可能會造成共振峰軌跡銜接不平順，降低合成聲音的流暢度。

除了PSOLA 的方式之外，還有語料庫為主(Corpus-based)的合成方式 [3]。其方法為先錄製大量的語料，然後在合成時根據演算法從許多候選單元中選出一組會讓合成音最為自然的組合。由於合成單元的選擇法並不會對錄製的語音作太多的信號處理動作，此外可供候選的合成單元數目很多，使得語音單元間的不連續被降低很多，因此合成音的自然度上是相當不錯的。在本文，我們簡化串接式語料庫為主的合成方式，改以引擎聲音來當作合成單元，因此可以原音重現，具有極佳的合成音質，進而合成出特定範圍的引擎聲。近年來，上述串接合成方式已應用在不少系統中且都有不錯的表現，如微軟亞洲公司之木蘭(MULAN)系統 [4]和訊飛中文語音系統。

2、引擎合成

在國外，諧波同步疊加法(Harmonic Synchronous Overlap and Add, HSOLA) [5]被使用來合成引擎噪音。此篇論文提到先採樣一個不斷變化預錄的引擎聲，然後使用諧波同步累加法的方式。該方法的目的主要是減少階段式的不連續性，使其聽起來更具有連續性。合成信號的和諧性被保留，提高了恢復原狀的音質。在其他的研究中發現到，車輛產生的聲波波形，是由兩個部份的總和所組成 [6]。第一個是由引擎旋轉部件所產生諧波相關的一連串音調，而第二個是由輪胎摩擦所產生的噪音。但在本文的引擎噪音合成裡，為了減少合成的複雜度，故不考慮輪胎摩擦所產生的噪音。

(三)、系統概述及研究方向

本文的研究重點是嘗試以繪圖的方式輸入所需要的資訊，希望能減少輸入資訊所需要的時間。也希望能更有彈性的，在特定轉速範圍間，能夠合成出想要的轉速音檔，本文中的轉速皆以每一分鐘的轉速(rpm)為單位。在此篇論文中，因為採用串接的方式，合成出來的聲音在音色的自然度上有不錯的表現。圖1為系統概述圖，一開始可以選擇兩種使用者介面來輸入所需要的資訊，分別是以文字的方式或是以繪圖的方式輸入資訊。文字輸入的資訊包括開始時轉速、結束時轉速和合成時間。繪圖輸入的資訊包括合成時間以及繪圖的曲線。採用繪圖輸入資訊的方式能更有彈性且快速的產生欲合成的音檔。

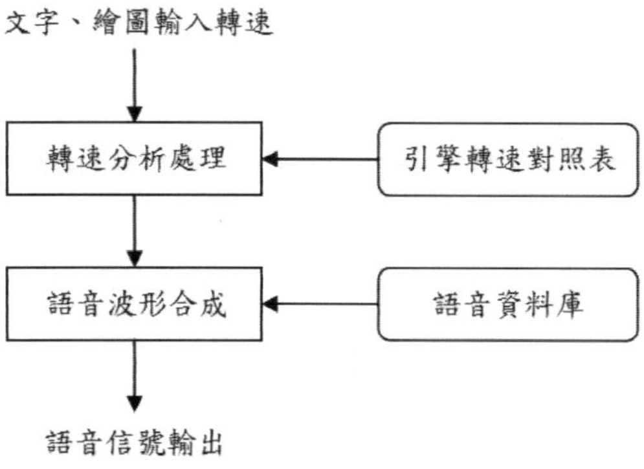

圖 1、 輸入轉速資訊和信號輸出系統架構圖

(四)、四行程引擎簡介

四行程引擎(Four Stoke Engine)完成一次循環，必須經過「吸入、壓縮、點火、排氣」四個步驟 [7]，其運作的程序分別是：

◇ 吸入行程：活塞往下，進氣閥打開，將空氣與燃料的混合氣吸入汽缸中。
◇ 壓縮行程：進氣閥關閉且活塞往上，壓縮此混合氣使體積變小。
◇ 點火行程：在壓縮的混合氣中點火，使氣體燃燒爆發並推動活塞往外作用。
◇ 排氣行程：此時排氣閥打開且活塞再度往上，將燃燒後之廢氣排出汽缸。

根據以上四個行程，可以發現到當完成一個循環時，引擎轉了兩次。

二、合成單元收集

由於引擎聲的轉速在時域上主要為遞增或遞減的連續性變化，故在錄製音檔時，盡可能的收錄大量的連續遞增或遞減音檔。在這一節裡主要是說明音檔的錄製、分析和合成單元產生的過程。

(一)、音檔錄製

本文所收錄的音檔為野狼125 檔車的引擎聲，音檔共分為兩個部份。第一個部份為一個長達3 分鐘左右遞增的引擎轉速音檔，將它令為*SetA* ；第二個部份為評測時所需要合成的測試音檔，將它令為*SetB* 。*SetA* 錄製的方式為，採用人為的方式來線性增加油閥的大小，以達到線性成長的轉速。但由於是以人為的方式來增加轉速，故很難達到線性增加轉速，所以合成單元無法依照線性的時間來做切割，故我們將在之後的章節來解決這個問題。*SetB* 為2 到16 秒共10 個不同轉速範圍的音檔，且轉速的變化為人為隨機產生。轉速的範圍介於1000 轉到3000 轉之間，其轉速變化與時間資訊如表1 所示。

編號	轉速範圍	秒數範圍
1	1000-2700	(0)-(16)
2	1160-2990-1530-2379-1250	(0)-(1.8)-(2.7)-(4.1)-(6.6)
3	1235-2783-1585	(0)-(3.4)-(8.8)
4	1454-1520-2961-2259	(0)-(3)-(3.8)-(4.1)
5	1030-2852-1113-2213-1208 -2786-1123-2570-1213-2790 -1206-2208-1310-2785-1630	(0)-(0.2)-(0.8)-(1.3)-(1.5)-(2.2) -(2.7)-(3.1)-(3.4)-(3.9)-(4.5) -(4.8)-(5.1)-(5.6)-(6)
6	1651-2772-1498	(0)-(1.6)-(5.8)
7	1635-1635-2901-1954	(0)-(1.5)-(1.9)-(2.6)
8	1628-1736-2493-1978	(0)-(2.3)-(3.5)-(4.3)
9	1972-1972	(0)-(2.1)
10	1111-2706	(0)-(2.7)

表 1、 *SetB* 音檔概要資訊

(二)、音檔分析

若將引擎的聲音以waveform 的形式表示，會發現到聲音的變換是非常具有規律性的。將此音檔改以在頻譜上顯示，更容易發現其規律性的變化，因此我們著重於頻譜的部份。圖2 為*SetA* 音檔其中一段引擎聲音的片段，所產生的waveform 和所對映的頻譜圖。

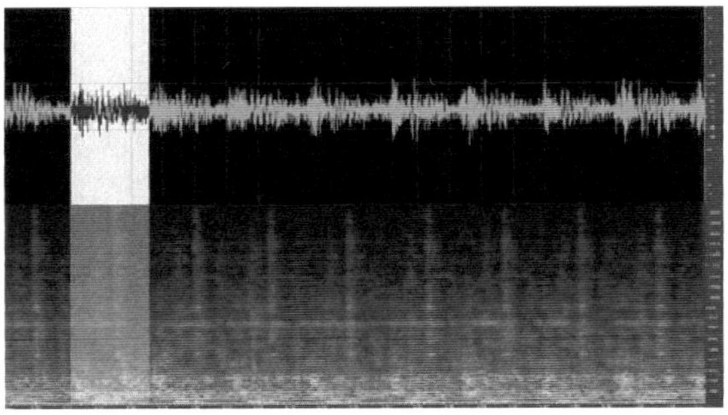

圖 2、 上半部為SetA 其中一片段的waveform ，下半部為其對映的頻譜圖。

根據之前四行程的引擎運作原理，我們發現到完成一次循環，引擎共轉了兩次。且此一循環也是引擎聲變換的一個週期，故我們可以根據此訊息來計算引擎的轉速。也就是說我們只需要計算一個週期當下的sample 數，就可以得知其當下的轉速，轉速的計算公式如下：

$$\text{cycle per minute} = \frac{\text{sample rate}}{\text{sample in the cycle}} * 2 * 60, \qquad (1)$$

其中，在本文裡的sample rate 為44100Hz ，cyclesamples 為一個合成單元的sample 數，cycle per minute 為此合成單元每一分鐘的轉速。

(三)、合成單元的產生

根據轉速計算公式，找出$SetA$ 音檔1000 轉到3000 轉的範圍，並以overlap 的方式切成2000 個一秒左右的片段。但為了方便起見，我們將其編號為1000 至3000 並且只選取以10 為單位的編號，共201 個片段。

接著將這些片段做頻譜的擷取來分析其頻率，如圖3(b) 所示。根據matlab 頻譜圖的色度表，能量大到能量小顏色的變化為紅色到藍色，其中引擎聲的能量都集中於黃色和紅色。黃色的色度值為-25 ，故我們將色度大於-25 的部份設為1 ，小於-25 部份設為0 。然後將縱軸上的值累加起來，重新產生一個根據能量分佈的曲線圖，如圖3(c) 所示。

之後，再根據此圖以人為的方式找出橫軸的切值。判斷的規則分別為要能切出最多週期，並且要能接近最大峰值。將大於此值以上的部份保留，小於此值的部份設為0 。並重新繪製出多個錐狀的圖，如圖3(d) 所示。

接著將每個錐狀體一開始非零的部分標記起來，最後將相鄰錐狀體標記的值相減，就可以得出此一編號多個合成單元。

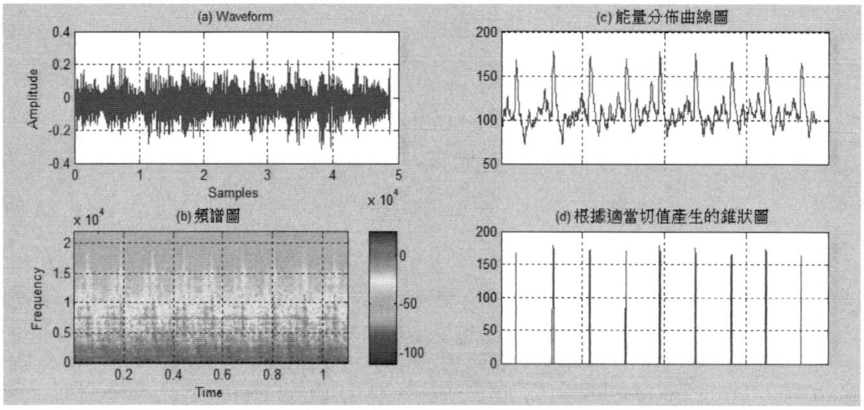

圖 3、 編號1000 的音檔片段所產生的waveform(a)，頻譜圖(b)，經由色度表重繪的能量分布曲線圖(c)，根據適當切值重新繪製的錐狀圖(d)。

經由以上的方法共切出2015 個合成單元。但根據轉速計算公式，因為重複的關係，只產生260 個不同轉速的合成單元。令其轉速為$U = \{u_i | i = 1, ..., 260\}$ 。接者，我們令V為欲找的轉速，如下式所示：

$$V = \{v_j | 1000 + (j-1) * 10, \quad j = 1, ..., 201\}, \tag{2}$$

之後再根據$|v_j - U|, \ j = 1, ..., 201$ 取差值最小的u_i 來代替v_j 。部分對映如表2 所示。且其轉速與sample 數的關係為近似一個如圖4 的反曲線。

表 2、 編號1 至編號10 的轉速對照表

編號	欲找轉速(V)	近似轉速(U)	編號	欲找轉速(V)	近似轉速(U)	...
1	1000	1003	6	1050	1048	...
2	1010	1008	7	1060	1058	...
3	1020	1022	8	1070	1069	...
4	1030	1032	9	1080	1080	...
5	1040	1042	10	1090	1091	...

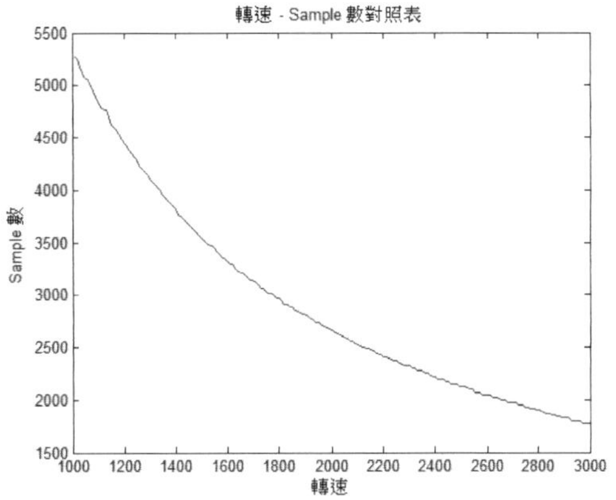

圖 4、 轉速與sample數關係圖。

三、系統架構

(一)、環境及介面

本文的引擎聲合成系統建構在matlab 環境中，其中有兩個使用者介面。第一個使用者介面為文字輸入介面，可以產生遞增或是遞減的合成引擎聲，如圖5 所示。第二個使用者介面為繪圖合成介面。當輸入完所要產生音訊的秒數時，會自動產生一個畫布，以供使用者來繪製引擎的轉速資訊。其中轉速的範圍介於1000 轉到3000 轉之間，如圖6 所示。

(二)、合成方式

在文字輸入介面，根據使用者輸入的開始轉速、結束轉速和時間來獲得合成所需要的資訊，接著我們將對應的轉速合成單元平均分配到適當的轉速範圍，分配方式如下：

◇ 若在時間內轉速變化大的話，則平均適當的挑選合成單元；
◇ 若在時間內變化小的話，則平均適當的重複挑選所需的合成單元；
◇ 開始轉速 < 結束轉速則為遞增，帶入遞增演算法；
◇ 開始轉速 > 結束轉速則為遞減，反向的帶入遞增演算法；

之後將所有的轉速單元串接起來獲得一個新的合成音檔。

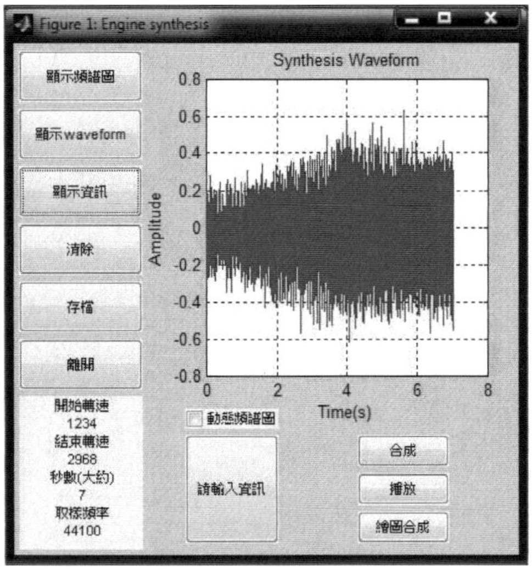

圖 5、 文字輸入介面

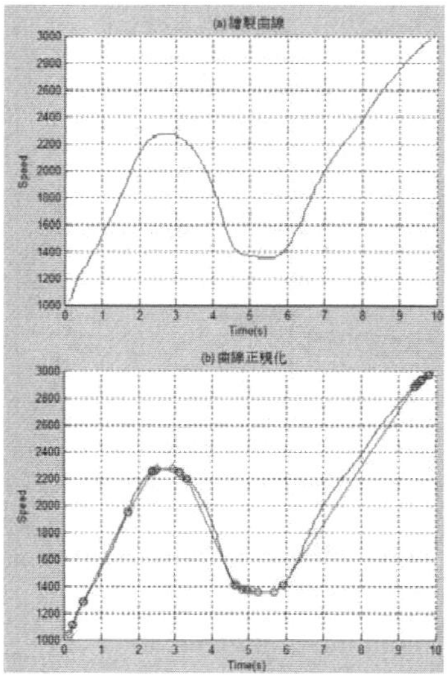

圖 6、 上半部為使用者繪製的曲線(a)，下半部將此曲線標示mark 並正規化(b)

在繪圖介面，使用者先輸入欲合成的時間資訊t 。之後會產生縱軸為轉速，橫軸為時間的繪圖介面，如圖6(a) 所示。我們令橫軸為t ，縱軸為y 。當使用者繪製完轉速曲線時，此時系統會根據以下的演算法將曲線正規化，如圖6(b) 所示。

- $t(start)$ 和$t(end)$ 標示為mark；

- 找出轉折點：
  - ◇ 若$t(i) > t(i-1)$ 且$t(i) > t(i+1)$ ，將$t(i)$ 標示為mark ；
  - ◇ 若$t(i) < t(i-1)$ 且$t(i) < t(i+1)$ ，將$t(i)$ 標示為mark ；
  - ◇ 若$t(i) > t(i-1)$ 且$t(i) = t(i+1)$ ，將$t(i)$ 標示為mark ；
  - ◇ 若$t(i) = t(i-1)$ 且$t(i) > t(i+1)$ ，將$t(i)$ 標示為mark ；
  - ◇ 若$t(i) < t(i-1)$ 且$t(i) = t(i+1)$ ，將$t(i)$ 標示為mark ；
  - ◇ 若$t(i) = t(i-1)$ 且$t(i) < t(i+1)$ ，將$t(i)$ 標示為mark ；

- 將相鄰的mark連接起來，產生欲合成的多個片段；

- 將所有片段根據文字合成的演算法串接成一個輸出音訊。

一、實驗與評測

在評測的部分主要分為聲音的自然度測試，和原始音檔的相似度測試，受測人數為10 人。在自然度測試中，根據MOS的5分評分制，每位受測者在聽完每句合成的音檔之後，隨即在聲音品質上的表現給予1 到5 分的分數。在相似度測試中，評分的規則也類似MOS 的5 分制度。但將其改成相似度的比較，評分標準如表3 所示：

分數	品質	註解	分數	品質	註解
5	優秀	聲音相當自然	5	優秀	聲音相當相似
4	很好	聲音自然	4	很好	聲音相似
3	普通	聲音品質可以接受	3	普通	聲音相似度可以接受
2	不好	聲音不自然	2	不好	聲音不相似
1	糟糕	聲音非常不自然	1	糟糕	聲音非常不相似

表 3、 左半部表格為MOS主觀評測標準表，右半部表格為相似評測標準表。

(一)、聲音自然度測試

在聲音的自然度測試上，我們根據曲線繪圖介面隨機產生8 個音檔。其時間為2 到10 秒不等，以便用來做聲音的自然度測試。8 個繪製曲線如下分類：

◇ 2 秒音檔：低轉-高轉、高轉-低轉，共兩個音檔。
◇ 5 秒音檔：低轉-高轉-低轉、高轉-低轉-高轉、低轉-低轉、高轉-高轉，共四個音檔。
◇ 10 秒音檔：多個上下起伏的轉速，共兩個音檔。

以上8 個音檔的曲線繪製和其編號如圖7 所示。

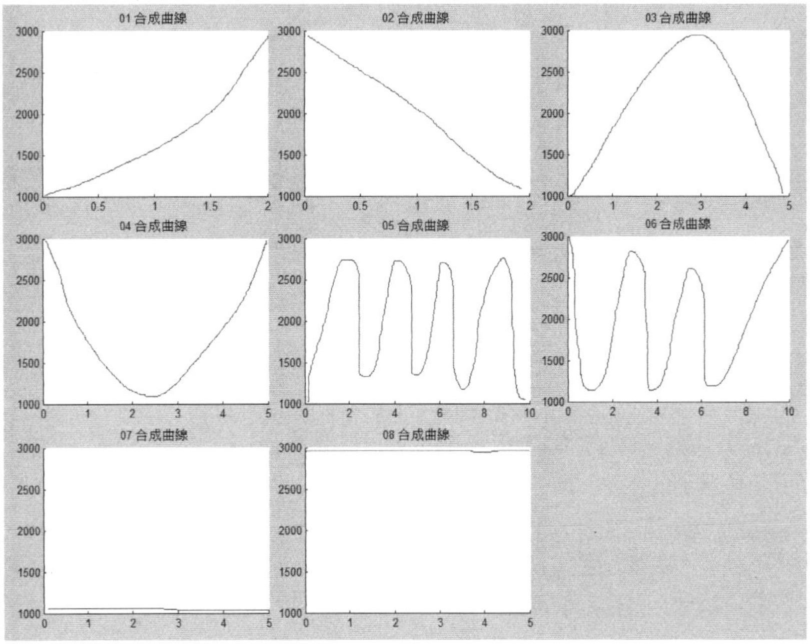

圖 7、 圖中為依序編號的曲線圖。橫軸為秒數，縱軸為引擎轉速。

(二)、聲音相似度測試

將$SetB$ 裡的10 個音檔做時間上轉速概要的分析，其資訊如表1 所示。根據這些測試音檔的資訊來產生合成的引擎聲，接著和原始的音檔做比較並且評分。

(三)、實驗結果

在自然度的測試上，我們可以發現到普遍都表現不錯，如表4 所示。但是編號7 和8 的音檔分數明顯的低落。分析其原因為，音檔7 為繪製低轉速的水平直線，音檔8 為繪製高轉速的水平直線，這將導致不明顯的轉速變化，進而使得合成的品質較為不好。在相似度的測試上，我們可以發現到分數也是不錯的，如表5 所示。但是編號7 和9 的音檔分數明顯的低落。分析其原因為，編號7 音檔前面部分的轉速變化較不明顯；編號9 音檔的轉速變化也不明顯，因而導致合成出來的品質較為不好。

編號	1	2	3	4	5	6	7	8
分數	4.7	4.3	4.1	4	3.5	4	2.8	2.7

表 4、 自然度評分

編號	1	2	3	4	5	6	7	8	9	10
分數	4	4.3	3.9	3.5	3.7	4.1	3	3.7	2.3	4.5

表 5、 相似度評分

五、結論與未來方向

本系統為基於串接式合成的引擎聲合成系統，並根據引擎轉速，且採用繪圖的方式來產生合成所需要的資訊。使用本系統能更有彈性的輸入資訊，且更能加快輸入資訊所需要的時間。在主觀實驗中，合成的聲音在自然度和原始音檔的相似度上，是令人滿意的。使用此合成系統，不只可以應用在引擎聲的合成，也可應用在在物理產生過程較為簡單的物件，例如雨聲、燒開水聲、海浪聲，甚至鼓聲等等。本系統在實作上也有幾個缺點，雖然串接式合成能有較佳的品質，但在音訊參數的調適上彈性較差。另外，使用本系統，在長時間相同轉速或者轉速變化較少的合成音檔裡，主觀評測的分數明顯較差。原因為，串接合成單元間的變化很小，導致音檔聽起來較不真實，這也是未來要克服的問題之一。在未來的方向裡，為了使合成單元能夠更為準確，在合成單元的產生部分，也可使用pitch mark 來偵測，以找出較準確的合成單元。另外，我們也可以將油門把手的資訊繪製成轉速曲線再進行合成，也就是說可以直接轉動把手來合成出想要的引擎聲，這些都是在可行的應用範圍之內。

參考文獻

[1] Carsoop, “Forza Motorsport 4: Heres how they record car engine sounds,” introduction: http://carscoop.blogspot.com/2011/06/forza-motorsport-4-heres-how-they.html, 2011.

[2] E. Moulines and F. Charpentier, "Pitch-synchronous waveform processing techniques for text-to-speech synthesis using diphones," *Speech Commun.*, vol. 9, no. 5-6, pp. 453–467, Dec. 1990.

[3] B. Ao, C. Shih, and R. Sproat, "A corpus-based Mandarin text-to-speech synthesizer," in *ICSLP'94*, 1994, pp. –1–1.

[4] M. Chu, H. Peng, Y. Zhao, Z. Niu, and E. Chang, "Microsoft mulan - a bilingual tts system," in *ICASSP 2003*, pp. 264–267.

[5] J. Jagla, J. Maillard, and N. Martin, "Sample-based engine noise synthesis using a harmonic synchronous overlap-and-add method," in *Proceedings of ICASSP 2012*, Kyoto, Japan, Mar. 2012, p. poster.

[6] Y. Ban, H. Banno, K. Takeda, and F. Itakura, "Synthesis of car noise based on a composition of engine noise and friction noise." in *ICASSP*. IEEE, 2002, pp. 2105–2108.

[7] V. Chen, "4-stroke engine," introduction: http://www.bizol.com.tw/video.aspx?cid=12, 2011.

Collaborative Annotation and Visualization of Functional and Discourse Structures

Hengbin Yan
Halliday Centre for Intelligent Applications of Language Studies,
Department of Chinese, Translation and Linguistics,
City University of Hong Kong
hbyan2@cityu.edu.hk

Jonathan Webster
Halliday Centre for Intelligent Applications of Language Studies,
Department of Chinese, Translation and Linguistics,
City University of Hong Kong
ctjjw@cityu.edu.hk

Abstract

Linguistic annotation is the process of adding additional notations to raw linguistic data for descriptive or analytical purposes. In the tagging of complex Chinese and multilingual linguistic data with a sophisticated linguistic framework, immediate visualization of the complex multi-layered functional and discourse structures is crucial for both speeding up the tagging process and reducing errors. The need for large-scale linguistically annotated corpora has made collaborative annotation increasingly essential, and existing annotation tools are inadequate to the task of providing assistance to annotators when dealing with complex linguistic structural information. In this paper we describe the design and development of a collaborative tool to extend existing annotation tools. The tool improves annotation efficiency and addresses certain difficulties in representing complex linguistic relations. Here, we adopt annotation based on Systemic Functional Linguistics and Rhetorical Structure Theory to demonstrate the effectiveness of the interface built on such infrastructure.

Keywords: Linguistic Annotation, Linguistic Visualization, Cross-domain References

1. Introduction

Recent years have witnessed an increasing need for large-scale high-quality annotated corpora on complex Chinese linguistic information where no automated annotators are available. Annotation on multi-level data complex structural relationships in such linguistic frameworks as Systemic Functional Grammar (SFG) [1] and Rhetorical Structure Theory [2] is a difficult task.

SFG investigates texts as intentional acts of meaning, organized in functional-semantic components known as "metafunctions". Three primary metafunctions, operating in parallel and each representing a layer of meaning with a set of options to language users, cover different functional aspects of human communication and expression: the *ideational*, *interpersonal* and *textual* metafunctions. For our purposes our discussion will focus on analysis and annotation of these three metafunctions in SFG.

Despite the fact that SFG is becoming increasingly influential among Chinese linguistic researchers, a large-scale, high-quality corpus annotated with SFG has yet to be developed [3]. Consequently, when trying to conduct corpus-based analysis using the SFG framework researchers must either 1) spend an enormous amount of time studying an unannotated corpus, 2) embark on the error-prone process of manually annotating a corpus on their own, or 3) rely on small corpora independently annotated by researchers which may not be particularly suited to needs of the tasks at hand.

The lack of high-quality Chinese SFG corpora is partly attributable to the lack of a competent SFG tagger capable of annotating large-scale corpora while ensuring quality. In developing such a tagger, a number of challenges need to be addressed:

1) Lack of an efficient and sophisticated storage scheme for storing such multilayered information with complex structures
2) Additional visual cues to facilitate the tagging process
3) Need for collaborative tasking (co-tasking) by different annotators

The most common method to annotate text includes the use of an open standard like XML document. Provided one possesses the prerequisite familiarity with XML conventions, the linguist-as-annotator inserts metadata most likely using a plain-text editor or generic XML editor. This method works well so long as the text is short, and the required linguistic information is relatively simple. While some special editing tools have been created which provide a graphical interface for linguists to tag texts, such tools, for the most part, tend to be stand-alone, primarily oriented to single users.

To facilitate efficient, high quality annotation of a large amount of Chinese text material by a team of co-tasking linguists, we have developed a new multi-user linguistic information annotator, which provides real-time cross-domain reference as visual "feedback", thereby assisting linguists to tag text data in a highly effective way. Multiple users can work at the same time on any portion of the text, with their annotations revealed (or selectively not) to other members as reference. Those responsible for verification, comparison, correction, and progress tracking can view the work even as it is being carried out. This design is intended to improve both the efficiency and quality of annotation, while enabling multi-user tagging of substantially greater text material in shorter time.

2. The Framework

Here, we first review existing tools for annotating texts before discussing the advantages of our new tool. We also present an application scenario of our tools for annotating text and explain how visualized cross-domain reference works.

A number of similar tools have been developed for various annotation scenarios. MMAX2 [4] is a customizable tool for creating and visualizing multilevel linguistic annotations that allows outputs the results of annotations according to predefined style-sheets. It supports tagging of part-of-speech tags, coreference and grammatical relations, but is not capable of representing and visualizing complex discourse level structures. SALTO [5] is a multilevel annotation tool for annotating semantic roles and Treebank syntactic structures. O'Donnell's annotation tool for Systemic Functional Linguistics, the UAM CorpusTool [6], is intended for annotating multi-layered Systemic Functional Grammar structures by a Single User. Both tools are restrictive in terms of functionalities and do not support collaborative annotation and provide no means of representing complex sentential structures.

Our representation model is built on the functionalities of Annotation Graph [7] and the underlying storage scheme is conceptually similar to Standoff XML format [9], but we opted for a relational database structure built with an object-oriented design for efficiency, reusability and versatility.

Several web-based annotation tools such as Serengeti [10], a tool for annotating anaphoric relations and lexical chains, are limited to a particular domain and cannot be used for annotating and visualizing complex structural information without substantial modification.

2.1 Web-based Collaborative Annotation

Traditionally, annotation processes that involve more than one annotator are often divided into multiple steps where one step is taken up and completed by one annotator before being passed on to another. This is adequate for small annotation projects where only a linear sequential procedure is involved. In recent years, however, the growing scale and complexity of annotation projects have necessitated the collaboration of different annotators who are often geographically dispersed. In view of these needs, we develop our application on a web-based infrastructure making it accessible from any web-accessible point and enabling collaborative annotation on the same data source either synchronously or asynchronously.

One problem that arises in collaborative annotation is that annotators often come with different sets of skills and have varying, sometimes overlapping responsibilities. Our goal is provide a user-friendly, intuitive interface, designed to reduce the drudgery of XML-based annotation, while enforcing annotating standards and quality functionalities for user management and versioning.

Each stage in the annotation process is divided into several hierarchically structured steps in which each parent step can spawn child steps to be taken up by one or more annotators. This gives the annotator fine-grained control over the annotating process and facilitates clear division of labor among different annotators. In addition, all annotators collaborating on the same step get notified of the relevant changes in annotation in real time once a modification has been made.

The tagger is built on a generic, multifunctional relational database similar to the annotation graph model [7] that has been demonstrated to be capable of representing virtually all sorts of common linguistic annotations. In the collaborative environment annotators can plug in certain linguistic resource that can serve as the standardized version assessable to all annotators, instead of each annotator keeping his own version, which may cause severe merging difficulties.

2.2 Representation of Complex Linguistic Structures and Relationships

The storage scheme for traditional annotation tools built using XML have been largely restrained by the inherent limitations of XML, which is suitable for storing written texts that are continuous, linear and single-layered. For non-continuous, overlapping and multi-layered linguistic information, XML-based tools typically rely on complex workarounds that unnecessarily overcomplicate the data model.

Most linguistic structures can be represented with an Annotation Graph interface. In annotating corpora with linguistic models such as Systemic Functional Grammar, where the linguistic information is structured in a multi-layered, overlapping hierarchy with references pointing to the linguistic elements, the underlying representation model must be carefully designed. The underlying data model of our platform is built on the same principles as Annotation Graph but adopts a modularized design to cover emerging use cases.

In annotating any sizable corpora, one recurring problem is representing the complex relations across various layers of linguistic elements. In this paper we have generalized common linguistic relations on three levels of linguistic elements, namely:

1) Unit Level: single linguistic elements (word, morpheme)

2) Segment Level: continuous range of linguistic elements (phrases, clauses, sentences, and paragraphs)
3) Group Level: groups of ranges of linguistic Elements (non-continuous grammatical units, i.e., clausal relations, hierarchical discourse trees in RST)

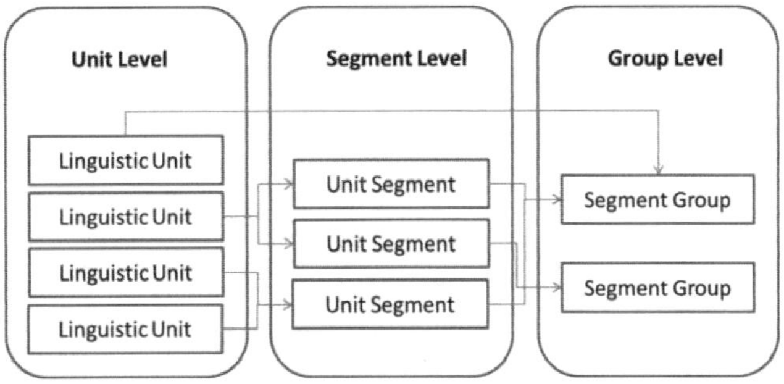

Figure 1: Three primary levels of linguistic relations.

Figure 1 illustrates a simplified abstract view of the three-level structure. At the Unit Level, the basic linguistic elements (e.g. words, morphemes) are either broken up into several separate linguistic segments, or joined together by an unlimited number of continuous units into a common segment. For example, the word *uncovered* can be made up of several morphemes (i.e., un + cover + ed), each represented by a single segment, or it can be joined together by another word (e.g. cases) to form a new segment (uncovered cases). At the Segment Level, segments (e.g. morphemes, words) can be part of a larger segment (e.g. clauses, paragraphs) in an indefinitely recursive and hierarchical manner. The Group Level is a generic structure that deals with relations among linguistic units and segments. For example, in RST there are different discourse relations (e.g. Antithesis, Condition) and roles (e.g. Nucleus, Satellite). Such relations in the data model are defined as groups, with one textual segment pointing to another and attaching a relation (function, tag, or role) to the pointed segment. Similar to segments, the number of segments in each group is unlimited and the group as a whole can in turn be pointed to by another group with an arbitrary depth of recursion and hierarchy, but unlike units in segments, the segments in each group can be non-continuous and overlapping, thus enabling any complex relations to be aptly defined.

In our application scenarios, we focus on annotating hierarchical discourse structures in RST and the three layers of metafunctions in SFG. These layers of linguistic units and the complex relations among them are represented using the proposed common structure.

In one-to-many and many-to-many relations, a sequence of ordered linguistic objects may be linked across different layers. Such interrelationships can form complex linguistic networks representing intricate linguistic meanings. Due to their inherent complexity, understanding such relationships can pose challenges to annotators, especially when such relationships are constantly added or removed in a collaborative annotating environment. The platform introduces real-time visualization of the structural relations as the annotation progresses, allowing the annotator to keep track of and make changes to annotations accordingly.

In annotating such structural relations, each unit is given a unique identifying number which we use for easy grouping of the units and to define the complex, often embedded interrelations between the units (e.g., in SFG these include logico-semantic relations such as *Parataxis* and *Hypotaxis*, *Elaboration* and *Extension* etc.).

2.3 Visualized Cross-domain Reference

While the past decade has seen significant advancement in the automatic annotation of functional structures, the automatic annotation of semantic and discourse information has been largely ignored. One difficulty has been the lack of high-quality corpora to bootstrap the automation, a time and cost extensive task that has to be done manually. In a collaborative environment, leveraging the resources of non-expert annotators can significantly boost the annotation efficiency, as has been demonstrated by recent experiments [11]. The lack of sufficient linguistic expertise, however, restrains non-expert linguistic annotators from engaging in more complex annotations. The annotation process can be significantly accelerated using assistance and reference tools such as a tag dictionary [12]. Different annotators may form different opinions on particular annotations based on their own reference to acquired linguistic knowledge. By unifying the source of such knowledge, we may be able to boost inter-annotator agreement on issues where they otherwise differ. Our annotation tool is built on a generic infrastructure compatible with various formats of linguistic information such as Treebanks, multilingual corpora, part-of-speech (POS) annotation and output from statistical syntactic parsers such as the Stanford parser. These additional corpora and annotations not only serve to enrich textual data with additional layers of linguistic information but can be potentially used to assist in annotation. In our current application scenarios, when annotating a corpus the annotator is often faced with the following tasks:

1) Divide the text into meaningful segments
2) Analyze the segmented texts for the internal structure, such as functional structure of a clause or sentence
3) Analyze the functions of each functional/semantic unit, such as the part-of-speech of each word
4) Refer to a previously annotated section similar to the one being annotated
5) Consult a thesaurus for entries to the words whose meaning is unclear
6) Consult a multilingual corpus parallel to or aligned with the corpus (when annotating a corpus in another language).

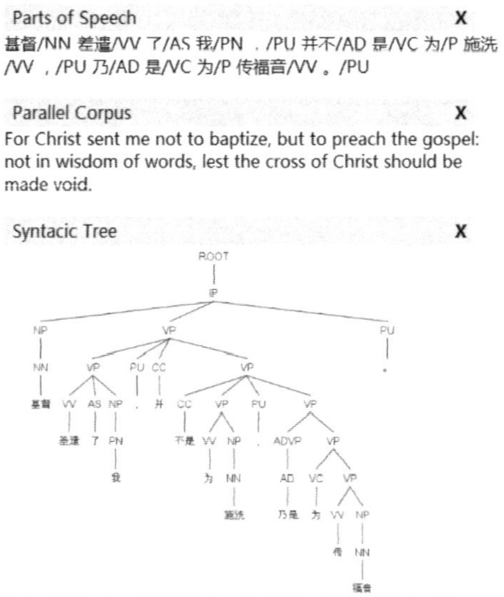

Figure 2: Automatically generated Reference Channels for annotation.

Figure 2 is an example of some of the available information that has been incorporated into our annotation platform to provide easy access for collaborating annotators. The panel is made up of three selected components that assist in the annotation task. The first section is produced from an automatic part-of-speech (POS) tagger (we use the Stanford POS tagger). The tagger reads raw text as input and yields the POS tags of each word. This information is useful as it provide basic disambiguation and guidance when annotating the text. Similarly, the third section is produced by a syntactic parser (Stanford Parser), which not only parses the text syntactically, but generates the complete tree structure of the parse. Glancing at the tree can provide helpful information in understanding the text at a syntactic level. Both the tagger and parser are highly generic and customizable. They can be used for tagging and parsing different languages after being trained on data of corresponding languages. The second section, on the other hand, is specific to texts with corresponding translations. The example is taken from a text from the Bible, which comes with many different versions that were aligned to each other using a special mechanism.

With such information integrated with the database, it needs to be easily accessible to aid in annotation and revision (correcting errors made in the annotation). Visualization has been found to be effective in helping users process new information [13] so introducing visualization techniques to our platform should enable users to more effectively process such information. Each of the above-mentioned layers of extra information is visualized in a windowed interface that can be customized for the needs of a particular task. The annotator can decide which of the available layers to use for reference, and at different stages of annotation different layers may be presented. The visualization is an automatic process requiring no manual intervention apart from initial settings. When the annotation moves on to the next section/stage, the contents of the visualization will be automatically updated.

When designing the annotation platform we have several goals in mind: it must be intuitive and easy-to-use. The learning curve must be kept to a minimum. We reduce the process of annotation to a two-step process: 1) define the annotation range 2) assign a label. We allow optional features such as defining the step hierarchy, placing labels in each step, visualizing and editing existing annotations, defining complex linguistic relations.

In addition, it must provide immediate feedback through visualization. In functional grammar systems such as Systemic Function Grammar when tagging a particular layer of meaning, the other layers as defined in the step hierarchy should be immediately visible in a multilayered structured format. These information layers provide additional references to the current layer being annotated, especially when they are closely linked in terms of function or meaning. When errors are made they are visible from the reference panel and appropriate actions such as deletion or modification can be taken. Figure 3 shows the annotation interface we designed to meet these requirements.

Figure 3 is an illustration of some of the functionalities currently implemented. The annotator starts by selecting a range of text to annotate. Visual channels appear to assist annotators in making the decisions more easily and with a higher degree of consistency. The channels on the right side of the interface provide a detailed collection of functional and semantic labels. The label structure for a particular annotation is shown at the bottom right where the structure of different metafunctions of the selected annotation is shown in a uniform way. The annotator can operate on the labeled structure directly by adding, removing and modifying the labels in the visual structure.

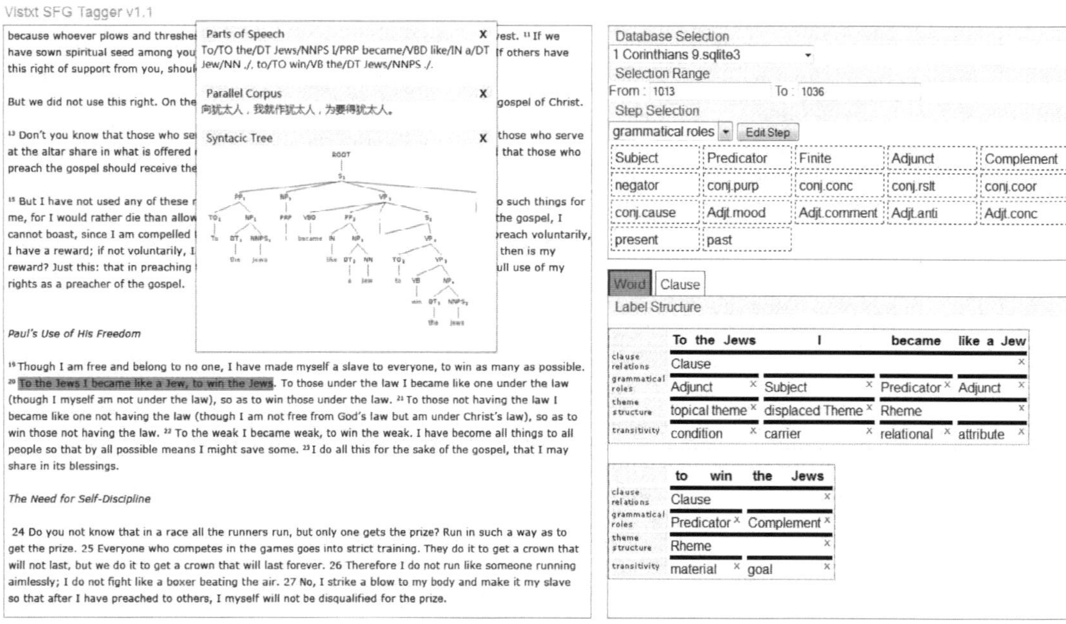

Figure 3: The web-based annotation interface.

3. APPLICATION

The tagger built on the proposed infrastructure can be used for visualizing various types of analysis. Rhetorical Structure Theory, for example, has been adopted for the tagger to help visualize the analysis of US President Obama's speeches.

Rhetorical Structure Theory (RST) is "an abstract set of convention" which "provides a general way to describe the relations among clauses in a text" [2]. This theory is widely used for text analysis for complex multilayer sentence and paragraph relations.

These sentence/paragraph relations are tagged using the proposed tagger, visualized and presented with the help of the "RST generator" which generates the RST figures, visualizing sentence/paragraph interpretation pictures.

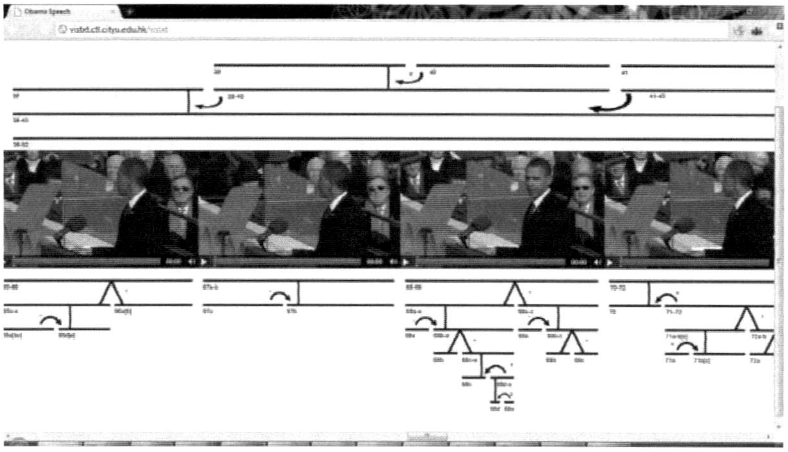

Figure 4: Visualized textual structures based on RST tagger outputs.

This annotating and visualizing method has already been applied in the analysis of Obama's inaugural and victory speeches, rendering 'the big picture' for how these speeches were constructed (Figure 4).

4. CONCLUSION

In this paper, we present a collaborative tool for Chinese and multilingual linguistic structure annotation with visualized cross-domain references. We begin by a discussion on current trends in annotating corpora and the requirements for developing a new annotation tool. A review of existing linguistics analysis tool is presented in our introduction.

We demonstrate with example applications that 1) a large collaborative annotation platform is necessary for speeding up large-scale manual or semi-automated Chinese linguistic annotation; 2) annotating complex linguistic information is a difficult and error-prone process; 3) visualized annotation references for language structures can help facilitate the annotation process, especially in a collaborative environment; and 4) cross-domain references can further assist annotators in making the right decisions.

Our tool is designed with collaborative tasking and cross-domain analysis in mind. All linguistic signals are converted into interoperable database structures in real time when users submit their input. Data obtained from different domains can be stored in the database structure and used to serve as the basis for cross-domain references. The use of our tools for handling these relationships requires a minimal learning curve. The same system may also be used for educational purposes like annotation training and examination marking for students. Usage examples may include exercises on identifying SFL constituents, translation alignment and other language analysis.

REFERENCES

[1] M. A. Halliday and C. M. Matthiessen, "An introduction to functional grammar," London: Edward Arnold, 2004.

[2] W. C. Mann and S. A. Thompson, "Rhetorical structure theory: Toward a functional theory of text organization," Text, vol. 8, no. 3, pp. 243–281, 1988.

[3] M. Honnibal and J. R. Curran, "Creating a systemic functional grammar corpus from the Penn treebank," Proceedings of the Workshop on Deep Linguistic Processing - DeepLP '07, no. June 2005, p. 89, 2007.

[4] C. Müller and M. Strube, "Multi-level annotation of linguistic data with MMAX2," Corpus Technology and Language Pedagogy: New, pp. 197–214, 2006.

[5] A. Burchardt, K. Erk, A. Frank, A. Kowalski, S. Pado, and M. Pinkal, "SALTO–a versatile multi-level annotation tool," in Proceedings of LREC 2006, 2006, pp. 517–520.

[6] M. O'Donnell, "Demonstration of the UAM CorpusTool for text and image annotation," Proceedings of the 46th Annual Meeting of the Association for Computational Linguistics on Human Language Technologies Demo Session - HLT '08, no. June, pp. 13–16, 2008.

[7] X. Ma, H. Lee, S. Bird, and K. Maeda, "Models and tools for collaborative annotation," Arxiv preprint cs/0204004, 2002.

[8] S. Dipper, "XML-based Stand-off Representation and Exploitation of Multi-Level Linguistic Annotation," German Research, no. 03.

[9] S. Dipper and G. Michael, "Accessing Heterogeneous Linguistic Data — Generic

XML-based Representation and Flexible Visualization," Computational Linguistics, 2004.

[10] M. Stührenberg, D. Goecke, N. Diewald, A. Mehler, and I. Cramer, "Web-based annotation of anaphoric relations and lexical chains," in Proceedings of the Linguistic Annotation Workshop on - LAW '07, 2007, no. June, pp. 140–147.

[11] J. Chamberlain, U. Kruschwitz, and M. Poesio, "Constructing an anaphorically annotated corpus with non-experts," Proceedings of the 2009 Workshop on The People's Web Meets NLP Collaboratively Constructed Semantic Resources - People's Web '09. Association for Computational Linguistics, Morristown, NJ, USA, pp. 57–62, 2009.

[12] M. Carmen, P. Felt, R. Haertel, D. Lonsdale, O. Merkling, E. Ringger, and K. Seppi, "Tag Dictionaries Accelerate Manual Annotation," Interface, pp. 1660–1664, 2006.

[13] C. Collins, "Interactive Visualizations of natural language," PhD thesis, 2010.

基於單語言機器翻譯技術改進中文文字蘊涵

Improving Chinese Textural Entailment by Monolingual Machine Translation Technology

楊善順 Shan-Shun Yang, 吳世弘 Shih-Hung Wu*
朝陽科技大學資訊工程系
Department of Computer Science and Information Engineering
Chaoyang University of Technology, Taichung, Taiwan (R.O.C)
{s10027619, shwu}@cyut.edu.tw
*Contact author

陳良圃
財團法人資訊工業策進會
Institute for Information Industry, Taipei, Taiwan (R.O.C)
eit@iii.org.tw
謝文泰
曹承礎
國立台灣大學資訊管理學系
Department of IM, National Taiwan University, Taipei, Taiwan (R.O.C)
wentai@iii.org.tw
chou@im.ntu.edu.tw

摘要

在本文中敘述了我們如何透過單語言機器翻譯提高中文文字蘊涵識別系統效能。在之前我們的做法是基於標準的監督式機器學習分類方法。我們整合單語言機器翻譯系統與其他可用的計算中文的自然語言處理的應用建設為語言資源處理系統。我們觀察訓練語料，並列出了所有可用的特徵。這些特徵包括表面文字，語義和語法的資訊，如：詞性標註、同義詞替換和上下位關係。從訓練語料中被標出特徵被應用於中文文字蘊涵識別的訓練分類模型之上。實驗結果表明單語言機器翻譯技術，可以提高我們的系統效能。

關鍵詞：中文文字蘊涵、 語言特徵、分類

一、緒論

文字蘊涵是一個重要的自然語言處理(NLP)問題，它有著許多方面的應用，例如問答系統、資訊抽取、機器翻譯[1]。截至 2011 年為止在中文領域缺乏認識文字蘊涵(RITE)的相關理論，所以現在很難評估它的效能。在 2011 年由 NTCIR-9RITE-1 提供繁體及簡體中文的共同任務中文文本蘊涵的數據集。該數據集包含一個分兩類(BC)和分多類(MC)的測試集。BC 子任務是假設為一個給定的文本對(T1,T2)，測試 T1 句子是否(推論到)T2

句子，MC 子任務將句子分類成 5 大類的方式來檢測是否有(正向/反向/雙向)蘊涵關係或沒有(矛盾/獨立)蘊涵關係[2]，在表一中舉出是否蘊涵的例子。

假設我們可以從 T1 的資訊得到 T2 相關資訊那麼我們可以認為 T1 與 T2 有蘊涵關係。在數據集中一些蘊涵的例子我們可以視為釋義[3]。也就是說，T1 和 T2 是描述同一件事，並有許多共同的字詞，這是比較容易檢測是否有意譯的關係在較複雜的蘊涵關係之上方法。在本文中，我們的分析著重於文字蘊涵問題的意譯部分。我們測試單語言機器翻譯技術的方式是否可能識別於中文蘊涵的數據集的正向蘊涵的意譯。

表一、蘊涵關係例句

類別	例句
蘊涵	T1：日本時間 2011 年 3 月 11 日，日本宮城縣發生芮氏規模 9.0 強震，造死傷失蹤約 3 萬多人 (Japan time March 11, 2011, Miyagi Prefecture, Japan, a magnitude 9.0 earthquake occurred, causing casualties of about 30,000 people missing or dead.)
	T2：日本時間 2011 年 3 月 11 日，日本宮城縣發生芮氏規模 9.0 強震 (Japan time March 11, 2011, Miyagi Prefecture, Japan, a magnitude 9.0 earthquake occurred)
獨立	T1：黎姿與”残障富豪”馬廷強結婚(Gigi married with the “disability rich” Mating Jiang married)
	T2：馬廷強為香港”東方報業集團”創辦人之一馬惜如之子(Mating Jiang is the son of Ma Xi Ru, one of the founders of Hong Kong, "the Oriental Press Group")

二、研究方法

在以前的文獻之中有許多不同的方法被應用在中英文文字蘊涵識別之上，如定理證明或使用 WordNet 等等不同的詞意語料資源[4]。我們的研究方法，嘗試使用單語言機器翻譯作為一個標準的監督學習分類系統[5]的特徵。我們透過觀察訓練語料，使用可用的計算中文的自然語言處理的應用建設成語言資源處理系統。發展過程如下所述，首先我們觀察到的訓練語料，然後列出的各種可用特徵。這些特徵包括表面文字、語義和語法的信息，如：詞性標註、命名實體識別(NER)標註和單語言機器翻譯特徵。然後，從訓練集我們執行了子系統提取到各個特徵。最後我們建立一個分類系統，使用將訓練資料分成 10 等份 9 等分用於訓練 1 等分用於測試，這樣不斷交叉測試稱為”10 倍交叉驗證”方法對訓練數據的特徵測試，並發現哪些特徵是文字蘊涵識別更為有用。

三、系統架構

我們的系統的系統流程圖如圖 1 所示。的基本組成部分”同義詞正規化”、”斷詞” 、”中文簡繁轉換”、”特徵提取”和”SVM 的分類”。

(一)、同義詞正規化

在這裡我們將 T1 和 T2 句子中具有相同的含義的字詞統一取代成相同字詞，因此在後續句子匹配步驟更容易執行。

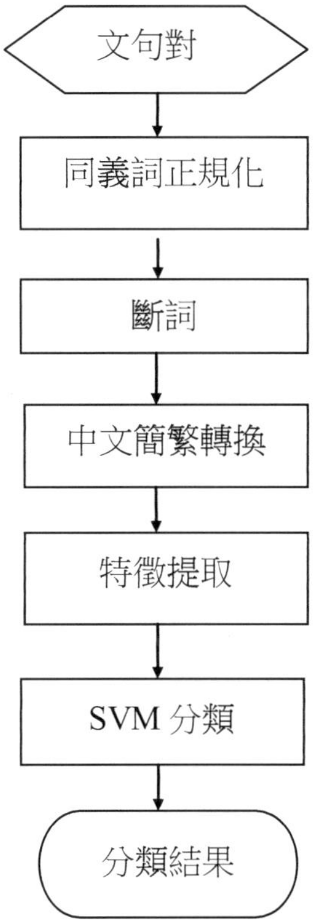

圖一、系統流程圖

1、 表示格式正規化

預處理的部份的第一個目標是句子中的符號正規化。在我們的系統，預處理模塊正規化中括號中的字可以視為一個在括號前字詞的一個代名詞。由於文件中括號通常表示在前面的括號一詞的音譯或翻譯。例如”車諾比核事故(切爾諾貝利核事故)”，括號中的字詞是翻譯另一個相同字詞”切爾諾貝利核事故”。時間表示方法也將正規化。如表 2 中所示的例子。在語料庫中有許多方式來表示語料庫中的日期或時間，正規化後的資料更容易被識別，在機器翻譯方面也更容易執行文字對齊。

表二、各種時間表示方式之例句

時間型態	時間表示方式
中文	一九九七年二月廿三日
數字全形	１９９７年２月２３日
數字半形	1997年2月23日
數字以「-」隔開	1999-05-07
範圍	1999年延長至2001年

2、背景知識的替換

預處理的部份第二個目標是代替它們的同義詞。從維基百科收集同義詞的資訊。明確的時間和地點資訊也視為同義詞替換的問題。

另外有關的時間表示的還有另一個問題在於中國或日本歷史上不同朝代的同一年的表示。例如”乾隆”是西元 1735 年和”昭和”是西元 1925 年。時間表示式需要背景知識才能正規化。

另一個類似的問題是需要擴展到文字匹配前的充分表示地點的縮寫。例如”台、印、美”是指”台灣、印度、美國”，因此將需要正規化為”台灣、印度、美國”。

3、 斷詞與中文簡繁轉換

我們的系統中使用的斷詞工具是 ICTCLAS 的斷詞系統，這是由中國科學院計算技術研究所提供。該工具包的功能包括斷詞、詞性標註、NE 識別、新字詞識別，以及自訂字典。由於我們使用的斯坦福剖析器只能處理簡體中文以及英文，我們必須將繁體中文文句對轉換成簡體中文文句，然後我們使用的簡繁轉換工具為 google 的線上機器翻譯系統。

(二) 特徵提取

在我們的系統中使用到的特徵在表三列出以前的文字蘊涵識別工作[9]大多數可用的特徵。而本篇提出的單語言機器翻譯將在下一小節描述。在前三個特徵測量T1和T2中根據一般中國類似的字元。unigram_recall、unigram_precision、unigram_F_measure可以視為在T1，T2的字元比例和幾何平均，我們的系統使用BLEU三個特點[7]。Bleu當初是被設計來測量機器翻譯(machine translation)的品質。一個良好的機器翻譯需要包含適當、準確以及流暢的翻譯，我們的系統會將其翻譯為原來的文字T1和T2得到log Bleu recall、log Bleu precision和log Bleu F measure values。

最後四個特徵是 T1 和 T2 的句子長度。我們的系統根據文字和字詞計算 T1 和 T2 的句子中長度的差異，並使用了這兩個特徵的絕對值在我們的系統中。

表三、我們使用到的特徵

編號	特徵
1	unigram_recall
2	unigram_precision
3	unigram_F_measure
4	log_bleu_recall
5	log_bleu_precision
6	log_bleu_F_measure
7	difference in sentence length (character)
8	absolute difference in sentence length (character)
9	difference in sentence length (term)
10	absolute difference in sentence length (term)
11	Sub-tree mapping
12	Time mapping

1、 剖析子樹匹配

一個句子的語法資訊也是一個重要的問題。在一個句子的依賴已用於識別意譯的關係[8]。以前的一些文獻表明以不同的方式來衡量兩個解析樹，如樹的編輯距離之間的相似性。子樹的匹配是通過比較兩個句子解析樹的方式來計算兩個句子之間的相似性。在之前我們相信子樹匹配是對系統有所幫助，然而在我們之後的實驗結果其使用後系統效能會略有下降。

2、 時間匹配

當我們觀察到的訓練集資料時我們發現，有許多文句對之中含有時間表示式，然而一些時間表示式是句子重要組成一部分。如表四所示我們分析分為四種類型的匹配。在 T1 和 T2 的時間表達方式可以是：(1)完全匹配、(2)部分匹配、(3)部分匹配、(4)完全不匹配。時間匹配和不匹配的是有用的訓練數據，然而在我們的實驗結果，此特徵沒有提高測試集效能。

表四、時間匹配度例子

匹配程度	例子
時間為完全匹配	t1：據他所知，這是查爾斯首度參加雪梨-荷芭特帆船賽，而查爾斯一向是注重安全、非常謹慎的人，他更想參加2000年雪梨奧運帆船賽。
	t2：2000年奧運在雪梨舉辦
部分時間匹配(1)	t1:若望保祿二世一九七八年十月十六日被選為教宗
	t2：若望保祿二世於1978年當上教宗
部分時間匹配(2)	t1：蘇哈托 1921年6月8日出生
	t2：蘇哈托（Suharto，民間常用「Soeharto」，1921年6月8日－2008年1月27日）
時間完全不匹配	t1：張藝謀1987年以「紅高粱」拿下柏林影展金熊獎
	t2：柏林電影節應該是張藝謀的福地。1988年，他執導的《紅高粱》贏得了最佳影片金熊獎，成為中國電影的首個金熊獎

3、 單語言機器翻譯

我們認為在系統中增加單語機器翻譯作為一項新的可用特徵是有意義的，這項新方法不同於以往的文字蘊涵識別系統。

在我們的實驗中，我們使用 GIZA++作為我們的單語機器翻譯的特徵工具。藉由 GIZA++對訓練集建立一個翻譯模型並計算測試集中文句對集對齊的機率。文字對齊是統計機器翻譯系統訓練很重要的程序。GIZA++[10]這是用於這樣工作的經典工具，GIZA++執行 IBM1-5 模型以及其延伸的的 HMM 模型和更複雜模型 6。產生的這些所有模型是不對稱的，也就說由選定的翻譯方向，讓他們多對一的進行對齊，但不是一對多的路線。通常進行訓練相反的兩種翻譯方向和對稱，產生字詞對齊提高字詞對齊的品質。兩個對齊模式訓練完全相互獨立，在 GIZA++使用到的 HMM 的對齊模型計算公式如下:

$$p_\alpha(t_1 \mid t_2) = \varepsilon(m \mid l)\sum_a \prod_{j=1}^{m}(t_\alpha(t_{1_j} \mid t_{2_j})a_\alpha(a_j \mid a_{j-1}, l) \qquad (1)$$

我們將 GIZA++計算出來的對齊機率應用於的分兩類的文字蘊涵任務中作為我們的第13 個特徵。在我們的系統所使用的計算公式如下：

$$p = \frac{\log\left\{\prod_{i,j=0}^{i,j=\max} p(t1_i \mid t2_j)\right\}}{n} \qquad (2)$$

在下面舉了一個例子說明文句對對齊的機率的應用：

T1:外交部長　胡志強　坦言　以　告　國人　，　台灣　外交

即將　面臨　暴風雨　。

T2:台灣　外交部長　是　胡志強　。

如表五所示為上面例子執行 GIZA++後計算出來的 T1 與 T2 對齊機率，經由公式(1)計算後就即是我們將增加系統的第 13 個特徵。

表五、GIZA++對齊機率例子

T1 單詞	T2 單詞	機率
外交部長	外交部長	0.9951
胡志强	胡志强	0.9512
坦言	台灣	0.2014
台湾	台灣	0.9812
台灣	是	0.0151

P=log(0.9951*0.9512*0.9812*0.0151)/4≒-0.46381736

四、實驗與討論

在這個章節中，我們報告的訓練集與測試集上進行的幾個不同的實驗設定的實驗結果。我們的系統在給定的 407 對訓練集和測試集做 10 倍交叉驗證訓練，並使用相同的系統處理另一個 407 對文句開放測試集。表六中列出的四個設定的實驗結果。在我們實驗結果中第二的設定得到最好的效能，其正確率為 0.69。

表六、實驗結果總表

	10 倍交叉驗證訓練	公開測試集

1~10 特徵 [9]	0.6560	0.6830
1~10 特徵與機器翻譯	**0.6658**	**0.6904**
1~12 特徵 [9]	0.6461	0.5577
1~12 特徵與機器翻譯	0.6560	0.5749

(一)實驗結果

如表七所示在第一個實驗中我們使用到表三 1 到 10 個特徵進行 10 倍交叉驗證實驗，接著我們加入單語言機器翻譯特徵如表八所示可以提昇其效能。

表七、使用 10 特徵 10 倍交叉驗證實驗結果

Predicted	**Actual**		**Total**
	Y	**N**	
Y	70	42	112
N	98	197	295
Total	168	239	407

表八、使用 10 特徵加入機器翻譯特徵 10 倍交叉驗證實驗結果

Predicted	**Actual**		**Total**
	Y	**N**	
Y	72	40	112
N	96	199	295
Total	168	239	407

如表九所示在第二個實驗中我們使用到表三 1 到 12 個特徵進行 10 倍交叉驗證實驗，接著我們加入單語言機器翻譯特徵如表十所示可以提昇其效能。

表九、使用 12 特徵 10 倍交叉驗證實驗結果

Predicted	**Actual**		**Total**
	Y	**N**	
Y	68	44	112
N	100	195	295
Total	168	239	407

表十、使用 12 特徵加入機器翻譯特徵 10 倍交叉驗證實驗結果

Predicted	**Actual**		**Total**
	Y	**N**	
Y	70	42	112

N	98	197	295
Total	168	239	407

如表十一所示在第二個實驗中我們使用到表三 1 到 10 個特徵與公開測試集進行實驗，接著我們加入單語言機器翻譯特徵如表十二所示可以提昇其效能。

表十一、使用 10 特徵公開測試集實驗結果

Predicted	Actual		Total
	Y	N	
Y	172	38	210
N	91	106	197
Total	263	144	407

表十二、使用 10 特徵加入機器翻譯特徵公開測試集實驗結果

Predicted	Actual		Total
	Y	N	
Y	174	36	210
N	89	108	197
Total	263	144	407

如表十三所示在第二個實驗中我們使用到表三 1 到 10 個特徵與公開測試集進行實驗，接著我們加入單語言機器翻譯特徵如表十四所示可以提昇其效能。

表十三、使用 12 特徵公開測試集實驗結果

Predicted	Actual		Total
	Y	N	
Y	126	43	169
N	137	101	238
Total	263	144	407

表十四、使用 10 特徵加入機器翻譯特徵公開測試集實驗結果

Predicted	Actual		Total
	Y	N	
Y	129	40	169
N	134	104	238
Total	263	144	407

(二)實驗討論

我們的系統的額外的機器翻譯新特徵提高了正確率，無論是的交叉驗證或是公開測試集的情況，實驗結果也證實第 11 和第 12 的特徵沒有改進我們的效能。從混淆矩陣我們可以發現，該系統是在數據分佈方面的強勁。yes/no 在訓練和開放測試集的分佈有很大的不同。該系統可以大多數識別正確。

五、結論

本篇報告改進我們參加 RITE1 的系統，我們增加了一個新的機器翻譯特徵到我們的系統中並取得了較好的效能，我們用機器翻譯方法來翻譯同一種語言作為一種方法來識別語言中的意譯。我們的系統是專門處理中文部份，然而同樣的想法以我們系統的基礎也可能應用在不同的語言。

從資料觀察得知，處理這個問題背景知識是最必要的條件，像中國或是日本人的朝代名稱，在時間匹配之前必須轉換成相同表示，地理知識也是必要的。這些需求是超出任何正常大小的訓練集和語言知識的內容。從 Web 挖掘需要的必要知識可能是一個有用的資源來源來。

在本篇我們提出了單語言機器翻譯來改進我們的系統，在實驗結果中發現這個新的方法的確可以改進我們的系統，但是改進的幅度並不高因為機器翻譯這個方法需要相當大量的訓練資料才能讓 GIZA++文字對齊效果更準確，所以在未來希望可以使用更大量的資料集來提昇文字對齊的精確度。

致謝

本研究依經濟部補助財團法人資訊工業策進會「100 年度數位匯流服務開放平台技術研發計畫」辦理。感謝國科會贊助部分研究經費，計畫編號 NSC- 100-2221-E-324 -025-MY2。

參考文獻

[1] Ido Dagan and Oren Glickman, Probabilistic textual entailment: Generic applied modeling of language variability, In Proceedings of the Workshop on Learning Methods for Text Understanding and Mining, Grenoble, France, 2004.

[2] NTCIR 9, Recognizing Inference in TExt task, http://artigas.lti.cs.cmu.edu/rite/Main_Page.

[3] Ion Androutsopoulos and Prodromos Malakasiotis, "A survey of paraphrasing and textual entailment methods", Journal of Artificial Intelligence Research, Volume 38, pages 135-187, 2010.

[4] Christiane Fellbaum, "WordNet: An Electronic Lexical Database", The MIT Press, 1998.

[5] Prodromos Malakasiotis, Ion Androutsopoulos, "Learning textual entailment using SVMs and string similarity measures", In Proceedings of ACL-PASCAL Workshop on Textual Entailment and Paraphrasing, pages 42–47, Prague, Czech Republic, 2007.

[6] Wan, S., Dras, M., Dale, R., & Paris, C., "Using dependency-based features to take the "para-farce" out of paraphrase", In Proceedings of the Australasian Language Technology Workshop, pages 131–138, Sydney, Australia, 2006.

[7] Kishore Papineni, Salim Roukos, Todd Ward and Wei-Jing Zhu, "BLEU: a method for automatic evaluation of machine translation", In Proceedings of the 40th Annual Meeting on ACL, pages 311–318, Philadelphia, PA, 2002.

[8] Prodromos Malakasiotis, "Paraphrase recognition using machine learning to combine similarity measures", In Proceedings of the 47th Annual Meeting of ACL and the 4th International Joint Conference on Natural Language Processing of the Asian Federation of Natural Language Processing, Singapore, 2009.

[9] Shih-Hung Wu, Wan-Chi Huang, Liang-Pu Chen and Tsun Ku. Binary-class and Multi-class Chinese Textural Entailment System Description in NTCIR-9 RITE, in Proceedings of the NTCIR-9 workshop, Tokyo, Japan, 6-10 Dec., 2011.

[10] F. J. Och and H. Ney, "A systematic comparison of various statistical alignment models." *Computational Linguistics*, vol. 29, no. 1, pp. 19–51,2003.